CONTENTS

ABOUT THE AUTHORS

TERRY SMITH was awarded a teaching scholarship in 1959 while matriculating at Unley High School. He began his teaching career at Port Augusta High School, where he taught woodwork and metalwork to primary, secondary and adult students.

On his return to Adelaide in 1966, Terry continued teaching Technical Studies at Thebarton Boys High School and in 1973 was offered a lectureship at what is now the University of South Australia. The next few years saw him committed to the professional development of trainee teachers of Technical and Technology Studies.

In 1986, following two overseas study tours, he was awarded a senior lectureship at the university, with responsibility for the Technology Department.

In 1991 he became Head of the School of Applied Science at the University of South Australia. Upon his retirement in 1996, he was offered a part time lectureship with Flinders University, training junior primary and primary teachers in Design and Technology.

He now acts as a consultant for the Senior Secondary Assessment Board of South Australia, and in this capacity has co-authored the Year 11 and Year 12 Design and Technology syllabus for the South Australian Certificate of Education.

Terry continues to maintain his enthusiasm for woodwork in a comprehensive workshop and is currently planning the design and building of a holiday home in a seaside town.

He holds an M.Ed.(Wales), Adv.Dip.T. (Tertiary) and Dip.T.

BRIAN HAINES Now retired, Brian continues to pursue his interest in woodwork, undertaking various woodworking and building projects for family and friends. Also, he has recently restored three classic motor vehicles, which reflect his skill and dedication to high standards of craftsmanship. Since retirement he has devoted more time to his interest in music, and regularly plays saxophone and clarinet in musical productions and stage bands. He also has a lively interest in art, particularly sketching and drawing, producing work which has been exhibited in the local community gallery.

His early training has enabled him to develop skills and experience in a wide range of areas, using a range of materials. He initially trained and worked as an engineering patternmaker. He also worked in a drawing office preparing engineering drawings. Brian was also able to learn cabinet making and carpentry skills in the family building business. He also served in the RAAF. He later trained as a technical studies teacher, educating secondary students in woodwork and metalwork.

Over the years Brian continued to study and develop his skills and retired from the University of South Australia as a lecturer assisting in the education of secondary teachers, TAFE teachers, adult educators and industrial trainers.

In addition to his trade qualifications, he holds a DipT,.Adv.Dip.T., B.Ed.

Terry Smith
& Brian Haines

THE COMPLETE BOOK OF
WOODWORKING
AND CARPENTRY

NEW
HOLLAND

In memory of Simon and Bill

Published in Australia in 2004 by
New Holland Publishers (Australia) Pty Ltd
Sydney • Auckland • London • Cape Town

14 Aquatic Drive Frenchs Forest NSW 2086 Australia
218 Lake Road Northcote Auckland New Zealand
86 Edgware Road London W2 2EA United Kingdom
80 McKenzie Street Cape Town 8001 South Africa

First published 1998 by Lansdowne Publishing Pty Ltd

© Copyright text: Terry Smith and Brian Haines

Set in Helvetica 8.5pt, tracked +2.5 units
and horizontally scaled to 102% in QuarkXPress 3.31.

Printed in China by South China Printing Company

National Library of Australian Cataloguing-in-Publication Data

Smith, Terry, 1942-.
The complete book of woodworking and carpentry.

Includes index.

1. Woodwork - Handbooks, manuals, etc. 2. Carpentry-
Handbooks, manuals, etc. I. Haines, Brian, 1938-. II. Title.

684.08

ISBN 1 74110 193 X

ACKNOWLEDGMENTS

We are indebted to our families, friends and colleagues for their willing assistance without which we would not have been able to complete this work. We further wish to acknowledge the assistance in the form of technical information, use of material, data, and photographs generously provided by the following companies and organisations:

Timber Development Association of S.A. Incorporated

Stanley Works Pty. Ltd.

Durden Machinery Company

David Trembath Agencies Pty. Ltd.

Australian Design Awards

Pine Australia

Sunlander Outdoor Products

Flintware

Hettich Australia

Selleys Chemical Co. Pty. Ltd.

3 M Australia Pty. Ltd.

Norman Turner & Nottage

Black & Decker (A/Asia) Pty. Ltd.

Otto & Co. Pty. Ltd.

S.A. Brush Co.

Tessa Furniture

Brady Billiard Tables

B.H.P. Building Products

Triton Manufacturing and Design Co. Pty. Ltd.

Woodfast Machinery Co.

Makita (Australia) Pty. Ltd

Plywood Association of Australia

Oil & Colour Chemists Association

Austral Engineering Supplies

Spear & Jackson

Guest, Keen & Nettlefold (Aust.) Pty. Ltd.

Lane Amalgamated Hardware Co.

Sidney Cooke Fasteners Pty. Ltd.

C.S.I.R.O.

Norton Pty. Ltd

Forestry S.A.

State Forests of N.S.W.

CSR Timber Products

Timber Preservers Association

Standards Association of Australia

Wattyl (S.A.) Pty. Ltd.

Patience & Nicholson Ltd.

University of S.A.

Lloyds Australia Ltd.

Formica Plastics Pty. Ltd.

INTRODUCTION

For centuries man has enjoyed the intrinsic qualities of timber—one of the world's most valuable natural raw materials still readily available. Qualities such as strength, workability, warmth, durability and lustre, to name but a few, have allowed craftsmen throughout the ages to manipulate this material into various artefacts of lasting beauty.

It is this sense of achievement and derived pleasure that prompts men and women of all ages to learn the skills associated with the working qualities of timber. These abilities may be used for such things as home improvements, wood turning and wood carving.

With these thoughts in mind we have endeavoured to communicate some of our ideas and experiences so that the individual, whether professional or hobbyist, may enjoy a greater sense of satisfaction.

During the preparation of this book we undertook to construct the majority of projects featured, thereby ensuring a comprehensive understanding of possible structure and components. Similarly, in gathering information and photographs, we made visits to most States and to New Zealand.

We also sought assistance from many individuals, organisations and industries. These people, who gave willingly of their time, provided information, drawings and photographs. Without their contributions our task would have been far more difficult.

We have endeavoured to produce a comprehensive volume catering for many levels of interest and skill in a variety of areas including hand tools, machines, home improvements and many other interesting facets of woodwork.

HANDTOOLS
...AND HOW BEST TO USE THEM

In an age where labour costs can exceed material costs many of us often feel the urge to design and construct our own furniture. In order to achieve a satisfying end result it is necessary to have an understanding of basic handtools and their applications.

The following chapter describes such tools and illustrates the ways in which they may be used. In conjunction with their applications are hints and suggestions enabling a more professional result to be attained.

MARKING OUT

As with all projects the initial planning and layout is the fundamental factor determining success or failure. An awareness for accuracy, ability to avoid defect timber, clear marking of waste material, and a means of checking prior to any cutting process are desirable. To this end, there are a variety of marking out tools having specific or multiple uses.

Pencil

For marking on planed stock an H or HB pencil, sharpened to have at least 6 mm of lead protruding, has proved most successful. For rough stock, i.e. off saw material, a rectangular shaped carpenter's pencil is necessary as the harder lead enables more accurate marking. A pencil should always be used in preference to a marking knife or marking gauge when laying out chamfers, bevels, or sloping edges since the mark left is easily removed at a later stage.

Marking Knife

This may consist of a small steel blade attached to a wooden handle. More sophisticated knives, however, have steel handles with retractable and removable steel blades. Basically, the marking knife is used in conjunction with a try square to sever the fibres *across* the direction of grain where saw cuts or planing are to occur. This eliminates the breaking or tearing of fibres due to the subsequent cutting actions.

To provide more accurate marking and a greater degree of safety, the length of blade exposed should be minimal.

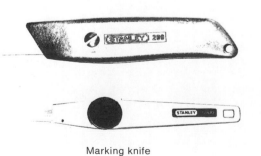

Marking knife

Use of marking knife and try square

RULES

Steel Rules

For general purposes a standard 300 mm steel rule calibrated in mm is adequate. However, they are also obtainable in 150 mm, 450 mm, and 600 mm lengths.

Besides measuring and checking short distances, the steel rule is used for testing flat surfaces and setting other marking out tools. To ensure accuracy, hold the rule on edge and sight the pencil or knife point down the calibration, thus avoiding the error of parallax.

Folding Rule

The most commonly accepted form of this rule consists of four pieces hinged together and usually made from boxwood or plastic. By nature of its construction its use is confined to general carpentry where accuracy is not as essential as it is in furniture construction.

Tape Rules

For distances exceeding 300 mm it is often convenient to use tape rules. These have flexible steel blades spring loaded and housed in a steel or plastic casing. Sizes range from 600 mm to 7 m in length with graduations in mm, cm, and m. The flexibility of the blade allows the measurement of circles, curves, and even circumferences. To assist in the visual transference of measurements the more modern tapes have coloured blades.

It is imperative that the rivets which attach zero hooks on tape rules are not fixed. Movement of this hook must occur to compensate for its thickness when measuring inside surfaces.

Straight Edge

The straight edge is made of spring steel and is usually 1 m in length. It has two straight, parallel edges which may be calibrated, and is used for testing straightness and flatness of large surfaces and edges as well as marking straight lines.

It is most useful for laying out projects on large sheet material.

Folding rule

Tape rule

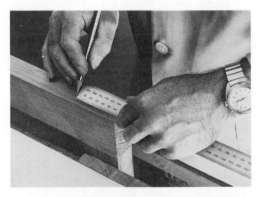

Marking out with pencil and steel rule

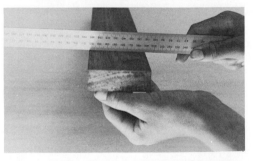

Testing flatness with steel rule

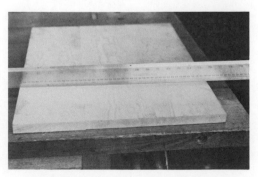

Steel straight edge to test wide board

Plumb bob
(using)

PLUMB BOBS

Plumb bobs are round sectional weights of brass or cast iron accurately machined to a perfect balance. Provision is made for attachment to a string line, so that when suspended from a pin, a true vertical may be obtained upon cessation of swinging.

Care should be taken when using a plumb bob that both the line and the bob are free to oscillate.

An alternative method is to attach the string line to a specially prepared length of machined timber stock. A rectangular hole, centrally located, is cut in the bottom end of the timber stock and accurately marked with a centreline. This centreline is continued to the top of the timber length at which point the string line is secured. Once the point of the plumb bob and the centreline align with one another, a true vertical may be marked from within the rectangular hole. (See left.)

Plumb bob

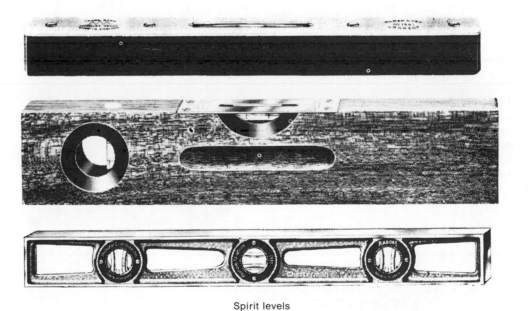

Spirit levels

LEVELS

Spirit levels are available with either timber, iron, aluminium, or plastic stocks, a varying number of adjustable or non-adjustable vials, which in turn may contain 'proved' or 'ground' glasses.

Proved glasses are made from glass tubing and are slightly bent so that the high point is exactly in the middle. These provide sufficient accuracy for the carpenter. Ground glasses, however, are straight on the outside with the inside ground barrel shape providing greater accuracy. For general purpose work, a metre aluminium stock level having three or four adjustable vials with proved glasses is most satisfactory.

To test the accuracy of the spirit level, place it on a surface to give a level reading and rotate it through 180° and check again for a level reading.

Use

For checking the accuracy of work in the vertical and horizontal planes.

Laser level and tripod

3

SQUARES

Try Square

The try square consists of two main parts, a parallel steel blade and a timber or steel stock. The stock and blade are attached by rivets to form an angle of 90°. Sizes of try squares are determined by the length of the blade and range from 100 mm to 300 mm. Basically the try square has two uses: first, for marking square lines across or around timber stock, and secondly, for the testing of internal and external angles of 90° (i.e. squareness).

When marking with a try square, the stock should be held firmly against the face or face edge. In the case of wide boards, hand pressure should be transferred from the stock to the blade to prevent slipping while marking is carried out. The positioning of the try square must allow for the blade to cover the material which is required, i.e. the waste is exposed.

The try square may be used in conjunction with a pencil or marking knife. A pencil line is used to establish layout. After checking the layout, a knife line may be used where cutting processes are to follow.

NOTE

(1) Try squares should be used from face and face edge surfaces wherever possible.

(2) When cutting timber stock it is essential to square and knife cut both sides of material to prevent chipping, particularly with sheet material.

(3) To test a try square for accuracy, draw a line along the blade from a straight edge, reverse the try square and check that the blade coincides exactly with the drawn line.

Mitre Square

This consists of similar parts to the try square but has the blade fixed at 45° to the stock. It is used for marking lines at 45° for testing the accuracy of mitres.

Combination Square

This tool combines try and mitre square, depth gauge, height gauge, marking gauge, level, and rule which may be used separately if required. The blade, ranging from 150 mm to 300 mm, is movable through the stock and is held in position by a spring and lock nut.

Sliding Bevel

This square, also known as an adjustable bevel, has a sliding blade which is adjustable to any angle with the stock. It is used for the setting out and testing of bevels and splays or where the joint line is other than 90° or 45°.

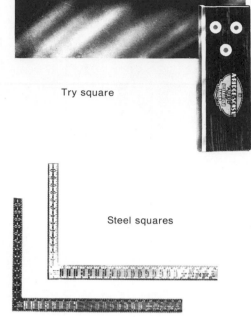

Try square

Testing edge for squareness

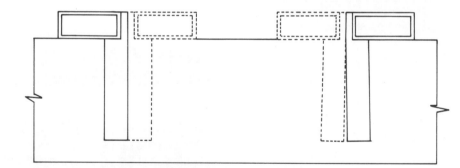

Steel squares

Marking a line with knife and try square

Checking try square for accuracy

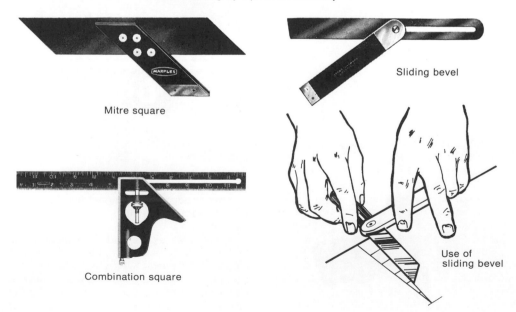

Mitre square

Sliding bevel

Combination square

Use of sliding bevel

GAUGES

Marking Gauge

The marking gauge is used for marking parallel distances along the surfaces of timber stock. To set distances the adjustable stock moves along the stem and is locked by means of a thumbscrew when the required measurement is obtained between the stock and fixed spur.

Modern marking gauges have brass wearing strips inserted on the face side of the stock.

Marking gauge

Method of Use

The marking gauge should be held by means of the 3–1 thumb grip. Pressure must be applied into the timber stock being marked in order to maintain a parallel line. Similar pressure is used to push the gauge away from the operator. On wide boards it may be necessary to hold the material in a vice and use both hands in order to maintain a mark parallel to the edge.

NOTE

(1) For continuity of accuracy the marking gauge should only be used with the stock held against the face or face edge.

(2) The marking gauge may be used for marking width, thickness, and depth of joints, but not for edge treatments such as splays, chamfers, or bevels.

(3) While one end of the stem holds a fixed steel spur, it is often useful to drill a small hole at the other end to accommodate a pencil. For edge treatment, since a gauge line is incorrect, the marking gauge may still be used, but with the pencil point marking the timber.

Mortise Gauge

This gauge is primarily used for the marking out of mortise and tenon joints. Its construction is similar to a marking gauge but has an extra steel spur attached to a brass slide. The slide is adjustable by means of a thumbscrew located at one end of the stem.

For the construction of mortise and tenon joints, the distance between the two spurs is determined by the appropriate mortise chisel. This provides for the marking of two parallel lines indicating the size of the mortise and of the tenon.

Gauging to width

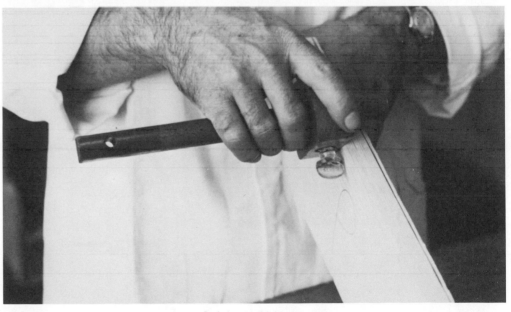

Gauging to thickness

Combination Gauge

As the name suggests, this gauge combines the attributes of both the marking and mortise gauges. At one end of the stem is a fixed spur while the other has both fixed and adjustable spurs. This is a most useful tool to include when compiling a tool kit.

Cutting Gauge

This is used mainly to mark out or cut lines on the face or edge *across* the gain. It may

Combination gauge

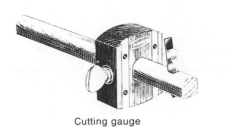
Cutting gauge

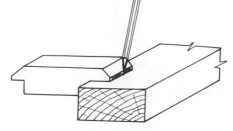
Pencil gauge

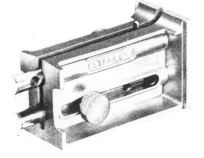
Butt gauge

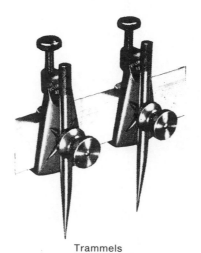
Trammels

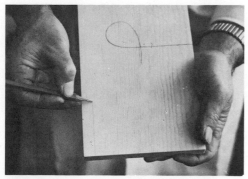
Use of a finger gauge

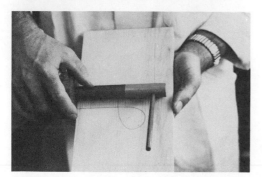
A hole drilled in stem of marking gauge makes excellent pencil gauge

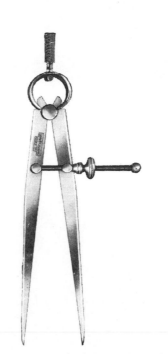
Dividers

also be used for cutting off strips of veneer or other thin material. An adjustable steel blade, held in position by a wedge, replaces the steel spur of other marking gauges.

Butt Gauge

This is a most useful tool for laying out butt mortises when hinging doors. The gauge is used to mark the position and thickness of the butt on the door and door jamb. It may also be used to mark the location of lock plates and strike plates.

Pencil Gauge

This consists of a small block of timber rebated to the size required for marking. The rebate shoulder is located against the face or face edge, a pencil placed against the end of the gauge and the block is moved along the material. A similar result may be obtained by using a pencil and rule. Using the left hand to hold the rule and act as a fence, the right hand holds a pencil firmly against the opposite rule end.

A further simplification is the finger gauge where the fingers of one hand hold the pencil and act as a fence. This method is often used to mark out chamfers and other types of edge treatments.

TRAMMEL POINTS AND TRAMMEL HEADS

These may be mounted on a beam of suitable thickness and provide an efficient and convenient means of laying out the distance between two points and for scribing arcs and circles outside the capacity of ordinary dividers. They are equally useful for metal, wood, and plastics and are therefore invaluable for patternmakers, joiners, and sheetmetal workers.

The hardened and ground points are eccentric so that final adjustment (within 8 mm) can be made before clamping the point to the body. The points can also be secured either vertically or at 45°, the angular setting being essential when marking under a ledge or similar obstruction. When required, a pencil can be used in place of the point.

DIVIDERS

These consist of two types, common dividers and winged dividers. The common divider has two tapered, pointed legs pivoted together by a riveted friction joint. The winged type has a quadrant arm connected to the legs to eliminate movement during use. They may be used for scribing curves and dividing and transferring measurements.

PLANES

The plane, evolving over many hundreds of centuries, has been one of the craftsman's most fundamental and important tools. This now sophisticated and precision cutting instrument has put accuracy and skill into the hands of craftsman and amateur alike.

Besides their basic function of planing timber stock flat and smooth, planes are now available to serve a multitude of purposes. Consequently, planes may be divided into bench planes, special purpose planes and multi-purpose planes. It is this understanding of function as well as method of use that will enable satisfying results to be achieved.

Bench Planes

Smoothing Plane

The No. 4 or smoothing plane is essentially used for cleaning up processes. The blade being ground square produces a shaving the full width of the mouth of the plane. This removes any 'high spots' that may have been left by the No. 5 or jack plane.

Smoothing planes, if used continuously for cleaning up, should be adjusted to allow a very small gap between the blade and the mouth of the plane.

This permits only a thin shaving to be removed and is therefore particularly useful where sloping grain occurs.

Uses

Cleaning up timber stock prior to sanding.
Removal of sloping grain—followed by scraping if necessary.
Cleaning up of joints on assembled frames or carcasses.
Cleaning up of applied timber stock to frames or carcasses, e.g. edge strips, mouldings.
Planing of end grain surfaces.

Jack Plane

This is a general purpose plane. As a result of the slight curvature placed on the blade during the grinding process, the removal of timber occurs across the centre section of the blade. Continuous planing across the surface results in a series of small hollows. Although not visible to the eye, they may be felt by touch. Because of this cutting action the jack plane is limited in respect to cleaning up processes. With the increase in length comes an increase in weight, both of which are useful in general work. The extra length enables the plane to produce flatter surfaces while the increased weight reduces the possibility of lifting from the surface.

Uses

General bench work.
Dressing of timber.
Preparation of timber stock.

Trying Plane or Jointer Plane

The further increase in length and weight enables this plane to produce long straight edges. However, due to its size and cumbersome nature it is not usual to employ this plane for general purposes. This may be refuted by 'old time' craftsmen who find the trying plane particularly satisfying because of the quality it can produce. With the introduction of man-made sheet material and the increasing use of power machinery, this plane has become redundant.

Use

Planing accurate and true flat surfaces.

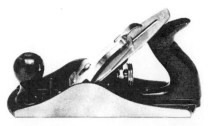

No. 4 smoothing plane

No. 5 jack plane

No. 7 trying plane

Long plane for long straight edges

Use of smoothing plane

Use of jack plane

Planing wide boards with trying plane

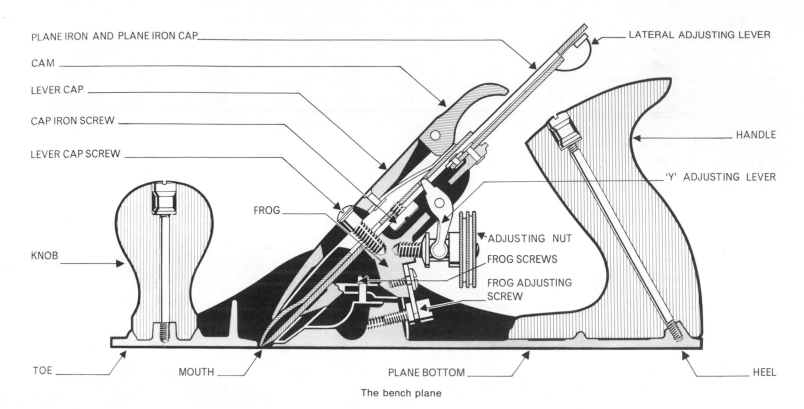

PLANE IRON AND PLANE IRON CAP

CAM

LEVER CAP

CAP IRON SCREW

LEVER CAP SCREW

KNOB

FROG

TOE

MOUTH

PLANE BOTTOM

LATERAL ADJUSTING LEVER

HANDLE

'Y' ADJUSTING LEVER

ADJUSTING NUT

FROG SCREWS

FROG ADJUSTING SCREW

HEEL

The bench plane

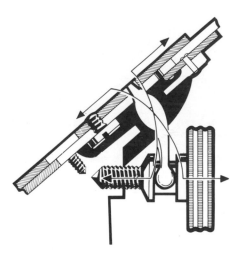

Action of thumb screw to adjust depth

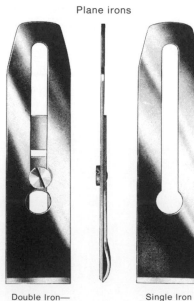

Plane irons

Double Iron— with cap iron and screw

Single Iron

Methods of Adjustment

FROG: The frog is attached to the body of the plane by means of two screws. Following loosening of these screws and the further screwing up or unscrewing of the frog adjusting screw, it is possible to close or open the gap in the mouth of the plane. This movement provides adjustment for the planing of timber with difficult grain.

The brass adjusting nut, attached to the frog, is also connected to the Y adjusting lever. This lever in turn fits into a rectangular slot in the cap iron. Since the cap iron and blade are held firmly in position against the frog by means of the lever cap, the screwing in or out of the brass adjusting nut will give an up or down movement of the plane blade. Hence it is possible for an accurate thickness of timber shaving to be removed.

The third means of adjustment attached to the frog is known as the lateral adjusting lever. As the name implies it is responsible for sideways movement of the plane blade. This adjustment enables timber shavings to be removed from either side or the centre of the mouth.

BLADE: To produce shavings the blade has a grinding facet of 20° to 25° and a honing facet of 25° to 30°. The honing facet may also be referred to as a whetting facet or sharpening facet.

Attached to the blade is a cap iron or back iron which is held in position by a cap iron screw passing through the long rectangular slot in the blade. The purpose of the cap iron is threefold. Firstly, it gives strength and rigidity to the plane blade. Secondly, the bottom end of the cap iron is curved so as to curl the shaving as it passes through the mouth. The shaving bends into a roll and finally breaks, hence keeping the mouth of the plane clear. Lastly, it provides the means by which the blade may be adjusted to depth.

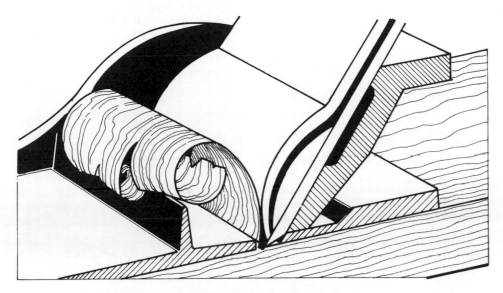

Cutting action of a plane

Adjusting to depth

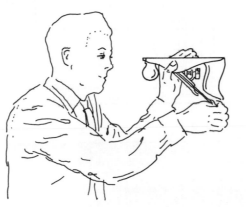

Use of lateral adjusting lever

Methods of Use

FACE PLANING (narrow stock): The timber stock should be securely located against a suitable support at an appropriate height. A comfortable stance should be adopted enabling a full stroke over the timber stock. The method of holding the plane may vary to suit the individual, but generally a 3–1 thumb grip is used. It is necessary to exert a downward pressure on the knob while a forward pressure is applied against the handle.

To maintain an even removal of shaving, the plane should be worked from one edge of the stock to the other and back continually. In the initial stages the depth of cut may be adjusted to allow a thick shaving. As the stock approaches the necessary requirements the adjusting nut should be altered to provide a fine shaving.

FACE PLANING (wide stock): If the stock to be planed exceeds 200 mm it may be necessary to traverse plane first. Instead of using the plane with the grain, it is used at an angle to the grain, planing from and working towards the opposite corners. Once flatness has been obtained planing along the grain occurs as with normal face planing.

EDGE PLANING (short stock): Locate the stock as low as practical in the vice and parallel to the bench surface to assist in planing accurately.

The 3–1 thumb grip on the handle is retained as is the forward pressure. If the thumb is placed on top of the front or toe of the plane and the four fingers located underneath on the sole to form a 'fence,' considerable assistance is given in holding the plane square to the face. It is essential that the plane remain parallel to the stock enabling full use of the length of the sole in order to maintain a straight edge.

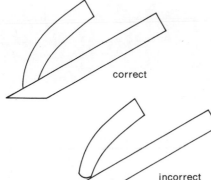

correct

incorrect

Cap irons

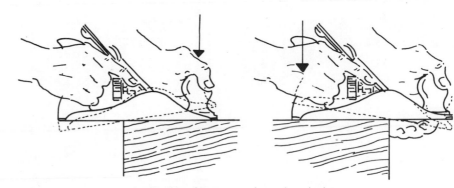

Application of pressure when edge planing

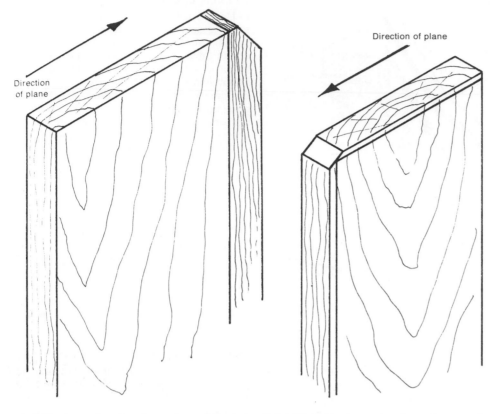

Direction of plane

Direction of plane

Left: Planing end grain using a piece of service material. *Right:* Planing end grain making use of excess width

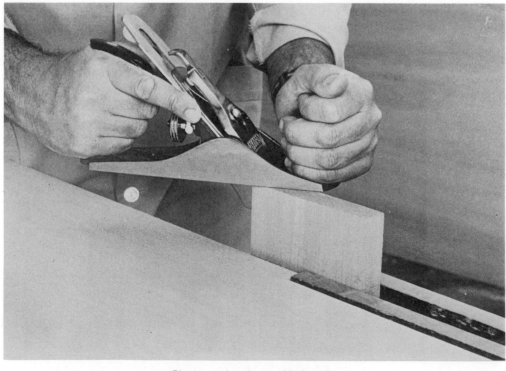

Planing end grain on wide boards

EDGE PLANING (long stock): For timber stock which exceeds 600 mm it is often necessary to support the stock from underneath by means of service material. This prevents undue bruising of the stock in the vice due to over tightening and steadies the end not firmly held.

Planing an edge

END GRAIN PLANING: While the grip and stance remain the same as for face planing, the plane is held at an angle to the stock to produce a slicing action. It is imperative that a downward pressure be maintained as the angle of the plane to the stock allows only a short section of the sole to be in contact with the timber surface.

NARROW STOCK: Since end grain planing involves cutting the fibres at right angles, it is possible for material to break away if the plane proceeds past the end. To prevent this, either the corner may be removed, provided it is in the waste section, or service material, with the corner removed, located against the end. Either method will now accommodate the plane passing over the end without damage occurring to the timber stock.

Planing end grain using waste on timber. The corner is cut off to prevent splitting

WIDE STOCK: Where the width of the timber stock prevents placement across the vice, it may be planed from either edge, i.e. planing occurs from each edge working towards the centre so that the blade does not pass more than two-thirds across the end of the stock from each edge. With all end grain planing it is *essential* that the fibres are severed by means of a knife cut line.

PLANING SHAPES

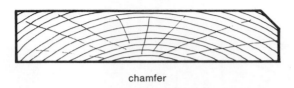

chamfer

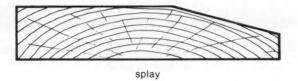

splay

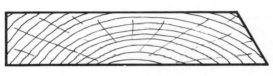

bevel

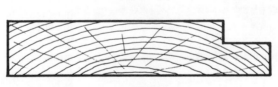

rebate

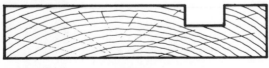

groove

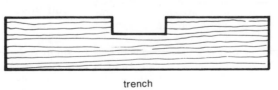

trench

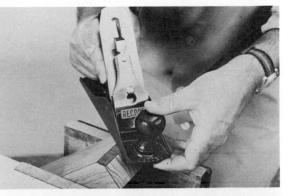

Planing a chamfer on the end grain

Planing a chamfer along an edge

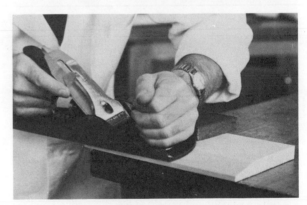

Planing a splay

Planing a bevel along an edge

11

SPECIAL PURPOSE PLANES

Rebate Plane

The rebate or fillister plane is used to cut rebates along the edges or across the ends of timber stock. A rebate may be defined as a rectangular recess along or across the timber edge.

The modern rebate plane consists of a cast iron body having two blade positions, one of which is adjustable, a movable side fence, and a depth gauge. Adjustment of the blade is made by a pivoted lever fitting into a series of slots in the blade. The blade is held in position by a cap iron and cuts with the honing and grinding facets facing down.

The movable side fence is adjustable by sliding along a steel rod, screwed to the body of the plane. The depth gauge should be set from the protruding blade edge to give an accurate indication of the depth of the rebate.

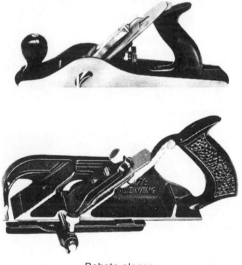

Rebate planes

Method of Use

The initial cut should be made at the front of the rebate with the plane held at a slight incline to the face of the timber stock. Gradually proceed backwards, lengthening the rebate each time until the full length of the rebate has been reached. It is then possible to remove a full length shaving of the rebate. If stopped rebates are required the blade may be moved to the front or bull nose position.

When planing a rebate *along* the grain it is sufficient to use the adjustable side fence or to clamp service material on to the timber stock against which the plane may be held.

For rebating *across* the grain, the timber stock must first be knife cut and sawn to depth.

Where possible, rebating should always occur *with* the grain. If in doubt as to the grain direction, a fine trial shaving is taken—the plane will dig in and tear opposing grain.

Planing a rebate

Side Rebate

This plane is used for side rebating in mouldings and grooves. It has two blades, one crossing the other, set at a low, oblique angle to allow for the trimming of tight corners and may be used in either direction.

The nose pieces are removable and the blades may be individually set.

Side rebate plane

Using side rebate plane to clean up a rebate

Router

The router is used to produce trenches of uniform depth. A trench may be defined as a rectangular recess running across the grain of timber stock. This plane, sometimes referred to as a Granny's Tooth, may also be used for backgrounds of relief carving and recesses for inlay work. For purposes of wide trenches, the sole of the plane has provision for an extra base to be attached. Similarly, for narrow trenches, the plane is provided with an adjustable shoe attached to a movable post.

Routers are supplied with two types of cutters, namely a spade-ended blade and a chisel-ended blade. The latter may be termed a general purpose blade while the spade-ended is used in sharp corners which will not

accommodate the chisel point. Also provided is a small adjustable fence which enables the router to produce grooves near the edge of timber stock while also being able to follow shallow curves.

Router plane

Method of Use

When cutting trenches using a hand router, the bulk of the waste material is first removed by using a chisel and mallet. The router cutter is then adjusted to the gauge line, indicating the trench depth. This is done by resting the router on the timber stock and easing or lowering the cutter until the cutter edge rests in the gauge line groove. Holding the router to give a slicing cut and working from both edges towards the centre, the trench bottom is levelled.

Using a router plane to clean up a trench

Bull Nose Plane

This is a useful plane for cleaning up stopped rebates, chamfers, and stopped chamfers. Approximately 100 mm in length and 25 mm wide it may be held and used in one hand.

The blade, which is the width of the body, is held at 15° with the bevel up. The method of adjustment may vary, some having an

Bull nose planes

adjustable blade while others have the nose detached. With the detachable nose, it is possible to use it as a chisel plane, thereby enabling use into stopped ends of rebates.

Using a bull nose plane to clean up a rebate

Bull nose plane with front removed cleaning up a stopped rebate

Shoulder Plane

The shoulder plane is mainly used for trueing up shoulders of tenons and rebates. This plane combines the functions of shoulder rabbet, bull nose, and chisel plane. In all aspects it is identical with the bull nose rabbet plane but with the addition of a detachable front extension.

Shoulder planes

Combination Plane

The combination plane may be used as a rebate or plough plane as well as a variety of moulding planes. It is, however, a complex tool. It can be adjusted for width and depth of cut as well as for blade setting. The cutters are also variable. To a large extent the combination plane has succeeded the traditional moulding plane because of its versatility. It is, by comparison, cumbersome, but does allow the cutting of a wide range of sections.

The combination plane encompasses such operations as ploughing or grooving, rebating, trenching, beading, and matching.

Combination plane

Block Plane

This plane is particularly useful for small end grain planing due to the low angle of the blade (20° to 12°). It may be held in one or both hands and is available either with an adjustable or fixed blade. For fine and more intricate work the mouth is also adjustable as well as the depth of cut and lateral movement. The blade is held in position with bevel uppermost.

Block plane

Plough Plane

'Ploughing' may be defined as producing a groove. The sash fillister or plough plane may be used to produce grooves as well as rebates. Its construction is similar to that of the rebate plane but the sole is generally thinner than the cutting edge. This enables the cut produced by the blade to accommodate the sole as the groove deepens.

The groove is cut by marking from the front towards the back as with the rebate plane. It is necessary to exert an inward pressure against the fence with the left hand to prevent the blade from following any grain movement. When cutting a groove wider than the blade, cut the groove nearest the timber edge first, otherwise the depth gauge cannot operate.

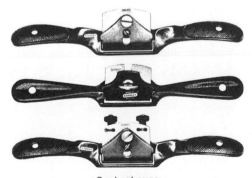

Ploughing a groove

Spokeshaves

Spokeshaves are short-soled planes used for cutting and smoothing curves. Metal spokeshaves are of two patterns, with a flat sole suitable for convex or outside curves, or a curved sole for shallow concave or inside curves.

The more accepted spokeshave has two adjusting screws which enable the blade to be finely set.

The spokeshave consists of a body or stock containing the mouth and short sole, either end of which are the two raised handles with thumb inserts at the rear. The adjusting screws fit through two slots at the top of the blade which is held firm by means of a cap iron.

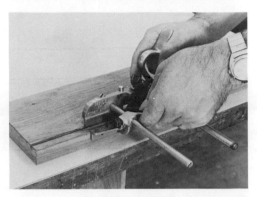

Spokeshaves

Method of Use

Holding the spokeshave with the 3–1 thumb grip and allowing the wrists to move freely, plane with the grain. For convex surfaces this means working from the centre towards the end, while hollows are planed from the end

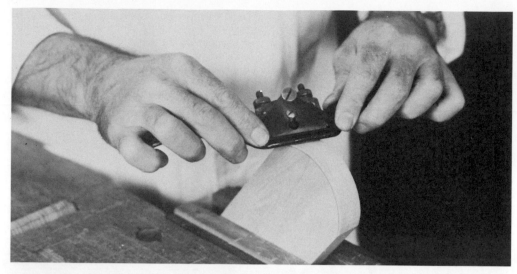

Using spokeshave to plane a curve

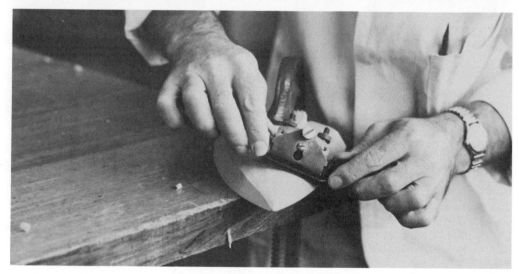

Using spokeshave to shape a bowl

towards the centre. It is important that the edges be kept square. To prevent 'chattering' or jumping the spokeshave may be held at an angle to provide a slicing cut and the sole wiped constantly on an oil pad.

Uses

Flat sole—cutting flat or convex narrow surfaces.
Curved sole—cutting concave (shallow) narrow surfaces.
Compound curves—stopped chamfers.

Compass Plane

This plane is similar in construction to most bench planes, with one exception, the flexible sole. By means of a large thumbscrew attached to the outside of the sole the curvature of the flexible sole may be changed from convex to flat or to concave.

The flexible steel base on this plane is adjustable for cutting regular convex or concave shapes. It is difficult to use but more effective than the spokeshave for long smooth curves. Work with the grain at all times when planing around a shape.

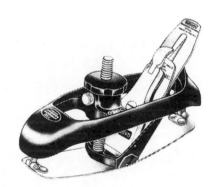

Compass plane

Surform Tools

These are in the form of many razor sharp teeth set at a scientifically developed angle in a hardened and tempered tool steel blade. This ensures controlled depth of cut. No clogging is possible because every tooth has an aperture through which all cuttings pass. Available as file, plane, and block plane.

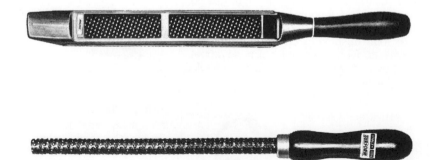

FILES

File Terminology

The vital part of a file consists of a number of teeth. The teeth form the cut. Differences in cut are termed single cut, double cut, rasp cut, diagonally milled teeth, and milled curved teeth.

How to order files

A file is designated by

Name or Number: The name refers to the shape, type, and use. Example: half round rasp, taper saw file, hand file, etc.

Length: Measured exclusive of the tang and as a rule given in mm.

Coarseness of Cut: The coarseness of cut is measured by the number of teeth per centimetre, measured perpendicularly to the tooth. Differences in coarseness are termed coarse, bastard, second cut, smooth, dead smooth.

Types

Half Round: This is a universal file for filing concave, convex, and flat surfaces. It is also suitable for filing large holes. Half round files are available from 100 mm to 400 mm in bastard, second cut, and smooth.

Round: These files are used for opening up holes and filing concave surfaces. Available in lengths from 100mm to 400 mm in bastard cut, second cut, and smooth, in lengths from 150 mm to 300 mm.

Triangular Taper Saw Files: These are designed for the exacting work of saw sharpening. The lengths vary from 75 mm to 200 mm in heavy taper, 75 mm to 250 mm in regular taper, 100 mm to 250 mm in slim taper, and 100 mm to 200 mm in extra slim taper. As a general rule, the side of the file selected should be slightly more than twice the depth of the saw teeth.

Use of file in wood sculpture

Rasps

Both the half round bastard rasp and the cabinet rasp may be used for the shaping of timber. However, the tooth shape produces a torn surface and care must be used to avoid splintering the edges. Consequently, it is necessary to use a file and abrasive paper following rough shaping with a rasp. They are available in regular and smooth cut and in lengths of 150 mm to 350 mm.

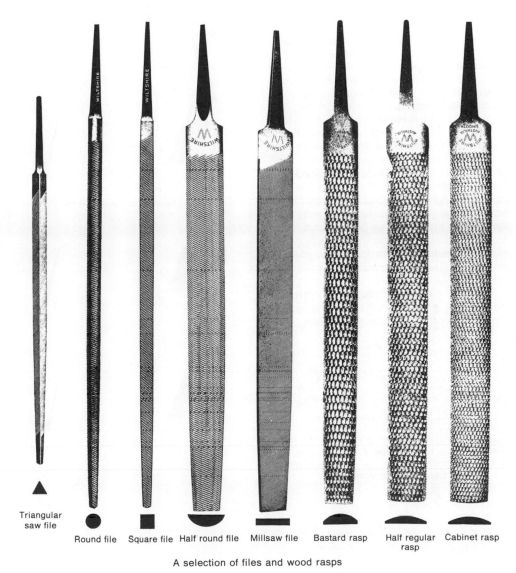

Triangular saw file · Round file · Square file · Half round file · Millsaw file · Bastard rasp · Half regular rasp · Cabinet rasp

A selection of files and wood rasps

Files Commonly Used on Different Saws

Rip Saw	3.5 to 5 point	200 mm Slim Taper to 175 mm Slim Taper
Cross Cut	6 to 8 point	175 mm Slim Taper to 150 mm Extra Slim Taper
Panel	8 to 10 point	150 mm Slim Taper to 125 mm Extra Slim Taper
Tenon	10 to 12 point	100 mm Slim Taper to 100 mm Extra Slim Taper
Dovetail	14 to 16 point	100 mm Slim Taper to 100 mm Extra Slim Taper

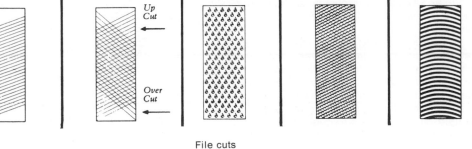

| Single Cut | Double Cut | Rasp Cut | Diagonally milled teeth | Milled curved teeth |

File cuts

15

SAWS

Saws may be classified into hand saws, back saws, and curve cutting saws, depending on the size and shape of the teeth. Rip saws, for example, are designed to sever fibres along or with the grain while crosscutting saws are used primarily across the grain. The teeth are measured by the number of points per 25 mm. Thus a 14 point saw has smaller teeth and produces a finer saw cut than a 6 point saw.

The majority of saws have adjacent teeth bent out from the blade in opposite directions. This is known as *set* and prevents the saw from jamming by providing clearance for the blade. To assist clearance further, quality hand saw blades are both skew backed and taper-ground. In these saws the thickness or gauge of the toothed edge is uniform throughout its length, but gradually tapers towards the back or top of the blade.

The saw cut thus produced by ripping or crosscutting and referred to as the *kerf* is slightly wider than the blade thickness.

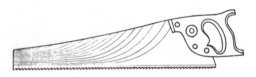

Diagram illustrates taper grinding. This radial grinding thin to back ensures clearance in the cut, permits minimum set on the teeth and makes sawing infinitely easier.

Number of points per 25 mm

Kerf

The cut produced by ripping or crosscutting is referred to as the saw kerf.

On all saws the kerf must be slightly wider than the thickness of the blade to avoid jamming.

To prevent this the teeth are 'set', i.e. alternate teeth are bent outwards very slightly so that the kerf will provide sufficient clearance for easy movement of the blade. To assist further in the clearance, blades are taper-ground. In these saws the thickness or gauge of the toothed edge is uniform throughout its length but gradually tapers towards the back or top of the blade.

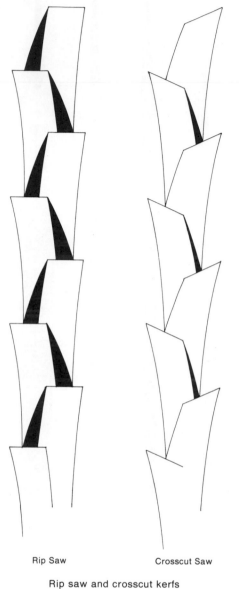

Rip Saw   Crosscut Saw

Rip saw and crosscut kerfs

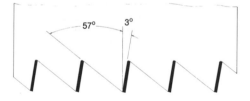

Crosscut Saw

clearance

knife points sever fibres

Kerf clearance

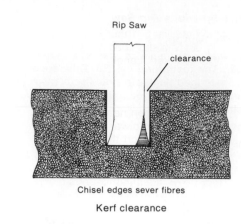

Rip Saw

clearance

Chisel edges sever fibres

Kerf clearance

Hand Saws

Rip Saws

These are distinguishable by the shape of the teeth, which are chisel like and sharpened at right angles to the length of the blade. They have been specifically designed to cut rapidly with the direction of the grain, hence the term 'ripping'. The length of the blade varies from 600 mm to 700 mm with 3 to 6 points per 25 mm.

Hand saw

57°   3°

Rip saw teeth

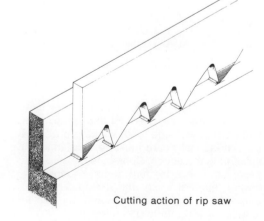

Cutting action of rip saw

Cutting with a Rip Saw

Using the familiar 3–1 thumb grip, commence the saw cut with short backward strokes. This will produce a kerf. Lengthen the strokes until the full length of the blade is in use. As the stroke is lengthened, maintain a cutting angle of 45° and apply only slight pressure on the forward stroke. When nearing the end of the saw cut reduce the forward pressure, the rate of cutting, and support the offcut material to prevent the tearing of fibre.

Short lengths of timber stock may be held in a bench vice and ripped by sawing halfway through and then reversing. Longer boards, however, will require laying on one or more saw trestles.

Rip saw cutting along the grain

Crosscut Saws

These are used for cutting across the grain of thicker timber and may be used for ripping thin material. They are similar in appearance to rip saws, but have slightly smaller teeth shaped like pointed knife edges. The length of the blade varies from 500 mm to 700 mm with 5 to 9 points per 25 mm.

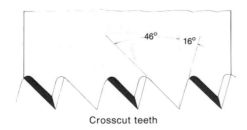

Crosscut teeth

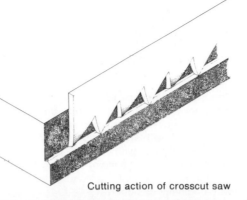

Cutting action of crosscut saw

Cutting with a Crosscut Saw

Holding the material firmly, commence the saw cut gently, with the saw held at a low angle to the timber stock. Having established a kerf, raise the saw angle to 30° and lengthen the stroke to use the full blade length. To maintain a square and straight cut, the elbow, hand, and saw blade must travel in the same plane. As with the rip saw, on nearing the completion of the saw cut the forward pressure and rate of sawing are reduced and support is given to the offcut material.

Using hand saw to cut across the grain

Panel Saw

This saw is the most versatile of the hand saw group. For all general purpose work, a panel saw 500 to 600 mm long with 10 to 12 points per 25 mm is most satisfactory. Generally the panel saw is used for finer work both along and across the grain. Again it is similar in appearance to the rip and crosscut saws but it is smaller and lighter and with teeth of the crosscut type.

The panel saw, having finer and smaller teeth than the ordinary crosscut saws, produces a clean and accurate saw cut when used on sheet material. It is also useful for cutting the cheeks of large tenons.

Cutting with a Panel Saw

When sawing sheet material across the grain it is necessary to knife cut both the top and bottom surfaces. This is particularly important when using veneered manufactured boards as the veneer layer is extremely thin and often brittle. For cutting with the grain a clear pencil line is sufficient. Supporting the sheet on trestles, hold the panel saw at a low angle and gently draw back just on the waste side of the line. The thumb of the supporting hand should be used as a guide while the kerf is being established. Use the full length of the blade, applying slight pressure only on the forward stroke.

When cutting sheet materials less than 6 mm thick a tenon saw should be used, as the smaller teeth provide a finer cut and the steel rib enables greater accuracy.

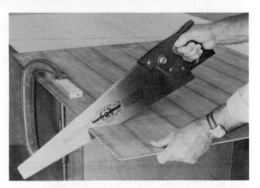

Panel saw cutting plywood panels

Back Saws

The tenon saw and dovetail saw belong to the group known as back saws because of the brass or steel stiffening rib attached to the back or top of the thin blade. This holds the blade rigid enabling accurate bench work to be carried out. The blade of these saws is rectangular in shape.

Tenon Saw

Tenon saws are used for general bench work and are available in 300 mm, 350 mm, and 400 mm blade lengths with 10 to 12 points per 25 mm. Since the tenon saw is designed to produce accurate bench work, it is essential that marking out across the grain be knife cut.

Tenon saw

Tenon Sawing to a Knife Cut Line

Secure the timber stock and place the saw blade against the thumb so that the teeth are just touching the knife cut line but the kerf is on the waste side. Holding the saw with the 3–1 thumb grip, lock the wrist so that the saw blade, wrist, and arm move in direct line. Taking the weight of the saw, gently make a few short strokes with the toe of the blade held at a slight angle to the timber stock. As the kerf is produced, slowly lower the saw blade until the kerf is the full width of the timber stock. Full blade length strokes may now be made with the blade moving parallel to the timber surface.

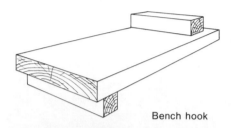

Bench hook

Holding a timber on bench hook

Tenon saw is used for general bench work and joint cutting

If stock is to be cut through, ensure that service material is located underneath to prevent the tearing of fibre.

The accuracy in starting a saw cut is essential. The closer the saw cut to a knife cut line or gauge line, the easier the final processes.

The following should be noted: *squaring to length*—the closer the removal of waste, the

less cleaning up required; *sawing tenons*—the greater the distance of the saw cut from the gauge line, the more paring required; *shoulder cuts*— require the knife cut lines to be split in half thus eliminating the need for paring.

Dovetail Saw

This is a smaller version of the tenon saw, with a thinner blade and finer teeth, and is used for cutting dovetails and other very fine, accurate work. The blade varies from 175 mm to 250 mm in length with 15 to 16 points per 25 mm. Because of the ease of handling it is often used in bench work for which the tenon saw was originally designed.

The teeth, although shaped like those of a tenon saw, are sharpened similarly to a rip saw. Consequently, when resharpening considerable skill is required to ensure that the shape and spacing remain even.

Dovetail saw

Mitre Box

Mitre boxes enable very accurate sawing of all angles between 45° and 90°. The back, frame, and graduated quadrant are cast in one piece and having a tie bar bracing the saw guides, absolute rigidity is provided.

The quadrant is graduated in degrees and numbered for sawing 5-, 6-, 8-, and 12-sided figures. The double locking, self clamping swivel is fitted with a pin which locks into any of the numbered index holes. In addition, the swivel can be clamped at any position between these holes. Stock guides, located on the base, hold all ordinary work tightly against the back. They provide support for curved and irregular shaped pieces. The length stop, attached to the front of the frame by a thumbscrew, allows for duplicate work

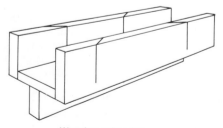

Wooden mitre box

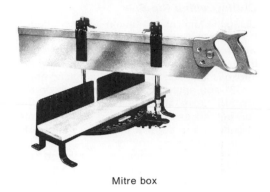

Mitre box

and may be used either on the right or left side. For longer members it may be fastened on the back of the frame with an extension stop attached.

Curve Cutting Saws

Coping Saw

This is considered the best all-purpose saw for cutting curves. It will cut almost any shape and is limited only by the distance between the blade and spring saw frame. The coping saw has a very fine crosscutting blade fitted between two retaining pins at each end of the frame.

Uses include cutting curves in thin timber, scribing on mouldings, and cutting curved shapes for templets.

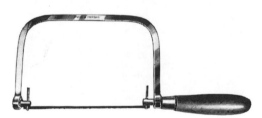

Coping saw

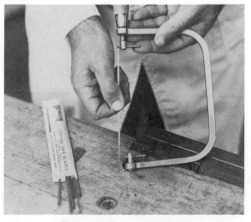

Fitting blade to coping saw

Bow Saw

The bow saw has a narrow parallel blade (6 mm) approximately 300 mm in length. It is limited to shallower curves than the coping saw but provides a faster cutting rate and is suitable for thicker material. The blade is held in a wooden frame with tension supplied by a string and twitching rod.

Compass Saw

This has an open-shaped handle with a stiff narrow tapering blade 300 mm to 450 mm long with 10 to 12 points per 25 mm.

It is used for cutting curved surfaces where a bow saw is inoperable. For internal cutting a hole may be required through which the blade may pass. Compass saws are also available as a 'nest of saws', having interchangeable blades.

Keyhole or Pad Saws

Keyhole saws have a tapering blade 250 mm to 300 mm long, held to the handle by two set screws. They are used for keyholes and small curves.

Hack Saw

This consists of an adjustable bow frame attached to a closed or pistol grip handle. The correct blade tension is applied by turning a thumbscrew at the open end of the bow frame. New blades should be replaced to have the teeth angle facing away from the operator, i.e. as with all saws, the hacksaw should cut only on the push stroke.

Use

For cutting softer metals.

Cutting curves with coping saw

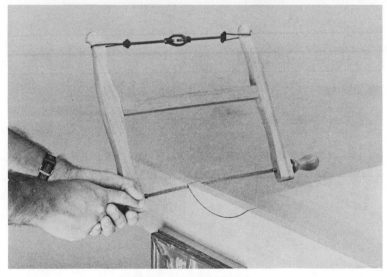

Cutting curves with bow saw

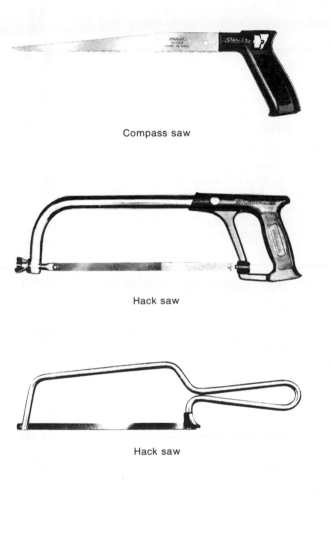

Compass saw

Hack saw

Hack saw

Keyhole or Pad saw

CHISELS

With the exception of the socket mortise, all chisels are similar in construction. They may be described as having a tool steel blade ground to a bevel at one end, with the other end fitting into a wooden or plastic handle by means of a square tapered tang. These are referred to as tanged chisels. In the socket type chisel, the handle is tapered to fit into a forged socket at one end of the blade.

Chisels may be classified into three main groups: firmer chisels, paring chisels, and mortise chisels.

Firmer Chisels

These are the most popular and widely used of the wood chisels. They are used in joinery, cabinet making, and bench work where accuracy is essential.

Plain Firmer

These chisels have a rectangular blade with a circular shoulder at the base of the tang. Sizes vary from 2 mm to 50 mm width of blade.

Bevelled Edge Firmer

This chisel allows easier cleaning up and there is less interference when paring. This is because of the bevels machined on the two long edges of the blade. However, the bevelled edged firmer is not as strong as the plain firmer. It is available in blade widths from 2 mm to 50 mm.

Butt Firmer

This is a short bevelled edge firmer, 60 mm to 75 mm in length and used for the accurate sinking of hinges, locks, and other similar fittings.

Registered Firmer

This chisel has a strong ferrule at the top and bottom of a wooden handle. A leather washer is located between the bottom ferrule and bolster to absorb the shock. The registered pattern is of robust construction for rough work in hard timbers where joiner's accuracy is not so essential.

Paring Chisel

This is similar in construction to the bevelled edge firmer but has a considerably longer blade. It is most suitable for all types of paring work and in particular the intricate shapes involved in patternmaking.

Mortise Chisel

Socket Mortise

The handle, which may be provided with a ferrule, is tapered to fit into a forged socket on the end of the blade. The blade is thicker and stronger than other chisels, permitting heavy blows with a mallet and enabling considerable leverage to be used.

Paring chisel

Paring gouge

Socket chisel

Firmer chisel

Firmer gouge

Butt firmer

Socket mortise

Registered firmer

Bevelled edge firmer

Scribing gouge

GOUGES

Gouges are a form of chisel with the blade curved in cross section.

Firmer Gouge

This gouge is ground and sharpened on the round or outside surface. It is used for carving, cabinetry, joinery, patternmaking, shaping, and sculpture.

Paring Gouge

This is ground and sharpened on the inside surface. It has a limited use but is handy where small convex surfaces are required. Patternmakers use it extensively.

The size of a gouge is determined by measuring across the blade.

Gouges are available in various curvatures and although they may be the same size they can produce different shaped curves. The curvature is indicated by a number.

Paring a Shoulder Cut

Knife cut the line to position using a try square and marking knife.

Firmly hold the timber stock to be pared by clamping to the bench top or placing in a vice.

Using a bevelled edge firmer chisel, position one corner of the blade 1 mm from the knife cut line and 1 mm below the top surface.

By raising the opposite corner 20° and paring across the timber stock an angular shoulder is formed.

Paring a Curve

Clearly mark the curve section on one surface of the timber stock.

Securely hold the material to the bench surface with service material underneath.

Holding the chisel vertically pare one corner to 45°.

Pare the opposite corner to 45°.

Maintaining the vertical chisel position, pare the corners left by the vertical cuts.

Continue this process until the curve consists of a series of small flats.

Finish by using a spokeshave or file.

Cold Chisel

A cold chisel is useful for cutting any material that is not tempered, e.g. rivets, steel, concrete, pipes, etc.

Quality cold chisels limit the amount of feathering at the hammer end, thus reducing the possibility of steel chips being thrown off. Similarly, they may be resharpened with a file, rather than a grindstone where there is the danger of drawing the temper.

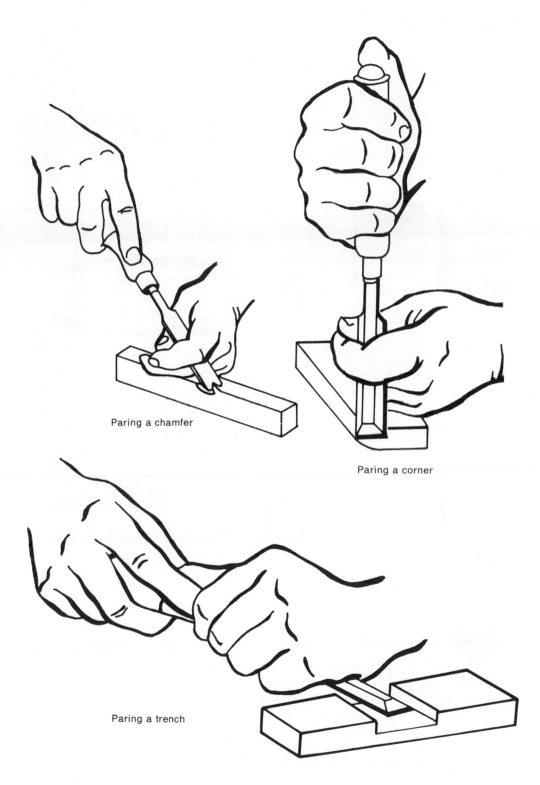

Paring a chamfer

Paring a corner

Paring a trench

Cold chisel

BORING TOOLS

Brace

The brace is used to hold and provide leverage for wood bits having a square tang. The size of the brace is determined by the sweep or the diameter of the circle when the bow is rotated through 360°. Modern braces are fitted with a ratchet enabling the bit to be rotated in either direction. This allows boring in confined spaces by moving the bow through an arc instead of a full sweep.

Brace

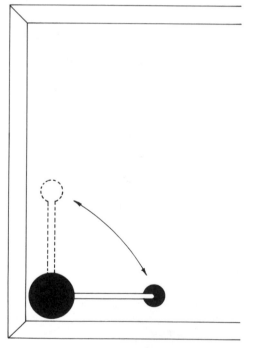

Using a ratchet brace in a corner

Method of Use

Fit the required bit between the alligator jaws by turning the chuck against the direction of bow rotation.

Where possible secure the material and bore in the horizontal position. This requires less effort and gives greater accuracy.

Locate the lead screw into position and apply a forward pressure by holding the handle against the body while turning the bow in a clockwise direction.

Fitting a bit into a brace

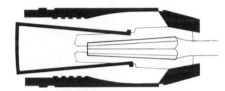

Sectional view of a brace chuck

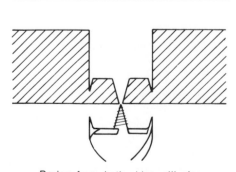

Boring hole using service material to prevent splitting.

Boring from both sides will also prevent splitting

Sight the bit for horizontal and/or vertical accuracy.

Continue boring until the lead screw point appears on the opposite side.

Continue clockwise rotation, but pull backwards on the brace.

To wind anti-clockwise will serve only to loosen the chuck.

Reverse the material and complete the hole.

Where boring is impossible from both sides secure a scrap block behind the hole and bore through into it.

Boring hole with brace and bit

Using a brace and countersinking bit

Counterboring using service material

NOTE

The basic function of the lead screw is to pull the bit through the timber. Consequently, once the lead screw is exposed, the cutting action relies on the push exerted on the brace. This may result in the excessive splitting of the wood fibre. It is therefore essential that boring occur either (a) from both sides, or (b) using a scrap block secured behind the hole.

If holes of a prescribed depth are required, as in dowel joints, depth gauges should be used. Manufactured varieties consist of a hollow steel tube and locking screw allowing for positive location at any depth. They may also be constructed by using a drilled piece of scrap timber cut to the necessary length or by wrapping masking tape around the wood bit at the required depth.

Hand Drill

The hand drill or wheel brace, although primarily designed for metal working, is widely used by woodworkers for such purposes as drilling and countersinking screw holes. Drive is provided through a pair of bevelled tooth wheels which serve to turn the direction of rotation through 90°.

The self-centring three jaw chuck is designed to hold plain cylindrical shank twist drills up to 8 mm in diameter. The majority of hand drills have a detachable side handle which is useful when more pressure or greater control is required.

Hand drill

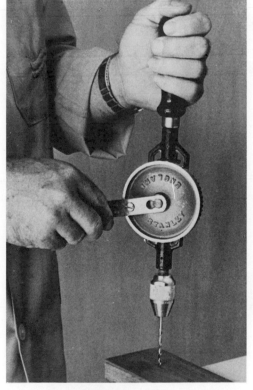

Using a hand drill

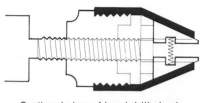

Sectional view of hand drill chuck

Bits

Auger or Twist Bits

Although auger bits have different patterns, their construction is basically similar. Each bit has a fine or coarse lead screw pulling it into the timber. The twisted shank provides for accurate deep boring and an exit for waste material produced by the two cutters. For boring in softwood it is recommended that the cutters be equipped with spurs. The Jennings pattern, generally associated with a double twist shank, and the Irwin pattern, having a single twist or solid centre, are the two most widely used patterns.

Jennings Nose: This is a general purpose bit used for boring soft to medium grained timbers.

Solid Centre Nose: Of general purpose design, but mainly used on softwoods.

Scotch Nose: Designed especially for boring all types of hardwoods and is obtainable with a coarse or fine thread.

Spur Nose: Often used for boring pored timbers requiring a neat, well-finished hole.

Speed Bore Nose: These bits have a cutting action similar to that of the centre bit and are ideally suited where the rate of boring is more important than the finish.

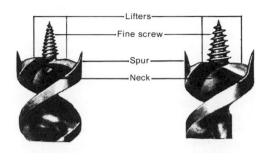

Jennings nose   Solid centre nose

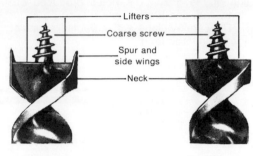

Spur nose   Scotch nose

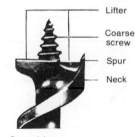

Speed bore nose

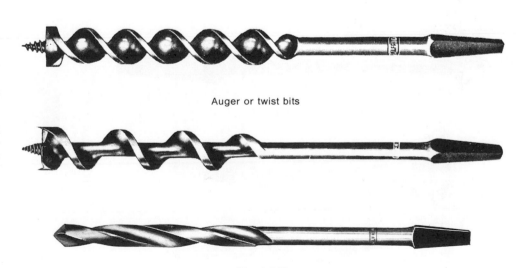

Auger or twist bits

Wood drill

Expansive Bit

This is similar to the centre bit in respect of form and cutting action, but allows variation of size. It is produced in two sizes to bore 12 mm to 38 mm and 22 mm to 75 mm. Each pattern is supplied with two interchangeable cutters graduated in size for easy adjustment.

Countersink Bit

This is available in two patterns, rosehead and snailhorn, and in sizes ranging from 6 mm to 25 mm. Used for chamfering holes to accommodate screw heads or dowels.

Forstner Bit

Unlike other bits the 'Forstner' is guided by its circular rim and is unaffected by knots or direction of the grain. The holes produced are clean, true and flat bottomed.

They are available with a parallel shank or square tapered fang.

Centre Bit

These bits differ in form from auger bits but have a similar cutting action. A centre point precedes the spur which cuts the extremity of the hole, followed by the cutter which removes the waste. Use is limited to boring shallow holes.

Dowel Trimmer

These are used for chamfering the ends of dowels to enable easier location when constructing dowel joints. They have an internal mouth diameter of 20 mm and are approximately 75 mm in length.

Dowel Jig

The dowel jig enables dowel holes to be bored in the edge, end, or surface of work with ease and accuracy. It may be used to make butted corners, mitre joints, butt joints, and is an excellent guide for mortising.

Graduations permit direct reading and accurate setting of the jig to the centreline of work. For the best result, Russell Jennings auger bits are recommended. A depth gauge may be used with or without the jig.

Screwdriver Bit

These bits allow greater purchase power and hence easier and faster screw insertion. They are particularly useful when screwing into pored timbers or where a large number of screws are required. They range in size from 6 mm to 25 mm.

Bradawls

The bradawl provides the starting holes for screws or drills. It may have either a square or tapered point. It should be used only with hand pressure in a back and forth motion and at right angles to the timber surface.

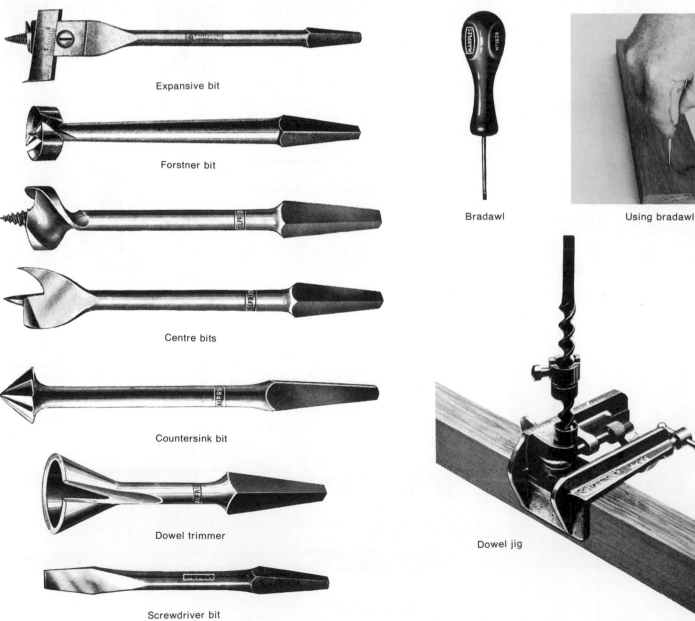

Expansive bit

Forstner bit

Centre bits

Countersink bit

Dowel trimmer

Screwdriver bit

Bradawl

Using bradawl

Dowel jig

SCRAPERS

Hand scrapers are used to produce smooth surfaces following planing and in particular for timbers with sloping grain.

Types

Rectangular scrapers consist of a small flat section of tool steel and may be used by a pushing or pulling stroke. Their use is limited to smoothing flat surfaces.

Pear shaped scrapers, so called by their form, are used for smoothing hollowed surfaces.

Cabinet scrapers have an adjustable rectangular blade held within a metal frame similar to that of a spokeshave. They are used where extensive scraping is required and cut only on the push stroke.

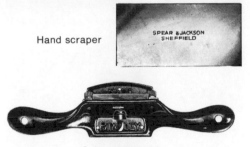

Hand scraper

Cabinet scraper

Method of Use

Hold the scraper in both hands with the fingers on one side and the thumbs towards the centre on the other. Exert a pressure on the thumbs to cause a slight curvature in the scraper, and push forward at an angle of 75° to the work. If the scraper is used with a pulling stroke the curvature pressure is applied by the fingers.

Using cabinet scraper to clean up drawer front

Using hand scraper

SCREWDRIVERS

The woodworker's basic screwdriver is of two types:
(1) the standard pattern which has a round blade and either a wooden or plastic handle
(2) the cabinet pattern which has a round blade with an oval wooden handle.

Quality screwdrivers have a bolster forged on the handle end of the blade to provide strength for turning. Similarly, the tips of the blades should be cross ground and tapered to allow holding power in the screw slots.

Ratchet screwdrivers have proved very popular and for some applications are almost a necessity. This form of screwdriver is available in various types from the small size, having a ratchet action only, to the larger spiral blade action types which drive the screw by a quick downward pressure, but without turning the handle.

The introduction of Pozidriv fasteners, replacing Phillips head fasteners, has provided an improved screwdriver shape. This has resulted in less damage to screw heads and consequently less damage to the screwdriver tip.

With the cross ground tip form of screwdriver it is important to touch up the shape continually using a file or grinder. This prevents the blade from slipping and spoiling both the screw slot edges and the tip. Care should be taken not to draw the temper if a power grinder is used.

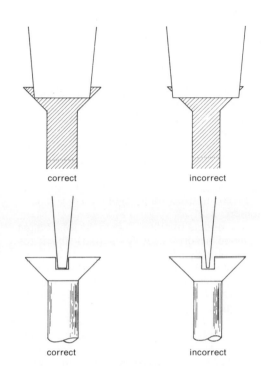

correct   incorrect

correct   incorrect

A correct fitting screwdriver is essential

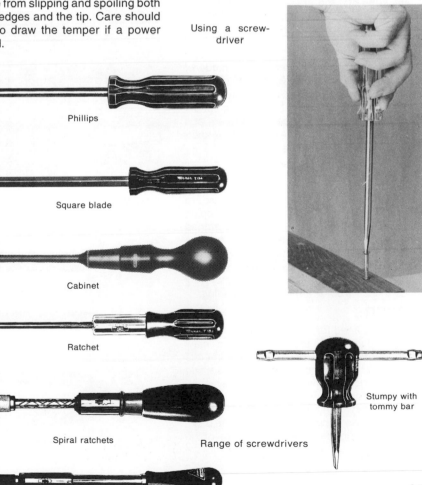

Using a screwdriver

Phillips

Square blade

Cabinet

Ratchet

Spiral ratchets

Stumpy with tommy bar

Range of screwdrivers

HAMMERS

The cabinetmaker, joiner or hobbyist generally has at least two types of hammers, a claw hammer and a cross pened hammer. By virtue of physical size the claw hammer is associated with the driving and removal of larger nails while the cross pene is useful for smaller nails and brads. When selecting a claw hammer consideration should be given to the following:

1. The hammer head should be of forged steel to prevent shattering and to protect the claws from breakage.
2. The claws should be uniformly split and bevelled to allow removal of the finest pins or brads.
3. Wooden handles should be of straight grained hickory, securely wedged to the heads and correctly balanced.
4. Steel shafts must be covered with a suitable cushioned grip which resists slippage.
5. The striking face should be slightly crowned.
6. Nail holder—to allow the user to drive nails overhead or in similar difficult positions.

For general purposes a 425 g to 560 g claw hammer is most satisfactory. The Warrington hammer, also known as a joiner's hammer, has a cross pene in place of a claw. This pene enables the starting of small brads and tacks held between the fingers. Warrington hammers vary from 112 g to 280 g.

MALLET

The carpenter's mallet has a head made of hard tough timber, Beech, Brush Box or Myrtle Beech. A tapered mortise is cut through the head to accommodate the handle. The handle is tapered to fit the mortise in the head, and shaped to suit the hand. Ash Beech or spotted gum would be suitable timbers.

NAIL PUNCH

This consists of a solid bar of high grade tool steel hardened at both ends. The heads are shaped to prevent hammer blows slipping from the tool. The shanks are machine knurled with the heads and tips polished. Punches are used to set the heads of nails below the surface of timber. The tips are cupped, chamfered, and heat treated for toughness. They range in size from 0.7 mm to 3.5 mm tips.

PINCERS

Pincers are used for removing brads or small nails in positions inaccessible to a claw hammer or when a Warrington hammer is being used. One pincer handle end has a fine claw enabling well-driven brads to be removed sufficiently for the jaws to grip.

There are two main types available—tower pattern and the Lancashire pattern—the basic difference being the square jaws shape of the latter.

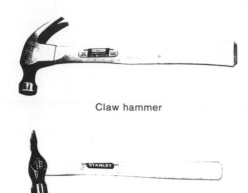

Claw hammer

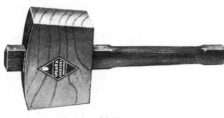

Warrington cross pened hammer

Mallet

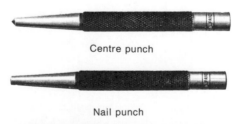

Using mallet to remove waste from a trench

Centre punch

Nail punch

Pincers

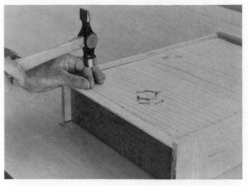

A cross pened hammer is ideal for fixing the bottom to a drawer

A claw hammer is essential for nailing heavy framing

Wrecking bar: Wrecking bars are manufactured from hexagonal sectioned steel, hardened and tempered and designed to provide maximum result with minimum effort. They are produced in sizes from 300 x 12 to 900 x 19. They provide effective leverage and are ideal for extracting nails.

Putty knife: These tools have blades of highly tempered steel, a ferrule and a quality timber handle. They are ideal for stopping screw and nail holes before surface finishing.

Pliers: These are drop-forged from fine quality steels, hardened and tempered with pipe grip and cutting edges, and finished to fine tolerances.

CLAMPS

Clamps are available in numerous types and sizes to suit many applications.

The G clamp is often used for holding timber stock firmly to the bench for the purpose of sawing, chiselling, or planing. It may also be used in the process of gluing small members.

Construction

G clamps consist of a malleable or dropped forge frame, with a machine cut screw thread and swivel button. Sizes range from 150 mm to 300 mm.

Quick Action Clamp

Although similar in function to the G clamp, the quick action clamp has the advantage of instant adjustment to the required capacity. Since it is self-locking with pressure adjustable by a plastic grip handle, it has proved a useful clamping medium for both carpenters and cabinet makers. Sizes range from 150 mm to 600 mm.

Joiner's Clamps

These include the *bar clamp*, consisting of a T bar with a fixed and movable shoe, and the *sash clamp*, similar in construction, but having a rectangular bar section. The malleable fittings of the bar clamp have been given increased length and are heavier in section around the T slot of the jaw castings where the strain is greatest. Standard sizes range from 600 mm to 2.4 m.

Both types of joiner's clamps are used for assembly and gluing of frames, carcasses, etc.

Mitre Corner Clamps

These are used for testing and gluing mitre joints as used in light frame construction. They are applied to the outside of the joint corner which fully exposes both sides of the joint.

Web Clamps

These consist of a webbing belt attached to a ratchet tensioning wheel usually tightened by means of a screwdriver. They are particularly adaptable for applying pressure in areas unsuited to normal clamping procedures, e.g. curved laminating projects, small picture frames, etc. To prevent the Web clamp adhering to the project, the glue contact areas should be protected by using metal corner brackets or waxed paper.

Edge Clamps

These are used for applying edging material to straight or curved surfaces where the opposite edge may not be accessible.

Pipe Clamps

These use a threaded length of water pipe as the bar section. A special spring-loaded shoe is adjustable to lock in any position along the pipe. These are particularly useful as their size is limited only by the length of pipe.

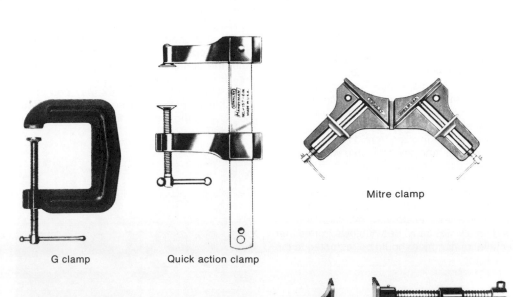

Mitre clamp

G clamp   Quick action clamp

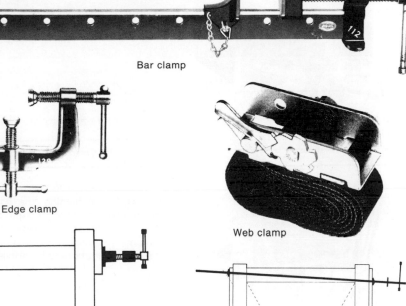

Bar clamp

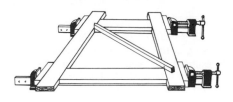

Edge clamp

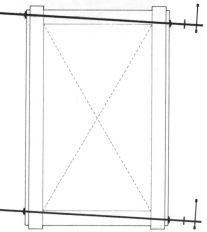

Web clamp

Clamp must be parallel to the rail to ensure squareness of frame

Squaring a frame

Squaring a frame by adjusting the bar clamps. Move the clamps in the direction of the long diagonal

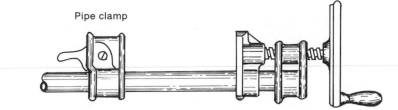

Pipe clamp

VICES

The woodworker's bench vice facilitates many basic operations, including planing, sawing, chiselling, and clamping. To this end it is advantageous to fit the largest vice possible in order to obtain the maximum grip over the biggest area.

Vices range in size from 175 mm to 250 mm openings and are available with or without quick action mechanisms.

The vice jaws should be fitted with wooden jaw liners to protect the material from bruising. Short material should be located centrally in the vice jaws to prevent overstraining the lead screw. Similarly, heavy blows from either a mallet or hammer should be restricted to the bench top.

Woodworker's vice

Woodworker's universal vice

TIMBER PREPARATION

Dressing of Timber

The following steps are indicative of basic timber preparation and are applicable for both hand and machine dressing.

Planing a Face

This involves the selection of the better of the two face surfaces and the establishment of grain direction.

Planing should continue with a reducing depth of cut until, when tested by means of a rule, the surface is found to be flat, straight, free from twists, and smooth to the touch.

At this point a face mark may be applied with the long tail pointing towards the face edge and the shorter indicating the grain direction.

Planing a face

a Select and plane a face

Planing a Face Edge

As with face planing, the selected edge is planed with a reducing depth of cut until testing shows it is square to the face, straight, and smooth. Having met these requirements a face edge mark may be applied.

b Plane and face edge

Gauging and Planing to Width

A marking gauge set to the required width and held against the face edge is used to gauge the width of the stock. A plane is then used to remove the waste accurately down to the line.

c Mark and plane to width

Ideally, the line or indentation should be split in half, but for appearance purposes it is just removed. This point is clearly visible because of the fibres which have been pushed into the stock by the spur of the marking gauge being released and thereby showing clearly as a furry edge. Once the gauge line has been accurately met on all four edges no testing is required. It must be square and straight.

Gauging and Planing to Thickness

The marking gauge is set to the required thickness and used against the face to gauge a line around the four surfaces of the stock. The waste is then removed by means of a plane with the same requirements applying here as they did in planing to width. At this stage the stock may be referred to as P.A.R., i.e. planed all round.

Mark and plane to thickness

Squaring Ends to Length

This involves the use of a try square used against the face and face edge and close to the end of the stock in conjunction with a marking knife. The knife is held firmly against the blade of the try square and made to cut through the top layers of fibres on the face and edge surfaces near the end. The stock is then held firmly in a vice and planed accurately to the knife cut line. From this squared end the length of the stock may now be measured and the process repeated as with the first end.

Square the end to length

Value of Face and Face Edge Marks

Once the face and face edge marks have been applied we know the following:
(1) The surfaces have been tested and found to be true and accurate.
(2) These are the only two surfaces from which marking out may occur. This simplifies the construction and assembly of jobs involving a number of members, i.e. all face marks located on the inside and all face edge marks downwards.

TOOL MAINTENANCE

To maintain handtools in good condition a number of special tools will be necessary.

Bench Grinder

A bench grinder, described in the section on Portable Tools, is a useful aid in any workshop and is essential if tools are to be kept sharp.

Bench grinder

Abrasive wheels

Suitable abrasive wheels are manufactured in aluminium oxide and silicon carbide. The wheels vary in diameter, thickness, and size of hole. They may be purchased to suit nearly any type of machine in a wide range of grit sizes and grades. When ordering a wheel specify the following detail:

1. Diameter of wheel.
2. Width of face.
3. Diameter of bore.
4. Shape.
5. Grain, grade, and bond.
6. Kind of abrasive.
7. Type of work.
8. Type of machine.

Care should be taken not to overheat the edge of cutting tools. They must be cooled regularly by quenching in water. All grinding wheels are breakable and must be installed and used correctly. A wheel breaking in operation can cause serious accidents.

Safety

- Visually inspect all wheels before mounting for possible damage in transit.
- Check maximum operating speed established for wheel against machine speed.
- Check mounting flanges for equal and correct diameter (should be at one-third diameter of the wheel and relieved around hole).
- Be sure work rest is properly adjusted (centre of wheel or above; no more than 2 mm away from wheel).
- Always use a guard covering at least one-half of the grinding wheel.
- Always wear safety glasses or some type of eye protection when grinding.
- Do not force a wheel on to the machine or alter the size of the mounting hole. If a wheel won't fit the machine get one that will.
- Do not tighten the mounting nut excessively.
- Do not grind on the side of the wheel unless wheel is specifically designed for that purpose.
- Do not stand directly in front of a grinding wheel when a grinder is started.
- Do not grind material for which the wheel is not designed.

There are three types of dressing tools in general use:
1. The industrial diamond mounted on a round steel shaft.
2. The abrasive sticks made of silicon carbide in a very hard bond.
3. The mechanical dresser, corrugated steel wheels mounted in a metal handle.

Industrial diamond

Abrasive stick

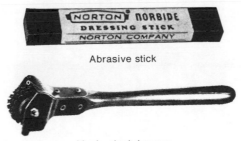

Mechanical dresser

Continued use of abrasive wheels will cause the cutting surface to become worn and clogged with metal particles. To reface the edge of an abrasive wheel the grinder is switched on and a pressing tool is held firmly against the circumference of the wheel and moved slowly across the width of the wheel. This process is continued until the surface of the wheel is true, and all particles have been removed. Safety glasses are essential.

Oilstones

Oilstones are used to put a keen edge on cutting tools. The process is called honing, whetting, or sharpening, and is carried out after grinding.

The most common stones are silicon carbide and aluminium oxide. Natural stones are also available, some being mounted in wooden boxes for protection.

Oil is used on the stone to float off particles of metal and to prevent clogging.

Oilstones must be kept clean and moist. It is desirable to store them in specially covered boxes. They may easily be cleaned with kerosene or turpentine.

Natural stone

Oilslips

These are specially manufactured in various shapes for honing gouges and carving tools, and other tools with curved cutting edges.

Oilslip

Grinding and Sharpening Plane Blades and Chisels

Plane blades and chisels as supplied by the manufacturer already have a ground facet. However, to obtain the most satisfying and accurate results, these facets are further sharpened using an oilstone. This results in two facets, referred to as the grinding facet and sharpening, whetting, or honing facet, being applied to plane and chisel blades.

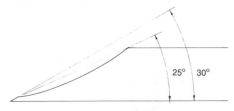

Grinding angle 25°
Sharpening angle 30°

Grinding

The most functional grinding angle has been found to be approximately 25°. This may be varied according to the work situation or the media being used.

Criteria for Grinding: The plane iron or chisel requires grinding when:
1. it becomes gapped due to contact with nails, grit, etc.,
2. the grinding facet becomes too short due to constant resharpening,
3. it becomes out of square or rounded due to poor sharpening.

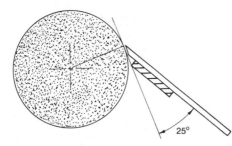

Grinding angle 25°. Rest set at the correct angle to make grinding easier

Grinding Procedure: Hold the blade lightly against the grinding wheel and move it back and forth to ensure even grinding.

To avoid overheating, frequently lift the blade and quench by dipping in water. Failure to do so will result in 'drawing the temper' of the blade, distinguishable by a blue colour.

Grinding should continue until a gap-free, square, and even facet appears across the blade.

The plane blade is held against the grinding wheel and moved to and fro to ensure even grinding

The most functional grinding angle has been found to be approximately 25°

Sharpening

Although the grinding facet is capable of producing a shaving, a keener and longer lasting cutting edge is produced by honing at an angle of 30°.

Honing Procedure: Holding the blade with the right hand, rest the back on the oilstone and remove any grinding burrs.

Turn the blade over, locate the grinding facet on the oilstone, and raise the back slightly. Since the grinding facet is 25°, this gives an approximate angle of 30°.

Rub the blade up and down the oilstone, using a figure 8 motion, until a wire edge is produced.

The blade is held at approx. 30° to the stone

Turn the blade over and lay it absolutely flat on the stone and lightly rub to remove the burr or wire edge.

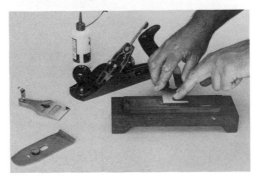

The blade must be absolutely flat on the stone to remove the burr

A final polish may be made by stropping the blade back and forth on a cloth or slicing the cutting edge across the end of a pored timber.

Sharpening a Gouge
Gouges are ground on the edge of an abrasive wheel and it is desirable to adjust the tool rest to the correct angle. They are difficult to grind and must be continually rotated against the wheel to maintain an even shape.

The gouge is honed on an oilstone using a figure 8 pattern. A slipstone is used to remove the wire edge. This is done by holding the gouge firmly against the edge of the bench, holding the stone flat on the inside of the gouge, and rubbing lightly until the burr is removed.

The gouge is ground on the edge of the abrasive wheel. The tool rest is set at the correct angle

The gouge is honed on an oilstone using a figure of 8 pattern

The gouge is held firmly against the edge of the bench and a slip stone used to remove the burr

Sharpening Scrapers

Sharpening a Rectangular Scraper: Holding the scraper in a vice, remove the old edge by draw filing, using a millsaw file.

The hand scraper is held in a vice and a new edge produced with a mill saw file

Remove the file marks by holding the scraper vertically and rubbing over an oilstone.

The file marks are removed by holding the scraper vertically and rubbing on an oilstone

Place the scraper flat on the oilstone and rub to remove any face burrs.

The scraper is held flat on an oilstone and rubbed to remove any burrs

Replace the scraper in the vice and using a burnisher flatten the edges.
Tilt the burnisher to approximately 8° to turn the edge, thereby forming a cutting edge.

Sharpening a Cabinet Scraper: File the blade to an angle of 45°.

Using an oilstone, hone the angle to remove file marks and burrs.

A burnisher is tilted at approximately 8° to 10° to turn over the edge and form a cutting edge.

The blade is filed to an angle of 45°

The blade is honed on an oilstone to remove file marks

The blade is held flat on an oilstone to remove the burr

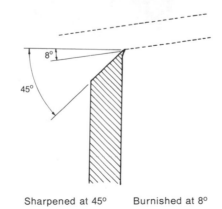

Sharpened at 45°   Burnished at 8°

Sharpening a Drill

The thumb and forefinger of one hand are used as a pivot while the shank of the drill is rotated. At the same time the drill is moved upwards against the rotation of the grinding wheel. Grinding pressure should be moderate and the drill frequently quenched to prevent overheating.

Position for sharpening a drill

General drilling   Plastic and wood

Cutting Edge
Point Angle
(LIP)

59°   59°

Point angle of 105°–118° is suitable for general purpose

Lip Clearance

8°–18°

This angle must be greater than rate of penetration

Sharpening Bits

It is essential that bits be cleaned carefully after use and preferably wiped with an oily rag, particularly after boring green or moist timber. Make sure that bits are kept in a dry place and avoid dropping them on concrete floors, as damage to the screw centre and spurs is difficult to repair. No attempt should be made to file or sharpen the screw.

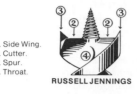

1. Side Wing.
2. Cutter.
3. Spur.
4. Throat.

SCOTCH PATTERN   RUSSELL JENNINGS

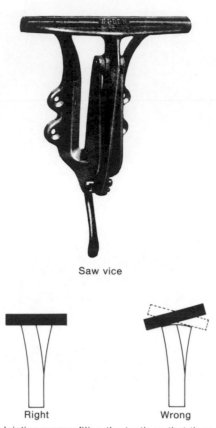

Saw vice

Saw set

Using a saw set

Sharpening Spurs: Hold the bit against the side of the bench with the screw pointing upwards and draw a smooth file across the *inside* of the spur, sharpening the front edge. Never file the outside of the spur, as this reduces the clearance and size.

Filing spurs

Sharpening Lifters: Hold the bit screw downwards on the bench and draw a smooth file lightly across the underside of the lifter until a sharp edge is obtained. On no account must the top of the lifter be filed.

Filing lifters

Sharpening a Saw

1. *Jointing:* The teeth must be of a regular size before the saw can be set. Jointing is the term used to describe the filing of the teeth so that they are equal in height. The saw is placed in a vice and a mill saw file passed lightly back and forth the length of the blade on top of the teeth.

Right   Wrong

Jointing means filing the teeth so that they are equal in height

2. *Shaping:* When jointing is complete the teeth must be formed to a correct and regular shape with gullets of equal depth. File straight across the saw at 90° to the blade. No attempt must be made to sharpen the teeth at this stage. Use a slim tapered triangular saw file and make sure it is held at the correct tilt to provide the appropriate tooth angle for each particular saw.

Teeth must be formed to the correct shape with gullets of equal depth

3. *Setting:* The teeth of a hand saw should be set before sharpening to avoid damage to the cutting edge. The purpose of set is to provide clearance for the blade in the saw cut. The depth of set should be no greater than half the length of the tooth.

When using a saw set the upper half of each alternate tooth is set away from the operator, and the saw reversed for setting the intermediate teeth. After setting, an oilslip should be rubbed down the face of the saw to remove any variation in setting.

After setting use oilslip to rub down the face of the saw to remove any variation in setting

4. *Sharpening:*
Sharpening a Rip Saw
Fix the saw in a saw vice with about 6 mm projecting above the vice jaws.
Use a 200 mm slim taper triangular saw file and press the file firmly into the gullet. Tilt the file to provide the correct angle on the front

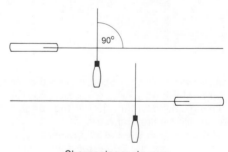

Sharpening a rip saw

edge of each tooth (0.3° of slope). Make one or two firm strokes in each alternate gullet, taking particular care to hold the file at the same angle for each stroke.

When filing from one side is complete the saw is reversed and the alternate gullets filed. The file must be held perfectly horizontal and at 90° to the saw blade.

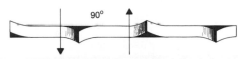

Teeth of a rip saw are filed at 90°

Sharpening a Crosscut Saw

Fix the saw in the saw vice as for the rip saw.

Use a 150 mm slim tapered triangular saw file. Press the file into the gullet and tilt the file to obtain the correct angle (14° of slope).

Keep the file horizontal and move the point of the file towards the point of the saw until

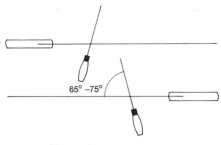

Sharpening a crosscut saw

the file makes an angle of 65° to 75° with the saw blade.

Make one or two strokes on each alternate gullet, always filing the front edge of each tooth set away from you.

When the end of the saw is reached, reverse the saw and file the gullets that were missed. In order to maintain the correct angle the file must swing towards the point of the saw.

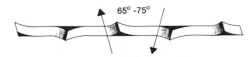

Teeth of a crosscut saw are filed at 65° to 75°

Using a slim taper saw file to sharpen a hand saw

SUGGESTED BASIC TOOL KIT

MARKING KNIFE	adjustable blade	CHISEL SET	6 mm, 12 mm, 18 mm, 25 mm firmers	PINCERS	tower pattern 200 mm
TAPE RULE	3 m	BRACE	300 mm ratchet	CLAMPS G	75 mm, 150 mm, and 200 mm
SPIRIT LEVEL	aluminium body 2 vials one plumb one level	AUGER BITS	6 mm, 9 mm, 12 mm, 15 mm, 18 mm, 25 mm	CLAMPS BAR	1 m, 2 m
COMBINATION SQUARE	removable 300 mm blade	HAND DRILL	double steel pinions 3-jaw chuck 8 mm capacity	VICE	plain screw 225 mm opening
TRY SQUARE	600 mm x 300 mm with mm graduations	SCREWDRIVER KIT	200 mm round blade ratchet, 25 mm pocket	TINSNIPS	straight cutting 250 mm
COMBINATION GAUGE	wooden stock and stem 3 spurs	CLAW HAMMER	425 g hickory handle	RIPPING BAR	goose neck 18 mm x 600 mm
SMOOTHING PLANE	50 mm blade	CROSS PENE HAMMER	220 g hickory handle	WOOD RULE	1 m folding
SURFORM FILE	multi-purpose type	ADJUSTABLE BEVEL	200 mm steel blade and handle	COMBINATION OILSTONE	fine and coarse 200 mm x 25 mm x 50 mm
CROSSCUT SAW	600 mm 10 points	BRADAWL	25 mm blade	PLIERS	combination 150 mm
TENON SAW	300 mm 12 points	PUTTY KNIFE	200 mm blade	WORK BENCH	1.5 m x 600 mm x 800 mm equipped with vice
COPING SAW	bow frame 125 mm deep	NAIL PUNCH SET	set of 3–0.7 mm, 1.4 mm, 2.8 mm cup point	CORDLESS DRIVER DRILL	7.2 volt, 10mm keyless chuck
HACK SAW	300 mm high speed blade				

Project 1

WORK BENCH

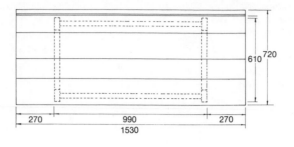

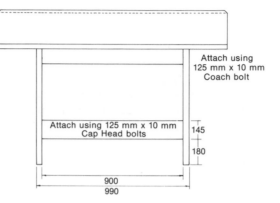

Attach using
125 mm x 10 mm
Coach bolt

Attach using 125 mm x 10 mm
Cap Head bolts

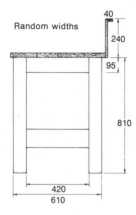

Random widths

CUTTING LIST Timber—Australian Oak

Item No.	Name	No. of	L	W	Th
1	Top	2	1.5 m	190 mm	45 mm
2	Top	2	1.5 m	140 mm	45 mm
3	Legs	4	770 mm	95 mm	45 mm
4	Top front and back rails	2	900 mm	95 mm	45 mm
5	Top end rails	2	420 mm	95 mm	45 mm
6	Bottom front and back rails	2	900 mm	145 mm	45 mm
7	Bottom end rails	2	420 mm	145 mm	45 mm
8	Tool rack	1	1.5 m	240 mm	20 mm
9	Tool rack	1	1.5 m	40 mm	20 mm

Construction

Lay out the position of the two edge and two side bolts on the four legs using a try square and marking gauge. Extra square lines to determine the position of top and bottom rails will be of considerable help.

Lay all four legs together and check their accuracy.

Using a 9 mm auger bit bore the holes through the legs.

Locate the centres for the bolt holes in the bottom and top rails. Number each butt joint.

Clamp the legs in their proper position to the front top and front bottom rails. Insert the auger bit through the hole that has been bored and make a small hole. This will give the centre for boring each hole in the rails.

Follow this procedure for each joint before boring holes in the rails.

Bore all holes in the rails as deep as the bolts, less the 45 mm thickness of the leg for front and back rails and less 95 mm for the width of the leg for the end rails (use a depth gauge).

Lay out the centres on the inside faces of the rails to bore 25 mm holes for the nuts.

NOTE

The holes for the machine bolts in the end rails are not as deep as in the front rails.

Place a bolt through one of the holes in a leg and determine where the hole should be put for the bolt nut.

Centre can now be located for the 15 mm holes to allow for expansion in the top rails for the coach bolts to fasten the top to the frame and the holes bored.

Short dowels 12 mm in diameter and 50 mm long should be provided in addition to bolts between all the rails and legs to keep the rails from turning. Lay out the centre for these dowel holes carefully and bore the holes to the desired depth.

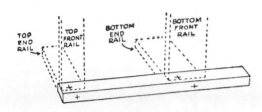

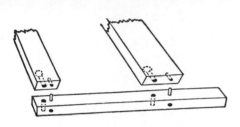

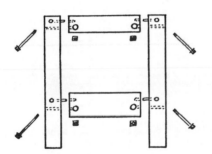

End frame construction

Assembly

The Frame

Place all four pieces for ONE END in position on the floor. Put the dowels in place, put a washer on each bolt and pass it into its hole.

Place a nut through the nut hole and turn the bolt until the leg and the rail are drawn tightly together. When all the bolts are in place assemble the other end unit in the same manner.

Place these end units on edge on the floor with the top and bottom back rails in place between them and assemble the rest of the frame.

Check the entire assembly for squareness using a steel square or tape.

Assembling end unit of work bench

Assembling top and bottom rails to end unit

Complete assembly of work-bench frame

The Bench Top

Lay out the pieces with the grains alternating and the best surface to the top.

Number these pieces and plane them straight and true so as to fit neatly together.

After all edges are true and matched to each other they are ready for gluing.

If required, holes may be bored for dowels.

Gluing may best be accomplished with clamps, but it can also be performed against other planks.

Apply glue to the edges of the boards and clamp them firmly together.

Remove excess glue before it hardens.

The top should now be planed and sanded to a good smooth surface.

Using the 15 mm auger bit locate the centres of the holes through the top rails marking the underside of the top.

Bore the appropriate size holes In the top for the coach bolts.

Do not bore through the top. Use a depth gauge for the depth of hole required.

Place the bench top flat on the floor with the underframe in the proper position. Turn the coach bolts through the rails into the top and drive them tight.

Turn the bench up on its legs and check that all joints are tight and that all arris edges are removed.

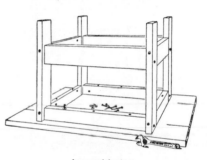

Assemble top

The Tool Rack

Take the two pieces cut for the tool rack and prepare the narrow top piece first to hold chisels, try squares, screwdrivers, etc.

Lay out the various holes and slots required for the tools along this narrow top piece, then bore, saw, and chisel these out.

Fasten the narrow piece along the top and at the back of the 240 mm panel with glue and screws. Drill the screw holes through the narrow strip and countersink them for CKS screws. Apply glue and assemble.

Locate a screw hole 75 mm from each end, and three more holes at regular intervals along the base at the back of the panel, 22 mm up from its bottom edge.

Drill the screw holes and countersink them for CKS 25 mm x 12 wood screws.

Place the panel in position against the back edge of the bench top and turn the screws through the panel into the bench edge.

Clean up the panel with garnet paper, remove all excess glue.

MACHINE TOOLS

...LARGE AND SMALL, SIMPLE & SOPHISTICATED

PORTABLE TOOLS

Portable Circular Saw

Portable circular saws are available in a variety of sizes and are designed for use away from the workshop. They may, however, be used in a workshop, but usually alternative, and probably better, methods of cutting are available.

These machines are widely used by carpenters on the job for framing, roofing, and flooring. The home handyman would also find extensive use for this machine. A range of blades are available for cutting a variety of materials.

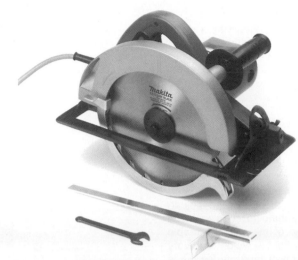

Circular saw (235 mm)

Specifications

Portable circular saws are designed to cut effectively at all angles between 90° to 45°. With a rip or crosscut saw blade fitted the machine will cut a variety of profiles, including rebates, chamfers, and grooves, in either hardwood or softwood.

With special blades fitted most machines are capable of cutting bricks, plastic, asbestos, non-ferrous metals, and steel.

The size of the portable circular saw is designated by the largest blade that may be fitted to the machine. This will vary from about 180 mm to 240 mm. The power will vary accordingly but is usually within the range 1020 watts to 2200 watts. The blade speed usually varies between 4000 to 5200 r.p.m. although this could be as low as 3000 r.p.m.

Operating Adjustments

Most machines are fitted with a fence to guide the saw while ripping a board. This device is easily adjusted and it is essential to make sure that the locking device is firmly clamped before operating the machine. The depth of cut is adjusted by moving the base so that the blade protrudes the required amount.

Bevel cuts are also possible by tilting the machine on its base so that the blade is set at the desired angle.

Portable saws are also equipped with spring-loaded blade guards. These guards must be adequately maintained in order that they operate effectively.

Because of the range of blades available and the necessity to select the correct blade for cutting specific materials, manufacturers provide a system of safe and quick blade replacement.

Using the Portable Saw

The base of the machine should be placed on the timber with the blade just clear. After switching on, allow the blade to develop full revolutions before attempting to cut.

As the blade enters the cut the spring-loaded guard is pushed back by the timber and when the cut is completed the guard returns to the safe position. After releasing the switch the saw is held until the blade is stationary.

It is desirable to use a fence to guide the machine, but the saw may be used freehand. If freehand cutting is attempted it is essential to align the guide mark on the base with the line on the work and feed the machine through the cut carefully following the line. Extra care must be exercised if this technique is adopted.

Holding the saw

Adjusting the base for angle cutting

Safety

- Eye and ear protection is essential.
- The timber must be well supported either with saw horses, or clamped to a bench.
- Make sure all adjustments are made before switching on and that all adjustment levers are tight.
- Always stand clear of the line of cut.
- Both hands must be used to guide the machine through the cut.
- Always disconnect the machine from the power when making adjustments.
- Never use a blunt saw blade or one that has no set.

Saw blades

Portable Electric Jig Saw

The portable jig saw, also known as a sabre saw, is widely used by craftsmen in many fields, it is used specifically for light work such as cutting thin sheet materials, plywood, sheet steel, and plastics.

Specifications

Modern portable jig saws are double insulated and are easy and comfortable to use. Good quality machines incorporate a tilting base for cutting angles, and many feature a variable speed control from 0 to 3200 strokes per min. Others feature straight and orbital reciprocating movements of the blade. These adjustments enable the machine to cope with the ever increasing range of materials. Portable jig saws are relatively light in weight and vary from 2 to 3 kg. The power input varies but is usually between 310 and 600 watts.

Operating Adjustments

The machines are designed for ease of adjustment and the manufacturer's specifications should be studied carefully in order that these procedures may be fully understood.

The method of inserting the blade will vary depending upon the make and type of machine. When cutting tight curves it is necessary to fit narrow blades. When cutting metal or plastics it may be necessary to use a lubricant to prevent abnormal overheating.

It is essential that consideration be given to the effective length, pitch, and set of teeth so that the blade may effectively cut the material whether it be wood, metal, or plastic.

Using the Portable Jig Saw

The machine is used to make straight or curved cuts. The cuts may also be bevelled by tilting the base.

The base must be held firmly on the surface being cut and moved at a rate depending upon the thickness and type of material.

The blade cuts on the up stroke and splintering is likely to occur in thin wood materials, particularly plywood. This must be taken into account when making finishing cuts.

Orbital blade action

0

Straight
Clean cutting of wood, plasterboard, mild steel, stainless and plastics

I

Small Orbit
Cutting of mild steel, aluminium, hardwood

II

Medium Orbit
High speed cutting of wood, plasterboard, mild steel and aluminium

III

Large Orbit
High speed cutting of wood and plasterboard

Cuts may be easily started from the edge of the material, but internal cuts may require the drilling of a starting hole. Most jig saws, however, are capable of direct piercing or plunge cutting.

Safety

- Eye and ear protection is essential.
- Loose clothing must not be worn.
- Make sure the switch is OFF before connecting to the power circuit.
- Disconnect the machine to change blades and make adjustments.
- Select the correct blade for the material being cut.
- Make sure the work is well supported or clamped to a bench or other suitable fixture.
- Do not bend or twist the blade while cutting curves.
- The base should be held firmly on the work before commencing the cut.

Guides and Accessories

Special shoes are available to prevent splintering on the upper edge of the material and must be considered as a worthwhile addition to the machine.

Adjustable circular cutting guides which are attached to the base allow accurate circle cutting and are readily available for most

Cutting curves with a jig saw

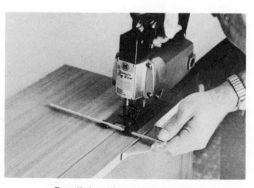

Parallel cutting using a guide

Plunge cutting

types. This guide is essential if accurate work is required.

Parallel cutting guides are also available and are highly desirable if long straight cuts are attempted.

Other useful accessories available from manufacturers include lubricating containers, saw tables, dovetailing attachments, and foam rubber cutters.

Adjusting the base for angle cutting

Using a circle cutting guide

Jig saw bench attachment

Type of blades

The Portable Router

Portable routers are versatile machines into which router bits of various profiles are fitted. The bits travel at high speeds to produce shapes and contours either along edges or on surfaces. The router is used to produce decorative work and to form joints for construction of furniture, patterns, or perhaps boats.

Specifications

A router is a relatively simple machine consisting of a body, which is essentially the power unit, housed in a router base. The router bits are held in position with a collet type chuck. The size of the router is usually designated by the power output which may vary from 1000 to 2300 watts. The motor travels at relatively high speeds varying within the range 22 000 to 27 000 r.p.m.

Operating Adjustments

Portable routers are designed for ease of adjustment, and most are similar in their construction. However, it is advisable to consult the manufacturer's specifications before making adjustments or installing bits.
INSTALLING BITS: This operation will depend upon the type and make of machine being used. But it is advisable to wipe all dust and wood chips from the chuck and collet before inserting the bit. Always use the correct

spanner and never overtighten. To clamp the bit in the collet the router is placed on the bench with the chuck away from the operator.

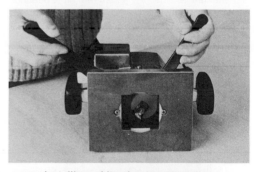

Installing a bit using two spanners

Installing a bit using one spanner against locking device in machine

DEPTH OF CUT ADJUSTMENT: This operation will also depend upon the type and make of machine, but generally involves placing the router on a flat surface and lowering the motor until the bit touches the surface. The motor is then locked in position. The locking lever must be tightened before commencing the cut.

Using the Router

It is important that the direction and rate of feed be carefully considered before commencing the cut. The correct relationship between the direction of feed and the rotation of the bit is shown, together with the position of the guide, in the diagram. The router is operated at high speed and must be advanced at a moderate rate of feed or burning will result.

It is advisable to make a sample cut on a scrap piece of timber before actually cutting the work. This will enable contours and dimensions to be checked.

The various bits available make possible an almost unlimited range of shapes and contours for decorative edges, panels, or joints. These bits, together with a wide range of accessories, increase the versatility of the machine.

Common router bits

Straight bit

Flush trim bit & bearing

Chamfer bit & bearing

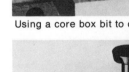

Roman ogee bit & bearing

Classic bit & bearing

Corner rounding bit & bearing

V-groove bit

Core bit & bearing

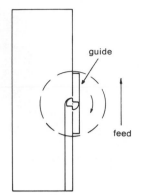

Position of router when using router guide

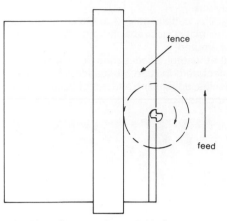

Position of router when using a fence

Moulding an edge using a shaped bit

Using a core box bit to cut a sail track in a mast

Cutting a groove using a flat bit

Joints

Tenon Cutting: Mark out the joints. The rails are clamped together face down on the bench.
- Select an appropriate bit, and install.
- A guide piece is clamped to the rails to establish the shoulder position.
- The cheeks of the tenon are determined by setting the depth of the router.
- A piece of timber the same thickness as the rails must be clamped to the bench to help support the machine.

Tenon cutting

Housing joints: Mark out the joints on the panels.
- The solid panels are clamped securely to the bench.
- Select an appropriate bit and install.
- Locate the position of the fence.
- Set the depth of the router.
- Feed the router through the material at a constant rate keeping the router base against the fence.

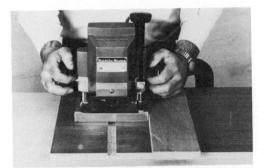

Cutting a trench for a housing joint

Safety

- Eye and ear protection is essential.
- Loose clothing must not be worn.
- Make sure the switch is OFF before connecting to power.
- Stop the motor as soon as the cut has been completed.
- Disconnect the router from the power circuit before removing or installing bits.
- The router must be securely held in both hands and located firmly on the work.
- Depth of cut and rate of feed must be regulated to suit the material.
- The correct relationship between the direction of feed, the rotation of the bit, and the guide is essential.
- Always use sharp bits.
- Make sure the work is firmly attached.

Attachments and Accessories

Guides: These may be of various types but are designed for attaching to the router for making straight cuts. Some guides may be in the form of a straight edge attached to the work. Guides may be adapted for cutting joints.

Cutting a rebate using an adjustable guide

Router table attachment

Trammel Points: By using trammel points attached to guide rods, circles can be cut with precision. The trammel point acts in a similar way to that of a compass point and the router is rotated around the point, producing perfect circles.

Fitting trammel points

Circle cutting with trammel points

Templets: Templet guides are available from most manufacturers and are readily attached to the router base. Duplication of shapes is possible by making a templet of 5 mm ply and guiding the router along the templet. This will reproduce the design exactly. A variety of decorative cuts are possible in this way.

Cutting a speaker box panel using a templet

Dovetail Attachment: This attachment is simply a plastic templet located on a fixture. The timber to be jointed is clamped into the fixture and by guiding the router along the templet the pins and sockets are formed simultaneously.

Setting up a drawer front and drawer side in dovetailing attachment. Drawer front is in horizontal position

This type of work requires careful setting of the router and fixture in accordance with the specifications. The ultimate fit of the joint depends on this accuracy.

To obtain the correct shape a dovetail bit is fitted to the router and in addition a templet guide is fixed to the router base so that the router may be used with the templet.

Complete cut showing pins and dovetails

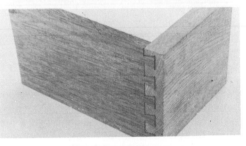

The assembled joint

Fluting and Beading: Flutes and beads may be cut using special fixtures to support the router while the work is supported in a lathe or special jig fitted with an indexing device.

Fluting legs using a small core box bit and parallel cutting guide

Safety

- Eye and ear protection is essential.
- The timber must be well supported or clamped to a bench.
- Make sure all adjustments are made before switching on and that all adjustment devices are tight.
- Ensure that the timber is sound. There must be no loose knots, splits, or nails.
- Check the grain direction and direction of feed to ensure a smooth surface.
- Both hands must be used to guide the machine through the cut.
- Always disconnect the machine from the power when making adjustments.
- Never use a machine with blunt blades.
- Make sure the machine has come to a dead stop before placing it on the bench.
- Avoid loose clothing.
- Disconnect the machine from the power supply when changing blades.

Portable Planers

Portable planers are available in many blade width sizes and are designed for use either in the workshop or out on a job. They are generally supplied with a steel carrying case and complete with a number of accessories.

These machines are widely used by carpenters, boatbuilders, cabinetmakers and are extremely useful for the home handyman.

Specifications

Generally the size of the blade width varies from 80 mm to 170 mm. Most machines have a maximum depth of cut of around 3 mm. The machines are relatively heavy and take a little getting used to. They may vary in weight between 2.5 kg to 8 kg. The power output also varies accordingly but is usually within the range of 600 watts to 1200 watts. The speed usually varies between 12 000 and 16 000 r.p.m.

Operating Adjustments

Most machines are fitted with a fence or planing guide and planing rebates of varying widths and depths for edge planing.

Guides can also be adjusted or removed for planing bevels, splays, and chamfers. The depth of cut can be easily adjusted simply by turning a knob controlling a mechanism linked to the cutting block (the front part of the sole).

Using the Portable Planer

To start the tool simply pull the trigger. Release the trigger to stop. Wait until the planer is running at top speed before bringing it into contact with the timber. Planing will be easier if the timber is held level, either in a vice or clamped firmly to a bench. Never plane uphill.

STARTING AND FINISHING WORK: Rest the front of the planer flat on the work surface, switch on and move the machine gently forward. At the end of the stroke apply pressure to the back of the tool and lift the front of the planer as the cutters pass over the end. For a fine finish the tool should be advanced more slowly over the work.

Planing an edge with portable planer using adjustable fence

Planing a rebate using a small machine

Planing a rebate using a large machine. Note the more rigid guide

REPLACING AND INSTALLING BLADES: When removing the blades from the planer make sure the power is disconnected.

Hold the machine upside down on the bench and remove the installation bolts with the spanner provided. This will loosen the clamp plate and allow the blades to be removed.

Removing bolts with spanner provided to allow removal of blades

Before installing new or sharpened blades clean out all chips and foreign matter around the cutting head.

Always use blades of the same dimension and weight otherwise vibration will result, eventually leading to tool breakdown.

To install a blade in the machine, the blade is first fitted to an adjustment plate which is slipped into a groove in the head. This assembly is then clamped firmly in position with a hexagonal head bolt.

When properly installed, the blades should be flush with the outside edges of the soles. For rebating it is desirable to allow the edge of the blade to protrude slightly outside (0.3 to 0.6 mm).

SHARPENING PLANER BLADES: Power planers considerably out-perform hand planes but the blades become dull relatively quickly. For safe use and ultimate performance the blades must always be kept as sharp as possible.

Most manufacturers provide a sharpening guide which holds the blade and allows it to be honed at a constant angle on an oilstone.

Proceed as with a blade from an ordinary hand plane.

For accurate grinding, when the blade becomes particularly worn, guides are available for small bench grinders.

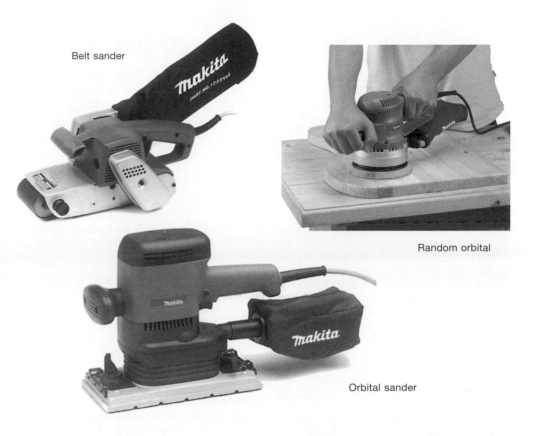

Belt sander

Random orbital

Orbital sander

Portable Sanders

The use of abrasives is indeed important if a project is to be correctly finished. Projects may of course be sanded by hand using a cork block and sanding with the grain. Hand sanding will provide an excellent finish but considerable time and effort will be required.

Two types of portable sanding machines are readily available and are almost essential if a professional finish is desired.

The Belt Sander is usually a heavy duty machine and with a coarse abrasive will smooth a rough surface very quickly. With a fine abrasive belt it can then be used to finish a project.

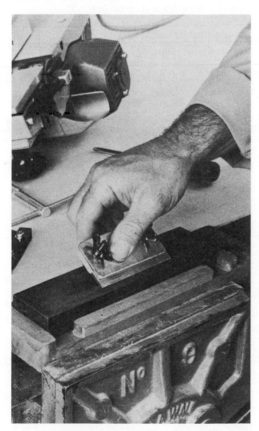

Honing planer blade

Abrasive belt

Using a belt sander

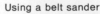

Fitting a sanding belt

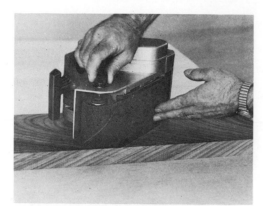

Adjusting sanding belt

The Orbital Sander is essentially a pad sander, the pad of which orbits around 10 000 times a minute to produce a fine finish.

Probably the orbital sander would be the most suitable for home workshop use. Abrasive paper of varying grades is easily attached to the pad making this machine the most versatile.

Orbital sanders are light and easy to hold and may be used on vertical surface, table tops, boats, etc.

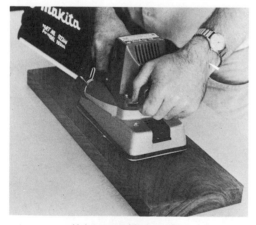

Using an orbital sander

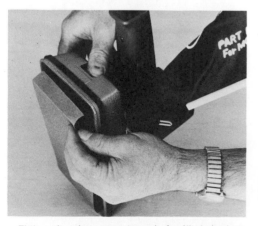

Fitting abrasive paper to pad of orbital sander

Portable Drills

Portable electric drills are available in a wide range of sizes and types. The home handyman will find extensive use for this type of tool, and there is available an almost unlimited range of accessories which increases the range of work that may be done with just one basic tool.

Specifications

Modern electric drills are usually double insulated, have a variable speed or an electronic speed feature, are reversible and may have a keyless chuck. Some drills may be classified as heavy duty and have one or two speeds. The common chuck sizes available are 6.5 mm, 10 mm and 13 mm.

Cordless drills (battery operated) have become increasingly popular with the handyperson and the tradesperson for the ease of use in many constructional tasks or where power is not readily accessible. There is an extensive range of cordless drills now available and standard features generally include variable speed, torque settings, two-speed gearboxes, keyless chuck and often a 1-hour, fast-charge battery. The type of drill (electric or cordless) selected for home use depends on many factors, but if the use of accessories is planned, or heavy duty functions are envisaged, a 10 mm two speed would be desirable. It may even be desirable to select a model with a 13 mm chuck, which will increase the range of work even further.

There are also available drills designed to drill concrete and masonry surfaces. These drills are known as hammer drills and are used widely by tradespeople. However, they may be uneconomical for the handyperson, as their use in the home would be limited.

Using the Portable Drill

For straightforward drilling jobs make sure the drill is inserted to the full depth and the chuck key removed before starting the machine. As a general rule holes larger than 13 mm should be drilled using the slow speed, although holes in steel or concrete require a slower speed than equivalent holes in wood.

The drill must be held perfectly straight or level to prevent bending or breaking the drill. It is desirable to centre punch the position of the hole to locate the drill accurately, especially in metal, concrete or masonry.

Safety

• Eye and ear protection is essential.
• Avoid loose clothing.
• Check the drill size–speed relationship. For drilling holes over 12 mm the slowest speed should be selected.
• The work should be securely clamped to prevent spin off.
• Insert the drill to the full depth of the chuck and remove the chuck key before starting the machine.
• Use only recommended drills. Bits with threaded lead screws should not be used since the cutting action is too fast.
• Feed pressure should be such as to produce shavings.

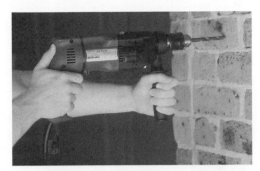
Using an impact drill with a masonry drill fitted to the chuck

DRILLING TO DEPTH: This is achieved by fitting a depth stop either to the drill or to the machine. With either method the drill must be continually 'backed out' to clear the shavings. Avoid drilling right through a piece of wood or splitting the reverse side. This splitting may be contained by either placing or clamping the work with a scrap piece of wood and drilling through into the scrap.

Using a portable drill with a depth gauge

Drills and Bits

Twist Drills: The straight shank type is recommended for use on all kinds of wood when the holes to be drilled are not very large or deep. The open formation of the flutes provide good chip clearance resulting in easy boring. When regrinding, the 60° angle of the point should be maintained. Sizes range from 0.8 mm to 13 mm.

Dowelling bits have a plain brad point and bore a smooth clean hole with or across the grain. Sizes range from 3 mm to 15.8 mm.

Machine Auger Bits: The solid centre machine bit is preferred in some areas of work due to its stiffness and strength and the extra chip clearance offered by the single twist. The solid centre gradually thickens in diameter towards the bottom of the twist, thus providing extra support at the point of strain. The single twist spur nose is especially suitable for boring wet, green, or knotty wood. The Jennings pattern machine bit is suitable for cabinet work and all smooth boring.

Machine bits having plain brad points are more easily controlled than the lead screw type. The rate of feed is proportional to the applied pressure, consequently there is no tendency for the bit to 'grab'.

Spade Bits: Spade bits cut clear, smooth holes and having a brad point allow for angle boring. These bits are suitable for use in drill presses and portable electric drills. Sizes range from 6 mm to 25 mm in increments of 1.5 mm.

The Machine Centre Bit: The machine centre bit is fast cutting, leaving a neat clean hole. It consists of a single cutting edge, spur, and brad point. It is recommended for boring to a depth equal to twice its own diameter. Sizes range from 6 mm to 50 mm with 1.5 mm increments.

Forstner Bits: A Forstner bit will bore any arc of a circle with its direction remaining unaltered by knots or difficult grain. Differing from other bits, it is guided by its circular rim and not by its centre point. The holes bored are clean, true, and flat bottomed. Sizes range from 9.5 mm to 75 mm with 1.5 mm increments.

Machine Countersinking: Countersinking cutters are used to make cone-shaped hollows suitable to accommodate the heads of a standard CKS screw. The included angle of the head is 90°. Countersinks made of carbon steel are suitable only for wood, while for metal countersinks containing 18% tungsten high speed steel are recommended.

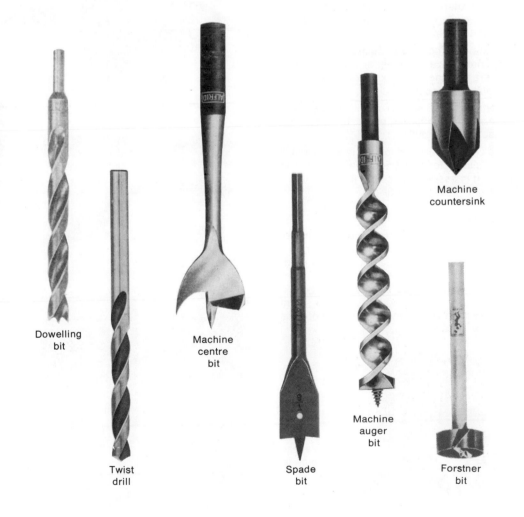
Dowelling bit

Twist drill

Machine centre bit

Spade bit

Machine auger bit

Machine countersink

Forstner bit

Combination Countersinking Cutters: Combination countersinking cutters provide a pilot hole for the screw threads, a clearance hole for the screw shank, a countersink for the screw head, and finally a counterbore producing a hole to be fitted with a plug.

Plug Cutters: Plug cutters are used in the manufacture of furniture where plugs have been used to cover counterbored screws. Types available include spiral plug cutter and tube type plug cutter, both producing parallel plugs, and the two winged cutter for making taper plugs. Sizes range from 8 mm to 20 mm diameter.

Glass Drills: Spear point glass drills are tipped with tungsten carbide. They are recommended for the rotary drilling of glass, china, and pottery with a hand drill or drill press at a slow speed.

Turpentine may be used as a cutting lubricant to provide clean accurate holes.

Masonry Drills: These drills are tungsten carbide tipped and are designed to drill bricks, stone, marble, concrete, and other masonry material. They are designed for use in cam-operated rotary impact portable electric drills, while others are designed for drilling bricks, tiles, and render.

Hole Saws: These are suitable for drilling wood, hardboard, sheetmetal, and fibreglass. They are designed for use in a power drill. The pilot drill is replaceable.

Surform Drum: This drum will shape most materials to the finishing stage. It is designed for use in power drills.

Circle Cutter: Designed for use in a bench drill only. Suitable for sheetmetal, laminates, and timber. It is essential to clamp the work firmly to the drill table while drilling.

Cordless Tools (including drills)

Recent innovations in the manufacture of cordless tools have seen the introduction of a new generation of DC (Direct Current) cordless motors. These longer life motors, in conjunction with improved battery capacity and reduced battery charging time, have resulted in an increase in the range of quality cordless tools now available.

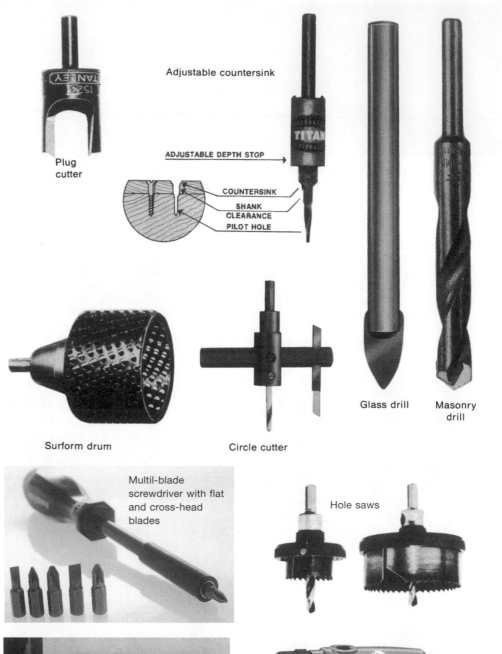

Adjustable countersink

Plug cutter

ADJUSTABLE DEPTH STOP

COUNTERSINK
SHANK
CLEARANCE
PILOT HOLE

Glass drill

Masonry drill

Surform drum

Circle cutter

Multil-blade screwdriver with flat and cross-head blades

Hole saws

10 mm Keyless chuck cordless driver drill

Above: Cordless hammer drill
Left: 9.6v Cordless driver drill using a spade bit

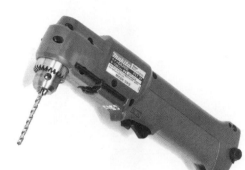

Cordless angle drill

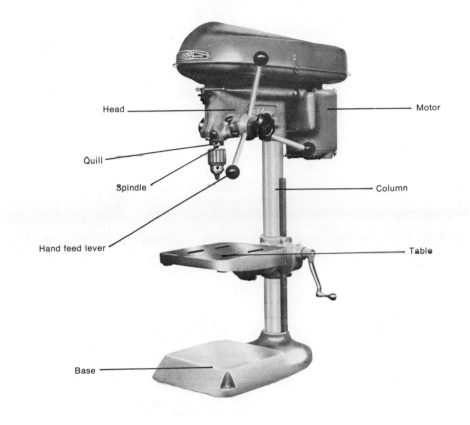

Head

Quill

Spindle

Hand feed lever

Motor

Column

Table

Base

Cordless angle grinder (100 mm)

Cordless saw (85 mm)

Cordless impact driver

Drill Press

The drill press is a most versatile machine, capable of working in wood, metal, plastics and composite materials. With the addition of attachments, the drill press may be used for mortising, sanding and routing, as well as its normal function of boring holes.

Boring is synonymous with producing holes in timber while drilling normally refers to producing holes in metal.

Drill Press: When selecting the correct machine bit consideration should be given to type of timber to be drilled, quality of work, depth of drilling, and the speed of the machine.

Drilling in soft open-grained timber requires a different drill than does a dense resinous timber. To prevent excessive strain a drill should never be used to drill in one operation a hole deeper than the length of the twist or flute. When high spindle speeds are used the lead screw is of little value, hence a brad point is more appropriate and easier to control.

Drilling a Hole

Mark out the position of hole or holes required in stock and indent with a bradawl or centre punch.

Select the wood drill of suitable type and size and mount it in the drill chuck. Adjust the belt for applicable speed.

Place the timber stock on the drill table with supporting service material underneath. The service piece prevents splitting of the underside of work as the drill passes through and it protects the top surface of the table.

Adjustable depth stop

Adjust the table height, affording initial wood drill clearance, and lock in position.

Set the depth gauge for the particular requirement, be it a through or stopped hole.

With the material firmly held or clamped, depending on type of drill and machine speed, feed the bit slowly through the timber. Reducing the rate of feed near the break-through point will minimise the splintering.

DRILLING TO DEPTH: This is achieved by adjusting the depth stop. Where the depth required is greater than the length of spindle, stop the machine, slip another service piece under the work or raise the table.

In either method the bit must be continually 'backed out' to clear the shavings.

Using twist drill

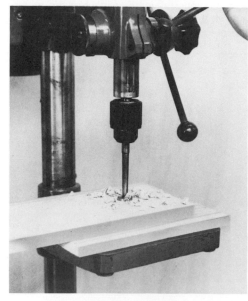

Using a Forstner bit

Drilling round stock

Table may be tilted for drilling holes inclined to a surface

MORTISING: The mortising attachment consists of a hollow square chisel containing an auger bit. The inner surfaces of the base of the chisel form cutting edges with slots in the sides to allow outlet for waste material. The auger bit has two scribing spurs, two cutting edges, and two spiral flutes pulling the waste material up to the outlet slots.

The mortising attachment

The chisel is attached to the drill press by means of a detachable bracket with the auger bit fitting into the chuck.

Fitting the Attachment

Adjust the depth stop, exposing sufficient quill to allow the attachment to be locked in position.

Locate the chisel in position with the slot parallel with the direction of mortise and a gap

of approximately 1 mm between the shoulder of the chisel and the base of the attachment. Lock in position.

Place the auger bit into the chuck with the spurs level with the points of the chisel. Lock in position.

Loosen the chisel and push the shoulder against the base of the attachment and lock in position. This provides the necessary clearance between the chisel and bit.

Locate the timber stock against the mortising fence and adjust the depth of cut.

Position the timber stock so that the first cut may be made at one end of the mortise and then clamp against the mortising fence.

Continue with cuts until the mortise is complete.

Safety

- Eye protection is essential.
- Avoid loose clothing.
- Check the drill size–speed relationship. For boring holes over 12 mm slowest speed should be used.
- Stock being bored should be mounted on service material to prevent damage to machined table surface.
- Small work should be securely clamped to prevent spin off from the table.
- Insert the bit to full depth in the chuck and remove chuck key before starting machine.
- Use V block for boring round stock.
- Use only the recommended bits for boring. Bits with threaded lead screws should not be used since the resultant cutting action is too fast.
- Feed pressure should be such as to produce shavings.

Bench Grinders

A small bench grinder is essential in a home workshop if cutting tools are to be maintained in good condition.

Sharpening cutting tools need not be a difficult job as many manufacturers provide a wide range of attachments and guides for various grinding jobs.

Safety

Bench grinders are a machine tool and should be treated accordingly.
- They must be securely bolted to a bench top, and plugged into a suitable power source.
- Guard and eye shields must be in position over the wheels.
- Eye and ear protection must be worn.
- The tool rest must be securely clamped and as close as possible to the wheel at all times.
- Avoid using the side of the wheel.
- When using attachments make sure they are securely clamped in position.

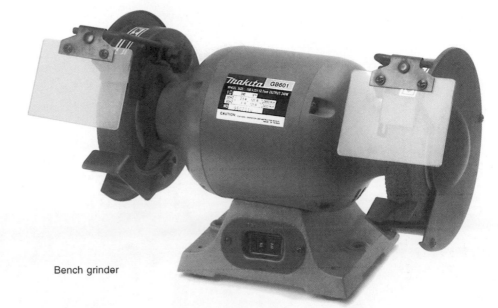

Bench grinder

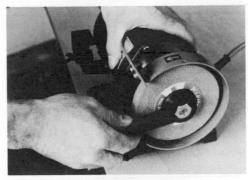

Abrasive wheels

Fitting an abrasive wheel

Sharpening attachments may be fitted to a bench grinder

Sharpening a portable circular saw blade

Grinding a planer knife

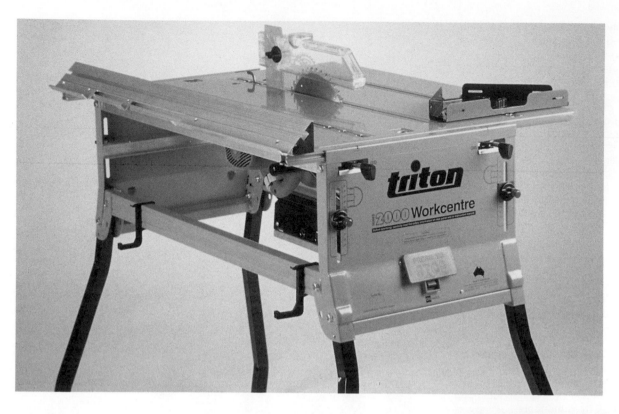

CIRCULAR SAWS

The circular saw is one of the oldest known power machines used for the breaking down of timber. Documented evidence records the use of reciprocating frame saws throughout Scandinavian countries during the 15th century. It was not until the 19th century, however, that the circular saw appeared, because of difficulties in the production of saw blades and arbor bearings. These were to evolve from the Pit Saw.

The first of these saws was constructed with a wooden table and supporting frame, with the blade mounted on an arbor so as to extend above the table. Following its acceptance into industry came modifications and improvements including rise and fall table, tilting saw, rise and fall saw, mitre gauge and extension tables.

From these modifications has evolved the present day circular saw capable of crosscutting, ripping, bevelling, chamfering, grooving, mitring, trenching, and tenoning. This type of saw, having one blade and one arbor, is perhaps the most common for home use. A further extension of the circular saw, and quite popular for home workshops, is the adaptation of 'portable power saws' for use with sophisticated table saw frames which allows all of the previously mentioned processes to be achieved, but also allows the 'saw' to retain its portability.

One such example is the Triton Workcentre, which, when used in conjunction with a portable power saw, can be adjusted for crosscutting processes or, alternatively, ripping processes using either solid timber or manufactured boards.

Safety
- Ear and eye protection is essential.
- Avoid loose clothing.
- Do not stand in line with the blade in case of kickback.
- Use a push stick where possible.
- Use a 'tailer out' when cutting long lengths.
- The overhead guard must be correctly positioned in relation to the operation being performed.
- Do not saw freehand—always use the rip or mitre fence.
- Always have the larger section between the blade and the fence.
- Do not reach over the saw blade.

Kickback: One of the often ignored dangers of operating a circular saw is that of material being thrown back with considerable force at the operator. Kickbacks, as they are known, often occur unexpectedly and are the result of:

1. Timber closing on the blade while cutting.
2. Insufficient set on the blade.
3. Sawing badly warped timber.
4. Timber touching the top of an unguarded blade.
5. Poorly set riving knife.

Using a push stick when ripping

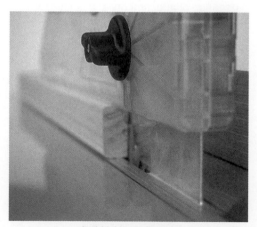

Anti-kickback fingers

50

Ripping

This refers to the sawing of timber lengthwise or parallel to the grain. It is necessary to ensure that a flat surface is placed on the saw table combined with a straight edge against the fence to prevent initial kickbacks.

Ripping Long Pieces

When ripping long pieces which will overhang the rear of the table by more than half their length, either have a friend help you, or rig up a 'tailer out' support.

Try to keep the workpiece moving, even slowly, during a long rip. Pauses can cause slight steps in the cut.

Ripping a long piece of timber

Ripping Larger Sheets

Have the overhead guard as low as possible. Push the work against the fence and into the blade with the left hand, and support the offcut with your right.

When ripping thin, flexible material wider than 500 mm, you will need additional support, such as the batten shown, to stop the front corner of the materiel becoming stopped by the rear fence arm.

For ripping very large sheets it is advisable to remove the saw from the chassis and use the saw in a hand-held position. Clamp a guide to the workpiece, to be used as a fence, and ensure the sheet is supported off the floor.

Ripping larger sheets

Ripping larger sheets (thin)

Ripping Thicker Wood

You can double the maximum depth of cut by turning the wood over, end for end, and making a second cut. If the blade is square to the table and the wood is dressed square, the two cuts should be in line.

The overhead guard must be removed for the first cut, but replaced for the second cut. When double ripping short or narrow pieces, use a push stick and a piece of scrap timber to form a guide for the workpiece.

Ripping thicker wood

Rebating

By lowering the saw blade and adjusting the fence, a wide variety of rebates can be made. The overhead guard must be removed when making rebates, so extreme care is required for hand positions.

Most rebates produce a narrow offcut. You should avoid trapping the offcut between the blade and the fence. If you can't do this, ensure you are not standing directly behind the blade as the offcut may be thrown towards you at high speed.

When rebating timber that is rectangular in section it is good practice to make the first cut with the timber on edge and the second cut with the timber on the flat. Otherwise, if rebating on a narrow piece of timber, the timber may be unsafely balancing on a narrow edge after the second cut.

Mark out the size of the rebate on one end of the timber and adjust the fence to the width of the rebate. Adjust the saw blade to depth and make a test cut. Make the initial cut and saw any other pieces having rebates of similar proportions. Readjust the fence position and depth of saw blade for the second cut. Complete the final cut and thereby the rebate.

A similar procedure is used for rebating across the grain except that the timber is held firmly against the protractor and the end is in contact with the fence.

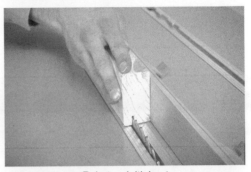

Rebate—initial cut

Rebate—second cut

Setting blade depth

Tongue and Grooving

Reference to rebating would indicate that if two identical rebates are made from opposite faces of the timber, you will be left with a central tongue.

Again, always make the first two cuts on the narrower edge of the timber and the final two cuts with the timber lying down flat.

To make the matching centralised groove, move the fence outwards by one blade thickness, and make two cuts from opposite faces.

Adjustable jig for tapers

Protractor for crosscutting

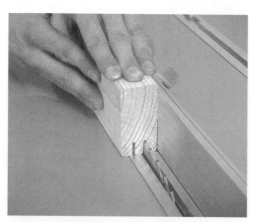

Narrow cuts of groove

Ripping a taper using a stepped jig

Protractor for crosscutting (reverse)

Crosscutting

When crosscutting on a table saw the timber should be of a manageable length and the offcut produced is well supported after the cut.

Ensure the protractor or mitre gauge slides freely in the slot, with both knobs tightened and the protractor set at 0°. Lubricate the slider strip, using a spray lubricant such as WD40.

Hold the timber firmly against the protractor and move it smoothly past the blade. Having the protractor behind the work is the preferred operating position, but it limits the crosscutting capacity to around 140 mm. Having the protractor in front of the work increases the width capacity to around 340 mm.

It should be noted that the fence should never be used as a stop as the off cut trapped between the blade and the fence is uncontrolled and will be flung outwards causing possible injury or damage.

Cutting tongue

Taper Ripping

For cutting tapers of different angles, make up an adjustable jig to angle the timber to the blade. Two pieces can be hinged at the front and then locked open at the desired taper angle.

An angled block holds the timber down and pushes it along. The jig is slid against the fence. Never angle the fence to the blade for taper ripping.

Never set fence as a stop

Crosscutting multiple pieces

Multiple Crosscutting

For crosscutting a number of short pieces to the same length, it is possible to use the fence as a stop, but there must be a spacer at least 19 mm thick attached to the fence. Set the fence to the required length of the pieces, plus the thickness of the spacer.

By using the spacer as a length stop, it is unnecessary to individually measure, mark and line up each piece.

By ending the spacer before the front of the blade, the cut-off pieces are not trapped between the blade and the fence.

Tenoning

The rip fence may be used as a stop for tenoning because the blade is lowered and is not cutting all the way through the timber—there is no solid offcut to become trapped between the blade and the fence.

Cutting a tenon

Place the end of the timber against the fence and hold it firmly against the protractor set at 0°. Make a series of cuts, moving the timber away from the fence by one blade width after each cut. Repeat this process on the other three sides to produce a perfectly central tenon.

If using a router to make the mortises, select the router cutter first (say 10 mm) and make the tenons 10 mm thick to suit. This means the mortising will be much easier—just one cut with a 10 mm bit.

An alternative method of removing the 'cheeks' of the tenon is to hold the timber in a 'cradle' or 'pusher' jig.

Attach a straight, wide board onto the rip fence, using countersunk bolts and nuts, for extra vertical support.

Construct a jig out of scrap timber, as shown, to slide along the top of the board. Use it to support the timber and to hold it square to the table as it is pushed past the blade. A clamp may also be used for further support.

Mitre Cutting

Set the protractor at 45°, make sure both knobs are tight and that the protractor slides freely. Hold a straight piece of timber against whichever face of the protractor best supports

Cutting tenon cheeks

the timber near the blade. The protractor can be used in either of the two slots and whichever way around best suits the job.

Cut about 150 mm off the end of a piece of scrap. Place the offcut against the main piece and see if they form a perfect right angle. If necessary, adjust the protractor angle slightly and repeat the above test.

Cutting mitre

Cutting mitre (other end)

Mitre Cutting Moulding

If the timber cannot be turned over (moulded picture frame or beading) cut the opposite mitres by making the first cut with the timber held against one fence of the protractor, and the second cut with it held against the adjacent face.

The protractor design on the workcentre allows mouldings to be cut with their flat base always resting against the table, and the taller edge against the face of the protractor.

Mouldings should only be cut in this manner, both for safety and as the moulded face is always upwards, less splintering occurs to mar the joint.

Because the two unnotched faces of the protractor form a perfect right angle, any piece cut on one face when placed against a piece cut on the other face will always form a perfect right angle, whatever the angle of the protractor. For example, if the protractor was accidentally set at 44°, the other face would give 46°.

Mitre cutting moulding

Mitre cutting moulding (behind protractor)

Mitre cutting to a length stop

Mitre Cutting to a Length Stop

To ensure perfect length accuracy when mitre cutting manageable lengths, fit an extension sub-fence to the protractor and clamp a mitred block to one of them.

Cut the first mitre against the fence that does not have the stop, and then place the mitred end against the stop on the other fence, for the reverse angle mitre. Both cuts can thus be made with the moulded face upwards.

Grip the timber firmly, as there is a tendency for it to 'creep' during the cut.

If square or rectangular frames are being made, cut all of the pieces to a length stop to ensure that each frame comes out perfectly square and with tight corners.

Jig Guides

Hold-Down Jig

Used to hold long narrow pieces when narrow ripping and can also be used as a side restraint.

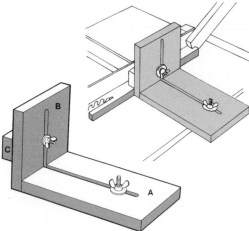

End Grain Jigs

Useful when working with timbers on end grain where good vertical support is required.

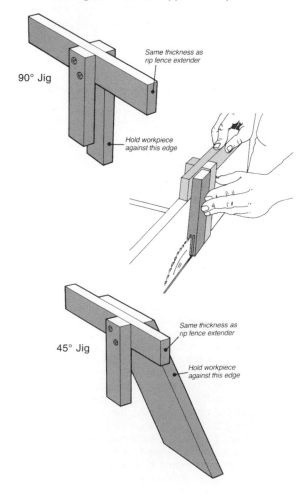

90° Jig

Same thickness as rip fence extender

Hold workpiece against this edge

45° Jig

Same thickness as rip fence extender

Hold workpiece against this edge

Alternative Operating Modes

Crosscut Mode

Mitre Saw—ideal for cutting precise mitres on long pieces such as architraves and large picture frames.

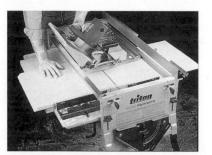

Bevel Saw—can bevel cut from 0–45° and cut compound bevel mitres by angling both the blade and the timber.

Overhead Router—will accurately crosstrench up to 600 mm and by angling the timber produce trenches for steps.

Multistand
Outfeed Support—very useful when ripping long lengths and no 'tailer-out', is available.

Tablesaw Mode

45° Bevel Ripping—the fence is reversible to provide a 45° face and work supports.

Shaper/Planer Table—by mounting a router upside down edge moulding, rebating, trenching and mortising can be professionally produced.

Jigsaw Table—a portable jigsaw mounted upside down will cut curves and intricate patterns.

Multistand
Outboard Support—provides support when crosscutting long, large sectional timbers.

Types of Circular Saw Blades

The shape of the teeth is determined by the type of work for which the saw is designed.

Rip Saw: For cutting with grain.

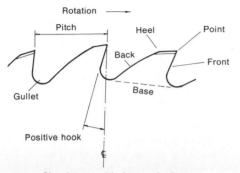

Circular saw blade terminology

Crosscut Saw: For cutting across the grain. Used for furniture manufacture or cutting ply panels.

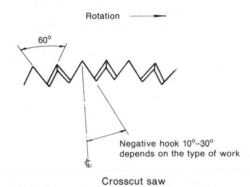

Crosscut saw

General Purpose or Centre Pitch Saws: The front of the tooth coincides with the centreline, i.e. it has neither negative nor positive rake. The teeth are usually filed with a top bevel and a front bevel. They are used for ripping and crosscutting.

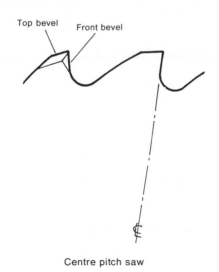

Centre pitch saw

Front Bevel: The angle at which the front of the tooth is filed. Crosscut saws are filed to produce a front bevel.

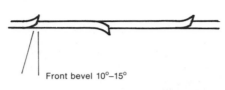

Front bevel 10°–15°

Clearance Angle: The angle formed by the top of the tooth and the cutting circle.

Positive hook 25°–30°

Tension: This is achieved by expanding the centre of a blade so that the cutting rim will remain taut or in tension. This tends to stiffen the blade and compensates for expansion of the rim during sawing operations. Tension is produced by hammering with a special hammer on a steel anvil.

Combination, Mitre, or Variety Saw: This blade has teeth in groups spaced by a deeper gulleted tooth with a positive hook. Used for crosscutting and ripping, it produces a clean finish.

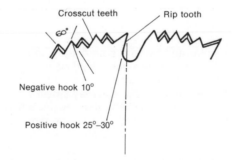

Combination, mitre, or variety saw

Tungsten Tip Saw: A shaped piece of tungsten carbide is brazed to each tooth. Tungsten carbide is hard and has great resistance to wear. The saw may be used for either ripping or crosscutting.

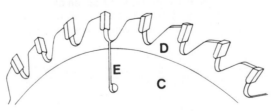

Tungsten Tip Carbide Saw
C – hardened steel plate
D – rim tensioned
E – expansion slots

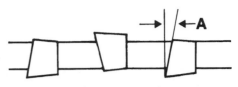

Bevel Faced Teeth
(angle A enables a slicing action when cutting)

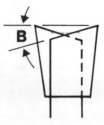

Alternate top bevel – angle B

Selecting a Saw Blade

A quality tungsten tipped carbide (TCT) blade is considered a good investment. Pressed steel blades, while quite good when correctly sharpened and set, lose their edge quickly, especially when cutting glue impregnated material, e.g. particle board.

The width of cut, or kerf, must be greater than the thickness of the riving knife.

Number of Teeth

For crosscutting, the more teeth available the better the cut. A 235 mm blade, for example, should have about 60 teeth. For ripping (cutting with the grain) fewer teeth more widely spaced are desirable, i.e. 16–24 teeth, to allow for better clearance of the sawdust.

Blade Quality

The following points should be considered when purchasing a saw blade:
- Check for flatness by holding a straight edge against the blade disc. No light should appear between the blade and the straight edge.
- On high-quality blades, faint grinding marks should be visible on the exposed faces of the teeth, along with concentric grinding marks on the blade disc. Beware of blades that have been painted.
- The blade disc should be hardened steel plate rather than sheet steel.
- Better quality blades are rim tensioned with larger blades having short expansion slots in the disc to cope with the difference in the heat build up between the rim and the centre of the blade—a common cause of blade buckling.

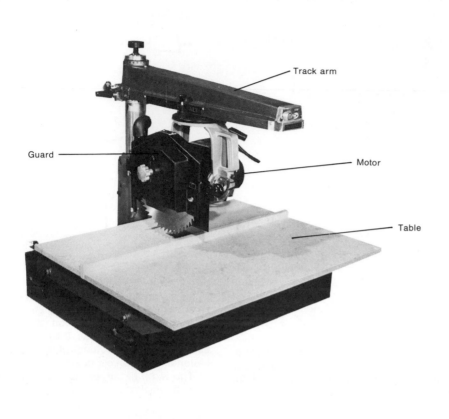

Track arm

Guard

Motor

Table

THE RADIAL ARM SAW

The Radial Saw has been developed from the earliest form of crosscutting saw bench, namely the Swing Saw. This consisted of a saw mounted on a long arm, the arm being attached to brackets which were in turn secured to a wall or ceiling.

The modern radial saw has the blade mounted on the motor shaft and is located on sides secured to a long arm running at right angles to the machine table. The saw assembly may be moved along the arm or carriage way producing vertical straight line saw cuts.

With correct adjustment, this precision machine may be used for crosscutting, ripping, mitring, bevelling, and compound bevelling. By the addition of various attachments it may be used for rebating, tenoning, trenching, and grooving.

Sizes and Types

Radial saw sizes, as with circular saws, are measured by the diameter of blade and vary from 200 mm to 500 mm.

Classification of radial saws is dependent upon the *overarm design*. The most common radial saw is the Stationary Overarm, where

the motor and blade are carried by an overhead arm while the stock is held stationary on the table. The arm is fixed to a vertical pillar at the rear of the table and may swivel 45° in either direction. Similarly the saw assembly may be canted through 45° in one direction only to provide for the cutting of compound angles.

The depth of cut may be controlled by raising or lowering the overarm.

The Travelling Head or Sliding Arm saw bench is similar to that of the radial saw bench with one advantage. Instead of a projecting arm the saw carriage is fixed to the arm and the whole assembly moves forwards and backwards through the pillar assembly.

Hydraulic Crosscut Saws are used for mass production work where sawing is confined generally to straight cuts. The saw carriage is fed forward with a predetermined length of stroke and rate of feed and with a constant return rate.

Specifications

The table consists of a series of flat boards of various widths held in position by thumbscrews. The guide fence is relocatable by virtue of the different width base boards and

provides support for timber during sawing operations. The base may be of steel or cast iron, and supports the table and radial arm. The yoke holding the motor and blade is suspended from the arm on a pivot enabling the motor to be rotated in a horizontal plane. The motor is also tiltable between the ends of the yoke. The track arm or overarm provides the carriage way for the yoke to move and is secured to a vertical column. It is adjustable to 45° in either direction and is the means of depth adjustment. The vertical column consists of a steel cylinder supporting the track arm and connecting the radial saw mechanism to the base. In some instances this column may be floor mounted.

The blade guards are freely adjustable with anti-kickback fingers provided for ripping operations.

Safety

• Eye and ear protection is essential.

• Avoid loose clothing.

• Stock must be held firmly against the fence.

• Return saw to rear of table on completion of cut and before removal of any stock.

• The supporting hand on the timber stock to be at least 100 mm from the blade.

• Remember to push back on the handle since the saw will pull itself into the work.

• If operating the saw left-handed, make sure that the right hand is not directly in line with or on the saw side of the handle.

• Anti-kickback fingers are *not* to be used for crosscutting and should be clear of timber stock.

• For ripping or ploughing make sure the saw blade rotates against the direction of feed of timber stock.

• If there is less than 75 mm between the blade and the fence it is better to use a push stick.

• The timber must be pushed past the anti-kickback bar before it can be removed.

• The guard should be lowered until it is about 3 mm above the timber.

Blade Mounting

1. Remove blade from table kerf by raising track arm.

2. Remove guard or guards.

3. Holding the arbor with spanner loosen the arbor nut with another spanner, remembering the left-hand thread.

4. Remove arbor nut, collar, and blade.

5. Replace new blade with teeth facing away from operator or in direction of arbor rotation.

6. Replace collar and nut and tighten.

7. Replace guards and lower blade 1 mm into table kerf.

Blade mounting

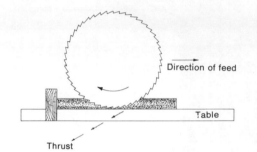

Direction of feed

Table

Thrust

Ripping

Right Hand: When the blade is between the motor and the fence.

The timber is fed from the right-hand side and pushed into the blade toward the left of the machine.

The teeth of the blade come up from the bottom and tend to push the timber back to the right. The anti-kickback bar should be set correctly, the points about 3 mm below the surface of the timber to prevent any kickback. Always check the kickback bar for proper adjustment before use.

It is *extremely dangerous* to feed the timber in from the left-hand side while the machine is in this position. The teeth would tend to pull the timber into the machine and out of your hands.

It is also desirable to use a push stick between the blade and the fence when cutting narrow stock.

Right-hand rip, where the blade is between motor and column

Left Hand: When the blade is on the outside, and the motor is between the blade and the fence.

With the saw in this position it is possible to rip wide boards.

Left-hand rip, where the motor is between column and blade

Crosscutting

This is the most basic of the operations on a radial arm saw as the machine was initially developed for this function. As the arm is adjustable to 45° in either direction the saw can crosscut at any angle within these limits. The saw carriage may also be canted up to 45° thus providing for bevelled crosscutting or compound crosscutting if required.

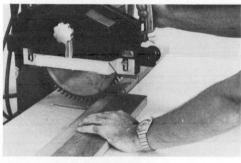

Crosscutting

Straight Crosscutting

Locate the radial arm at right angles to the guide fence, check by means of a try square, and lock in position (refer to graduated 0° scale).

Adjust the depth of cut by turning the elevating handle to allow the saw teeth to just scratch the top of the table.

Place the timber stock against the guide fence and adjust the guard and kickback fingers; kickback fingers 2 mm above stock being cut.

Begin the saw cut with the blade behind the guide fence and pull the saw through in a steady movement.

Return the saw to its starting position and switch off before removing the timber stock.

For crosscutting similar lengths a stop may be clamped to the guide fence.

Right-hand Feed: When using the right hand for pulling the saw through, the longer length

of material is held firm by the left hand and is on the left of the saw blade. This method is acceptable when cutting a 'free' end.

Left-hand Feed: This is preferred when cutting to length using a stop clamped to the guide fence. The stop is clamped to the right of the saw blade, with the right hand holding the stock against the stop and guide fence. The left hand is used to pull the saw through. With the right hand holding the stock firm, there is no possibility of 'jamming' occurring between the saw blade and stop as the blade is returned.

Mitring

Move the radial arm to the right or left of the column, lock in at the 45° notch and check the angle using a mitre set (refer to graduated 0° scale).

Adjust the depth of cut by turning the elevating handle to allow the saw teeth barely to touch the table surface (if required to cut completely through).

Place the timber stock against the guide fence and adjust the guard and kickback fingers; kickback fingers 2 mm above material being cut.

For right-hand mitring hold the timber stock with the left hand and pull the saw through with the right hand.

Return the saw to its original position behind the guide fence and switch off before removing the timber stock.

For left-hand mitring repeat as above, holding as for left-hand crosscutting.

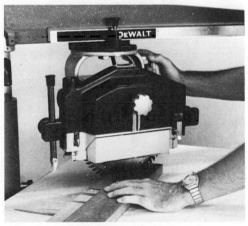

45° right-hand mitre

Crosscutting Bevels

Boards may be crosscut in two ways: by the movement of the arm from the right-angle position (left or right) and keeping the saw blade at 90° or by moving the saw blade from the right-angle position and keeping the arm at 90°.

Machine Adjustment (for bevelling)

Raise the machine to provide blade clearance as the motor is swivelled within the yoke.

COMPOUND SAWS

Compound mitre saws and compound slide saws are portable, lightweight and perfect for use in any workshop or on any worksite.

Compound mitre saws consist of a calibrated swivel base, a one-piece guide fence and a pivoted guarded blade housing and motor.

Slide compound saws have an additional feature of carriage slide arms allowing for an increased width-cutting capacity.

Both types of saws are particularly accurate and provide a high quality finish for everything from skirting boards to picture frames.

Cutting Mitres

The cutting of left- or right-hand mitres is achieved by loosening the grip and turning the base until the pointer indicates 45°. In these positions, as with the 90° position, a sprung loaded pin positively locks the base. Angles between 90° and 45° are obtained from the calibrated scale and the base is locked in position by tightening the grip.

Compound slide saw

Cutting Bevels

Tilt the blade to the required bevel angle. Where possible clamp the work piece in position and gently lower the saw until the cut is complete. Wait until the blade has come to a complete stop before returning the blade to the elevated position.

Safety

- Ear and eye protection is essential
- Avoid loose clothing
- Do not operate saw without guards in place
- Ensure that the base is positively secured
- Remove all chips from table top before operating
- Ensure the blade is not in contact with work piece before starting

BANDSAWS

Initially bandsaws were used only to cut irregular shapes and curves in flat stock. However, industrial requirements have produced heavy duty bandsaws capable of straight sawing and resawing of thick round stock into thinner pieces. These are known as Band Mills and Band Resaws, respectively.

The Band Scroll Saw, ranging from 360 mm to 1060 mm, generally used in school and industry where curve cutting is predominant, can also be used for straight cutting where great accuracy is not paramount. The saw itself is a continuous flexible band of spring steel with teeth cut on one edge.

Bandsaws are considered safe in comparison with circular saws since they have a cutting action perpendicular to the stock surface thereby eliminating the possibility of kickback.

Sizes and Types

The size of a bandsaw is measured by the diameter of the wheels around which the band runs. A 360 mm bandsaw has 360 mm diameter wheels. The cutting capacity is measured by the maximum stock thickness that may be cut, and thus the throat capacity is determined. For classification purposes bandsaws may be grouped into four categories: Band Scroll Saws, Band Resaws, Band Bevel Saws and Band Mill Saws.

Specifications

The band scroll saw consists of two rubber tyred wheels mounted in a G-shaped frame. The frame is in the form of a metal casting, ribbed for strength, and supported on a base. For some bandsaws the base is a separate enclosure, while for others it is an integral part of the design. Within the base are contained the motor, pullies and belt adjustment mechanism.

The lower wheel, connected to the upper wheel by means of the continuous blade, provides the driving power and is fixed in position. The upper wheel is mounted in slides within the main frame in such a manner that an arrangement of springs keeps it pushing upwards against the saw blade, thus maintaining the tension of the saw. The upper wheel may be raised or lowered by means of the tension adjustment handwheel in order to accommodate varying blade lengths. To assist in this fitting, a canting or tilting knob is provided to enable the blade to track in the correct position on the upper wheel. Both the upper and lower wheels are rubber faced to provide blade protection and to prevent the blade from slipping.

Between the two wheels is mounted a table which serves as a work support and may be canted up to 45° to the right and 10° to the left. Guides are fitted above and below the table to keep the blade from twisting, thereby ensuring accurate cutting. The upper guide is attached to the guide post to allow for the thickness of cut. Fastened to the upper blade guide is the blade guard.

Blades: The two most used bandsaw blades are the Standard and the Skip Tooth, both of which may be classified as general purpose blades. The skip tooth blade has the advantage of faster cutting since its design eliminates sawdust clogging.

The width of blades used on band scroll saws varies from 4 mm to 20 mm, resulting in variation of tooth pitch. For example, if a large tooth were used on a narrow blade the resulting depth of gullet would produce a very weak blade likely to crack under cutting load. This leads to the number of teeth per 25 mm varying from seven on narrow blades to four on wider blades.

The length of a blade is calculated by adding together the circumference of one wheel and twice the distance between the wheel centres.

The thickness of bandsaw blades is determined by giving .025 mm for each 25 mm of the diameter of the wheels on which it runs.

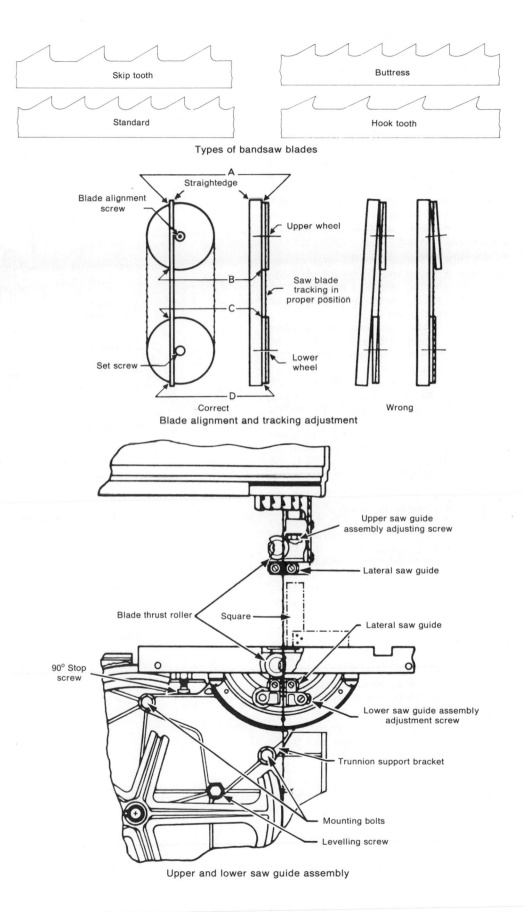

Types of bandsaw blades

Blade alignment and tracking adjustment

Upper and lower saw guide assembly

Operating Adjustments

WHEELS: Frequent checking of the rubber surfaces of the wheels for resin or gum deposits will promote longer blade life since it minimises the strain caused by flexing and consequent cracking of the blades.

The tilting device attached to the upper wheel enables the blade to run with its centre corresponding to that of the centre of the wheel. It is important that each blade mounted is set similarly as this will not only enable the blade to run and cut correctly but will also spread the wear caused by the set of the teeth, hence reducing grooves on the rubber tyres. This adjustment and positioning of the blade is known as 'tracking'.

SAW GUIDES: Because of the large diameter of the wheels there is considerable distance between the points of contact of the blade and wheels, leaving large sections of the blade unsupported.

Two saw guide assemblies are therefore fitted to the machine to provide lateral and back support to keep the blade running accurately.

The upper guide is attached to the adjustable guide post and consists of two brass jaws to prevent the blade from twisting and a ball bearing thrust wheel to support the back of the blade while sawing. The lower guide assembly, located directly beneath the saw table and having the same parts as the upper guides, is bolted to the bandsaw frame.

POSITIONING JAWS: Having placed the blade on the machine, adjust the tension wheel and the tilting wheel so as to provide the correct tension, and locate the blade centrally on the wheels. It is important that these adjustments be made simultaneously since one is dependent upon the other.

Each saw guide assembly is positioned so that the front edge of the jaws are behind the gullets of the saw teeth. The brass jaws are further adjusted, allowing 0.05 mm clearance between each face of the jaws and the saw blade.

Rotate the saw by hand, checking the clearance of the blade between the jaws and the position of the gullets in relation to the jaws.

SETTING THRUST WHEELS: Following the correct adjustment of the jaws the thrust wheels are moved forward until they are within 1 mm of the back of the blade. Free rotation of the thrust wheels will prevent grooves from forming on the faces through contact with the blade. Poorly adjusted thrust wheels are the main reason for saw breakages.

MOUNTING BANDSAW BLADES: Isolate the machine and remove the guards.

Lower the upper wheel by releasing the tension and remove the blade.

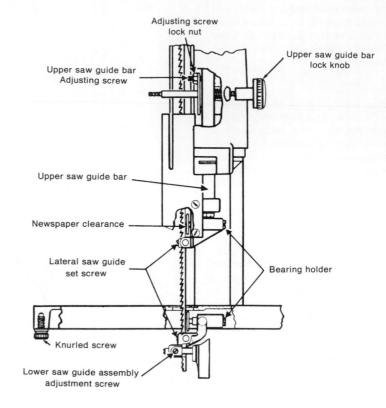

Upper and lower saw guide assembly

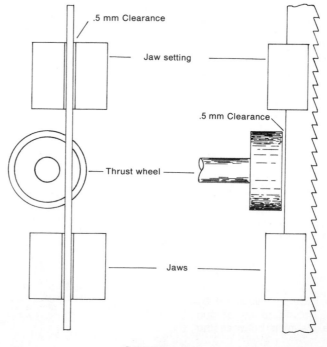

Guide assembly

Place the new blade on the wheels.

Adjust the tension and locate the blade centrally on the wheels.

Relocate the saw guides to their correct position.

Adjust the thrust wheel to its correct position.

Replace all guards.

Blade precautions

1. Check the tension.
2. Check the condition to ensure there are no cracks—indicated by a rhythmic click.
3. Check the position of the blade with respect to jaws and thrust wheels.
4. Check the blade sharpness.
5. Check the blade size in relation to diameter of cuts to be made.

Safety

• Eye and ear protection is essential.
• Avoid loose clothing.
• All guards must be positioned correctly and firmly fastened.
• Allow the saw to reach full speed before commencing the saw cut.
• Keep hands at least 50 mm away from the blade and not directly in line with the teeth.
• Avoid 'backing out' of curve cuts where possible.
• Cylindrical stock should not be cut unless mounted in a suitable jig.
• Switch off to make any adjustments.
• Isolate the machine from the power circuit when changing a blade.

Straight Sawing

Freehand: Raise the guide post to provide 6 mm clearance of work.

Slowly feed the stock past the saw using one hand as a guide and the other for pushing the material.

Ensure the saw cut is approximately 1 mm on the waste side of the line.

Ripping: This may be carried out freehand or with the aid of a fence.

Attach a rip fence to the saw table in the desired position, allowing 1 to 2 mm clearance for dressing.

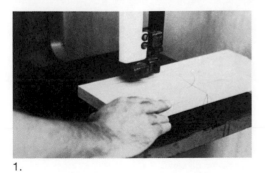

1.

Holding the timber stock firmly against the fence, feed in past the saw blade.

Square stock may be ripped diagonally by holding it firmly against the fence and canting the table to 45° or by passing the stock through a suitable jig held against the fence.

Round stock may also be cut by using this same jig.

Care should be taken when using a wooden fence that it is fixed parallel to the blade otherwise the stock will not be sawn straight and parallel.

Crosscutting: As with ripping, timber stock may be crosscut freehand or by using a mitre gauge.

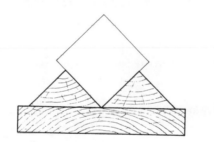

Round stock

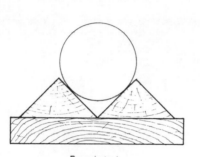

Square or rectangular stock

Locate the mitre gauge in the machined slot and check for squareness against the blade.

Holding the timber firmly against the mitre gauge feed in past the saw blade.

Wide stock may be crosscut by reversing the mitre gauge, thus providing better support.

NOTE
The use of the ripping fence and mitre gauge should be severely limited where access is available to machines specifically designed for ripping and crosscutting.

Curve Cutting: For normal bandsaw work it is necessary to observe a number of basic rules to understand the manipulation of both the blade and the stock.

Cutting round stock

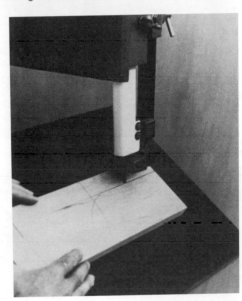

2.

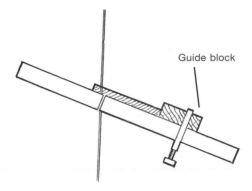

Guide block

Bevelling on the bandsaw

Cutting should not commence until the blade is running at full speed.

Where a curve is required, too small for the blade to accommodate, a series of radial cuts should be made.

For cutting irregular curves make a number of straight cuts to free the blade, thus eliminating the need to 'back out'.

When cutting into a sharp corner, a series of saw cuts should be made for blade manoeuvrability.

Multiple Sawing: Mark out the required shape on the top member.

Attach further required pieces by means of nails driven into the waste timber.

Care should be taken to ensure the nails are driven vertically and a sufficient distance from the marked line.

The total height of the nailed blocks should not exceed 100 mm in case of 'run in'.

Compound Sawing: This is to saw to an outline from two adjacent surfaces on a piece of stock, e.g. cabriole legs.

Using a narrow blade start the saw cut on one of the marked surfaces.

Sawing on the waste side of the line carry the saw cut through to within 6 mm from the end and stop.

To remove the waste completely would also remove the markings on the adjacent side.

Proceed with and complete the cuts on the adjacent side and remove the waste.

Return to initial cut and complete.

SCROLL SAW

Scroll saws are used mainly to fine curved saw cuts and are able to do 'inside' cutting or 'piercing' work.

They are generally a small bench machine with a cast iron frame, a table and an arm or gooseneck extending over it.

A steel rod that moves up and down between two vertical slides connects a wheel driven by a motor. The blade is held between a lower and upper clamp with the latter being tensioned to prevent the blade from buckling. The table, similar to that of a bandsaw, is able to tilt 45° to the left and 15° to the right.

Using the Scroll Saw

Blades are fastened in the clamps with the teeth pointing downwards and the guide plate positioned behind the blade. Check that the slot is wide enough to allow free movement of the blade.

Position the guide post so that the hold down foot rests lightly on the work being sawn. (This prevents the work being lifted off the table on the upstroke.)

General cutting is technique is similar to that of using the bandsaw. Although it is easier and safer to 'back out' of a cut than it is for a bandsaw, the scroll saw tends to 'roughen' the edges of the cut.

Piercing

Holes are bored in the parts to be pierced using a twist drill a little larger in diameter than the blade width. Raise the guide post and insert the blade through one of the holes and secure the blade to the upper clamp.

A piece of waste material clamped to the back of the timber stock will avoid roughening the edges around the hole on the underside.

If several pieces of the same shape are to be sawn, nail them together and markout the design on the top piece.

3.

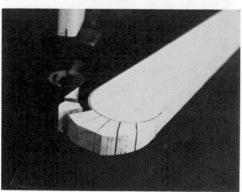

4.

Basic bandsaw operating techniques
1. Ripping through stock (see page 61)
2. Ripping a bevel using the tilting table (see page 61)
3. Crosscutting can be done either freehand or using a mitre gauge
4. Curve cutting with the aid of a series of saw cuts
5. Cutting a regular curve
6. Multiple cutting—note the nails driven through the waste timber of the top member
7. Compound sawing by sawing to a line on two adjacent surfaces

5.

6.

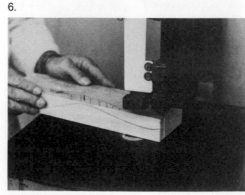

7.

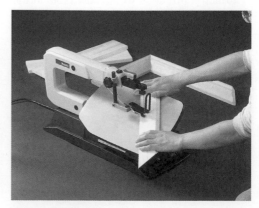

Using a scroll saw

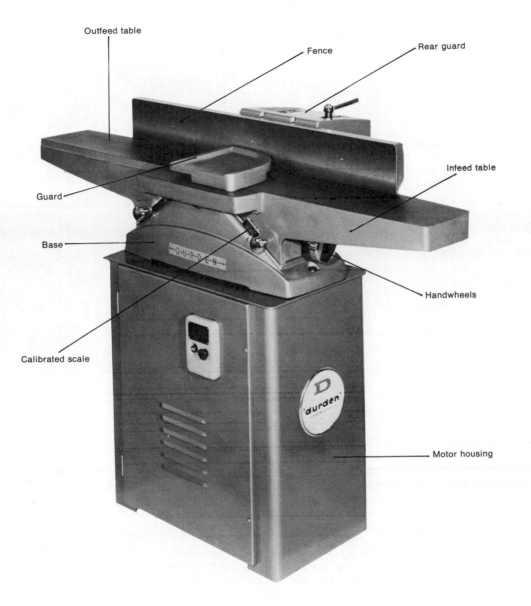

Outfeed table

Fence

Rear guard

Guard

Infeed table

Base

Handwheels

Calibrated scale

Motor housing

Planer Jointer

Jointers are planing machines designed to produce one surface straight, true and flat, and one edge straight, and at 90° to the flat surface. These planed sides provide the 'true' surfaces for further operations whether by hand or machine.

The jointer may also be used for planing bevels, chamfers, tapers, and rebates on previously 'dressed' timber stock.

Types and Sizes

The size of the jointer is determined by the lengths of the knives used in the cutter head. These may range from the small bench jointers of 100 mm, 150 mm, and 200 mm to the 600 mm industrial machines.

Since the planing is performed by means of rotary cutters the surface produced cannot be classified as 'flat'.

The surface, in fact, must be composed of

minute parallel hollows known as cutter marks. The average cutter head rotation is between 4000 and 4500 r.p.m. The rate of feed and the speed of rotation of the cutters determine the quality of surface finish. For the standard finish grade, eight cutter marks per 25 mm are acceptable while up to sixteen are required for top quality cabinet work.

Specifications

Parts and Uses: The major parts of the jointer are the base, tables, fence, cutter head, guards, and motor.

Cutter Heads: By regulation these must be cylindrical in cross section following the prohibition of square cutter heads exposing an unduly large gap between the cutter head and table.

The cutter head contains machined slots for holding 2, 3, 4 or 6 high speed steel or tungsten carbide knives. The two basic methods of holding the knives in position are referred to as the Cap and the Moving Plate Method.

For the best cutting action, knives are mounted at a slight angle to provide a shearing cut. For general purpose work in both hardwood and softwood this cutting angle is approximately 25°.

Modern jointers are being constructed with at least four knives in the cutter head which produce a better finish at a faster rate of feed than two cutter machines.

Similarly, research has demonstrated the larger the diameter of the cutter head the flatter the cutter to the timber and the better the finish, since the peripheral speed has been increased without increasing the r.p.m. of the cutter block.

Tables: Mounted on either side of the cutter head are the accurately machined tables. Each table may be raised or lowered independently by means of handwheels or levers and dovetailed ways.

The front table or infeed table controls the depth of cut by reference to a calibrated scale located on the side of the table. The rear table or outfeed table is adjusted to be perfectly level with the cutter head at the peak of its cutting circle. The rebate table is attached to the infeed table and provides support for material being rebated.

NOTE

For this purpose the knives must extend slightly beyond the rebated edge of the outfeed table to allow clearance.

An essential principle of this machine is that whatever the relative position of the two tables, they must always be parallel to each other.

Fence: This is generally attached to the infeed table and may tilt in both directions and be secured at any angle by a locking device. For ease of adjustment some jointers have stops located at 45° and 90°. The section of fence covering the outfeed table contains an adjustable plate to supply support for thin stock.

Base: This is generally of heavy cast iron construction enabling good support for front and rear tables. Bench models may be bolted to

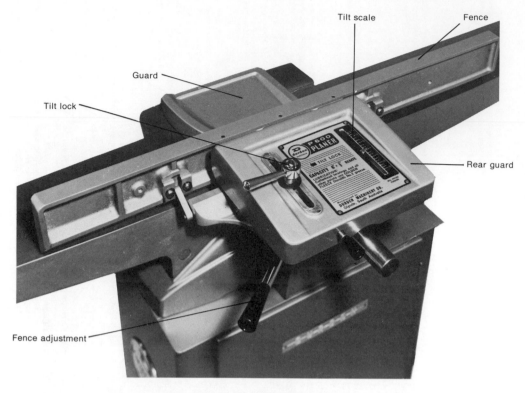

Detail of tilting mechanism

open steel stands or enclosed cabinets.

Guards: There are various types of guards available but generally they are classified as bridge guards or leg of mutton guards. The bridge guard has a rise and fall movement enabling variations in stock thickness and sideways adjustment to cover the cutters completely at all times.

The leg of mutton guard, so called because of its shape, covers the cutter head only in its closed position. With the cut near completion the cutter head becomes completely exposed and consequently manufacturers are tending to supply bridge guards for improvement of safety standards.

Motor: For the average 150 mm to 200 mm machine a 700 to 1400 watt electric motor is used with up to 3720 watts for 300 mm to 400

mm machines. The optimum r.p.m. has been found to be in the vicinity of 4000 to 4500 with some belt driven machines attaining 6000 r.p.m.

Safety
- Eye and ear protection is essential.
- Avoid loose clothing.
- Keep the guards correctly positioned and adjusted.
- Check grain direction—always cut with the grain.
- Use push block for planing short or thin stock.
- Check accuracy of fence and see that it is firmly locked in position.
- Check depth of cut.
- Attain the correct stance for comfortable use of machine.

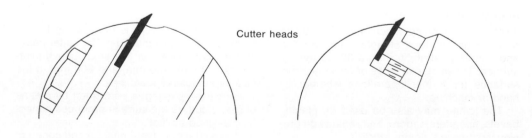

Cutter heads

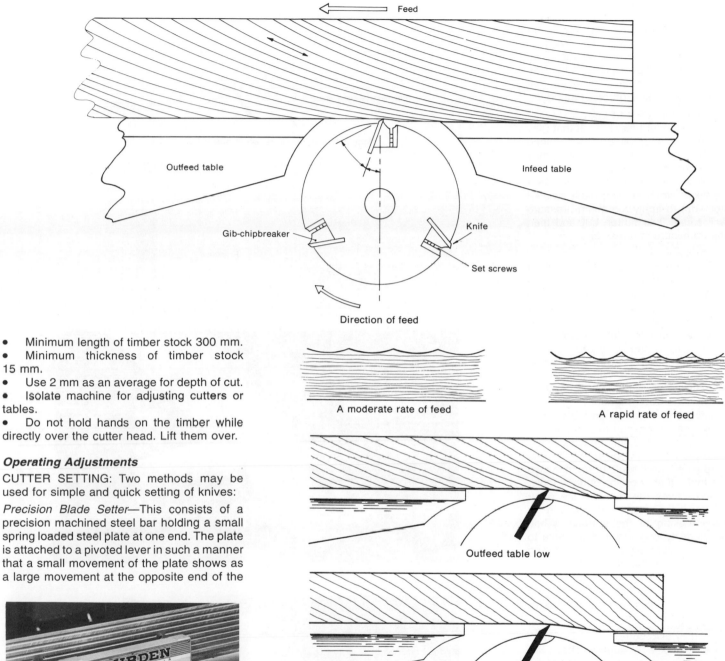

Feed

Outfeed table

Infeed table

Gib-chipbreaker

Knife

Set screws

Direction of feed

A moderate rate of feed

A rapid rate of feed

Outfeed table low

Outfeed table high

- Minimum length of timber stock 300 mm.
- Minimum thickness of timber stock 15 mm.
- Use 2 mm as an average for depth of cut.
- Isolate machine for adjusting cutters or tables.
- Do not hold hands on the timber while directly over the cutter head. Lift them over.

Operating Adjustments

CUTTER SETTING: Two methods may be used for simple and quick setting of knives:

Precision Blade Setter—This consists of a precision machined steel bar holding a small spring loaded steel plate at one end. The plate is attached to a pivoted lever in such a manner that a small movement of the plate shows as a large movement at the opposite end of the

Precision blade setter

lever. The free end indicates on a calibrated scale variations between cutter settings.

Timber Straight Edge—A piece of timber stock approximately 375 x 38 x 10 mm is prepared as a straight edge and two marks 6 mm apart are made about 75 mm from one end. The cutters are placed in the cutter head protruding 1.5 mm from the end of the cutter head to allow for clearance.

Place the straight edge on the outfeed table with the first mark resting on the lip of the table. Rotate the cutter head so that the cutter lifts the straight edge and moves it forward on to the second mark. Adjust the cutter by means of a wooden mallet until this forward movement is accurate. This procedure is carried out across the full width of the blade and repeated for the other cutters. When found to be correct the holding nuts are tightened working from the centre.

TABLE ADJUSTMENT: The setting of the outfeed table on the jointer is most critical since it must accept the planed surface at the exact height of the cutter head periphery.

If the outfeed table is low, the timber stock drops on to the cutters as it leaves the infeed table. This produces a dip in the end of the timber.

If the outfeed table is too high the cut reduces, thereby producing a taper.

To adjust the outfeed table pass a piece of timber stock over the cutters until it just protrudes over the outfeed table. This table can now be adjusted so that it just touches the timber stock. Check on completion of cut that the stock has not tapered off or 'dropped in'.

Planing a Face Surface and Edges

The maximum width of timber stock that may be planed on the planer jointer is determined by the length of the blades. Face planing may involve the removal of twists or winds, hollows, high spots, and surface roughness. Care should be taken when planing badly twisted timber stock not to apply too much pressure as this will cause it to flatten out and then return when pressure is released.

Planing a Surface

Adjust the infeed table to provide a depth of cut of approximately 2 mm. Position the fence to allow a full width cut and raise the bridge guard to provide underneath clearance for passage of timber stock.

Examine the stock for defects and grain direction. If hollow, the concave surface should be planed first to prevent stock being unstable on the infeed table. With both hands in contact with the material, move the stock forward at an even rate of feed.

When sufficient material is on the outfeed table the left hand is passed from the infeed table over the guard to the outfeed table where a downward pressure is applied. As the end of the board is reached the right hand is also transferred to the timber on the outfeed table. As one hand leaves the material the other should control it for weight and pressure to prevent any rocking of the surface. When using the bridge type guard it is possible to 'slide' the hands over the guard without losing complete contact with the stock.

Continue this process until a satisfactory surface has been produced, checking to ensure the timber is not rendered undersize.

Planing an Edge

This process may also be referred to as *jointing* an edge. Using a try square, check the angle between the fence and table. Adjust the depth of cut to approximately 2 mm by lowering the front table. Position the fence to accommodate the thickness of timber stock and adjust guards to cover exposed blades. Re-position the front guard to provide clearance for the passage of material over the cutters. Placing the previously machined face against the fence on the infeed side and applying an inward pressure coupled with a downward pressure, feed the stock forward at a constant rate.

For longer stock it is important to maintain pressure near the cutter head, changing the position of the hands when necessary.

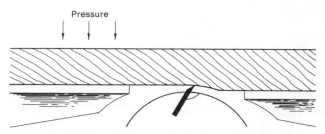

Application of pressure when planing surfaces

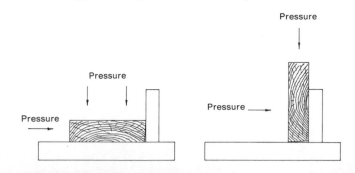

Method of planing surface

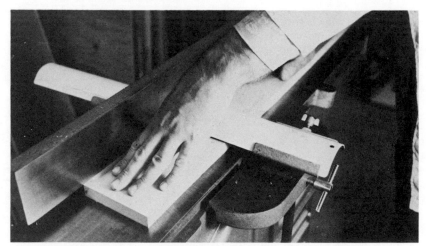

Method of planing an edge

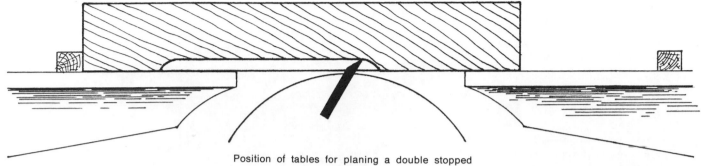

Position of tables for planing a double stopped
chamfer

Planing Chamfers, Bevels, Rebates, Tapers, and Tenons

In addition to normal surface planing, the jointer, in collaboration with specialised jigs, may be adapted to plane chamfers, bevels, rebates, tapers, and tenons. Consequently this machine is most versatile for home and school use.

Planing a Chamfer

Adjust the angle of the fence and lock in position at 135° or 45°. For safety reasons an angle of 135° is preferred since the material and work edge are visually acceptable. Adjust for the required depth of cut by raising or lowering the infeed table. Position the rear bridge guard so as to be in contact with the fence. Locate the front guard allowing adequate clearance for the machining of the stock. Using a test piece and holding similarly to when jointing an edge, make a trial cut to check the angle and depth of cut. Plane the chamfer as shown.

The same procedure may be adopted in planing a bevel, the only difference being if the angle is any other than 45° or 135°.

The fence is tilted to plane chamfers, bevels and splays

For Single Stopped Chamfers, the machine is adjusted as for through chamfering, with the exception of the front guard. Determine the position at which the blade ceases cutting. Position the timber stock so that the run out point of the chamfer coincides with the cutter

cessation point and clamp a stop to the outfeed table. Replace the front guard, providing enough clearance for stock to be machined.

For Double Stopped Chamfers adjust the infeed table to the required depth of cut then *lower the outfeed table* to be level with the infeed table. Position the fence at 135° and slide the rear guard so as to be in contact with the back of the fence. Locate the position at which a cutter begins and ends its cutting action. Affix stops to the infeed and outfeed tables enabling the chamfer to be stopped at the appropriate positions. Replace the front guard, providing sufficient clearance for stock to be machined.

As a safety precaution, one end of the stock should be placed against the stop on the *infeed table* and slowly lowered until in full contact with both tables.

Splaying

This requires the attachment of an extension fence providing longer support for timber stock. Adjustment of the fence may be made by either the tilting scale or using a sliding bevel. The total depth of cut is determined by measuring the vertical distance from the corner of stock to the splay line. It may be necessary to consider a number of cuts to meet the required depth since a maximum of 2.3 mm should be observed. If the timber stock is narrow, a push block should be used.

Rebates

These may be cut on the jointer as follows. Remove the front guard and adjust the position of the fence and infeed table to desired locations. The fence position may be achieved by measuring its distance from the edge of a cutter. For this method it is advisable to make sure that all cutters protrude a similar distance in the cutter block. Adjust the rear guard so

Planing a rebate

as to be in contact with the fence, thereby covering the exposed blades. Using a test piece, make a trial cut to check the width and depth of rebate. Adjust if necessary and make required cut or cuts as in edge jointing.

NOTE

The front guard must remain out for rebating. For single and double stopped rebates the procedure is the same as for single and double stopped chamfering, the only difference being that the angle of the fence for rebating must be 90°.

Taper Planing

When tapering, the infeed table should be lowered to the required depth. Place one end of

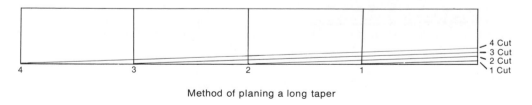

Method of planing a long taper

the stock on the infeed table and lower the timber to the outfeed table and pass it over the cutters. The lowering position, determined by the coinciding of the highest cutter point with the beginning of the taper, is marked by a stop block clamped to the infeed table.

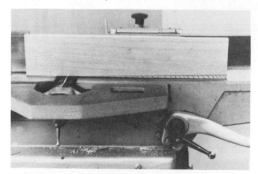

Planing a taper. Note position of stop clamped on to infeed table.

For tapering long lengths the method used is to divide the length and depth of the taper into equal parts. For a 1200 mm long 12 mm taper the length may be divided into four parts each of 300 mm and the depth into four parts each of 3 mm. The timber stock is then marked accordingly and the depth of cut set. Locate mark 1 over the cutters, lower and cut, repeating for marks 2, 3, and 4.

Tenoning

Using the circular saw bench, produce the shoulder cuts. Lower the infeed table of the planer jointer to the required depth and attach an extension fence. With a squared timber block run a short rebate and check for accuracy of width and depth.

Holding the end to be tenoned against the fence and using the squared block as a back up member, feed in to produce one cheek of the tenon. The timber stock is turned over to complete the tenon.

Position for cutting a tenon. Note use of a push block

COMBINATION MACHINE

Combination woodworking machines have been developed over many years to meet the

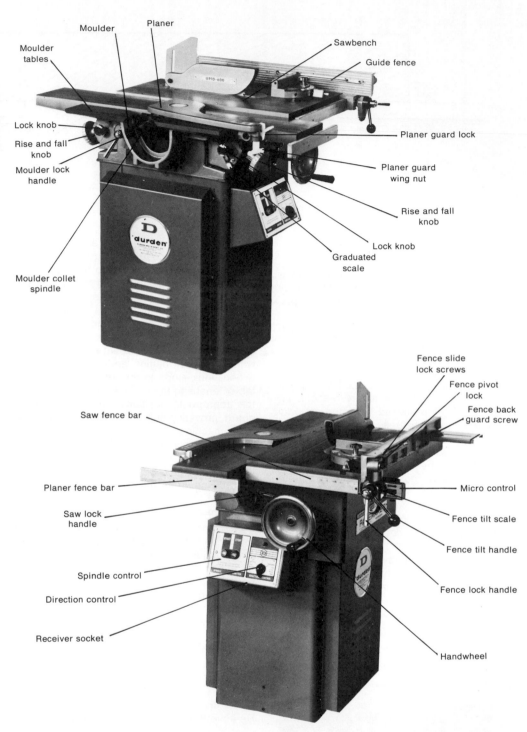

needs of the home owner, small tradesman, and the professional craftsman.

Many of the features incorporated in these now sophisticated machines are the direct result of suggestions made by owners over the years.

Specifications

Saw Bench: The handwheel is used to position the saw table height in relation to the saw blade. The saw lock handle locks the saw table slide and no attempt should be made to operate the handwheel while this lock is engaged.

Planer: The rise and fall knobs are used to position the table surfaces in relation to the cutting line of the blades. The graduated scale fitted to the front planer table indicates the depth of cut. The lock knobs lock the tables in any position on the scale. The planer guard lock is pushed forward to prevent the guard from opening or is drawn full back when automatic guard operation is required. The planer guard wing nut is loosened to remove the planer guard when necessary.

Moulder: The planer rise and fall knob is used to position the moulder tables in relation to the moulder collet spindle and the graduated scale on the planer can be referred to for moulding operations.

The moulder lock is used to lock the moulding tables prior to any moulding work being performed and it is quite important that this lock be released before any attempt is made to operate the planer rise and fall knob.

Fence: The fence lock handle locks the whole fence assembly to the fence bars while the fence tilt handle enables the fence to be tilted over to any angle shown on the fence tilt scale.

The fence pivot lock allows the fence to be aligned to an angle across the table while the fence slide lock screws are loosened when it is required to draw the fence back for rip sawing work. The fence back guard screw can be locked to contain the length of the back guard where necessary. The micro control will move the whole fence assembly along either fence bar providing the fence lock handle is loosened.

Saw Bench

Types of Saw Blades: There are many types of saw blades available for various uses, but the most important is the Rip Blade which is used for all 'along the grain cutting'. Second choice should be a Crosscut or Fine Tooth Blade for clean and square cross grain cutting. The Planer Blade, which is hollow ground and uses a tooth form of unique design, may be used for both ripping and crosscutting but its cutting speed is not as fast as ordinary blades.

Ripping: The saw bench is probably used more for ripping wide timber into narrower sections than any other operation which may be performed on it. To facilitate these operations more efficiently the following simple rules should be observed:

Never use the guide fence in its fully extended position when ripping. Adjust the fence so that the end does not extend more than 75 mm past the gullet of the saw teeth. This eliminates jamming of the material between the back of the saw blade and the fence if the fence is left in an extended position.

Make sure the fence is running parallel to the saw blade.

To avoid unnecessary friction, adjust the saw blade to maximum height. This allows the blade to cut on the down revolution, thereby producing a cleaner saw cut.

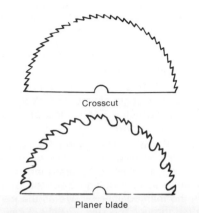

Crosscut

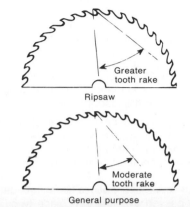

Ripsaw — Greater tooth rake

Planer blade

General purpose — Moderate tooth rake

Types of saw blades

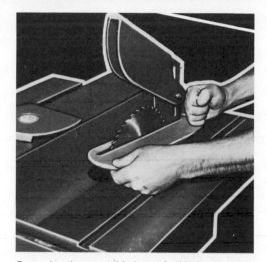

Removing the saw table insert for blade changing.

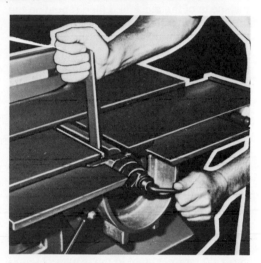

Spindle holding bar for the removal of the saw blade

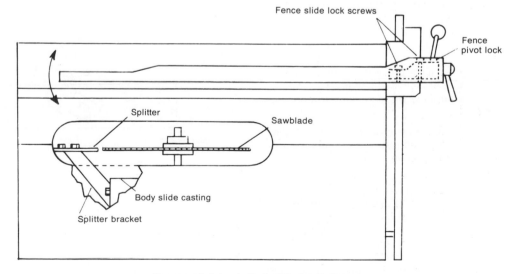

Fence slide lock screws

Fence pivot lock

Splitter

Sawblade

Body slide casting

Splitter bracket

Fence and riving knife (splitter) adjustment

Unless it is impractical, always leave the saw guard and riving knife on the machine. This assists in preventing the material binding on the saw blade and consequent kickback occurring.

When ripping material where the distance is less than 75 mm between the blade and the fence, a properly made 'push stick' should be used to finish the last of the cut.

Resawing: The cutting of material which, in the first instance, is greater in thickness than the maximum cutting capacity of the saw blade also comes under the heading of ripping.

This operation necessitates the material being passed over the saw blade twice, first to a depth of cut a little greater than half the thickness of the stock and then repeating the procedure after having reversed the timber in an end for end motion.

Angle Ripping: This is accomplished with the guide fence tilted to the right to the required angle. The same rules that apply to ordinary ripping should be observed.

Crosscutting and Mitring: The accuracy of the work produced when crosscutting depends on the following factors:

For best results use a crosscut or fine tooth blade.

A mitre quadrant, providing accuracy and stability, should always be used when crosscutting or mitring is to be performed.

To increase the useability and accuracy of the mitre quadrant it is advisable to attach a piece of PAR hardwood approximately 360 mm x 60 mm x 20 mm to the working face of the quadrant by two CKS screws.

A greater crosscutting capacity can be achieved by reversing the mitre quadrant in its machined guide track.

When crosscutting material which is less in thickness than the depth cutting capacity of the machine it is useful to raise the table to allow the blade to be the same height as the timber thickness plus the depth of the saw teeth blades. This provides a larger working area in front of the blade and allows the operator a better view when working to pencil or scribed lines.

Dadoing and Grooving: For most operations of this type it is necessary to remove the saw guard and riving knife.

Example—a 30 mm x 12 mm trench may be cut in the following ways:

Raise the table to allow the blade to protrude through the required 12 mm.

With the mitre quadrant adjusted square to the blade, cut the two extremes of the 30 mm trench section.

With successive cuts either remove the waste completely or cut sufficiently to allow cleaning up with a wide chisel.

Grooves may be cut by raising the table to expose the correct amount of saw blade and then adjusting the guide fence after each cut so that the waste is removed. This fence movement is continued until the desired groove width is obtained.

Cove Cutting: This is the operation of cutting a radius in the length of timber stock as seen on 'Scotia' sections. For cutting procedure refer to Circular Saws.

Wide Sheet Sawing: The ripping down of large sheets such as plywood, hardboard, particle board, etc., is achieved by first marking out the sheet and then cutting freehand by following the marked lines by eye as the material is fed through the saw. For sheet sawing a fine toothed saw should be used.

Planer

Face Planing: This is achieved by having the rear table surface perfectly level with the uppermost cutting line of the revolving blades. The desired depth of cut is obtained by means of the rise and fall knob attached to the front table. As a general rule the depth of cut should be limited to approximately 2 mm. However, this will vary according to the width of the material.

When planing timber wider than 30 mm the adjoining saw table edge can be used as a guide rather than the guide fence which can be left set for use on the saw side.

NOTE

It is imperative that the saw table be fully raised and the saw guard in position when using the planer.

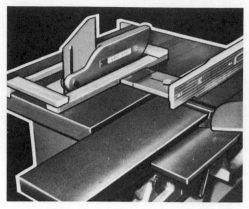

Planer set up ready for use

Face Edge Planing: This operation is usually carried out after the wide or face surfaces of the material have been planed. The guide fence should be adjusted to keep the material at right angles to the cutting blades, with the planed face held against the guide fence.

The depth of cut for edge planing may exceed that of face planing but again this depends on the thickness of the material. The lighter the cut the better the finish on all planing operations.

Bevel Planing: To perform bevel planing tilt the guide fence to the required angle and then proceed in the same manner as in edge planing. For obvious safety precautions the fence should always be tilted to the right.

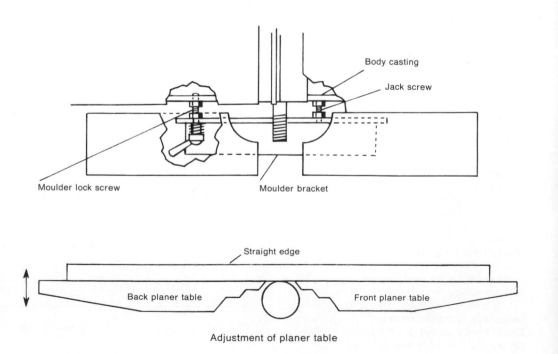

Adjustment of planer table

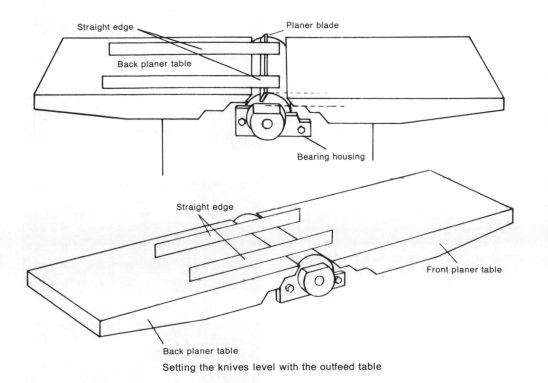

Straight edge

Planer blade

Back planer table

Bearing housing

Straight edge

Front planer table

Back planer table

Setting the knives level with the outfeed table

Rebating: This operation may be carried out by:

Removing the planer guard.

Positioning the guide fence to the desired width of the rebate and ensuring the back guard is covering any exposed cutting blades.

Lowering the front table to the required depth.

Double Stopped Rebating: This type of rebating may be referred to as 'blind' as the rebate does not run through the entire length of the material but starts some distance from the leading edge and finishes before the trailing edge passes the cutter head. For procedure details refer to Double Stopped Chamfers in the Planer Jointer section.

Back Planer Table   Front Planer Table

Table adjustment for a double stopped rebate

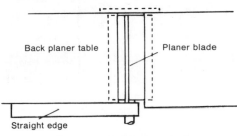

Back planer table

Planer blade

Straight edge

Adjustment of table for rebating

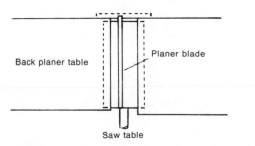

Back planer table

Planer blade

Saw table

Moulder

The moulder most commonly used is of the horizontal twin cutter type. This allows a wide variety of shapes to be produced without any special skill on the part of the operator, the work being passed over the cutters in a similar manner to a planing operation.

Cutting the Mould: As with the planer, the method of holding the work and feeding over the blades should be even, with a good 'downward and toward the fence' pressure being applied throughout the cutting operation. The feed should be no faster than that which the cutters will allow, and where this is very slow, consideration should be given to taking two cuts. This will, of course, necessitate the raising and lowering of the tables.

Angle Moulding: This is carried out with the guide fence tilted either to the left or right, whichever is the most convenient for the particular operation. This method of moulding is extremely useful where it is necessary to let ply or the like into a rail at an angle other than 90°.

Fly mould

Splay

Groove or Rebate

Broad cove

Edge mould

Screen bead

Quad

Scotia

Parting bead

Chamfer

Stop bead

Unique

Tongue

Groove

Dust proof

Flute

Types of moulding cutters

Grooving: The moulder is extremely adaptable to this operation and with cutters ground to the required groove width, finished grooves can easily be produced. The necessity to have an extensive range of grooving cutters can be overcome by the use of the Wobble Saw.

Rebating: While this operation is often carried out on the planer, the moulder has the advantage of being able to produce rebates longer than the planer's capacity.

Attachments

1. *Borer—Sander.* This useful attachment allows the following operations:

Boring or *Dowelling*—using spiral fluted dowel drills ranging in size from 4 mm to 18 mm and having a 12 mm parallel shank.

Mortising—using straight fluted mortise drills. These drills have their edges relieved along the entire cutting length to facilitate the cutting action when the workpiece is moved sideways to produce the slot known as the mortise.

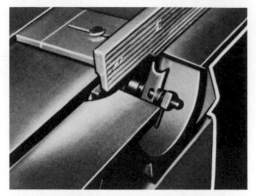

Adjustment for spindle moulder

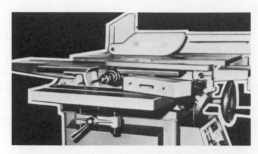

Boring or dowelling attachment

Use of disc sanding attachment

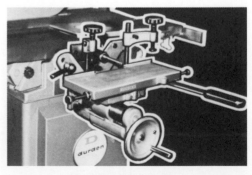

Table adjustment for disc sanding

Disc Sander—allows all types of disc sanding using a 200 mm diameter aluminium disc.

2. *Mechanical Mortiser:* This attachment is intended for use where larger quantities of mortised work are required than would be practical to produce by the hand method described under the Boring and Sander section.

Action of the wobble saw

Minimum

Maximum

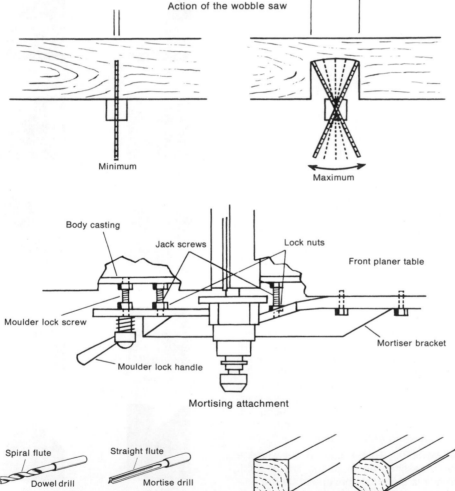

Body casting

Jack screws

Lock nuts

Front planer table

Moulder lock screw

Mortiser bracket

Moulder lock handle

Mortising attachment

Spiral flute

Straight flute

Dowel drill

Mortise drill

Boring bits

Shape prior to turning

Mortising attachment

THICKNESSER PLANER

The Thicknesser, as it is commonly known, is used for planing timber stock to specified sizes. It is general practice to use the planer jointer in conjunction with the thicknesser. Timber stock with defects such as cupping, winding or 'off saw' surfaces need to have these conditions removed on the planer jointer to enable a flat and true surface to be presented to the thicknesser table.

Thicknessers are manufactured in a wide range of sizes. Large industrial machines are capable of handling stock up to 1500mm x 225mm, while smaller lightweight machines that plane a maximum dimension of 300mm x 150mm are found in schools, colleges and more so now in home workshops.

Specifications

Feed Mechanism: This includes the feed rollers, pressure bars, cutter block and outfeed roller.

Feed Roller: The purpose of the feed roller is to pass the timber stock through the machine at a predetermined speed. In industrial machines the feed roll is made from steel and has machined serration's to enable it to grip the timber. Smaller lightweight machines have composition rubber feed rollers where the roller compresses when gripping the timber.

Outfeed Roller: In larger machines this is smooth and highly polished as it is in continual contact with the timber. For smaller lightweight machines the outfeed rollers are comprised of composition rubber.

Pressure Bars: Located between the feed rolls and the cutter block, these bars firmly hold the timber stock being planed against the machined table surface so that a positive feed is obtained.

Cutter Block: This is generally circular with the blades or cutters being held in machined slots by steel 'gibs' that are secured by case hardened screws. In the lightweight machines the cutter block rotates around 8000 r.p.m. against the infeed direction of the timber.

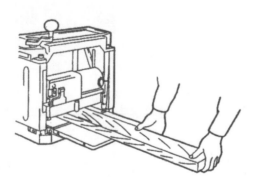

Passing timber stock through thicknesser

Planing to Thickness

Prior to passing the timber stock through the thicknesser, a face surface should be planed using the planer jointer. Adjust the height of the table so that the calibrated scale indicates 1mm to 2mm less than the thickness of the timber stock.

Examine the timber stock for warp, defects and grain direction. The grain direction should be running towards the operator in relation to the rotation of the cutter block (remember the cutter block is on top of the material). This will enable the cut to be made with the grain. Engage the machine and place the end of the stock 'face' down on the table. The push forward to make contact with the feed roll. Support should be given to the stock until it has past the outfeed roller. Further support the board as it comes from the rear table.

If when one surface has been planed, it is desirable to plane the other, the board should be turned 'end for end', thus maintaining grain direction.

Timber stock less than 300mm in length should not be passed through the thicknesser.

NOTE: The above procedure applies equally to the method of planing to width.·

The width should always be prepared first since it already rests on a narrow surface to be further reduced by thicknessing. Consequently, since the board is under pressure when the machine is operating, there is the possibility of tilting due to the narrow contact area.

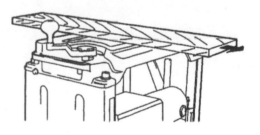

Rollers supporting timber stock for easy return

Safety

- Ear and eye protection is essential
- Avoid loose clothing
- Check timber for defects and grain direction
- Minimum length of material should be 300mm
- Maximum depth of cut should not exceed 2mm
- Always operate the machine standing to one side to avoid the dangers of kickback
- Always plane the width before planing the thickness

JOINTS

...ALL THE TYPES YOU WILL EVER NEED

Joints may be defined as the connecting medium between pieces of material orientated to distribute load, resist separation, and maintain the individuality of separate components.

With the advent of synthetic resin glues the implications of advances in metal fasteners have not been as severe on the furniture industry as they may be in the future. The majority of cabinet furniture produced is dependent upon the strength of glued joints. The individual strength factor of each joint is further dependent on the glue contact area. Consequently, joints serve to increase the strength and durability of members by providing greater gluing area.

Stress values indicating the operational forces to which the joint may be subject will influence the type, size, and positioning of joint proportions. The magnitude of the force may well dictate the finished size of some members. The forces of bending, shear tension, and compression may require further consideration, depending upon the joint application.

The aesthetics or general appearance of the finished joint should be considered in respect to function.

The innovation and wide acceptance of man-made sheet materials has necessitated the introduction of a new range of joint structure. In particular, K.D. (knockdown) connectors provide the professional and amateur alike with a simple, strong, and aesthetic alternative to traditional joint procedures.

Joints may be classified into three broad categories: Carcass Joints, Framing Joints, and Widening Joints.

CARCASS JOINTS

Carcass joints are associated with boxlike constructions and have members joining with their faces at right angles. They may be subdivided into:
1. Corner Carcass Joints.
2. Divisional Carcass Joints.

Corner carcass joints—include those used in the construction of solid carcass units using either solid timber or sheet material. They relate specifically to the construction of right-angled corner joints.

Butt Joint

This is the simplest form of joint construction. The end of one member is squared and butted against the other and nailed, screwed and/or glued. It is commonly used in cheap construction, such as boxes, or where a covering material is to be applied.

Construction

Square the ends of the members to be joined using either a saw or plane.

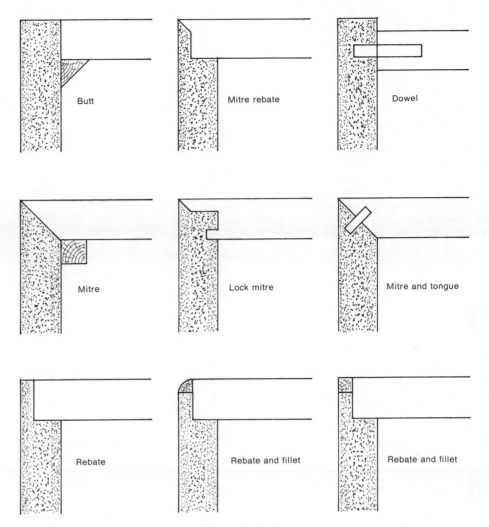

Recommended joints

Using a marking gauge and pencil, set to half the material thickness and mark a line around the end of one member.

Using this line, position and bore the required holes for nailing or screwing.

If screwing, holes should be countersunk.

Position the end of the bored member to be flush with the sides of the other member. Support if necessary.

Glue and fasten, using nails or screws.

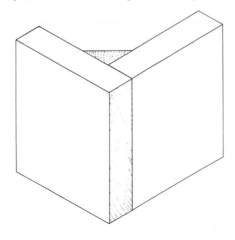

Butt joint with corner block

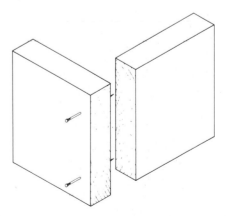

Common butt joint

75

Check for squareness of internal angle.
Flush off the joint using a smoothing plane.

NOTE

Where only glue is to be used pressure must be applied by clamping, and corner blocks inserted to provide greater strength.

Rebated Butt

The squared end of one member is accommodated into the rebate on the end of the other. This increases the contact gluing surface and provides positive location. The depth of rebate is two-thirds the thickness of the member on which it is placed. Used for the cheap construction of boxes, drawers, plinths, and cabinets.

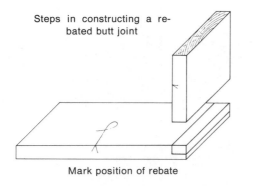

Steps in constructing a rebated butt joint

Mark position of rebate

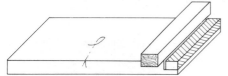

Saw cut rebate to depth

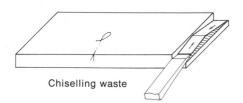

Chiselling waste

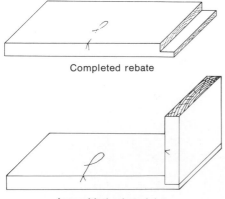

Completed rebate

Assembled rebate joint

Marking: Pencil mark the rebate shoulder on the face surface and edges.
Gauge the rebate depth.
Knife cut all lines to be saw cut.

Cutting: Saw cut the rebate to depth on the shoulder line by resting the saw in a pared groove *or* clamp a service member accurately on the shoulder line to provide saw support.

Remove the bulk of the waste material with a mallet and chisel, working from either side.

Use a bull nose plane to finish on the gauge line.

Assembly: Assemble using adhesive, nails, or screws depending on application.

Tongue and Trench

A bareface tongue is produced on the end of one member to fit the appropriate trench on the face of the other member. Uses include box and solid carcass construction and drawers.

Tongue

Plane the end square.
Pencil gauge the tongue length to one-third the material thickness.
Gauge the tongue width to one-third the material thickness.
Knife cut all lines to be sawn.
Saw cut the tongue shoulder to depth by resting the saw in a pared groove *or* clamp a service member accurately on the shoulder line to provide saw support.
Remove the bulk of the waste using a mallet and chisel, working from either side.
Use a bull nose plane to finish on the gauge line.

Trench

Plane the end square.
Pencil gauge the position of the trench—two-thirds the material thickness from the squared end.
Gauge the trench depth—one-third the material thickness.
Knife cut all lines to be sawn.
Saw cut both shoulder lines to depth by resting the saw in a pared groove *or* clamp a service member on the shoulder lines to provide saw support.

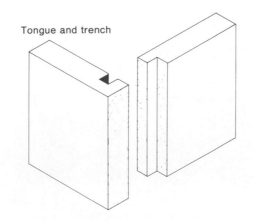

Tongue and trench

Pare out the waste material, chiselling from both edges.

Rebate and Fillet

This joint may be described as a rebated butt produced with the fillet strip concealing the exposed ends of the sheet material. Used in the construction of solid carcass cabinets (in particular with particle board).

Steps in constructing a rebate and fillet joint

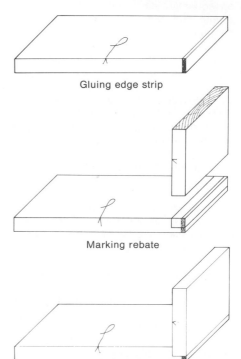

Gluing edge strip

Marking rebate

Completed joint

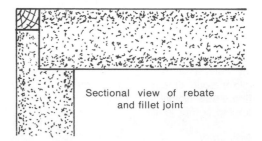

Sectional view of rebate and fillet joint

Construction

Square the ends of both members.
Prepare an edge strip equal in width to the material thickness and 1 mm thicker than one-third the material thickness.
Glue and clamp the edge strip to one end of the vertical member allowing 1 mm overhang on the outside surface.
Mark the rebate width. From the glue line pencil square a distance equal to two-thirds the material thickness and on the inside face.

Gauge the rebate depth—two-thirds the material thickness.

Knife cut all lines to be sawn.

Cutting: Saw cut the rebate to depth.

Remove the bulk of the waste material using a mallet and chisel working from either side.

Use a bull nose plane to finish on the gauge line *or* adjust an electric router to the required depth and remove the rebate waste with one pass.

Assembly: Assemble using clamps and adhesives.

Check for internal squareness.

NOTE

The 1 mm allowance on the side and top of the fillet may be removed by planing and/or scraping.

Mitre Joint

Similar to a simple butt joint, except that each end is bevelled to 45°. The strength characteristics are poor but may be increased by the insertion of 'keys' or 'feathers'. This joint, however, does provide the simplest means of covering end grain. It is frequently used for plinths and small boxes.

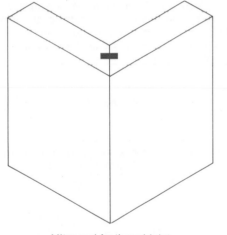

Mitre and feathered joint

Construction

Using a mitre set, pencil mark an angle of 45° on one edge at the end of each member.

Where this angle meets the material corners square two pencil lines to the opposite edge.

Join these two lines, again using the mitre set.

Cutting: Securely fasten the member to a mitre planing jig.

Using a No. 5 jack plane in a slicing position, plane down to the pencil lines.

On nearing completion the mitre jig provides an accurate plane support.

It is important that the angle produced while planing remains parallel to the pencil lines at all times.

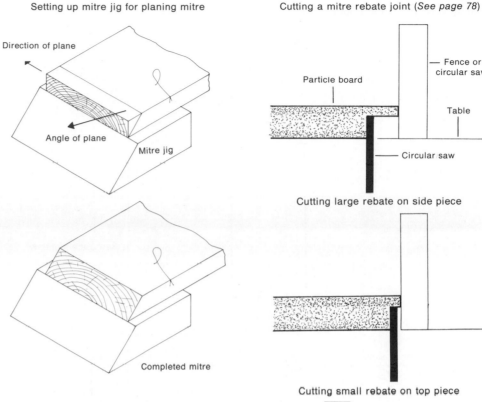

Setting up mitre jig for planing mitre

Direction of plane

Angle of plane

Mitre jig

Completed mitre

Dovetail or skew nailing a mitre joint

Assembly: Assemble using clamps and adhesive.

Check for internal squareness.

Rebate and Mitre

The end of each member is rebated and mitred (bevelled at 45°) thus providing rebate joint advantages and the concealment of end grains. Used in box, cabinet, and buffet construction (top corners, joints). Particularly applicable when using particle board.

Due to the shortness of the 45° bevel it is essentially a machine-constructed joint.

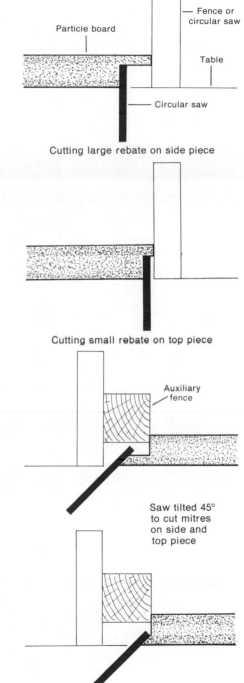

Cutting a mitre rebate joint (*See page 78*)

Fence or circular saw

Particle board

Table

Circular saw

Cutting large rebate on side piece

Cutting small rebate on top piece

Auxiliary fence

Saw tilted 45° to cut mitres on side and top piece

Dovetail Joints

These are the strongest of all carcass joints used in furniture construction. The joint consists of a series of 'dovetails' cut on the end of one member fitting into a series of sockets cut on the end of the other member.

Cutting a single dovetail joint

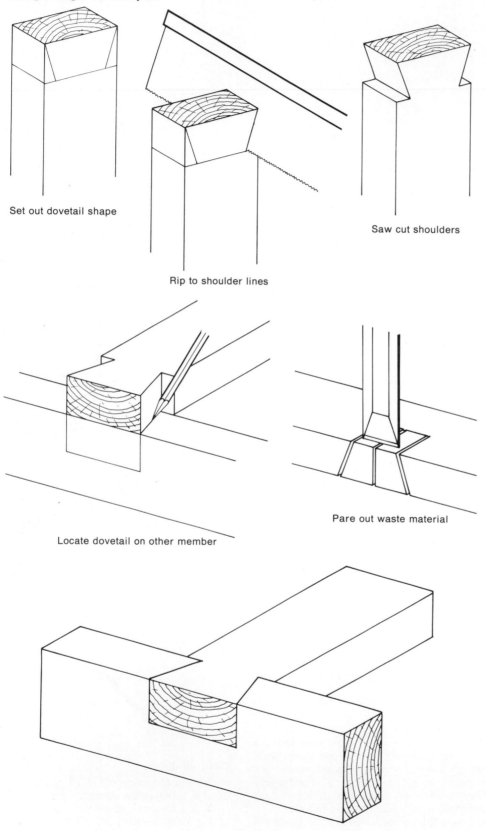

Set out dovetail shape

Rip to shoulder lines

Saw cut shoulders

Locate dovetail on other member

Pare out waste material

Individually, each dovetail is wedgelike in shape, allowing removal from one direction only. When used in multiples, the many gluing surfaces provided, coupled with the interlocking action of the tails and pins, make the dovetail joint a necessity if strength is of prime importance.

Single Dovetail Joint

Lay out the position of the dovetail on the end of one member. Allow 2 mm waste on this end.

Set out the dovetail shape on both sides of the material, using a slope of 1 in 6.

Rip the sides of the dovetail to the shoulder lines using a dovetail saw.

Saw cut the shoulder lines.

Locate the dovetail in position on the end of the other member and mark out the dovetail socket.

Square the sides of the sockets from the end on both sides to the depth line.

Rip the sides of the socket, sawing on the waste side of the lines.

Pare out the waste material by chiselling vertically and then obliquely until halfway through. Turn the member over and repeat the process.

Common or Through Dovetail

This consists of two or more dovetails and exposes end grain on both sides of the joint. Uses include strong box construction and drawer construction (fixing drawer backs to sides).

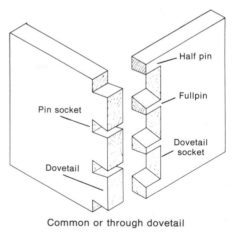

Common or through dovetail

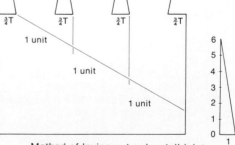

Method of laying out a dovetail joint

Construction

Square the ends of both members since all marking is done from the ends.

Lay out the joint position by squaring a pencil line around the end of both members. For through dovetails the depth of the squared line equals the thickness of the material.

Lay out the dovetail shape on the face side of one member.

Proportions—The width of the widest section of the half pin is usually three-quarters the thickness of the material ($\frac{3}{4}$T). The slope or pitch of the dovetail is generally 1 in 6. The half-pin size may range from $\frac{1}{2}$T to $\frac{3}{4}$T while the slope may vary from 1 in 4 up to 1 in 8.

Refer to the diagram illustrating the method of setting out to obtain equal size dovetails.

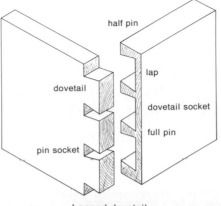

Lapped dovetail

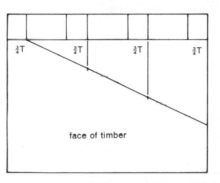

Method laying out the pins on a lapped dovetail

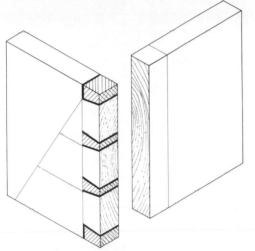

Sawcuts on waste side of material

Knife cut the pin sockets.

Saw cut the sides of the dovetails leaving the waste section in the pin sockets.

Remove the waste between the dovetails.

Mark the shape of the pins. Locate the dovetails accurately over the end of the other member and mark between the dovetails.

Pencil square the sides of the pins down both surfaces and knife cut the dovetail sockets.

Remove the waste from the dovetail sockets.

An alternative method is to cut the pins first, using them as templets to mark the dovetails.

Lapped Dovetail

Although similar to the through dovetail, a lap one-third of the timber thickness is left on the front member to cover the end grain of the dovetails. Used for drawer construction for attaching the sides to the front.

Construction—alternative method

Square the ends of both members.

Pencil gauge a lap of three-quarters the material thickness on the end and sides of the front member.

Lapped dovetail joint

Gauge this same distance around the end of the side member.

Lay out the socket shapes on the face side of the front member.

Knife cut between the pins and clearly indicate waste.

Secure vertically in a vice and, using a dovetail saw, cut out the pins—the saw kerf on the waste side of the line.

Remove the waste using a bevelled edge chisel, remaining short of the line until the bulk is removed.

Position the front member on the side member and mark out the pin sockets.

Square these lines across the end of the side member and clearly indicate the waste.

Saw cut the sides of the dovetails using a dovetail saw.

Remove the waste material between the dovetails using a bevelled edge chisel and working from both sides towards the centre.

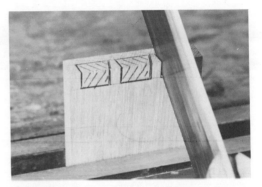

Sawing the pins. The saw cut should be made carefully against the line. Very little paring should be necessary

A block of service material will act as a guide ensuring accurate cut when removing waste from dovetail sockets

Use a bevelled edge firmer or bevelled edge paring chisel to remove waste from socket

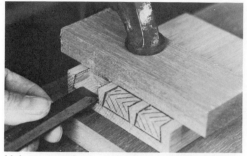

Make sure socket is perfectly clean and square and that dovetails retain an even shape

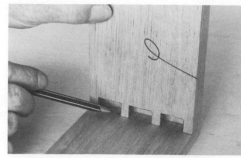

Use sharp pencil to mark out pin sockets

Be sure to saw into waste when cutting pin sockets. The saw cut should be accurate, requiring little or no paring

Most of the waste in sockets can be removed with saw

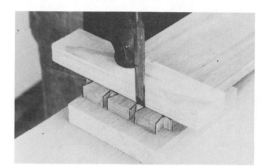

A piece of service material makes an excellent guide when paring out the pin sockets

Once shoulders have been cut work in from end with small chisel to remove waste

Secret Dovetail

Provision is made for a lap on both members which is mitred to conceal all end grain. When assembled, appearances would indicate a plain mitre.

Used for high class cabinet work where strength and appearance are required.

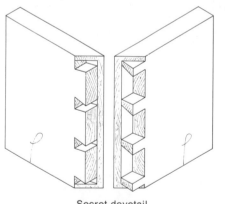

Secret dovetail

Divisional Carcass Joints—occur where the internal members meet with their faces at right angles.

Housing Joints

These consist of the end of one member fitting into a trench on the face of another member. The depth of the trench is universally accepted as being one-third the thickness of the accommodating member.

These joints are commonly used for bookcase divisions, shelving, and stair treads.

Through Housing

The full width of one end is housed into a through trench in the other member. Joint detail is visible from both sides.

Housing Joint
Marking: Using a pencil, position the trench on the face and edge surfaces.

Method of cutting a housing joint

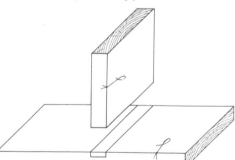

Marking out housing joint

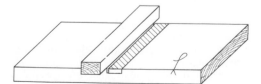

Saw cut using service material as guide

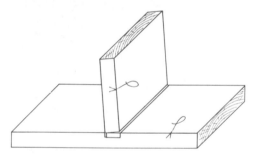

Positioning vertical member in first saw cut

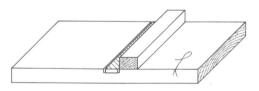

Second saw cut using service material as guide

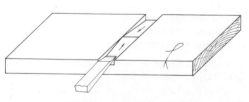

Chiselling to remove waste

Gauge the trench depth to one-third the material thickness from the face side.

Knife cut *one shoulder line only*.

Cutting: Saw cut the *knifed* shoulder line to depth. Rest the saw in a pared groove *or* clamp a service member accurately on the shoulder line to provide saw support.

Locate in the saw cut one edge of the member being housed and mark the thickness.

Saw cut the shoulder line to depth.

Pare out the waste material, chiselling from both edges.

For wide trenches a router may be used to obtain a level bottom.

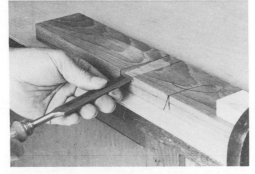

A trench marked out on the face and edge

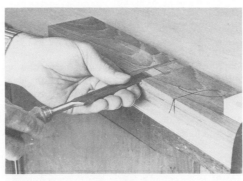

Sawing across the knife cut shoulder line to depth

Paring out the waste material from the first side. Work up toward the face

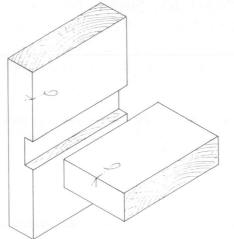

After paring from the other side pare the trench until the bottom is flat. This may be tested with a steel rule

A router plane may be used to obtain an even depth

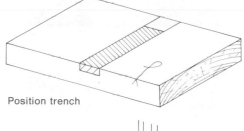

Through housing

Stopped Housing

The trench is stopped short of the front edge with the incoming member notched accordingly to provide a butt appearance. Used in better class work where some strength and visual qualities are required.

Construction

Using a pencil, position the trench on the face and edge surfaces.

Gauge the trench depth to one-third the material thickness on the edge only.

Pencil gauge the required stop from the opposite edge.

Knife cut and pare the shoulder lines.

Chisel out a small recess 2 mm from the stopped end, the exact width of the trench and about 20 mm in length.

With the saw resting in the pared grooves and the recess acting as a stop, saw cut the sides to the required depth.

Pare out the waste using a bevelled edge chisel and/or a router plane.

Clean up the stop by paring vertically.

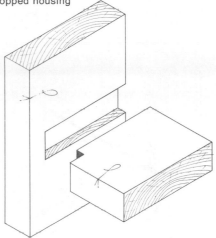

Stopped housing

Method of cutting stopped housing

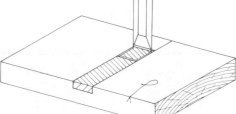

Position trench

Chisel out small recess

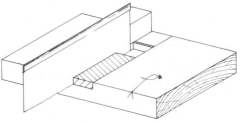

Saw cut using recess as a stop

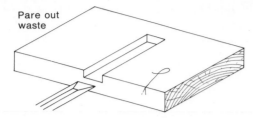

Pare out waste

Notching

Position and mark the size of the notch. Knife cut all lines across the grain.

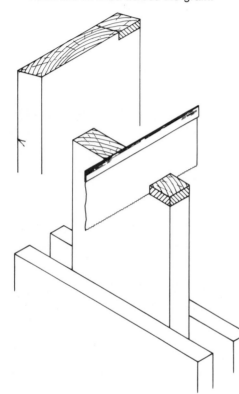

Remove the notch by using a dovetail saw and ripping to the depth line followed by cross-cutting the shoulder.

Double Stopped Housing

The trench is stopped short of both the front and back edge. This joint is used where

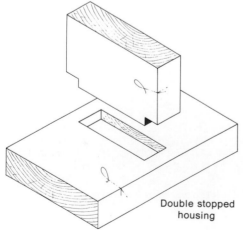

Double stopped housing

appearances may dictate, e.g. room divider or free standing bookcase.

Dovetail Housing

The end of one member is dovetailed on one or both sides and fitted into a dovetail trench. This joint is used where greater strength is required and is generally of the through housing type. Where one side only is dovetailed it may be referred to as a bareface dovetail housing.

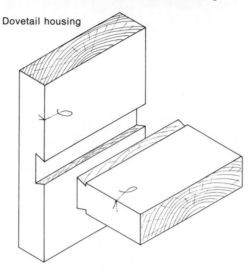

Dovetail housing

FRAMING JOINTS

These may be classified as those where the members meet edge to end to generally form a right angle. Uses include framed carcass construction chairs, leg and rail construction, doors, and picture frames.

Halving Joints

As the name implies, half the material thickness is removed from each piece, enabling the surfaces to finish flush.

Tee Halving

This is used where an internal rail meets a

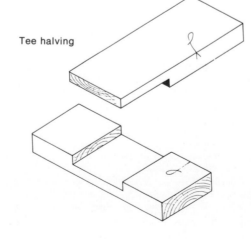

Tee halving

stile. The halving socket may be stopped to cover the end grain of the rail.

Marking: Position the socket or trench by marking pencil lines squared across the face surface and *halfway* down the edges.

Mark the length of the pin on the edge of the other member, allowing 2 mm for cleaning up.

Adjust the marking gauge to half the material thickness and gauge the socket depth and thickness of the lap.

All gauging must be done from the face surface. Indicate all waste material.

Knife cut one socket shoulder.

Knife cut the lap shoulder.

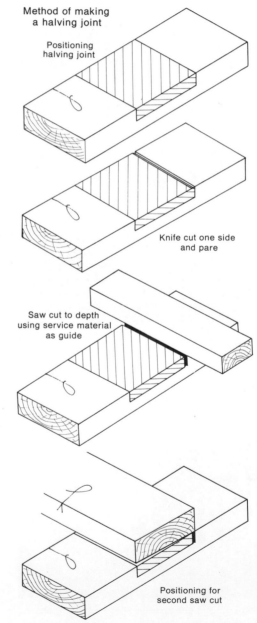

Method of making a halving joint

Positioning halving joint

Knife cut one side and pare

Saw cut to depth using service material as guide

Positioning for second saw cut

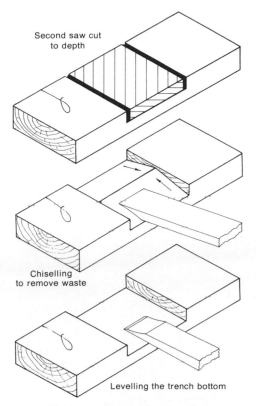

Second saw cut to depth

Chiselling to remove waste

Levelling the trench bottom

Cutting: Socket or trench. Suitably secure the material and saw cut the knifed shoulder line to depth by resting the saw in a pared groove or by using a service member accurately clamped on the shoulder line to provide saw support.

Locate one edge of the lap member in the saw cut and mark the width of the socket or trench.

Knife cut and saw the shoulder line to depth.

Pare out the waste material, chiselling from both edges.

Lap: Saw cut the cheek or thickness of the lap, allowing the kerf to remain in the waste material.

Saw cut the shoulder line to depth.

Fitting: Assemble the members and square the waste material from the lap.

Cross Halving

This is a double tee halving used where

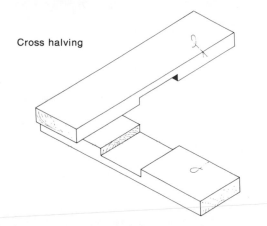

Cross halving

members are required to cross each other maintaining a flush face. Commonly used for crossed stretcher rails in table construction.

The marking and waste removal on both members occur as for the socket section of the tee halving.

Corner Halving

This joint is suitable for members having their ends meeting to form an angle as in light frame work.

The marking and waste removal on both members occur as for the lap section of the tee halving.

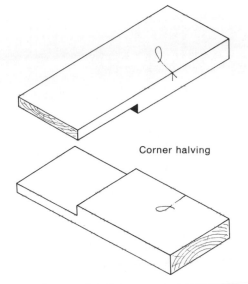

Corner halving

Mitre Corner Halving

Although this joint is similar to a corner halving, only a mitred section of each member is removed. This is the weakest form of halving because of the decreased gluing surfaces. However, it does provide coverage for the end grain of one member.

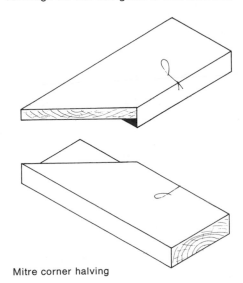

Mitre corner halving

Dovetail Halving

This joint resembles the tee halving but the dovetail shape of the lap increases the strength substantially. The dovetail socket may be stopped to hide the end grain of the rail. A commonly used joint in small boat building.

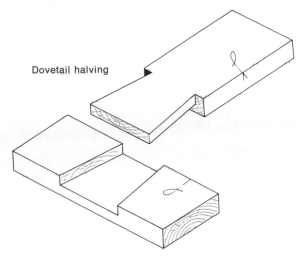

Dovetail halving

Construction

Mark the position of the socket on the face of one member.

Lay out the length of the pln (allowing 2 mm waste) from the end of the other member.

Set out the dovetail slopes on the pin.

Adjust the marking gauge to half the material thickness and gauge the depth of the socket and the pin thickness, gauging from the face side only.

Saw cut the pin thickness, saw kerf on the waste side of the gauge line.

Saw cut the dovetail slope, saw kerf on the waste side of the pencil lines.

Knife cut the shoulder on the reverse side and also both edges.

Saw cut the shoulder on the reverse side to the gauge line depth.

Saw cut the edge shoulders to the dovetail slope.

Position the pin over the socket location and scribe one edge of the dovetail slope.

Knife cut this shoulder line across the face and to depth.

Saw cut the shoulder line to depth.

Pare out waste material, chiselling from both edges.

MITRED JOINT

For framing application the mitre is cut across the width (face) of the timber. The two mitred ends are butted together and secured by nailing or gluing. To increase the strength, dowels or feathers may be inserted. Uses include picture frames, edge treatments, and architraves.

Mitred picture frame held with mitre clamp while glue sets

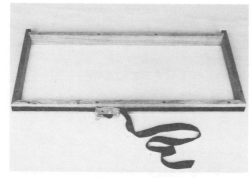

Use of web clamp to hold mitred base of a cabinet while glue sets

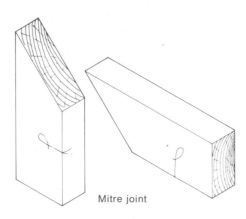

Mitre joint

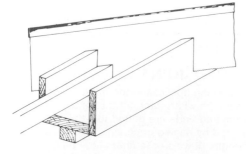

Cutting a mitre joint using mitre box and tenon saw

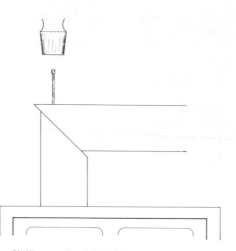

Nailing a mitre joint with allowance showing for slippage

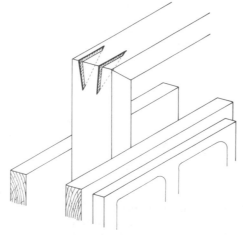

Mitre joint showing feathers—note dovetailed angles

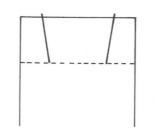

End view of mitre joint showing dovetailed feathers

DOWELLED JOINT

This is basically a simple butt joint strengthened by the addition of dowels. Dowels may be described as smooth or grooved cylindrical sticks of hardwood. They are used extensively in modern furniture construction and at times act as a substitute for the mortise and tenon joint. Patternmakers also use dowels in the construction of split patterns. Used extensively in leg and rail construction.

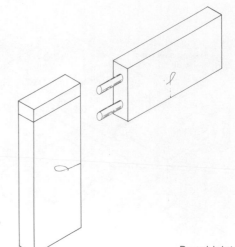

Dowel joint

Dowel joint—edges of holes are chamfered to allow for excess glue that may squeeze out. Ends of dowels are also chamfered to assist fitting

Mark position of rails on legs or stile. Use the actual rail

Mark positions of dowels on ends of rails initially

Secure with clamp and mark the centre line on each leg or stile and transfer the position of dowels from end of rail

Marking out completed

Dowel Joint—(Framing)

Marking: Lay out the position of the joint.

If occurring at the end of a member a waste section of 20 mm must be left to act as a horn.

Gauge centrelines in the ends and edges of the members to be joined, from the face surfaces.

Locate the position of the dowels.

Using a marking gauge mark across the centrelines on the ends of the rails working from the face edge.

Transfer the positions from the rails to the stiles and square across the centrelines using a try square.

Bore holes the same size as the dowels at the intersection of the gauge and pencil lines.

The dowel diameter should be from one-third to half the thickness of the material.

A depth gauge should be used to enable the correct depth of the hole to be bored.

The length of the dowel pin should be three times its diameter into each member.

Slightly countersink the holes. This provides a small reservoir for adhesion.

Chamfer the ends of the dowels, using a dowel rounder.

Assemble by gluing the dowels into the rails and gluing and clamping the rails into the stiles.

When using a dowelling jig, marking out is as indicated in the diagram.

The dowelling jig is adjusted to centre on half the material thickness. The inside or outside datum line is then aligned with the pencil mark.

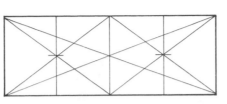

Setting out dowel joint—end view

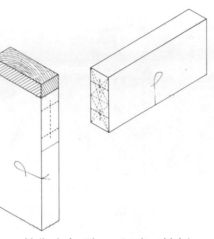

Method of setting out a dowel joint

Countersunk holes and chamfered dowels

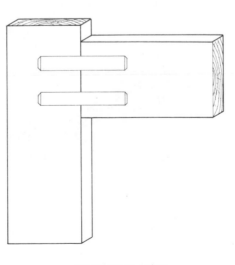

Dowel joint section

When using dowel jig be sure to line up gradation on jig with mark representing position of dowel

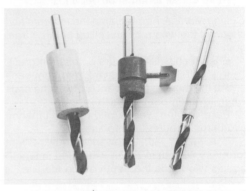

It is essential to use a drill stop to establish holes at correct depth

MORTISE AND TENON JOINTS

These are the strongest type of framing joints and are used where the stress loadings are known to be considerable. Panelled door frames, table and chair construction, and framed carcasses for cabinet construction are common uses for this joint. They provide many supporting shoulders and have a number of large glue contact areas.

Proportions

Experience has provided joint proportions for the many variations of mortise and tenon joints. However, deviation from the norm is also acceptable as member sizes may necessitate altering joint proportions to obtain maximum results. It should be realised that the mortise and tenon joint proportions indicated are the accepted guidelines and must be altered where the need arises.

Through Mortise and Tenon Joint

This is used where the members (rail and stile) are of the same thickness. The tenon is full rail width and passes completely through the stile. To obtain further strength the joint may be wedged or, if used in exposed conditions, pinned by passing a dowel through from the face surface.

Proportions

Tenon thickness is the equivalent of one-third the thickness of the rail.

Tenon width is equal to approximately six times the tenon thickness. Where the width of rail is excessive, use should be made of the double tenon. Uses include internal door rails and cabinet frames.

Marking Out: Lay out the position of the mortise by squaring pencil lines across the face and edge surfaces.

Lay out the length of the tenon, allowing 2 mm for waste.

Set a mortise gauge to the selected chisel and gauge the mortise width and tenon thickness working from faces and face edges.

Knife cut all tenon shoulder lines.

Cutting Mortise: Firmly clamp the material and chop out the waste by chiselling halfway from both edges.

Ensure chiselling occurs across the grain.

In the first instance leave 2 mm from each end of the mortise to prevent bruising the ends when levering out the waste.

Pare out the wedge allowances tapering two-thirds through the mortise.

The wedge width allowance equals 2 mm for every 40 mm in tenon width and in length equals two-thirds the depth of the mortise.

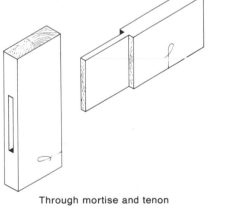

Through mortise and tenon

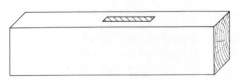

Marking out mortise

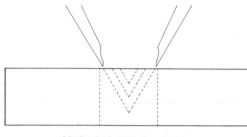

Method of cutting a mortise

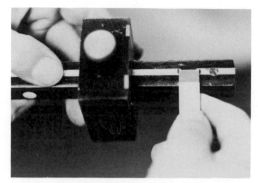

The mortise gauge is set to the selected chisel

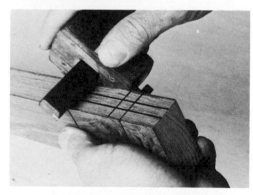

Gauge the mortise from the face

Cutting out waste from a mortise using registered firmer chisel

Cutting Tenon: Saw cut the tenon cheeks to the shoulder lines.

Saw cut the shoulders.

Rest the saw in a pared groove *or* clamp

a service member accurately on the shoulder line to provide saw support.

Assembly: Fit together with adhesive and wedges and remove tenon waste by planing.

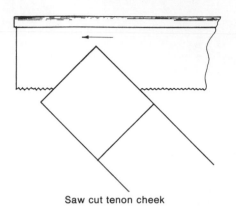

Saw cut tenon cheek

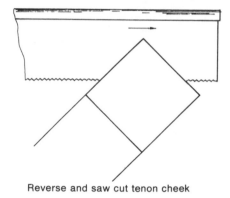

Reverse and saw cut tenon cheek

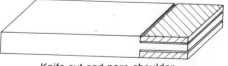

Complete cheek cut to depth

Knife cut and pare shoulder

Saw cut shoulder

Four Shoulder Mortise and Tenon

This\ is similar in all respects to the through mortise and tenon but has an additional top and bottom shoulder. These provide complete coverage of the mortise when the joint is assembled. The tenon may be 'through' or 'stub', depending on the application.

Proportions: The tenon thickness is equal to one-third the thickness of the rail.

The top and bottom shoulders may vary between 5 mm and 10 mm, depending on the rail width.

The length of the tenon, if a stub, should be two-thirds of the stile into which it is located.

An accepted joint for table and chair construction when used on spreader rails where strength and appearance are required.

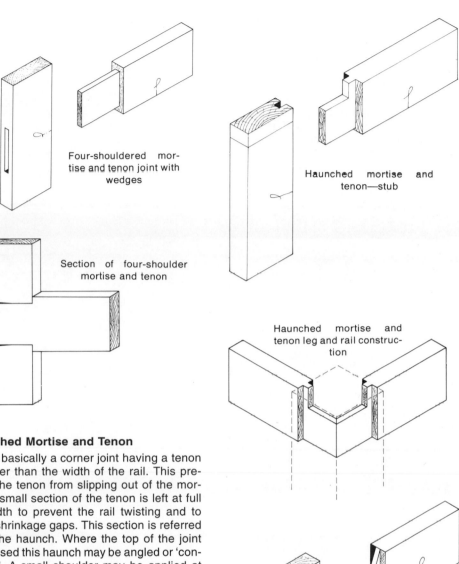

Four-shouldered mortise and tenon joint with wedges

Haunched mortise and tenon—stub

Section of four-shoulder mortise and tenon

Haunched mortise and tenon leg and rail construction

Four-shoulder mortise and tenon joint

Foxtail mortise and tenon

Foxtail mortise and tenon section

Haunched Mortise and Tenon

This is basically a corner joint having a tenon narrower than the width of the rail. This prevents the tenon from slipping out of the mortise. A small section of the tenon is left at full rail width to prevent the rail twisting and to avoid shrinkage gaps. This section is referred to as the haunch. Where the top of the joint is exposed this haunch may be angled or 'concealed'. A small shoulder may be applied at the base of the tenon to improve the appearance. The tenon may be a through or stub.

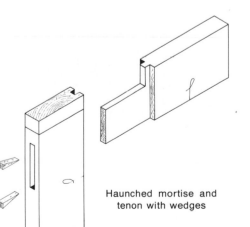

Haunched mortise and tenon with wedges

Concealed haunch mortise and tenon with wedges

Proportions: Tenon thickness is one-third the thickness of the rail.

The tenon width is equal to approximately two-thirds the width of the rail.

The tenon length, if stubbed, is two-thirds of the stile width; if through, it is full width of stile.

This is a commonly used joint for table frames, panelled doors, and sashes.

Sawing the haunching

Pare out waste

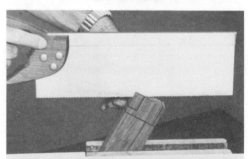
Ripping the cheeks of the tenon

Ripping the cheeks to the shoulder line

Complete all ripping cuts before cutting shoulders

Cutting the shoulders

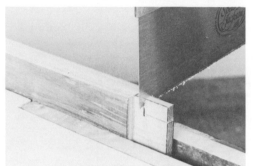
Cutting the haunch

Haunched mortise and tenon joint

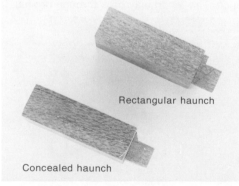
Rectangular haunch

Concealed haunch

Long and Short Shoulder Mortise and Tenons

These are applicable where the rails and stiles are rebated for panels. The inside tenon shoulders are cut longer to fill up the rebates on the stiles. The tenons are generally stubbed and haunched with the proportions similar to those of the haunched mortise and tenon joint.

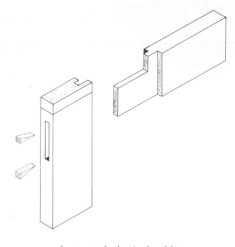
Long and short shoulders —mortise and tenon

Bareface Mortise and Tenon Joint

This is used where the rail is of thinner material than the stile. To provide optimum strength the tenon is left at half the rail thickness and has only one shoulder. The tenon may be the full rail width, haunched, with or without a bottom shoulder.

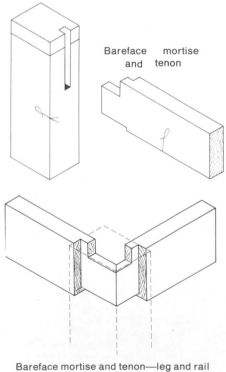
Bareface mortise and tenon

Bareface mortise and tenon—leg and rail construction

Double Tenon

Where a rail is particularly wide it is convenient to construct two tenons applying the formula of each tenon width not exceeding six times the tenon thickness. This eliminates problems caused by large tenons shrinking or weakening the stile. The tenons may be haunch and/or shouldered. Useful for rails in door construction.

Twin Tenons

These are used for thick material requiring a strong joint. The rail thickness is divided into five equal sections. The tenons may be full width, haunched or shouldered.

Compound Tenons

These are applied where the material is both wide and thick. It is a combination of the double and twin tenons.

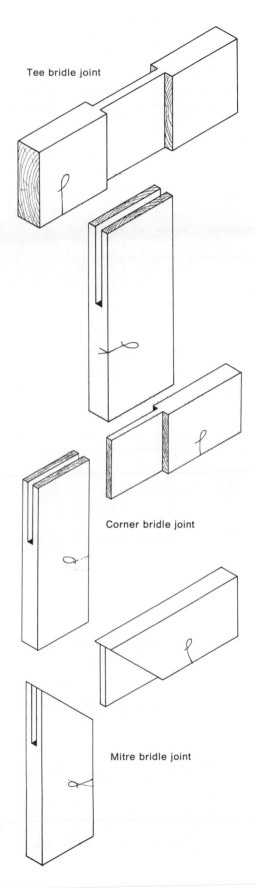

Tee bridle joint

Corner bridle joint

Mitre bridle joint

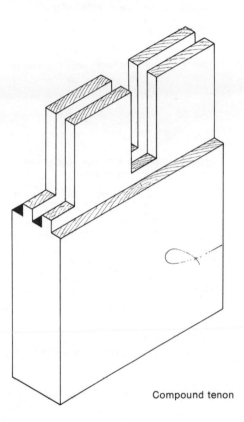

Double tenon

Compound tenon

Twin tenon

BRIDLE JOINTS

These joints are mortise and tenons in reverse. In place of the tenon an open slot is formed on the end of the rail to accommodate a pin made on the stile by trenching from either side. The joint proportions of the pin and slot are generally one-third the material thickness.

Tee Bridle Joint

This may be used for joining through rails to legs as in cabinet construction. The pin may not extend the full width of the rail if the end grain requires coverage.

Corner Bridle Joint

This is sometimes used in place of a haunched mortise and tenon joint or dowelled joint. May be used for general corner joint construction as in chair backs and seats.

Mitre Corner Bridle Joint

This is used where greater strength is required for picture frame moulding as in mirror frames.

WIDENING JOINTS

Widening joints are used for increasing the width of boards in the same plane by joining narrow boards edge to edge.

Butt Joint

This is the most common and simplest form of widening joint. The edges may be planed square and straight or square and hollow, and glued and/or clamped. Corrugated box fasteners (wiggle nails) may also be used, depending on the joint application.

Methods of butt jointing 1—to produce a flat surface

Methods of butt jointing 2—to produce an even curve

Rubbed Butt Joint

Marking: Lay out the boards and establish the following criteria:

Face grain running in the same direction.

Growth ring structure alternating *or* growth ring structure similar.

Place a locating mark across the edges of the boards to be joined.

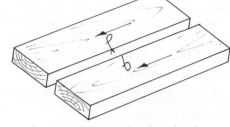

Arrows to indicate direction of grain

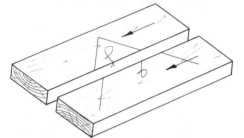

Application of face with face edge marks and location mark

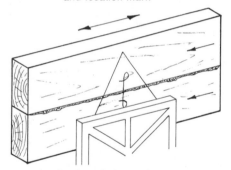

Application of glue and pressure

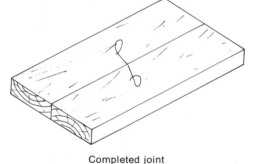

Completed joint

Cutting: Secure the boards together in the vice and plane the edges using a trying plane.

Test by placing the boards together.

Use a straight edge to ensure the face surfaces are in the same plane.

Hold the boards to the light and check the fit of the edges.

Assembly: Secure one member in the vice and apply adhesive to both edge surfaces.

Attach the other member and allow to dry.

Apply a downward pressure when edge contact is made, coupled with a short back

and forward movement. This removes any air locks and excess glue.

Flush the joint line and remove excess glue using a damp cloth.

Clamped Butt Joint

Marking: Layout follows the same procedure as in the rubbed butt joint.

Cutting: Secure the boards together in the vice with the two joining edges level and uppermost.

Using a No. 7 plane commence in the middle and with lengthening strokes plane progressively towards each end.

Continue until testing indicates a 0.5 mm hollow in each edge.

It is important to retain the squareness of each edge.

Place the boards in a bar clamp and tighten.

Check that the slight hollow in the joint line disappears with reasonable pressure.

Firmly strike the ends of the faces to ensure no slippage occurs due to insufficient hollowing.

Test for flatness using a straight edge.

Assembly: Apply adhesive and reclamp.

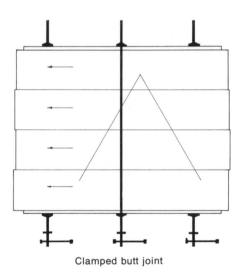

Clamped butt joint

Dowelled Butt Joint

This is used extensively in modern furniture construction for reinforcing boards glued edge to edge. The dowels range in diameter from 4 mm to 25 mm and are not generally applied in timber less than 12 mm in thickness.

Uses include table tops and wide flat surfaces.

Dowel Joint—(Widening)

Marking: Clamp the members together with the faces outwards and square pencil lines across the edges indicating the dowel spacing. The distance between the dowels is approximately 200 mm to 250 mm, starting one dowel length in from each end.

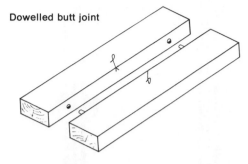

Dowelled butt joint

Adjust the marking gauge to half the material thickness and gauge the dowel centre, marking from either face surface.

Bore holes to three times the diameter of the dowel, using either a brace and bit or a power drill. Slightly countersink hole.

Cut the dowels to length and chamfer the ends, using a dowel rounder.

Apply adhesive to the dowels, holes, and edges. Assemble and clamp, using a bar clamp.

Groove and Feathered Joint

This is used where the material thickness exceeds 25 mm. The joining edges are grooved to an approximate depth of 12 mm and a tongue is inserted. The width of the groove is approximately one-third the material thickness. Uses include table and benchtops.

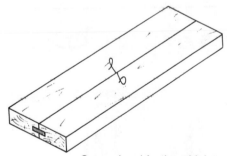

Grooved and feathered joint

Tongue and Grooved

A tongue prepared on the edge of one member is fitted to a corresponding groove on the edge of an adjacent piece. It is a commonly used joint for flooring boards and match boards.

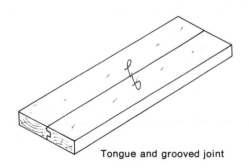

Tongue and grooved joint

Rebate Joint

This consists of a rebate planed on the edges of each member followed by gluing and clamping. This provides a gluing area approximately one and a half times greater than a simple butt joint. Used for table tops and shelving.

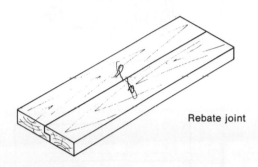

Rebate joint

Biscuit Joiners

An innovative alternative to joining timber using other than nails, screws or traditional hand or machine joints is to use a biscuit cutter or joiner system. The biscuits are pieces of uniformly compressed wood (just under 4 mm) which fit into grooves produced by portable or fixed machines. When the biscuit is inserted into the groove or slot the moisture from the glue swells the biscuit, locking the timber joint firmly together.

This technique has proven to be easier and stronger than traditional dowel joints, for example, and can be used for framing, widening or carcass joints. Biscuits are available in three standard sizes.

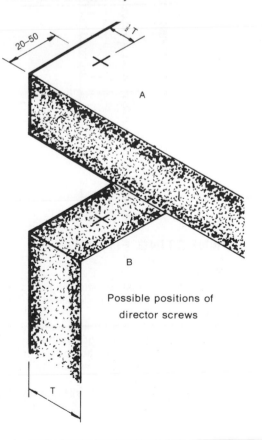

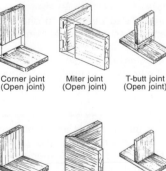

Corner joint (Open joint) Miter joint (Open joint) T-butt joint (Open joint) Edge-to-edge joint (Open joint)

Corner joint (Closed joint) Miter joint (Closed joint) T-butt joint (Closed joint) Edge-to-edge joint (Closed joint)

KNOCKDOWN FITTINGS

The increase in production of knockdown furniture has produced a new dimension in joint structure. The use of metal and plastic connectors enables furniture to be transported in a knockdown condition and assembled either by unskilled labour or by the consumer.

Moreover, the handyperson and hobbyist, using basic woodworking equipment, can lay out and assemble complete furniture units using a selection of connectors.

ASSEMBLY AIDS

CONNECTING SCREWS

Direkta

These are specially designed threaded screws which allow the angle-butt jointing of timber and, in particular, particle board and medium-density fibre board.

Plastic caps are available to neatly cover the screw heads.

Assembly

Drill a 5 mm hole in panel B to the required length.

Drill a 7 mm hole through panel A.

Ensure the ends of both panels are square to each other and screw in the connecting screw with an allen key.

Possible positions of director screws

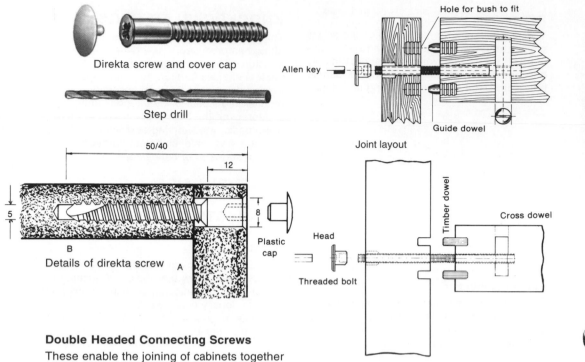

Direkta screw and cover cap

Step drill

Hole for bush to fit

Allen key

Guide dowel

Joint layout

50/40

12

5

8

B

Details of direkta screw   A

Plastic cap

Head

Threaded bolt

Timber dowel

Cross dowel

Combifix fittings

Thread

Threaded bolt

Heads

Collar

Cross dowels

Ø 6
Ø 8
10,5

Ø 6
Ø 8
11
18

Guide dowels

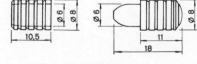

Double Headed Connecting Screws

These enable the joining of cabinets together in either a vertical or horizontal situation. They are suitable for wood thicknesses between 34 mm and 41 mm.

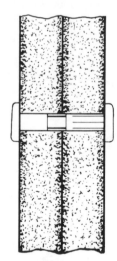

CONNECTING FITTINGS

Combifix

The once difficult task of attaching rails to chairs and tables has been simplified by the introduction of Combifix.

A metal dowel is located in a hole drilled in the rail and pulled tight against the leg by using a threaded bolt which has a decorative brass head. This method eliminates the need for clamping and gluing.

To assist in preventing the rails from twisting, wooden dowels or brass guide dowels may be used.

Assembly

Position and lay out the joint. (See joint layout)

Using a bradawl or small nail and hammer, make a small indentation for the drill bit at the centre of each of the hole positions.

Drill 10 mm holes to the required depth in the rail or the horizontal member to accept the metal cross dowels, using a depth stop on the drill bit.

Drill 10 mm holes, 10 mm deep into the leg or vertical member—again using a depth stop—to accommodate the sleeve of the brass head.

Using the above hole as the location point, drill 6 mm holes through the legs or vertical members.

Drill 8 mm holes for the brass guide dowels, 10 mm deep, in both the horizontal and vertical members, ensuring that the drill is kept vertical.

Cut 6 mm threaded rod to the required lengths and locate the metal dowels in the horizontal members.

With the brass head attached to one end of the threaded rod, screw the other end into the metal dowel.

Remove the brass head, assemble the joint and re-screw the brass head until the joint has pulled up tight, using an allen key.

NOTE

The use of brass guide dowels and bushes is more costly than wooden dowels and is generally used where considerable knockdown and knockup requirements are involved. Moreover, due to the accuracy involved with guide dowels and bushes, jigs are generally required to ensure ease of assembly.

Detail of joint layout for guide dowels and threaded bolt

Trapez Fittings

No longer is it necessary to use screwed wooden blocks in an attempt to construct right-angle carcass butt joints. By using Trapez fittings, it is now possible to assemble and disassemble angle carcass butt joints by the removal of a single screw.

Assembly

Position part A on the vertical panel and part B on the horizontal panel. The Trapez fitting should be a minimum distance of 30 mm from the panel edge.

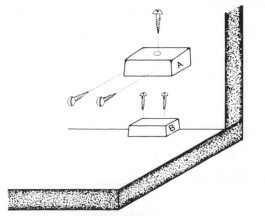

Trapez fitting

Remove the bottom metal section and attach it to the horizontal panel using the screws provided.

Attach the plastic cover section to the vertical panel and connect the two sections together using the larger screw as provided.

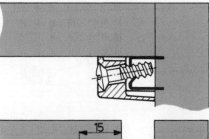

Trapez connecting fitting

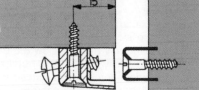

Assembly detail—trapez connector

Rastex

These are a concealed assembly aid for butt-joining panels. Operating on an eccentric cam system, the assembly aid acts like a clamp and can be easily knocked down for removal. They are available in 25 mm, 15 mm and 12 mm diameter casings.

The only tools required for Rastexs are a drill, an 8 mm drill bit, a Krefting cutter and a screwdriver.

Rastex 25   Rastex 15 with   Rastex 12
                 torque support

Assembly

Position and lay out the joints.

Drill 8 mm hole, 11 mm deep, in the vertical panel A.

Using a hammer, knock in the plastic socket and screw in metal dowel.

Drill 8 mm hole, 30 mm deep, horizontally into panel B.

Using a Krefting cutter, drill a 25 mm hole also into panel B, 12 mm in depth.

Position panels together, locate cam and lock up using a screwdriver.

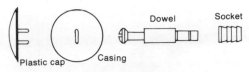

Rastex 25—components

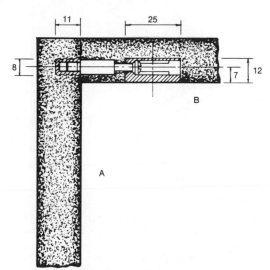

Assembly detail for Rastex 25—sectional

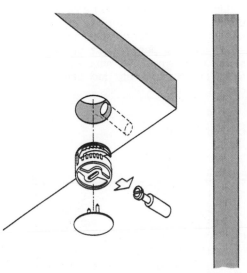

Exploded view—assembly details for Rastex 25

93

Eccentric Connectors

These are a range of eccentric cams, similar to Rastexs, but housed in a plastic casing which also has a 10 mm locating pin for further stability.

Suitable for 16 mm manufactured boards, these concealed assembly aids are an excellent means of joining adjustable shelves and side panels.

Based on System 32, these connectors are ideally suited for use in conjunction with simple drilling jigs which may provide drill bit support at 32 mm centres.

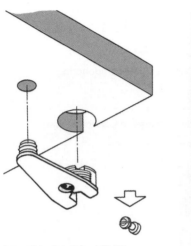

Assembly detail for VB 36

Assembly

Mark out the position of the connectors with each connector being no closer to the panel edge than 40 mm.

Using a jig that has a 32 mm-wide timber hinged to a fixed fence, drill a 20 mm hole 12.5 mm deep using a Krefting cutter or Forstner bit.

Lift the hinged timber up and holding the panel against the fixed fence, drill a 10 mm hole 11 mm deep for the locating pin.

On the side panels mark out and drill a series of 5 mm holes 13 mm deep and 32 mm apart to accommodate the screw-in steel dowels.

Drilling jig for VB 36

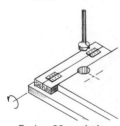
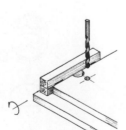

| Boring 20mm hole using a Forstner bit | Drilling a 10 mm hole for locating pin |

OTHER CONNECTING FITTINGS

Snap-Caps

These are available in a range of types, colours and sizes to decoratively cover the heads of nails, screws, bolts, or even rivets. Their use provides a professional finishing touch to any project.

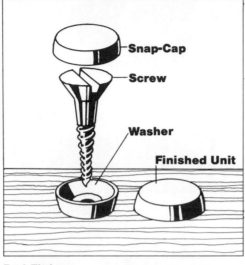

Bed Fittings

This is a particularly useful assembly aid used for locking the sides and ends of bed bases and plinths. Not only does it allow the unit to be quickly and easily dismantled, but it eliminates the need for complicated joint structure.

Note that where these fittings are used in conjunction with steel framed spring mattresses, they should be located sufficiently down from the top edges as to not interfere with the angle frame of the mattress.

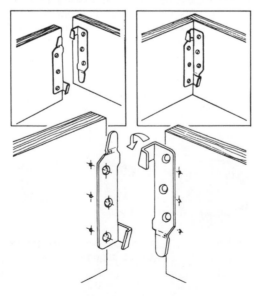

Use of bed fittings

Leg Truss

This simple assembly aid makes table and chair construction particularly easy. They provide rigid support yet allow easy detachment of legs and rails for convenient transport and storage.

These knockdown trusses, available in a range of sizes, are specially shaped steel plates with pre-drilled holes which support the two rails against the leg by means of a leg screw.

They are suitable for application in the construction of chairs, occasional tables, stools, and plinths and are equally suitable for use with round or square legs.

Assembly

A full-size working rod of one of the corner joints being assembled will provide the necessary measurements for the position of the trenches for the location of the leg trusses.

Having laid out the position of the trenches, use either a power saw or hand saw to cut the trenches.

If the top of the leg-rail structure is to be covered, the saw cuts may be the full rail width. However, if the legs and rails are to be exposed then it is essential that the saw cuts be stopped. The metal truss can, in this instance, be used not only to hold the frame together, but if the frame is to form a chair the seat base can rest on top of the corner truss.

Locate the position of the leg screw in the leg and drill a hole equal in size to the core diameter of the wood-thread section of the leg screw.

To assist the drilling of this hole the leg can be supported in a cradle and the edge of the leg, if square, can be chamfered to prevent splintering of the timber. By using two nuts locked against each other, screw the leg screw into each leg.

Attach the metal trusses to each rail by fitting the flanges into the prepared trench and screwing through the pre-drilled holes.

Attach the legs by placing the leg screw through each leg truss and tighten using a wing nut or hexagon-head nut. Check for firmness of joint and fit of leg against the rails.

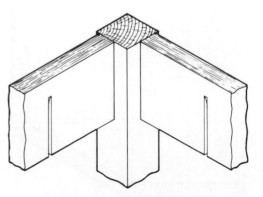

Saw cuts to accommodate leg truss

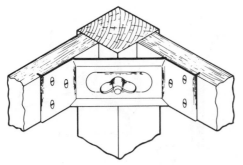

Leg truss

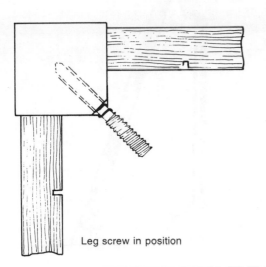

Leg screw in position

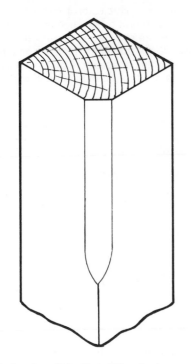

A chamfer will facilitate fitting the leg screw

HINGES

Concealed Hinges

The introduction of fully concealed hinges has eliminated the end grain problems of particle board and medium-density fibreboard where traditional butt hinges simply do not work.

Concealed hinges are now available with 90° to 170° arc openings, have a snap on, clip on or slide on facility, can have an adjustable closing force and may also be fitted to glass doors and corner cabinet doors.

All concealed hinges have 3-D adjustment—that is, for door straightness, height and distance between the door and side panel.

Concealed hinges are available as either STRAIGHT for mounting doors externally on carcasses or CRANKED for mounting doors internally.

Mounting Concealed Hinges

Select a suitable mounting position on the door and, using a 35 mm Krefting cutter, drill a hole for the hinge cup, 3 mm from the door edge and 11 mm deep.

Insert the round hinge cup into the hole, square the hinge wings to the door edge and screw the 'wings' to the door using the holes provided.

Secure the 'winged' mounting plates to the side of the cabinet carcass at the specified distance (usually 37 mm) from the inside face of the door using the screws provided.

Locate the hinge arm over the mounting plate and slide, clip or snap the hinge in position. Adjustment may then occur to correct any variations in height, straightness or gap between the carcass and door.

'Snap on' concealed hinge

fall overlay   inset

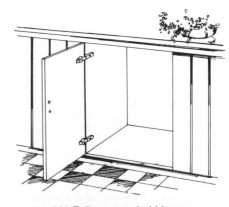

90° Fully concealed hinges

170° Fully concealed hinge

170° Fully concealed hinges

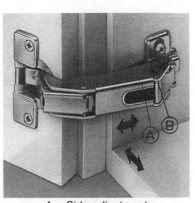

A = Side adjustment
B = Depth adjustment

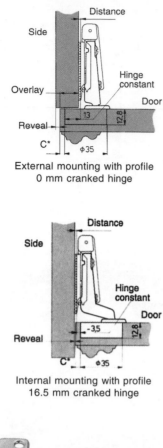

External mounting with profile
0 mm cranked hinge

Internal mounting with profile
16.5 mm cranked hinge

'Clip on' straight hinge

10 mm cranked hinge

Flap Hinges and Flap Stays

These are fully concealed plastic hinges, easily fitted by using a Krefting cutter and suitable for use in cocktail cabinets, writing bureaus or other cabinet constructions where flap-down doors have application.

It is advisable to use flap stays in conjunction with flap hinges to prevent the flap-down doors opening beyond 180°. Flap stays are now available having both a braking mechanism as well as an in-built catch. For mounting instructions refer to the manufacturer's recommendations.

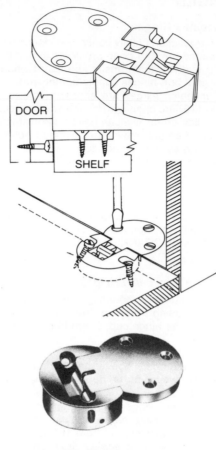

Flap hinges

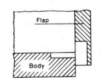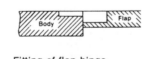

Fitting of flap hinge

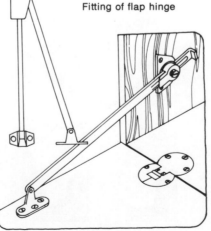

Use of flap stay

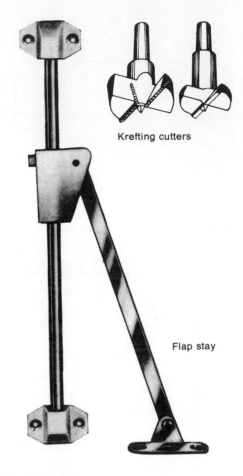

Krefting cutters

Flap stay

Pivot Hinges

These hinges, suitable for 4 mm and 6 mm glass, are attached by two tightening screws, so no holes are required to be drilled through the glass. Since the hinge operates on a pivot action it is only necessary to drill two holes in the cabinet for the internal fitting of the door.

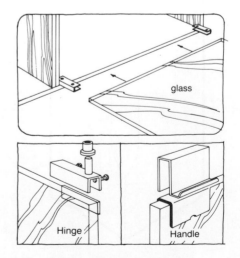

Fitting of glass door hinges

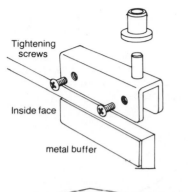

Tightening screws

Inside face

metal buffer

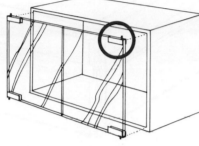

Details of glass door hinge

Semi-concealed Hinges

These hinges have been designed to fit 18–20 mm particle board and are often used where economy is of concern.

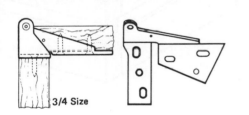

3/4 Size

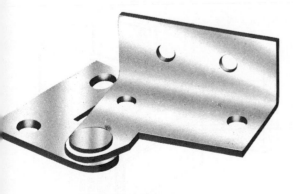

Semi concealed hinges

Piano Hinge

Piano hinge or continuous hinge has suitable application for use on the edges of particle board (particularly using long thread screws) where numerous screws can be located to further assist the strength. Exposing the hinge pin the full length of the door rarely looks good.

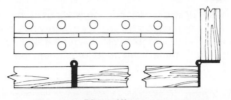

Piano Hinge
Available in 1.8 m lengths or 30 m coils.

Butt Hinges

These hinges, be they extruded brass or mild steel, are generally confined to use with solid timber.

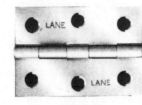

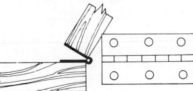

Butt Hinge
For use with natural timber

SHELF SUPPORTS

Shelf supports are available in a variety of materials, sizes, and shapes. By the drilling of a few equally spaced holes in a vertical line, flexibility of shelf heights is easily obtained. The overall lengths of adjustable shelving should be considered in conjunction with the type of shelf support being used, as the allowance will vary with the type of shelf support.

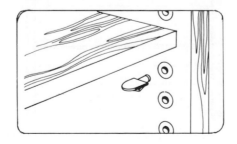

WARDROBE TUBE HOLDER

To prevent the sagging of wardrobe hanging rails, plastic robe hangers can provide support where it is needed in the middle. You should also provide locations at each end of the wardrobe panels.

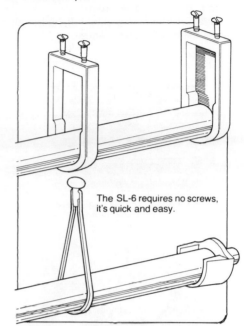

The SL-6 requires no screws, it's quick and easy.

IRON-ON EDGING

As the range of pre-finished melamine particle boards increases, the necessity to easily and quickly cover the exposed edges with similar material also increases. The 19 mm wide, pre-glued melamine edging may be ironed on to provide a perfect edge.

Similarly, paint-bond edging, iron-ons for raw-particle board also eliminate the need for filling and sanding edges prior to painting particle board.

P.V.C. Edge Trimmer

Using 'supports' of plastic material, in angles of 45° and 30°, the edge trimmer removes surplus edging material to produce a neat bevelled edge.

Depth of cut can be adjusted by sliding the plastic supports further apart.

It is ideal for trimming plastic edging but also may be used on natural veneer.

Using edge trimmer with fence

Using edge trimmer with 45° jaws

MAGNETIC CATCHES

These not only operate as a means of holding doors closed but also as a stop to position the door evenly in the door opening. They are available in a range of strengths, sizes, and colours.

Magnetic catch

DRAWER SYSTEMS

Drawer construction has always been a most difficult task in the home workshop. However, with the introduction of a range of vinyl-wrapped, mitred drawer-frame systems, previous difficulties have been eliminated.

Types

These drawer systems, consisting of high-density particle board wrapped with vinyl, not only provide a most hygienic and durable surface but eliminate the need for sanding, painting, or polishing.

Assembly

Placing the supplied plywood bottom panel in the prepared groove, fold the pre-cut vinyl-wrapped frame around the bottom panel. A smear of P.V.A. glue on each of the three mitre joints and the dowel joint will ensure that the drawer frame remains assembled.

Care is needed when tapping in the dowels as excess glue or excessive pressure may result in one side of the dowel holes breaking away.

To enable the drawer to be used widthwise as well as lengthwise, a small section of the drawer runner groove, at the dowel joint corner, may be removed. Although timber runners may be used for the drawers to slide on, specially designed and easily fitted nylon runners provide the best results. To ensure smooth drawer action when using nylon runners, an allowance of 16 mm must be made between the exterior width of the drawers and inner surfaces of the cabinet.

Full-length drawer handles are available to fit neatly into the runner groove on the drawer front. Alternatively, a 'false' front may be attached to the drawer by screwing through the drawer front into the 'false' front.

Sizes

Common fold-up drawer sizes include:
100 mm x 400 mm D x 350 mm W
100 mm x 400 mm D x 400 mm W
120 mm x 400 mm D x 350 mm W
120 mm x 400 mm D x 400 mm W
140 mm x 400 mm D x 350 mm W
140 mm x 400 mm D x 400 mm W
200 mm x 400 mm D x 450 mm W

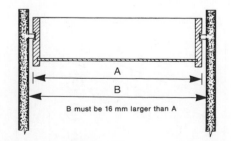

B must be 16 mm larger than A

Allowances for fitting a fold-up drawer in a cabinet

Accessories

A vacuum-formed, washable styrene cutlery drawer insert is available to suit a variety of drawer sizes.

Wire baskets are also available in compatible sizes with fold-up drawers and are useful additions to wardrobes and large kitchen cupboards.

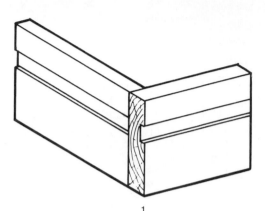

1

Conversion for sideways use

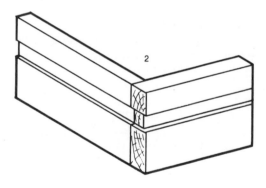

2

False front for fold-up drawer

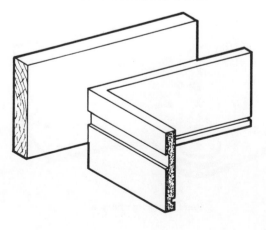

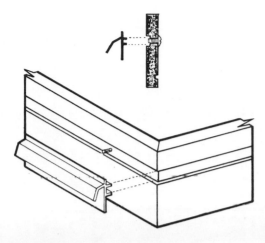

Metal handle for fold-up drawer

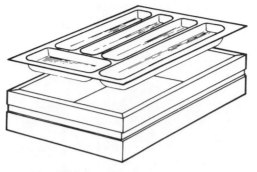

Plastic cutlery insert

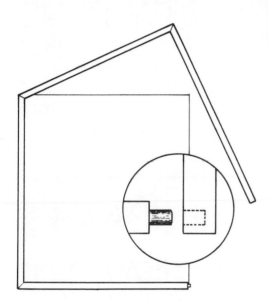

Jointing of fold-up drawer

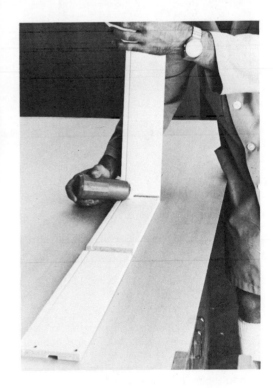

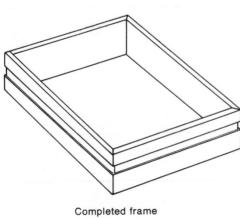

Completed frame

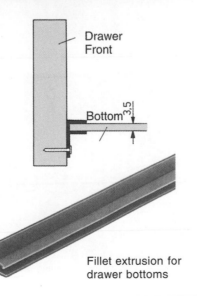

Drawer Front

Bottom 3.5

Fillet extrusion for drawer bottoms

SYSTEM 32

System 32 was developed in Germany during the early 1980s in collaboration with manufacturers of particle board, drilling machines and cabinet furniture.

The aim was to unify the manufacturing of cabinets, taking into consideration the construction of the cabinet and the positioning of different cabinet hardware items.

What is System 32?

System 32 provides a drilling pattern for vertical cabinet members. The multiple holes are drilled at 32 mm centres, they are 5 mm in diameter and in general have a depth of 13 mm for most material thicknesses.

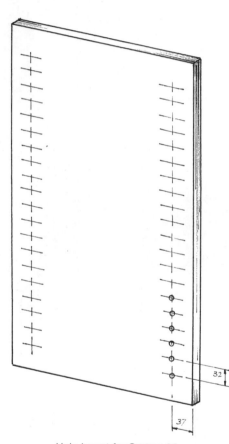

Hole layout for System 32

The typical hole pattern consists of two hole lines, one on either side of the cabinet side. The first hole line is centred 37 mm from the front edge of the cabinet side and the second hole line is a multiple of 32 mm depending on the cabinet depths.

System 32 can be readily adapted by the home handyperson by purchasing manufactured drilling jigs or constructing simple drilling jigs for one-off productions. (See drilling jig for eccentric connectors, page 94.)

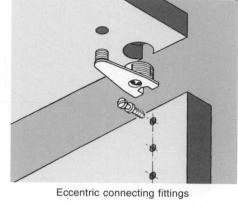

Eccentric connecting fittings

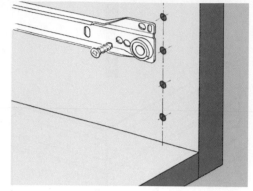

Drawer runner

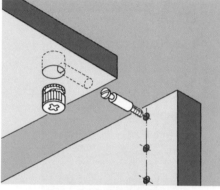

Eccentric connecting fittings

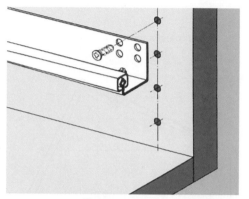

Runner system

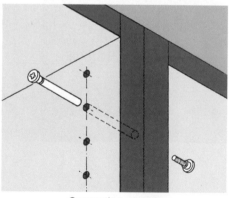

Connecting screws

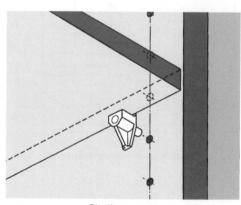

Shelf supports

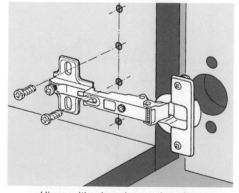

Hinge with winged mounting plate

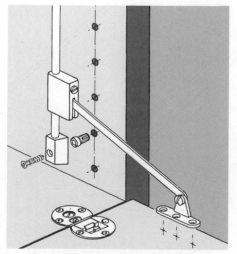

Flap stays, flap supports, flap hinges

FASTENERS & CABINET HARDWARE

...A CLOSE LOOK AT WHAT THEY REALLY DO BEST

WOOD SCREWS

The screw may be defined as an inclined plane, spirally wound around a cylinder or cone. Scientifically, the screw is classified as a simple machine. Although the inventor of this ingenious fastener remains anonymous, Archimedes is reputed to have invented the spiral about 250 BC. Historical evidence indicates that ancient screw threads were applied to cylinders and not cones.

Roman type screw

The first recorded reference to wood screws dates to the 15th century where iron screws were used in lieu of iron nails in the construction of bellows. Screw production remained a cottage industry until the beginning of the 19th century when automated lathes enabled mass production.

Wood screws are preferred in timber constructions where assembly and disassembly may be necessary. Like nails, wood screws may be classified as semi-permanent fasteners. However, they provide greater joint strength than nails and permit removal without further internal or external damage. Their use is limited to relatively light work, including frame construction, cabinet work, attachment of cabinet hardware, and architectural joinery.

Method of Production

Wood screws are most commonly produced from steel and brass, but other metals include bronze, aluminium and stainless steel. Prerequisites for all drawn wire used in screw manufacture are close dimensional tolerances and specific tensile strengths.

Structure of Screws

Screw Heads

These may be flat, round, or raised and either slotted or recessed for a special screwdriver.

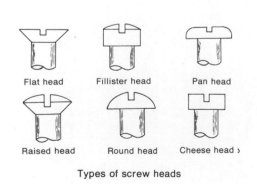

Types of screw heads

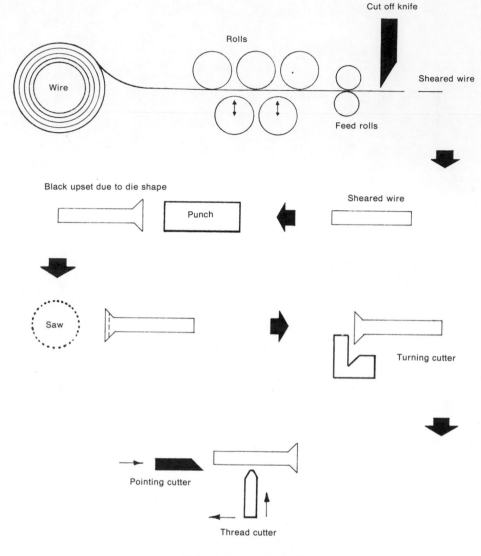

Method of screw production

Flat and raised head screws are bevelled under the head to accommodate a countersunk hole. Round head and raised head screws should be used where an aesthetic appearance is desirable. Other types of heads include Cheese head, Fillister head, Pan head, Phillips head and Posidriv.

Shank

The shank is located immediately below the head and has some two-thirds of its length threaded to a point. It is this section of the screw which designates its diameter or gauge (Standard Screw Gauge or S.S.G.).

Thread

This is the spiral part projecting from the shank or cylinder. As the screw is rotated one full turn it travels from crest to crest of the thread. The distance between the crests is called the pitch.

Points

These are generally of the gimlet type but some screws are produced with a drill point for high speed assembly—Posidriv screws are available in 'header point' and 'cone point' for quicker location.

Metal Composition

This includes steel, brass, aluminium, stainless steel, silicon, bronze, and monel, each

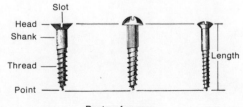

Parts of screw

102

type having different attributes in strength, corrosive resistance, appearance, and cost.

Metal Finishes

Wood screws may be bright or blued; nickel, copper, chrome and cadmium plated; galvanised and phosphated and oiled. This range of plated finishes allows for the varied screw fixtures now available (antique brassed, black japanned, oxidised).

Common Types of Screws

Flathead or Countersunk

This is the most common of all screws and for general purpose work it is made of mild steel. When used in moist conditions it is expedient to use CKS screws made from brass or copper or steel screws, plated with a rust resistant metal.

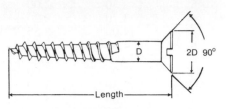

Countersunk head screw

Uses may be defined as general purpose and where the head is required to fit slightly below the top surface. With the underside of the head bevelled, a greater holding power results because of the lesser frictional resistance offered by the head. Common usage includes attaching pieces of wood together as in tables, chairs, cabinet frames, and for securing metal fixtures such as hinges.

Round Head

These screws have a flat surface underneath the head and expose the whole of the screw head above the timber surface. They are usually made from steel, brass, aluminium, or stainless steel, with steel and brass round heads available in nickel and cadmium plate, galvanised and antique copper.

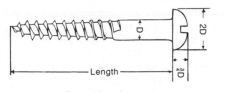

Round head screw

Uses are confined to situations where the head is required to be visible or where the material thickness does not permit countersinking. Zinc plated cone head roofing screws are available for fixing roofing iron.

Raised Head

These screws combine the strength of the countersunk screw with the appearance of the round head screw. They are available in sim-ilar metals and finishes as round head screws but being countersunk possess greater holding power.

They are used for securing metal fittings to timber where both strength and ornamentation are required. Raised head screws in conjunction with cup washers are used extensively in the motor body building industry.

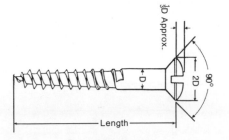

Raised head screw

Special Purpose Screws

Coach Screws

Available in sizes up to 25 mm in diameter and 300 mm in length, they have a square or hexagonal head. Sometimes called 'lag screws', they are normally used for structural work and they may be galvanised when used in exposed situations.

NOTE

Coach screws need to be driven with a spanner and are measured in mm.

Coach screw

Long Threads

These screws have been designed to provide greater holding power in manufactured board and as such have a full-length self-tapping thread with a gimlet type point. They are available in countersunk, point, or Posidriv head and in sizes varying from 9.5 mm to 50 mm.

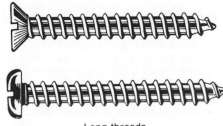

Long threads

Screw Hooks and Screw Eyes

Although 'headless', these do possess screw threads. They are extensively used as supporting fixtures for various items and are available in a range of sizes and finishes.

Self-drilling Screws

These have a section of the thread ground away forming a cutting edge. This type of fastener is available in standard sizes with flat, round, raised, or variant head shapes. Used for attaching plastics.

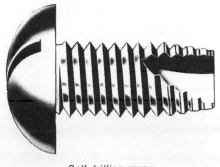

Self-drilling screw

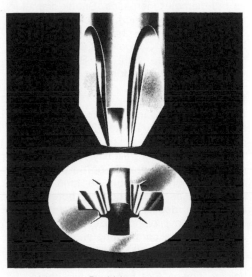

Posidriv screw

Self tapping screws   Wood screws   Machine screws

Posidriv screws

Posidriv

The Posidriv pattern has been developed to replace the old Phillip recess pattern which, although distinctly better than the long accepted single slot type, still had some disadvantages.

Posidriv screws provide a more complex recess, having vertical driving faces into which Posidriv screwdrivers firmly fit for the entire driving operation.

Advantages of Posidriv include: greater control over driving, especially at acute angles, greater reductions in operator fatigue, less work damage as a result of virtual elimination of driver slip, cam-out of the driver is reduced as the driving faces of the recess are almost vertical.

Posidriv fasteners are available in all types, sizes, and head forms of self-tapping screws, wood screws, and machine screws as previously available with Phillip recess.

Screw Statistics

The length of a screw is measured from the point to the section of head flush with the material surface.

When selecting the length of a screw, penetration into the second piece of material should be at least seven times the screw diameter for pored timber and ten times the diameter for non-pored timber.

The gauge or diameter of shank is indicated by a screw gauge number, increasing as the diameter increases. Shank diameters range from 0 (1.6 mm) up to 24 (9.5 mm). Screw gauges are based on a unique Standard Screw Gauge (S.S.G.) and should not be confused with the Standard Wire Gauge (S.W.G.) used for nails.

Installing Screws

A series of boring and countersinking operations are necessary to facilitate correct driving procedures.

A clearance hole, slightly larger than the screw shank diameter, is bored through the attaching upper member. A smaller hole, referred to as a pilot hole, is bored to the appropriate depth into the attached lower member. The pilot hole size is equal to the average of the core diameter of the screw being used. It must allow full thread depth fibre penetration for the screw to attain maximum holding power. Flat head screws should be countersunk so that they are slightly below the surface or counterbored to allow the use of plugs or buttons.

For non-pored timbers it is necessary to bore a clearance hole only and countersink if required.

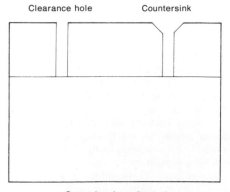

Screwing in softwood

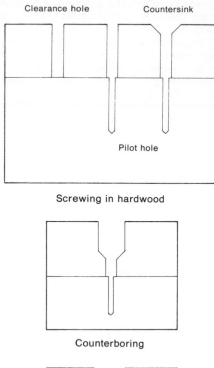

Screwing in hardwood

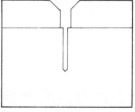

Counterboring

Countersinking

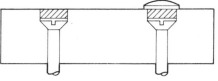

Counterbored and plugged   Counterbored and wood button

For pored timbers both a clearance hole and a pilot hole are necessary because of timber density and fibre compactness.

Screws should be driven with a correctly fitting screwdriver and never a hammer as this causes a severance of fibres and consequent reduction in holding power. Similar problems may arise if the screw is 'over driven'.

The application of soap or wax prior to screw insertion facilitates easier driving, particularly in hardwoods.

The holding power of screws is dependent upon two factors:

The accuracy of the clearance hole—if bored too large the screw head has little or no

resistance, or if undersize, the shank interference inhibits the natural spiralling action of the thread; the accuracy of the pilot hole, which must be such that the wood fibres are entwined to the full depth of the screw thread. The depth of the pilot hole should be slightly less than the screw depth.

A professional appearance is obtained if all screw slots are aligned parallel to the grain. This is referred to as 'heading the screw'.

Screw gauge	Clearance hole	Pilot hole
0	1.60	0.85
1	2.00	1.10
2	2.40	1.40
3	2.65	1.50
4	2.95	1.70
5	3.30	2.00
6	3.70	2.20
7	4.00	2.55
8	4.30	2.80
9	4.60	2.85
10	4.90	3.00
11	5.30	3.50
12	5.60	3.80
14	6.20	4.60
16	6.90	4.90
18	7.70	5.20
20	8.20	5.40
22	8.70	5.80
24	9.60	6.20

Recommended Hole Sizes

BOLTS

Small bolts are used in general joinery construction for ease of dismantling, as in knock-down furniture. Larger bolts are used wherever joints may be under structural load, as in long span roof trusses or bridges.

Carriage Bolts

These have a mushroom-shaped head with either a cut or rolled thread. Beneath the head is a short square section embedded in the pre-bored hole and preventing the bolt from turning during tightening. Although the size of the bolt is designated by the thread diameter, for a rolled thread bolt this may be larger than the shank diameter. Carriage bolts for timber are usually made of steel and may be galvanised to prevent discolouration.

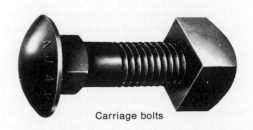

Carriage bolts

CONNECTORS

Masonry Anchors

This is a term applied to a number of special fasteners for timber structures. They are used where:

1. high loadings would require an excessive number of nails or screws.
2. there is a significant need for a more rigid joint, and
3. prefabrication may be further simplified.

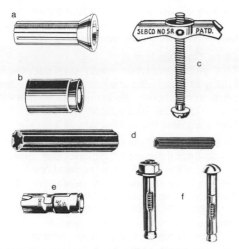

(a) 'Scuin' use with wood screws, ideal in concrete, brick, plaster. (b) 'Tampin' use with machine screws or bolts, ideal where shallow holes for installation are necessary. (c) Toggle bolt for hollow walls. (d) Nylon anchors work efficiently in concrete, brick, plaster. (e) 'Loxin' when properly installed is a very secure fitting, tapped into the hole with a hammer. (f) 'Dynabolts' tightening of the nut forces the expansion of the outer sleeve over a tapered portion of the bolt.

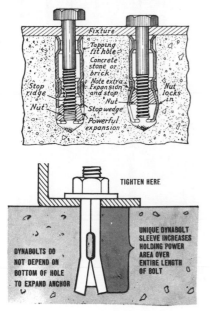

Toothed Plate Connectors

These are specially designed for use in low density timbers.

Bulldog Connector

These are pressed from sheet steel with teeth cut alternatively around the periphery. The connectors are embedded into the timber by tightening the central bolt. No joint preparation is required. They are available in 50 mm and 63 mm diameters with a 12 mm bolt.

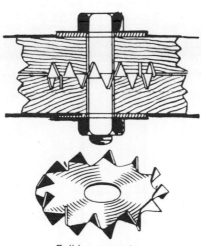

Bulldog connector

Nail-on Plates

A second type of toothed plate connector, also made from sheet steel, has a series of teeth punched over the whole surface. This form of toothed plate connector is used in the mass production of light timber trusses where they are pressed in by a hydraulic press.

Smaller nail-on plates are also used for joining low density timbers where it is possible to use a 400 g to 500 g claw hammer to attach the nail-on plate.

Nail-on plates

Split Rings

These are steel rings sprung into grooves cut into adjacent faces of timber members using a special tool. A central bolt holds timbers firmly together and the split ring carries the load. The special wedge shape of the ring sec-tion provides maximum tolerance for easy insertion, at the same time ensuring a tight fitting joint when the ring is fully seated in the conforming groove.

Split rings

Angle-shaped Plates

Made of galvanised sheet steel bent to various shapes, these are prepunched ready for nailing. They are used wherever two pieces of wood are joined, as in roof, wall, and floor framing, and provide a stronger and more efficient connection. Angle-shaped plates are particularly suitable where wind lift is a problem. Since nailing occurs at right angles to their axis the joints are firmer than the commonly accepted skew-nailed joints.

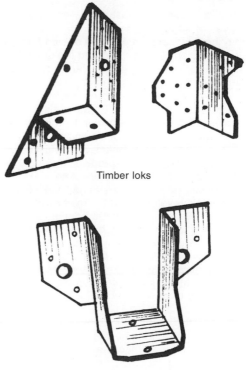

Timber loks

Joist support bracket

Uni-tie

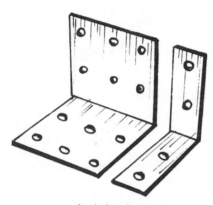

Angle brackets

NAILS

Nails are used for fastening two or more pieces of timber or composite material. They may be described as a length of wire formed to a sharp point at one end and the other end shaped to form a head. Nails are driven into timber by means of a hammer.

Wrought nails were in common use during the Roman occupation of Britain. This forging process of nails remained an industry of some consequence until the beginning of the 18th century. With the invention of sophisticated machinery designed to produce a variety of nails this process became obsolete.

The introduction of wire for nail making has completely revolutionised the method of manufacture. Nails manufactured from drawn wire may be made so cheaply that their purchase price is almost that of the wire from which they are drawn. Although cut nails are still being manufactured from flat plates, the volume produced is insignificant when compared with round wire nails.

Method of Production

Wire nails are formed by a cold heading process. The nail machine consists of four basic parts: a hammer mounted in a cross head capable of a reciprocating action via a connecting rod and crank shaft, a set of cam-actuated slides containing case-hardened tools for forming the point and cutting the nail after heading, a further set of cam-actuated slideholding discs for gripping the round wire and acting as an anvil for head formation, and a reciprocating feed table straightening the correct length of wire for each nail.

Structure of Nails

Nail Points
These may be shaped for specific purposes. The centre or diamond point is the most common but may cause splitting. Shear or flat points, although commanding lower holding powers, reduce the tendency to split. Other special shapes include the chisel point and bifurcated point.

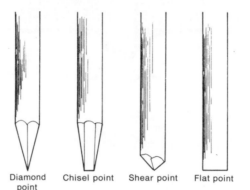

Diamond point   Chisel point   Shear point   Flat point

Nail points

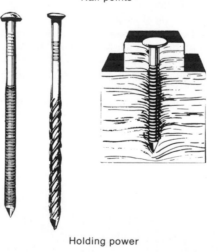

Holding power

Nail Shanks
These consist of various cross-sectional forms. Shank deformation includes twisted and barbed for greater holding power and annular groove and helical groove for improved holding power over longer periods.

Annular ring nails are most effective for fastening softwoods. The annular threads wedge into the wood fibres and holding power actually increases as the wood seasons.

Helical threaded nails for hardwoods and particle board have up to five times the holding power of equivalent plain shank nails. The nails actually turn as they are driven, cutting a thread as they go. The mating threads strongly resist any tendency to withdraw.

Nail Heads
These may be classified into three types: flat, countersunk, and round. These shapes provide the basis for further modification where special requirements are needed.

Flat head nails, as used in general construction work, provide limited withdrawal capacities, while brad or countersunk head nails designed to be punched below the surface have little withdrawal resistance.

Metal Composition
This includes carbon steel, stainless steel, brass, bronze, aluminium, monel, and other metal alloys. In the use of non-ferrous metals, the advantages in application must be balanced against the additional costs.

Various Nail Finishes
These offer increased functional and appearance qualities in particular applications. Nails are available as 'bright' (untreated) or treated thus imparting greater holding power, more resistance to corrosion, and a range of colours. Nail finishes may include blue flashing, nickel plating, zinc plating, cadmium plating, cement coating, and hot dipping (galvanised).

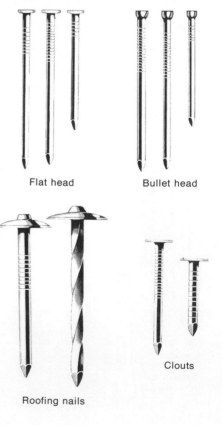

Flat head   Bullet head

Roofing nails   Clouts

Common Types of Nails

Flat Head (also known as Common nail or Box nail)
This is a round wire nail of low carbon steel having a flat head which makes it difficult to pull through the timber. Box nails are similar but made of smaller gauge wire for comparative sizes.

Uses
General construction in softwoods, particular sheet materials, and packing cases.

Standard sizes range from 20 mm x 1.25 mm to 150 mm x 5.6 mm.

Flat head nails for normal use are bright finished, having a diamond or centre point. However, they may also be obtained in various compositions and finishes.

Bullet Head, Jolt Head or Round Head (also known as Finishing nail)
This is a general purpose nail used in carpentry where the head is to be driven below the surface. Similar in formation to a brad but longer and of heavier gauge.

Uses
General construction work, fixing flooring boards and wall linings.

Sizes range from 15 mm x 1 mm to 150 mm x 5.6 mm.

Available in bright steel, galvanised, and cadmium plated, all with a diamond point.

Wire Brads
These are similar in construction to the equivalent sized jolt head or bullet head nail. They are made from very thin gauge wire ranging from 1 mm to 30 mm. Wire brads are commonly used for attaching decorative mouldings and panelling. Available in bright or cadmium plate finish.

Roofing Nails (Spring Head)
These nails have a plain, twisted, or helical threaded shank and are made of iron with a hot-dipped galvanised finish. The curved spring head acts as a self-sealer moulding to the corrugated iron profile to give a watertight seal. The helical threaded roofing nail with neoprene washer providing a waterproof seal is used in applications which would otherwise require roofing screws.

Roofing nails are available in sizes ranging from 40 mm x 3.75 mm to 65 mm x 3.75 mm.
Aluminium: Roofing nails with imitation spring head are also obtainable in the standard size 65 mm x 5 mm.

Panel Pins
These provide the ideal nail for fixing the various types of timber sheets generally used for interior walls. Construction is of thin wire with an inverted cone-shaped head allowing clean timber entrance.

Uses
The securing of wall panels, framed panels, and the application of various mouldings.

Sizes vary from 12 mm x 1 mm to 50 mm x 2.5 mm.
Available in bright steel or cadmium plate.

Clout Heads
Available in bright steel or hot-dip galvanised, these are used for fixing fibrous plaster sheets and in similar applications where head pull through is a problem. These nails are similar in formation to round flat head nails but are normally shorter with a larger flat head.

Standard sizes vary from 12 mm x 2 mm to 50 mm x 3.75 mm.

Annular threaded clouts are also available in bright steel, cadmium or zinc plated.

Fibro-Cement Nails
A form of clout but with a shear point (blunt) to reduce the tendency to fracture, they are for securing asbestos-cement sheets.

Available in standard sizes of 25 mm x 2 mm to 50 mm x 2.5 mm.

Special Purpose Nails

Hardboard Nails
Available in bright steel or cadmium plated, these are designed for fixing various timber sheets used in interior walls. Plating is recommended to prevent staining, which mars the finish and can also show through subsequent paintwork.

Standard sizes range from 20 mm x 1.5 mm to 30 mm x 1.8 mm.

Particle Board Nails
These are helical threaded and made from bright steel. They have been specially designed to overcome the problems caused by the low holding power of plain shank nails not suitable for this type of man-made board.

Usual sizes 25 mm x 2 mm to 50 mm x 3.15 mm.

Drive Screws
Generally hot-dip galvanised with a flat countersunk head and helical thread, these are used for roof deck and similar applications where greater holding power is required.

Also available with round, raised flat, countersunk, or pan heads.

Standard lengths 25 mm to 65 mm in diameter of 4.5 mm, 3.75 mm, and 3.15 mm.

Duplex Nails
These are the correct nails for form work which has to be removed later. Provide secure clamping during concrete pouring as they can be driven home completely. Save time and waste as the double head allows them to be quickly and easily withdrawn without damaging the timber.

Boat Nails
These are made from non-corrosive monel metal, silicon, bronze, or brass.

Copper boat nails are available in countersunk or rose head with a square shank. The tendency for nails to pop when the structure is twisted is reduced with square shanks.

Annular nails range from 12 mm x 1.6 mm to 75 mm x 3.15 mm while copper nails vary from 12 mm x 1 mm to 150 mm x 5.6 mm.

Escutcheon Pins
Small brass, blued, or nickel-plated nails, these have a dome-shaped head. They are used for securing ornamental plates such as escutcheon plates used over keyholes.

Obtainable in lengths from 12 mm to 125 mm.

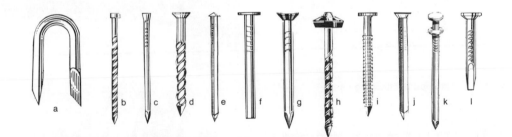

Special purpose nails (a) Fencing staple (b) Particle board nail (c) Panel pin (d) Drive screw (e) Copper boat nail (f) Asbestos cement nail (g) Plaster board nail (h) Holdfast roofing (i) Boat nail (j) Copper boat nail (k) Duplex nail (l) Splayed clout

Nail Statistics

The length of the nail used must provide maximum penetration into the member receiving the point. For medium to high density timbers this should be at least half the nail length and for low density timbers at least two-thirds the nail length.

The gauge or diameter of the nail should be proportional to the load requirements of the joint application. The choice of nail gauge is critical with respect to splitting. To reduce splitting, the minimum diameter nail which can be driven without bending should be used.

Nails are subjected to operational forces acting in either of two directions: (1) the resistance to separation of one member from another as applicable in packing case construction, and (2) the prevention of movement of one member past another as in the construction of roof trusses.

Driving Nails

Holding the hammer near the end of the handle, and using a wrist action for smaller nails or an arm to shoulder action for larger nails, drive the nail home to within 1 mm of the top surface. Using a nail punch, set the nail head a small distance below the surface (1 to 2 mm) allowing the hole to be stopped up with an appropriate filler. Fissile timber will require a hole slightly less than the nail diameter and so will nailing close to end grain.

Avoid nailing in a continuous line running with the grain. Staggering the nails will help reduce splitting problems.

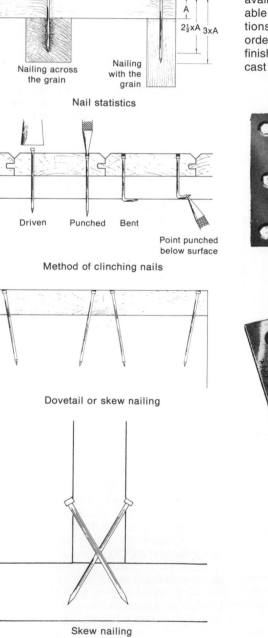

Nail statistics

Method of clinching nails

Dovetail or skew nailing

Skew nailing

Hardware

This term generally applies to the metal and plastic fittings and trim screwed or glued to an article of furniture. The selection of such items is vital to the ultimate finish and appearance.

The furniture designer carefully studies the range of fittings available and will make a selection based on the material used to make the fitting (steel, brass, plastic, aluminium), how it is made (cast, pressed), the type of finish (nickel plated, galvanised, enamelled, etc.), and the function and position of the fitting.

Hinges

There is an almost endless variety of hinges available for every hinging problem. It is desirable to consult the manufacturers' specifications when ordering special hinges. For ordering butt hinges the length, material, finish, and whether the hinge is pressed or cast is essential information.

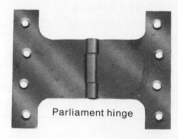

Parliament hinge

Face frame hinge

Strap hinge

Tee hinge

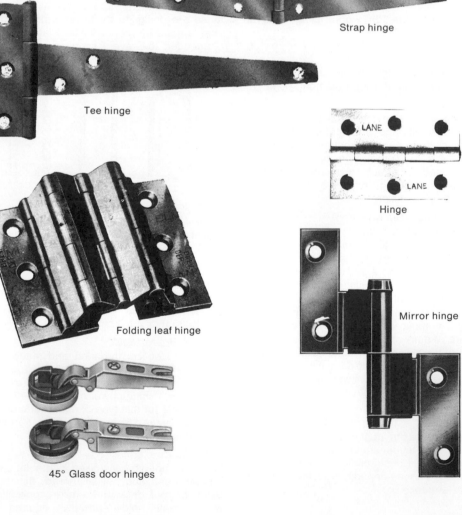

Folding leaf hinge

45° Glass door hinges

Hinge

Mirror hinge

Snap-on corner unit concealed hinge

Slide-on corner unit concealed hinge

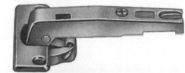

Locks and Catches

Locks are used for cabinet doors and boxes and it is desirable to consult a manufacturer's catalogue and select one suitable for the particular job in hand.

Catches may be classified as those that open and close merely by pushing the door shut and pulling it open (ball catches, magnetic catches, roller catches), and those that need to be operated by pushing a button to release a mechanism.

Sash lock

Chain door guard

Magnetic catch

Pivot hinge

Door knob

Rim night latch

Hasp and staple

Invisible hinge

Mortise lock

Push button catchset

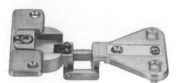

180° Single pivot hinge

Escutcheon plate

Roller catch

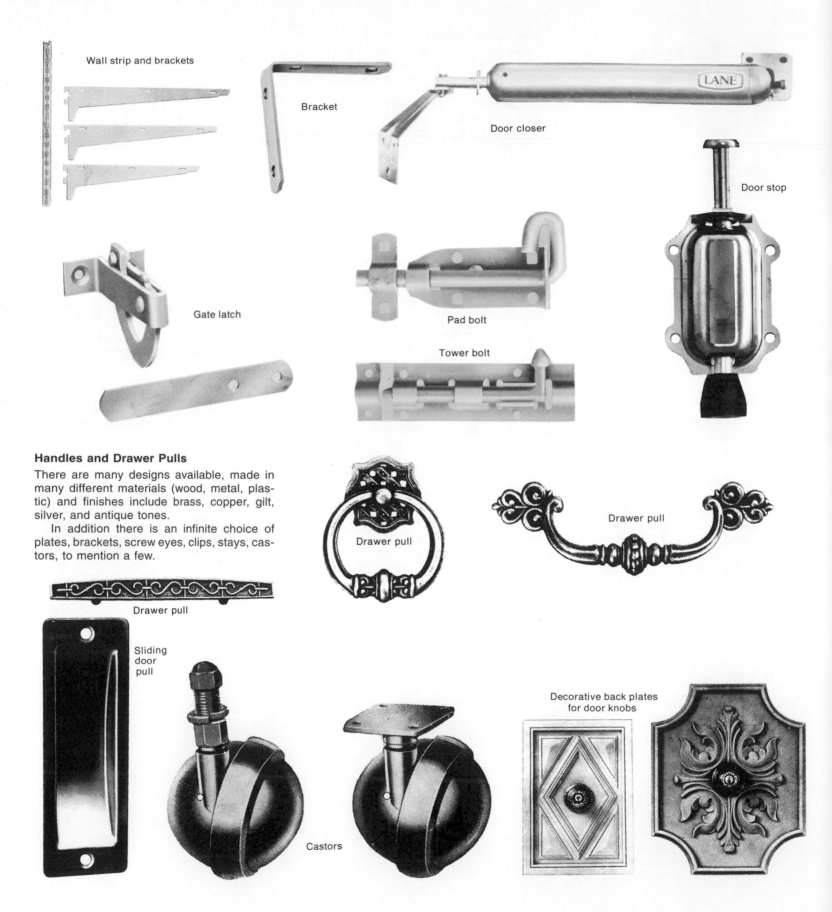

Wall strip and brackets

Bracket

Door closer

Door stop

Gate latch

Pad bolt

Tower bolt

Handles and Drawer Pulls

There are many designs available, made in many different materials (wood, metal, plastic) and finishes include brass, copper, gilt, silver, and antique tones.

In addition there is an infinite choice of plates, brackets, screw eyes, clips, stays, castors, to mention a few.

Drawer pull

Drawer pull

Drawer pull

Sliding door pull

Castors

Decorative back plates for door knobs

ADHESIVES

...CHOOSING THE RIGHT KIND

The term adhesive may be defined as a substance capable of holding materials together by surface attachment. It is generally taken to mean a wide range of glues, pastes, and cement.

It is well established that adhesion between two solids may be of two kinds.

1. Mechanical adhesion, which means that the adhesive has obtained a key by filling pores or cavities in adjacent surfaces.

2. Natural adhesion, which is produced by molecular forces similar to those holding the molecules of any solid.

Many adhesives combine both systems of adhesion to produce a bond that has a shear strength greater than that of wood.

The many adhesives now available make it difficult to select the best glue for a specific purpose. Many factors, such as cost, materials to be glued, whether indoors or out, type of timber, must be considered before final selection is made.

Types of Adhesive

Animal glue

This is made from protein material extracted from animal tissue such as bones, hides, etc. The adhesive is fawn in colour and obtainable in the form of cakes, flakes, pearls, powder, or jelly. The glue may be stored indefinitely in suitably closed containers.

The glue is prepared by soaking the pearls or whatever in water and heating to between 60° and 70°C. The glue must be used at this temperature and is applied with a brush or roller.

Assembly time is limited usually to only five or six minutes. The glue sets by cooling, combined with the loss of water.

Clamping time depends on the air temperature and can vary from one hour to eight hours.

This adhesive is the traditional woodworker's glue and there exists evidence of its use by ancient civilisations. It has very good gap-filling qualities, high strength and good creep resistance. However, it has low water, heat, and fungus resistance.

Casein glue

This is a mixture of protein material precipitated from cow's milk and alkaline materials. It is in the form of a cream powder, with a storage life of around twelve months. The glue is prepared by mixing the powder with water.

It is applied with a brush or roller and has an assembly time of up to forty minutes. The glue sets by chemical action combined with the loss of water and usually requires up to four hours' clamping at room temperature. Clamping time may be reduced if the temperature is increased.

The glue has good gap-filling qualities, high strength, and good creep resistance.

Water and heat resistance is low and there is little resistance to fungi.

P.V.A. (polyvinyl acetate)

This is a thermoplastic synthetic resin usually containing some polyvinyl chloride fillers and plasticisers. The mixture is a dispersion which sets by loss of water. It is in the form of a white viscous liquid.

The glue has indefinite storage life and no preparation is required before use. The glue is generally applied with a brush, roller, or squeeze bottle.

Assembly time is generous, usually up to ten to fifteen minutes, with clamping time up to two hours at room temperature.

The glue has excellent gap-filling properties, with a high bond strength. Being a thermoplastic material, the glue will soften with heat. Creep resistance is low, and water resistance is poor. The glue is limited to interior use, mainly for the assembly of furniture. It is clean and convenient to use.

Urea Formaldehyde

This is a thermosetting synthetic resin, a combination of urea and formaldehyde to which a catalyst is added to set the glue by polymerisation.

The adhesive is available as a white liquid or powder to which a liquid or powder hardener is added. The resin has a limited storage life, about three to six months for the liquid resin and about two years for the powder.

The adhesive is prepared by mixing the resin and hardener, but they may be used separately. The powder resin must be mixed with water before application.

The adhesive may be applied with brush, roller, or spray. Assembly time is generous, usually around half an hour, but clamping time at room temperature will vary up to about twelve hours.

The adhesive has high strength, and heat resistance is good. Water resistance, however, is low.

The adhesive is used extensively in the manufacture of plywood and particle board, radio-frequency gluing, furniture assembly, and veneering.

Melamine Formaldehyde

This is a thermosetting synthetic resin produced by reacting melamine with formaldehyde. It is in the form of a white powder with a liquid hardener. Storage life is limited to about two years. The glue is prepared by mixing the powder with water and adding the hardener, although they may be applied separately.

Assembly time is generous, with a clamping time of up to twenty-four hours. Gap-filling properties are good, with high strength. Heat and water resistance is also very good. The adhesive is used for plywood production, joinery, and boat building.

Resorcinol Formaldehyde

This is a thermosetting synthetic resin produced by reacting resorcinol with formaldehyde. The adhesive is a reddish brown liquid with a liquid or powder hardener. Storage life is limited, around three to six months.

The adhesive is prepared by mixing the resin and hardener. It is applied with brush, trowel, or roller, and for better results, to both surfaces of the joint line.

Assembly time is generous, but work must be left in clamps for about twenty-four hours.

Gap-filling qualities are good, with a high bond strength. Heat and water resistance is excellent.

Epoxy Resin

This is a thermosetting synthetic resin. The resin is a honey-like liquid with a liquid hardener. It is a universal glue, highly resistant to chemicals, and is used extensively for bonding wood to wood, wood to metals, and for glass and ceramics.

Storage life is in excess of six months. The adhesive is prepared by mixing the resin and the hardener. It is applied with a brush or a trowel.

Assembly time is generous, usually around one and a half hours, and the work must be left clamped for forty-eight hours at room temperature. Clamping time may be reduced if the temperature is increased.

Gap-filling qualities are excellent, with high bond strength, and the adhesive has excellent water and heat resistant properties.

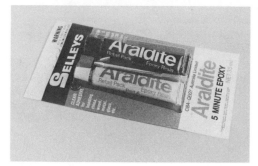

A clear epoxy resin, sets in 5 minutes, cures in 30 minutes

Contact Adhesives

These are solutions of natural or synthetic rubbers known as elastomeric materials, with highly volatile solvents. The adhesive sets by loss of the solvent. It is a creamy, yellow-coloured liquid requiring no preparation. Storage life is in excess of twelve months.

Contact adhesives may be applied with a serrated edge trowel, roller or spray gun. It is desirable to coat both sides of the glue line.

Drying time is from ten to twenty-five minutes, depending upon atmospheric conditions. When the film of adhesive becomes dry to touch the two surfaces should be combined. After contact of the two coated surfaces the bond will have around 70% of its ultimate strength, the full strength being developed over the following seven days. Clamping is not necessary.

The bond strength is lower than the other woodworking adhesives mentioned, and the bond is likely to deteriorate after a prolonged period.

Considerable precautions must be observed as the adhesive is very inflammable and it must be used only in well-ventilated areas.

The adhesive is used for bonding panelling, laminated plastics, glass, ceramics, and metals.

Contact adhesive, bonds without pressure, designed for fixing laminated plastic sheeting

Timber Preparation

Before actual preparation of the timber surface it is essential to consider the quality of the timber. Knots, cross grain, gum veins and the presence of extraneous substances will seriously affect the strength of joints. In addition, it is important to ensure the uniformity of the moisture content of the timber to be glued. The maximum moisture content must not exceed 13% if maximum strength of the bond is to be achieved.

Accurately machined surfaces free of dirt and oil are desirable. For reasons not yet fully understood, it is also important that the time lapse between surface preparation and the application of the adhesive be as short as possible or the strength of the bond may be affected. Timber treated with preservative should be machined immediately prior to the application of adhesives.

Joints are fully discussed in a previous section but it is as well to mention here that the bond between side grain surfaces is extremely strong. The glue line is generally as strong as the wood itself. On the other hand the bond between end-grained surfaces,

even with the utmost care and control during preparation and application, will develop only very low strength. It may be assumed for all practical purposes that the joints have no tensile strength at all.

Application

Adequate precautions should be taken during assembly to ensure that any surface that is to be clear surface finished is kept free of glue. Glue that is allowed to spill on to the surface will effectively seal the grain, and will be noticeable once the work is stained or clear finished.

The glue should be applied carefully and evenly so that there will be a minimum of 'squeeze out'. Any adhesive which does squeeze out should be removed with a damp rag or sponge.

A brush or roller is generally desirable for the even application of adhesive, although this depends on the type of glue and the size of the work.

Using a brush to apply P.V.A. glue

CONSTRUCTION ADHESIVES

Surface preparation for woodworking joints needs to be carefully considered. Accurately machined surfaces free of dirt and moisture are essential if strong, long lasting joints are to be achieved. However, in the building and construction field, it may be necessary to bond rough, ill fitting surfaces, such as wood to metal, concrete or brick, using products known as building or construction adhesives. These adhesives are produced using polymers such as polyurethane and silicone. They are suitable for many building applications including fixing wallboard and panelling to wood or metal frames, concrete or brick walls.

Construction adhesives are also ideal for fixing solid flooring to joists, and fixing skirting and other trim pieces, and can also be used with timber products like particleboard and M.D.F. The adhesives are suitable for interior or exterior application and are noted for their gap filling qualities and generally may be painted when dry.

P.V.A. glue may be applied with a squeeze bottle and spread with a towel. Contact adhesive on the other hand must be spread with a serrated trowel. Most of the adhesives may also be prepared for application by spray gun, a method often used in industry.

Removing excess glue using a damp cloth

Using a squeeze bottle to apply P.V.A. glue

The products are available in cartridge form, and are designed for use with a caulking gun. It is recommended that careful selection of the adhesive be made to ensure compatibility with the materials being used. All products have comprehensive instructions on the pack, which clearly specifies its application and clean-up methods. A nozzle is fitted to the end of the cartridge and the end of the nozzle is cut to an opening of about 5mm-6mm in diameter. When fixing wallboard or panelling a bead of adhesive is directed along the length of the frame or stud. On flat surfaces, like concrete or brick walls it is best to apply a bead of adhesive about every 400mm It is generally advisable to allow the adhesive to set before removing any temporary fastenings or clamps. Some products may be fast setting. Check the instructions.

These adhesives are excellent for their recommended uses, however, they are not suitable for cabinet or joinery work, where good quality joints are required.

ABRASIVES
...ALL THE SANDING MATERIAL YOU SHOULD BE AWARE OF

A coated abrasive may be defined as a multipoint cutting tool consisting of natural or synthetic abrasive grain bonded to a flexible backing with a suitable bonding agent.

ABRASIVE GRAIN

Abrasive grains used in the production of coated abrasives may be classified into two main categories:
1. Natural minerals.
2. Synthetic minerals.

Two important characteristics of abrasive grain are hardness and toughness. Besides being tough enough to resist shearing forces set up during abrasion, the grain must be hard enough to penetrate the material.

Grain Shape

As well as being hard and tough the abrasive grain should be shaped to provide a wedge-shaped cutting surface. This will allow the abrading required and re-fracture after wear to produce a new cutting point.

Natural Minerals

Flint: (Greyish-white in colour and similar in appearance to white sand).

Flint paper is actually quartz and is the mineral on the cheaper 'sandpaper'. While flint fractures into a sharp-edged grain it lacks hardness and toughness and therefore economical use of flint sandpaper is confined to the leather and hatting trades.

Garnet: (Reddish brown in colour).

Of the seven known forms of this mineral only two have been used to any extent for coated abrasives, namely almandite and rhodolite. The hardness and toughness of garnet is increased by heat treatment at high temperatures to various colour standards. For example, the scale of hardness used for abrasives is referred to as the 'Moh scale' with the diamond rated the highest at 10. The garnet mineral almandite, considered the best type of garnet, ranges from 6.5 to 7.5 on this scale. It fractures along the clearage planes, presenting new cutting surfaces with very sharp edges. All these factors make garnet a very useful abrasive and far superior to flint.

Synthetic Minerals

Aluminium Oxide: These man-made abrasive crystals are produced in electric furnaces by purifying bauxite mixed with titania for extra toughness. This produces a grain which is tough and durable with long lasting cutting edges, able to withstand the most severe working strains.

Aluminium oxide has a more 'chunky' grain shape than silicon carbide and is well suited to sanding operations on hardwoods. It has often been described as the 'work-horse' grain.

Aluminium oxide is produced in two forms:

(a) *Brown or reddish colour*—This common form has a massive, chunky, wedge-shaped grain and is very hard and tough.

(b) *White Aluminium Oxide*—This is a purer form than the brown, and while not as tough or as hard, the shape produced is a sharper wedge type. Suitable for use on timber and softer metals.

Silicon Carbide: The electric arc furnace, using coke and sand as the principal materials, produces another crystalline form known as silicon carbide.

The product is an iridescent, blue-black, hard and sharp crystal, with a hardness demonstrated by the fact that it was originally used for polishing diamonds and other gems. It is in fact rated second only to the diamond, being 9.5 to 9.9 on the Moh scale, depending on purity. However, it is a relatively brittle material compared with aluminium oxide and breaks into rather long crystals, but nevertheless it is superior in its ability to penetrate and cut rapidly under light pressure. Consequently this abrasive is compatible with high speed sanders and the 'scuffing' back of lacquers and enamels.

Diamond: The hardest known substance, this is now being manufactured for use in the coated abrasive field, but because of its high initial cost manufacture has been limited.

Grading

Screens are used to separate the crushed minerals into individual grades.

Numbers are used in classification, the number indicating the number of apertures per lineal 25 mm on the mesh.

There are three main Grade Standards systems:
1. American Standards—U.S.A. specification.
2. European Standards—F.E.P.A. system—designated 'P'.
3. Japanese Standards—similar to U.S.A.

The Australian standards follow U.S.A. standards. Reference may be made to Australian standard B279—1968 for Technical Coated Abrasives.

Backings

There are three basic materials used for coated abrasive backings: paper, cloth, and fibre.

Paper Backings

These are available in three types: rope paper, kraft paper, and jute paper. They may be further divided depending upon usage, e.g. (a) hand sheets, (b) use by specially designed machines.

Paper backings are now classified by letters according to weight, the standard weights being:

A wt	68	measured in grams per square metre
C wt	120	
D wt	153	
E wt	220	

The lighter the paper the more flexible it is.

The hand sheets are A, C, and D wt papers.

A wt paper: is used generally with fine grades for hand finishing. Its extreme flexibility allows for operator 'feel'.

C and D wt papers: are less flexible than A wt and are generally used with the coarser grades.

E wt paper: has high tensile strength, lacks flexibility, and is essentially used on sanding machines for flat surfaces.

Cloth Backings

These are produced from cotton yarns, the two most common types being Drills, designated 'X' wt, and Jeans, designated 'J' wt.

The drills cloth is made from heavier threads, thereby producing a heavier and stronger cloth than the jeans. Drills, therefore, are mainly used for heavy work and for coarse grades, whereas jeans are preferred where considerable flexibility is required.

Fibre Backings

Vulcanized fibre is a strong, flexible backing produced by treating a cotton rag base paper with zinc chloride. This fibre has the highest strength of any of the coated abrasive backings and is used mainly as a backing for resin bonded discs for use on heavy duty portable sanders.

Paper–Cloth combination consists of a light-weight cloth united with paper to give a non-stretch, durable type of backing.

Fibre–Cloth combination uses an X weight cloth combined with fibre, predominantly for the production of discs.

Coating Densities

Two types of coating densities are used: Closed Coat and Open Coat. A closed coat is one in which the abrasive grains completely cover the surface of the backing whereas in the case of the open coat about 50% to 70% only of the surface is covered.

Using a drum sander fitted to a drill to sand a canoe frame

Using Abrasive Paper

HAND PROCESSES: Despite the development of complex machinery, hand sanding is still important in the use of coated abrasives. Moreover, there are certain polishing operations that require the 'feel' of a skilled worker's hands on the abrasive sheet.

An old hack-saw blade screwed to a board makes a handy tool for tearing abrasive paper

Full sheets of abrasive paper (275 mm x 225 mm) require tearing into smaller pieces for convenience and economy of use. The majority of the modern abrasive papers do not require 'breaking of the grain' because of the quality of backings and bonding agents.

However, for coarser grits it may be necessary to give greater suppleness and flexibility of backings when used with a sanding block. To break the grain, grip the sheet diagonally and roll over a sharp edge. To complete the process, grip opposite corners and repeat. This has the twofold effect of removing any abrasive grains which may be poorly secured and giving more flexibility to the backing.

An orbital sander

A belt sander

The sanding block may consist of cork, rubber, felt, or soft board attached to a wooden block. Before sanding, all work with cutting tools should have been completed, since abrasive grains may lodge in the fibre.

Papering with the grain, the wood on the bench against a bench stop

It is most important that all sanding should be done *with* the grain to obtain the best results.

Abrasive grain will cut faster across the timber grain. If the need arises for this treatment, e.g. blemish or defect, care should be taken to remove cross grain scratches by much sanding with the grain.

Grit sizes

Recommendations for use

The grade is clearly displayed on the back of individual sheets. The lower the number the coarser the grade. 80 grit is probably as coarse as you will need, and 240 grit is sufficient for sanding surfaces prior to finishing.

Since both pressure and motion are required for the abrasive paper to cut, the article may need to be firmly held. This may be done with a bench vice, a G clamp to a bench top or, if large enough, against a bench stop, again on a bench top. If fixing is necessary, previously sanded surfaces should be protected by means of felt pads or low density fibre boards.

Excessive sanding, particularly on woods with prominent growth rings, may produce a wavy surface. Similarly, the fine, sharp edge produced where two angular surfaces meet—the arris—should be removed with one or two light strokes of fine abrasive paper. This has a twofold purpose: to reduce the chance of feathering or splintering, and to assist in the holding of finishing material.

Using a belt sander

Hardwood

	Type of Grit	Grade	Use
Portable Belt Sander	Aluminium Oxide	80–100	Removing material
Portable Orbital Sander	Aluminium Oxide Garnet Silicon Carbide	120–150	General sanding prior to finishing
Hand Sanding	Garnet or Glass Silicon Carbide	100–240	Finishing—sanding between coats of surface finish

Softwood

	Type of Grit	Grade	Use
Portable Belt Sander	Aluminium Oxide	100–120	Removing material
Portable Orbital Sander	Garnet Silicon Carbide	120–220	General sanding between coats of surface finish
Hand Sanding	Garnet or Glass Silicon Carbide*	120–240	Finishing—sanding between coats of surface finish

* Silicon carbide 300–600 may be used to rub back between coats of surface finish to obtain a smooth finish. Manufacturers have developed a self-lube paper, with a powder substance between the grains to reduce scratching and clogging. This type of paper is also suitable to use with orbital sanders. A range of grades is available.

Backings

Hook and loop type backings have been developed for easy changing of sheets on portable machines.

Abrasive paper folded around a small piece of ply for finishing a narrow edge

Abrasive paper folded around a felt pad for sanding a curved edge

A sheet of abrasive paper taped to a flat surface for sanding small objects

The progression of abrasive grit size should always move from the coarsest to the finest, since each grit must remove the scratch marks left by the preceding particles. The removal of dust particles from both the abrasive paper and work will lengthen the life of the paper and improve the quality of surface finish.

Using an abrasive disc to true up a mitre

Using an abrasive disc to square an end

Prior to application of finish, a damp cloth may be wiped over the surface to remove any remaining dust and to raise any small fibres not previously cut through by abrasive paper. This procedure is known as 'raising the grain'. Once the surface has dried, these fine whiskers may be removed with a few light strokes of fine paper.

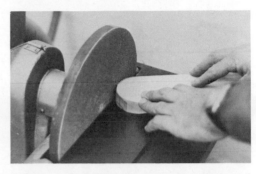

Using an abrasive disc to shape the end of a piece of timber

Using an abrasive disc to true up a compound angle

Comparative Grit Sizes

'P' Graded and Mineral graded to the Federation of European Producers of Abrasive Products. 'P' Grading is the system now being adopted by most coated abrasive manufacturers. In equivalent grit sizes 'P' grading is slightly 'purer' than the U.S. grading.

General	P. Grade Reading	Silicon Carbide Equivalent	Garnet Aluminium Oxide	Glass Paper	Flint Paper
Extra fine	P 1200	600			
	P 1000	500			
	P 800	400			
	P 600	360			
	P 500	320			
	P 400	280	280 8/0		
	P 320	240	240 7/0	00	
	P 280	240	240 7/0	00	
	P 240	220	220 6/0	0	
	P 220	220	220 6/0	0	
Fine	P 180	180	180 5/0		V. Fine
				F	
	P 150	150	150 4/0		
				1	
	P 120	120	120 3/0		Fine
	P 100	100	100 2/0		
Medium				F2	
	P 80	80	80 1/0		Medium
	P 60	60	60 1/2	M2	
	P 50	50	50 1	S2	Coarse
Coarse	P 40	40	40 11/2	21/2	
	P 36	36	36		V. Coarse
				3	
	P 30	30	30 21/2		
Extra Coarse	P 24	24	24 3		
	P 20	20	20 31/2		
		16			
		12			

FINISHING

...HOW TO BRING OUT THE BEAUTY OF THE WOOD

More than anything else it is the design and quality of the wood finish that provides the initial appeal to the potential customer in a furniture showroom. Manufacturers spend considerable time developing finishes that are going to complement various timbers and designs so that furniture sales may improve. This, however, is only one reason why wood finishing is so important.

Small amounts of 'movement' in timber during changes in climatic conditions are often observed, maybe a door or drawer does not close or open easily. This phenomenon is due to the hygroscopic nature of wood. Sealing the surface will limit this movement, and also assist in preventing splitting and warping.

Clear surface finishes are used to enhance the grain. Timber in the 'raw' is often dull in appearance and quite often the full beauty of the grain is only evident when the wood has been finished.

Timber left in its natural state is very difficult to clean. Many homes in the 19th century had kitchen table tops of raw timber, and these required vigorous scrubbing in order that they be kept clean. Modern finishes provide hygienic, readily cleaned surfaces. Finishing material is also used as protection against weathering, insect and fungal attack.

In order that timber may be correctly finished it is essential to have an understanding of its properties, the characteristics of the finishing material, and a thorough understanding of the methods and equipment necessary for application of the finish.

BRUSHES

The application of wood finish with a brush is perhaps the oldest and most widely used method, the quality of the finish depending largely upon the brush. Generally, finishing materials for brush application are air drying and are used predominantly in the home and on building construction sites.

Good brushes are designed so that there are more air spaces between the bristles of the tip than at the stock, that is they will hold more paint at the tip. Brushes are made from horse hair or special nylon fibre, but the best brushes are made from Chinese hog bristles. These brushes produce a more even spread of finishing material because the ends of the fibre are split or splayed, allowing greater contact with the surface.

Advantages of Brush Application

1. More economical in terms of paint usage.
2. Versatile—brushes can be used in almost any situation.
3. There is no contamination of adjacent areas.
4. Brush application may be used either in or out of doors under a wide range of conditions.

Brush application is relatively slow and in terms of labour rather more costly than other methods.

It is also essential that finishing materials designed for brush coating have properties that allow easy application and good flow over a broad temperature range.

Taking Care of Brushes

Brushes that are used regularly may be left suspended in the appropriate thinner. Avoid standing the brush on its bristles.

To clean a brush thoroughly, as much as possible of the finishing material must first be removed. The brush is then washed carefully in the appropriate thinners until all trace of finishing material is removed. When the brush is dry it may be stored away to await further use.

Brushing Techniques

The selection of the brush is important. It must suit the size of the work to be coated and the surface finish that is to be used. It is desirable not to use the finishing material from the container in which it is delivered, especially if it

Brush towards the end

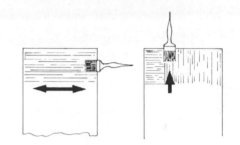

Brushing technique

happens to be rather small. It is better to pour some of the contents into a large container to prevent damage to the brush.

It can be assumed that if brush coating, the surface finish will be relatively slow drying. It is important then that brush coating be carried out in a dust free environment.

When using the brush it is dipped into the finish material to only about one-third to one-half of the bristle length. Rather than draw the brush over the edge of the can, which has the effect of removing most of the paint from the brush, it is more effective to tap the point of the brush lightly on the side of the can. This technique leaves the brush 'loaded' and the finishing material will flow more easily.

It is essential to use only the tip of the brush and apply the finishing material with long strokes. To ensure 100% coverage, brush the material first in one direction and then lay off at 90° to the brush marks.

When coating a large surface with a brush it is desirable to start in one corner and cover an area that can be easily handled and lay off so that the brush marks all run the same way. It is then desirable to coat a similar area adjacent to the first and blend in the brush marks as you lay off.

It is not good practice to keep going over the work already finished. This practice tends to 'tear up' the work, giving a rough appearance. Modern finishing materials flow readily and it is almost impossible to detect brush marks once the surface has dried.

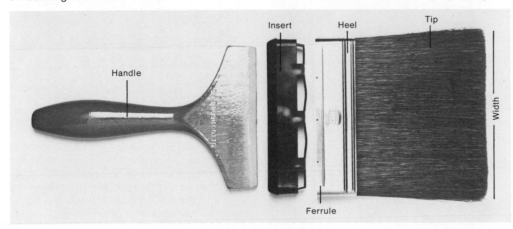

Parts of a brush

SPRAY APPLICATION

Spray application of surface finishes was first used by furniture manufacturers around 1907. Its use was rapidly developed in the early 1920s following the development of nitrocellulose lacquers.

The basic principle of spray application is to atomise the finishing material into a fine spray, the spray then being directed on to the object being finished. Various pieces of equipment are necessary to supply compressed air, regulate its flow, and filter the system.

Hand spray guns are by far the most common form of application. They allow the operator control over the film thickness and the nature of the finish. This is particularly important in furniture finishing where it is possible to allow for colour and grain variations of the timber by varying the quantity of surface finish deposited on the surface.

Equipment used for spray application of finishes is determined by the type of work being coated.

For use in the home, and other small operations, a suction feed spray gun, a small portable compressor, and a length of hose are all that is necessary.

Spray Guns

A spray gun is a sophisticated piece of equipment designed to atomise the finishing material and apply it to the surface with the

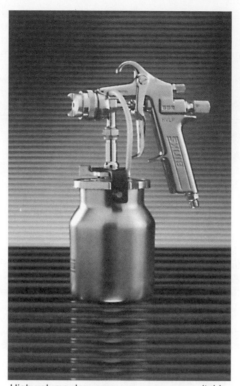

High volume, low pressure spray gun suitable for use where the finest standards of finish are required

assistance of compressed air. The air and the finishing material enter through separate passages a specially designed cap where they are mixed and expelled in a controlled pattern.

Types of Spray Guns

Bleeder Type Gun

This type of gun does not have an air valve. The compressed air passes through the gun at all times, preventing pressure build-up. The trigger controls only the amount of fluid at the tip.

Non-Bleeder Type Gun

This type of gun is designed with an air valve. The trigger controls both the fluid and the air supply. It is essential to use this type of gun wherever pressure-controlling devices are installed on the compressed air system.

Gravity feed spray gun

Operation of the Spray Gun

Pulling back slightly on the trigger opens the air valve to allow only air to pass through the nozzles. This action clears the area in front of the gun. In this position the trigger does not actuate the fluid needle and no fluid flows. As the trigger is further retracted, it unseats the needle in the fluid nozzle and the gun starts to spray. The amount of finish leaving the gun is controlled by the pressure on the container, viscosity of the finish, size of the fluid orifice, and the fluid needle adjustment.

High volume, low pressure syphon feed spray gun suitable for clear coats and most other finishes

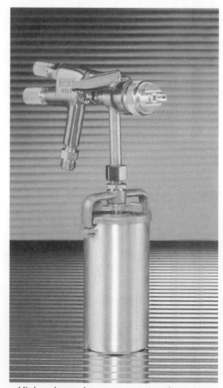

High volume, low pressure touch-up gun suitable for touching up fine, accurate work

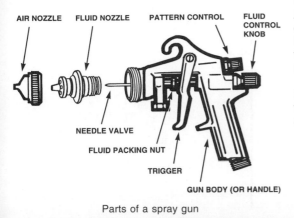

Parts of a spray gun

AIR NOZZLE · FLUID NOZZLE · PATTERN CONTROL · FLUID CONTROL KNOB · NEEDLE VALVE · FLUID PACKING NUT · TRIGGER · GUN BODY (OR HANDLE)

Air Nozzle

The air nozzle directs compressed air through the horn holes into the finish stream with the air jets atomizing the finish and directing the flow of particles into the desired spray pattern.

Fluid Nozzle

The function of the fluid nozzle is to meter and direct the finish into the air stream. It also forms a set for the fluid needle to shut off fluid flow.

Fluid Needle

The fluid needle shuts off the passage of finishing material through the fluid nozzle, and in siphon feed systems only, regulates the flow of finishing material passing through the fluid nozzle.

Trigger

The trigger operates the air valve and fluid needle.

Fluid Adjustment Control

This control is used only with siphon feed and adjusts the volume of the finishing material.

Air Valve

This mechanism controls the air flow through the gun. It is operated directly by the trigger and when the trigger is released the air valve moves to the closed position, stopping air flow.

Methods of Feeding the Material to the Cap

Suction Feed Gun

In this type of gun a stream of compressed air creates a vacuum, allowing atmospheric pressure to force the finishing material, in an attached container, to the cap.

Pressure Feed Gun

In this type of gun the air enters the container and the finishing material is forced up to the cap. This type of gun is generally used when fast application is required, e.g. production spraying, or when the materials are too heavy for the suction type to handle.

External and Internal Mixing Caps

An internal mix gun refers to the cap which is designed to mix the finishing material and air inside the cap before ejecting the spray. This type of cap is used for slow-drying finishing materials and where low pressures are used.

The external mix cap is designed to atomise the finishing material outside the cap. This type of cap is particularly suitable for lacquers and other fast-drying materials.

Mixing caps

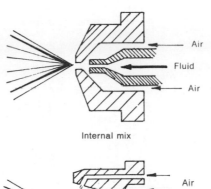

Internal mix

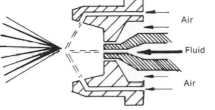

External mix

Fluid Tip

The fluid tip is the component directly behind the cap. Its function is to meter and direct the material into the air stream. The fluid tip is made of hardened stainless steel and forms a seat for a metering needle which controls the flow of finishing material. The fluid tips are available in many sizes and must be selected carefully so that they may adequately handle the type and volume of finishing materials that may be required at any one time.

Selection of Caps and Fluid Tips

Manufacturers' catalogues provide the technical information needed to make a proper selection and will refer to the following:
1. The amount of air available (litre per minute).
2. Air pressure (kilopascals)
3. Feeding system—whether suction, pressure, or gravity.
4. Material to be sprayed.
5. Volume of material to be sprayed.
6. Section of fluid tip in accordance with the required flow and viscosity of the finishing material.
7. Nature of the object to be sprayed.

Maintenance of the Spray Gun

Cleaning

When spraying is complete, empty out the remaining finishing material and replace it with a small amount of solvent. The solvent is then sprayed through the gun to flush out the passage ways. The cap is removed and immersed in the solvent. If the small holes remain clogged, a piece of soft material, such as a match, is used to dislodge the offending material. Wire and nails should be avoided as they may damage the cap permanently.

Lubrication

One or two drops of light oil are required occasionally around the metering needle packing, the air valve packing, and the trigger bearing screws. The metering needle spring should be lightly coated with petroleum jelly.

Spray Pattern

The cap is responsible for atomising the finishing material and directing it on to the work in the form of a spray. The cross-section of the spray is called the pattern and it will vary with the type of cap.

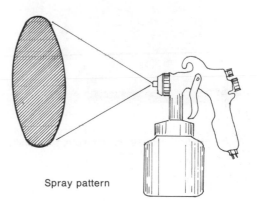

Spray pattern

Air Compressors

An air compressor may be described as a device that raises the pressure of air above atmospheric pressures. Compressors may be classified as a piston or diaphragm type.

Piston Type

In this type of machine the pressure is developed by the action of a reciprocating piston. The air is drawn through an intake valve, compressed, and expelled through an exhaust valve to the air line. This unit is available in a variety of types and sizes depending upon the volume and pressure needed. These machines are used for heavy duty requirements, such as furniture finishing, automotive refinishing, service stations, and large industrial plants.

Diaphragm Type

This type of compressor is small and portable and develops pressure through a reciprocating flexible disc attached to an eccentric shaft. This type of device is limited and only provides sufficient air for small work. It is suitable for use in the home.

A diaphragm type compressor of up to 70 litres per minute and up to 275 kPa.

Light weight portable unit operates on a high-volume principle, virtually no pressure, so virtually no mess.

Spraying Techniques

The gun should be held at right angles to and about 200 mm from the surface being sprayed. The gun is moved in such a way that it is kept parallel to the surface. If arcing is allowed to occur, uneven application will result and in particular excessive overspray will be evident at the end of the stroke. It is also important not to tip the gun. The gun must be triggered before beginning the stroke and released before the end. Each stroke must be lapped over the preceding stroke otherwise streaks will appear on the surface. The gun must be moved at a constant speed as the finishing material is being delivered to the surface at a constant rate.

When spraying furniture where two surfaces meet at right angles it is desirable first to spray the edges of the article, then holding the spray gun pointed at the corner, spray both surfaces at once. Each side may then be sprayed taking care to blend into the coated area.

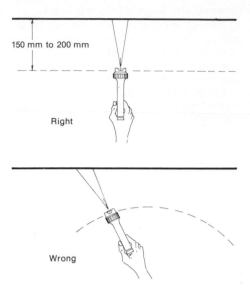

150 mm to 200 mm

Right

Wrong

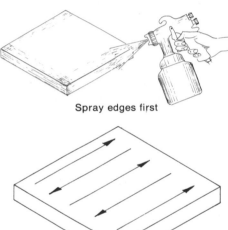

Spray edges first

Spray sequence

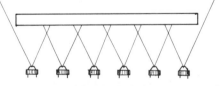

Each stroke must be lapped over the preceding stroke

Some Other Problems Associated with Spray Finishes

Runs

This can be the result of too much finishing material being applied to the surface, or it may mean that the finishing material is too thin. It is generally caused by tilting the gun or holding the gun too close, or moving too slowly, causing finishing material to build up and run.

Orange Peel

This is a defect, so called because it resembles the texture and appearance of orange

Hold gun perpendicular to surface. If the gun is tilted it may cause runs

peel. It may be caused by pressure, either too high or too low, or the gun being held too close or too far away from the work. Incorrect thinners or inadequate preparation of the surface may also be the cause.

CLEAR FINISHING FURNITURE AND PANELLING

Preparation

Planing

Any rough areas or torn grain should be planed out using a No. 4 smoothing plane. For this type of cleaning up the frog should be adjusted to leave only a small gap between the blade and the mouth. This allows only for a very small shaving. The blade must be very sharp and uniformly flat. The cap iron must be as close as possible to the cutting edge (see section on Handtools).

Scraping

The scraper is generally used as an intermediate stage between the plane and abrasive paper. The scraper gives a fine finish, removing plane marks and cutting curly grain without tearing the surface.

The scraper is generally only used on timbers with difficult grain. It could damage the fibres of some high grade furniture timbers.

Success in using the scraper lies in the correct sharpening process. (This is set out clearly in the section on Handtool Maintenance.)

There are two types of scrapers suitable for furniture.
1. The rectangular scraper is a piece of tool steel of thin gauge sharpened to form a cutting edge and held directly in the hands. Inexperienced users would be well advised to practise first on a scrap piece of timber.
2. The cabinet scraper is much easier to use, and consists of a rectangular piece of tool steel held within a metal frame. (Details of the tool in Handtools and Processes.)

Use of Abrasive Paper

(Details of abrasive paper and its use are set out in the section on Abrasives.)

Fine sanding follows the scraping process. It is most important that all sanding be done 'with the grain'. Scratches across the grain are very hard to remove. This also applies to orbital sanders which sand across the grain for part of each revolution. Hand rubbing, using a cork block with the grain, is the safest way of ensuring a perfect surface. A brush is used for removing the dust as the work proceeds.

Removal of Dents

It is most annoying to dent a surface already prepared for coating, but it can so easily happen, perhaps by careless handling, or the dropping of a tool or other equipment on the prepared surface.

Dents can, however, be easily removed. A damp cloth is placed over the offending area and a hot household iron or soldering bit is placed on the cloth. This action will generate steam and the wood being hygroscopic in nature will swell back to its original size. The surface is allowed to dry and is then refinished with abrasive paper.

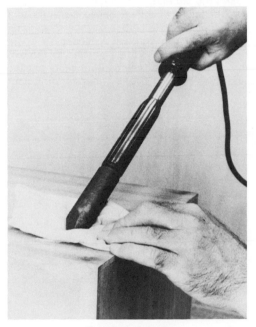

Removal of dents

Stopping

Holes and cracks must be stopped before the surface is stained or filled. Many types of stopping are available in a wide range of colours for use with various finishing materials.

For clear wood finishes, lacquer putties, available in a wide range of colours, are desirable. They can be used with shellac, nitro-cel-lulose lacquer and modern plastic finishes. The putty requires about one hour to dry before fine abrasive paper can be used to level off the surface.

For pigmented finishes a neutral coloured stopping may be used, and is generally applied after priming. A wide range of putties or 'plastic woods' are available for this purpose.

The correct putty or wood stop is essential for a first class finish

Tools Used For Stopping

A plasterer's small tool is ideal for stopping but a modified knife blade with a rounded edge will serve adequately.

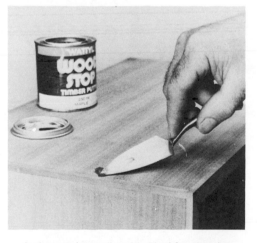

A plasterer's small tool is ideal for stopping

STAINING

Staining of timber requires some careful consideration. First the work must be carefully and perfectly finished or the stain will appear blotchy. Secondly, if applied too heavily it will appear dark, and it is very difficult to scrape out the dark stain. In many cases timber is best left in its natural colour. Always try the stain on a test piece, allow to dry, and give it one or two coats of finish to make sure it does not change colour.

There are many types of wood stain available but basically they may be described as a staining solution made up of a solvent in which colouring matter has been dispersed.

Penetrating Oil Stain

These stains are purchased ready for use and are available from a large range of manufacturers. The stain is prepared by dissolving coal-tar dyes in naphtha, benzine or turpentine. A variety of shades are available, and retailers are able to supply colour cards to assist in the selection of required shades.

This type of stain is easy to apply, soaks into the timber surface very quickly, and allows the grain to show through clearly. In addition it will not raise the grain.

Application
It is of the utmost importance to inspect the surface carefully before the stain is applied. It should be free of all imperfections. Stain should be applied in well lighted areas.

The stain is applied with a brush using long even strokes in the direction of the grain. The excess is removed with a clean cloth wiped in the direction of the grain.

Pigmented Oil Stain

These stains are purchased ready for use and are available in a wide range of colours. The stain consists of insoluble particles of colouring matter suspended in a vehicle of drying oils.

The stain is easy to use and dries rather more slowly than the others. It does not need to be applied so quickly.

Application
The stain may be applied with either a brush or cloth. Because it is slow-drying, a reasonable period of time must elapse before wiping off the excess. In order to show off the wood grain it is important to wipe off all the excess as this type of stain does not possess the transparency of other stains. The stain must be allowed to dry for at least twenty-four hours before coating with finishing material.

Spirit Stain
These stains are also readily available commercially and are manufactured by dissolving powdered dyes in alcohol. They are very quick-drying indeed and may be applied directly over a sanded surface, giving a beautiful transparent finish. Because the stain dries rapidly it is difficult to apply to a large surface area. It is almost impossible to apply without visible streaks or marks.

Application
The stain may be brushed on using the widest possible brush. It is applied quickly with long strokes. Avoid going over the work just stained.

Water Stain

This stain is actually coloured water prepared

by dissolving coal tar or vegetable dyes in water. Water stain penetrates deeply and is very transparent. However, when applied to the surface it raises the grain, necessitating further papering before applying the surface finish.

Application

The stain is brushed on using long even strokes in the direction of the grain. The surface must be left for about six hours before recoating.

Care must be taken to ensure that the finishing coat will be compatible with the stain.

SEALING

Sealing depends on the timber species. Porous hardwoods and many of the pines may require sealing. If the timber surface feels rough it may be advisable to apply a sealer coat, and when dry, rub down with wet and dry paper about 200 (used dry). This will produce a smooth surface for subsequent coats.

Sealers

Sealers may be described as a clear filling undercoat. They are specially formulated to give maximum build and have free sanding qualities. They are transparent and will not obscure the grain of the timber and in many cases are used directly on to the surface without the use of grain filler. They may also be applied after staining or filling to seal or fix the surface.

The sealer is applied directly to the surface either by spray or brush and permitted to dry. Sealers manufactured for use under nitrocellulose lacquers and modern plastic finishes usually have a plastic base. They dry in three to five minutes and are ready to sand in about twenty minutes. Other material such as shellac, varnish and lacquer may be used as sealers.

FILLERS FOR FURNITURE FINISHING

Grain fillers are used to fill the pores in a timber surface and to provide a level base on

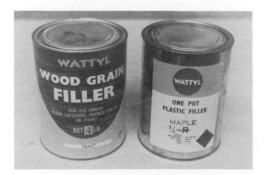
Grain fillers are used to fill the pores on a timber surface

which to apply finishing coats. Grain fillers are desirable where a high gloss finish is required. If an open grained appearance is required grain filler is not used. There are two types of grain filler available commercially.

Linseed Oil Paste Fillers

This type of filler is produced by mixing finely ground crystal quartz, known as silex, with boiled linseed oil to form a paste. Driers are added and the paste coloured.

Plastic-based Paste Fillers

This type of grain filler cures chemically and is designed for use under nitro-cellulose lacquers and plastic finishes such as polyesters and polyurethane. This type of filler may be either supplied with a hardener or may have its own inbuilt catalyst. It is applied in the same way as ordinary fillers, but it is advisable to read carefully the manufacturer's specifications.

Application of Grain Fillers

The filler is first thoroughly mixed and thinned to a consistency that resembles a thick cream. This will to some extent depend upon the texture of the timber.

Filler is applied in a circular motion

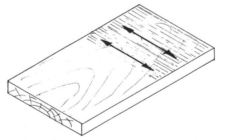
Excess filler is removed by rubbing across the grain

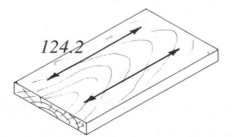
Cross streaks are removed by rubbing lightly with the grain

A piece of hessian about 200 mm square folded into a pad is ideal for applying the filler. The paste is applied freely to the surface in a circular motion.

The filler is allowed to stand for about five to ten minutes until the wet or shiny appearance goes dull.

The surplus filler is wiped off with a clean piece of hessian, taking care to work across the grain.

When the surplus has been removed wipe the surface with a clean soft cloth and allow the filler to dry.

Plastic fillers dry quickly and may be sealed after about four hours' air drying, but linseed oil-based fillers need up to twenty-four hours' drying time.

CLEAR FINISHES

Shellac

Shellac traditionally holds a very important place in the field of wood finishing. It is one of the oldest types of finishes known to man. It is fast drying, long lasting, and still compares favourably with some of the more modern rapid-drying finishes.

Shellac is an organic material manufactured from the exudations of a small red bug called the lac bug, from India.

The natural colour of shellac is orange, and when applied to a timber surface it will tend to discolour the surface. A bleaching agent may be added to orange shellac to remove the colour. This is then sold as white shellac and does not significantly change the colour of the timber.

Uses

Sealer

Shellac is an excellent sealer. It gives a hard transparent undercoat, allowing all types of finishes to be applied over it, from lacquer to enamels.

A Final Finishing Material

Four or five thin coats of shellac rubbed back with steel wool produces a beautiful desirable finish. This type of finish is not used industrially but is popular with amateurs. Shellac may be coloured by adding dyes and in this form is a desirable finish for patternmakers.

French Polish

This is the ultimate in wood finish. It is the traditional method used by the old French masters during the 17th and 18th centuries to create the still beautiful finishes seen on pieces of antique furniture exhibited in museums.

The shellac is applied to the surface with a pad made of lint-free linen. The shellac is built up slowly until a required body is reached and a high smooth gloss is obtained.

Shellac is a very durable material and will last indefinitely. It is not, however, waterproof and must not be applied to a surface that is to be exposed to the elements. It is not heat resistant. Also it should not be applied to furniture likely to be associated with the serving of liquor. Shellac is made with alcohol and any liquor spilt will dissolve the finish. Shellac can be brushed or sprayed with equal success.

Varnishes

Varnish has been used for thousands of years. It was used by the Greeks as a preservative for their sailing vessels, and earlier by the Egyptians to decorate their tombs. It is still used extensively today as it possesses many desirable characteristics. It is hardwearing, will withstand moisture, and can be polished to a high gloss.

A varnish is composed of a resin, a solvent which dries by evaporation, a vehicle such as linseed oil that dries by oxidisation, and driers that hasten the drying process.

Varnish resins are commonly classified into natural and synthetic resins.

The natural resins and gums are obtained as exudations of trees or from the ground where past exudation has been buried (Kauri gum). A natural resin commonly used is wood rosin. The rosin is extracted from pine tree stumps.

Natural resin varnishes are readily available in flat, semi-gloss, and full gloss, and they are extremely easy to apply. Varnishes should not be stirred as this will cause air bubbles which will mar the surface.

Synthetic Resin Varnishes

Commonly called plastics, synthetic resin varnishes are available from most hardware stores in flat, semi-gloss, or full gloss finishes. Manufacturers' instructions must be followed carefully, particularly with a two-part variety where a catalyst has to be added to set it.

Synthetic Resins

Synthetic resins may be produced by natural substances or by a wide range of chemicals derived from petroleum and coal. Resins have been developed in recent years which have led to the development of varnishes that combine the characteristics of the older type varnishes with the ability to dry rapidly. A scientific approach to varnish-making is now established and the modern varnishes can be manufactured to meet the needs of a specific problem. They can be produced to suit interior, exterior, and marine finishing.

Polyester Resins

Polyester coatings have been used mainly for wood finishes on furniture. They require a two-component system which to some extent has limited their use in industry. Electron beam radiation and ultra violet radiation are new methods of cure currently under development. Finishes prepared with polyester resins may be brushed, dipped, or sprayed. Special guns can be used to mix the two components as they leave the nozzle.

Urea Resins

Urea was first synthesised over a hundred years ago and first used in 1936 for organic coatings. Urea pre-catalysed resins are widely used for wood finishes either as clear lacquers or pigmented enamels. They have excellent adhesion to wood and provide an adequate gloss. Their exterior durability is inferior and their chemical resistance is fair.

Polyurethane Resins

These resins have been used for surface finishes for about twenty-five years but their development was retarded because of a two-component system. Recent developments include a one part polyurethane, and their use in industry is increasing. One of the most outstanding advantages of polyurethane is its hardness and resistance to abrasion. They are also tough and flexible.

Epoxy Resins

These resins were introduced into Australia in the late 1950s and since then have become firmly established in industry. Epoxy resins have good adhesion to a variety of materials: wood, metal, glass, ceramics. The resins are tough, flexible, and resistant to abrasion. The paint industry, producing special types of surface finishing, is one of the main users of epoxy resin. Two-pack solvent-based paints can be applied by brush or spray and are obtainable as clear or pigmented. They can be applied to wood, steel, concrete, asbestos, and many other surfaces.

Nitro-cellulose Lacquers

These lacquers are known as non-convertible coatings and dry through solvent evaporation. No significant chemical change takes place. These lacquers remain soluble in the solvent used in their preparation and are easily removed by the application of such solvents.

Nitro-cellulose lacquer is made from purified cellulose from natural cotton or wood pulp. The cellulose is treated with a nitrating mixture of nitric and sulphuric acids.

Nitro-cellulose lacquers are used extensively for the surface finishing of furniture. To obtain a desirable finish a number of important steps are necessary.

The surface must first be stained to achieve the desired colour. Water-, spirit-, or oil-based stains may be used. The grain must be filled and a sealer used as a base coat. The lacquer may be applied by either brush or spray. More than one coat is necessary to achieve a high quality finish, usually about eight coats.

A felt-faced block is used to cut back the surface using wet and dry paper 320–600. Mineral turps or kerosene is used as a lubricant.

A specially selected solvent blend is prepared and applied with a French polisher's pad. This technique softens the lacquer, allows the material to flow, removes any cutting marks, and produces a high gloss.

To obtain a maximum gloss the surface is burnished and polished. During this stage a special burnishing liquid is applied with a pad of flannelette. It is rubbed vigorously over the surface in straight line motions. This may need to be repeated several times until the desired effect is achieved.

Some Advantages and Disadvantages of Lacquer

Perhaps the most significant advantage is that the drying time is very short. Several coats may be applied within hours. On the other hand, lacquer is difficult to apply with a brush. For better results spraying is essential.

Wax Finishing

Wax finish will produce a soft mellow finish. There are a number of products readily available but a satisfactory product can be made from beeswax thinned with mineral turpentine. Shredded beeswax is melted in a vessel suspended in hot water while an equal part of turpentine is added.

Wax may be applied directly to the timber or after a shellac or varnish finish. It is applied with the aid of a piece of soft cloth and polished off with a fresh piece of soft cloth.

Where a wax finish has been used no other finishing material can be satisfactorily applied over it.

FINISHING EXTERNAL TIMBERS

Natural Finishing of External Timbers

Varnishes and synthetic resin finishes are not recommended for general external use but they may be used with reservation in small well protected areas. These finishes generally begin to deteriorate within twelve months of application, and maintenance usually involves the complete removal of the film by sanding. If regular maintenance is neglected the timber will stain in an uneven and patchy manner.

Exterior timbers recommended for natural finishing include Western red cedar, Californian redwood, Douglas fir, or treated Radiata pine.

When specifying timber for exterior use, timber with a rough-sawn surface will tend to conceal scuff marks and will hold stains and other penetrating finishes longer.

Bleaching Agents to Achieve a Weathered Look

Bleaching agents contain a small amount of grey pigment and an ingredient that actually bleaches the wood. When first applied the oil gives a delicate grey tone but gradually changes the colour of the raw wood to a natural driftwood grey.

Linseed Oil-based Stains

These finishes allow the grain of the wood to show through and should only be applied to new timber or for refinishing previously stained surfaces.

Oil-based stains have a low cost in both initial application and subsequent maintenance.

The use of pure, raw, or boiled linseed oil for an exterior finish is not recommended as it causes considerable darkening and tends to attract and hold dust.

Creosote-based Stains

These stains are economical and are intended for use on external rough-sawn timber surfaces, e.g. fences, pergolas, etc. They have a high creosote content which provides protection against decay and insect infestation. Two coats are recommended to achieve the required penetration. The stains are not intended for internal application because of the objectionable smell of creosote in confined spaces.

Solvent Type Preservative Treatments

Pentachlorophenol in Oil

This finish is basically a preservative treatment and offers resistance to decay but will not prevent discolouration from sun and rain. It is a cheap finish marketed as a brush application protective finish for fences.

Water-Repellent Preservatives

Timber treated with water-repellent preservatives is resistant to end-grain splitting, surface checking, mould growth, insect attack, and decay. The timber is effectively sealed and water absorption will be greatly lessened, reducing dimensional changes in the timber.

These preservative treatments are primarily intended to protect joinery from the effects of water during delivery and on-site installation.

Pigmented Finishes

Pigmented finishes are used for a variety of reasons, from a purely visual or decorative use, to coatings that are designed to give protection. Many wood products can be made more attractive with pigmented finishes. Surfaces are easily cleaned and are durable.

Pigmented finishes for outside use are designed not only to give lasting protection to exterior surfaces but also to provide colours that enhance the building.

General Composition of Pigmented Surface Coatings

Pigments

Pigments are powdered substances that remain insoluble. They have to be carried to a surface, hence the term 'vehicle', which is the medium that performs this task. Their principal function is to supply colour and opacity to the film. They also provide additional properties such as control of flow, increased resistance against light, heat and solvents.

Inorganic pigments may be broadly classified into white and coloured varieties and include white lead, zinc oxide, titanium oxide, iron oxide, and lead oxide, to mention only a few.

Vehicle, Media, or Binders

This is the component that binds all of the other ingredients together. It also carries the pigment to the surface and is the film-forming portion that remains after drying. It dries by evaporation of solvents, or by polymerisation with oxygen from the air, or by the use of a catalyst.

Solvents

The type of solvent will depend largely upon the vehicle. Generally solvents are blended to provide a balance between drying time and application properties. Solvents commonly in use are hydrocarbons, ketones, esters, alcohols, glycol esters and water.

Plasticisers and Auxiliaries

Plasticisers are used to impart a degree of flexibility to the dried film. In addition, other materials are added in small amounts such as driers, fungicides, anti-skinning agents and thickening agents.

Pigmented Finishes

Application of Pigmented Finishes

Before painting it is important that all grease, dust, and dirt be removed. This may be done by washing down with a liquid detergent in water. All loose peeling and flaking material is best removed with a scraper, wire brush, or abrasive paper.

It is also advisable to sand glossy painted surfaces until all the gloss is removed.

On exterior surfaces holes and cracks should be filled with linseed oil putty *after* the application of the primer. For interior surfaces a woodstop putty may be used before applying the undercoat.

On previously painted work in good condition the finish is applied directly. No undercoat is required.

On new timber for interior use, two coats of undercoat are desirable before the application of the surface finish.

On new timber for exterior use, one coat of primer is recommended followed by one coat of undercoat before applying the surface finish.

It is also recommended that the primer and undercoat be allowed twenty-four hours to dry. It is then advisable to sand lightly before applying the finish.

Two coats of the surface finish are generally desirable for an acceptable surface.

Stripping

It may be necessary to strip off completely any previously painted surface before refinishing. This will depend largely on the condition of the surface and the type of finish to be applied.

Clear surface finishes will allow any imperfections to show through, while opaque finishes can usually be successfully applied over old finishes provided they are sound and can be sanded smooth.

If the surface has been stained with a penetrating stain, no stripper will remove the colour.

The stripper is applied with an old paint brush and the surface allowed to soften before removing with a paint scraper. The surface must be washed thoroughly with turps and allowed to dry before sanding.

Paint scraper

Antique Finishing

This type of finish offers a variety of distinctive effects from French Provincial and early American finish to strong bright colours and wood tones.

On old furniture antique finishes can be applied over paint or varnish provided the finish is sound. It may also be applied to new timber not suitable for clear surface finishing.

Preparation

Old surfaces, if basically sound, must be clean. Traces of oil or furniture polish may be removed by rubbing down with fine steel wool and mineral turps and wiping off with a clear dry rag. It is then advisable to sand lightly with 240 grit abrasive paper before applying the base coat.

Application

Antique finishing requires three processes—base coat, toner, and clear surface finish.

The Base Coat

A full base coat is brushed on and allowed to dry. It may be necessary to wait up to twelve hours before applying the toner.

The Toner

The toner application determines the end result which will depend on the way the toner is wiped. Cloth of different textures, face tissues, and brushes will produce many different effects.

To produce timber grains wipe lightly leaving fairly heavy streaking of toner. Let the grain curve gently as does the grain of natural timber.

The toner dries slowly, giving time for experiment to achieve the desired effect. The toner must be allowed to dry, usually for twenty-four hours, before application of the clear surface finish.

FINISHING AND CARING FOR TIMBER FLOORS

Timber is an ideal flooring material. It is hard-wearing, resilient, attractive, and a good insulator of heat and sound. Timber is available in a wide range of species, colours, and patterns, but needs the protective and preservative action of a properly applied finish.

Preparation of the Timber Floor

Unless 'secret nailed' it will be necessary to fill the spaces left above the nail heads when they have been punched below the surface.

The filling should be done before the final sanding operation. There are a large number of proprietary woodstopping plastic woods and fillers available, coloured to match the various timbers.

When the filler has dried out thoroughly, rub the surface smooth and sweep or vacuum all the dust from the room to prevent its spoiling the appearance of the final finish.

Do not attempt to fill any hairline cracks that may occur between the boards.

Sanding

It is necessary to bring the flooring to a uniform level by scraping and sanding. Most levelling is done with electric sanding machines. These machines are readily hired.

The floor is traversed diagonally with a coarse grade of paper until the boards are level.

The machine is then run straight up and down the length of the boards with successively finer paper until a smooth shiny surface is obtained.

It may be necessary to level 'hard to get at' corners with a hand scraper and a small portable sander.

After completion of sanding, sweep the floor and inspect the surface for scratches. All scratches across the grain must be removed as they will be accentuated when the surface finish is applied.

Staining

In most cases it is not necessary to alter the colour by staining. Staining is not recommended where there is a likelihood of excessive wear. Uniform colour does not penetrate deeply and it is difficult to repair a severely scuffed area to match the rest of the floor.

Oil-based stains are considered best for softwood.

Timber is an ideal flooring material

Oil and water stains are suitable for hardwoods.

Oil stains do not raise the grain of the timber, but water stains are more permanent and penetrate more deeply.

The stain is applied in the direction of the grain with a soft bristle brush and allowed to dry for twenty-four hours.

Any raised grain may be removed by carefully sanding with fine abrasive paper.

Surface Finish

The amount of gloss desired on a floor varies according to individual taste. The somewhat matt appearance of a freshly waxed timber floor is often considered to be ideal. A high gloss finish immediately after application will often wear within a few weeks to an ideal semi-matt appearance. A matt finish may be obtained by light abrasive action using wire wool.

Natural resin varnishes are easily applied but are rather slow drying, and the floor should not be walked on for several days to allow the surface to harden. They only have moderate

wear resistance and require regular waxing.

Synthetic resin finishes, often referred to as plastic finish, give a high gloss, are harder, and more resistant to scratching and spilt liquid. They are, however, more expensive.

They are generally supplied in two separate containers, one of which is a hardening chemical.

Mixing is done to the manufacturer's specifications immediately prior to application and the mixture should be used immediately.

General Maintenance

Regular sweeping and wiping over with a dry cloth should be sufficient. If quantities of dirt have to be removed a damp cloth should suffice. Never scrub the floor with water.

An easily removable film, such as wax, is recommended as a protective coating against wear.

Waxing is successfully carried out with paste or liquid floor wax and a good electric polishing machine.

DESIGN & PLANNING

...HOW TO DECIDE ON THE RIGHT DESIGN FOR YOUR PURPOSE

Design is an accepted and integral part of our daily lifestyle. Consequently, the need to be aware of good design is important if we are to accept such things as mass production, new and innovative materials and new styles, so necessary in a rapidly changing world. The problems associated with furniture design, in fact any design, are clearly illustrated by a chapter from the book *Design as Art* by Bruno Munari. Using the chair as the focal point, he demonstrates the complexities facing both the designer and consumer when required to make decisions.

While there are certain prescribed basic design principles, it becomes obvious that the selection of design is personal, and limited only by education and experience.

'A very thorough market research campaign on people's taste in chairs has established that they must answer the following requirements: they must be comfortable, luxurious, rustic, fanciful, strictly technical and functional, broad, narrow, high, low, hard, soft, flexible, elegant, rigid, compact, large and impressive, cheap, good value, obviously expensive and socially impressive, made of one single material, made of a variety of materials, while the favoured materials are rare and rough, as well as refined and crude.

'So there we are. Chairs must be made for indoors and out, for the drawing-room, the office, the waiting room at the doctor's or at the railway station, for playing cards in, for taking tea in the garden, for lunch, for the seaside, for holidays in the mountains (a vast range), very low with a very high back, very high with no back at all (for the bar), for boutiques, for buses, for churches, for camping.

'They can be made of carved wood, curved wood, pressed wood, plasticised wood; they can be dovetailed, screwed, glued or pegged; they can be sandpapered, stained, painted, varnished, matt, semi-glossy or perfectly dazzling. And all this goes for all kinds of wood from poplar to ebony.

'Or they can be made of iron or steel, welded, bent, burnished, enamelled, chromium plated, nickel plated, pressed, magnetised, plated with brass or copper. They can be extruded, tubular, in square section or in oblong, in U-section, E-section, X.Y.Z.-section.'

From: Bruno Munari's *Design as Art*.

Comfortable chair on wood swivel base

FURNITURE STYLES

History contains recorded evidence of the development of furniture styles and periods. Furniture 'styles' refer to distinctive characteristics pertaining to the design form and were often named after craftsmen (Chippendale), periods (Tudor), movements (Renaissance), and monarchs (Queen Anne). The three most popular furniture styles in vogue today may be classified as Traditional, Provincial, and Contemporary.

Traditional

Traditional furniture includes designs inspired by such craftsmen as Chippendale, Sheraton, Hepplewhite, and the Adam Brothers. This period, the middle 18th century, reflected in some degree the preceding periods of Queen Anne and Louis XV. The furniture style was formal, gracefully refined, and pleasing in form.

Characteristic ornamentation included open fretwork, claw and ball feet, gilding, heavy and elaborate carving, and lavish fabrics. Possibly the most distinguishing feature of traditional furniture has been the slender and well proportioned cabriole leg.

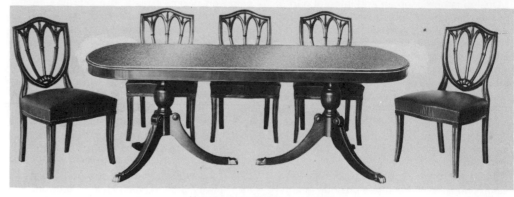

Hepplewhite dining room suite

Hepplewhite sideboard

Chippendale writing bureau

Antoinette suite

Provincial Furniture

Although of Louis XV persuasion, provincial furniture developed a personality distinctly different from earlier furniture designs. Ornamentations gave way to more flowing contours and pleasing proportions. The graceful curved leg and scroll foot became its hallmark. French Provincial styles, particularly bedroom suites, gained notoriety with their off-white painted finishes and plain gilded relief.

Contemporary Furniture

This has evolved from the 'Modern Movement' which began during the mid-19th century under the auspices of William Morris, an architect and artist. It was during this period, one of industrial upheaval, that the stimulus was provided for a protest against Victorian ornamentation and opulence. It was the considered opinion of reformers that the evolving industrial techniques were incompatible with existing furniture designs. The outcome was a simplification of shape, form, and construction. Honest use of materials and quality craftsmanship provided the basic principles of 20th century furniture design.

The Modern Movement also gave rise to others, including the Art and Craft Movement, the Art Nouveau Movement and, in particular, the Bauhaus.

The Bauhaus, a school founded by Walter Gropius in Germany during the early 1900s, applied industrial techniques to create a more humane environment. Many of the designs

TIME	ENGLAND	FRANCE	AMERICA	OTHER COUNTRIES
16th century	Gothic Renaissance Tudor (1485–1558) Elizabethan (1558–1603)	Renaissance (1500–1610)		Early Renaissance (1500–1610) Italy, Germany, Holland
17th century	Jacobean (1603–1649) Early Jacobean (1603–1649) Commonwealth (1649–1660) Late Jacobean (1660–1688) William & Mary (1689–1702)	Louis XIII (1610–1643) Louis XIV (1643–1715) Early French Provincial (1650–1700)	Early Colonial (1620–1700)	Late Renaissance Italy, Germany, Holland
18th century	Queen Anne (1702–1714) Early Georgian (1714–1740) Late Georgian (1740–1810) (1) Chippendale (1745–1770) (2) Hepplewhite (1760–1790) (3) Adam Bros (1760–1790) (4) Sheraton (1790–1806)	French Regency (1715–1723) Louis XV (1723–1774) Louis XVI (1774–1793) Directoire (1795–1804) Early French Provincial (1700–1800)	Late Colonial (1700–1790) Duncan Phyfe (1790–1839)	European designs influenced by English, French and Dutch craftsmen
19th century	Regency (1800–1850) Victorian (1837–1900)	French Empire (1804–1815) Late French Provincial (1800–1900)	Federal (1795–1830) Victorian (1830–1900)	Biedermeier (1800–1850) Germany
20th century	Arts & Crafts (1882–1910) Modern Initiated by W. Morris— 1850	Art Noveau (1895–1910) Modern	Mission (1895–1919) Modern	Modern

Based on Seng Co. Chronological Table of Furniture Periods and Styles

Dining

Utility

LIVING ROOM

Office

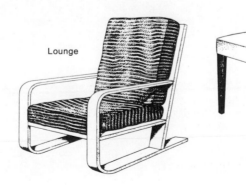

Lounge

Bedroom

Kitchen

produced at the Bauhaus were aesthetically pleasing and have become well-known examples of classic simplicity and function.

At present, new mass production techniques and new materials are imposing continual changes in furniture design. However, emphasis is being given to function, comfort, simplicity of line, and sound construction. Evidence of this is to be seen in products and designs emanating from such design-conscious countries as Sweden and Denmark.

131

DESIGN IN AUSTRALIA

Traditionally, design in Australia has copied often poorly designed overseas models and reproduced them under licence. Consideration of environmental factors, living standards, life styles and similar criteria influencing design have been noticeably absent. The outcome has been a conglomerate array of internationally accepted styles but nothing that may be acclaimed 'Australian'.

Australia is now facing an increasingly competitive and demanding global marketplace. To compete successfully in this marketplace requires the development of better designed and more innovative products

Within the last three decades, furniture design in Australia has developed from its embryonic state. This growth has been due to a number of factors. People are being educated to discriminate between good and bad design, changes have occurred in social and economic standards, and the resultant expanding markets have provided a need for good designers. Moreover, manufacturers are becoming increasingly aware of the advantages of employing full-time design staff.

Since 1957, Australian Design Awards have been promoting and encouraging the use of industrial design to improve the quality of manufactured products. The Australian Design Awards, a division of Standards Australia, actively promotes and rewards design excellence.

One of the requirements of Standards Australia's charter is to '… assist enterprises to improve economic efficiency and international competitiveness … and provide the wider community with a safer, more pleasant environment'.

Consumers, therefore, are assured that products exhibiting the Australian Design Award reflect the highest standards of product design, including aesthetic and user consideration, functionality in design and are appropriately engineered for economical manufacture.

It is evidenced by the number, range and quality of designs entered in this year's Australian Design Awards that the creativity and innovativeness of Australians is meeting the challenge of the global marketplace.

The beauty of well-designed furniture, having quality in function, materials and construction combined with easy maintenance and value for money

DESIGN FUNDAMENTALS

Basic Factors of Furniture Design

Factors affecting furniture design may be divided into two basic and interrelated groups, namely Efficiency Requirements and Visual Requirements. It is important that the analysis of these requirements be both sequential and cyclic in nature.

Efficiency requirements include the resultant ability of the article to perform its function and be ergonomically and/or structurally sound.

Visual requirements refer to the appearance relationship with the immediate environment, and include shape, texture, colour, balance, and decoration.

Efficiency Requirements

Efficiency is dependent upon:

Function

Function or purpose may be defined as 'how the artefact meets human requirements' and is the most basic factor affecting design.

Due consideration must be given to the requirements and needs the design is expected to fulfil. As well as meeting these needs, factors such as safety, hygiene, and serviceability to users, to name but a few, must also be taken into account.

The functional aspects of furniture design have led to a series of studies, collectively known as Bionics. This involves indepth research into all areas imposing on man, both mentally and physically.

Ergonomics

The essential nature of ergonomics is the convergence of the disciplines of human biology, especially anatomy, physiology, and psychology, on the problems of people at work. Ergonomics influences form, proportions, positioning of members, and explains the psychological use of colour. A chair, for example, is said to be ergonomically sound if its form complements the form of the occupant. Ergonomics is often categorised as 'the measurement of man'. Anthropometry, the study dealing with the measurement of the human body, is but one aspect of this science.

Materials

Awareness and understanding of the properties of the materials being used are desirable if a solution to the problem is to be achieved. The appropriate use of material, relative to its inherent qualities, is both structurally and visually important. The most economic use of material is often reflected in the most efficient solution.

The introduction and acceptance of new materials has influenced furniture design. Plastics, for example, demonstrate man's ability to shape materials to exacting dimensions. This provides the maxim that 'design affects the material' rather than 'material affects the

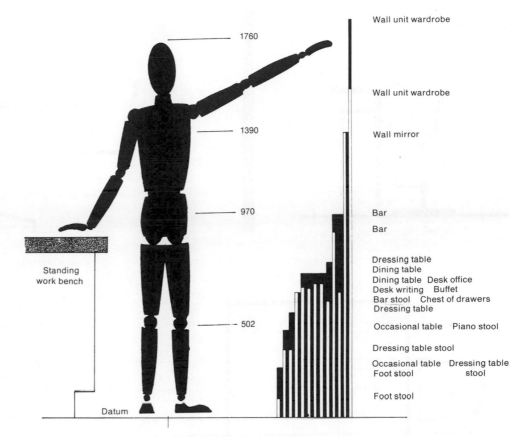

Furniture heights relative to man

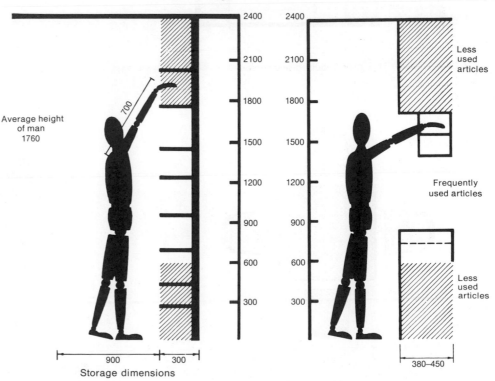

Storage dimensions

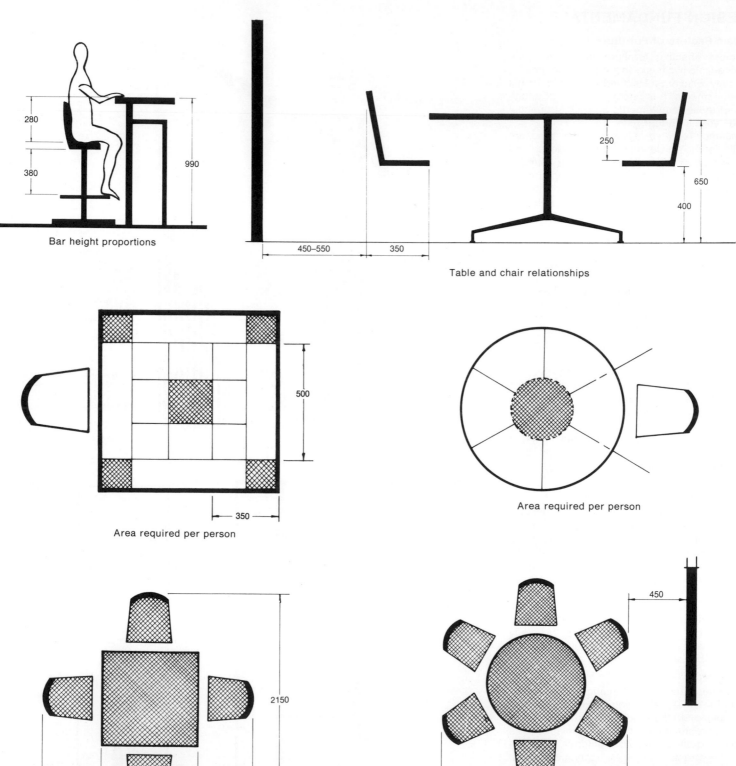

Bar height proportions

Table and chair relationships

Area required per person

Area required per person

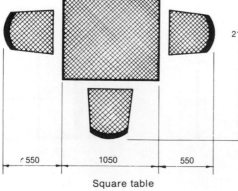

Square table

Round table

design'. The use of synthetics has been most spectacular in chair design where the carcass may be moulded in one piece or cut out of one homogeneous material.

Manufactured boards, which are not truly compatible with the traditional wood joints, have likewise led to new forms in storage and knockdown furniture.

Production Techniques

This involves a knowledge of joint structure and processes, the availability of tools and machines, and a depth of experience associated with both the materials and equipment. With the inception of synthetic resin glues the 'production line' manufacture of furniture has evolved. In many instances the intricacy of joint structure has given way to the strength factor of synthetic glues.

The innovation of knockdown furniture has required the development of new forms of connectors suitable for continual reassembly.

Yet another development, using man-made sheet material, is the folding system, where V grooving, followed by folding and gluing, allows the construction of intricate shapes.

Visual Requirements

Shape and Form

Shape refers to the relationship between the material and the method of production.

Form relates to the shapes which have occurred on the material due to external forces.

Consequently, in furniture design, it is necessary to understand the manufacturing techniques used in construction as well as the intrinsic properties of the material.

New shapes will evolve from the use of new materials and production methods.

In determining the shape and form qualities of an article consideration must be given to:

- Functional requirements.
- Honest use of materials.
- Appropriate construction relative to the material.
- Visual appearance of line, proportion, and colour.

Proportion

The unconscious comparison of shapes and forms constituting our environment and referred to as proportions may be expressed as ratios. Proportion enables a sense of balance and harmony between the individual parts of a unit and the unit as a whole.

The Golden Mean Rectangle provides a simple formula for obtaining units which have a proportional relationship to one another. Lay out a square of x units and bisect one side. Scribe an arc about this bisection point to form a rectangle. The sides of the rectangle thus formed and the original square have a ratio of 1.618 to 1. Continuance of this process will provide further rectangles having similar proportions.

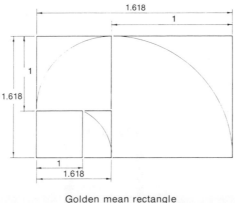

Golden mean rectangle

Balance

Proportions appearing out of balance become disturbing. However, balance need not be obtained by equality of parts. Designs pertaining to a centreline, as in turnery, are symmetrically balanced. Designs having unequal parts not symmetrically distributed about a centreline, yet retaining a sense of balance, are referred to as asymmetrical designs.

Social Factors

These involve the location of the article within the environment and the changes which occur due to economic and social reform. People are becoming more nomadic in their habits, and consequently their furniture must similarly be capable of adjustment and relocation.

BASIC FURNITURE DIMENSIONS

Reference Table

The following table is based on measurements derived from the average man. Where great variations in body size occur or when the utmost comfort is required, custom built furniture may be made to suit individual requirements. *All dimensions are in mm.*

TABLES	Height	Length	Width
Dining	710–760	915–1830	760–990
Occasional	355–560	460–1830	300–610
Desk (office)	710–735	1220–1980	610–915
Desk (writing)	685–710	760–1220	460–840
Dressing Table	610–810	760–1450	430–535

STOOLS			
Foot	100–255	255–380	180–300
Dressing Table	380–460	380–460	300–315
Piano	560	460–610	380
Bar	660	300–380	square or circular

STORAGE	Height	Depth	Width
Chest of Drawers	660–1065	405–460	610–1015
Wall Cabinets			
Buffet	685–735	405–610	990–1830
Bars	990–1065	300–405	915–1525
Wardrobes	1730–1980	460–610	760–1830
Bookshelves	180–255 wide shelves, 200–300 apart with vertical supporting division 600–750 apart		

SEATING	Seat height front	Lower seat height rear	Width of seat	Depth	Height of back	Angle of back
Dining (straight chair)	430	0–50	460–560	405–510	810–840	100–105
Office	380–460	0–25	430–480	300–380	660–735	100–110
Lounge Upholstered	355–430	0–100	510–610	460–585	760–990	105–115

FURNITURE PROPORTIONS

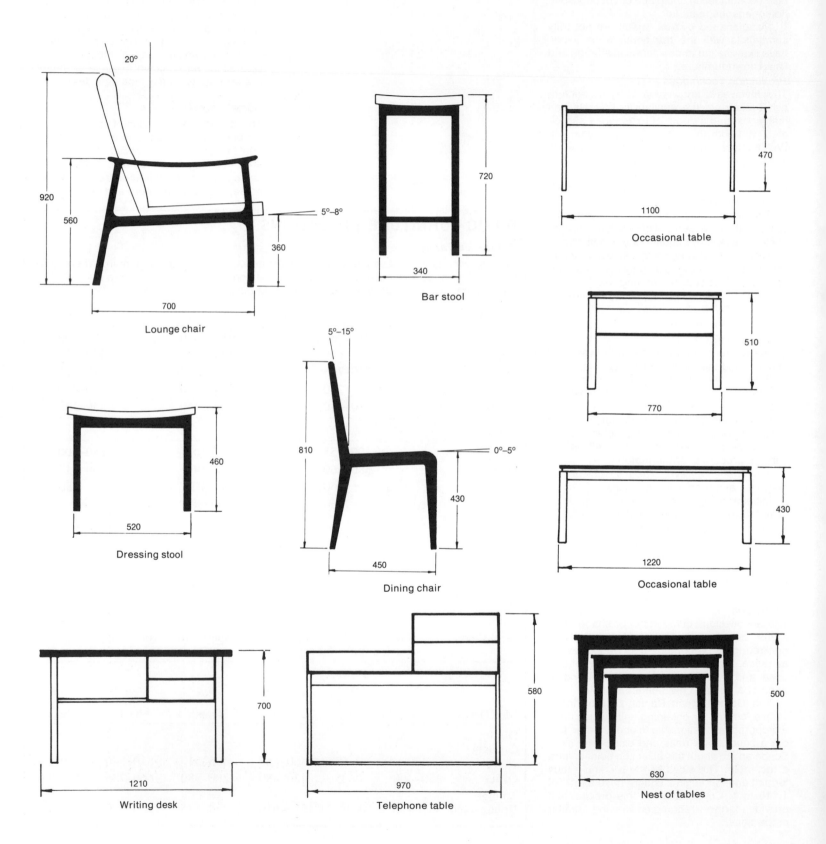

20°

920

560

360

5°–8°

700

Lounge chair

720

340

Bar stool

470

1100

Occasional table

510

770

460

520

Dressing stool

5°–15°

810

430

450

0°–5°

Dining chair

430

1220

Occasional table

700

1210

Writing desk

580

970

Telephone table

500

630

Nest of tables

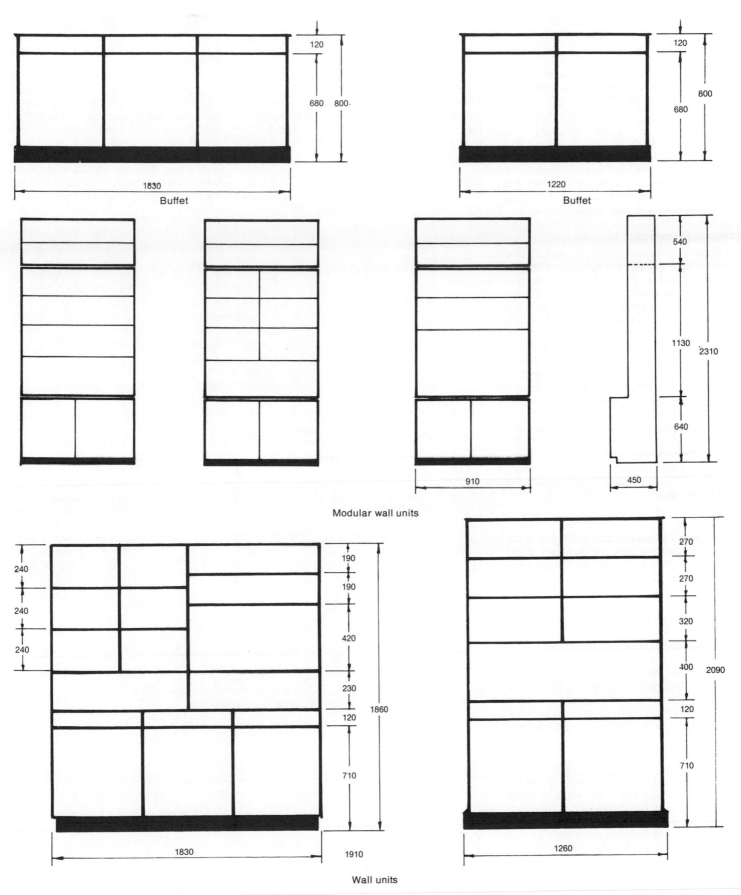

Buffet

Buffet

Modular wall units

Wall units

Changes in furniture design are not only attributable to new materials and new methods, but also reflect the social attitudes of the period.

Modular furniture is an example of social factors, economic factors, and new materials combining to provide one of the present day furniture requirements.

Fashion

Fashions provide comparisons of present needs, materials, and production methods with derivative styles from bygone eras. Such factors as decoration, styles, and trends are terms commonly applied when rationalising problems associated with fashion.

Designing Process

The function of design is not necessarily one of producing originality but rather deciding on the best solution to the design problem. It is a dubious point whether there is such a thing as original design. Most original design is the blending of current ideas and principles into a new situation.

The designing process provides for a systematic approach to the solving of design problems. These problems are characterised by the need to reconcile a number of factors by means of value judgments and the incorporation of the solution in an identifiable end product. The designing process may require the application of knowledge from the many facets of technology.

The schematic diagram illustrates, in a simplified form, one method of disseminating the design process.

Investigating

It is necessary to detail a statement about the need or problem and any expectations about the solution. This statement or *design brief* should outline:

- the task to be undertaken
- any constraints involved and
- the performance requirements expected.

The design brief should establish the parameters constituting the design problem. This stage also includes investigating as many solutions to the design brief as possible. An idea for a likely solution requires expansion and further research. For example, an idea involving a certain material may need information about costs, sizes, availability and properties.

Devising

This stage requires choosing, refining and trialling the best idea from the range of ideas considered from the investigation. It is important that all working drawings and notes that will enable production be completed at this point.

Producing

This is the 'making' part of the design process that results in the construction of the solution as specified by the design brief.

Evaluating

The final outcome is evaluated in relation to the design brief. How well the outcome meets the constraints and performance requirements as given in the brief determines its success or otherwise.

Communication

Closely associated with the designing process is the need for communication. The formulation of the design brief, constraints, performance requirements and the identification of a possible solution involves observation and experimentation.

The gathering of statistical information as required for such factors as ergonomics, economics and environment must be transferred from one stage to another. Similarly, visual relationships, involving proportions, balance, and finish become useful only if applied throughout the design process.

Material science provides the craftsman with detailed characteristics of the possible mediums which may be applicable to the design.

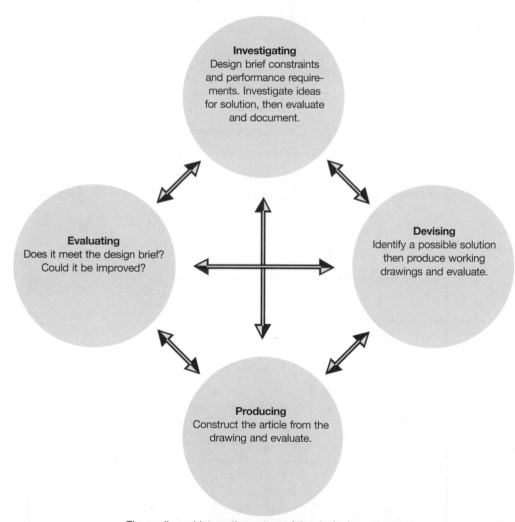

The cyclic and interactive nature of the designing process

However, if this knowledge is isolated, solutions to the problem can become obscure. Methods of production, likewise, unless considered throughout the stages of planning may also inhibit the final design.

The most dominant method of communication, in any design process, is that of drawing. Drawing is the clarification channel used by designers and craftsmen alike to communicate their ideas and problems to themselves and others. To this end various types of drawings may be used.

Drawing

Freehand pictorial sketches, including oblique, isometric, and perspective, give a quick and simple picture of the design. These may be visuals of complete projects or alternatives of various components, or both. *Working Drawings* are used to relay the final design decisions to those having to implement the design. They may be in the form of fully dimensioned *pictorial* or *orthographic* drawings or a *working rod*, laid out in full size but having no dimensions.

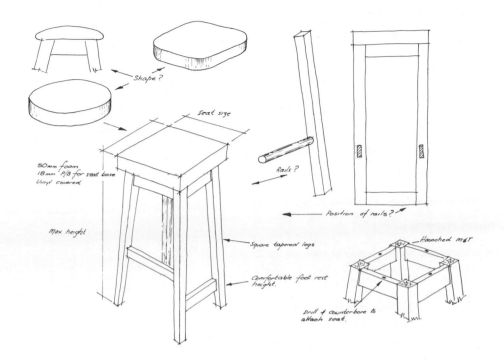

CUTTING AND COSTING

Cutting List

This is a brief of the materials required for a specific project. It is obtained by reading or 'Taking off' from the working drawings or rod the sizes of individual members.

A suggested *Cutting List* layout may be as follows:

Item Number	— refers to the corresponding part number on the drawing or rod.
Number Off	— indicates the number of particular parts required.
Part Name	— identifies the item number.
Finished Sizes	— length, width and thickness are shown—all in mm.
Material	— specifies the type of matieral to be used for each item.

CUTTING LIST			PROJECT—STOOL				COSTING				
Item No.	**No. Off**	**Part Name**	**Finished Sizes**			**Material**	**Unit Cost**	**Rough Size**				**Item Cost**
			L.	W.	Th.			L.	W.	TH.		
1	4	Legs	650	35	35	Blackwood	$800/m^3	700	40	40	Cost L.m. x W.m. x TH.m. x Cm.^{3} .7 x .04 x .04 x 800	$3.52
2	4	Top Rails	230	60	19	Blackwood	$800/m^3	300	70	25	.3 x .07 x .025	$1.60
3	2	Bottom Rails	258	35	19	Blackwood	$800/m^3	300	40	25	.3 x .04 x .025	$0.48
4	2	Bottom Rails	265	35	19	Blackwood	$800/m^3	300	40	25	.3 x .04 x .025	$0.48
5	1	Seat Base	265	265	19	Raw particle board	$4.80/m^2	300	300	19	.3 x .3	$0.37.
6	1	Seat Filling (Foam)	265	265	75	Low density foam	$2.10/m^2	300	300	75	.3 x .3	$0.29
7	1	Seat Covering	320	320	H/D	Elastic back vinyl	$3.20/m	380	380	—	.38 x .38	$0.36

MEASUREMENT

Solid Timber

Linear Measurement
This method provides for length measurement only, with width and thickness being disregarded. It is used where the cross-sectional area of boards is the same as in milled or moulded timber.

The price is calculated per 100 metres, including machining costs.

Calculation
Length (m) x number of pieces x cost/100 m.

Sheet Material (area)
The unit measurement for plywood, hardboard, particle board, or any sheet material is the square metre (m²). The *referred* length, width, and thickness are all referred to in millimetres (mm).

The cost is quoted per square metre for a given thickness.

Calculation (thickness disregarded)
Length (m) x width (m) x cost/square metre.

Cubic Measurement
This unit of measurement is generally applied to sawn timbers not classified as 'milled'.

Calculation
Length (m) x width (m) x thickness (m) x cost/m³.

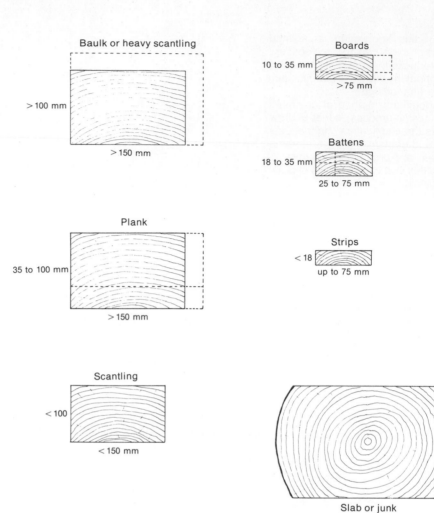

MARKETING TIMBER

Glossary of Trade Terms
Timber may be classified as wood suitable for use in construction, joinery, and cabinetmaking or for further breaking down for manufacturing processes.

For terminology classification, this section has been subdivided into three areas: sizes, manufacturing, and grading.

Sizes
Log—a length taken from the bole or large branch of a tree from which timber may be produced.
Slab, junk, or flitch—a section of sawn log, usually of large dimensions and intended for further breaking down. A flitch has at least two sawn surfaces.
Baulk or heavy scantling—are large rectangular pieces of sawn timber greater than 150 mm in width and 100 mm in thickness used for heavy structural work or intended for further resawing.
Plank—may be sawn or dressed timber rectangular in cross-section, ranging from 35 mm to 100 mm in thickness by more than 150 mm in width. Load expectations on face surfaces—e.g. scaffolding.

Scantling (light)—usually less than 100 mm thick and less than 150 mm wide. Uses include framed structures, rafters, and studs.
Boards—may be sawn or dressed and are greater in width than thickness. They may be used for joinery and furniture construction.
Battens—sawn or dressed timber, rectangular in section, generally between 18 mm and 35 mm in thickness and between 25 mm and 75 mm in width. May be used as supporting members for roof sheathing or wall linings.
Strips—pieces rectangular in section, sawn or dressed, under 18 mm in thickness and up to 75 mm in width. Often used as separation strips in the seasoning process.

Manufacturing
Round timber—logs used for converting into sawn timber and veneers or used in the round for posts and poles.
Rough sawn—timber having sawn surfaces. Often used green or partially dried for heavy constructional work or timber framing. For further processing, it is necessary to dry or season by kiln drying (K.D.), air drying (A.D.) or a combination of both.

Dressed timber—refers to seasoned timber which has been finished to a smooth surface on one or more surfaces by means of planing machines.
Abbreviations used include:
P1S — planed one side
P2S — planed two sides
P2E — planed two edges
P1S1E — planed one side, one edge
P2S1E — planed two sides, one edge
P1S2E — planed one side, two edges
PAR — planed all round

Timber specified as 'dressed' will always be less than the ordered size unless the prefix 'F' follows each size.
For example: An order for timber 150 mm x 25 mm PAR would be received as 145 x 20 PAR. This is allowing approximately 2 to 3 mm per side for planing. If specifically required at 150 mm x 25 mm the order would have to read 150 mm F x 25 mm F. However, this would be most uneconomical since it would have to be obtained from 175 mm x 35 mm.

FURNITURE CONSTRUCTION

...BUILDING THE THINGS YOU WANT IN A WAY YOU'LL BE PROUD OF

Furniture is the term generally used to describe articles such as cabinets, chairs, tables, desks, beds, and other items used to furnish rooms in homes, offices, schools, and public buildings.

Cabinetmakers, woodmachinists, joiners, shopfitters, and chairmakers are the skilled craftsmen who produce today's furniture, which is largely produced in factories set up for mass production, although some items are still made in small cabinet shops.

A sound knowledge of design principles, materials, construction methods, finishing materials and techniques, and cabinet hardware is essential if high quality furniture is to be produced.

Use of a Set Out Rod

When the design of a piece of furniture has been developed and the working drawings completed, it is essential to plan the construction. A specialised full-size working drawing is set out from the details and specifications supplied. This drawing is known as the rod, and is usually drawn on a piece of 4 mm plywood of suitable length and width.

The rod must show the height, width, and depth of the piece of furniture to be made and indicate clearly all joints, rebates, grooves, trenches, chamfers, and the positions of blocks, screws, and brackets.

The rod should be easy to read and show clearly all necessary information. No dimensions are required. The possibility of error is reduced as lengths and shapes can be checked immediately. Members may also be marked directly off the rod. A cutting list may be compiled by working directly from the rod.

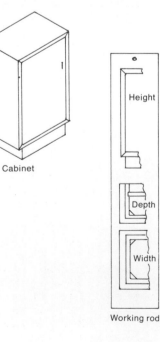

Cabinet

Working rod

Construction Method

Furniture construction may be divided into several convenient areas.
- *Frame construction* for basic items such as mirror frames or picture frames.
- *Leg and rail construction* used for such items as tables, chairs, and bases for cabinets.
- *Carcass construction*, which in turn may be divided into three different types of construction:

Framed carcass construction, a skeleton of rails and stiles covered with a sheet of material such as ply.

Solid end carcass construction, where the ends are of solid wood or particle board with cross rails dovetailed at the top and bottom. Other members may be fixed with stub tenons or housed into position.

Solid carcass construction, for which veneered particle board is generally used. The top, bottom, ends, shelves, and partitions are solid.

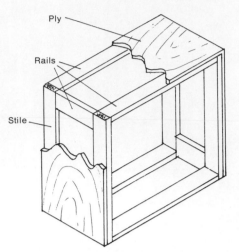

Framed carcass construction

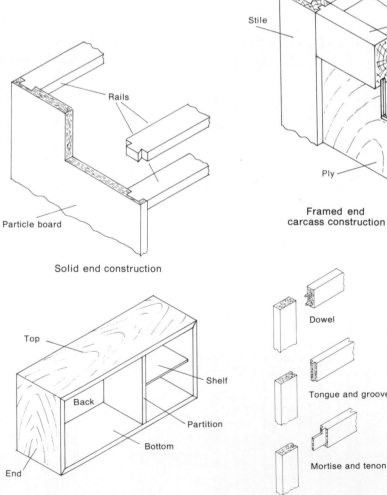

Solid end construction

Framed end carcass construction

Solid carcass construction

Framing joints

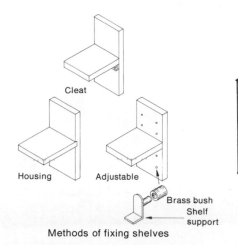

Cleat

Housing

Adjustable

Brass bush
Shelf
support

Methods of fixing shelves

Mitre rebate

Butt

Rebate with
corner mould

Tongue
and
trench

Rebate

Housing

Carcass joints

Plinth screwed to bottom of cabinet

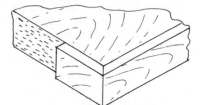

Solid wood edging

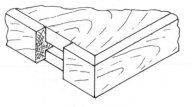

Solid wood edging

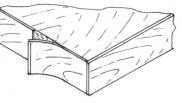

Veneer edging

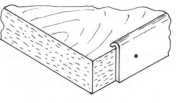

Metal edging

In many cases it is desirable to construct a base on which to stand the carcass. A base may be described as a frame which supports the weight of the cabinet. The base of a cabinet is sometimes called a plinth. Bases may be of two types:

1. Box construction.
2. Leg and rail construction.
- *Shelves* may be fixed or adjustable.
- *Edge treatment* is essential if manufactured boards are used either in framed construction or solid construction. Edge treatment may be classified in three groups:
1. Solid wood edging.
2. Veneered strip edging.
3. Metal or plastic edging.

Metal and plastic edging are made in a variety of shapes and sizes and if their use is contemplated it would be advisable to obtain a catalogue from a supplier.

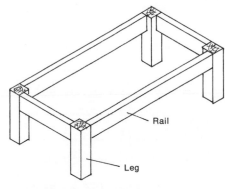

Rail

Leg

Leg and rail base

DRAWER CONSTRUCTION

Traditional joints for drawers are lapped dovetails for the front to sides, and common dovetails for the back to sides. Because of the lapped dovetail the front is made of thicker material, usually 19 mm to 20 mm thick, and planed to fit the opening in the carcass. The *sides* are usually of 9 mm to 12 mm thick mate-

rial and at least 12 mm shorter than the drawer space, and planed to a hand tight fit between runners and kickers. The *back* is the same thickness as the sides, and the same length as the front, but the width depends on the height of the groove in the sides. The top edge of the back is rounded for appearance, and is about 2 mm lower than the sides. The same sizes and proportions may be used if alternative joints are selected.

Setting Out

When setting out the joints, place all pieces in position on the bench with face sides in and face edges down. Mark clearly all parts to be joined. Set out the joints and mark the position of the grooves.

The joints are cut first and then the grooves ploughed.

Before assembly clean up the inside faces of all pieces.

Slide the drawer bottom into position.

When the glue is set, clean up the sides and edges until the drawer fits neatly into the drawer space.

The drawer bottom may be made of plywood, hardboard, or particle board. It is held in grooves in the front and sides or in special slips glued and nailed to these parts.

The bottom is nailed to the underside of the drawer back.

The drawer sides and front project beyond the drawer bottom and the sides slide on wooden runners which form part of the carcass.

Other members, called kickers, are fixed above the drawer sides to prevent the drawer from tilting or dropping in the open position.

A member which prevents lateral movement is known as a guide.

The drawer is made to stop in the desired position by the use of plywood stops fixed to the drawer rail. The inside of the drawer front strikes the stop.

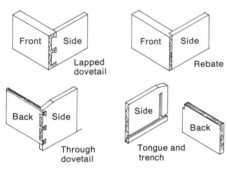

Traditional drawer construction

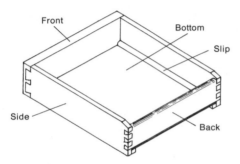

Joints used in drawer construction

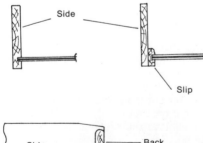

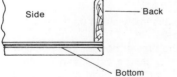

Nylon and ball bearing runners are available and desirable especially where it is necessary to use large drawers.

Aluminium drawer slide

Drawer pulls may be made of wood, plastic, or metal. They may be screwed to the front or let in to create a flush fitting effect. Finger grips may be machined on the edge of the drawer front.

To suit the design of the piece of furniture or cabinet to which it is fitted, a drawer front may be flush fitting as in traditional type furniture, or it may overlap along the top or bottom edges. False fronts may be added.

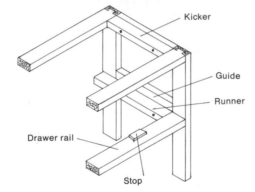

Frame showing runners, guides, and kickers

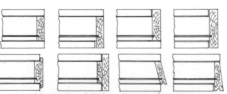

Methods of fitting drawer fronts

Fitting a drawer front

Fitting drawer sides

Fitting a completed drawer

Modern knock down drawer system:

Vinyl-coated, particle-board drawer sides ready for assembly

Gluing mitre joints as the sides are folded together

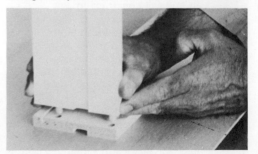

Drawer assembly completed by gluing locating dowels

DOORS

Generally, cabinet doors are of two types, either sliding or swinging. Construction varies and may depend upon the size of the door. Cabinet doors may be of solid particle board trimmed with solid wood or veneer edging. To reduce weight, framed and panelled construction would be desirable, or perhaps a light frame covered with ply. Solid natural timber doors are never used, as excessive clearances would need to be provided for timber movement.

Swinging Doors

Swinging doors may be hung with a variety of hinges in a variety of ways. Doors may be flush fitting, rebated, or may overlap the opening. The flush fitting door is probably the most commonly used in cabinet work and is fitted with butt hinges.

The door is carefully fitted to the opening, leaving approximately 1 mm clearance on each edge. Hinges are selected carefully. Generally two are sufficient but three may be necessary on large doors. As a general rule, hinges are fitted either one or two hinge lengths from the top and bottom of the door.

There are two methods of fitting a butt hinge to a door. One requires that both door and frame are checked out to accommodate the hinge. This has the effect of breaking the clean lines of the edging framing the door. The second method requires that the door only is checked out to the full thickness of the hinge. This allows a clean unbroken line around the door.

To hinge a door successfully it is essential that a logical sequence is followed.

The door should be carefully fitted to the opening, leaving approximately 1 mm clearance on each edge. The door may then be removed and held in a vice in a vertical position with the edge to be hinged uppermost, and the face of the door out. The position of the hinge is marked on the edge, usually one or two hinge lengths from the top or bottom, depending on the size of the hinge and the door.

A marking gauge is set from the edge of the flange of the hinge to the centre of the pin. The gauge is then used to mark the width of the hinge on the edge of the door.

The gauge is then set to the thickness of the hinge less 1 mm (to allow for clearance) and the thickness is marked along the face of the door.

Before the waste is removed with a bevelled edge firmer chisel it may be desirable to make the shoulder cuts with a tenon saw.

The method of checking out for a hinge is clearly indicated in the diagrams.

Care must be taken not to go beyond the lines. The hinge may now be fitted and it is desirable at this stage to use only one screw

Concealed hinges

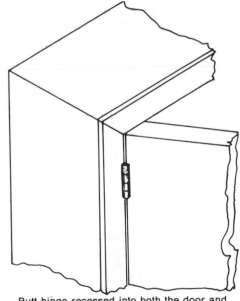

Fitting a door to the opening, leaving approximately 1 mm clearance on each edge

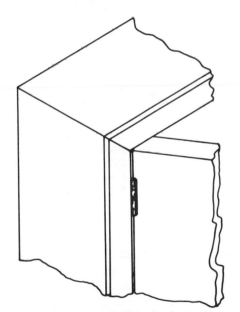

Butt hinge recessed into the door only

Butt hinge recessed into both the door and the stile

in each hinge as it will be necessary for the door to be removed for finishing.

The door can now be placed back in the opening, making sure that it is packed up at the bottom to ensure a 1 mm clearance.

Check the clearance on the other edges by using a piece of veneer about 1 mm thick as a feeler gauge.

The position of the hinges are marked on the cabinet.

The door is removed and the cabinet carefully placed on its side with the side to be hinged down on the bench. The hinge position marks are squared across the inside of the cabinet for about 25 mm from the front edge.

The marking gauge is set approximately 1 mm greater than the distance from the edge of the flange and the centre of the pin, and this distance is marked in between the marks indicating the position of the hinges. This will ensure

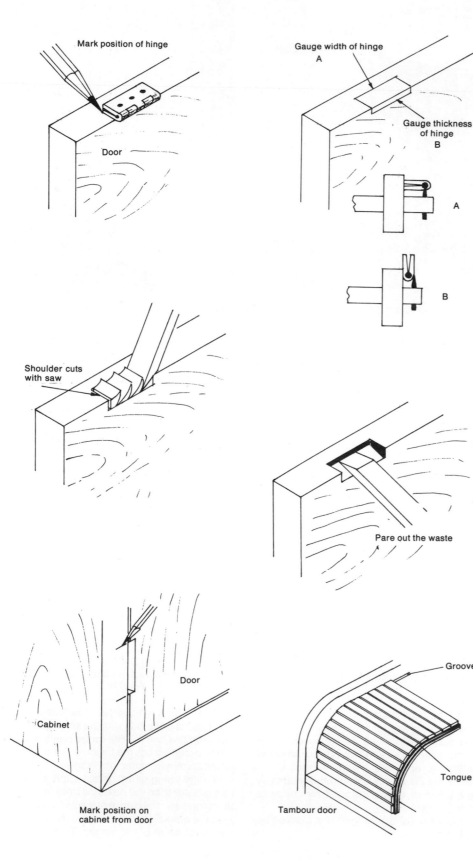

Mark position of hinge

Door

Gauge width of hinge
A

Gauge thickness of hinge
B

A

B

Shoulder cuts with saw

Pare out the waste

Cabinet

Door

Mark position on cabinet from door

Groove

Tongue

Tambour door

that the door will sit back slightly from the edge, as it is extremely difficult to fit a cabinet door so that it is perfectly flush with all edges.

So that the hinge will be positioned correctly, the chisel is gradually angled from the hinge centreline (1 mm in from the cabinet face) so that the thickness of the flange is removed at the gauge line. This will provide positive location.

With the waste removed, the door may be fitted into position. One screw in each hinge is again sufficient. Stand the cabinet upright and test the swing of the door. It may be necessary to plane a slight bevel on the edge opposite the hinged edge to ensure smooth operation.

Stops are fixed to locate the door in the desired position. They may be fixed on all edges, but generally on the lock or catch slide. Sometimes the catch may act as the stop.

Sliding Doors

Sliding doors may be accommodated by grooving the carcass before assembly and rebating the top and bottom edges of the doors to match the grooves. With the many plastic and aluminium tracks available, however, it is desirable to select the type that best suits the cabinet as they are much more efficient. If large heavy doors are contemplated, as in a wardrobe, overhead aluminium track and rollers are essential for proper operation.

Silent glide cupboard track

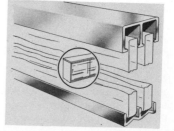

Aluminium head guide with brass pyramid track

Tambour Doors

These doors are constructed of strips of wood, with grooves or tongues machined on the ends, glued to a heavy cloth backing. These doors are flexible and are often used for curved top desks.

LEG AND RAIL CONSTRUCTION

Tables

Usually tables are framed with legs and rails. Mortise and tenon joints provide the most effective means of jointing and are generally selected for this type of work.

In addition a block is glued and screwed into the corners as an added precaution against the breaking of the joints.

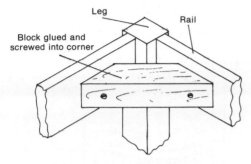

Method of securing corner block

Table Tops

There are two distinct methods of fixing table tops. If solid natural timber is used, allowance must be made for movement of the timber. If a manufactured board is used, no allowance for movement is necessary.

Extending Tables

The drawings indicate the two methods commonly used for increasing the length of a table top.

Drop centre construction

This type of construction features a folding leaf arrangement concealed beneath a pair of sliding tops. The table is extended by sliding back the tops and folding out the extension pieces to form a flat surface.

The pivot centres are located midway between the underside of the sliding tops and the top of the folding leaf in the closed position. When looking down at the top of the table, with the sliding tops open, the pivot is seen to be midway between the centreline of the table and the hinged edge of the extension piece. The pivot position should be clearly marked when drawing up the working rod.

Extending leaf construction

This type of construction features a top which is essentially of a double thickness when in the closed position. The bottom centre piece is fixed to the under frame while the top centre piece is free to move up (located by a central pin) as the extension leaves are withdrawn. The extension pieces are fixed to slides that are inclined at a slight angle to the top. The slides are free to move between guides screwed to rails that run the length of the table. The position of these rails and the angles of the slides are determined when laying out the working rod.

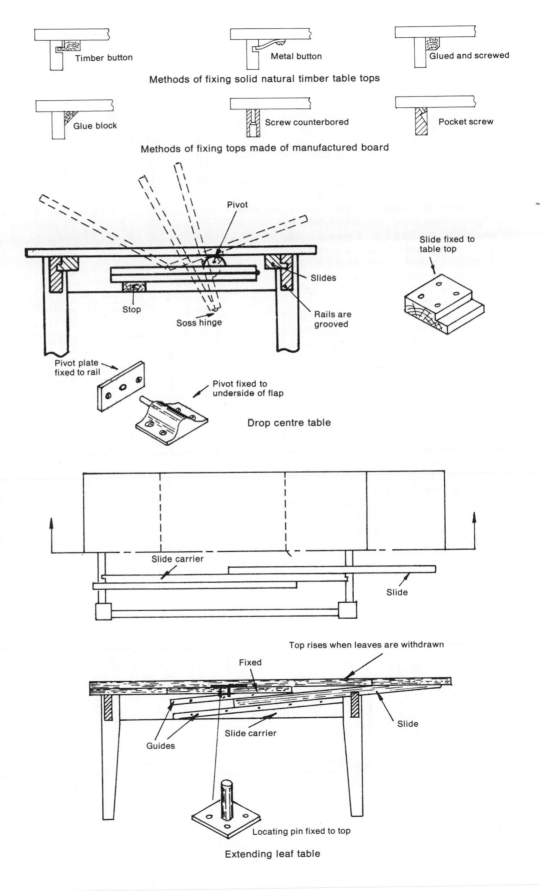

Methods of fixing solid natural timber table tops

Methods of fixing tops made of manufactured board

Drop centre table

Extending leaf table

147

Chairs and Stools

Chairs and stools are designed to support human individuals and must be constructed accordingly. Jointing should be a major consideration of the designer, and as with the table, mortise and tenon joints provide the most effective means of jointing legs and rails. Blocks are glued and screwed to the corners to provide additional support and strength.

In the case of lounge-room chairs the side frames, including arms, are made first. The two side frames are later joined by cross rails. Separate seat and back frames may be desirable. Rubber webbing can be used to support fabric-covered rubber cushions.

Similarly, dining chairs can also have their side frames constructed first. These two side frames are connected by top cross rails that may be shaped or left square, depending on the design of the chair. Lower cross rails are sometimes also included to provide further strength and rigidity.

A separate seat frame or a piece of laminated plywood that has been upholstered can be attached to the cross and side rails.

A supporting back member, often also shaped and upholstered, is attached at the same time as the cross rails.

Ergonomics plays an important role in chair design. It is essential, for example, in a lounge chair, to consider the appropriate angles required for the slope of the seat and the slope of the back. The height of the seat and width of the chair are also important if the chair is to be comfortable and complement the form of the user.

Reference to any reliable basic dimension furniture chart will provide a list of the essential sizes and angles for different types of chairs (see page 135).

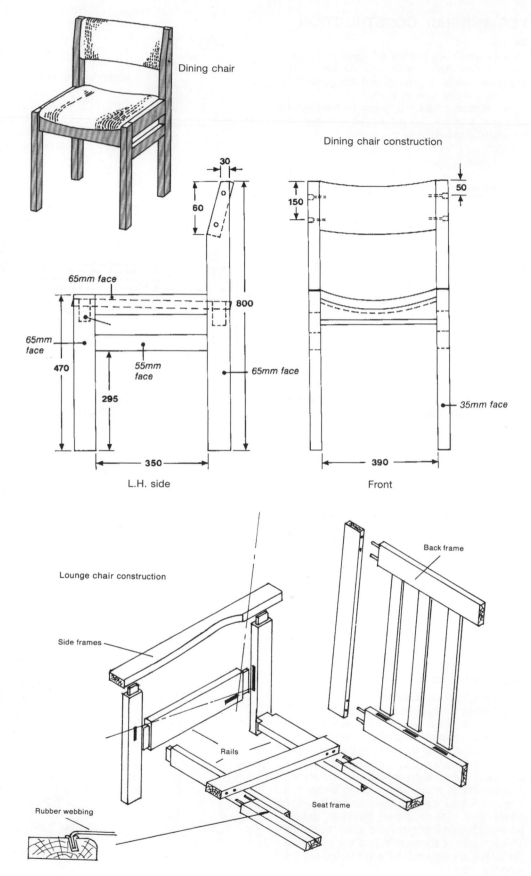

Dining chair

Dining chair construction

L.H. side

Front

Lounge chair

Lounge chair construction

Side frames

Back frame

Rails

Seat frame

Rubber webbing

148

Project 2

OCCASIONAL TABLES

Occasional tables come in a variety of shapes, sizes, materials, and colours. They have a multitude of uses, including: display, magazine storage, food serving, and, with special treatment, they can become 'games' tables. The tables need to be designed in sympathy with the surrounding furniture. They can be used in groups as a 'nest' of tables, or placed individually where needed to separate chairs, or placed at each end of a lounge where table lamps may be required.

The following occasional table designs highlight many of these features.

Procedure for Design 1

The suggested design of this table incorporates the use of square timber sections for legs attached to a top by means of timber cleats. Although the drawings suggest four square sections per end the number used can be a personal decision.

Legs

Using fully dressed material (P.A.R.), cut to length the number of pieces of square material required to serve as legs. Due to the size of each leg (suggested—90 mm x 90 mm) they may be treated individually rather than by clamping together. Care should be taken that they are all of equal length and that both ends are square. To prevent splintering on the bottom end of the legs it is good practice to plane a small (2 mm x 2 mm) chamfer.

Cleats

The cleats should be prepared from material similar in width to the leg material and the length determined by the amount of overhang required on the two long edges of the table top. The thickness of the cleats should be taken into consideration when determining the overall height of the table.

The position of each leg should be laid out on both cleats with the outside legs flush with the ends of the cleats and with equal spacing between the internal legs.

Mark out the required number of holes in each cleat necessary to attach the legs to the cleats, and the cleats to the table top. Drill and countersink these holes to accommodate 8-gauge C.S.K. screws. Note that the countersinking of the holes for attaching the cleats to the table top should be on the opposite side to the countersink for the legs.

Table Top

If a pre-finished board is used the edges should be treated with an appropriate plastic edging. Where a veneered particle board top is desired the raw edges may be covered with timber veneer or solid timber of a compatible species.

Accurately position the cleats on the underneath side of the table top and using a bradawl, initiate the screw holes for attaching the cleats.

Cleaning Up

The legs, cleats, and table top should all be sanded using between 180-grit and 240-grit abrasive paper. All arris should be removed and care should be taken where veneered particle board is used, not to sand through the thin veneer surface. A little extra effort may be required on the ends of the cleats to keep them square and obtain a suitable finish for polishing.

Assembly

The legs should be attached to the cleats ensuring that the ends of the cleats are flush with the outside surfaces of the legs and the edges of the cleats are flush with the inside surface of the legs. The cleats are then screwed to the underneath of the table top so as to be equidistant from the ends and equidistant from the edges.

Finishing

The completed unit should be given two or three coats of a suitable clear finish with a light 'scuff' back occurring between each coat. Since the distance between each of the squared timber sections comprising the legs is small, it would be prudent to either brush or spray finish these components prior to assembly.

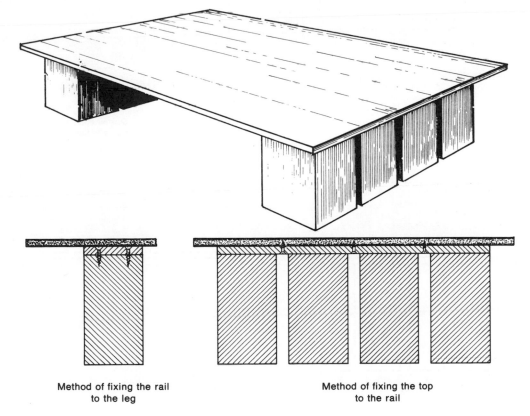

Method of fixing the rail to the leg

Method of fixing the top to the rail

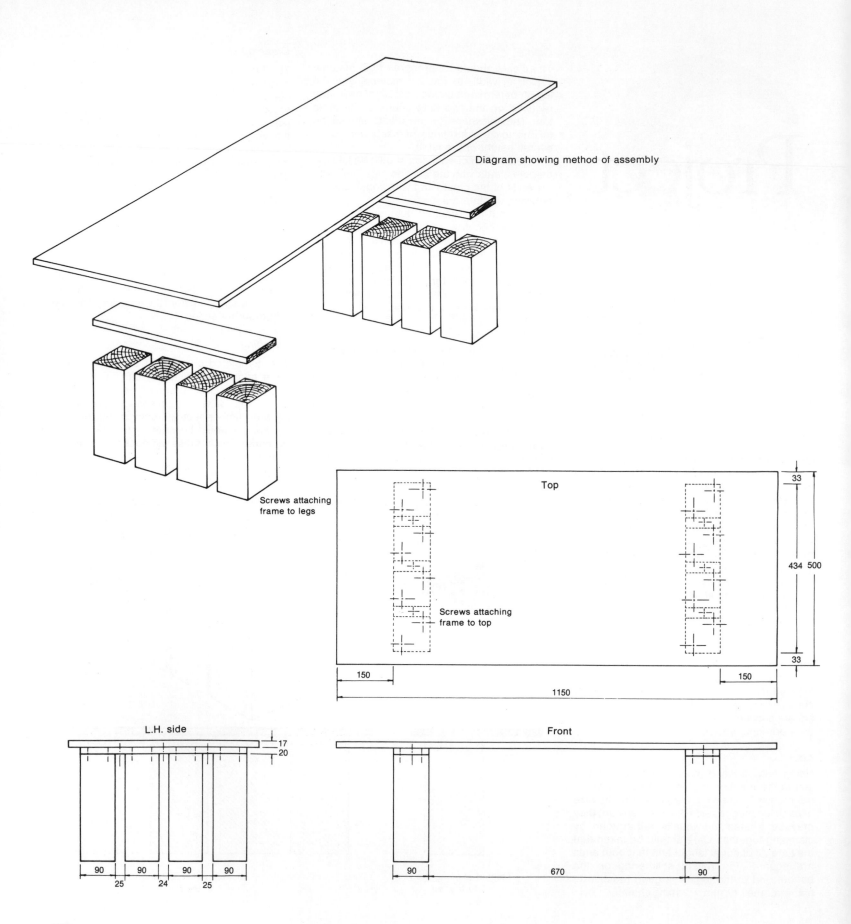

Diagram showing method of assembly

Screws attaching
frame to legs

Top

Screws attaching
frame to top

33

434 500

33

150

150

1150

L.H. side

17
20

90   90   90   90

25   24   25

Front

90   670   90

Procedure for Design 2

An interesting feature of this table design is the use of readily available picture-frame moulding which provides a ready made rebate for particle board, glass, mirror, or mosaic tops. Individual mouldings can also be made using the portable router and various shaped cutters.

Legs

The four legs should be dressed—that is, planed all around and cut to the appropriate length. Each leg should be squared at both ends. This process is best achieved by using a sharp smoothing plane in a circular motion on each leg end.

At this point, having the four legs equal in length and with square ends, variation of design can occur. The working drawing, for example, shows a mitred frame connecting the four legs together, and used for attaching the table top. This frame may be prepared by using a mitre jig to cut the mitre joints on each frame member and the frame then glued together and finally screwed to the top of each leg. Alternatively, having cut each member of the frame to the required length (and mitred), they can then be placed individually in the correct position on the top of each leg and attached by screwing.

Top

The top is then cut and planed to size and treated with the appropriate edge strip material. Pre-finished boards, for example, should have their edges treated with plastic edge strip or, if veneered particle board is used, a similar timber veneer or solid-timber edge strip should be applied.

Assembly

With the top located in the correct position on the mitred frame, join these two sections by screwing through the mitred frame into the table top.

Finishing

Prior to the application of finishing material, all components of the table should be individually sanded using 240-grit abrasive paper (except for pre-finished boards). Apply two or three coats either by brush or spray of a suitable clear finish over all sections of the table which have not been previously finished.

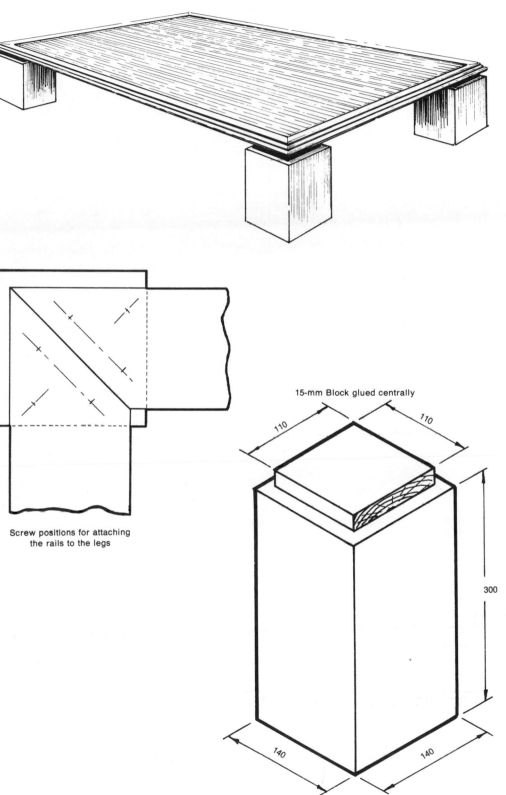

Screw positions for attaching the rails to the legs

15-mm Block glued centrally

110

110

300

140

140

Alternative leg design

151

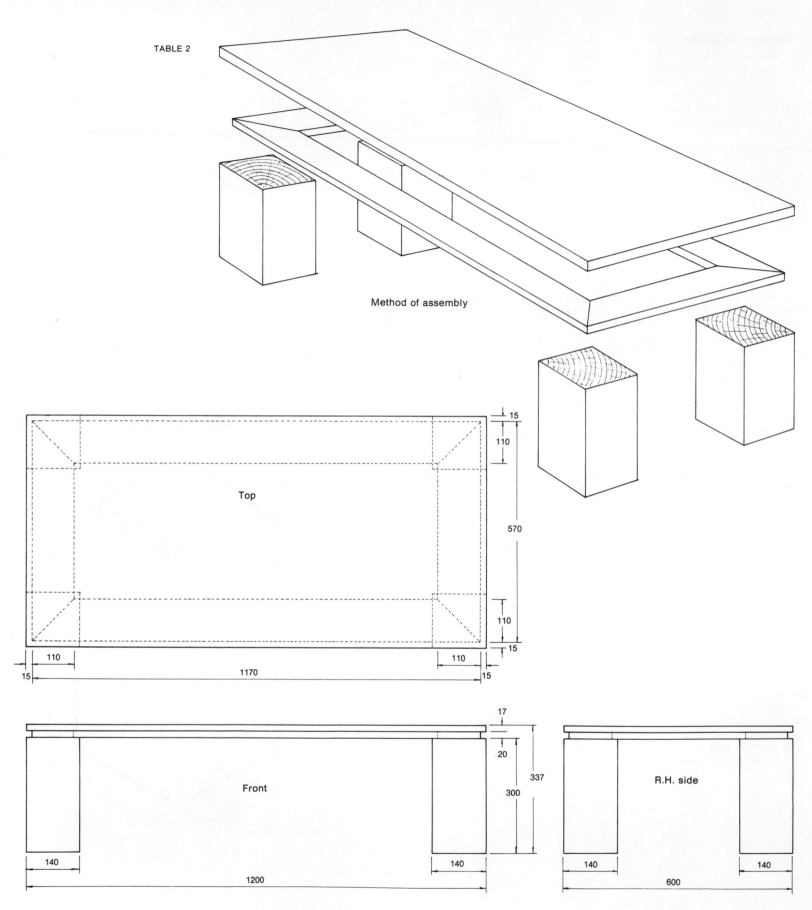

TABLE 2

Method of assembly

Top

15
110
570
110
15
110
110
1170
15
15

17
20
337
300

Front

R.H. side

140
1200
140
140
600
140

152

Alternative to Design 2

This alternative makes use of small sections of timber attached to the top of the table legs but having smaller dimensions than the legs (see diagram). Prior to fixing to the leg, these small sections of timber are attached to four sections of framing material of a predetermined size, thereby forming a rectangular frame (see diagram).

The framing material used to form the frame should be mitred in each corner and positioned over the small timber block as illustrated.

Screws are then used, passing through from the underneath of the timber block, to attach the mitred frame to the small timber sections.

Assembly

In the process of assembly, these various members may also be glued.

The finished size of the framing material is dependent upon the material to be used for the table top. It may be pre-finished or veneered particle board, glass, or mosaic tiles. It is also dependent on the size of picture-frame moulding which it is suggested should be used to form the edges of the table top.

From the sectional sketches it can be seen that the moulding should sit on top of the small timber sections, butt against the framing material, and have its rebate section flush with the top of the framing material. The depth of the rebate, as previously mentioned, is determined

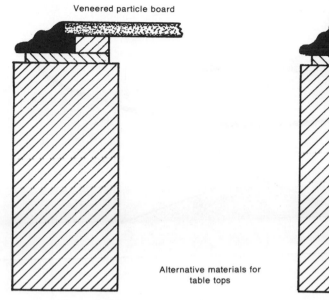

Veneered particle board

Alternative materials for table tops

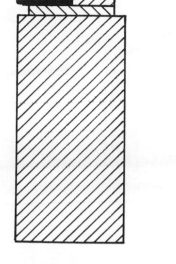

Mirror

by the thickness of the table top material.

The small timber blocks with the attached mitred frame are centrally located and screwed to the top of each table leg. This then allows the picture-frame moulding to be accurately mitred to fit around the outside of the framing material. The outside edge of the picture-frame moulding should be flush with the leg or extend a small distance beyond.

Having fitted the four mitre joints on the picture-frame moulding, thereby forming a

frame, this frame may now be glued to the framing material and small timber blocks. The top is fitted and if screwing is required this is best achieved by drilling and screwing through the framing material between the legs.

Finishing

All timber surfaces should be sanded using between 180-grit and 240-grit abrasive paper and then clear-finished using an appropriate finish.

Procedure for Design 3

This table is particularly easy to construct, consisting of only two separate panels joined to form 90°. The top is of 10 mm glass either plain or coloured with a polished edge. The finished table looks very attractive indeed.

Panels

The panels, if made from pre-finished manufactured board, would need no further surface finishing. It is suggested that the panels be prepared to width as one long board. This would ensure identical pieces.

Once the width is determined, the separate panels may be cut to length. Care must be taken to ensure that the ends are square to the edges. Finally clamp the pieces together to check that they are exactly the same.

Joint

While the panels are clamped together the

joint may be marked out. The joint is not difficult, but care is needed.

Initially, mark the centre and square a line across the top edges. The thickness of the material can then be set out 9 mm each side of the centre line. With the panels still clamped together, square these lines down the outside faces. The panels can now be separated and the lines squared down the other faces and across the bottom edges. A marking gauge is used to mark the middle of the panel, but care must be taken to gauge from the top edges of both the panels.

When removing the waste material from the joint it must be remembered that on one panel the waste will come from the top and on the other the waste will come from the bottom portion of the panel. It is also a good idea to cut the lines with a knife to prevent any tearing of the surface when sawing down the line. Once the waste has been removed

assemble the joint. If it is satisfactory it may be glued into position.

Edges

To complete the project it will be necessary to trim the raw edges of the board. This is best done using an appropriate plastic edging. Once the edging is positioned and trimmed, no further surface finish of the panels is required.

Fitting the Top

When the glass top is ordered from the glass supplier, small, circular rubber pads can be purchased. These pads can be located on the top edges of the panels. They have a cushioning effect and will prevent the top from sliding about.

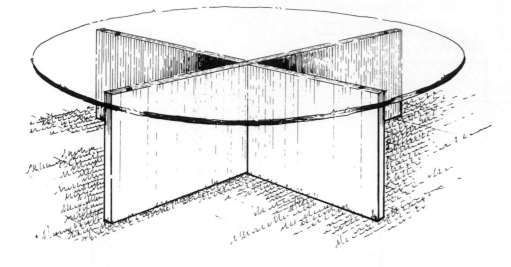

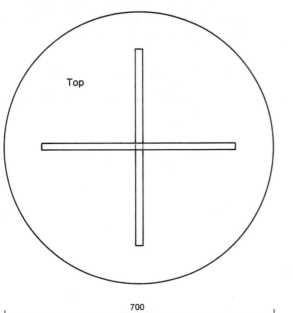

Top

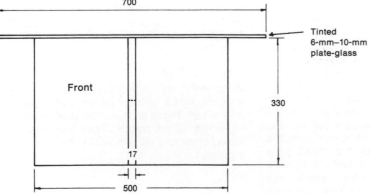

700

Front

Tinted
6-mm–10-mm
plate-glass

330

17

500

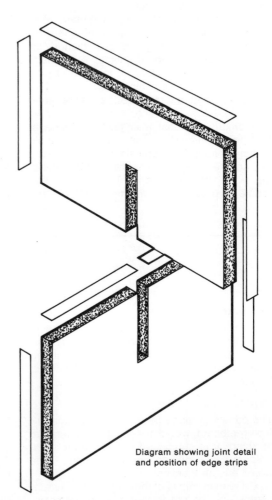

Diagram showing joint detail
and position of edge strips

Procedure for Design 4

The use of mosaics for table tops provides not only durable and serviceable surfaces but with thoughtful selection of tone and design, they can be most pleasing in appearance. They do, however, require edge treatment to cover tile edges and cement grouting.

Sides and Ends

From the selected sheet material mark out and cut the four panels forming the sides of the base section of the table. The ends, being the same size, should be clamped together and planed to produce square and parallel edges. The sides are prepared in the same way.

While the sides are still clamped, mark out and drill the four holes required for the screws used to attach the sides to the ends.

Cleats

To enable the top to be secured to the base section, small 30 mm x 20 mm cleats are screwed to the inside of the two end panels and two side panels. The cleats on the side panels should be short by twice the combined thickness of the cleat and panel and located centrally on the side panels.

Top

The material for the top of the table may be the same as that used on the base or, as in the sketch, raw-particle board with mosaic tiles applied. The size of the top is then dependent upon the finished size of the mosaic tiles.

Where tiles are used, contact adhesive should be applied to attach them to the particle board and then tile cement, of appropriate colouring, used to fill the gaps between the mosaics.

Edging

Prior to the application of the tile cement, it is good practice to attach an edge strip, mitred in the corners and level with the mosaic tiles, to the edge of the raw-particle board top. The finished sizes of the edge strip are for personal choice but should be considered in the initial planning of the table. Once the edge strip is in position it then provides a definitive edge against which the tile cement may be placed. To this end, the edge strip should be covered with masking tape to prevent any staining occurring from the tile cement. Alternatively, the edge strip may be given two coats of the intended finishing material.

Assembly

Attach the sides to the ends using screws. The ends must have a pilot hole drilled 50 mm deep where each screw is inserted to prevent the sheet material from splitting.

Lay the table top upside down and centrally position the assembled sides and ends ready for attachment.

Drill clearance holes and countersink them through the cleats to accept 8 gauge screws.

Screw the base to the top via the cleats. Cover the screw heads with the appropriate colour snap-caps.

Finishing

If the base is of pre-finished material, the only finishing required may be the edge strip around the mosaic tile top. If veneered particle board has been used for the base material then both the base and edge strip may be given two or three coats of a suitable clear finish. A light scuff back between coats enhances the overall finish.

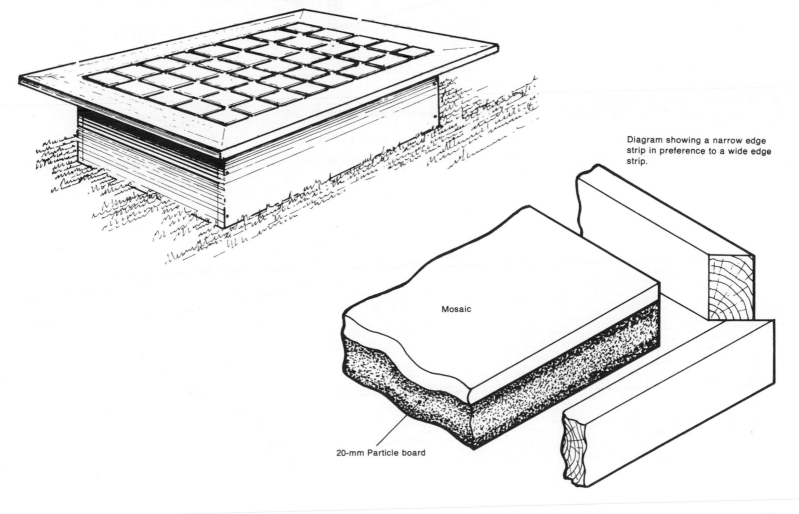

Diagram showing a narrow edge strip in preference to a wide edge strip.

Mosaic

20-mm Particle board

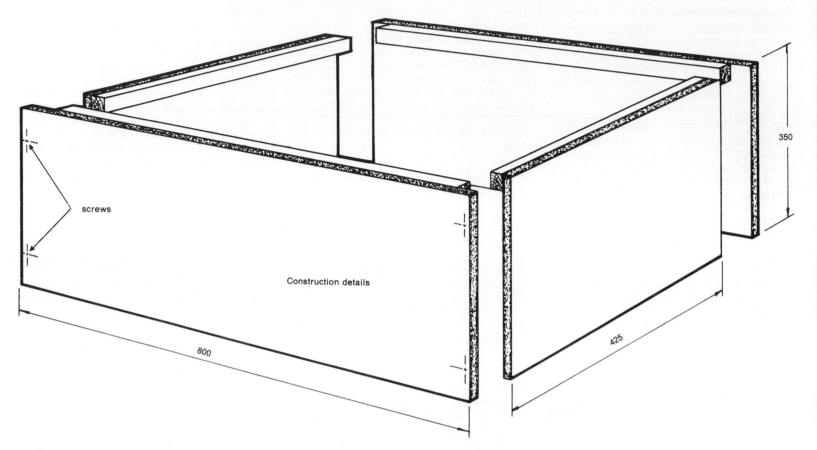

screws

Construction details

350

800

425

NOTE
- All sheet material 20 mm thick.
- Table top not dimensioned—this will depend on the type and size of the ceramic mosaics selected.
- Refer to section on knockdown fittings for details of suitable connector screws for joining the sides to the ends.

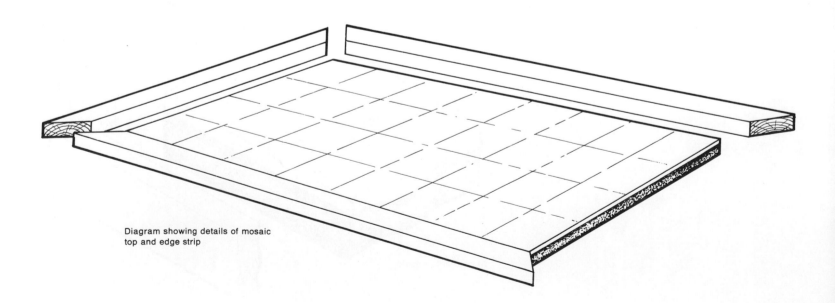

Diagram showing details of mosaic top and edge strip

Procedure for Design 5

The addition of castors in this table design further adds to its functions. Besides having a surface to act as an occasional table, the lower shelf provides a storage area and the castors, of course, provide mobility.

Panels

From a sheet of manufactured board, mark out and cut out the appropriate panel sizes, leaving sufficient waste material between panels for saw cuts and giving consideration to continuity of grain—particularly the top and sides.

To ensure squareness and equality of length, clamp the end panels together and the top and bottom panels together and using a No. 5 jack plane correct any irregularities which may have occurred during sawing.

To prevent the chipping of veneer when sawing it is good practice to knife-cut the saw-cut line rather than just using a pencil line.

Joints

The panels may be easily assembled using specially designed manufactured-board screws (see chapter on joints). The positions for these screws are marked out on the end panels, and the top and the bottom panels.

Using a specially prepared jig which can be clamped into position to provide for greater accuracy, the clearance holes and pilot holes are independently drilled in the appropriate panels.

Alternatively, the panels may be clamped together to form the table, and using a specially designed drill, the clearance and pilot holes are drilled together.

Assembly

The table is then assembled, using appropriate screws, and each panel checked for flushness of fit against the others. If inaccuracies are apparent, they may be easily remedied by using a No. 4 smoothing plane.

All exposed edges should then be covered using either iron-on edge strip or solid-timber edge strip.

If the top surface is required to be level, allowance must be made for the thickness of the edge strip.

Hardware

Attach to the underneath of the table base (using round head screws) four half-ball castors with metal plates.

Finishing

Using 240-garnet paper clean up all surfaces and apply a suitable clear finish.

If raw-particle board is used a suitable stain or opaque finish would be more appropriate.

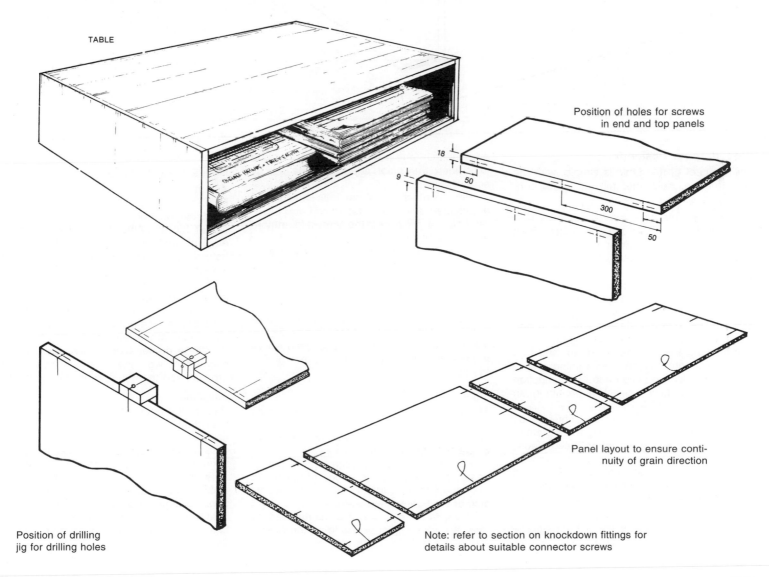

TABLE

Position of holes for screws in end and top panels

18

9

50

300

50

Position of drilling jig for drilling holes

Panel layout to ensure continuity of grain direction

Note: refer to section on knockdown fittings for details about suitable connector screws

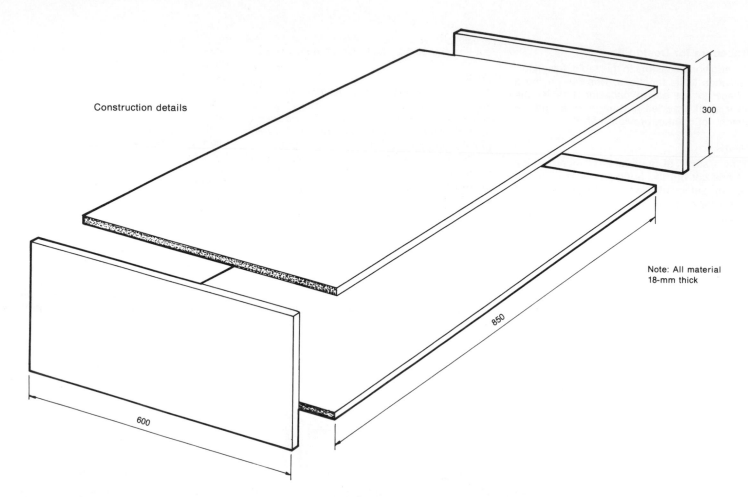

Construction details

300

Note: All material
18-mm thick

850

600

Procedure for Design 6

The concept of this table is simple, with the leg structure, rails, and top, all being connected by screws.

Legs

The legs for this table are constructed from rectangular timber stock and may be joined by rails or corner blocks which in turn are attached to the table top. It is essential to square the ends of each leg, preferably to a knife-cut line, to ensure a suitable result finish in both appearance and stability. This may be achieved by squaring one end of each leg individually, clamping all the legs together, and then planing the other ends square and to a common length. A sharp smoothing plane, used with a slicing action and in conjunction with an oil pad, will assist in providing an excellent end-grain finish.

Further decoration may be achieved by rounding the corners by making a template of one leg and marking the others accordingly. In this instance the corners may be removed by a disc sander or alternatively, a flat-soled spokeshave. Each leg should then be individually sanded and all arris removed.

Rails and/or Corner Blocks

When using rails to join the legs and table top together, they should be saw cut to the appro-

priate length, and using either a mitre or butt joint where they meet, attached to the legs by screws.

Prior to attachment these rails should have a suitable number of holes drilled and countersunk ready to accept the screws for attaching the table top.

Corner blocks are also attached by screws; however, it will be necessary to counterbore where the blocks are too wide to accommodate average length screws. Similar to the rails, the corner blocks should be drilled and countersunk in at least two positions, to facilitate the attachment of the top. To provide further strength, P.V.A. glue may be used where the rails and/or corner blocks are attached to the legs.

Table Top

The table top may be made from veneered manufactured board or pre-finished board, having the edges covered with timber veneer or plastic edge strip respectively.

Prior to applying the edge strip it is necessary to check that the edges of the board are square to the surface and that the overall size of the board is accurate.

If the table legs are to be connected by rails, allowance must be made on the overall size of the table top to include the edge strip.

This is necessary as the table top is to fit inside the leg and rail structure.

Assembly

Using the appropriate size screws and P.V.A. glue, join the legs together either with rails or corner blocks. Where one leg overlaps the edge of another it is suggested that screws be inserted to provide further strength for the leg structure.

The screw heads should be covered with plastic snap caps.

In the case of the leg and rail structure, the table top is located in position and screwed down against the rails.

Where corner blocks have been used to connect the legs, the individual leg structures are screwed to each corner of the table top.

Finishing

Prior to the application of any surface finish, individual components should be cleaned using 180-grit to 240-grit abrasive paper. Once assembled, the unit should have a final sand to remove any remaining blemishes or arris. Two or three coats of an appropriate clear surface finish are then applied using spray equipment or brushing. Between each coat of surface finish, scuffing back with very fine garnet paper will ensure a very smooth finish.

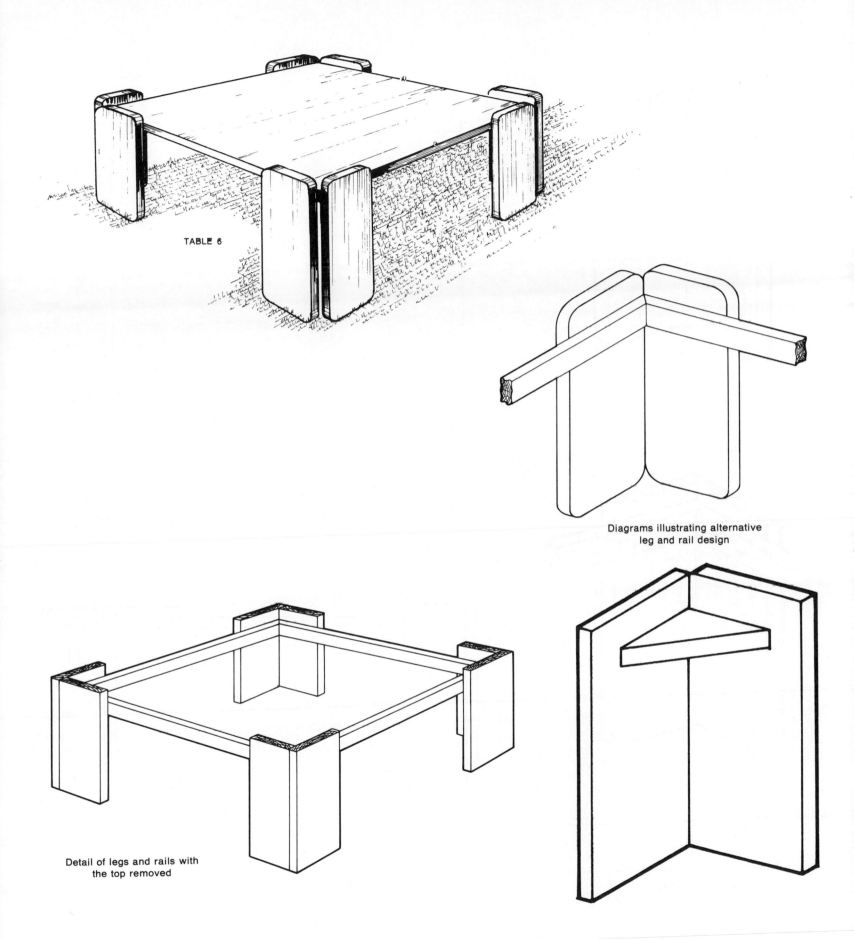

TABLE 6

Diagrams illustrating alternative
leg and rail design

Detail of legs and rails with
the top removed

159

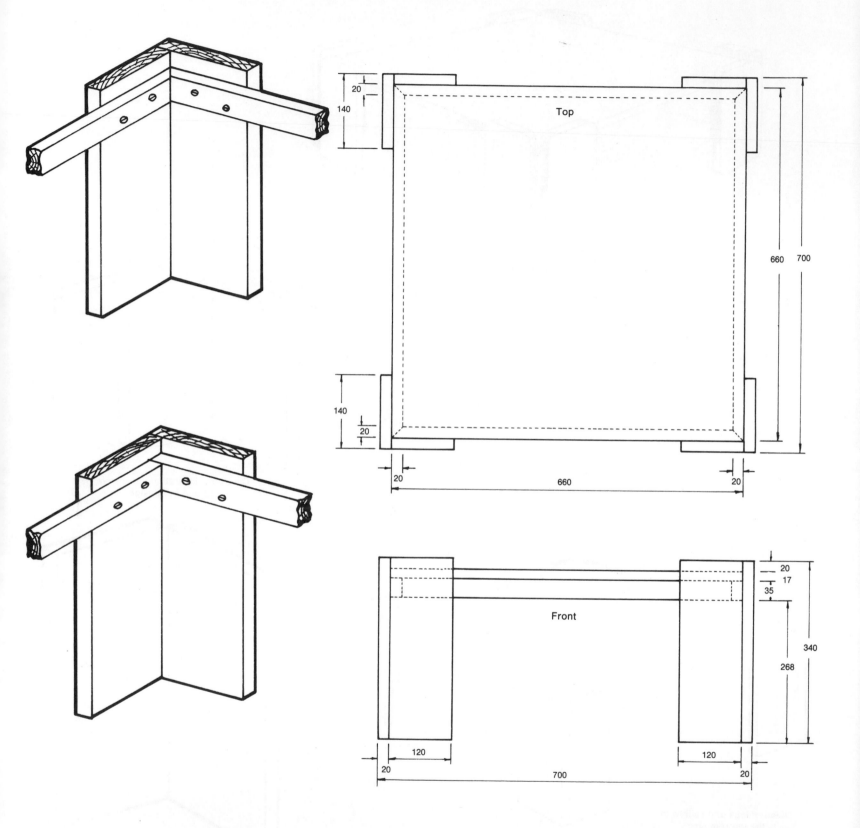

Top

20

140

660 700

140

20

20

660

20

Front

20
17
35

340

268

120

120

20

700

20

Procedure for Design 7

This table features a veneered manufactured board top and, for ease of construction, the frame is assembled using metal corner trusses. The frame is constructed of solid timber.

Frame

Before beginning this table read carefully the section on assembly aids, with particular reference to the use and fitting of leg trusses. It would also be an advantage to purchase the trusses before beginning the construction.

Legs

The legs are cut from 45 mm x 45 mm stock and may be cut exactly to length. It is a good idea to clamp the four legs together to ensure that the lengths are identical.

Rails

The rails are of 45 mm x 20 mm stock and may be cut to length. Keep the rails in pairs and ensure that the lengths are identical. It could be difficult to keep the outside faces of the legs and rails flush. To overcome this problem it is a good idea to plane a small chamfer or radius on the ends of the rails and make a feature of the joint.

When the components are carefully prepared, including a good rub with abrasive paper, the trusses may be fitted to each corner. This process is explained in the section dealing with assembly aids.

Assembly

When attaching the trusses, check the frame for squareness by measuring the diagonals. When the frame is square and sitting perfectly on a flat surface, tighten the bolts on the trusses.

Top

The top is of natural timber-veneered particle board. It is cut to the outside dimensions of the table frame. The raw edges of the board are covered with natural timber-veneer edging. This type of veneer is best fitted using contact adhesive. The edges of the veneer can be easily trimmed using abrasive paper around a cork block.

The top is secured to the frame by wood screws fitted through the rails. Care must be taken to select screws of the appropriate length to avoid damage to the top surface. It is best to remove the top when finishing the surface and refit it when the finish is dry.

Finishing

The frame and top will need at least two or three coats of clear surface finish with a careful rub down between each coat with a fine abrasive paper. Once the surface is dry the top can be reassembled and the table is ready for use.

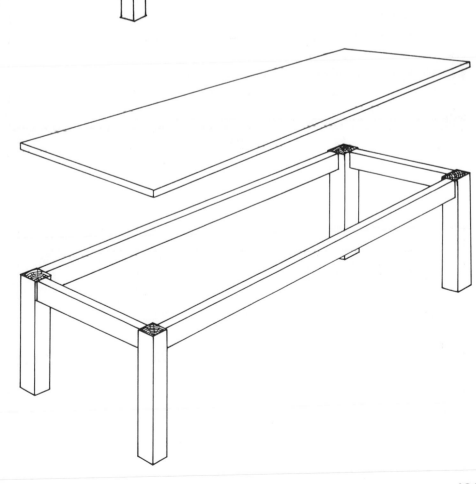

TABLE

Note: Refer to section on knockdown fittings for details about leg trusses.

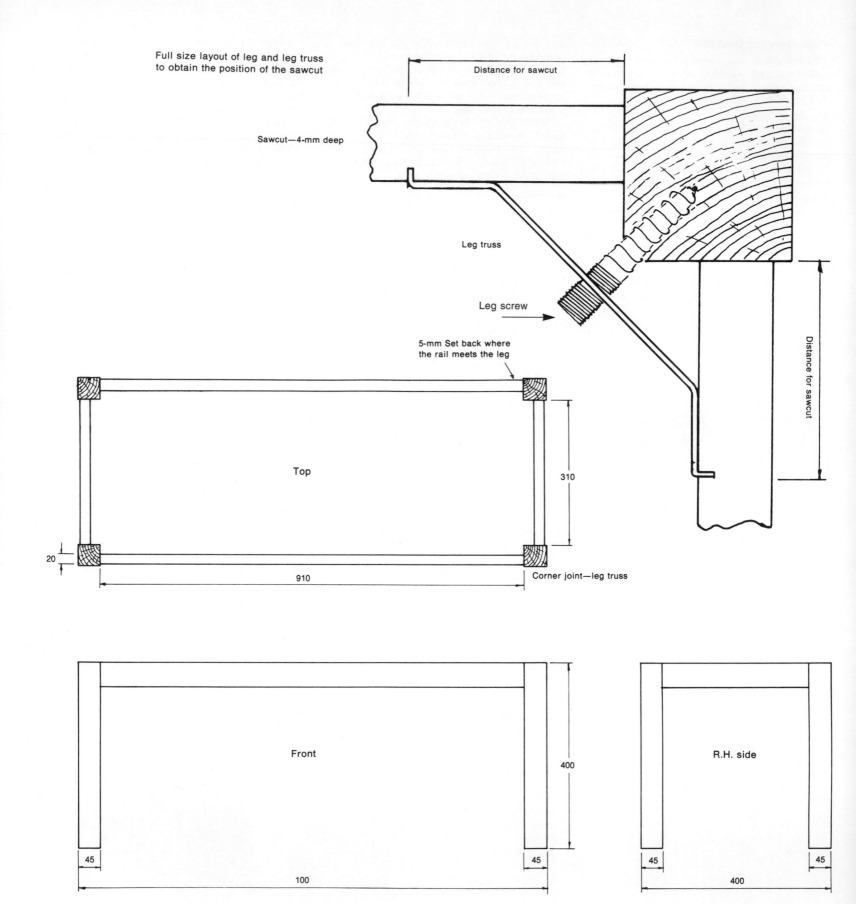

Full size layout of leg and leg truss
to obtain the position of the sawcut

Distance for sawcut

Sawcut—4-mm deep

Leg truss

Leg screw

5-mm Set back where
the rail meets the leg

Distance for sawcut

Top

310

20

910

Corner joint—leg truss

Front

400

45

45

100

R.H. side

45

45

400

162

Procedure for Design 8

This delightful little table is particularly elegant and would go well with any contemporary setting. It is constructed with solid timber, legs and rails being connected with threaded bolt, guided-dowel and cross-dowel guide assembly aids. The top is of 10 mm glass with the polished edges finishing flush with the outsides of rails.

Frame

Before beginning this table read carefully the section on assembly aids with particular reference to the use and fitting of threaded bolts, guide dowels and cross dowels. It would also be an advantage to purchase the assembly aids before beginning construction. The project 'Bar stool' also uses this method of construction and is well detailed.

Legs

The legs are cut from 40 mm x 40 mm stock and may be cut exactly to length. Clamp the legs together to ensure the lengths are identical.

Rails

The rails are also cut from the same stock and may be cut exactly to length. Keep the rails in pairs to ensure that the lengths are identical. At this stage the legs and rails may be marked out and drilled to receive the metal fittings. Details for this process are set out clearly in the section on assembly aids. Again refer to the 'Bar stool' project. In addition, the manufacturer of the fittings will have the specifications clearly set out, with step-by-step instructions.

Assembly

After carefully fitting the metal dowels and bolts to the legs and rails, tighten the heads locking the frame together. Before finally tightening the head nuts, ensure that the table is square by checking the diagonals.

Top

The top is of 10 mm-thick glass finished with polished edges. The glass top may be clear or coloured. It is also a good idea to purchase some rubber pads, usually circular in shape. These little pads are located on the rails and cushion the glass against the timber and prevent the top from sliding around.

Finishing

The timber components will need at least two or three coats of clear surface finish, with a careful rub down with a fine abrasive paper between each coat.

TABLE

Note: Refer to section on knockdown fittings for details on threaded bolt and guide dowel assembly aids.

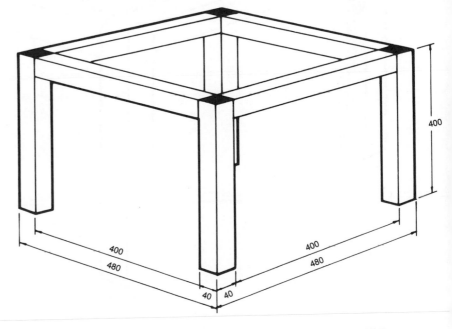

Procedure for Design 9

This attractive table is constructed using solid timber. The legs and rails are connected using dowels, while the top is of raw-particle board covered with ceramic tiles. Bar clamps will be necessary to adequately clamp the joints during assembly.

Top

Before deciding on the final dimensions of the table it is suggested that the tiles that are to be used for the top are purchased. Once the tiles have been selected lay them out on a bench or floor and carefully measure the outside dimensions. Cut the piece of raw-particle board to these dimensions.

Make sure the surface of the particle board is free from grease and dust and, using a saw-tooth trowel, spread the ceramic tile adhesive evenly over the surface. The tiles must be placed firmly in position carefully lined up with the outside edges. Make sure also that the joint lines are straight and even. Allow to dry for about twelve hours.

Select a coloured grout to match the tiles and mix it into a thick paste. Work the grout into the joints with a rubber grouter. The excess may be removed with a damp sponge and the surface finally polished with a dry cloth.

Frame

The length of the rails are marked from the top. Allow 2 mm longer to ensure that the top will fit neatly between the rails when the frame is glued together. The rails must be cut and squared accurately to length. The legs are cut 10 mm longer than the indicated length and only one end is squared. The length is marked from the squared end and a line scribed around the other end at the indicated length.

Refer to the diagram indicating the relationship of face and face edge marks for setting out. It is suggested that reference is made to the chapter on joints before setting out the dowel joints.

The dowels are glued into the ends of the rails and all of the inside edges are cleaned up before final assembly.

Assembly

The end frames are assembled initially. Take particular care to ensure that the legs are square to the rails and that the legs are not twisted. When the end frames are dry they may be connected by the long rails. Particular care must be taken to ensure the table is square and not twisted.

The joints are strengthened by four corner blocks. These blocks also support the top. When preparing them make sure the grain of the timber is parallel to the long edge.

The corner block is fitted flush with the underside of the rails. These blocks must be glued and screwed. If desired, a cleat, the same thickness as the corner blocks, may be fitted to the long rails.

With the corner blocks in position the tops of the legs may be planed flush with the rails and any joints that are out of line may be trued up. When all planing is complete use a fine abrasive paper to clean up the table ready for surface finishing.

Finishing

Three coats of clear surface finish should be adequate and when dry, the top may be placed into position and the table is ready for use.

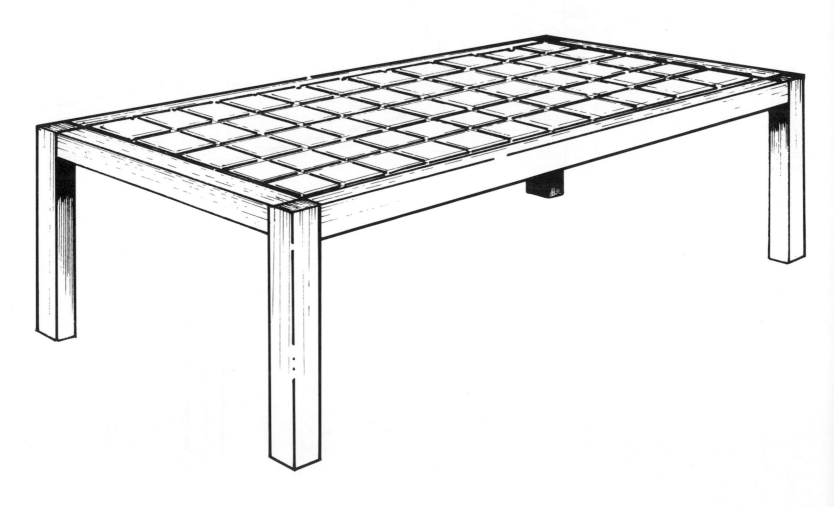

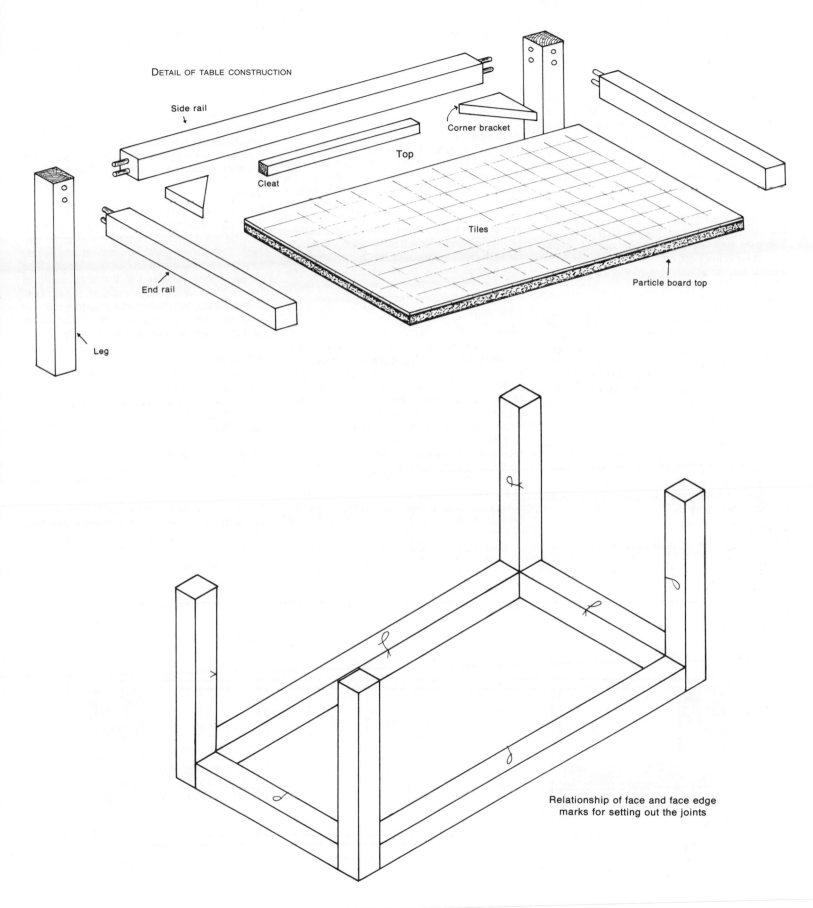

DETAIL OF TABLE CONSTRUCTION

Side rail

Corner bracket

Top

Cleat

Tiles

Particle board top

End rail

Leg

Relationship of face and face edge
marks for setting out the joints

Procedure for Design 10

This table has been designed to provide storage and mobility.

Top and Bottom

Mark out and cut from pre-selected sheet material the bottom member and top section of the table. These two components, being of the same dimensions, should be clamped together and planed accurately to size. Once the edges have been checked for squareness they should then be covered using the appropriate edge strip.

On the bottom panel, mark out and drill the six holes to accommodate the screws which will hold the vertical divisions in position. Similarly, on the top and bottom panels, mark out and drill the eight holes for the screws necessary for the attachment of the four vertical posts.

Vertical Divisions

From the same or similar sheet material, cut out the two vertical divisions. Again, these members, being identical in size, are best clamped together and planed to have square and straight edges. Since the long edges of these vertical members will not be exposed it is necessary only to cover the four front edges with edge-strip material.

In order to attach the top to these vertical members, two cleats 30 mm x 20 mm should be screwed to the inside surface of the vertical divisions to be flush with the top edges. The length of these cleats is optional, but must be shorter than the division to allow the doors to close (see sketch).

Vertical Posts

These square sections of solid timber should be accurately cut to length and have both ends checked for squareness. The centre of each end is found and a pilot hole is drilled in each end to accept the threaded section of the screws. These posts may be shaped if further decorative treatment is required (such as chamfers).

Assembly

Attach the vertical divisions to the bottom panel by inserting the screws. Similarly, the four posts may be screwed to the bottom panel. To prevent the posts from rotating, a further 30 mm x 6 mm countersunk head screw should be inserted into each post from underneath the bottom panel. The top is then positioned and secured by screwing internally through both cleats and finally inserting the screws into the top of the vertical posts. The exposed heads of the screws on the top panel are covered by using the appropriate coloured snap-caps.

Doors

Again from the same or similar sheet material, mark out and cut the four panels to become the four doors—the grain direction should be vertical. Once again, these panels, being all of the same dimension, may be clamped together while the edges are planed square and the panels brought to a size being 1 mm less all round than is the opening formed by the vertical divisions, top and bottom.

Attach an appropriate length of piano hinge to the shorter edge of each panel—the flange of the hinge being flush on the inside of the door. Each door is then attached to one of the vertical divisions being set back at least 1 mm to 2 mm from the edge.

Each door should be pushed firmly against the top edge when screwing to the vertical divisions as it will drop due to its own weight.

Having checked for clearance all round on each of the doors, appropriate edge strip should be applied to the top and opening edge of each door. A tip catch can be applied to each door in which case no handles are required. Alternatively, a magnetic catch, which serves both as a stop and a means of holding the door can be applied. In this case handles of some description will be necessary.

Base

Using either solid timber or similar sheet material as used in the table, a small plinth or base can be constructed on which the table can rest. The corner joints are mitred and joined together by means of corner glue blocks. The plinth is then attached to the underneath of the table bottom by means of screws. Alternatively, four heavy-duty castors may be attached to the underneath of the table bottom, thereby providing for mobility.

Finishing

When pre-finished material is used, little finishing is required other than for the four vertical posts. These should be sanded using 240-grit abrasive paper and coated with a suitable clear finish.

If veneered manufactured board has been used then it is necessary to use 240-grit abrasive paper over the whole unit and then apply two or three coats of an appropriate clear finish which may be brushed on or sprayed. It is good practice to clean up individual components, as the unit is assembled with a final clean-up as a fully assembled article just prior to the application of the finishing material.

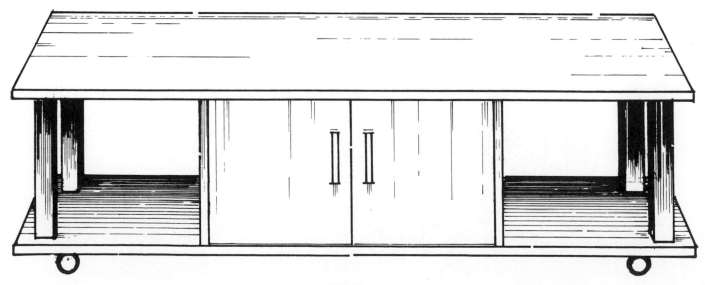

TABLE 10

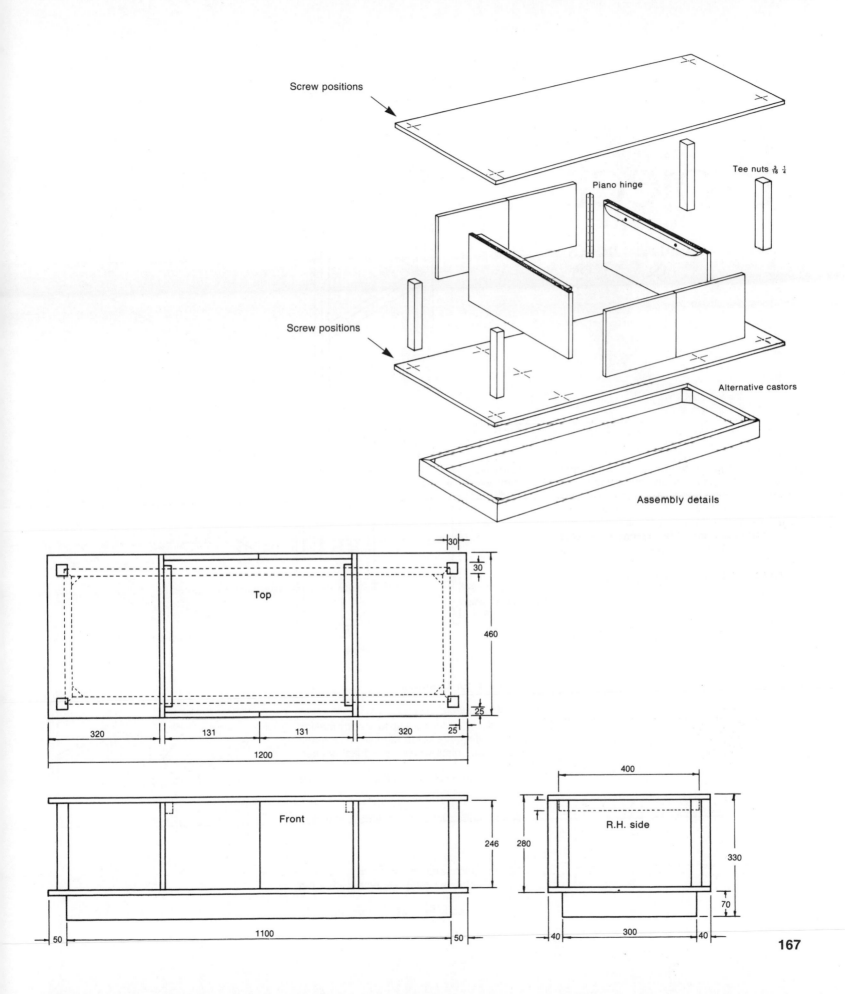

Screw positions

Piano hinge

Tee nuts $\frac{3}{16}$ $\frac{1}{4}$

Screw positions

Alternative castors

Assembly details

Top

30

30

460

25

320   131   131   320   25

1200

Front

400

R.H. side

246

280

330

70

50   1100   50

40   300   40

167

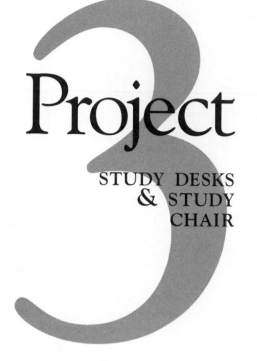

Project

3

STUDY DESKS & STUDY CHAIR

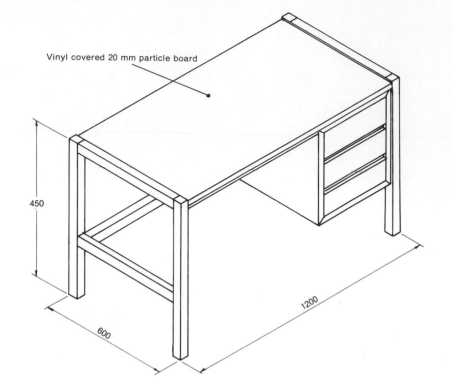

Vinyl covered 20 mm particle board

450

1200

600

These desks illustrated have been designed for ease of construction, and make use of pre-finished manufactured board panels, vinyl tops, and solid timbers. Some of the designs use only particle board or medium fibre density boards, and could be described as solid construction. Two of the designs make use of solid timber in various sections and could be described as framed construction.

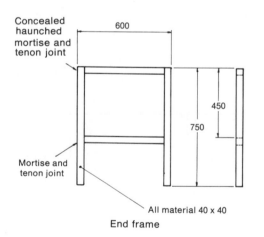

Concealed haunched mortise and tenon joint

600

450

750

Mortise and tenon joint

All material 40 x 40

End frame

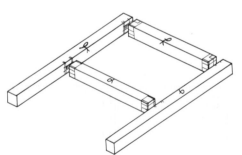

Set out on the bench top to mark out the joints

Procedure for Design 1

The Leg Assembly

The legs and rails are cut to length making suitable allowances for mortise and tenon joints. Dowel joints would be a suitable alternative.

The legs and rails are laid out on the bench to set out the joints.

Cut the joints and check the fit.

Apply adhesive and assemble the end frames.

Clamp the end frames together and mark the position of the back rail.

Cut the joints and check the fit.

Apply adhesive and assemble the leg assembly.

Clean up ready for surface finishing.

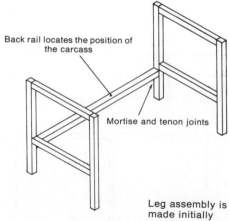

Back rail locates the position of the carcass

Mortise and tenon joints

Leg assembly is made initially

The Cabinet Assembly

The cabinet assembly of the desk may be classified as solid end carcass construction. The ends are made of 17–20 mm veneered manufactured board, joined with a number of rails. Drawer runners are screwed to the sides flush with the drawer rails.

The sides are cut initially, clamped together and planed accurately to size.

Rebate the back edges to accommodate 4 mm plyback.

Set out the joints for the long top rails. Make allowance for the rebate at the back.

Set out the joints for the bottom rails.

Set out the joints for the drawer rails.

Cut and fit all joints.

When satisfied with the assembly, apply adhesive to the bottom and drawer rails only and assemble the carcass as indicated.

Set out and make the dowel joints at the end of the top rails.

Apply adhesive to these joints and clamp up independently of the carcass.

When the adhesive is set apply adhesive to the top joints and fit the top rails, completing the carcass assembly.

Screw the drawer runners to the inside of the carcass, making sure they are square and flush with the drawer rails.

Fit the ply back.

Fit and clean up the edging at the front and back of the cabinet.

Clamp up ready for surface finishing.

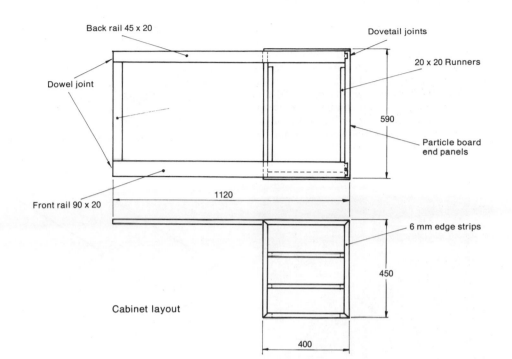

Cabinet layout

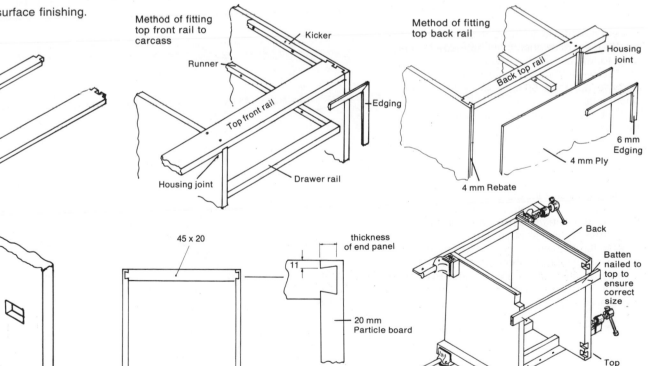

Bottom rails are dovetailed into the ends

169

The cabinet may now be fitted to the leg assembly.

Screw holes are drilled through the panel at one end, and the rail at the other, and the cabinet is glued and screwed from the inside to the end frames. It is advisable to clamp the two parts securely until the screws are fitted.

The drawers may now be fitted, and this operation is fully described earlier in the chapter. If drawer pulls are not to be used, finger grips must be machined along the top or bottom edges of the drawer front.

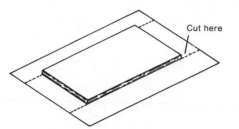

Glue vinyl to top and cut along dashed line

Fitting the leg assembly to the cabinet

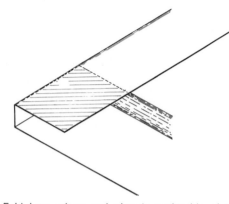

Fold long edges and glue to underside of top; remove surplus material

Top

Cut the manufactured board to fit between the end frames. Allowance must be made for the vinyl to fold around the ends.

Cut the vinyl to fold around the edges and ends so that about 50 mm can be glued to the underside.

Glue the vinyl to the desk top, and cut along the lines indicated.

Fold the long edges around and glue them to the underside of the top. Remove the surplus material indicated.

Fold the ends around, over the side pieces and with a sharp knife cut an angle of 45° from the corner, through both thicknesses of vinyl. Remove the bottom piece, and glue the end fold to the underside of the top.

Fold the flap left on the front piece around to the end, and cut through the two thicknesses of vinyl with a sharp knife. Remove the bottom piece and glue the top piece into the space.

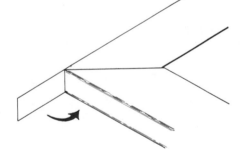
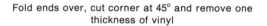

Fold ends over, cut corner at 45° and remove one thickness of vinyl

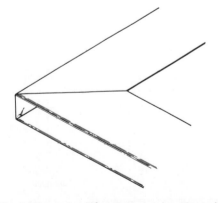

After folding, cut at 45° and glue into position to form a neat corner

170

Procedure for Design 2

Initial Planning

This desk is designed around standard Radiata pine sizes. All framing timber shown is 70 mm x 35 mm. The top is 18 mm manufactured board covered with vinyl on a suitable pre-finished board. The components are connected using 75 mm x 10 mm countersunk-head wood screws, with the heads covered with plastic snap-caps.

End Frames

Standard Radiata pine sizes are P.A.R. so all that is required is careful cutting to length. After trimming the legs and rails to length, clamp the legs together and mark out the holes for the screws.

Mark out the centre for the clearance holes in the legs as shown.

The rails may also be clamped together and marked out for the pilot holes. To ensure accuracy it is suggested that a drill guide be used when using a portable electric drill.

Spreader Rails

As with the end frames the spreader rails are 70 mm x 35 mm and must be carefully cut to length, ensuring that the ends are square. It is intended that 75 mm x 10 mm countersunk screws be used to fix these components to the end frames.

The top and bottom rails of the end frames can be clamped, marked and drilled with clearance holes as shown.

The spreader rails can now be marked and drilled with a 6 mm hole ready for fitting.

Assembly

Before assembly carefully clean up the surfaces with abrasive paper. It is suggested that the end frames be assembled first, and when locked in position attach the spreader rails. To complete this section of the desk it is desirable to drill four screw holes in the top spreader rails to fix the top.

The Top

The top may be made from pre-finished board or 18 mm-thick manufactured board covered with a coloured vinyl and edged with 35 mm x 19 mm Radiata pine as shown to give the appearance of a thicker top.

The top is screwed to the frame from underneath using 75 mm x 10 mm countersunk head screws.

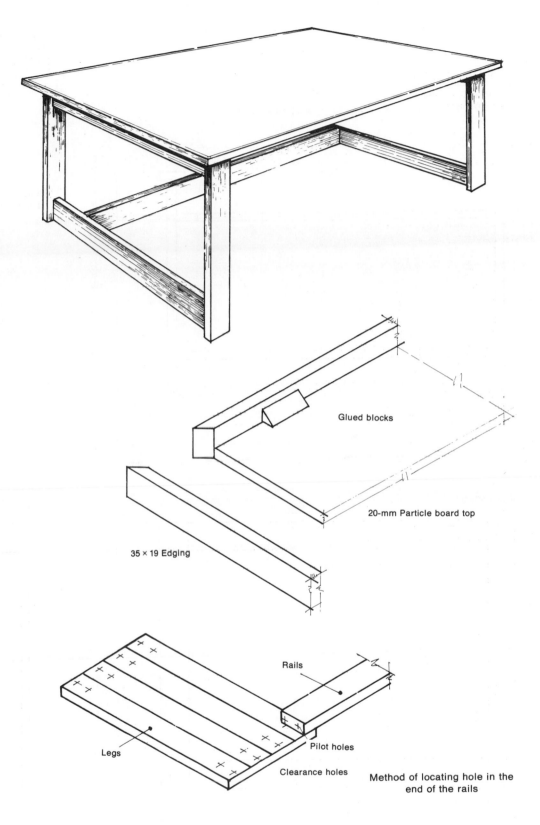

Glued blocks

20-mm Particle board top

35 × 19 Edging

Rails

Legs

Pilot holes

Clearance holes

Method of locating hole in the end of the rails

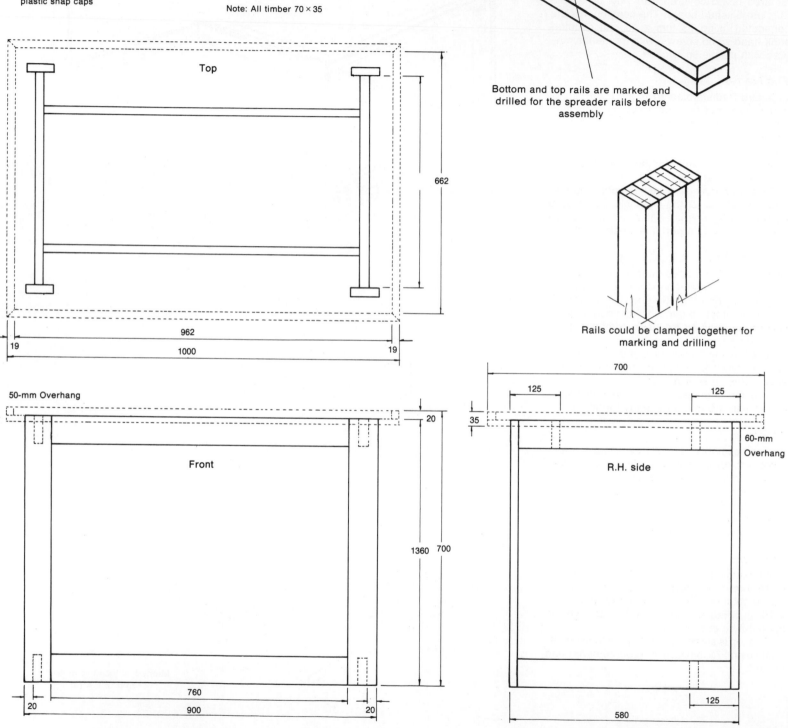

Legs and rails are connected by 75 × 10 countersunk head wood screws—covered by plastic snap caps

Note: All timber 70 × 35

Top

662

962

19   19

1000

Bottom and top rails are marked and drilled for the spreader rails before assembly

Rails could be clamped together for marking and drilling

700

125   125

35

60-mm Overhang

R.H. side

580   125

50-mm Overhang

20

Front

1360   700

760

20   20

900

Procedure for Design 3

This desk is also designed around standard Radiata pine sizes. Members are connected with screws, covered with plastic caps for a neat appearance.

End Frames

These simple frames consist of one vertical and two horizontal pieces, one at the top, and the other at the bottom.

The vertical piece is a standard Radiata pine size 190 mm x 30 mm, and all that is required here is careful cutting and squaring to length. The horizontal cross pieces are standard Radiata pine sizes 90 mm x 35 mm, and once again careful cutting and squaring to length is all that is required. When these components are prepared, they can be glued and screwed together, as indicated in the drawing. It is a good idea to drill the holes in the top members for connecting the spreader rails.

Spreader Rails

These members are cut from standard Radiata pine size 70 mm x 35 mm, and carefully squared to length. It is again intended that connector screws are used to assemble the desk. The end frames can be clamped together for marking and drilling of the holes. The spreader rails can also be clamped together for marking and drilling the smaller hole.

Assembly

Before assembly carefully clean up the surfaces with abrasive paper. Take particular care when finishing the end frames as this will be an attractive feature. When satisfactory attach the rails to the end frames. Make sure the holes are drilled in the rails to fix the top.

Top

The top may be made of pre-finished manufactured board, or 18 mm particle board covered with a coloured vinyl and edged with Radiata pine 35 mm x 19 mm.

The end frames can be clamped together to mark and drill the holes.

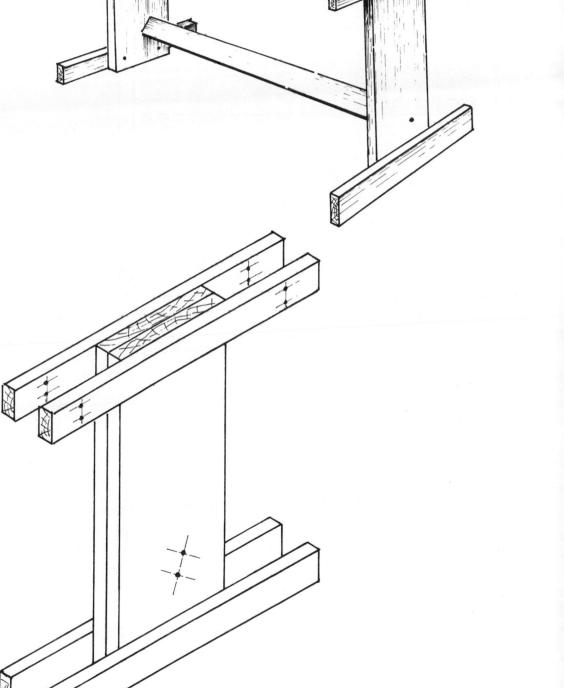

Right: The end frames can be clamped together to mark and drill the holes

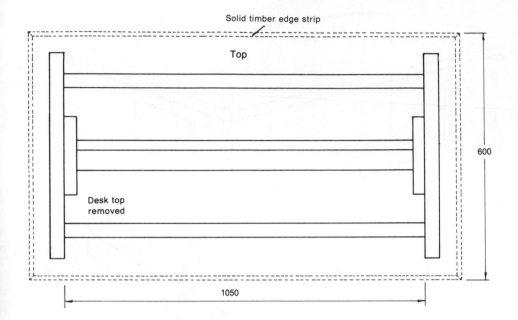

Solid timber edge strip

Top

Desk top removed

600

1050

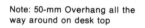

Note: 50-mm Overhang all the way around on desk top

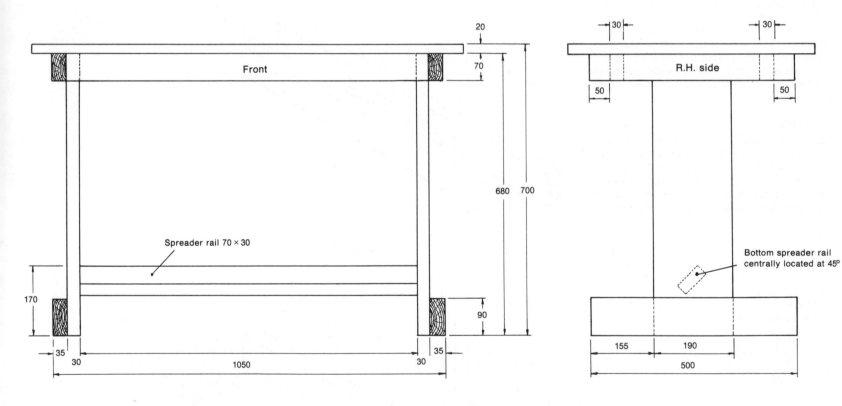

Front

20

70

Spreader rail 70 × 30

170

90

35

30

1050

30

35

680   700

R.H. side

30

30

50

50

Bottom spreader rail centrally located at 45°

155   190

500

Procedure for Design 4

This desk is designed to make use of Radiata plywood panels, joined with Radiata pine spreader-rails using screws covered with plastic caps for a neat appearance.

End Panels

The end panels are from 20 mm-thick plywood. The rectangular cut out is marked out on the face surface of each panel and after drilling a hole in one corner, a jig saw with a fine blade is used to carefully cut out the shape. The edges can be cleaned up with a bastard grade file and abrasive paper. It is intended that the outside edges and inside edges are carefully cleaned up to feature the ply on the edge of the panel.

It is important that the panels are clamped together when shaping to ensure that they are identical.

When the end panels are shaped and cleaned up, and while they are clamped together, the holes for the screws can be marked out and drilled.

Spreader Rails

The spreader rails are cut from Standard Radiata pine size 70 mm x 35 mm. Two rails are cut to support the top and are fitted at floor level. Care must be taken to ensure the ends are square. When satisfied the rails can be clamped together and the holes marked and drilled for the screws to match the direction of the holes in the ends.

Assembly

Before assembly carefully clean all surfaces with abrasive paper. When satisfactory attach the rails to the end frames. Make sure holes are drilled in the top rails to secure the top.

Top

The top may be made of pre-finished particle board edged with the appropriate plastic edging. Or if desired, a vinyl top may be adhered to 18 mm manufactured board. If a thicker appearance is required glue a piece of 35 mm x 17 mm timber along the front and back edges and cover with the vinyl.

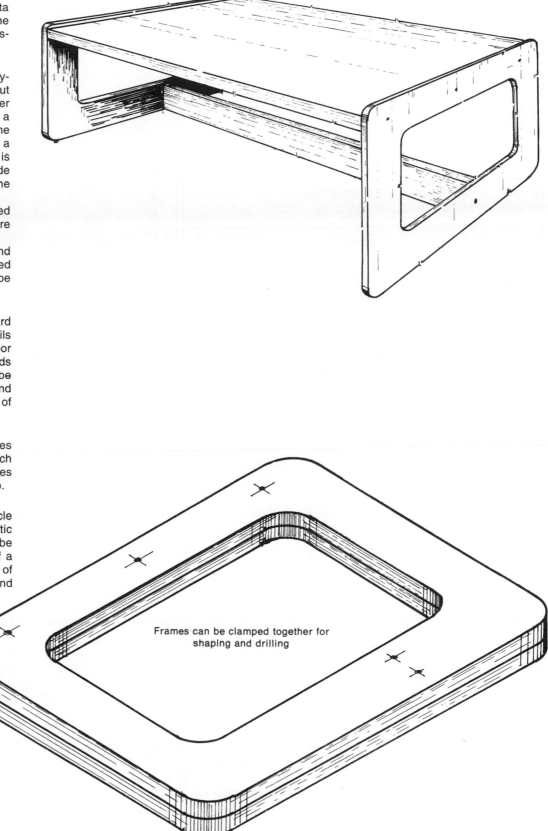

Frames can be clamped together for shaping and drilling

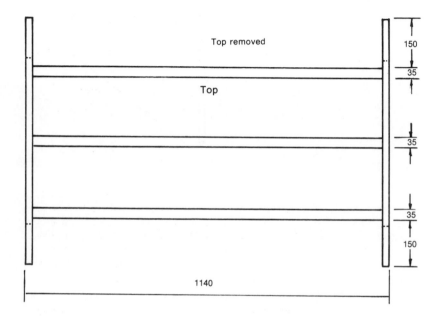

Top removed

Top

150

35

35

35

150

1140

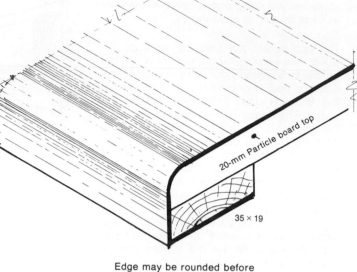

20-mm Particle board top

35 × 19

Edge may be rounded before
attaching the vinyl top

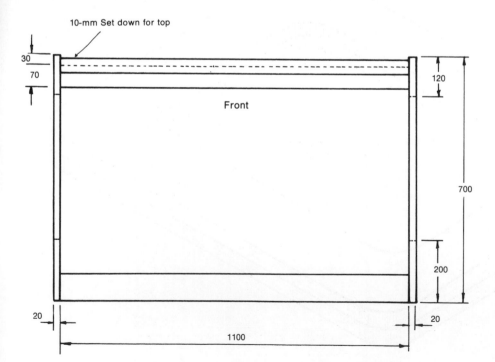

10-mm Set down for top

30

70

Front

120

700

200

20

20

1100

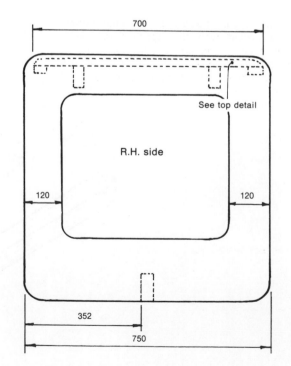

700

See top detail

120

R.H. side

120

352

750

176

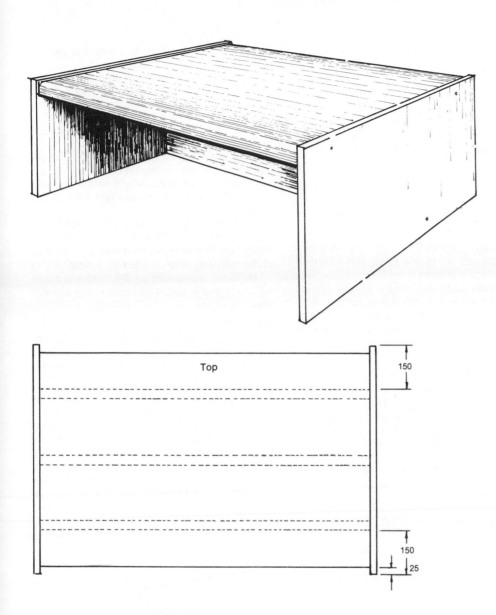

Procedure for Design 5

This desk is similar in its construction method to the previous design, but instead of plywood ends, pre-finished manufactured board is used, connected with screws.

End Panels

This time the end panels are prepared from 18 mm pre-finished board. After carefully cutting the panels place them together to ensure identical sizes. While they are clamped together, mark out and drill the holes for the screws.

The plastic edging can now be applied.

Spreader Rails

The spreader rails should be prepared from a natural timber that best matches the chosen pre-finished panels. After careful dressing to the size indicated, cut to length. When satisfied the rails can be clamped together and the holes marked and drilled for the screws, to match the position of the holes in the end panels. The rails can also be drilled to accommodate screws for attaching the top.

Top

The top is of 18 mm manufactured board with the front and back edges built up to give a thicker appearance. The front and back edges are also rounded. This can be achieved by rubbing the edge of the board with abrasive paper wrapped around a cork block. The top is cut to fit between the end panels.

Assembly

Carefully fit the spreader rails to the ends and tighten the screws. Fit the plastic caps. The top can now be attached to the rails.

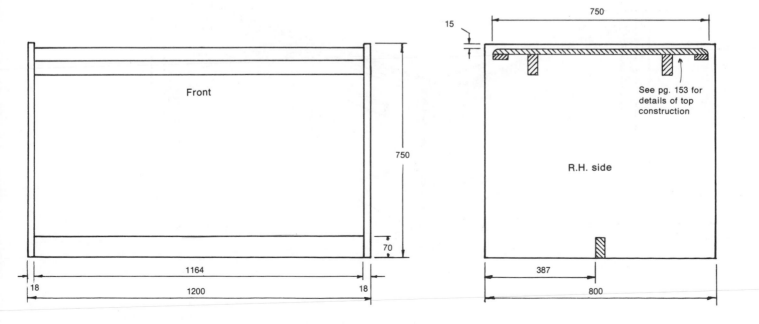

Top

150

150

25

Front

750

70

18   1200   18

1164

15

750

See pg. 153 for details of top construction

R.H. side

387

800

Procedure for Design 6

This desk is similar in construction method to the previous design, but solid timber legs have been screwed to the outside of the panels, and a two-drawer cabinet has been fitted to one end. A modesty panel has also been included.

The end frames, cabinet, drawer fronts, and modesty panel are prepared from 18 mm pre-finished manufactured board. The legs and spreader rails are prepared from timber that matches the choice of the pre-finished panels. Plastic caps can be fitted to the screws for a neat appearance.

End Frames

It is desirable to cut and prepare the end panels initially. Place them together to ensure identical sizes. The front and back edges are trimmed with the appropriate plastic edging.

At this stage it is desirable to mark and drill the holes for the screws. This is best achieved by clamping the panels back to back and drilling together. The legs, 45 mm x 42 mm, are screwed flush with the front and back of the end panels. The legs must be cut to length, cleaned up, and surface-finished before being fitted. It will be necessary to drill and countersink from the inside of the panel, and use three 35 mm x 8 mm countersunk head screws in each leg. If desired, the screw holes can be counterbored, and fitted with a neat plug.

Spreader Rails

The spreader rails should be carefully squared to length, marked, and drilled to accept the screws. In addition, top and bottom rails will need to be drilled ready for the attachment of the modesty panel.

Modesty Panel

This panel is prepared to the same length as the spreader rails. There is no need to apply edging as none of the edges are visible. Do not fit this panel until the cabinet has been fitted.

Assembly

Using screws attach the end panels to the spreader rails. Leave the frame at this stage and construct the cabinet and drawers.

Cabinet

The cabinet is constructed using pre-finished manufactured board and fitted with a Hettich mitred-drawer system.

It is recommended that the drawer system be purchased prior to the laying out of a working rod to establish finished sizes. This cabinet is designed around the 100 mm profile 400 mm x 400 mm drawer system.

Ends of Cabinet

The ends are first squared to length and width. It is a good idea to clamp the panels together to ensure identical shapes. The edges should be square to the faces before applying plastic edging to the top and front edges only. The 8 mm holes can now be marked out and drilled to accommodate the screws. The drawer runners can also be fitted at this stage.

Top and Bottom of Cabinet

The top and bottom need to be carefully prepared to suit the width of the drawer system.

Again it is a good idea to clamp the pieces together to ensure accuracy.

The holes can be drilled into the ends of the top and bottom to match the holes in the end panels. Plastic edging will need to be applied to the front edges only.

When the holes are drilled the carcass can be assembled.

Before cutting the top and bottom to length construct the drawer system, and add 2 mm for clearance on to the length of the top and bottom. This will ensure easy operation of the drawers.

Once assembled check the fit of the drawers. If satisfactory the drawer fronts may be fitted. The drawer fronts overlap the front edge of the carcass, and also act as a stop.

No back is required as the modesty panel will perform this task when completely assembled.

Top of Desk

The top is made of manufactured board, 18 mm thick, covered in vinyl, and screwed directly to the spreader rails from underneath.

Final Assembly

The cabinet can now be fitted to the initial assembly. Clamp it in position under the spreader rails and mark their position. Remove the cabinet from the desk and drill four screw holes through the top of the cabinet. The cabinet can now be clamped back in position while it is screwed on to the rails. When the cabinet is in position, fix the modesty panel. The final task is to fit the top, which is attached to the spreader rails, by four screws.

WORKING DRAWING FOR DESIGN 6

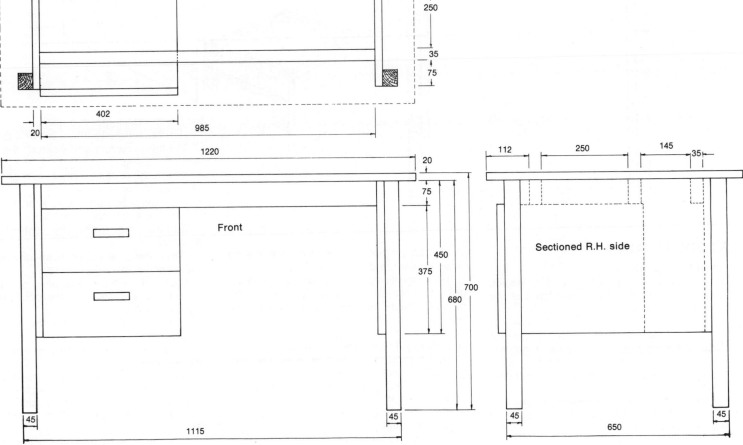

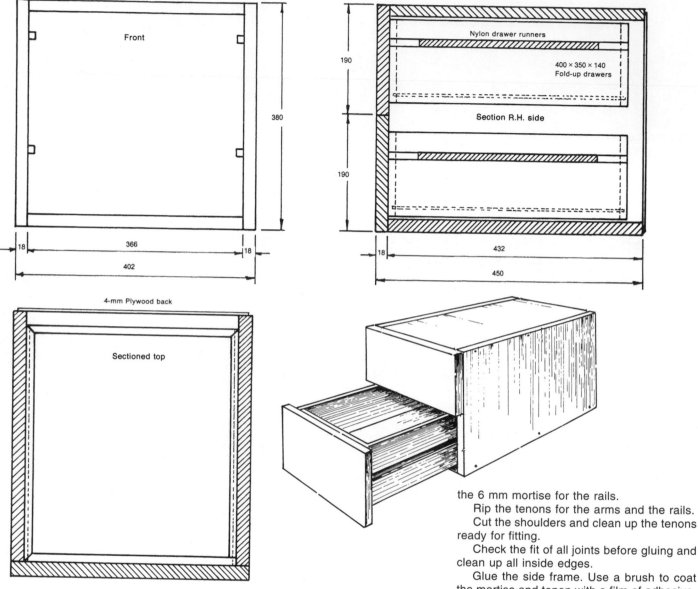

Front

380

18 | 366 | 18

402

4-mm Plywood back

Sectioned top

Nylon drawer runners

400 × 350 × 140
Fold-up drawers

Section R.H. side

190

190

18 | 432

450

STUDY CHAIR

Timber Preparation

Cut and plane the back legs to the finished length and plane the taper on the top. Drill the holes for the backrest.

Mark the front legs to length but plane only one end. Leave a horn on the top. This will be planed off when the frame is glued together.

Cut the arms to length, including tenons.

Cut the side rails to length, including tenons.

Cut the front and back rails to length.

Joint Preparation (see Mortise and Tenon Joints)

Clamp the legs together and mark the position of the mortises.

Use an arm or rail to determine the width when marking out.

Use a mortise gauge, taking care to gauge from the face, and mark the position of the mortise. Shade the waste. Don't forget there will be a right- and a left-hand arm.

Clamp the arms together and mark the shoulder for the tenons. Use a knife line.

Use a mortise gauge and mark the position of the tenon (see Joints).

Clamp the side rails together and mark the shoulder length.

Use a mortise gauge and mark the position of the tenon.

Mortise the legs (see section on Joints). Cut the 13 mm mortise for the arms first, then the 6 mm mortise for the rails.

Rip the tenons for the arms and the rails.

Cut the shoulders and clean up the tenons ready for fitting.

Check the fit of all joints before gluing and clean up all inside edges.

Glue the side frame. Use a brush to coat the mortise and tenon with a film of adhesive.

Square the frame by checking the diagonals.

When the glue is set, flush off the joints and clean up the side frames.

Mark out for the dowel joints on the front and back rails and transfer the locations to the legs (see Joints).

Use a dowel jig and drill the holes (see Dowel Joints).

Glue the dowels into the rails and remove excess glue.

Spread the glue evenly into the dowels on the legs and clamp the chair together.

Prepare the four corner blocks and glue and screw them in position. Remove the clamps.

Flush up all joints and clean up the chair with abrasive paper ready for surface finishing.

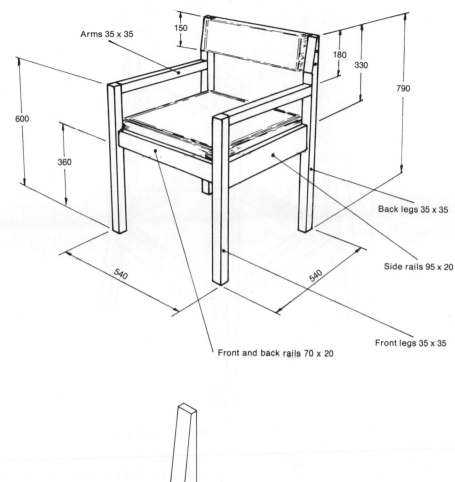

Arms 35 x 35

150

180

330

790

600

360

540

540

Back legs 35 x 35

Side rails 95 x 20

Front and back rails 70 x 20

Front legs 35 x 35

Seat

The seat consists of a seat base made of 20 mm particle board and a piece of 50 mm foam covered with vinyl.

Prepare the seat base to the size indicated.

Drill the air holes in the base.

Cut the foam slightly larger than the seat base.

Prepare the seat back in the same way.

Sewing the Seat Covers

Mark out the vinyl as indicated on the back side.

Hold the corners together and along the line from the edge to the corner. Double stitch at the ends.

Trim the corners.

Fold the cover so that the good side is on the outside.

Place the foam and base into the cover.

Fold the corners neatly and staple or tack the cover to the underside of the base.

In the case of the back rest, a plywood panel is cut and neatly finished with rounded corners and fixed to the back rest with nickel-plated raised head screws and cup washers.

The back rest is attached to the chair using nickel-plated raised-head screws and cup washers screwed into the manufactured board base.

The seat simply fits between the rails and rests on the corner brackets.

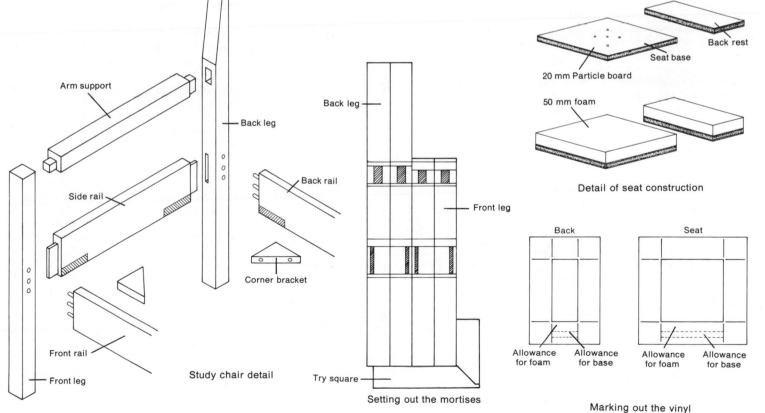

Arm support

Back leg

Side rail

Back rail

Back leg

Front leg

Corner bracket

Front rail

Front leg

Study chair detail

Try square

Setting out the mortises

Back rest

Seat base

20 mm Particle board

50 mm foam

Detail of seat construction

Back

Seat

Allowance for foam

Allowance for base

Allowance for foam

Allowance for base

Marking out the vinyl

181

Project 4

STOOLS

The following designs of stools not only illustrate the various uses for stools but also show a variety of simple construction methods. Associated with the making of stools is the need for upholstery skills. While these techniques may appear difficult, the application of a few simple procedures makes upholstering both simple and rewarding, be the material leather, fabric, or vinyl.

Top rail

Legs 35 mm square tapered on the inside edges to 25 mm square

Intermediate rail

Bottom rail

Leg

BAR STOOL

Procedure for Design 1

This project will provide some interesting setting out as the legs of the stool are tapered. This means that the shoulders on the rails are not square, and all angles must be taken from the rod, using a sliding bevel.

It is essential to draw an accurate full-size working drawing, or rod, on a sheet of ply. This will enable the angles to be accurately transferred.

The legs should be prepared so that they are square in the first instance. Mark the face and face edge. This face will be the outside edge. Taper the inside of the legs only.

Don't try to angle the top and bottom of the legs at this stage. This can be done when the stool is assembled.

Clamp the legs together and set out the position of the rails. *Mark one set of bottom rails only*. The position of top rails can be marked on each piece, and on both inside edges.

Be sure to square from the face or face edge.
Set out and cut the mortises.
Prepare the timber for the top rails.
Mark the shoulder angles and lengths from the rod.
Set out the tenon using a mortise gauge.
Rip the tenon and check the fit.

Drill the screw holes.

Prepare the timber for the bottom rails.

Mark the shoulder length and angles from the rod.

Set out the tenons.

Rip the tenons and check the fit.

The two frames may now be assembled. Clean up the inside of the frames before gluing. Wipe off all excess glue.

Don't try to glue the stool together as a single unit.

It is best to assemble two separate end frames and then join the frames with the intermediate and top rails.

When the glue is dry, clamp the end frames together and mark the position of the intermediate rail.

Remove the clamps and square the lines on the inside edges of the frames.

Use a mortise gauge and mark the mortise.

Mortise the legs.

Mark the shoulder length and angles from the rod on the intermediate rails.

Gauge the position of the tenon.

Rip the tenon and check the fit.

Clean up all inside edges before assembly.

Carefully brush glue into the mortises and on the tenons and assemble the stool.

Clamp the stool together and wipe off all excess glue.

When the glue is set, flush off the top of the legs.

Stand the stool on a flat surface and mark

a line around the bottom of the legs.

Remove the waste with a saw and clean up with a plane, taking care not to split the timber (see Planing End Grain). Remove the sharp edge around the bottom with a piece of abrasive paper.

Assemble the seat (refer to study chair) to the dimensions indicated.

Clamping the stool

Using a templet to drill airholes in the seat base

Mark the position of the intermediate rails on the two assembled frames

Top rail

Leg

Bottom rail

The end frame, mortised and ready for final assembly

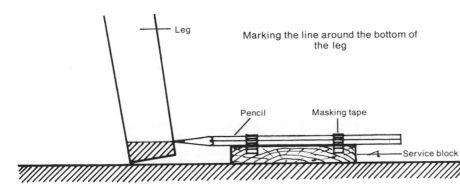

Leg

Marking the line around the bottom of the leg

Pencil

Masking tape

Service block

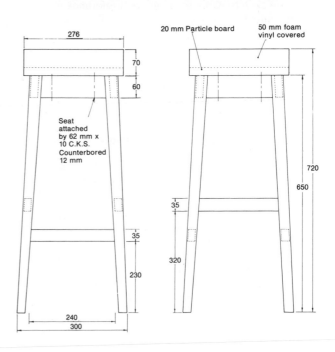

276

70

60

Seat attached by 62 mm x 10 C.K.S. Counterbored 12 mm

20 mm Particle board

50 mm foam vinyl covered

720

650

35

35

230

320

240

300

Procedure for Design 2

This easily constructed, yet most aesthetic bar stool is designed around assembly aids: in particular, cross dowels, guide dowels, threaded bolts, and brass heads. With the aid of a few boring jigs it is a simple procedure to construct a set of six or more stools to complement any bar setting.

Legs

Using the desired 35 x 35 P.A.R. timber stock, mark out and cut the four legs. Square the bottom end of each leg using a smoothing plane, clamp all four legs together and square the other ends to length. It is good practice to cut the ends with a knife when squaring to length to ensure a good finish from the plane.

Lay out the legs in pairs and clamp (see sketch) ready for the marking out of the positions of top rails and lower rails.

From the top end, square a pencil line across the legs down the width of the top rails. While still clamped in this position, mark the position down from the top end of the bottom rails and square two lines across.

Re-clamp the legs to mark the second set (see sketch) and repeat the marking out process as before, except the position of the bottom rails will be slightly higher.

Rails

The four top rails should be marked out, cut, and planed square to length from 45 x 35 P.A.R. timber stock. Similarly, the four lower rails should be marked out, cut, and planed square to length but from 35 x 35 P.A.R. timber stock.

Marking Assembly Aid Positions

The ends of the top rails need to have their assembly aid positions marked out in pairs (see sketch). Consequently, with reference to manufacturer's specifications, mark out the positions for the holes to accept the dowel guides and threaded bolts in each end of the top rails. Note that these positions must be offset in each pair of rails to enable the bolts to clear each other in each leg.

The ends of the four lower rails are similarly marked out except there is no requirement for offsetting.

The top rails and lower rails should now be clamped together with the underneath sides uppermost. Two lines should then be squared across 20 mm from each end to indicate the position of the cross dowel. To positively locate this position in each rail a centre line should be drawn across each of these rails (see sketch).

One pair of top rails should now have their assembly aid positions transferred to one set of leg pairs. Similarly the other pair of top rails should have their assembly aid positions transferred to the second set of leg pairs (see sketch).

Each pair of lower rail markings are likewise transferred to the appropriate set of leg pairs.

Drilling the Assembly Aid Holes

Clamping all legs securely, drill holes to the required depth to accept the shanks of the sixteen brass heads. Using the appropriate drill and again clamping the legs securely, drill all the holes for the threaded bolts. These holes are in the same position as the shank holes and pass through the leg. Using the same drill and with the rails clamped firmly in a vertical position, drill all holes in the rails for the threaded bolts, to the required depth.

Reference to the manufacturer's specifications will provide details as to the drill sizes and depths required for the holes in the legs and rails for the guide dowels and bushes.

Lastly, on the underneath side of all rails, drill the required size holes to the appropriate depths to accommodate the cross dowels.

Assembly

Locate and secure all the guide dowels and bushes in the rails and legs respectively.

Attach all the threaded bolts to the cross dowels in the top and bottom rails. This is best achieved by using one of the heads screwed to the threaded bolts to allow for easy rotation of the bolt into the cross dowels.

Attach the appropriate two legs, top rail and lower rail and lock up in position using the brass heads.

Repeat this process for the other two legs, top rail and lower rail.

Complete the frame assembly by joining these two assembled frames with the remaining two top rails and lower rails.

Check the frame assembly for squareness and adjust if necessary, by releasing the brass heads, re-aligning the rails, and re-tightening the brass heads.

Cleaning and Finishing

Having checked that the frames have pulled up squarely and all rails are meeting the legs neatly, the stool frame can be dismantled and each individual component sanded all around, using 240-grit abrasive paper. The bottom end of each leg should be chamfered to prevent splintering if the stool has occasion to be dragged over the floor. The stool frame should then be re-assembled, each joint again checked for flushness of fit and all arris removed.

Two or three coats of a suitable clear finish, preferably applied by spraying, should be sufficient to provide protection and a pleasing appearance.

Seat

The seat base may be adequately provided for by using 18 mm-thick manufactured board cut to slightly overhang the outside dimensions of the stool frame. Using the base as a template, cut a piece of 50 mm or 75 mm high density foam, 3 mm larger all around than the base.

Making the allowances as shown in the working drawing, cut out the desired material for the seat covering. Stitch along the edges shown using an ordinary household sewing machine—reversing the stitch further aids in holding the material together.

Fit the seat cover over the foam and base board and staple to the underneath as shown in the sketch. Neatly cover the underneath of the seat by stapling the calico, set 10 mm back from all edges.

Secure the seat to the top rails by one screw centrally located in each of the rails.

Note: Refer to the section on knockdown fittings for details of assembly aids—bolts and guide dowels.

Traditional joints, such as mortise and tenon or dowel joints may also be used. See section on furniture construction.

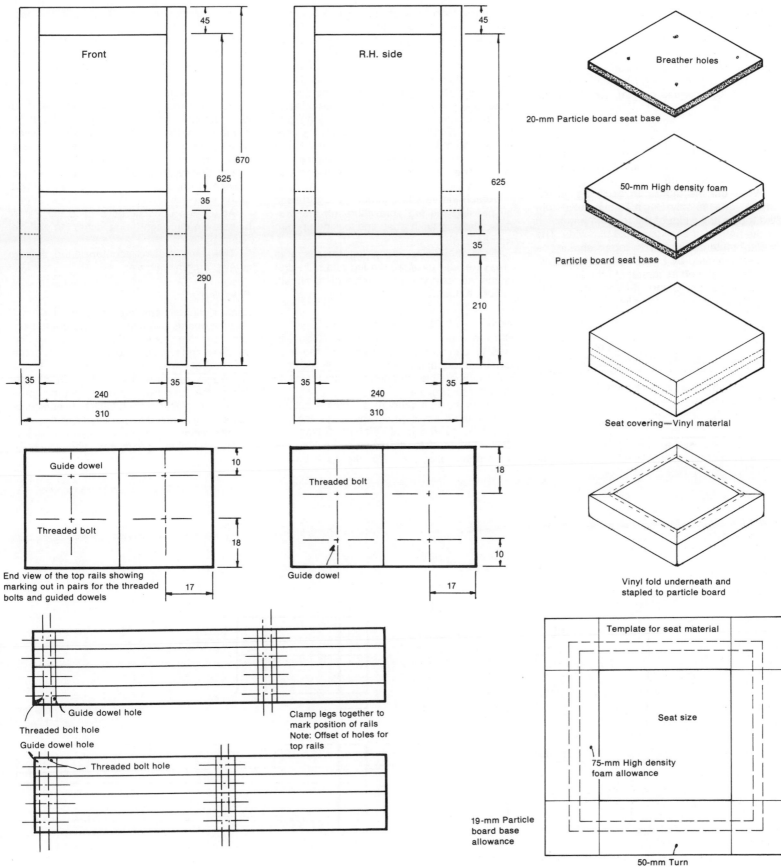

Front

R.H. side

Breather holes

20-mm Particle board seat base

50-mm High density foam

Particle board seat base

Seat covering—Vinyl material

Vinyl fold underneath and stapled to particle board

Guide dowel

Threaded bolt

End view of the top rails showing marking out in pairs for the threaded bolts and guided dowels

Threaded bolt

Guide dowel

Guide dowel hole

Threaded bolt hole

Guide dowel hole

Threaded bolt hole

Clamp legs together to mark position of rails
Note: Offset of holes for top rails

Template for seat material

Seat size

75-mm High density foam allowance

19-mm Particle board base allowance

50-mm Turn under allowance

185

PIANO STOOL

Procedure for Design 1

In this design the seat appears to be a fixture, but the attachment of two butt hinges to the seat base and a plywood bottom under the rails quickly provides a most useful storage area.

Legs

Using 45 x 45 P.A.R. timber stock of the desired species, mark out and cut the four legs to the required length.

Mark out the tapers on each leg on the inside surfaces only. Begin 70 mm down from the top (or the width of the top rail) and finish at the bottom of each leg at 25 mm wide. The waste material on each taper should be quickly removed by a hand saw or bandsaw and finally planed accurately to the line.

Note that tapers should only occur on the two inside surfaces of any leg.

Rails

Again using P.A.R. timber stock of the appropriate size and species mark out and cut the four rails. The two long rails may be placed together and the ends squared to length. Similarly, the short rails.

Assembly

Since it is intended to use leg trusses to hold the legs and rails together, it is necessary for a full-size plan view of one leg meeting two rails. This enables the positions of the trenches in which the leg trusses sit to be determined and consequently measured.

These trenches are marked on all four rails and cut using either a power saw or hand saw. Attach the rails together by screwing the leg trusses in position on the ends of each rail.

The position of the leg screw in the leg is then determined and a hole, equal to the core of the diameter of the wood thread section of the leg screw, is drilled to an appropriate depth. The leg screw are then screwed into each leg.

Attach the legs to each of the leg trusses by passing the leg screw through the pre-drilled hole in each truss and locking up with a metal nut.

Note that when fitting leg trusses it is always easier to offset the leg and rail—that is, the face surfaces of the leg and rail should never be flush.

Seat

Cut out a raw-particle board panel equal in size to the outside dimensions of the legs forming the piano stool frame. Drill six centrally located holes through the panel to allow the seat to 'breathe'.

Using the seat panel as a template cut out a piece of 50 mm high density foam—leaving a 3 mm overhang all around. Select the desired material for the covering, making the appropriate allowances for the base board, foam, and overlap and cut out (see the section on the bar stool).

If the material is to be pulled down tight, as illustrated in this design, begin stapling from the centre of the edges and work towards each corner. Finally, work each corner until all material is secured.

For best results the seat should be held firmly upside down by means of a 'holdfast' clamp, so that when released, the foam, being under pressure, helps to remove any wrinkles in the material.

For that really 'professional' finish, staple a piece of white calico to cover the underside of the seat—set back 10 mm from the edge.

Attach the upholstered seat to the frame by screwing through the rails into the particle board base.

This may require counter-boring if long screws are unavailable.

Finishing

Each of the rails and legs should be individually cleaned up, working from 180-grit to 240-grit abrasive paper. All arris should be removed and sanding should occur only in the direction of the grain. Using a suitable finish, the frame, either assembled or in pieces, should be given two or three coats by spray gun or brush. A light scuff back between coats helps remove any dust particles and provides a better finish.

Re-assemble if in pieces, and screw on seat.

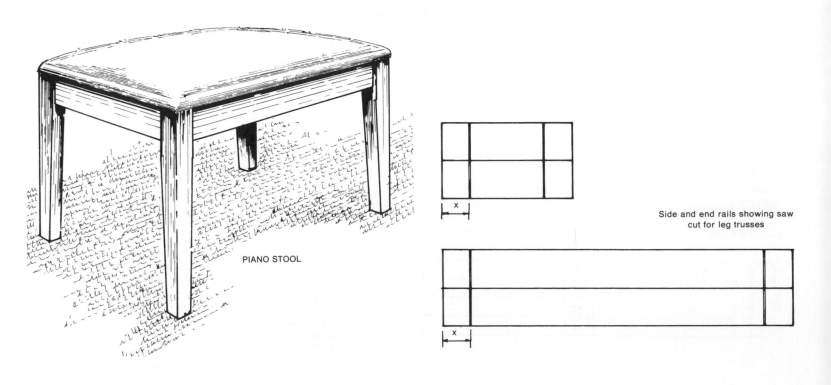

PIANO STOOL

Side and end rails showing saw cut for leg trusses

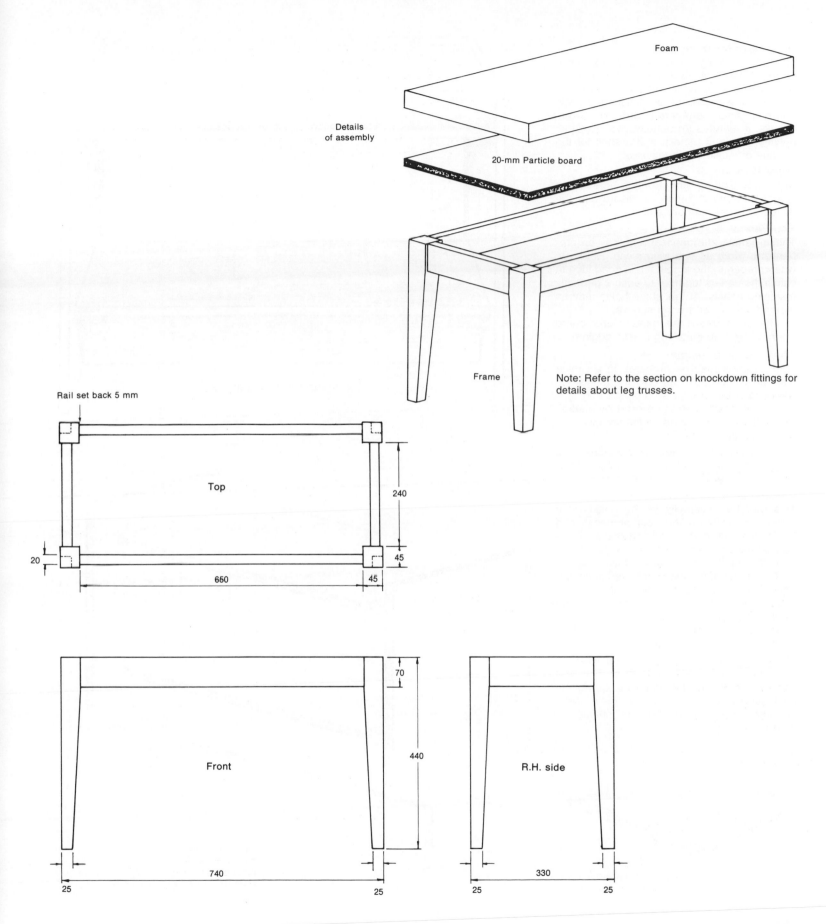

Foam

Details
of assembly

20-mm Particle board

Frame

Note: Refer to the section on knockdown fittings for
details about leg trusses.

Rail set back 5 mm

Top

240

20

45

650

45

70

Front

440

R.H. side

740

330

25

25

25

25

Procedure for Design 2

The stool is designed specifically to be used while playing a piano or organ, though obviously it may be used for other purposes.

It is constructed of pre-finished particle board panels connected with easy-to-fit screws. It features an upholstered top, fitted between the end panels, and a shelf for the storage of music or magazines.

Initial Planning

Before beginning construction check the height of piano or organ to ensure that the dimensions set out here suit.

End Panels

These panels are identical and may be prepared to width as one long piece. However, when preparing the length it is a good idea to clamp the panels together to ensure perfectly matching panels. At this stage holes may be marked and drilled for the screws.

The raw edges of the manufactured board are covered with matching plastic edging.

Shelf and Seat Support

These panels may be prepared in a similar manner to the ends, but only the long edge will need to be covered with plastic edging.

The ends will need to be carefully marked and drilled to accommodate the screws.

Shelf Support

This panel is the same length as the shelf and will give the stool stability, so it must be cut accurately to ensure a good fit.

Assembly

This can be accomplished by holding the panels vertically on the floor or bench and butting the ends of the shelf and seat supports against the end panels, so that the pre-drilled holes line up.

The screws can then be inserted and tightened. Before finally tightening the screws check for squareness. The appearance can be improved by covering the screw heads with plastic snap-caps.

Seat

The method of constructing the seat is set out in detail in the project study chair. The seat can be secured to the frame by drilling the seat support and fitting wood screws from underneath. About four screws should be sufficient.

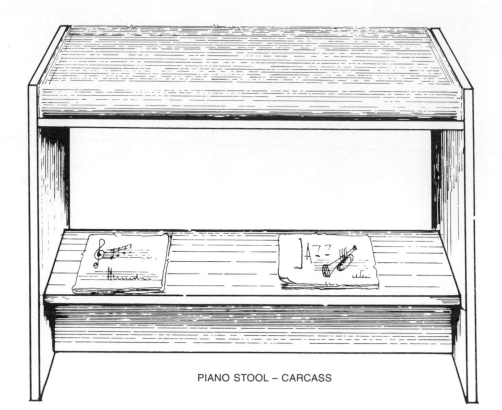

PIANO STOOL – CARCASS

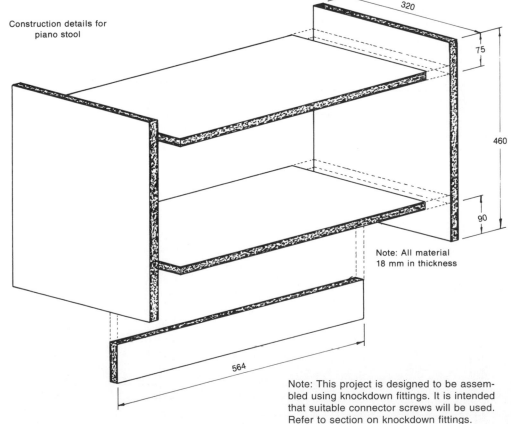

Construction details for piano stool

320

75

460

90

Note: All material 18 mm in thickness

564

Note: This project is designed to be assembled using knockdown fittings. It is intended that suitable connector screws will be used. Refer to section on knockdown fittings.

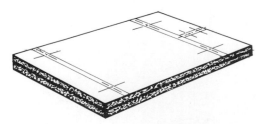

Layout for the position of the holes on the side panels

FOOT STOOL

Procedure for Design 1

Although the design of this foot stool may be termed 'rustic', the addition of a cushion, held on by tapes underneath each slat, would provide for more enhancing lines.

Vertical Supports

From the appropriate P.A.R. timber stock mark out and cut two sections to serve as the vertical support pieces for the seat slats. Clamp these two pieces together and plane the ends square to the required length.

Horizontal Slats

From similar P.A.R. timber stock, although smaller in section than the vertical supports, mark out and cut three pieces to act as the horizontal members. These three pieces may be clamped together and planed square to length, or treated individually.

Assembly

Mark out on the horizontal slats and as indicated on the sketches, the positions for the screw holes. Note the two outside slat markings differ from those on the centre slat due to the overhang on each side of the foot stool. Drill all the holes in the horizontal slats to provide clearance for 8-gauge screws.

Locate each horizontal slat in position over the vertical supports and attach by screwing. If the timber stock chosen is a pored timber then it is good practice to drill a pilot hole into the vertical support before inserting the screws.

Finishing

All components of the foot stool should be individually sanded and all arris removed, using 180-grit to 240-grit abrasive paper. Particular attention should be given to the end grain of all members. Secure all members together and spray or brush two or three coats of a suitable finish over the whole of the assembled foot stool. Scuff back lightly between each coat.

Cushion

For those wishing to make the foot stool appear a little more inviting or perhaps double as a seat, a small cushion may be made with similar dimensions to the top area of the foot stool. Reference to the bar stool and study chair will provide the necessary details for the cushion construction.

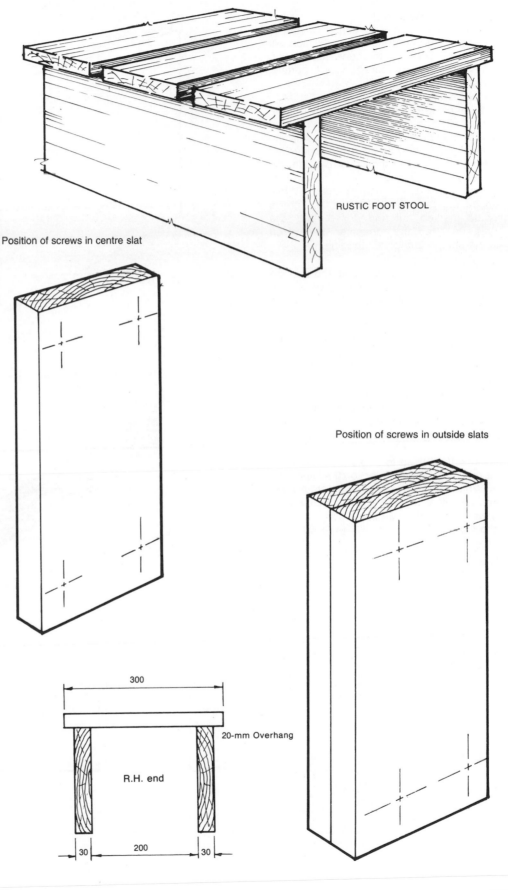

RUSTIC FOOT STOOL

Position of screws in centre slat

Position of screws in outside slats

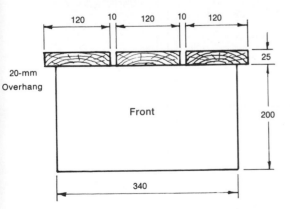

Front — 120, 10, 120, 10, 120 / 25 / 20-mm Overhang / 200 / 340

R.H. end — 300 / 20-mm Overhang / 30, 200, 30

189

Procedure for Design 2

This little stool is easy to construct and is designed so that an upholstered cushion will fit into the recessed top. It is constructed using pre-finished, manufactured board panels, connected with screws.

Vertical Panels

These panels are identical. They may be prepared initially by cutting a strip to the indicated width from a larger sheet. From this strip the individual panels may be prepared. Once they are cut from the strip they may be clamped together while squaring the ends. This practice will ensure identical panels. While clamped together, the holes for the screws may be marked out and drilled. With the panels separated, the edges can be covered with the appropriate plastic edging.

Horizontal Panels

These panels are also identical and may be prepared similarly to the vertical panels. The corners of these panels are visible, so it is suggested that the raw edges of the manufactured board be covered with plastic edging. Once the panels are edged they could be carefully marked out and the holes drilled to accommodate the screws.

Assembly

The assembly of this project simply requires that the vertical panels be screwed to the horizontal panels. Once the screws are tightened, plastic caps may be used to cover the screw heads.

The method used to make the seat cushion is described in the project on the telephone seat. When making the seat for this stool, however, make sure there is adequate clearance to enable the seat to fit between the four vertical panels.

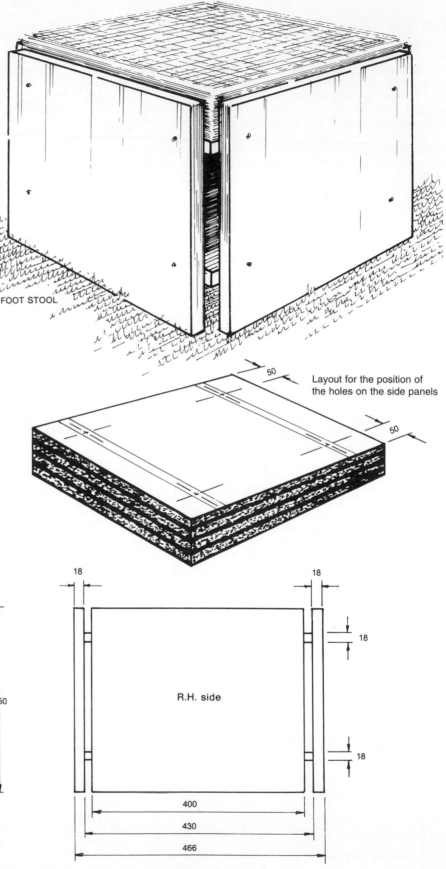

FOOT STOOL

Layout for the position of the holes on the side panels

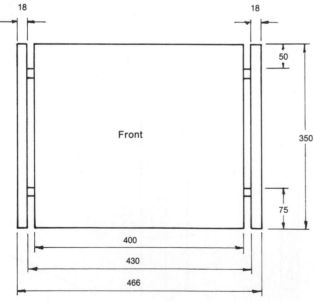

Front
50
350
75
18
18
400
430
466

R.H. side
18
18
18
18
400
430
466

Note: This project is designed to be assembled using knockdown fittings. It is intended that suitable connector screws be used. Refer to the section on knockdown fittings.

190

Project 5

BAR & WINE STORAGE

This design is a free standing unit, intended for serving drinks, and the storage of glasses and bottles. Pre-finished manufactured board is used in its construction with panels being connected with screws.

It is strongly recommended that a working rod be prepared for this project, so that sizes of the various panels may be determined accurately.

Procedure

Ends

These panels could be prepared initially. It is recommended that they are clamped together while they are squared to length and width in order to ensure identical panels. The position of the top, bottom, and shelves could also be set out, and the position of the holes marked and drilled to receive the screws. The edges could be trimmed with the appropriate edging. If a wood-grain pattern is used it is suggested that the end panels be oriented so that the grain is in a vertical direction.

Top

The top is made of 18 mm manufactured board covered with vinyl. It is first prepared to the length and width indicated. To give the appearance of a thicker edge along the front, a strip of timber 40 mm x 32 mm is glued to the front edge as indicated. The front and back edges of the top are rounded.

It is suggested that the vinyl top is glued to the top, but be sure to smooth out all air bubbles to ensure a nice flat surface. If desired the vinyl can simply be stapled or tacked along the undersides of the top. This will also give a satisfactory finish to the bar top. The holes can also be carefully aligned and drilled to receive the screws.

Foot Rest

While working with vinyl it would probably be a good idea to cover the foot rest. This is readily made from a piece of solid timber 42 mm x 35 mm with a radius planed on the corners. 12 mm foam plastic could be wrapped around this piece and stapled underneath. Vinyl could then be stretched around the foot rest. This would then match the top.

Front Panel

This panel is of pre-finished board with three additional smaller panels arranged evenly and screwed to the front.

The panel must be prepared carefully, as much will depend on the accuracy of this panel. The holes on the ends will need to be carefully aligned and drilled. In addition the position of the middle and bottom shelf and division will need to be marked and holes drilled for the screws.

The 'plant on' panels can be clamped together and prepared to ensure identical sizes. The edges of these panels can be trimmed with the appropriate plastic edging. It is also suggested that if wood-grain patterns are used that the grain be oriented in a vertical direction on all pieces making up the front panel. The small panels can be attached to the larger panel with countersunk-head wood screws from the inside of the front panel.

Middle and Bottom Shelf

These panels are identical, and may be clamped together to prepare the length and width, and to drill the holes for the division. The holes along the back edges will need to be carefully aligned with the holes in the front panel and drilled accurately to receive the screws. The holes in the ends will need to be aligned from the end panels.

Division

This vertical panel is the same width as those previously mentioned and fitting between them. When the panel has been carefully prepared to width and thickness, the holes in the end can be aligned and drilled. The position of the small shelves can be carefully marked and the holes marked and drilled.

Small Shelves

These three panels are identical and can be clamped together to prepare length and width. The 5 mm holes can be carefully aligned and drilled to receive the screws.

Kickboard

This piece can be made of pre-finished board and screwed to the bottom shelf using counter-sunk-head wood-screws and plastic snap-caps to cover the screw heads. The ends are fixed to the end panels with connector screws.

Assembly

It is suggested the middle and bottom shelves be joined initially to form a sub-assembly. The kickboard can also be fitted to the bottom shelf.

The front panel can then be fixed to this subassembly. At this stage be sure all of the ends are flush. If satisfactory the end panels can be fixed. The top can be placed on this and fixed into position.

Now locate and fix the small shelves, and then all that remains is to fit the foot rest.

Make sure all visible edges have been trimmed with the appropriate edging, cover the connector screws with the plastic caps and the bar is ready for use.

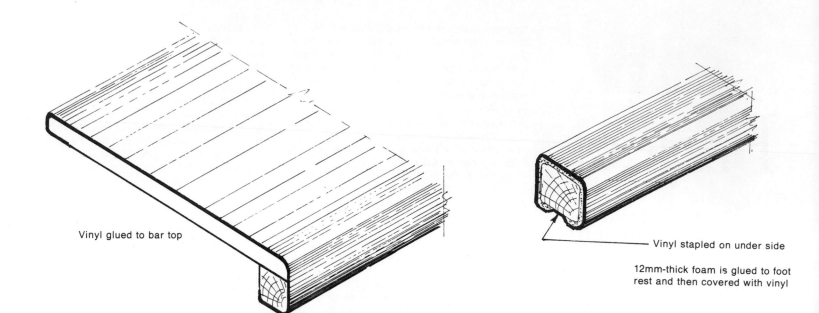

Vinyl glued to bar top

Vinyl stapled on under side

12mm-thick foam is glued to foot rest and then covered with vinyl

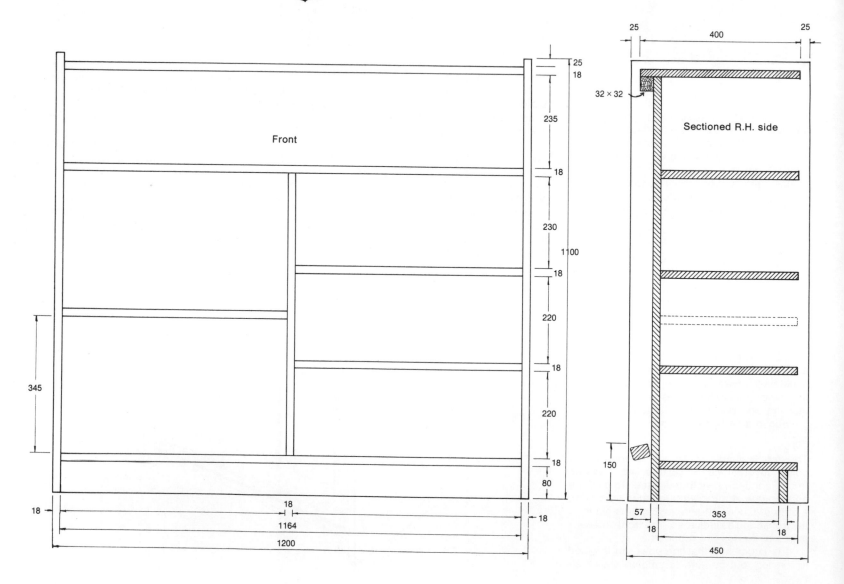

Front

1100

345

25

18

235

18

230

18

220

18

220

18

80

18

1164

1200

18

18

25

400

25

32 × 32

Sectioned R.H. side

150

57

18

353

18

450

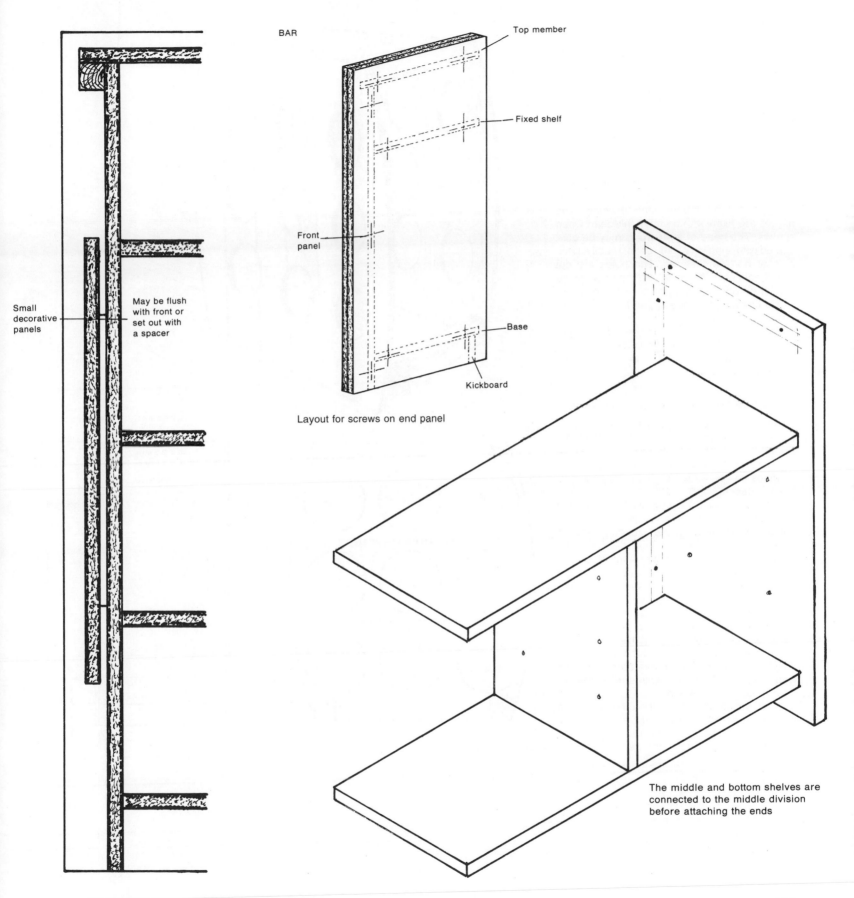

BAR

Top member

Fixed shelf

Front panel

Small decorative panels

May be flush with front or set out with a spacer

Base

Kickboard

Layout for screws on end panel

The middle and bottom shelves are connected to the middle division before attaching the ends

193

WINE STORAGE

The units illustrated are intended to be used for the storage of bottles. The designs incorporate the use of a variety of materials, and feature easy-to-construct methods.

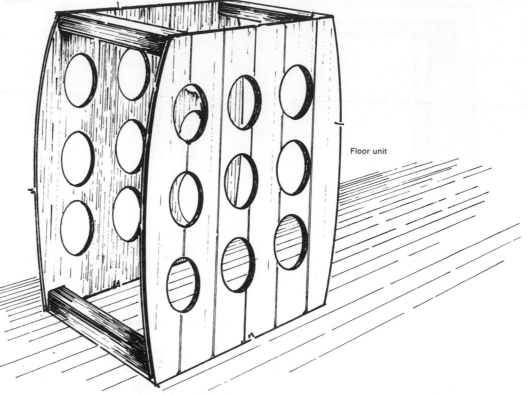

Floor unit

Procedure for Design 1—Floor Unit

The first design consists of two pre-finished plywood panels joined by solid timber sections as indicated on the working drawing. The panels are fixed with countersink-head wood screws. The head of the screws may be concealed with snap-on plastic caps, readily available at hardware stores. The holes are cut with a hole saw. When cutting the holes make sure the panel is clamped to a flat piece of waste timber, good side up, and select a slow speed on the portable drill.

If offcuts of pre-finished plywood wall panelling are available they would be quite suitable and quite decorative if random grooved pieces are used.

Procedure for Design 2—Modular Unit

This modular wine storage system is intended to be constructed from a solid timber like Radiata pine. It is designed as a stackable unit, and would be ideal in a cellar. Additional modules can be added as the number of bottles increases.

The ends could be prepared initially. It is suggested that a number of pieces could be placed together and the trenches cut to accommodate the rails. The trenches could be cut by hand or using a router as illustrated.

The rails would best be shaped by using a hole saw fitted to a drill press or a portable drill mounted in a drill stand. The holes can initially be cut in a board 150 mm wide. After the holes have been cut the board can be sawn down the centre to form the rails for one module. A radius would need to be formed on the corners as indicated, this could be done with a file and cleaned up with abrasive paper prior to surface finishing.

To complete the rails a trench needs to be cut near the ends to locate it on to the ends. Once again it would be desirable to place a number together to form the trench.

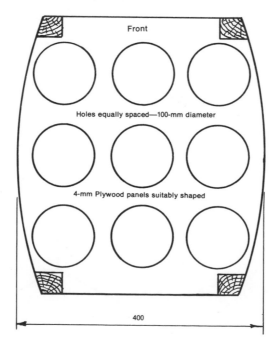

Front

Holes equally spaced—100-mm diameter

4-mm Plywood panels suitably shaped

400

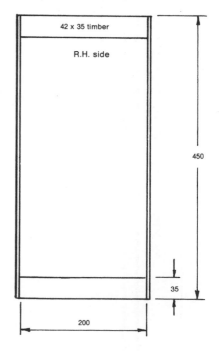

42 x 35 timber

R.H. side

450

35

200

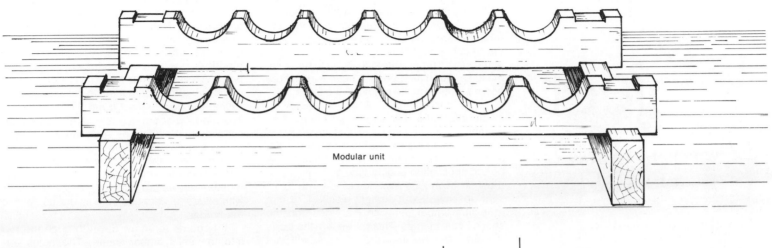

Modular unit

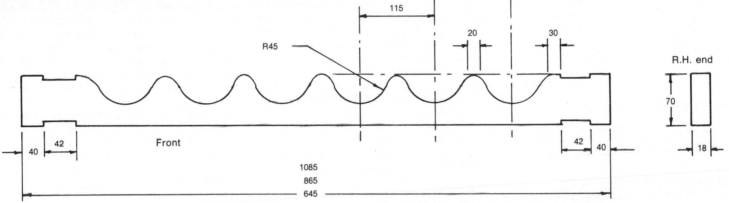

R45

115

20

30

R.H. end

70

Front

40   42

42   40

18

1085
865
645

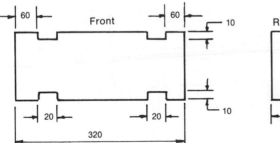

60   Front   60

10

R.H. end

90

20   20

40

10

320

Modular unit

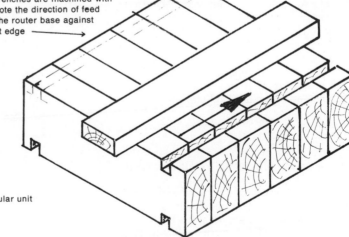

Ends can be clamped together
while the trenches are machined with
a router. Note the direction of feed
and keep the router base against
the straight edge

Rails can be shaped by using a hole
saw. After the hole is cut, the board
can be sawn down the centre to form
the rails for one module

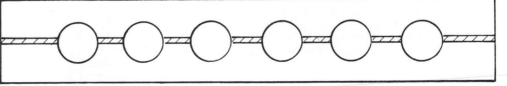

Project 6

POOL TABLE & ACCESSORIES

POOL TABLE

The billiard table has become increasingly popular in the home, and building your own table is not difficult and will provide many hours of interesting work in construction and many more hours of entertainment when complete.

The table consists of a top, covered with felt and supported by an underframe, designed to give rigidity and stability to the top. Four solid legs bolted to the underframe provide support for the table. Adjustable feet are bolted to the legs to provide ease of levelling.

The cushion blocks are screwed to the cushion sides, which are screwed to the sides and ends of the table.

There are no complicated joints, but the result is a table of professional appearance and outstanding rigidity and stability.

Procedure

The Top

The top is made of 32 mm particle board. This thickness will provide a relatively stable surface.

Templets for the centre and corner pockets are made from pieces of 4 mm ply. The templets are used to mark out the shape of the pockets. A portable jig saw is used to cut the shape, care being taken to cut approximately 6 mm away from the line to allow for a taper.

The pockets are tapered, using a half-round file or a surform tool.

Radius the top edge of the pocket to about 6 mm. Clean up the top and edges carefully with abrasive paper.

Underframe

Pair off the sides and ends and pair off the intermediate bearers.

Clamp the sides together and mark out the housing joints (see the section on joints) and rebates. Clamp them flat on the bench and cut the trenches and rebates.

Mark out and groove the sides to accommodate the leg support members. Tongue the leg support member to fit the groove in the sides.

Eight bar clamps will be necessary to clamp the frame. The use of nails is not recommended as they spoil the final appearance.

It is best to clamp the frame together dry and check the joints and the squareness before application of glue. The glue should be brushed evenly on each joint.

If possible use a straight piece of 75 mm x 50 mm timber between the sides and the shoes of the clamps. This will ensure the sides remain straight and the clamps will not damage the surface. Check for squareness by checking the diagonals. If out of square the clamps may be adjusted to bring it back into square. (Again see the section on joints.)

Glue-blocks about 100 mm x 30 mm x 30 mm may be added to each corner. These will improve the rigidity of the frame. Remove all the excess with a damp cloth. The clamp must not be removed until the glue is set.

The top of the frame must be perfectly flat to receive the top. A long straight edge is used to check the work. If planing must be done it is best to use a long soled plane such as a No. 6 or No. 7. Do not use a smoothing plane.

The rebate joints may be flushed up with a sharp smoothing plane, and the outside of the frame cleaned up with abrasive paper ready for surface finishing.

If required, a bead may be added around the bottom of the frame, as a form of decoration. Various sections are available and can be purchased from most joinery or handyman stores. The bead, depending on the profile, may be glued and clamped to the side or glued and bradded to the bottom. While the frame is in this position drill the 13 mm holes for the leg support to receive the bolt attached on the legs.

Fitting the Top to the Frame

The particle-board top could of course be screwed to the frame by screwing through the frame and into the particle board. While this may look neat, the holding power of screws is not as good in particle board as in solid timber and the screws are likely to pull out or loosen with seasonal changes in moisture content of the timber.

It is better to screw down through the top into the solid timber frame. The holes are easily stopped with a plastic filler, which can be flushed off perfectly, having no effect at all on the playing surface. Place the top upside down on the bench and place the frame on top. Locate the frame centrally on the top and mark its position on to the top.

Remove the frame and mark the position of the screw holes with six screws along the side, and three along each end and centre member. Holes should be equally spaced. Drill the holes to accommodate 10 g screws.

When the holes are drilled turn the top over and countersink the holes so that the screw is well below the surface. The top is then located on the frame ready for fixing.

Clamp the top firmly to the frame and drill a thread hole (see the section on screws).

The screws are best fitted with a ratchet screwdriver. A little lubrication on the thread is also desirable. With the screws fitted the holes must be stopped with a plastic filler, and sanded level. Care must be taken to ensure a flat surface. At this stage it is a good idea to apply a sealer to the top.

Legs

The legs are constructed of solid timber, tapered on all four sides. The decorative moulding at the bottom is made separately and screwed to the bottom of the leg.

The flutes are optional and are machined on the sides using a portable router, and a special jig. A metal plate on to which a 12 mm bolt is welded is screwed to the top of the leg. This method provides ease of fitting as well as rigidity. Special plastic fittings are used at the bottom of the leg for an adjustable foot. The legs are first dressed perfectly square and planed accurately to length.

The legs may now be tapered by the amount indicated. If a planer-jointer or a portable electric planer is available this process will be easy. The taper may, however, be planed by hand. It may take a little longer, but the finished job will be just as good. The legs may be fluted using a special jig and a portable electric router. The legs then must be cleaned up with abrasive paper before fitting the decorative piece to the bottom.

The decorative piece on the bottom of the legs is rounded on all four edges. This is best done by planing a small chamfer along each edge and sanding with abrasive paper. Take care to finish along the grain to remove any scratches.

Drill and countersink the piece for 2/25 mm x 10 mm. Countersink head screws and glue and screw the piece on the bottom of the leg. The bottom of the leg may now be drilled to receive the plastic fitting. These are press-fitted in an 18 mm hole. The adjustable feet will screw into these fittings. Screw the metal fitting to the top of the leg and clean up ready for surface finishing.

Cushion Blocks

The cushion block ends are shaped as shown in the drawings and a rubber moulding is glued into a rebate locating its position. Once the glue is set the cushions are shaped to a special templet, designed to fit the centre and end pockets. (See the drawings for templet layout.)

Dress the timber to the required dimensions.

Plane a rebate along the top edge. This will locate and accommodate the rubber cushion. Cut the ends of the blocks to 45° and simply blend a radius on the corner as shown.

Glue the rubber in position using contact cement. When the glue is set the rubber may be shaped to the templet. It may be necessary to trim the rubber with a sharp knife before final shaping. A sanding disc, orbital

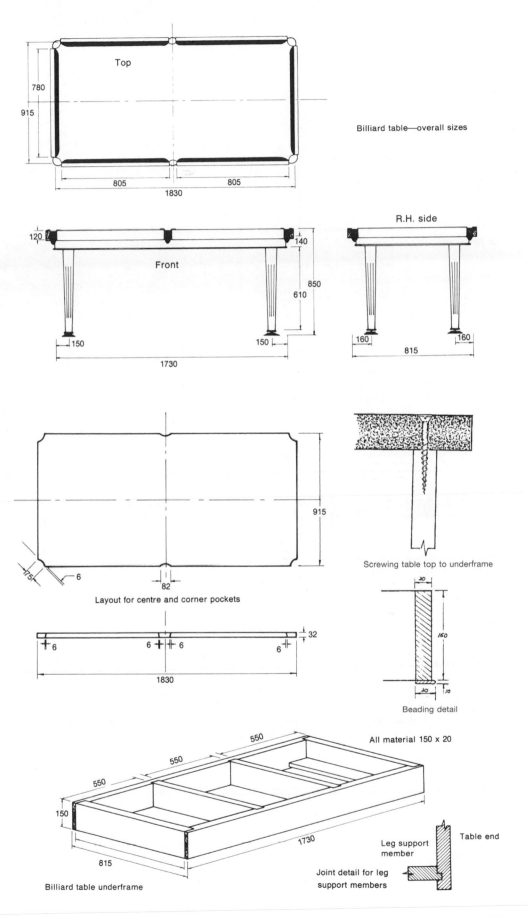

Billiard table—overall sizes

R.H. side

Front

Layout for centre and corner pockets

Screwing table top to underframe

Beading detail

All material 150 x 20

Billiard table underframe

Leg support member

Table end

Joint detail for leg support members

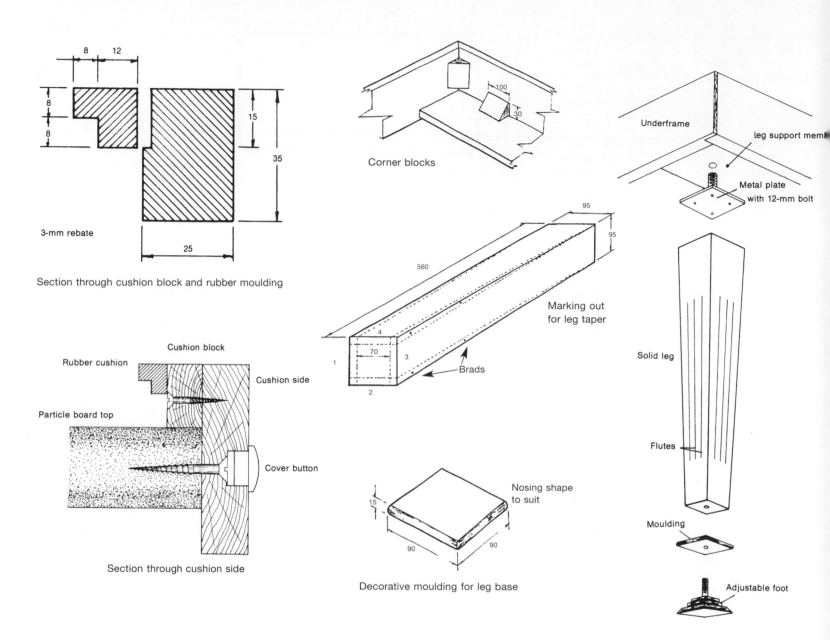

8 12

8

8

15

35

25

3-mm rebate

Section through cushion block and rubber moulding

Corner blocks

100

30

Rubber cushion

Cushion block

Particle board top

Cushion side

Cover button

Section through cushion side

560

95

95

4

70

3

1

2

Brads

Marking out
for leg taper

15

90

90

Nosing shape
to suit

Decorative moulding for leg base

Underframe

leg support mem

Metal plate
with 12-mm bolt

Solid leg

Flutes

Moulding

Adjustable foot

Detail of leg assembly

sander, or a file is satisfactory for this purpose.

Finally, clean up carefully, leaving all surfaces smooth and ready for fitting the felt.

Cushion Sides

The cushion sides may be left plain or moulded on the edges. Dress the material accurately to size and plane a 15 mm chamfer on the ends as indicated. Screw the cushion blocks to the sides. Three screws should be sufficient.

Locate the sides and blocks on the table and mark out the screw holes. Four screws in each side and end will be required. This time it will be necessary to counterbore the

hole for the screws as the hole will be plugged with a button. Once the holes have been drilled remove the cushion blocks and clean up the sides ready for surface finishing.

Covering a Billiard Table

The cloth is laid out on the table with the nap side uppermost and running towards the 'spot' end. Adjust the cloth to have an even overhang on both sides and at each end. Beginning with the centre of the 'D' end, locate four staples through the cloth and into the underside of the top at approximately 75 mm spaces. Moving to the opposite end, pull the cloth as tight as possible and staple in a sim-

ilar manner as for the 'D' end. Moving to either of the centre pockets, the cloth is pulled across sufficiently to provide a reasonable overlap for stapling to the base frame. Stapling should occur only around the centre pocket.

At the opposite centre pocket, place the left hand in such a position to assist in the removal of any folds. Grip the cloth with the right hand and pull as tight as possible into the pocket recess.

Ensuring no folds have resulted, the left hand is manoeuvred over and under the centre pocket to hold the cloth in position while it is stapled to the underside of the top. Sufficient staples should be inserted around this pocket to prevent any tearing of the cloth.

Tight folds will now appear in a diamond shape along the table, but the inside centre of the centre pocket should be smooth. Working to the left of the centre pocket, stretch the cloth across and around the left side with a curving action until sufficient cloth appears for stapling.

Ensure all creases have been removed.

Repeat this process for the right side of the pocket.

Move to the other centre pocket, remove the initial staples and repeat the above operation, keeping in mind that the cloth must be pulled as tight as possible. Moving to either of the corner pockets at the 'D' end, grip the cloth in both hands and, flexing as tightly as possible, pull diagonally from the centre point. Maintaining this tension, staple the cloth to the underside of the top approximately 50 mm from the corner of the pocket and on the *end* of the table.

This process is repeated for the other side of the same pocket. Stapling occurs along the underside of the table.

The complete procedure is repeated for the pocket at the other end but on the same side of the table.

Moving to the opposite side of the table and again starting from the 'D' end, staple the cloth around the pockets as previously described. To stretch the cloth into each of the corner pockets, pull down over each pocket as tightly as possible, turn the cloth under, and staple it to the underside of the table. At this point the cloth should be tightly stretched over the table and around the pocket areas.

General fixing may now proceed, working from between any two pockets outwards.

After fitting the two end cushions the table is marked out as indicated in the chart.

Covering the Cushions

Lay the cloth over the cushion with the nap side uppermost and running from the 'D' end.

Staple the cloth to the centre of the back of the cushion. Pulling the cloth as tightly as possible from the centre, staple to within 50 mm of one end. Stretch the opposite side from the centre and staple in a similar manner.

It is essential that the cloth be stretched at this stage, almost to the point of tearing.

Screw the cushion to the cushion side. Lay it upside down and with the left hand pull the cloth tightly over and staple it centrally to the underside of the cushion. Working from one end and the centre, pull the cloth tightly over the cushion and staple it.

Repeat this process for the other side of the cushion.

Neatly fold each end of the cloth under and, using upholstery pins, fix to the ends of the cushion sides.

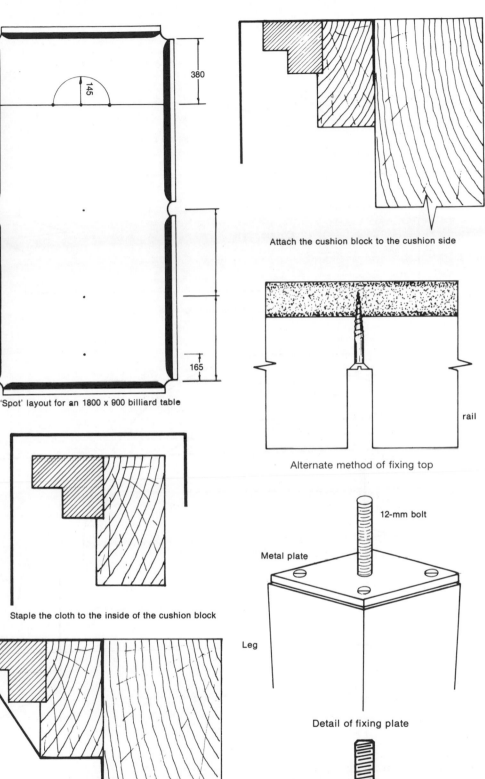

'Spot' layout for an 1800 x 900 billiard table

Staple the cloth to the inside of the cushion block

Staple the cloth to the back of the cushion block

Attach the cushion block to the cushion side

Alternate method of fixing top

rail

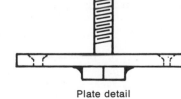

Detail of fixing plate

12-mm bolt

Metal plate

Leg

Plate detail

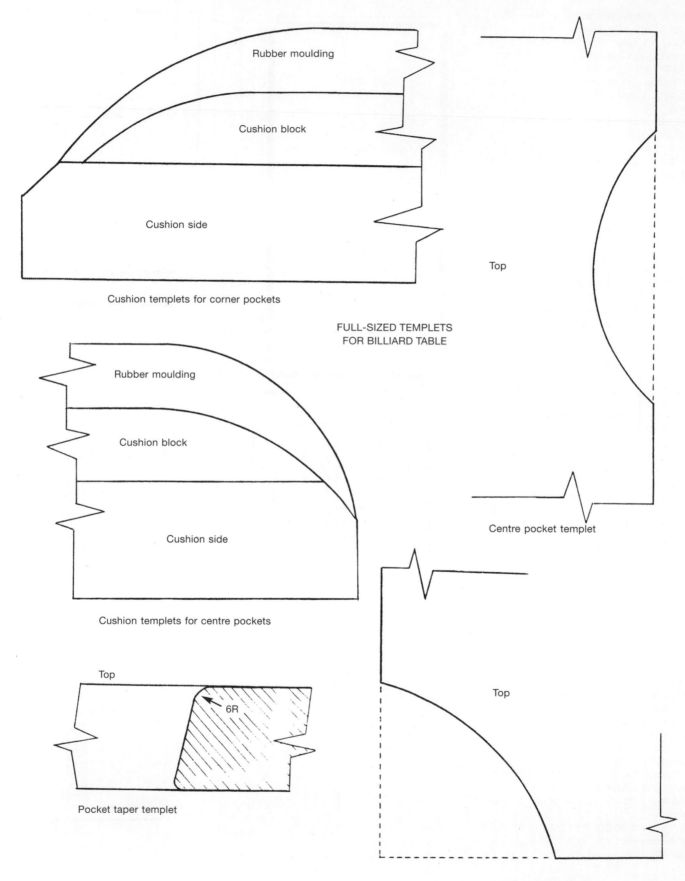

Rubber moulding

Cushion block

Cushion side

Cushion templets for corner pockets

FULL-SIZED TEMPLETS
FOR BILLIARD TABLE

Rubber moulding

Cushion block

Cushion side

Cushion templets for centre pockets

Top

6R

Pocket taper templet

Top

Centre pocket templet

Top

Corner pocket templet

SCORE BOARD

This simple project is intended to be wall-mounted. It is constructed using a piece of pre-finished 18 mm manufactured board, preferably a wood-grain pattern, with a matching timber frame. The holes are drilled to two-thirds the depth of the board, and the markers are different coloured golf tees. The numbers can be applied easily and will look very professional by using a readily available transfer lettering system.

Procedure

The board is firstly squared to length and width. Care must be taken to ensure the edges are square with the face. The holes can be carefully marked and it is a good idea to lightly centre punch the holes. This will ensure the drill doesn't 'run'.

To drill accurate holes it is suggested that a drill stand be used, rather than using the portable drill freehand. However, whatever method is used a suitable stop will need to be utilized.

The holes for wall mounting can also be drilled. It is recommended that countersunk wood screws are used here with 'Hettich' plastic snap-caps to conceal the screw heads.

The illustration indicates that the board is framed. This is easily achieved by using a piece of flat material 25 mm x 6 mm or similar. However, the board would look effective with the raw edges of the manufactured board covered with appropriate plastic edging. If the board is to be framed, a mitre box will be needed to prepare the corner joints. It is suggested that the two long edges be fitted initially and the end piece carefully fitted between them, making sure of a good joint. The framing material can be easily fixed using P.V.A. glue and three 20 mm beads along the long edges and two along the short edges.

The timber used for the frame will need to be surface-finished. To match the pre-finished board it may need to be stained. Two coats of clear surface finish carefully applied to the framing material should prove adequate.

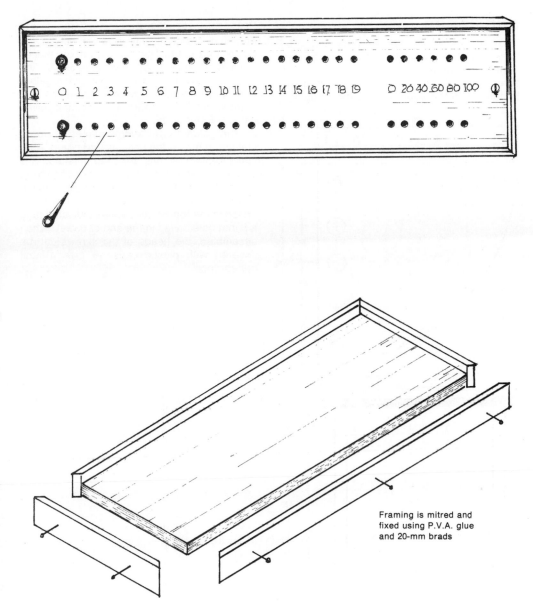

Framing is mitred and fixed using P.V.A. glue and 20-mm brads

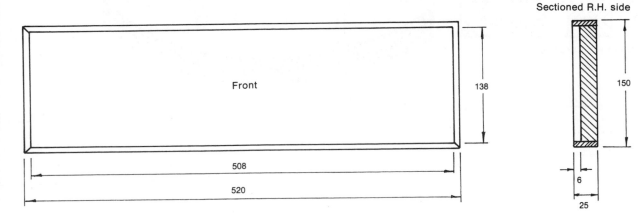

Front

138

508

520

Sectioned R.H. side

150

6

25

CUE RACKS

The two racks illustrated are designed to be constructed using pre-finished manufactured board, with components being connected with screws. All visible edges of the board are trimmed with the appropriate plastic edging.

Procedure for Design 1

The first design is intended for use in the corner of a room. The top and bottom pieces are a quarter circle. When shaping and drilling it is suggested that they are clamped together to ensure identical parts. The holes are marked out as indicated and are best drilled using a Forstner bit.

The columns are simply pieces of dowel stained to match the pre-finished board. After staining, the columns are clear finished. This process is explained in the chapter on finishing.

The top and bottom quadrants are attached to the columns with screws. The holes are drilled in the top and bottom as indicated, and a 5 mm hole drilled in the end of dowel. When assembled, the heads of the screws can be covered with plastic caps, to give a neat appearance.

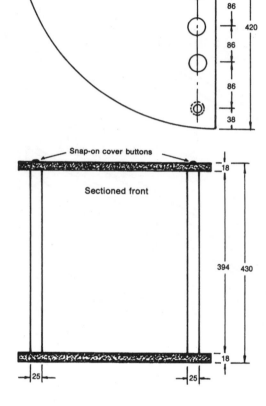

Top

Sectioned front

Snap-on cover buttons

Section through shelves to show depth of holes

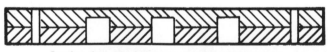

Clamp shelves together for marking out and drilling

Procedure for Design 2

The second design is intended as a wall rack. It can be free standing or if desired, mounted on a wall above floor level.

The ends can be prepared initially, taking care to clamp them together to ensure identical panels. The holes for the screws can also be marked and drilled. Visible edges can be trimmed with plastic edging.

The shelves can also be clamped together to ensure identical length and widths. While together the holes for the cues can be marked and drilled. An appropriate Forstner bit is ideal for this job. After drilling the holes the shelves must be separated and the holes in the top shelf cut out toward the front edge. This can be achieved with a fine toothed saw taking care to cut accurately and not to tear the surface of the pre-finished board. Once cleaned up with a file and abrasive paper, the slots can be trimmed with plastic edging. The front edges of the shelves can also be trimmed. To mark out the holes on the ends of the shelves for the screws, mark the centre line on the ends, and then place the end of shelf adjacent to the holes in the ends. The position can then be marked on the ends of the shelf from the existing holes, thus ensuring accurate location.

After accurate drilling of the holes in the ends of the shelves the unit can be assembled. No further surface-finishing is required.

If the rack is to be fixed to a wall, an aluminium angle section can be screwed to the underside of the top and bottom shelves at the back. This bracket can then be drilled to accept the appropriate masonry anchoring or screws, as indicated in the diagram.

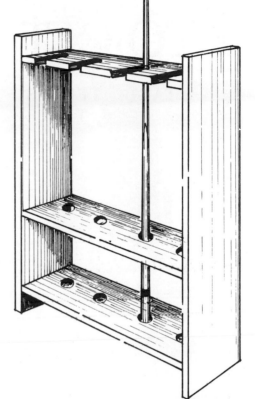

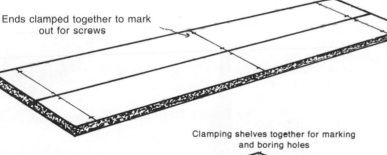

Ends clamped together to mark out for screws

Clamping shelves together for marking and boring holes

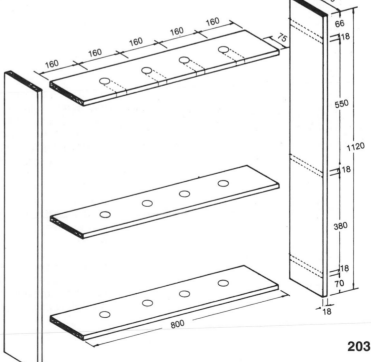

Holes for wall screws

Aluminium section screwed to underside of shelf to facilitate attachment to wall

203

Project 7

TABLE TENNIS TABLE

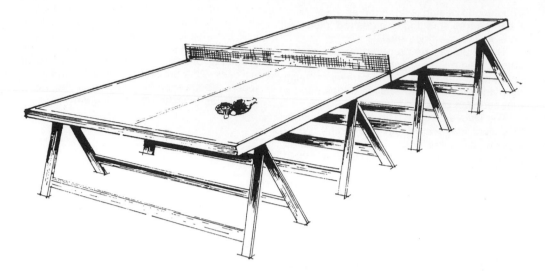

The top is constructed of 12 mm thick particle board. The boards are manufactured in 2700 mm x 1500 mm sheets especially for table tennis tables.

The sheet is initially cut in halves, making two equal 1500 mm x 1370 mm pieces. This is primarily to facilitate storage and for ease of handling.

The particle board top is edged with 42 mm x 19 mm Radiata pine framing material, mitred in the corners for neatness. It may also be desirable to glue two pieces of 42 mm x 19 mm, on the flat, equally spaced on the underside to provide additional support.

The frame may be nailed or screwed and glued from the top. Holes should be stopped with a plastic putty and sanded back to a smooth surface.

There are many ways of fastening the two halves together to form a playing surface. They may be hinged, but the combined weight of the two pieces is considerable and is difficult for one person to handle when assembling or storing the table.

It is preferable to bolt the pieces together using wing nuts, or make or purchase catches that screw to the side of the table to hold the two halves together while in use.

The top will need at least three, preferably four, trestles for support. These may be easily and quickly constructed using 42 mm x 19 mm framing material.

Dowel joints provide probably the quickest and strongest method of construction.

It is best to cut all of the legs, and then all of the rails, to the exact length. Select the better faces and apply face marks.

Set out each frame as indicated with the face marks up and face edges in.

The holes are marked on the ends of the rails and transferred to the legs (see dowel Joints). Number each joint.

When marking is complete use a dowel jig and drill the holes in the ends of rails and in the legs to approximately 30 mm deep, making sure the face of the dowel jig is held against the face of the timber in each case. This will ensure a flush fitting joint. Bevel the top of each hole with a countersinking bit held in a brace.

Edging the particle board top with framing material

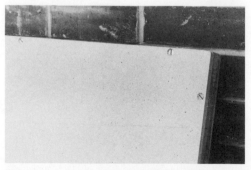

The framing material is screwed through the top and holes are stopped with plastic filler

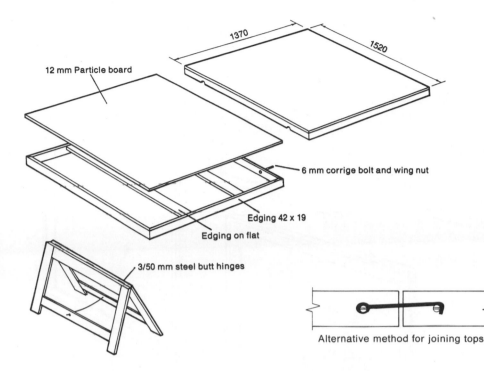

12 mm Particle board

1370

1520

6 mm corrige bolt and wing nut

Edging 42 x 19

Edging on flat

3/50 mm steel butt hinges

Alternative method for joining tops

frames, and screwing the hinge into position. A bradawl is best used to make a pilot hole for the screws.

So that the frame will not spread in use, a piece of 6 mm rope is threaded through the holes in the bottom rails and knotted at both ends.

The top is given two coats of dark green chalkboard paint. A white line 20 mm wide is painted around the perimeter of each top piece and a centreline is marked out carefully and painted also on each piece. Masking tape is ideal for providing straight lines while painting.

Method of attaching hinges

Cut the dowels 55 mm long and bevel the ends.

Drive the dowels into the ends of the rails and wipe off the excess glue.

Treat each frame individually and assemble the rails into the stiles. Use a bar clamp and pull up the joints. Check each frame for squareness and winding. Let the glue set and

remove the clamps.

The frames are flushed up with a smoothing plane and finally cleaned up with abrasive paper ready for hinging.

They are attached with two or three steel butt hinges. This is done by laying the frames on a flat surface, end to end, lining up the centre of the hinge with the joint line of the

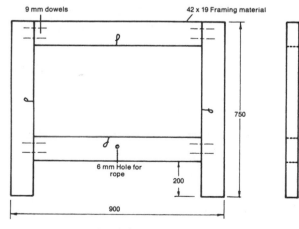

After painting is completed, the table is lined

Inserting the dowels into the rails

Checking the squareness of the assembled frame

Applying the adhesive to the stiles ready for assembly

The frames are flushed up with a smoothing plane

9 mm dowels

42 x 19 Framing material

750

6 mm Hole for rope

200

900

Trestle detail

Project 8

FRAMES & PELMETS

FRAMES

Good quality paintings and prints can add a good deal of interest to any room. There are many galleries around the country selling a wide range of styles, including landscapes, seascapes, and portraits. It is no secret, either, that framing is very expensive. It may be an advantage to buy the canvas or print and make the frame yourself.

There is a wide range of moulding, including pre-finished sections, available from handyman stores. Many manufacturers also market picture framing material in kits.

It is recommended that nailing be avoided as this tends to split the ends and even at best remains unsightly.

With modern adhesives such as P.V.A. it is possible to obtain an excellent bond on the end grain.

Special tools needed include a mitre box, a tenon saw, and a suitable clamp. Sophisticated mitre boxes may be purchased but they can be fairly expensive.

Procedure

Place the moulding on the mitre box and cut a mitre at one end.

Place the moulding on the picture to be framed, as indicated in the diagram, and measure back the width of the rebate on the right-hand edge.

With a mitre-set mark the 45° and cut the moulding. Make another piece exactly this length.

Repeat the process for the ends.

When all four corners are cut, there is no need to plane the ends. A sharp saw will produce a satisfactory cut. Lay the four pieces on the bench and check the fit of the corners.

Fit a web clamp around the frame and tighten the screw. If the joints are satisfactory the frame may be glued. Glue must be spread evenly on both surfaces and the excess removed with a damp cloth after clamping. When set, remove the web clamp.

The corners may now be strengthened with a small piece of veneer fitted into a saw cut made on the corner. Note the grain direction of veneer. Spread glue evenly on the veneer and in the saw cut.

When the glue is set the piece of veneer may be trimmed and the frame cleaned up with abrasive paper.

The frame may now be finished as desired.

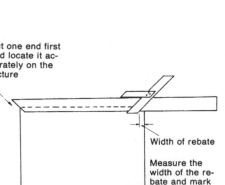

Cut one end first and locate it accurately on the picture

Width of rebate

Measure the width of the rebate and mark the angle

Marking out the length and the position of the mitre from the picture

206

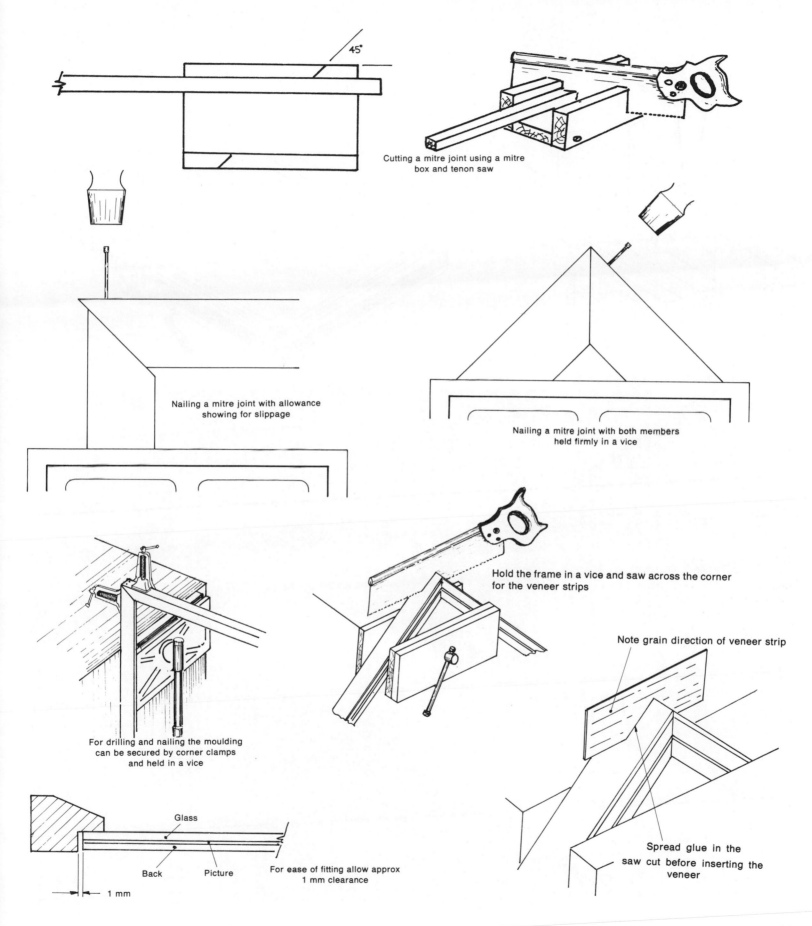

45°

Cutting a mitre joint using a mitre box and tenon saw

Nailing a mitre joint with allowance showing for slippage

Nailing a mitre joint with both members held firmly in a vice

For drilling and nailing the moulding can be secured by corner clamps and held in a vice

Hold the frame in a vice and saw across the corner for the veneer strips

Note grain direction of veneer strip

Spread glue in the saw cut before inserting the veneer

Glass

Back   Picture

For ease of fitting allow approx 1 mm clearance

1 mm

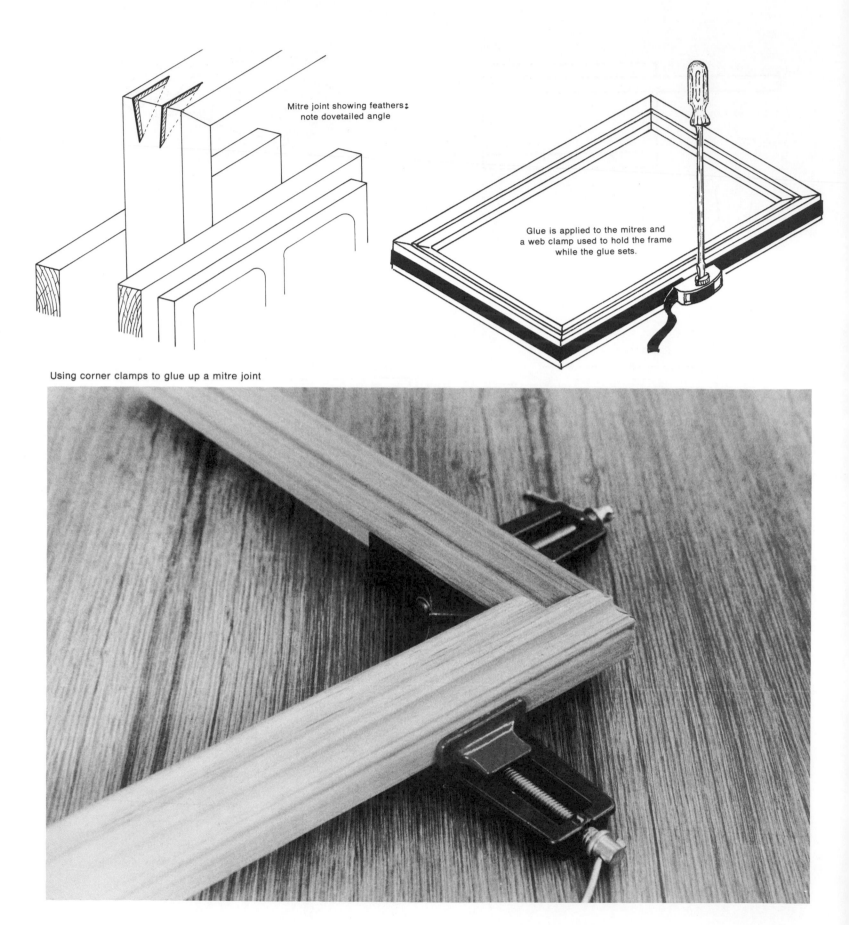

Mitre joint showing feathers:
note dovetailed angle

Glue is applied to the mitres and
a web clamp used to hold the frame
while the glue sets.

Using corner clamps to glue up a mitre joint

PELMET

Timber profiles can be readily obtained from timber suppliers and handyman stores for the construction of pelmets. Pelmets need to be well made as they usually have to support the weight of curtains which run on tracks installed in the pelmet. Pelmets can also be used to conceal lighting systems.

The pelmet described here is constructed of a solid timber profile.

The thickness of the material could vary from 12 mm to 18 mm and the width could also vary from between 100 mm to 150 mm or greater, depending on the size of the window opening and the effect required. In determining the length it is suggested that the pelmet overlap the window opening by at least 150 mm at each end.

Procedure for Design

The top of the pelmet is of 18 mm-thick material which will allow the fitting of curtain tracks. This member is carefully squared to length and width. Care is essential as the other members are fixed to this piece, and a good square piece here will ensure good fitting joints.

The front is then mitred to length, and fitted to the top. If the pelmet is to be painted the front could be nailed carefully into position with 35 mm round-head nails. If, however, a clear finish is desired, gluing and clamping would be sufficient.

When the front is fitted, the ends could be mitred and fixed. Care must be taken to apply glue to the mitre joint and to make sure it is correctly aligned, before driving in the nails.

Finishing

If the pelmet is to be clear-surface finished it is recommended that nail holes be stopped with a matching wood stop putty. Two or three coats of clear surface finish, with a light sanding between each coat, should be sufficient.

If the pelmet is to be painted it is suggested that an undercoat be applied initially. When dry, the surface could be lightly sanded, and the holes stopped. Two coats of pigmented finish could then be applied.

Installation

The installation procedure will depend upon many variables, including size of window, type of dwelling, etc. However, wherever the pelmet is going to be fixed to it will need to be fixed securely. If it is to be fixed to a masonry wall it is suggested that a wall plate be firmly screwed to the wall with masonry anchors. The pelmet will then fit over this wall plate and can be fixed securely to the plate with wood screws.

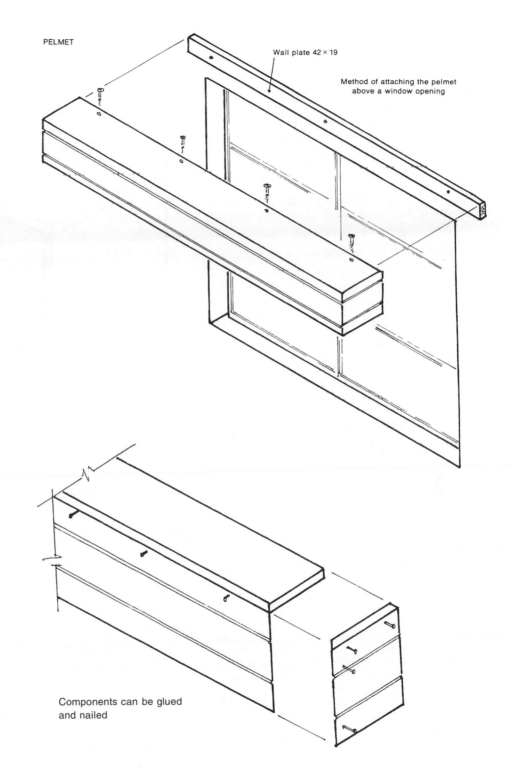

PELMET

Wall plate 42 × 19

Method of attaching the pelmet above a window opening

Components can be glued and nailed

Project

STORAGE

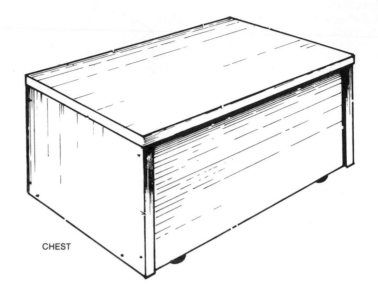

CHEST

CHEST

Procedure

This storage unit is constructed using pre-finished particle board with panels being connected with director screws.

Castors are fitted to the base to ensure ease of movement and the lid is fitted with an appropriate stay.

If a wood-grain pattern is used it is suggested that the grain be oriented in the horizontal direction on the end and side panels. The grain on the lid should run lengthways.

Ends

The ends can be prepared initially, and it is recommended that they be clamped together to ensure identical panels. After squaring to length and width the edge can be trimmed with the appropriate plastic edging.

In addition the position of the sides and bottom can be located and the holes for the connector screws marked and drilled.

Sides

The sides are also identical and could be clamped together to prepare length to width. In this case only the top and bottom of the panels need to be trimmed with plastic edging.

The 8 mm holes can be marked and drilled along the bottom of the sides while the thread holes must be carefully aligned with the holes in the end panels.

Bottom

This panel must be prepared carefully as much depends on the accuracy of this piece. The holes must be carefully aligned and drilled to ensure accurate fitting of the connector screws.

Assembly

It is desirable to screw the sides to the base initially. To this the ends can be attached. Make sure the edges around the top fit flush so that the lid will sit flat.

Lid

The lid overhangs the front and ends by some 10 mm but fits flush with the back. All of the edges are trimmed with plastic edging. Concealed hinges would be satisfactory for this function. They are easily fitted and adjusted, but manufacturer's instructions must be followed carefully if satisfactory results are to be achieved.

A continuous hinge would also be suitable. It would also be desirable to fit a stay to prevent the lid from being pushed back too far. Once again this sort of fitting is readily available, and manufacturer's instructions need to be carefully followed.

Castors

Castors are readily available in a wide range of styles and types. It is suggested that when selecting a set of castors the load likely to be placed in the chest is considered.

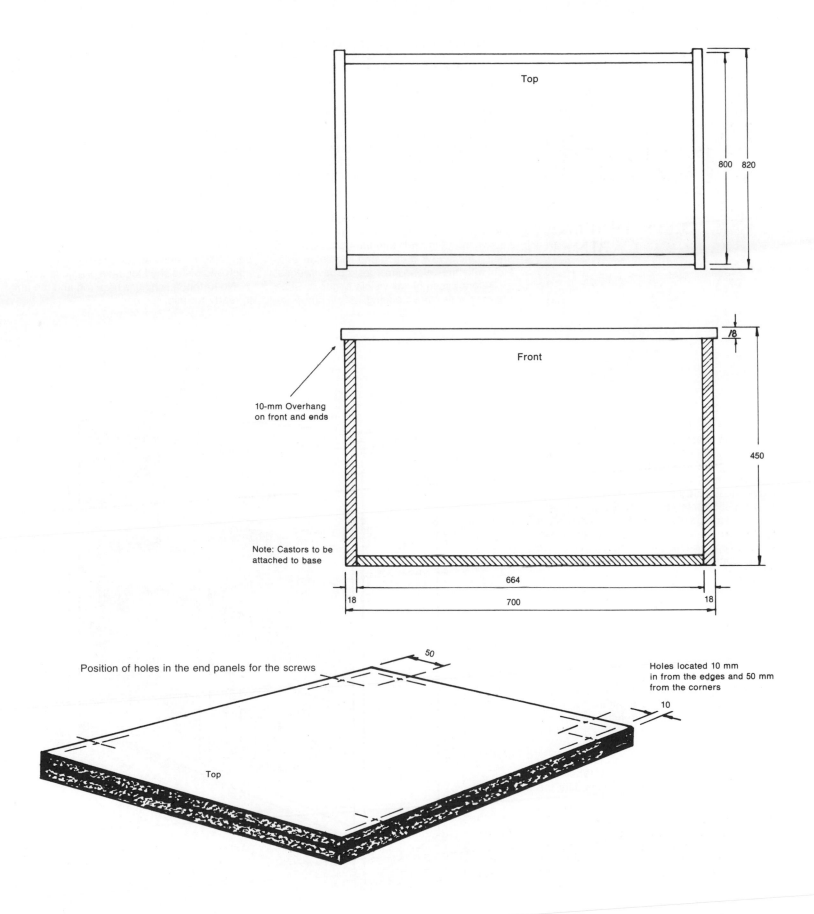

Top

800   820

Front

18

10-mm Overhang
on front and ends

450

Note: Castors to be
attached to base

18   664   700   18

Position of holes in the end panels for the screws

50

Holes located 10 mm
in from the edges and 50 mm
from the corners

10

Top

Project 10

OPEN DISPLAY CABINET

This versatile unit is constructed without a back and can be adapted for a number of purposes. It has adjustable shelves that can be arranged in a variety of positions. It would be suitable as a small room-divider in which articles of interest may be tastefully displayed. The cabinet could also be used against a wall for display purposes or for the storage of books, magazines, or other household artefacts. The unit is easy to construct using pre-finished manufactured board panels connected with screws.

Procedure

All of the panels are the same width. Pieces may be cut from a large sheet to the common width before marking out the various panels to length.

Ends

The ends could be prepared initially. The panels are best clamped together to ensure they remain identical while they are being squared to length. While together the holes for the screws may be carefully marked out and drilled.

Top and Bottom

These panels are identical and may be prepared in a similar way to the ends. When they are to length the holes to accommodate the screws can be marked and drilled.

Middle Division

This panel must be carefully cut to fit between the top and bottom. When square the holes may be drilled in the ends for the screws.

To accommodate the adjustable shelves holes need to be drilled for shelf supports.

These are brass fittings, generally manufactured to suit 6 mm holes. It is desirable to make a plywood template the same size as the middle division. The holes can then be set out and drilled in the required position in the plywood template. The template can then be clamped to one panel while the holes are drilled, and then transferred to another. This will ensure accurate positioning of the holes, essential if the shelves are to appear level. A drill stop will be required to ensure a hole of the correct depth and prevent damage to the panel.

Bottom Support Rails

These rails are of pre-finished board cut to fit under the bottom shelf. They are fixed with screws from the ends and through the bottom shelf. One screw in each end should be sufficient with three along the front and back edges.

Before assembly all visible edges must be trimmed with plastic edging.

Assembly

With the major panels complete, the unit may be assembled. This is best done by laying the panels on the floor and connecting the ends to the top and bottom. The middle division can then be fitted, followed by the support rails underneath the bottom shelf. Care must be taken to ensure that all edges are flush and that the cabinet is square before finally locking the screws. Plastic snap-caps can be used to conceal the screw heads.

Adjustable Shelves

These panels are the same width as the other components, but only the front and back edges need to be trimmed with plastic edging. It is also desirable to allow about 2 mm clearance on each end of the shelf for ease of adjustment.

No further finishing is required and the unit is ready for use.

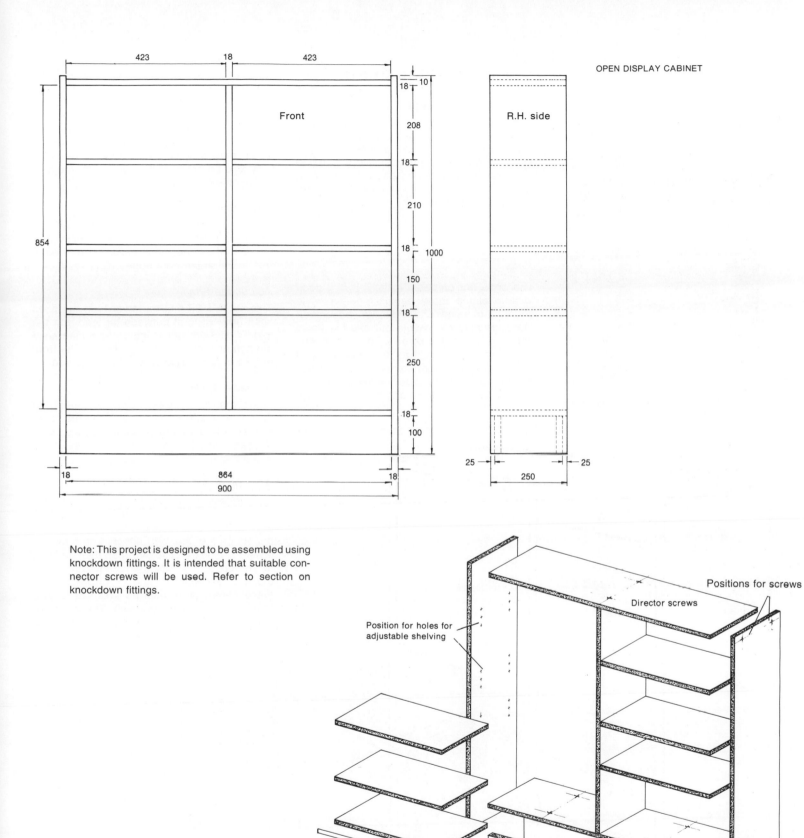

423   18   423

Front

854

18

900

864

18

18   10

18

208

18

210

18   1000

150

18

250

18

100

OPEN DISPLAY CABINET

R.H. side

25   250   25

Note: This project is designed to be assembled using knockdown fittings. It is intended that suitable connector screws will be used. Refer to section on knockdown fittings.

Positions for screws

Director screws

Position for holes for adjustable shelving

Veneer edge strip applied to all exposed edges

Positions for screws

Project 11

CHILD'S STORAGE UNIT

CHILD'S STORAGE UNIT

Procedure for Design 1

The unit illustrated is assembled using screws to connect carefully prepared panels. The panels are of pre-finished manufactured board edged with the appropriate plastic strip. It features seven drawers and a cabinet, ensuring ample storage. In addition a roll-out bin is provided, ideal for toys.

Procedure

Ends

The ends are prepared initially. It is a good idea to clamp these panels together while squaring to length and width. While together, the ends may be marked out and the holes drilled to accept the screws. The middle division is the same width as the ends but is 18 mm shorter. The front edges of these panels can be trimmed with plastic edging. It is also a good idea to mark out and drill the holes for the shelf supports to accommodate the adjustable shelf in the cabinet.

Top

The top is prepared to the sizes indicated and after edge treatment, the holes may be drilled in the ends to accept the screws. The holes may also be drilled in the centre for attaching the middle division.

Fixed Shelf

The fixed shelf is fitted between the end and the middle division. It must be carefully prepared to the dimensions indicated with edge treatment on the front edge.

Adjustable Shelf

This shelf is 25 mm narrower than the fixed shelf and cut to fit between the end and the middle division with at least 2 mm clearance at each end for ease of adjustment. The front edge can also be covered with plastic edging.

Spreader Rails

These members are of solid timber, prepared to the dimensions indicated. They are fitted with screws, so that holes can be accurately marked and drilled to match the holes in the end panels.

Assembly

It is suggested that once the above-mentioned members are prepared, the unit can be assembled. This is best done by laying the panels on the floor and attaching the middle division to the top. The ends can then be fitted to the top, and the fixed shelf fitted between the end and middle division. When assembling these panels care must be taken to ensure that the front edges are flush. The spreader rails at the bottom of the drawer space can also be fitted.

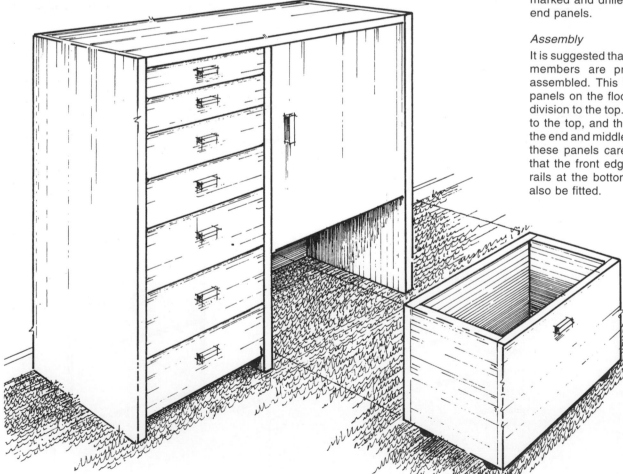

Back

The back is of 4 mm ply. The ply is attached using 20 mm flat-head nails about 75 mm apart. It is suggested that the edge of the ply is set back about 6 mm from the outside surfaces of the ends and top panels for appearance. The ply back will give the unit strength and rigidity and allow for easy fitting of the door and drawers.

Drawers

The drawers intended for use here are 'Hettich' mitred-drawer frames. Details of sizes, profiles, and assembly are clearly indicated in the chapter on joints and assembly aids.

After folding up and gluing, endure that the frame is square before attaching the front. The drawer fronts are cut to fit between the end and middle divisions and are screwed to the drawer frame from the inside.

If pre-finished board is used it will be necessary to trim the raw edges with plastic edging, however, solid timber may be preferred. If solid timber is used, ensure that the species selected matches the colour of the pre-finished board.

The drawer runners can be fitted to the inside surfaces of the unit. The drawer-frame system comes complete with detailed instructions for this procedure.

Door

It is intended that the door is made of pre-finished manufactured board prepared to the dimensions indicated, with plastic edging applied to all edges. The door is intended to be flush fitting. It is suggested that approximately 1 mm clearance be left all the way around to ensure adequate clearance. Concealed hinges are most appropriate for fitting this type of door; however, manufacturer's instructions must be carefully followed.

When the door is attached a magnetic catch could be fitted on the middle division

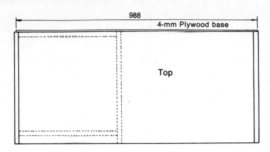

near the door handle. A suitable door handle may be purchased and screwed to the outside of the door in a position indicated by the sketch.

Roll-out Bin

This unit is designed to finish flush with the front of the cabinet. It is intended for the storage of toys and is mounted on castors for ease of movement. It is constructed of pre-finished manufactured board panels which are connected with screws. All visible edges are trimmed with plastic edging.

It is suggested that the ends, front, and back panels be prepared to width initially. The ends can then be squared to length. They are best clamped together to ensure identical panels. The front and back are prepared in the same way. After marking out and drilling for the screws, the panels may be connected. Once assembled the bottom can be marked to suit, and then cut and fitted. Castors are then fitted to the underneath side and the unit is ready for use.

Finishing

No further surface-finishing is required although, if desired, plastic snap-caps could be used to conceal the heads of the screws.

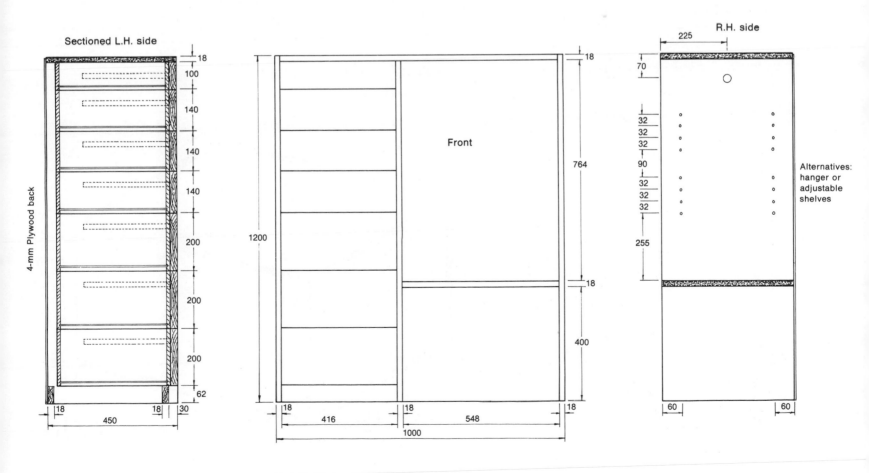

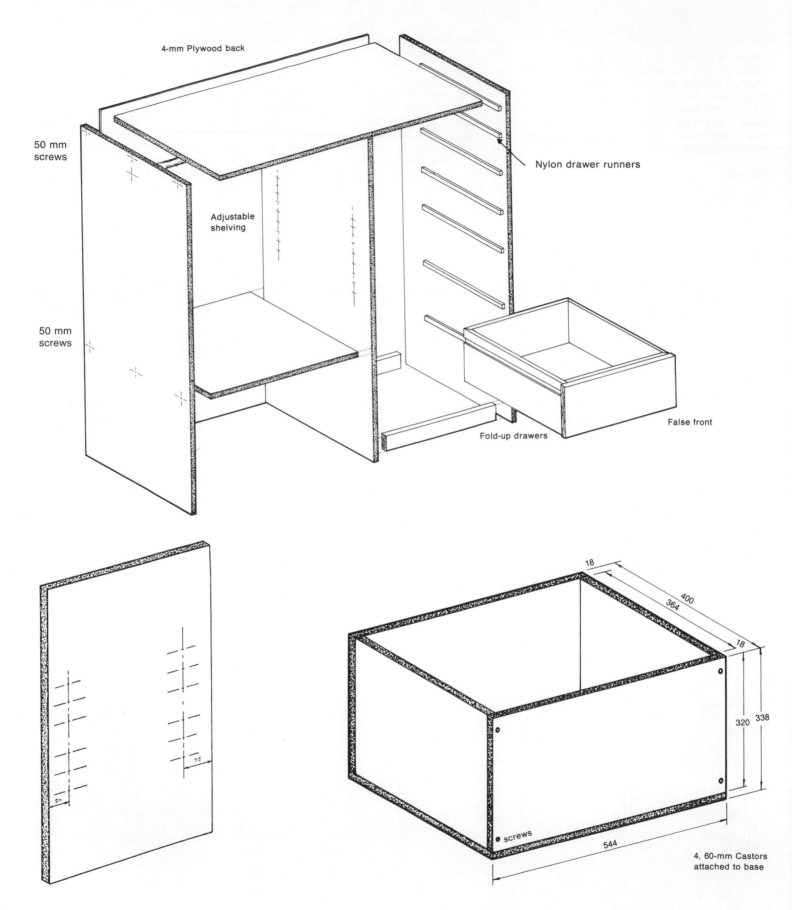

4-mm Plywood back

50 mm screws

50 mm screws

Adjustable shelving

Nylon drawer runners

Fold-up drawers

False front

18

400

364

18

320

338

544

75

5n

screws

4, 60-mm Castors attached to base

CHILD'S STORAGE UNITS

The individual modules are designed to be stacked into any desired arrangement and used in a variety of ways: as storage systems, room dividers, or book shelves.

Procedure for Design 2

The modules are intended to be constructed of pre-finished manufactured board, with the panels connected with screws.

The four panels are all the same width. However, the lengths will vary. It is suggested the end panels be prepared initially, carefully squared, and edged with the appropriate plastic edging. While together the holes may be drilled for the screws. Care must be taken in marking out and drilling as it is intended that the surface of the top and bottom panels will finish flush with the edges of end panels.

The top and bottom can also be placed together for preparation to ensure identical panels. It is also practical to mark out and drill the holes for the screws. Here care must also be taken to ensure that the holes are accurate. They are best marked from the end panels. The front and back edges only need to be trimmed with plastic edging. When the holes have been drilled the modules may be assembled.

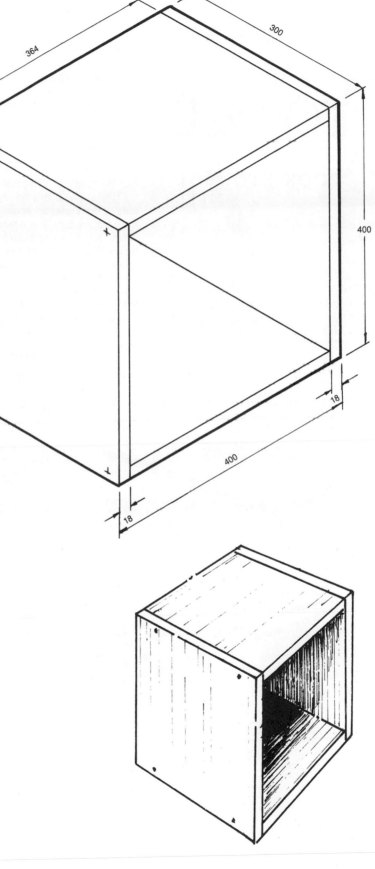

Child's storage unit

Project 12

BOOK STORAGE UNITS

Procedure for Design 1

The unit illustrated is the traditional type of book shelf consisting of end panels connected with shelves varying distances apart. It is intended that 18 mm pre-finished manufactured board is used, and that the panels are connected with screws. The back is of 4 mm plywood.

It is suggested that the end panels be prepared initially. To ensure accuracy clamp the panels together. While together the position of the shelves could be set out and the holes marked and drilled.

The top and front edges of these panels can be trimmed with plastic edging.

The shelves are all the same width and length, and plastic edging is applied to the front edges only. It is a good idea to mark the holes from the end panels. When drilling the holes in the ends of the shelf, a drill guide should be used to ensure accurately positioned holes. After drilling, the shelves can be attached to the end panels. After assembly the toe board can also be fixed. This is easily carried out by clamping it in position and drilling for screws. One in each end and two through the shelf should be sufficient.

If adjustable shelves are desired (and these can be a real advantage, making the unit much more versatile) only the top and bottom shelves are fixed with screws. However before assembly holes need to be drilled in the ends to accommodate shelf supports. Shelf supports are brass fittings readily available at hardware stores, and are generally manufactured to fit into 6 mm holes.

It is desirable to make a plywood template the same size as the end panel with holes set out in the required positions. The template is clamped to one end while the holes are drilled, and then transferred to the other to ensure accurate positioning of those holes. A drill stop will be required to ensure a hole of the correct depth.

Back

The back is of 4 mm plywood. The edge of ply is stopped back from the top ends at least 6 mm for appearance. The panel can be attached using 20 mm brads about 75 mm apart.

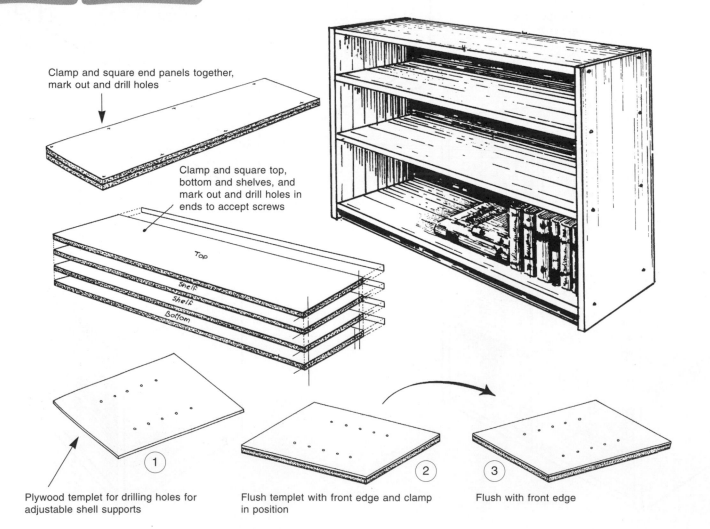

Clamp and square end panels together, mark out and drill holes

Clamp and square top, bottom and shelves, and mark out and drill holes in ends to accept screws

Top

Shelf

Shelf

Bottom

① Plywood templet for drilling holes for adjustable shell supports

② Flush templet with front edge and clamp in position

③ Flush with front edge

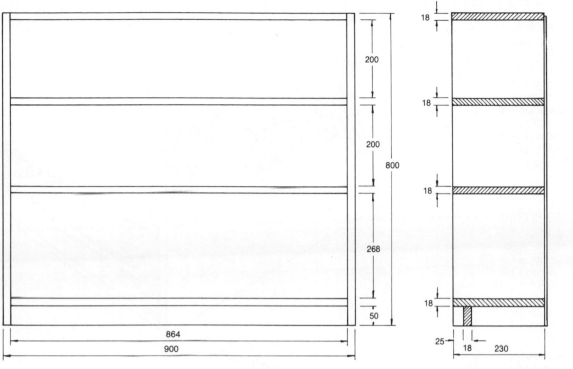

200

200

800

268

50

864

900

Front

18

18

18

18

25   18   230

Sectioned R.H. side

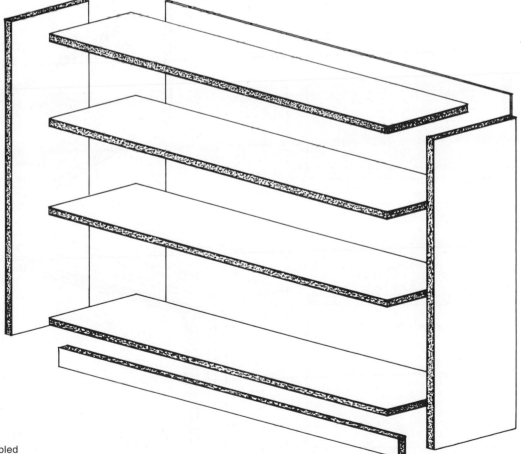

Note: This project is designed to be assembled
using knockdown fittings. It is intended that suitable connector screws will be used. Refer to section on knockdown fittings.

219

Procedure for Design 2—Book Storage

This book storage unit consists of two identical modules. As well as storage for books and magazines the unit can also serve as a table. It is designed to be constructed using pre-finished manufactured board, looking equally effective with brightly coloured panels, or the more traditional wood grains.

The end panels are prepared first, and trimmed all around with the appropriate plastic edging. This may also be marked out and holes drilled ready for fitting screws.

Shelves

After carefully preparing the shelves to identical dimensions, plastic edging may be attached to the front and back edges. After carefully marking and drilling the holes to match the holes in the ends, the unit can be assembled ready for use.

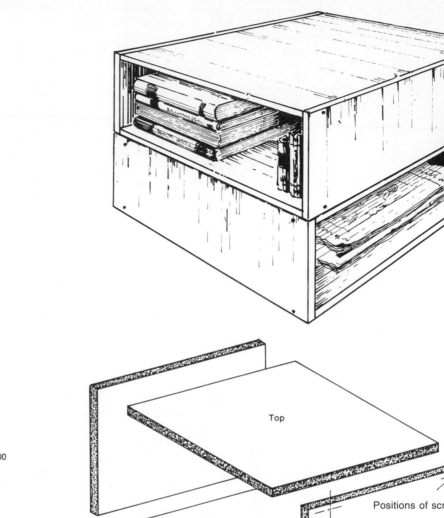

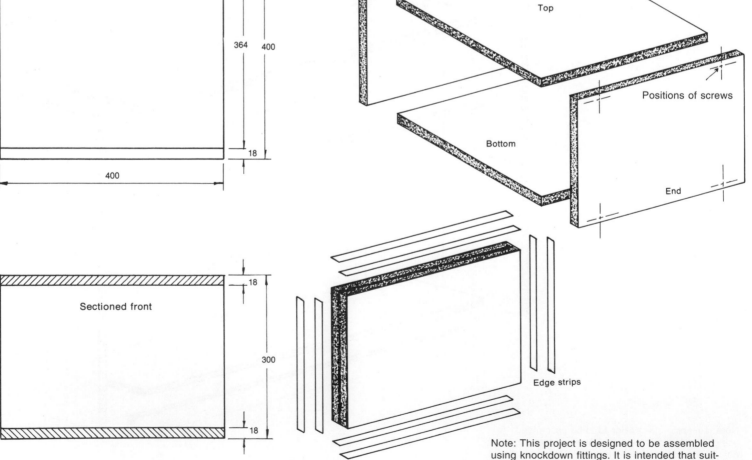

Note: This project is designed to be assembled using knockdown fittings. It is intended that suitable connector screws will be used. Refer to section on knockdown fittings.

220

Procedure for Design 3

This unit is made up of identical modular units arranged as indicated in the illustration, or may simply be stacked one on top of another to form a unit of a suitable safe height. The unit is designed to be constructed of pre-finished manufactured board.

In this project the top and bottom panels can be prepared initially, and plastic edging may be applied to all edges. The holes can also be marked and drilled ready for the screws. As the screws are being fitted through the top and bottom it is important that the screw heads finish flush with the surface. This can be accomplished by lightly countersinking the top of the hole.

The back is the full length of the top, and after trimming the end edges with plastic edging should finish flush with the edges of the top and bottom.

The end panel is cut to fit in between the back panel and finish flush with the front edges of top and bottom. The front edge of the unit will need to be trimmed with plastic edging.

After careful marking and drilling of the holes the unit is ready for assembly.

At the open ends of the unit a solid-timber column, in a similar colour to the pre-finished board, is fitted. The column is the same height as the back and end panels, and fits between the top and bottom. Before fitting the column it will need to be surface-finished.

When all panels have been carefully prepared and the column surface-finished the modules can be assembled. After arranging the modules into a unit to your satisfaction, plastic snap-caps can be inserted into the head of the exposed screws. The unit is now ready for use.

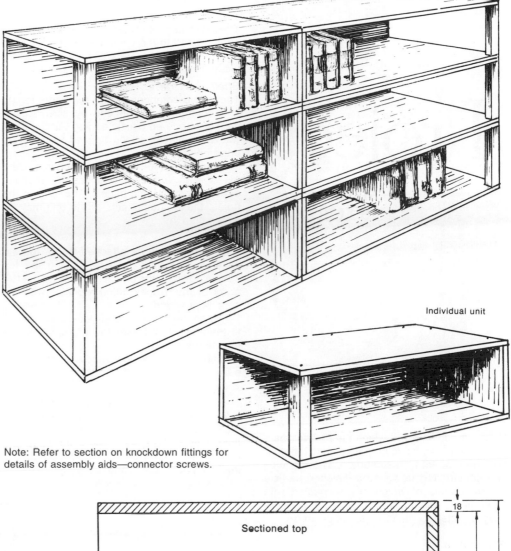

Individual unit

Note: Refer to section on knockdown fittings for details of assembly aids—connector screws.

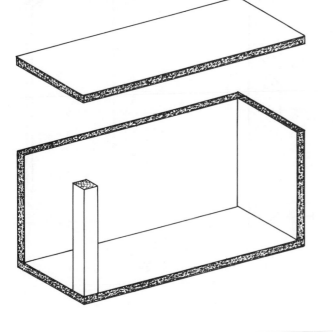

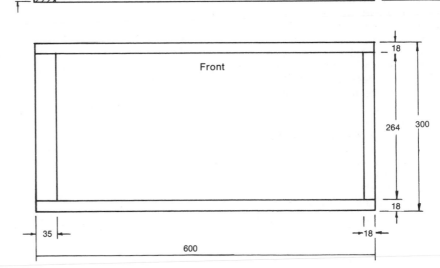

Sectioned top

18

182 200

35

Front

18

264 300

18

35 18

600

221

Project 13

MODULAR STORAGE UNIT

These modules are designed to be used as a single unit or with two or more placed together to form a buffet or a sideboard. The modules are constructed using a pre-finished particle board, panels of which are connected with appropriate assembly aids. Drawers or doors may be fitted to the carcass as desired.

Procedure

The drawings give the dimensions for the construction of a module design around 400 mm x 400 mm x 140 mm drawer system. It is suggested that, the basic drawer frame be purchased initially, and perhaps even assembled to ensure that panels are cut to the correct widths and lengths. This will ensure good fitting drawers.

It is intended that the top be connected using 'Hettich' Trapez fittings to ensure a clean top surface to the unit. Screws are used to connect the bottom shelf and drawer rail.

End Panels

The end panels are prepared first. When accurately cut and trimmed to size the front edge can be edged with the appropriate plastic edging. The end panels can now be marked out and drilled for the screw holes.

The Trapez fitting can also be positioned and fixed to the inside of the end panels.

Top

The top is carefully prepared to size and plastic edging fitted to the ends and front edge. The second part of the Trapez fitting can now be located and screwed to the inside of the top.

Shelf and Drawer Rail

These two components are the same length and connected to the end by screws. The drawer needs no plastic edging but the shelf will need plastic edges applied to the front edge only.

The centres for the holes to accommodate the screws are best obtained by marking directly from the end panels. After drilling the holes, these components of the unit may be assembled.

Assembly

The ends should be attached to the top initially. This is best done by placing the top upside down on the bench and locking the two parts of the Trapez fitting together with the screws provided.

When the top is securely locked in position fit the shelf and drawer rail into position and fix using a screw.

The carcass is now ready for fitting the back.

Back

The back is of 4 mm ply and is fixed directly to the back of the module with 20 mm brads. The back is cut so that the edges of the ply are not flush with the outside surfaces of the top and ends. The back will give the carcass stability for the fitting of the doors and drawers.

Drawers

As mentioned earlier the drawers intended for this unit are 'Hettich' mitred-drawer frame systems. Both drawers can be folded up and glued so that they are square, and the drawer bottoms fitted. At this stage the runners can be screwed into place on the inside surfaces of the ends, and the drawers placed into position to check the fit. If satisfactory the drawer fronts may be attached, by fitting screws from the inside of the drawer. The drawer fronts are designed to fit over the outside edges of the end panels and to overlap the drawer rail as indicated on the working drawing. It is desirable that plastic edging be applied to all four edges of each drawer front.

Door

The door is of pre-finished manufactured board and cut to fit over the edges of the end panels, but under and flush with the front edge of the top. The door may be attached with either continuous hinge or concealed hinges. It is suggested that a magnetic catch be fitted to the inside of the end panel located near the handle.

As indicated in the working drawing the back edge of the drawer fronts are chamfered. This is intended to act as a drawer pull, in an attempt to preserve a clean uncluttered appearance to the modules. However, drawer pulls of an individual's choice may be attached to the drawer front to match the door handle, if the modules are to be used as indicated in the sketch.

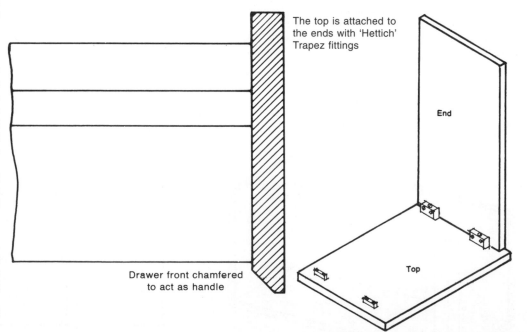

Drawer front chamfered to act as handle

The top is attached to the ends with 'Hettich' Trapez fittings

End

Top

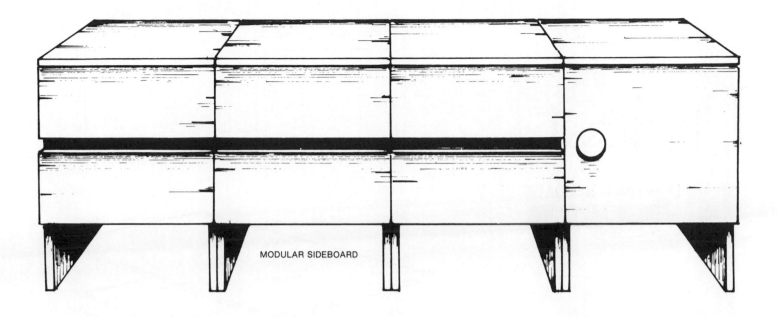

MODULAR SIDEBOARD

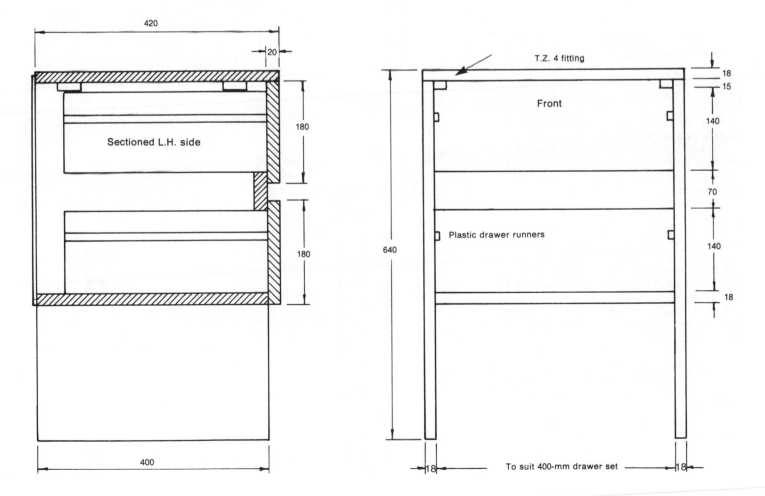

420

20

Sectioned L.H. side

180

180

400

T.Z. 4 fitting

Front

18

15

140

70

Plastic drawer runners

140

640

18

18

To suit 400-mm drawer set

18

223

Project 14

DINING ROOM TABLE

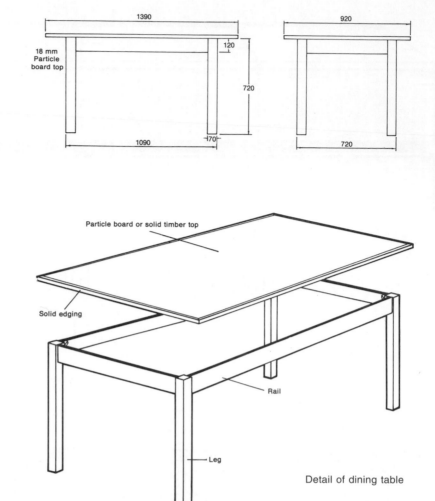

Detail of dining table

The table illustrated is a basic unit, featuring a veneered manufactured board top with solid timber edging and supported by a frame of legs and rails.

Frame

A set out rod must be prepared to establish the rail lengths and joint detail.

The legs are cut to length, allowing approximately a 6 mm horn on the top. The bottom of the legs are cleaned up and a small chamfer is planed around the end. This will tend to prevent splitting when the table is in use. Mark the face and face edge marks.

The rails are cut to length, allowing for tenons, or if dowels are used, cut exactly the length between the legs.

Clamp the legs together and mark the position of the rails. The rails are used as guides to mark the width across the legs.

Scribe the lines around the insides of the legs, i.e. on the face and face edge, and set out the joints (see Joints).

Set out the joints on the rails, either a tenon or the position of dowels.

When the joints have been cut, check the fit and clean up the inside surfaces ready for assembly.

Legs could also be tapered on the inside to give a splayed effect and turned legs provide a further option

Apply the glue evenly to the joints with a small brush and assemble the end frames. Remove excess glue and check for squareness.

When the end frames are dry, glue and clamp the side rails to the end frames. Remove all excess glue and check for squareness.

The corner blocks are prepared and screwed into each corner. They are essential if dowel joints are used.

Clean up the top of the legs so that they are flush with the rails, and clean up the sides of the joints if they are out of true.

Finally clean up with abrasive paper ready for surface finishing.

Veneered Manufactured Board Top

The top is cut to the dimensions indicated. It may be desirable to knife-cut the top surface to avoid any unsightly splintering.

The solid timber edging is prepared to the dimensions indicated.

The edging is best glued and clamped in position as rails tend to detract from the finished appearance. Nailing the edging into position is satisfactory for work that is to be painted, but not desirable for clear-finished projects.

It is best to fit the edging to the ends initially and then to the sides.

Cut one mitre first, and place the edging against the ends. Mark the exact length and cut the second mitre. When satisfied with the fit, glue and clamp both ends using two or three bar clamps. Make sure the edging is flush with the top.

When the ends are dry, cut the sides to fit in between the mitres on the ends. When satisfied with the fit, glue and clamp the side pieces of edging in position.

When the glue is dry, a scraper is used to flush up the edging. Care must be taken not to damage the thin layer of veneer on the top.

Finish off with abrasive paper ready for surface finishing.

Fitting the Top to the Frame

The rails are drilled and counterbored as indicated to accommodate a suitable screw. Care must be taken when selecting the screw that it is not too large as it may damage the surface. The rails are probably best drilled before assembly.

Carefully lay the top face down on a bench and locate the frame so that it is the correct distance from the edges.

A pilot hole will not be necessary; just apply a little pressure to the screwdriver as it is turned. Care must be taken not to overtighten the screws.

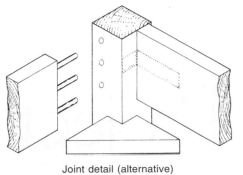

Joint detail

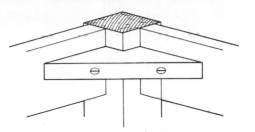

Joint detail (alternative)

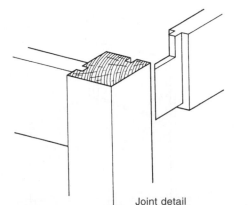

Corner block detail

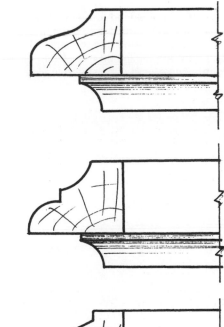

Fit sides after ends have been fitted

Fit end first

Fitting edging to the particle board top

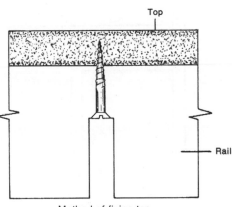

Top

Rail

Method of fixing top

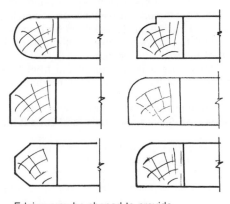

Edging may be shaped to provide a decorative appearance.

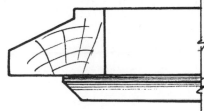

Moulding could be fitted to the underside for a very pleasing effect.

225

Project 15

DINING ROOM CHAIR

The chair is designed to be used with a dining table. The rails may be mortised and tenoned or dowelled into the legs. The seat and back are laminated from 4 mm ply to form a curve, and upholstered in vinyl.

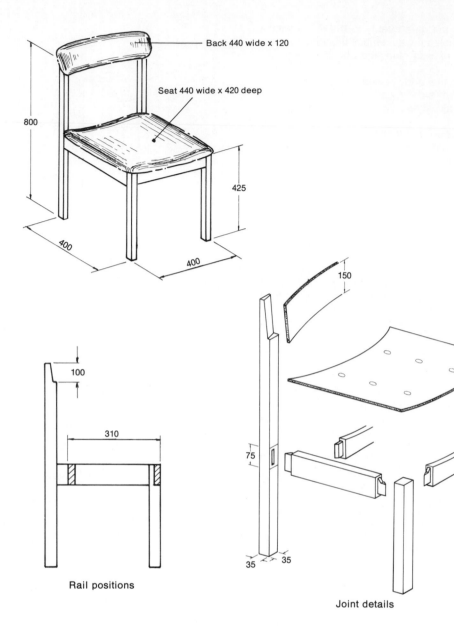

Back 440 wide x 120

Seat 440 wide x 420 deep

800

425

400

400

150

100

310

75

35   35

Rail positions

Joint details

Frames

Prepare the material for the legs and side rails.

Mark out the position of the mortises on the front and back legs. These must be clamped together to ensure that the lengths and position of the joints will match.

Square the line around on the front legs and mark out the position of the mortises for the front rails.

Clamp the side rails together and mark out the mortise for the back rails, and set out the tenons.

Clamp the front and back rails together, set out the tenons, and mark the curve for the seat.

When all setting out is complete, cut and fit the joints.

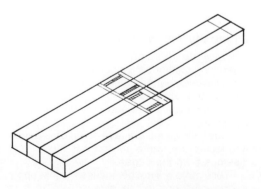

Setting out the positions of the mortises

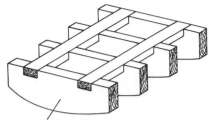

Particle board formers

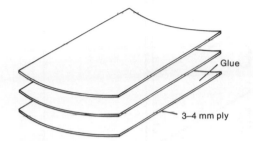

Glue

3–4 mm ply

G clamps to press shape while glue dries

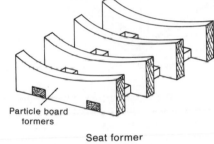

Particle board formers

Seat former

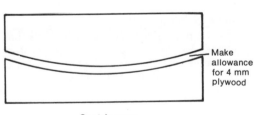

Make allowance for 4 mm plywood

Seat former

Foam to overhang 6 mm all round

25 mm Foam

Covering the back

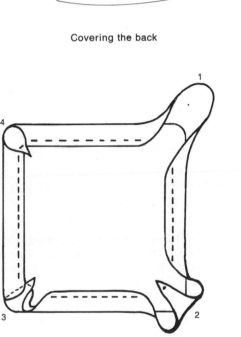

Method of folding corners

Full Back
The top of the leg Is tapered to obtain a suitable angle for support. Screw the back to the legs

Fitted Back
The back rest is fitted between the legs. Screw back into position from the sides

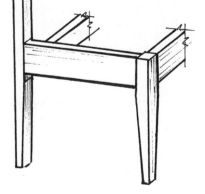

Taper inside legs for a splayed effect

Shape the front and back rails.

Shape the back legs to accommodate the back rest.

Clean up all inner surfaces and glue up the side frames. When dry, flush up the joints.

Join the side frames with the front and back rail.

Screw corner brackets into the corners for added strength. When the glue is dry, flush up the joints.

Seats and Back Rest
A simple former is constructed for the curve in the seat and back rest.

Three pieces of 4 mm ply are pressed together, and when the glue is dry they will retain the curved shape.

The seat is trimmed to size, air holes drilled, and cleaned up ready for upholstery.

The back is made by the same method, using the same former.

When upholstery is complete, the seat and back may be attached to the frame.

The back of the seat may be trimmed, using 4 mm ply, in a face veneer to match the timber used for the construction of the chair.

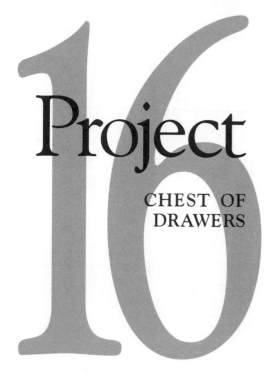

Project 16

CHEST OF DRAWERS

Procedure

It is recommended that a set-out rod be prepared to establish actual material sizes in relation to the definite dimensions of the purchased components. The set-out rod is a good idea, as definite lengths, widths, heights, and position of assembly aids can be established before actually cutting expensive panels, and sizes can be checked as work on the unit progresses.

Ends

The ends are first squared to length and width. It is a good idea to clamp the pieces together while squaring-up, setting out, or shaping the panels. The edges should be square before applying the plastic-veneer edging. Contact adhesive is ideal for this task. The adhesive is applied to both surfaces, care being taken not to spread it on the face surface.

Set out and drill holes for the screws. Make sure the centre line is square to the face edge.

Top and Bottom

These panels are the same length. Where possible clamp them together to ensure identical length and width. Only the front edges need to be edged. A centre line is marked or gauged along the ends of these panels and they are placed on the end panels to locate the position of the holes. When satisfied that all holes align, drill the holes to suit the screws.

Assembly

Once the holes in the ends have been drilled the carcass may be assembled. Fit the plastic caps over the screws for a neat appearance.

Base

It is sometimes desirable to construct a base on which to stand the cabinet. This is a good idea as it prevents the end panels from being kicked or damaged.

The base is best constructed from solid timber, mitres at the front, and strengthened with glue blocks. The back is generally housed into the sides.

Drawer

It is intended that 'Hettich' mitred drawer systems are used in the units illustrated. The dimensions shown suit drawers available at retail outlets. If other dimensions are required check the sizes of drawers available.

The drawer runners are of solid timber planed to fit the recess in the drawer side. These runners are best fitted, using countersunk head screws, to the inside of the end panels before assembly. They may be cut the full width of the end panel.

Assemble the drawer as indicated, and check the fit in the cabinet.

The drawer fronts are all the same length and width and overlap the front edges of the carcass. The fronts are screwed to the drawers from the inside. The fronts are of the same material as the carcass, with the grain pattern either vertical or horizontal and the raw edges covered with plastic or wood-veneer edging.

Fit the drawer pulls.

Cabinet Backs

The 4 mm ply back fits directly on to the back edges. To ensure the edge of the ply is not visible the panel is cut so that the edge is set back 6 mm to 8 mm from the edge.

The ply is then fixed using 20 mm brads about 75 mm apart.

Finishing

If pre-finished boards are used no other finish is required.

If timber veneer is used the cabinet should be sanded using 240-grit abrasive paper, before applying two or three coats of suitable clear finish. Scuffing back between coats will ensure a smooth finish.

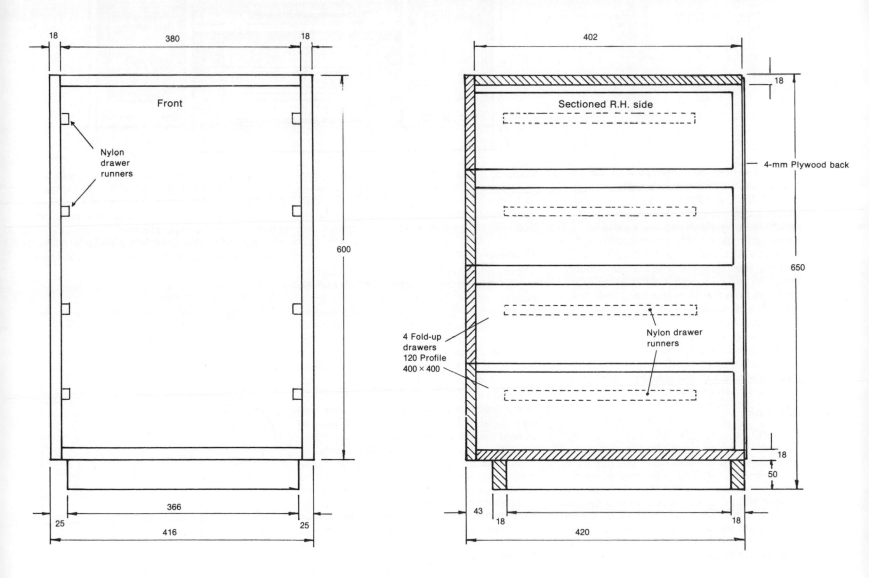

Front

Nylon drawer runners

Sectioned R.H. side

4-mm Plywood back

4 Fold-up drawers 120 Profile 400 × 400

Nylon drawer runners

18

380

18

600

366

25

416

25

402

18

650

18

50

43

18

420

18

Project 17

ENTERTAINMENT UNIT

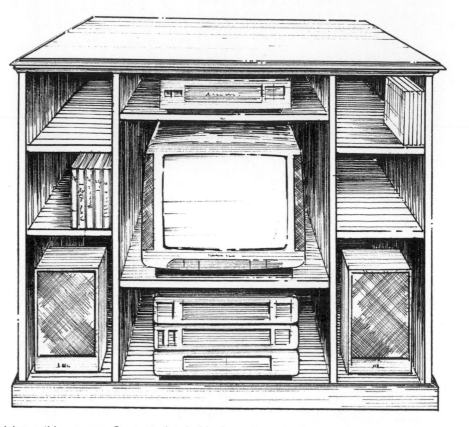

This unit is designed to house a 51 cm TV unit, a mini system with tuner, cassette desk, C.D., 2 speakers, and a V.C.R. The unit has been designed for ease of construction using either veneered particle board or medium density fibre-board, and assembly aids. Before proceeding it is strongly recommended that the components are purchased, or definite dimensions are obtained from the manufacturers' specifications. The dimensions may need to be adjusted to suit components purchased.

It is also suggested that the section on Assembly Aids is read and that a suitable connector screw is selected. It is recommended that Direkta Screws are used for this project—note the position of the holes.

Procedure

Planning

It is strongly recommended that a working rod is prepared to accurately determine panel size and shape before cutting expensive boards. Refer to the section on Furniture Construction.

The design consists basically of a carcass made up of two ends and a number of shelves to support various components. The raw edges of the manufactured board are trimmed with veneer strips.

Ends

The ends are first squared to length and width. The front edges should be square before applying a thin veneer. Contact glue is ideal for this task. The adhesive is applied evenly to both surfaces. Set out and drill the clearance holes for the connector screws, to accommodate top, bottom and shelves.

Partitions

These panels are the same width as the ends, but fit between the top support panel and the bottom panel. Veneer the front edges. Carefully mark out the position of the shelves and drill the clearance holes for the connector screws. It is a good idea to clamp the partitions to the ends to ensure the holes are aligned, to make sure all shelves are level.

Top Support Panel and Bottom Panel

These panels are the same width as the end panels, and fit between the end panels. Veneer the front edges. Drill the thread holes for the connector screws, taking care to ensure that they align with the clearance holes in the end panels. Mark out the position of the partitions, and drill the clearance holes for the connector screws. Transfer the centres to the partitions and drill the thread holes for the connector screws. Drill 4 mm clearance holes, in the top support, for 8 g screws, so that the top can be attached during assembly.

Top

This panel is edged with solid timber 18 mm x 18 mm, glued and clamped into position, along the front and ends. Use P.V.A. glue for this task. The top should overhang the basic carcass on the front and ends by approximately 20 mm. The back fits flush with the back of the top support panel.

When the glue is dry use a router to shape a moulding around the front edge and the two ends.

Moulding (under top)

This may be made using a suitable router cutter, or purchased as a moulding.

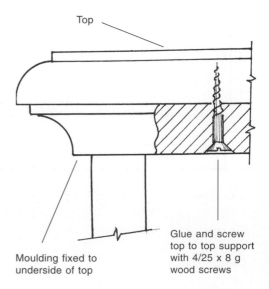

Top

Moulding fixed to underside of top

Glue and screw top to top support with 4/25 x 8 g wood screws

Shelves

Prepare the shelves, as indicated in the drawing, to fit between the partitions. Mark out the connector screw holes from the partitions to ensure positive alignment of the clearance and thread holes.

Ply Back

4 mm plywood—best cut and fitted after the assembly of the carcass. Leave about 4 mm from the edge of the carcass, so the edges of the plywood cannot be seen.

Base

The base is made of solid timber 70 mm x 18 mm. Shape the top edge of the base using a router, as shown in the drawing. Mitre the corners. Cut the centre and back support as shown, and prepare the support cleats. Use P.V.A. glue and brads to assemble the base as shown. Attach the cleats with wood screws and glue. Drill and countersink clearance holes for 8-gauge wood screws to attach the carcass as shown.

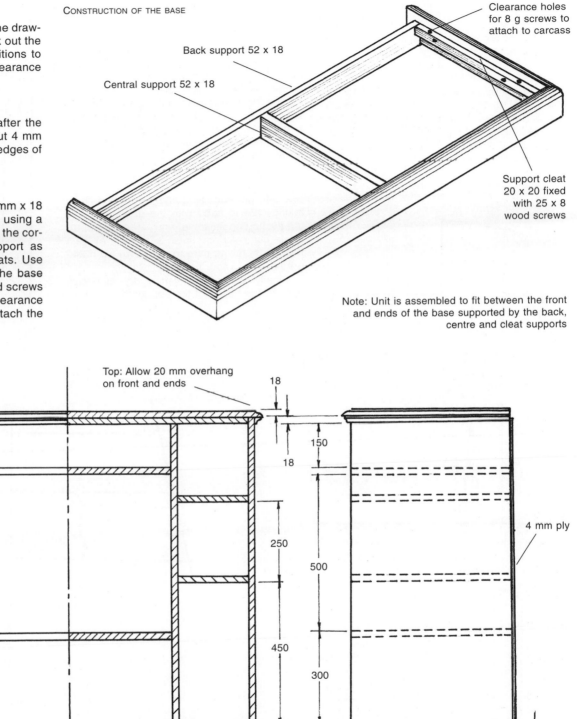

CONSTRUCTION OF THE BASE

Clearance holes for 8 g screws to attach to carcass

Back support 52 x 18

Central support 52 x 18

Support cleat 20 x 20 fixed with 25 x 8 wood screws

Note: Unit is assembled to fit between the front and ends of the base supported by the back, centre and cleat supports

Top: Allow 20 mm overhang on front and ends

18

150

18

250

500

450

300

1000

18

650

1200

20 x 20 Cleats

70

18

4 mm ply

52

18

30

500

231

Assembly

Using the assembly aids:

- First assemble the carcass, top support, two end panels and bottom.
- Fit the partitions and shelves, ensuring that the front edges are flush.
- The 4 mm plywood back may be fitted at this stage, as shown in the drawing. Use 20 mm brads about 75 mm apart. Note that the back is fitted about 4 mm in from the outside edges of the panels.
- Fit the base to the carcass as shown. The carcass is supported by the back, centre, and the cleats attached to the inside of the base.

Use 25 mm x 8 gauge screws and P.V.A. glue to secure the base to the bottom of the carcass.

- Screw on the top panel with the moulded edge to the top of the carcass, using four 25 mm x 8 g screws. Screw from underneath, through the top support panel.
- Fit the decorative moulding to the underside of the top as shown. Mitre the carcass, and glue and brad into position.
- Stop any brad holes with stop putty ready for finishing.

Finishing

Use 240 grit abrasive paper, and hand finish taking care to sand with the grain. Refer to the section on finishing, and select an appropriate clear surface finish and apply at least two coats, taking care to rub down worn 240 grit paper to ensure a smooth finish.

Finally, when the finish is dry, fit plastic caps to the heads of the connector screws.

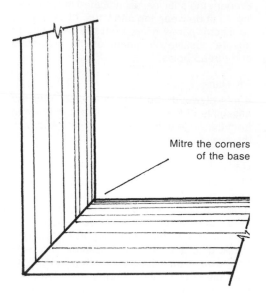

Mitre the corners of the base

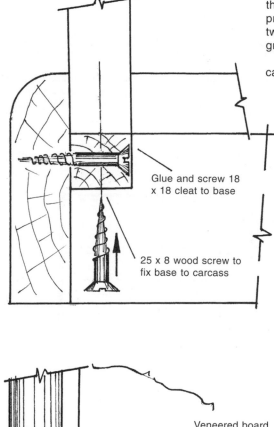

Glue and screw 18 x 18 cleat to base

25 x 8 wood screw to fix base to carcass

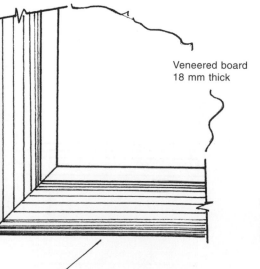

Veneered board 18 mm thick

18 x 18 solid edge glued and clamped to the front and ends of top. Mould with suitable router cutter

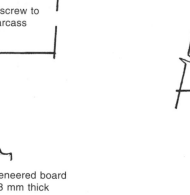

Top

Moulding

Top support

Glue and brad the ply back 4 mm from edges

Profile of moulding

Project 18

MODULAR WALL UNIT

This particular design for a wall unit is comprised of three individual modules—a buffet, a middle unit with adjustable shelves, and a top unit having a fixed shelf. In line with the basic concept of modular furniture, the individual units can be used as separate items of furniture, inter-changed with other modules of similar dimensions, or simply re-arranged.

Procedure—Buffet

While the suggested buffet can be most economically obtained from two 1800 mm x 900 mm sheets of the desired material, a sketch similar to the working drawing will allow personal dimensions to be accommodated.

Top and Base

Lay out one sheet as shown and cut it into four to produce the top, base and two sides of the buffet. As the top and base are of the same dimensions, they are best clamped together when the edges are planed square and to equal width and length. The position of the central division is then located on the top and base and two holes, 45 mm in from each edge, are drilled through each of these members. These holes are to accommodate the screws holding the central division in position. Using the appropriate edge strip, cover the front edges of the top and base panels.

Sides

The sides similarly may be clamped together and the edges squared and the panels planed to equal length and width. The width must be equal to that of the top and bottom panels. Lay out the position of the top and base panels and drill four holes centrally, 50 mm in from each edge through each side panel, to accept screws. (This may be done while the two sides are still clamped together.)

Lay out and cut the recess for the front plinth on the two side panels. Using the appropriate edge strip, cover the front edges of the two side panels—including the recess section.

If the buffet is to be used as a separate article of furniture two solid-edge strips may be glued the full length of the top edge on each side panel.

Alternatively, the edge strip may extend to cover only the exposed section of the side panel when the middle unit is in position.

Central Division

The second 1800 mm x 900 mm sheet should be marked out as shown and cut to produce the central division as well as the shelves and doors. The central division should then be square and fitted between the top and bottom panels when they are in their correct position against the side panels. Edge-strip the front edge only.

233

Mark out and drill the holes for the adjustable shelf on the central division and the left-hand side panel and similarly for the shelves on the central division and the right-hand side panel. Secure shelf bushes into these holes.

Shelves

Once again, since these panels are all of the same dimension, it is good practice to clamp them together to plane them square and equal in length and width. Allowance must be made in length for the shelf supports and similarly the shelves must be narrower than the sides to allow for the thickness of the doors. The shelves should be edge-stripped on all sides but the back.

Plinths

Using solid timber, the front member being of the same colouring as the sheet material, prepare two plinths the same length as the base panel and the same width as the height of the plinth-recess in the side panel. These are best attached by screwing through the plinth into the base panel. This generally requires the plinth to be counter-bored rather than merely

countersunk.

Assembly of Carcass

In the ends of all panels where screws are to be used, pilot holes 50 mm deep should be drilled (in the appropriate position) to prevent splitting the sheet material.

The central division is then connected to the top and base panels using screws. The two side panels are then attached to the ends of the top and bottom panels respectively.

Cover the heads of the screws using the appropriate colour plastic snap-caps. The front plinth is screwed to the underneath of the bottom panel to be flush with the recess section on the side panels. The rear plinth is similarly attached and finishes flush with the back edges of the side and bottom panels.

Back

A plywood back 4 mm in thickness and set back from all edges (except the bottom) by 6 mm, should now be attached by small brads to provide complete rigidity of unit.

Doors

The doors illustrated in this design are

intended to fit inside the carcass. However, by using different hinges and allowing for the thickness of material used in the carcass, the doors may also fit externally.

It is suggested that the two doors be clamped together and planed square to width and height.

Allowance for a plastic or timber edge-strip on the top and two sides of each door should be made as well as a 1 mm clearance all around on each door.

If concealed hinges are to be used then a cranked hinge would be necessary as the doors are to be fitted inside the carcass. (For fitting details see joints.) Where the doors are fitted externally, straight hinges would be required.

In the absence of handles from the doors, tip catches serve as a means of holding the door closed, opening the doors, and act as a stop for the doors. If handles are required, magnetic catches will hold the doors shut and act as a stop.

Further decorative treatment to the buffet may be by the addition of mouldings to the door fronts.

Note: This project is designed to be assembled using knockdown fittings. It is intended that suitable connecting screws be used. Refer to the section on knockdown fittings.

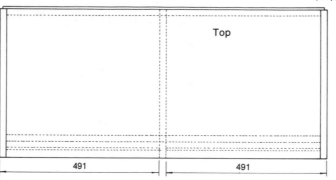

4-mm Plywood back
(stopped back from edge)

491   491

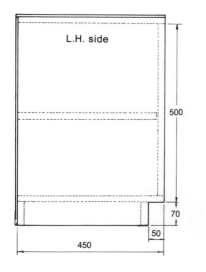

L.H. side

500

70

50

450

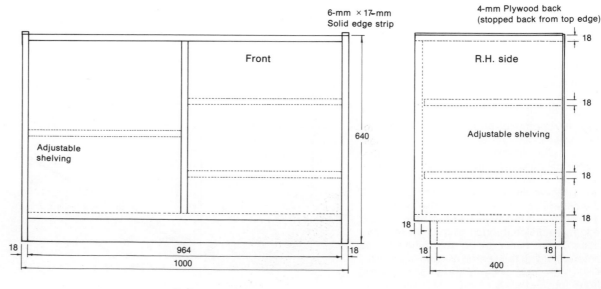

6-mm × 17-mm
Solid edge strip

4-mm Plywood back
(stopped back from top edge)

Front

Adjustable
shelving

640

18

18

18

18

R.H. side

Adjustable shelving

18   18   18

964

1000

400

Buffet

234

The shelves are now located inside the buffet and rest on the shelf supports.

Finishing

Where pre-finished boards have been used, no finishing other than the front plinth is required. Where veneered manufactured board has been used, a light sand using 240 grit abrasive paper over the whole unit prior to the application of any surface finish is recommended.

It is suggested that two or three coats of a suitable clear finish be applied to the whole unit with scuffing back in between each coat to remove any dust particles. This provides an excellent finish. To maintain the unit in new condition, a light rub with any oil-based conditioner is recommended.

Procedure—Middle Unit

Top, Bottom, and Shelves

From a sheet of material similar to that used in the buffet, lay out the top, bottom, and shelves as shown in the sketch. Cut out these five panels, clamp together, and plane square to length and width using either a smoothing plane or a planer-jointer. The front edge of each panel should be edge-stripped using the same edging material as that on the buffet.

Sides

The two sides are best obtained by purchasing a panel 2400 mm x 300 mm of the same material as the shelves, as too much waste would occur from a full-size sheet unless an alternative use could be found for the offcut. The panel should be saw-cut in half, clamped together, and planed square to the correct width and length.

While the drawing provides dimensions for each of the shelf positions, they are in fact adjustable and can be placed at will.

With the two sides still clamped together, mark out the position of the top and bottom panels and drill four holes 50 mm in from the front and back edge on both panels (see sketch).

Lay the two side panels side by side with the two inside surfaces uppermost and mark three centre lines across both panels to indicate the positions of the adjustable shelves. Drill two stopped holes, 50 mm back from each edge, along each centre line to accommodate the adjustable shelf guides.

Edge-strip the two front edges of the sides using the same edging material as used on the top, bottom, and shelves.

Assembly

In both ends of the top and bottom panels drill holes 50 mm deep and on the same centres as the holes in the side panels. These pilot

holes are necessary to prevent the sheet material from splitting when inserting the screws.

Attach the top and bottom panels to one side panel and then the other side panel using the appropriate length connector screws.

Back

From a sheet of 4 mm decorative plywood cut out a panel, the face grain running vertically, to fit the overall size of the unit. The two side edges and top edge of the plywood panel should be short of the carcass edges by 6 mm. This is to prevent the edge of the plywood back from being readily visible. Position the plywood over the carcass and attach using 20 mm x 18 mm brads.

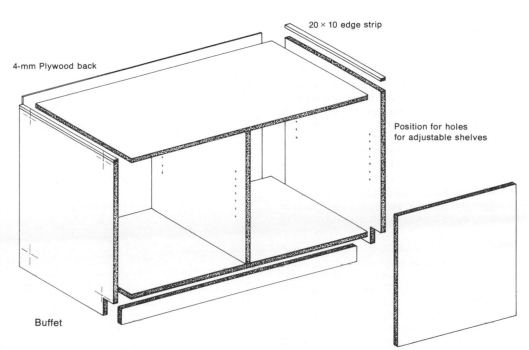

20 × 10 edge strip

4-mm Plywood back

Position for holes for adjustable shelves

Buffet

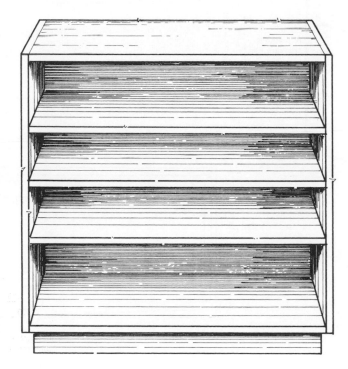

Middle unit showing optional plinth

Plinth

If the unit is required to be free standing a plinth can be readily made from the offcut material as shown in the sketch.

Three strips, the appropriate width, are cut, two to serve as the long sides, the other to be cut in half for the two short sides of the plinth. The ends of each piece are mitred and the rectangular frame, so produced by joining the mitres, is glued and clamped using a webb clamp. To further strengthen the plinth, corner blocks are cut and glued into each corner. The plinth is attached by screwing through the frame into the under side of the bottom panel. A suggested size and position of plinth can be obtained by reference to the working drawing.

Finishing

If the sheet material which has been used is pre-finished, no finishing is required other than for the plywood back. Where veneered manufactured board has been used a light cut-back with 240-grit abrasive paper should be all that is required prior to the application of a surface finish. Two or three coats of a suitable clear finish, sprayed for best results and scuffed back between coats, should provide a most durable and pleasing finish.

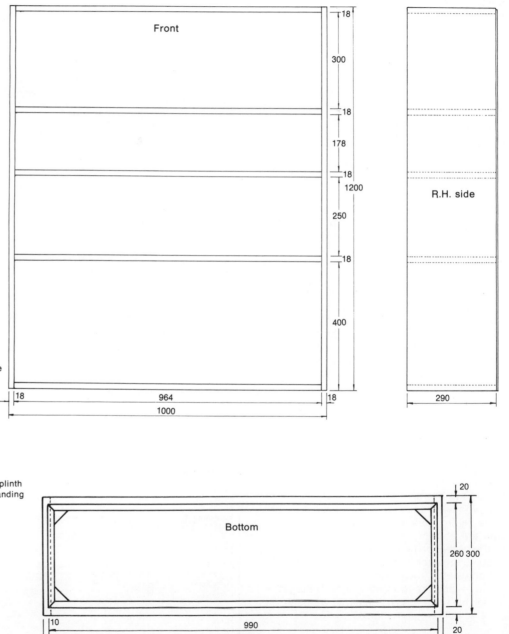

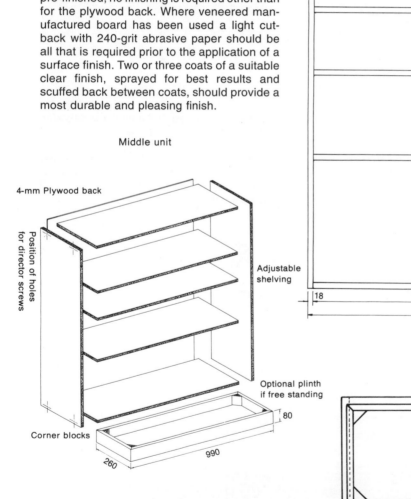

Middle unit

Bottom

Positioning of optional plinth
(Underneath view)

236

Procedure—Top Unit

Top, Shelf, and Bottom

Using an 1800 mm x 900 mm sheet lay out the top unit as shown. Cut out the top, bottom and shelf; clamp together and square to length and width. The front edge of each panel should be edge-stripped using the appropriate material (same as buffet and middle unit).

Sides

From the remainder of the sheet prepare the two side panels to the appropriate dimensions. This is best achieved by clamping the two sides together and planing them square to length and width. With the sides still clamped mark out the position of the top, shelf, and bottom on one side only. Drill six holes 50 mm in from each edge on both side panels ready to accept connector screws (as shown in sketch). Edge-strip the front edge of both side panels.

Assembly

In the appropriate position on the ends of the top, shelf, and bottom, mark out and drill pilot holes 50 mm deep to prevent the connector screws from splitting the sheet material.

Using the appropriate length connector screws, attach the top shelf, and bottom to one side panel and then the other side panel.

Ensure that the edges which have been edge-stripped are all towards the front. Cover the screw heads with the correct colour snap-caps.

Back

From a sheet of 4 mm plywood of a colour and grain that matches the carcass, cut a panel to fit the back of the top unit that is 6 mm short all round with the exception of the bottom. The back is then secured in position using 20 mm x 18 mm brads evenly spaced approximately 80 mm apart.

Finishing

Where pre-finished boards have been used, there is, of course, no finishing required. For veneered manufactured board, it should be necessary for only a light sand using 240 grit abrasive paper followed by two or three coats of a suitable clear finish. For best results a spray application is recommended with a light scuff back between each coat.

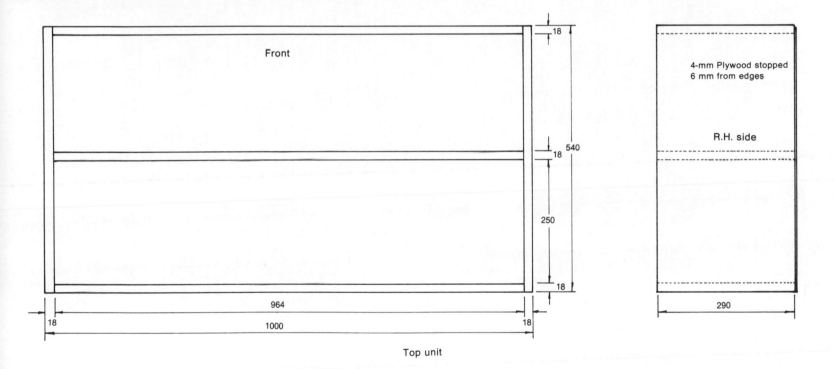

Top unit

WOODCARVING & SCULPTURE

...APPROACHES THAT HIGHLIGHT THE INHERENT QUALITIES OF THE WOOD

WOOD CARVING

Historically, wood carving has been concerned with symmetry of design, intricately applied to various utilitarian articles. Wood sculpture on the other hand, exhibits an uninhibited, tradition-free approach dependent upon the inherent qualities of the material itself.

It is obvious, however, that wood sculpture cannot exist without wood carving. Consequently, it is sufficient to say that whereas carving is an imposed formal method of decoration, sculpture may remain informal and free, often reflecting the spirit of the time.

Wood Carving Tools

Similar tools are used for both wood carving and wood sculpture, although carving may demand a greater variety of wood chisels.

The following chart suggests a range of chisels useful for both wood carvers and wood sculptors.

To prevent the chisels from being damaged, they are stored in a 'carvers roll'—a canvas roll with sewn pockets preventing the tools from touching.

Wood Carving Techniques

For wood carving it is essential for the beginner to be initiated into the traditional processes by means of simple exercises. With the acquisition of manipulative skills and an understanding of the basic designs, it is possible to develop a distinctive style and handle more complex designs.

The series of simple exercises that follow have been devised to highlight the shaping techniques, use of correct tools, and difficulties that may be encountered. The combination of these simple processes could, for example, culminate in a nest of claw and ball tables. Although these exercises may be considered more appropriate to 'applied' motifs, that is, a motif glued on to an article, the processes involved develop the necessary techniques for 'set in' motifs as well.

'C' Scrolls and 'S' Scrolls

The initial design, drawn full size to establish a flowing movement, is best laid out over a series of squared lines or a 'grid'. The shape may be developed freehand or by using a series of French curves. This method allows individual variations, but it is suggested that beginners use traditionally accepted designs. The design is transferred to the timber by using carbon paper. The paper templet is folded over the edges of the timber as a means of location while the marking out is done. As these processes constitute simple exercises, the timber need not be of final project choice. Rather, a straight-grained, evenly textured timber, such as Jelutong allows the processes to be carved with few problems.

The basic outside shape is accurately cut out by using a bandsaw. This is then glued to a small section of 4 mm plywood with cartridge paper used as a means of separation. Where practice is required, two or more shapes may be attached to the same plywood section. Clamping the plywood to the bench top, a straight gouge of suitable curvature is used to produce the outside convex curve to depth. A pencil line indicating the finished depth of carving is drawn around the cut out shape.

No.	Type of Tool	Size (mm)
1	Straight chisel	2 3 6 13 19 25
2	Skew chisel	6 13 19
3	Straight chisel	3 13
4	Straight chisel	6 19
5	Straight chisel	4 10 16
6	Straight chisel	4 8 13 19
7	Straight chisel	4 6 8 13
8	Straight chisel	3 4 11 13 16
9	Straight chisel	3 4 6 8
10	Fluters	3 8 11
11	Veiners	4 13 16
39	Parting tools	3 8 11
41	Parting tools	3 6 8
45	Parting tools	3 5 8

Macaroni Fish tail Spoon gouge	—chisels of limited use
Gouges Fluters Veiners Parting tools	—available in curved or front bent
Gouges	—available in back bent
Number	—designates the curvature of the blade, e.g. No. 6, 4 mm straight gouge has the same curvature as No. 6, 19 mm straight gouge.

Selection of wood carving tools

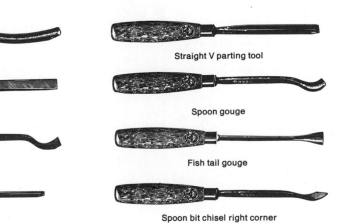

Curved gouge

Straight chisel

Spoon bit chisel

Veiners

Straight V parting tool

Spoon gouge

Fish tail gouge

Spoon bit chisel right corner

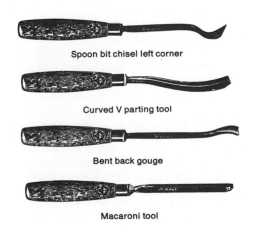

Spoon bit chisel left corner

Curved V parting tool

Bent back gouge

Macaroni tool

Using a series of straight gouges, gradually shape the volutes at each end. Care is needed, as too heavy a blow will split the short grain. With a further straight gouge, shape the inside hollow curve to the required depth. The volute is pared off both internally and externally using a straight chisel.

With 'S' scrolls there is a central transition from a convex to a concave shape. Care is required that this occurs without a visual line of distinction.

The straight gouge is used vertically to mark the spiral on each volute

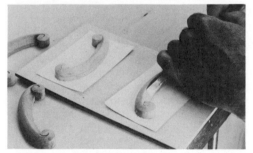

Using a straight gouge on the inside concave surface of a 'C' scroll

Little sanding will be necessary if all cutting processes have been carried out with sharp tools. However, it is important that the cleaning up process be done with very small sections of abrasive paper to ensure that the sharp, distinctive edges remain intact.

'S' Scroll and Shell Motif

As with the 'C' scrolls, the design is developed by means of a grid and transferred to the timber in a similar manner. The motif is cut out and attached to a plywood base, thereby providing rigidity for the carving operations that follow.

The suggested scroll provides a design variation requiring a more deft use of the straight gouge. This occurs at the extremities where the volute becomes enclosed, thereby necessitating a change in shape from a near horizontal hollow curve to a vertical shoulder. As this change takes place over a very short distance, grain direction may cause difficulties.

Using a straight gouge on the inside convex curve of an 'S' scroll. Note the central transition from a curve to a hollow

The outside of the enclosed volute is pared to shape using a straight gouge to blend with the outside convex curve. As with the 'S' scroll, a mid-way transition from a hollow to a radius occurs. The volutes attached to the shell motif are shaped similarly to those for the 'C' scrolls.

Using a parting tool, lay out the curves indicating the shape of the shell. With the appropriate straight gouge pare each section of the shell to its finished size. The initial section, closest to the volute, should be hollowed while the rest are rounded. A pencil line indicating the finished depth of carving, and if possible the actual curvature, should be drawn around the cut out shape. It is important that each of the three sections are clear in definition in order to retain their identity. As these shapes get more complex it becomes obvious that sanding processes are limited, and therefore the work needs to be finished as near as possible with the cutting tool.

Leaf Scroll

Lay out the design and attach it to a plywood

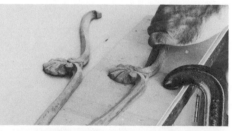

Using a straight gouge to clean up the concave curve leading into the volute on a scroll and shell motif

Using a straight gouge to pare a convex surface on the shell motif

base as previously described. A pencil line is drawn around the cut out shape to indicate the depth of carving. For this particular motif the depth line should taper to suggest a more realistic form.

This taper should have its highest point at the beginning of the scroll and radiate downwards to the point of the leaf.

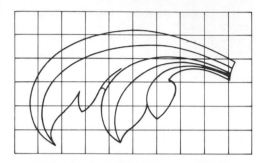

Traditional leaf design laid out over a grid

Using a straight gouge to pare a hollow on a leaf scroll. Note the taper radiating from the scroll

Using a curved parting tool to place V-shaped cuts on the leaf scroll

The internal sections of the leaf are shaped with a straight gouge giving a concave curvature. The outside sections, however, should be formed to a convex shape by using a straight gouge or chisel. The internal section of the volute, initially only marked with the appropriate sized straight gouge, becomes deeper as it radiates out until it blends into the internal curvature of the leaf. With a parting tool, two or three V cuts are placed on the larger leaf, suggesting the rib structure of a growing plant.

Scroll, Leaf Scroll, and Shell Motif

This exercise combines the simple scroll, leaf scroll, and shell into one pleasing design. As with the other designs, the shape is laid out and transferred to the material using carbon paper. The cutting out process becomes a little more involved because of the tight curves around the leaf scroll. If using a bandsaw, a narrow blade will facilitate the greater accuracy that is required. In view of the more complex outside shape, it is also suggested that any irregularities in the profile be filed smooth before attaching it to a plywood base. A series of pencil lines indicating the various depths of the different sections should be drawn around the outside shape before carving.

Using the appropriate straight gouges, carefully pare the first concave section of the leaf scroll approximately to shape. This is followed by paring approximately to size the larger concave section of the leaf scroll. The single scroll is then pared close to the depth line where it joins the outside curve of the leaf scroll. Remember that the single scroll has both a concave and convex section at this point. By giving definition to this shape, the outside convex curvatures of the leaf scroll may be made.

Using a straight gouge and mallet, carefully run a chisel cut where the shell and leaf scroll join. The shell area is then pared approximately to shape and depth. As this relief is relatively deep, a number of vertical chisel cuts may be required. With this section relieved, the outside convex shape of the leaf scroll can be completed. Replace the pencil lines on the shell and using a parting tool, give them definition by a slight curvature of each section. Complete the inside curves of the leaf scroll to depth.

The closed volute of the scroll is then completed. Be sure to take into consideration the problems of short grain. Finally, with a parting tool, run four short grooves in the outer sections of the shell.

The surfaces are then sanded carefully so as not to remove any of the crisp defining edges.

Using a small section of abrasive paper to clean up finished surfaces

Relief Carving

The series of exercises so far can now be collectively incorporated into the rail design of the nest of tables. The basic difference is that the carving is 'relieved' into the rails instead of formed for use as in 'applied' carvings.

The rails are prepared for assembly as a finished unit. That is, the tenons have been cut and fitted and any face shaping necessary has been made. For this particular design the rails are slightly bevelled. The designed motif is again transferred to the rails using carbon paper, each table requiring two proportionally differing rail length designs. The underneath of the rails are cut to the appropriate shape, using the bandsaw, and accurately cleaned up with a file.

The design illustrated includes a central simplified shell design attached to an S scroll, having a partial scroll V tooled and running out on to the shaped leg.

Indicate the depth of the carving on the shaped edges of the rails with a pencil line. Using a parting tool establish the initial internal position of each of the scrolls. With a straight gouge, make a series of vertical cuts along this carved V line. This allows the hollow to round section of the scroll to be pared accurately to depth. It must be remembered that there is a change of shape from one volute to the other on each of the scrolls. The external hollow to round shape of the S scroll is then carved in conjunction with the spiral on each of the volutes.

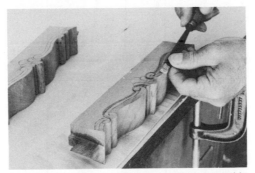
A straight gouge is used to pare the outside curvature of the 'S' scroll being relieved into the table rail

The central shell motif is relieved in a similar manner to that of the scrolls. Use a parting tool to establish the shape, then pare vertically with the appropriate straight gouge. This method establishes a clear and decisive outline of the finished shapes. Further decoration may be made on the shell itself by applying a few parting tool V cuts. The partial scrolls are completed only up to the volutes and spiral curves. The rest of the shaping is done when the leg and rail are joined.

Shell and Husk Motif

This traditional motif is applied to the top of the shaped cabriole leg. The top outside sections of the leg are left oversize to accommodate the raised section of the design. The previously drawn up motif is applied to the leg, about a centreline which coincides with the corner edge of the leg, by means of carbon paper.

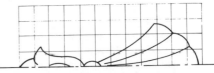
Traditional shell and husk design laid out on a grid

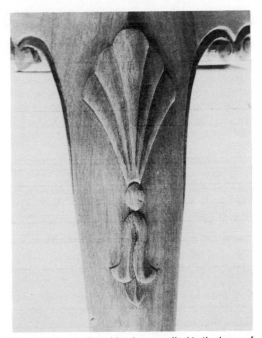
Detail of the shell and husk as applied to the knee of a cabriole leg

Grounding In

First the material around the design is removed with a large straight gouge. The depth and shape of the removed timber should be such that it blends to the shape of the incoming rail and also blends to the lower portion of the cabriole leg. Final cleaning up of this area is done when the rails are joined.

To remove this material, first gouge around the shape some 2 mm away from the line, ignoring fine detail. Use a small straight gouge. This defines the area to be left proud and indicates the material to be removed with the large straight gouge.

To complete the grounding in, go around the outline with straight gouges of the appropriate curvature and cut in with a vertical action. This permits a further cleaning up of the flat area around the raised motif. A small 150 mm rule used as a straight edge may be applied to the surface to test for flatness.

241

With a parting tool, define the various sections of the shell pattern working from the base towards the top. Select a flat straight gouge and pare each section towards the V cuts made by the parting tool. During this stage of initial shape formation the outline may be slightly changed. This can be corrected by lightly cutting in along the parting tool lines to give an accurate definition of shape.

The bell motif attached to the base of the shell is shaped with a straight chisel and a small straight gouge. To represent further the husk on which the design is based, the centre section is undercut to suggest an overlap on one side. This is achieved by a vertical cut with appropriate sized straight gouges, followed by undercutting back into this vertical edge.

Final cleaning up is done with abrasive paper when the legs and rails have been glued together. This allows the flushing of the relieved section of the leg and incoming rail to be accurately made. Similarly, the area around the husk should be sanded so as to harmonise with the flowing lines of the cabriole leg.

Lastly, the partial scroll on each of the rails is completed with a straight gouge to run out the hollow on the inside of the legs and a parting tool to run out the convex curve on the face of each leg.

Cabriole Leg with Ball and Claw Foot

Although there are many variations to the basic shape of the cabriole leg it is important to avoid a bandy-legged appearance. To this end, the knee should be kept high to allow a flowing taper from the knee to the ankle. From below the ankle it may vary according to the shape of the foot.

For the purposes of the shell motif and the ball and claw the carving detail is ignored, but sufficient material must be allowed for the carving which is to follow.

In carving detail there are also many variations. The knee may remain plain or relieved with shell, leaf, or lion head motifs while the foot may be plain turned, scrolled foot, hoof foot, lion's foot, or claw and ball. With the exception of the turned foot, the cutting out procedure is similar for all types of cabriole legs.

Marking Out: Develop a plywood templet of the desired leg shape using the grid system to obtain flowing and harmonious lines. It should be remembered that for knee decoration, such as the shell and husk, and foot decoration, such as the claw and ball, the templet outline must include these projections. For example, in developing the outline around the claw and ball, it is suggested that a sectional plan view be drawn to provide a full outline detail. Similar sectional views should be made at other necessary positions through the leg.

Using the appropriate sized square material, the templet shape is marked out on two adjacent surfaces. With a bandsaw, straight cut the leg to size. To assist this procedure, each of the two saw cuts on the initial surface are taken to within 2 mm of completion. This provides a flat and square surface for the following saw cuts on the adjacent side. Alternatively, the initial cut out sections may be replaced in position while the remaining adjacent sections are removed. In either situ-

Section through A-A

Section through C-C

Section through B-B

Section through D-D

ation, the first cut out sections must be located so as to act as a 'cradle' to allow an accurate saw cut on the adjacent side.

Shaping: The majority of the shaping may be done with a spokeshave while the leg is held firmly in a bar clamp. With the bar clamp secured in the bench vice the leg can be constantly rotated, thereby assuring a complete visual awareness as the shaping progresses. Continual reference should be made to the various cross sectional views as the shaping continues, keeping in mind the circular shape at the ankle, developing to an angular shape and finally an almost square section at the knee.

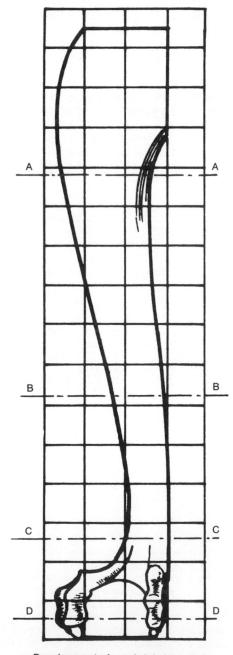

Development of a cabriole leg using the grid system

Method of holding the cabriole leg while carving is done. Note the depth of relief for the shell and husk motif

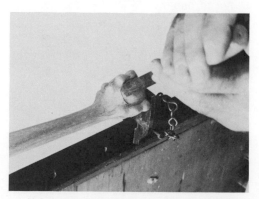

Using a straight gouge to undercut the ball

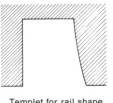

Templet for rail shape

Templet for the knuckle on each claw

Templet for curvature of the ball

A half round file is then used to remove the many small facets left by the spokeshave. Final cleaning up is done with abrasive paper, although work is limited at this stage until the knee and foot decorations have been applied.

A straight gouge is used to blend the ankle into the hollow of the claw

Where a number of similar sized legs are to be made it is advantageous to make a metal gauge of the ankle diameter to ensure uniformity. To assist uniformity further, it is suggested that similar legs are worked as a group and not as individuals.

Timbers

Timber offers the sculptor a material with a number of basic inherent qualities. Figure characteristics, a term encompassing grain, texture, and colour, provide unlimited possibilities for the creation of new forms. The intricacies of growth rings, medullary rays, and interlocking grain suggest many flowing movements and shapes for the sculptor to develop and enhance. Similarly, the multitude of colours, virtually embracing the spectrum, gives rise to a further variety of ideas. Also, within timber occur natural embellishments which the astute sculptor will often seek out and display.

There is one quality of timber that is sometimes forgotten; it may be worked on in a most rudimentary manner and with a very basic kit of woodworking tools.

It is these characteristics that provide the material with its appealing warmth and sense of belonging that we all too often accept when discussing sculptures.

In general, timbers for wood carving need to be close-grained hardwoods. They should possess qualities which produce a clear crisp cut without any 'woolliness' of appearance, yet not be unduly hard.

In the case of wood carving consideration of figure characteristics is not as important as it is in the case of sculpture since the finished article may be stained, pore-filled, painted, or gilded. The following table suggests a range of timbers with suitable qualities for both wood carving and wood sculpture.

Timber	Botanical Names	Features	Availability
English Lime	Tilia vulgaris	Yellowish white in colour, occasional brownish tinges. Has indistinct grain pattern. Carves exceptionally well with sharp tools.	Limited
Honduras mahogany	Swietenia macrophylla	Reddish brown in colour. Generally close and straight-grained.	Limited
English oak	Quercus robur	Pale brown, generally straight-grained, with coarse texture. Distinctive ray figure. Fairly easy to work, tough and elastic.	Limited
Japanese oak	Quercus mongolica	Similar to English oak but more open-grained.	Reasonable
Teak	Tectona grandis	Golden brown colour, darkens on exposure, coarse uneven texture. Often irregular grain. Resinous. Carves well but dulls cutting edges. Excellent for sculpture.	Readily
Queensland maple	Flindersia brayleyana	Pinkish brown in colour, decorative figure. Non-fissile. Works well and is fairly soft.	Readily
Queensland walnut	Endiandra palmerstonii	Brown to chocolate-brown with high silica content. Works well with handtools but dulls cutting edges.	Limited
Blackwood	Acacia melanoxylon	Golden brown coarse texture. Generally straight-grained. Works well and is moderately soft.	Readily
Red cedar	Cedrela toona	Light to dark red soft and coarse texture. Easy to work. Produces excellent sculptures due to interesting grain formations.	Readily
Myrtle beech	Nothofagus cunninghamii	Reddish brown with fine uniform texture. Fairly hard but cuts very cleanly with sharp tools. Accepts stains and fillers well.	Limited
Douglas fir	Pseudosuga menziesii	Pale yellow to reddish brown. Generally straight-grained with distinctive growth rings. Suitable only for sculpture work.	Readily

Carved table

243

Sculpture based on the human form

SCULPTURE

To some the art of sculpture represents a form of livelihood while to the majority it may mean a most pleasant form of relaxation. While some deem it necessary to have a technical understanding of constructional methods related to timber, others find satisfaction from the inherent beauty of the material itself.

It is the development of this creative desire that the majority of people, both amateur and professional alike, find most difficult yet most rewarding.

Sculpture provides experiences with the elements of nature which in turn may stimulate a broader imagination. Basically, nature is the master sculptor, and as such should be the focal point when developing free form sculptures. It may be that the natural qualities of the material being used dictate the form of the sculpture, or conversely, the shape may be developed from an object previously imposed on by nature.

Sculpture also provides an understanding and an awareness of material characteristics. In respect of timber it becomes apparent, as skills develop, that certain qualities may be highlighted by particular processes. Similarly, one becomes aware of the limitations of the material.

Allied to this awareness of the material's qualities is the development of basic hand skills. As the progression from the simple to the involved sculpture occurs, so does the appreciation of what the material will and won't do, when certain tools and processes are used. One problem facing all enthusiastic sculptors is the ability to communicate their ideas in some form of drawing. Initial planning may involve some form of line-work to be placed on the material in order to develop a pleasing shape.

Tools and Processes

Initially, a most basic set of woodworking tools will allow the enthusiastic sculptor to become familiar with the necessary processes. With the development of skills and the desire to 'create' rather than 'follow' it may be advantageous to acquire such items as portable power tools, wood turning lathes, and so on.

Chisels and Gouges

Cutting tools—those that produce a shaving—should be used wherever possible. Not only do they remove waste material quickly, they also leave a surface which requires little cleaning up. A range of four or five chisels varying from 25 mm to 10 mm would prove most adequate. A similar set of gouges would also accommodate the majority of basic processes.

Mallet

Tradition suggests that the sculptor's mallet

should by cylindrical, consequently having no specific striking face. Its weight should enable a good blow to be delivered but permit use for a considerable length of time.

Rasps and Files

As it is often necessary to shape internal and difficult curves, a range of abrading tools is more than useful. A 200 mm half round cabinet rasp provides a quick and efficient method of waste removal. However, care should be observed as the sharp protruding teeth may tear the grain more deeply than required.

Following the use of a rasp, a second cut half round file removes any torn grain and leaves a surface suitable for abrasive paper.

Surform Tools

Surform tools lie midway between chisels and rasps. While looking like rasps, the cutting edges produce shavings. Moreover, they are available with a flat, half round, or round blade and fit a variety of holders.

The success of surform tools in sculpturing is twofold. First, they allow shaping to occur swiftly but without the problems of over-enthusiastic chisel work, and secondly, the surface finish is suitable for sanding.

Holding Devices

Many holding methods may have to be devised as the sculpture develops. It is essential that the material be securely held while shaping operations are occurring. To this end a bench vice, bar clamps, and G clamps will fulfil the basic requirements. The use of protective materials such as low density fibre board is necessary when other than waste material is in contact with the holding mechanism. For circular shaped objects it may be necessary to construct a square or rectangular 'cradle' in which the object is housed but allows itself to be clamped.

Abrasive Paper

The adage 'the right tool for the right job' is particularly applicable when discussing sanding. Abrasive paper should be used only to present a surface-finish suitable for polishing. Not only is it expensive to use abrasive paper where perhaps a file is needed but it also becomes tedious and laborious.

Garnet paper, although costly, has good wearing qualities and is available in a variety of grades. The sheet should be reduced to a number of smaller pieces and wrapped around a cork block or felt pad depending on the area of contact. All papering should be done with the grain and proceed from the coarsest to the finest.

It should be remembered that the total aesthetics of the finished form not only relate to the visual sense but also to the sense of touch.

It is not intended to present a series of instruction sheets providing a step-by-step method of construction of the sculptures depicted. Rather, it is hoped that the illustrations will suggest ideas for development and experimentation in finding new approaches.

Cut Out Sculptures

Using a pleasing rectangular shaped block of wood, sections are cut from the outside edges and re-located on the face surfaces. All members may be sanded prior to gluing, and once assembled, polished with two or three coats of clear finish.

Alternatively, the cut out sections may be applied directly and the whole sculpture slightly burnt with a blowtorch. A wire brush is then used to produce a textured surface.

Douglas fir has particular application to this method as the softer spring wood burns most readily, leaving the autumn wood proud. To further highlight the shadow areas apply two or three coats of clear finish. It is suggested that paper templets be used to develop the cut out shapes which should be elongated rather than symmetrical.

To provide a sense of balance the cut outs should not proceed past the vertical centre-line nor should they be horizontally opposite each other.

The shape remaining following the removal of cut outs should suggest a vertical movement.

This form of sculpture can be free-standing or attached to a base member.

A further extension of this theme may be seen in the form of a totem pole. This involves removing shaped forms from one surface and applying them to others: for example, holes replaced by dowels, grooves replaced by beading, etc. The addition of coloured paint may highlight the overall effect.

Block Sculpture

Using the Golden Mean rectangle as a basis, an interesting wall sculpture may be developed by using proportional rectangular blocks. Starting with one member of unit size, prepare a number of other pieces each having a proportional relationship in length, width, and thickness.

These may be laid on top of each other to build up a larger rectangle and glued and screwed together. To provide variation in depth and figure the smaller members may be turned on their edge or end. By using templets of the rectangular shaped blocks it is possible to relate the shapes between the blocks to the Golden Mean. Care should be taken not to develop too many or too small a rectangle as this may cause confusion of shape.

Tangram

This ancient Chinese puzzle provides another form of geometrical sculpture. One large square is divided into seven parts consisting of one small square, five right-angled triangles, and a parallelogram. From these various members an infinite number of shapes may be made.

To construct a tangram, lay out two 150 mm squares on paper and divide them as shown in the diagram. Using these as templets, set out the various shapes in timbers of differing colour and approximately 10 to 15 mm in thickness. Develop an interesting shape using the various pieces and construct a backing member to which the pieces may be attached. The use of dowels as the attaching medium allows the shapes to be periodically altered.

Block sculpture based on Golden Mean rectangle

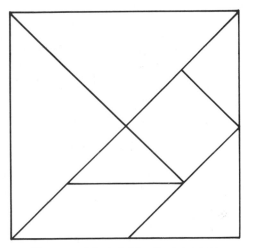

The geometrical division for a tangram

It is necessary that the geometrical shapes make an exact square when re-assembled to allow precision fitting when constructing other representational forms.

Cellular Structures

Combinations of geometrical shapes and the intricate cellular structure of plants provide many shapes and forms for interesting sculptures. Cell structure may be achieved with the use of drills, cubes and rectangles with basic handtools, and spheres with a wood lathe.

The 'golf trophy' is representational of a square to round movement and the holes are suggestive of cell structure and the dimples on a golf ball. The sphere, turned on a wood lathe, has the head stock and tail stock ends left intact. That is, the sphere is turned to within 20 mm of the central spindle, sanded and removed from the lathe. The two unparted ends provide support and location for the sphere when it is mounted in a 'cradle' ready for drilling. Using various size drills a number of holes are bored towards the centre. The sphere is rotated in its cradle to allow holes to be bored at different angles. The supporting ends are sawn off and two holes bored in their place.

A further variation involves the representation of a leaf cell structure applied as a 'totem pole' effect. Three flat rectangular sections of timber are glued together using cartridge paper between the joints to allow separation. The position of the holes are located and bored using the appropriate variation in drill size. The rectangular shapes are separated, cleaned up, and glued together in a vertical position.

Turned Sculptures

The acquisition of a wood lathe to provide an initial symmetry of design may prove very useful. One such interpretation of a turned sculpture can be seen in a ceiling mobile.

Using a square section of material, e.g. 300 mm x 300 mm x 15 mm, locate the centre by using a 2 mm drill through the full thickness. Divide the circle into an appropriate number of parts and using a portable router cut a series of shapes on both sides. Bandsaw to the outside circle. With a false face plate, mount the disc on the wood lathe and using a parting tool, divide it into a series of rings. The rings are separated and pivoted together with 2 mm diameter brass rod.

A small brass screw eye and a length of piano wire are used to suspend the hanging.

Mask

A different yet often startling sculptured 'hanging' is to be seen in the many and varied mask sculptures. For realism, research into ancient civilisations provides a wealth of information and ideas for this form of sculpture. As well as revealing different concepts and materials, the gathered data indicates various methods

Sculpture showing use of the Chinese trangram to achieve an animal shape in walnut and silver ash

Cellular sculpture—square to round movement

A group of tactiles pleasingly arranged

of sculpturing. For instance, while some cultures developed intricate and finely finished replicas of their own form, others stylised and approximated to the extent of revealing how the sculpture was achieved, e.g. gouge marks. This method has become an accepted form of sculpture.

Gouged Dish

Sculptured forms are often concerned only with the visual aspects of design. However, there are forms which combine function as well as aesthetics. The gouged dish, for example, is one such article.

A free form of representational shape is

applied to a suitably sized block of timber. Within this shape is another, providing the hollow or gouged area of the dish. It is important that the shape made by the outside and internal shapes is aesthetically pleasing. A depth hole is located in the hollow and the waste material is removed with a gouge. Clean up the hollow shape with scrapers and abrasive paper and, finally, with the sensitive touch of the fingertips to indicate any imperfections.

The dish is reversed, clamped to the bench top and shaped on the outside using spokeshaves, rasps, and files. A flat section, centrally located, is left to provide stability. The final process of cleaning up is again done with abrasive paper and with the fingertips, to determine the evenness of wall thickness and uniformity of shape. Consequently, the gouged dish not only develops an appreciation of visual concepts of line and form but also imparts a sensitivity of touch.

Free Form Sculpture

With the use of the human form as a basis, many varied ideas may evolve. This is to be clearly seen when, as with the 'mask' sculpture, history has recorded man's attempts to symbolise his own three-dimensional image. Today, as then, the sculptor creates his ideas of human form.

Similarly, free form animal sculptures can be developed. Using a most simplified outline, perhaps sufficient to suggest a particular animal, the shape is cut out and rounded with rasps and files. The final cleaning up is done with abrasive paper, and two or three coats of clear finish are applied. Animal sculptures are best represented without the addition of a base member.

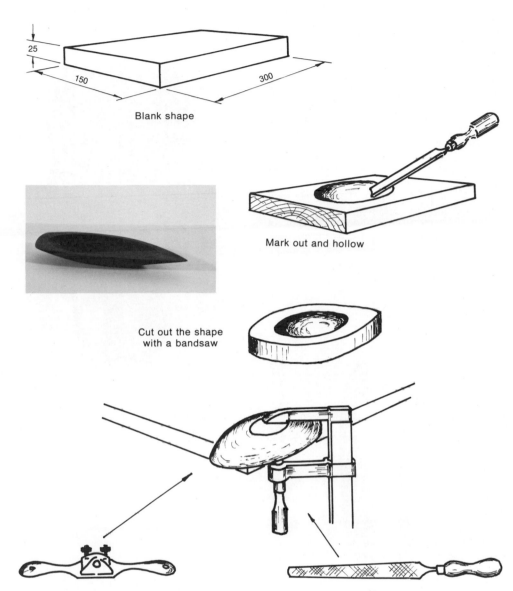

Blank shape

Mark out and hollow

Cut out the shape with a bandsaw

Clamp the dish to the bench and shape the back. Place a piece of low density fibre board inside the dish when clamping to the bench. Finish with abrasive paper

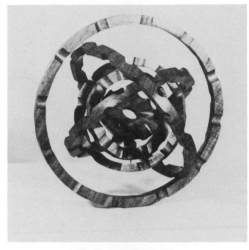

Circles—blackwood

The sculptures discussed thus far have been based essentially on some preconceived idea. While free form or abstract sculpture may be similarly conceived, it can also develop as the sculpture progresses. To initiate a feeling for this type of sculpture, 'tactiles' provide an excellent starting point.

These involve small sections of quality timber that are shaped with the use of spokeshaves, rasps, files, and abrasive paper. Shaping continues until the blocks of timber possess pleasant forms and a sense of touch in as many positions as possible.

A number of 'tactiles', each of handling size, may be made and placed in a turned bowl. When mixed with other objects an interesting talking point is created.

Continuing this theme, use a length of square material to produce vertical sculptures. A suitably shaped line is drawn along two adjacent surfaces which in turn are bandsawed. Placing each of these sections in turn in a bar clamp and shaping with rasps and files as dictated by grain, line formation, movement of shape, or balance, a 'group' sculpture may be evolved. This is one where all of the finished shapes relate to each other.

Yet another type of free form sculpture involves developing a preliminary model based on some interesting object, preferably a natural one (bones, stones, etc.). The model should be made of a soft material, easily and quickly shaped to determine the overall visual appearance of the form.

The transference of these shapes on to the actual material may further vary depending on grain characteristics, colour, and change in proportions. The end result may reflect little resemblance to the initial object.

The collection of materials used in formulating ideas for abstract sculpture often form interesting sculptures themselves. This is particularly true where nature has imposed her whims and fancies in the shaping process.

An example of natural sculptured forms are seen in the 'Burl and Shell'. The burl, of Queensland red cedar, is nature's way of healing a wound, in this case, a covering over a previously lopped branch. The shell, long since uninhabited, reflects the continual abrading, shaping, and smoothing action of the sea. While each may be used independently, together they present an unusual sculptured feature.

Stylised mask using gouged effect

Stylized mask using gouge marks for effect

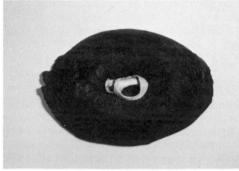

'Burl and Shell'

Group sculpture

Dice

Totem pole

248

WOODTURNING

...SHAPES THAT COME FROM KNOWING YOUR LATHE

THE LATHE

A lathe may be described as a machine for turning wood. The wood is held in a horizontal position between centres and rotated. Tools of various shapes are held against the rotating article to produce the desired profiles.

Description of Parts

The *bed* is the solid base of the lathe. Made of cast iron, it is accurately machined and supports the head and tail stocks.

The *head stock* is fixed to the left-hand end of the bed. It houses a hollow spindle supported by two bearings. A cone pulley system is usually mounted on the spindle to provide a range of speeds.

The *hollow spindle* is threaded at both ends for attaching face plates. The spindle is tapered internally to take the tapered shank of a spur centre. The hollow spindle also facilitates the removal of tapered shanked attachments with a drift bar.

The *tail stock* is mounted on the bed. It is movable and can be locked in any position along the bed. The tail stock has a hollow spindle, tapered at one end to receive the tapered shanks of various centres and attachments. The spindle length protruding from the tail stock can be adjusted by rotating the tail stock spindle wheel.

The *tool rest* is held securely in a tool rest bracket which is clamped to the bed. The tool rest can be adjusted up and down and to any position along the bed.

Turning Tools

A comprehensive set of tools includes about six different shapes, although it may be desirable to have wide and narrow tools of similar shape.

The *gouge* is a hollow-bladed chisel, ground on the outside, and honed to produce a sharp cutting edge. It is desirable to have two or three different sizes. The gouge is used for roughing outs and for cutting various curves or coves when turning between centres.

The *skew chisel* is flat and ground on both sides, and honed to produce a sharp cutting edge. The skew chisel is used to smooth cylindrical work and to cut shoulders and beads. The gouge and the skew chisel are often referred to as cutting tools, and once their use has been mastered the woodturner can produce a quality finish straight off the tool requiring little work with abrasive papers.

The *round nose*, *square nose*, and *spear point* are flat chisels and have only one grinding bevel. Their cutting edge is not honed and they are known as scraping tools. The bevel provides clearance, and the tools are held at centre height so that the work revolves against them. This method of turning is much easier than the cutting method and may be mastered very quickly indeed. The scraping tools are also used for extremely accurate work, such as specific and critical diameters that may be required for patternmaking.

The *parting tool* is ground on both edges so that a point is formed along the centreline. It is used for preparing work to specific diameters for parting off and cutting to length.

The *outside* and *inside callipers* are precision tools that are used to test specific diameters.

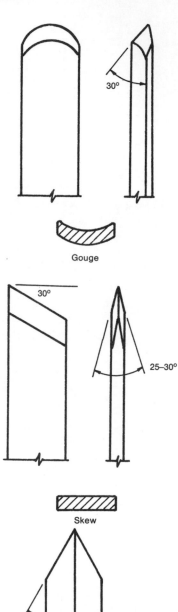

Gouge

Skew

Parting tool

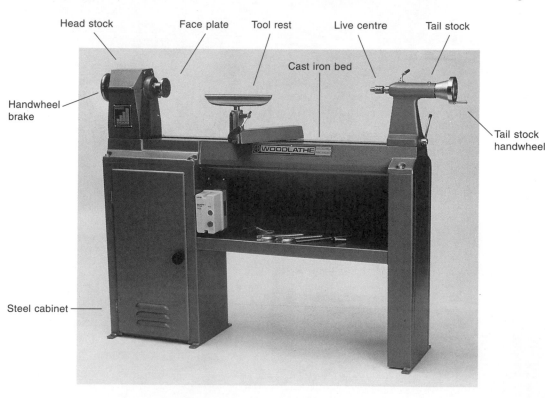

Head stock — Face plate — Tool rest — Live centre — Tail stock

Handwheel brake

Cast iron bed

WOODLATHE

Tail stock handwheel

Steel cabinet

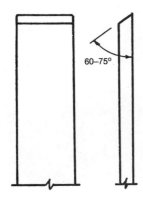

60–75°

Square nose

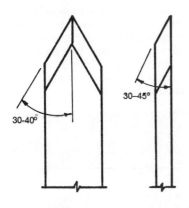

30–40°   30–45°

Spear point

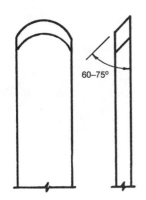

60–75°

Round nose

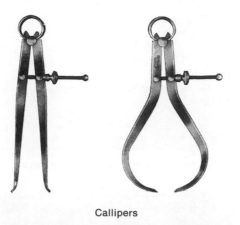

Callipers

Sharpening Turning Tools

Special mention must be made of the fact that woodturning tools must be kept sharp.

They are ground on the edge of a grinding wheel and it is desirable to adjust the tool rest to the required angle. This will assist in the maintenance of a constant angle. Gouges and round nose tools are difficult to grind and must be continually rotated against the wheels. Care must also be taken to maintain an even shape.

The gouge and skew chisel are finely honed and the wiry edge carefully removed. A special stone called a slip is used to remove the wiry edge from the inside of the gouge. Scraping tools are only honed for finishing cuts as the burr left by the grinding process is not detrimental to the roughing cuts and can in fact be of some advantage.

Grinding a gouge

Lathe Speeds

The diameter of the work to be turned is perhaps the most important consideration when selecting lathe speed. Judgment in selecting proper turning speed will be developed by experience. It is always good practice to make roughing cuts at relatively low speeds (600 to 1000 r.p.m.) and when the work is running true increase the speed to suit the diameter of the work being turned.

Lathe Safety

- Eye protection is essential.
- Avoid loose clothing, such as sleeves and ties.
- Check the timber for splits and knots and make sure all glue joints are sound.
- Be sure the work is securely fastened between centres or firmly fixed to a face plate.
- Make sure the tail stock and tool rest are securely clamped.
- Rotate the work by hand to check the clearance of the tool rest. The rest should be as close to the work as possible. Always stop the lathe before making adjustments.
- Before starting the machine select the appropriate turning speed. A slow speed is desirable until work is cylindrical.
- Make sure the lathe tools are sharp.
- The tool rest must be removed when using abrasive paper.
- The floor area around the lathe must be kept clear.

Turning Between Centres

Preparation for Turning Between Centres

The timber should be carefully selected, avoiding splits and knots. The timber to be turned should be approximately square in section and slightly longer than the finished size. The ends are squared and diagonal lines drawn across the corners to locate the centres. A circle of the largest possible diameter is scribed on the end of the timber. A tenon saw is used to make saw kerfs along the diagonal lines on one end only to accommodate the spur centre. It is also an advantage to drill a small hole at both ends to locate the centres accurately. Before mounting the timber in the machine remove the corners with a hand plane, or if large enough with a planer jointer.

Use a mallet to drive the spur centre firmly into one end and insert the spur centre, with the work attached, into the hollow spindle.

The tail stock is moved along so that the centre locates neatly into the centre mark on the timber. The tail stock is locked and the spindle is adjusted by turning the handwheel so that the timber is firmly held between the spur centre at the head stock and the centre at the tail stock. If a dead centre is used it should be lubricated with oil or wax.

The lathe is rotated by hand to ensure the work spins freely. The tail stock spindle is locked with the lever provided. The work should be checked continuously to make sure the centre is not overheating. Regular checks should also be made to make sure the work remains securely fixed between centres.

Using Cutting Tools

The tool rest is adjusted so that it clears the work by about 6 mm and is about 10 mm above the centreline.

Scribe the largest possible diameter on the end of the timber

Saw kerfs to accommodate a spur centre

The spur centre is driven into one end before mounting on the lathe

With due consideration to the appropriate speed the lathe is set in motion. For roughing cuts a large gouge is held firmly on the tool rest with the right hand gripping the handle, while the left hand guides the tool along the tool rest.

For finishing cuts a skew chisel is used. The tool rest is adjusted so that it is parallel to the work, and the lathe speed is increased. The skew chisel is held in much the same way as the gouge, making sure the heel of the cutting edge rather than the point is used so that digging in may be avoided. The shearing cut made by the skew chisel produces a good quality finish that requires little sanding.

Check clearance between work and tool rest before switching on

Using a gouge

Using a skew chisel

Using Scraping Tools

The height of the tool rest is adjusted so that the cutting edge of the chisel is at centreline height, and so that it clears the work by approximately 6 mm. The chisel is held firmly on the tool rest, the handle held in the right hand and the blade in the left. The tool is held horizontally, with the cutting edge against the rotating work. For roughing cuts a large round nose chisel is moved along the tool rest with the thumb located near the cutting edge to deflect the shavings. When the cylinder has been formed the speed may be increased and a square nose chisel used for the finishing

Using a round nose chisel

Using a square nose chisel

cuts. To obtain a first class finish considerable effort with abrasive paper will be necessary.

Setting Out and Turning to Size

Various lengths and positions are marked when the work is stationary. There are many ways of marking out. The parting tool is used to cut positions and turn diameters. It is essentially a scraping tool. Work may be turned to size holding the callipers and parting tool as shown in the illustration. It is essential to provide a clearance for the parting tool to prevent overheating of the chisel.

Marking out from a set out rod

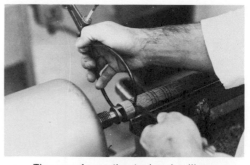

The use of a parting tool and callipers

Turning Coves and Beads

The easiest way to turn these shapes is to use scraping tools. The spear point, round nose, and parting tools are used, but the process is relatively slow, and considerable papering will be required.

Much better results, requiring little sanding, will be produced if the cutting tools are used. When using the skew to cut beads the point is used to mark the position and make vee cuts. The heel of the chisel is then held so that it is rotated towards the vee cut. This is repeated until the required shape and depth is reached. The other half of the bead may be formed by reversing the tool and repeating the procedure.

A gouge may be used to cut a cove. The cove is first set out, and the gouge is used so that it cuts from one side to the centre. Then repeating the process by cutting in from the other side of the contour, the desired shape may be formed.

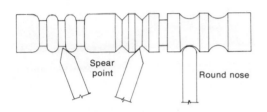

Scraping beads, vees, and coves

Turning Tapers

The length of the taper is set out and a parting tool used to turn the diameters at each end. A round nose is used to make the roughing cuts to within 2 mm of the finished size. A square nose is then used to make the finishing cuts. The shoulders may be squared with a parting tool.

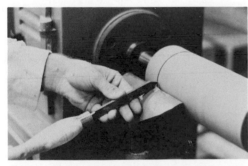

Using a parting tool to establish the position of the cup chuck

Using callipers to check the smaller diameter of the cup chuck taper

Turning the taper to fit the cup chuck

Use of a Cup Chuck

A cup chuck is a hollow receptacle slightly tapered so that work may be fitted and held while turning. The work is carefully prepared by turning between centres, particular attention being given to the fit of the cup chucks. The grain of the timber is parallel to the axis of the cup chuck. Cup chucks are used for turning and hollowing small articles such as egg cups, small handles and knobs, sugar basins, etc.

When 'deep turning' in a cup chuck it is best to use a skew chisel as a scraping tool and work toward the head stock, 'stepping' out the waste as shown in the illustration. Finishing cuts may be made with appropriate scraping tools.

Work supported by tail stock while outside shape is being turned

Deep turning using a skew chisel

Use of Mandrels in Woodturning

Mandrels are generally turned to fit articles so that they may be more effectively finished. Mandrels can be made to fit a cup chuck, the morse taper in the hollow spindle, or held between centres or even in a large three jaw chuck. Articles may be pre-drilled on a drill press and fitted to a mandrel for completion on a lathe. Salt and pepper shakers may be turned in this way.

To suit hollow spindle

Mandrel

Article may be pre-drilled to suit mandrel

Article may be turned to desired shape on the mandrel

Face Plate Turning

Face plate turning is essentially done using scraping tools. The use of the gouge should be avoided.

Whatever the method of chucking to be used, the timber must be carefully selected and cut so that it is approximately square. One surface is then planed so that it is flat. Diagonal lines are drawn from the corners to locate the centre, and the largest possible circle scribed with dividers. The circle is then cut on a bandsaw. When these preliminary steps are completed the work may be mounted on a face plate.

The face plate is screwed on to the spindle until it fits tightly against the shoulder. This gives positive location and allows the work to spin accurately. The tool rest is set just below centre height and parallel to the axis of the lathe so that the outside diameter may be turned. The lathe is spun by hand to ensure adequate clearance.

Scribing the largest possible circle

The diameter is turned using a round nose and spear point chisel. When the specified diameter has been obtained and the work is running true the tool rest is shifted so that it is at right angles to the axis of the lathe and across the face of the work. A round nose and square nose can be used to true this face. A rule and pencil may be used to mark out a specific diameter on the face of the work.

Preparation for Face Plate Turning
A face plate may be described as a circular metal plate which screws on to the spindle. The face plate has a number of holes drilled in it so that the work may be attached for turning. The timber is fixed so that the grain is at right angles to the axis of the lathe.

Bandsawing to the line before mounting on the face plate

Mounting Directly on to a Face Plate
This method is used when the screw holes will not detract from the finished article. Better quality work is always mounted so that screw holes are avoided.

One of the simplest methods of attaching work to a face plate is to use a screw centre. This method is used for small turned articles such as teapot stands, small bowls, etc. Large platters may also be turned using this method but special face plates with a number of screws located around the circumference of the face plate are used to apply pressure once the timber has been attached with the central screw. The outside of the platter is turned first, then reversed so that the inside may be completed.

Face plate screwed directly to work

True up the outside shape initially

Turning the inside

Turning the outside shape

Use of Intermediate Face Plates
Paper Chucking: An intermediate face plate is prepared on a bandsaw; 20 mm particle board is ideal as both surfaces are flat and true. Glue is first spread evenly on the intermediate face plate and a sheet of paper, cut slightly larger, placed on the glued surface. Glue is then spread on the paper. The intermediate face plate with paper is then located and clamped centrally on to the work. When the glue is set a metal face plate is screwed securely to the intermediate face plate. When the article has

been turned the intermediate face plate is easily removed by inserting a wide chisel between the plate and the work and tapping it lightly with a mallet, making sure the intermediate face is supported on the edge of a bench.

Apply glue evenly to the intermediate face plate

Place the paper on the intermediate face plate and apply the glue evenly to the paper

Intermediate face plate clamped centrally in position

Special face plate with a single centre and tension screws

Ring Chucking: Where both sides of an article are to be turned, as in the case of a bowl, it is essential to provide some form of location so that when the article is reversed it will still spin perfectly true.

The wood is first attached directly to a metal face plate. The outside of the bowl is turned, incorporating a standing ring. This ring can be used as a locating device, fitting neatly into a corresponding recess turned out in an intermediate face plate. A little glue is smeared around the ring and the intermediate face plate clamped in position. When the glue is set the inside of the bowl may be turned.

To facilitate removal of the intermediate face plate it is advisable to make the circumference slightly larger than that of the ring. This will allow the plate to be levered off with a wide chisel.

Turning the outside shape and standing ring

Apply a thin film of glue to the standing ring

Clamp securely into position

The ring can then be cleaned up with a sharp smoothing plane.

Deep Turning

Deep turning, say in a large bowl, will present many problems if conventional scraping tools and methods are used. It is essential that the cutting edge of the chisel is supported at all times, and never allowed to 'overhand' too far. Special tool rests may be made up to follow the contour of the article being turned and may in fact be the only solution to a particular problem.

It may also be desirable to reduce the cutting edge in contact with the work. This has the effect of reducing 'drag', and will often provide easier cutting. Never hesitate to modify the angles, or the shape of a turning chisel, if it will provide a more effective cutting surface.

Quite often it is better to use a skew chisel and work towards the head stock. The chisel is held in a horizontal position and the point is used to remove the waste by pushing the chisel towards the head stock. The waste is more or less removed in steps. The surface can be finished evenly with an appropriately shaped chisel.

Alternatively, a bowl gouge may be more appropriate, particularly if turning 'green' timber. Bowl gouges are available in sizes ranging from 6 mm to 20 mm, and consist of round sections of high speed steel which have a milled flute along the length of their blade.

For best results bowl gouges are used on their side (about 15°–20° off the vertical), with the flute pointing in the direction of the cut.

One advantage of bowl gouges over traditional turning tools is the thickness and thereby rigidity of the blade. This feature is most noticeable when deep turning with respect to the length of blade which may safely protrude past the tool rest. However, it remains good practice to minimise tool overhang where possible by keeping the tool rest as close to the work as practical.

When turning bowls or other hollow receptacles it is advisable to use a chisel ground to a smaller diameter than the curve eventually required. The chisel is moved around the curve, shaping the curve by moving the chisel. Never try to cut a radius identical with the curve of the chisel. This practice will more often than not result in the chisel 'digging in', due to the large amount of cutting surface in contact with the work.

When sharpening bowl gouges a 45° grinding facet will assist in limiting the possibility of 'digging in' caused by the two outside corners of the flute being too vertical.

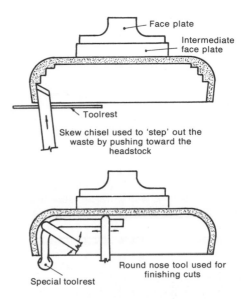
Skew chisel used to 'step' out the waste by pushing toward the headstock

Round nose tool used for finishing cuts

Special toolrest

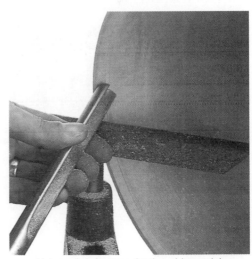
Using a bowl gouge (notice side angle)

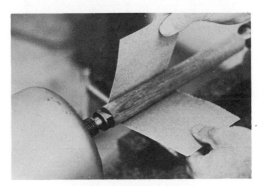
Sanding between centres

Use of Abrasive Paper on the Lathe

Considerable care must be exercised in the use of abrasive paper on the lathe. The paper must not be allowed to overheat and clog up. Pressure and movement of the paper over the work are important. If too much heat is generated the paper will glaze, reducing the cutting effect, and this in turn will cause the timber to dry out rapidly, creating splits and checks visible on the surface of the work. It is generally safer to reduce the speed of the lathe when using abrasive paper.

When using paper between centres it is often advantageous to use strips of paper looped under the work, making sure that the paper is continuously moved so that the dust may be cleared. Felt pads may be used under the paper to distribute the pressure more evenly, but it is still essential to move the pad continuously. Felt pads are particularly suitable for curved surfaces. Most work will need rubbing with the grain so that scratches may be removed.

Sanding inside using a specially-prepared sanding block

Special Jigs and Tools

There are many jigs and aids which can be purchased or made up for use with a lathe. These jigs in effect increase the versatility of the machine.

A variety of chucks may be purchased, ranging from a large three jaw to small collett chucks for holding knobs and buttons.

Screw Cup Chuck

The screw cup chuck is one of the latest concepts in cup chucks currently available. While screwing the job onto the chuck, a thread is cut onto the spigot of the workpiece, prior to locking against the front flange or shoulder, thus providing extra stability and reducing vibration, especially on larger turnings.

This technique eliminates the traditional cup chuck problem of throwing the job out of true when excess (side) pressure is applied or when tool dig-ins occur.

Screw cup chuck

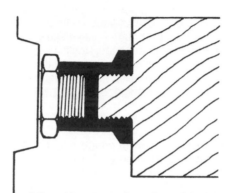

A thread is cut onto the spigot of the job

Screw Spigot Chuck

The screw spigot chuck allows the work to be screwed onto the chuck. This is achieved by cutting a thread into the bore of the workpiece, prior to it locking against the rear flange. As with the screw cup chuck, this technique provides extra stability and reduces vibration, especially on larger turnings. This method has the added advantage of eliminating the traditional pin chuck problem of jamming in hardwoods or jobs slipping from oversize bore holes in softwoods.

Screw spigot chuck

Accurate end for ending made simple

Super Chuck

The Woodfast super chuck provides a quick and easy method for mounting timber blanks when faceplate turning. For example, the timber blank, seasoned or green, is clamped to the base of a drill press where a recess is drilled using the appropriate size cutter.

The super chuck assembly is then hand screwed into the recess by turning the chuck and the timber blank against each other. The complete assembly is then screwed on to the lathe spindle.

When turning green timber, for example, the super chuck is particularly useful as it will readily accommodate any shrinkage that occurs as the timber is 'seasoned', e.g. by placing the timber bowl in a microwave oven.

A Woodfast super chuck

1. Turn recess in lathe with conventional turning tools or use optional cutter in tail stock or drill press.
2. Screw the chuck assembly into the recess.
3. Screw the loaded chuck onto the lathe spindle and commence turning.

Stages for mounting a super chuck

256

Drilling jigs (also known as boring jigs) are easily made to slip into tool rest brackets. They are adjustable and can be made to fit any size of drill.

Jigs can be made to take a router for machining flutes along turned legs. The jig is bolted to the bed and the indexing head used to lock the work while the router is operated.

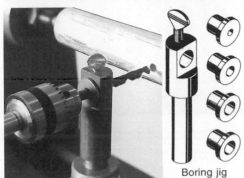

Using a drill bit in conjunction with a boring jig

Boring jig

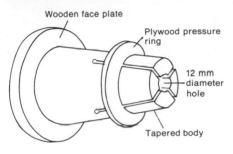

Ringed collet chuck

- Wooden face plate
- Plywood pressure ring
- 12 mm diameter hole
- Tapered body

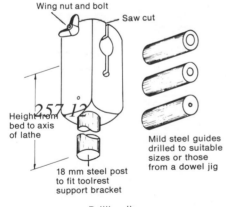

Drilling jig

- Wing nut and bolt
- Saw cut
- Height from bed to axis of lathe
- 18 mm steel post to fit toolrest support bracket
- Mild steel guides drilled to suitable sizes or those from a dowel jig

A variety of gauges for making out or testing can be purchased or made to suit a particular task. These are essential for repetition work.

Double ended inside/outside calipers

Most lathes have provision for attaching a sanding disc. This accessory is extremely useful and parts are readily available.

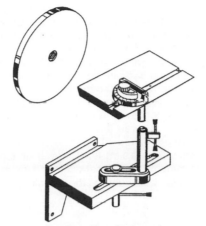

Sanding disc attachment

With a suitable table usually fitted to the tool rest bracket, and a suitable chuck on the head stock, the lathe may be used to drill dowel holes or cut mortises.

Lathe Centres

Revolving cone centre

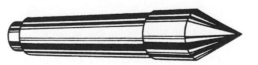

Cup centre

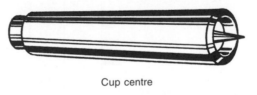

Cone centre

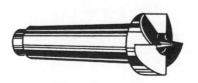

25 mm Spur centre

Lathe chucks

3 jaw self-centring chuck

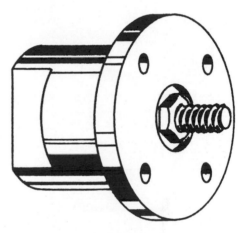

Screw point chuck

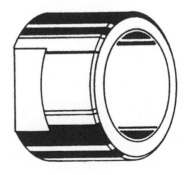

Cup chuck

Jacob's drill chuck

257

Project 19

SALT & PEPPER SHAKERS

The salt and pepper shakers are prepared from 50 mm square stock.

Cut the stock to 100 mm and carefully square one end.

Locate the centre on the square end by drawing the diagonal and drill holes as indicated in the drawing. The drilling is best done on a drill press, with the work held securely in a vice clamped to the table. Drill the 35 mm diameter hole to 8 mm deep initially, then drill the 25 mm hole to 70 mm deep.

Use a piece of 25 mm diameter steel about 150 mm in length as a mandrel and support one end in a three jaw chuck on the lathe. Slide the pre-drilled stock on to the mandrel. This should be a firm fit. If it is at all loose, centre punch a ring of marks around the mandrel. This will tighten the stock on the mandrel.

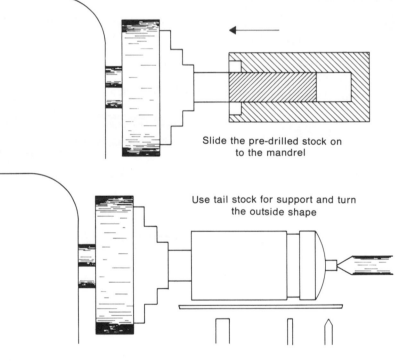

Slide the pre-drilled stock on to the mandrel

Use tail stock for support and turn the outside shape

After sanding remove the work from the mandrel and mark out the holes on the top. The hole can be drilled using a drill press.

A base piece is inserted into the shakers to accommodate the cork. This is made by preparing a piece of timber to 3 mm thick.

Turn to the desired shape using a round nose tool. It may be desirable to support one end with the tail stock. The tail stock can be removed to finish off the end when all other work is finished.

Mark out and cut the circles as indicated in the diagrams.

Glue the base pieces into the shakers.

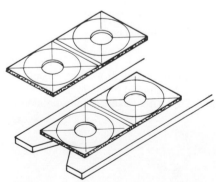

Marking out the circular base pieces

Project 20

TABLE LAMP

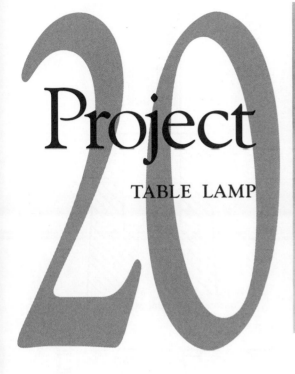

The procedure shown here for turning a lamp base may be adapted for a variety of shapes and sizes.

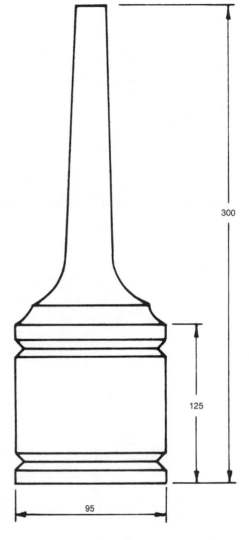

Lamp base

Step 1

Prepare two pieces of timber to the 350 mm x 100 mm x 50 mm and plane one face on each piece.

Using a circular saw cut a groove 12 mm x 6 mm along the middle of each piece. This will allow for a piece of flex to run down the centre of the lamp.

Spread glue evenly on both surfaces and, taking particular care to line up the grooves, clamp the pieces together.

Step 2

Before the glue is set and while still in clamps drive plugs about 25 mm long into each end of the grooves to fill the holes. Flush the end carefully.

The work should now be carefully prepared for turning between centres.

Step 3

Using a gouge and round nose tool turn the work to the largest diameter. Use callipers to check the work.

Use a pencil and rule or working rod and carefully mark off the lengths on to the cylinder.

Step 4

A parting tool is used to turn the smallest diameters at points A and B. Check with callipers.

The waste is removed with a gouge or round nose chisel and finished with a square nose to ensure a flat surface.

Step 5

The parting tool is used to square the ends as far as possible without striking the centres.

Use a spear pointed chisel to shape the vee indicated in the drawing.

When the shape has been turned accurately the surface must be finished with abrasive paper.

Remove the lamp base from the lathe and level off the top and bottom. This can easily be done on a disc sanding machine or alternatively held in a vice, with suitable packing to prevent damage, and carefully planed using a smoothing plane.

Step 6

The top may now be drilled to accommodate a 12 mm ferrule which should be a firm fit in the hole. The ferrule will support a plastic socket which is screwed directly on the top.

Drill a hole in the base, attach the wire to the socket, thread it through the base and attach a plug.

All that is necessary now is a shade and the lamp is ready for use.

Step 1

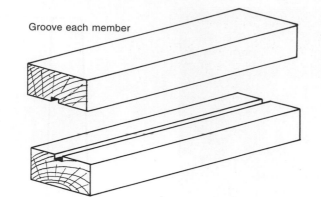

Groove each member

Step 2

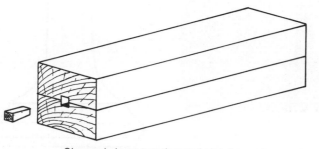

Glue and clamp together and plug the ends

Step 3

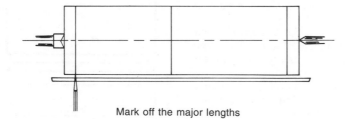

Mark off the major lengths

Step 4

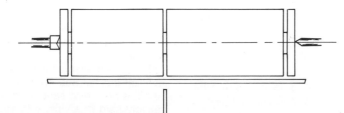

Turn the smallest diameters with a parting tool

Step 5

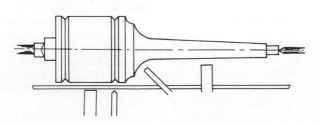

The various tools used to shape the lamp base

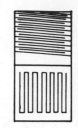

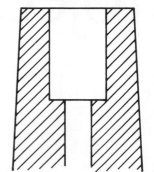

Top drilled to accommodate a 12 mm ferrule

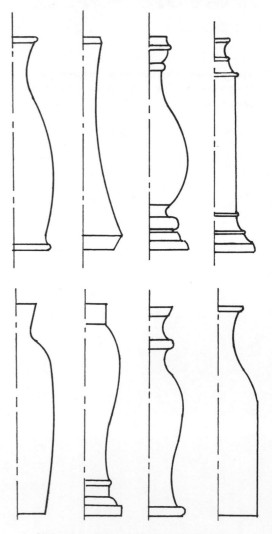

Alternative shapes suitable for a table lamp

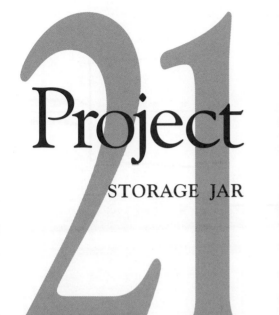

Project 21

STORAGE JAR

Step 1

Prepare a piece of timber 200 mm long x 100 mm square for turning between centres.

Turn between centres and prepare both ends for a cup chuck, one end for the lid, the other for the storage jar. Must be a firm fit in the chuck.

Drive one end of the cylinder into the cup chuck and part off the lid end.

Turn the outside shape.

Step 2

Hollow the container, using the deep turning technique. The container is only 70 mm deep and should not present many problems.

Clean up both inside and outside surfaces with abrasive paper. Use a parting tool and square the base.

Step 3

Turn the lid to fit the recess around the top of the jar.

Turn the outside shape of the lid and check the fit.

Hollow the inside of the lid.

Clean up both the inside and the outside of the jar with abrasive paper.

Use a parting tool to square the top. Take care when parting off, it may be advisable to use a saw.

When the parts are removed from the cup chuck carefully clean up the top and bottom using abrasive paper on a flat block.

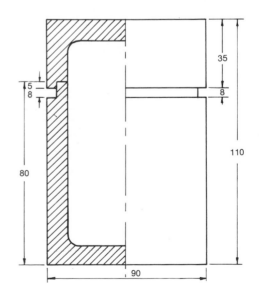

Step 1

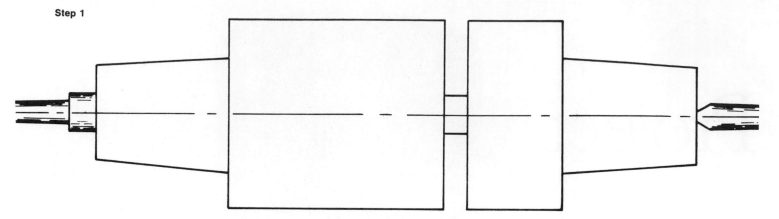

Turn both ends to suit a cup chuck

Step 2

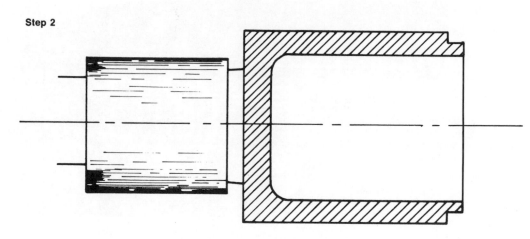

Deep turn the container

Step 3

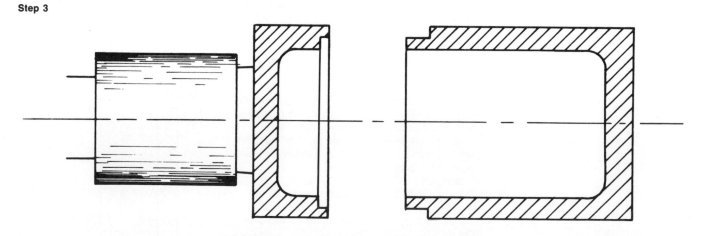

Shape the lid to fit the recess around the top of the jar

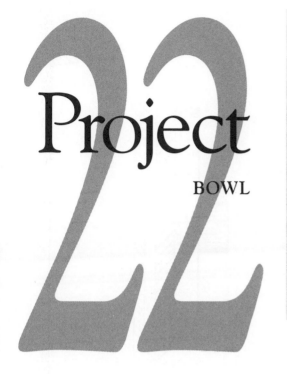

Project 22
BOWL

Examples of bowls

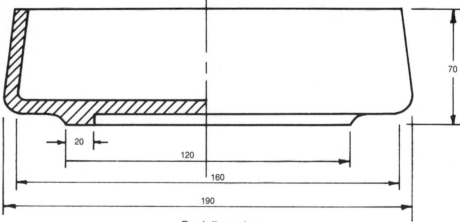

Bowl dimensions

BOWL

It is not advisable to mount the work directly on to a face plate as the screw holes will detract from the finished article. A much better job will result if an intermediate face plate is used in conjunction with ring chucking. Ring chucking is used where both sides need to be turned, and the ring provides the method of relocation.

Prepare a piece of timber 200 x 200 x 75 mm for face plate turning.

Mount the circular piece of timber directly on to a face plate and turn the outside shape, including the standing ring.

Finish with abrasive paper and remove from the face plate.

Secure a disc of 20 mm particle board 150 mm in diameter to the metal face plate and turn a recess to accommodate the ring. The recess should be 2 mm deep and a neat press fit with the bowl base.

A little glue is smeared around the ring and the intermediate face plate is clamped in position.

When the glue is set the bowl is remounted on the lathe and the inside turned. Deep turning techniques will be necessary to remove the waste.

Use abrasive paper to clean up.

To facilitate removal of the intermediate face plate it was made slightly larger than the ring. This will enable the use of a wide chisel to lever the particle board away from the bowl.

The bottom of the ring should only require cleaning up with abrasive paper before surface finishing.

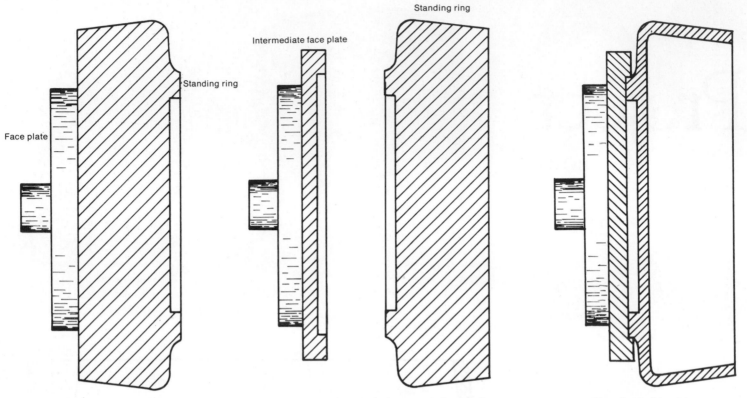

Turning the outside shape and standing ring

Turn the intermediate face plate to suit the standing ring

Turn the inside shape

PLATTER

It is not advisable to mount the work directly on to the face plate as the screw holes will detract from the finished article. A much better job will be made if an intermediate face plate is used (see Intermediate Face Plates, use of).

Make up an intermediate face plate 150 mm diameter from 20 mm raw particle board.

Using a 300 mm wide board 300 mm x 25 mm thick, plane a face on one surface.

Find the centre by joining the diagonals and scribe the largest possible circle. The circle may then be cut either on a bandsaw or using a portable jig saw.

Glue the intermediate face plate to the timber using a paper joint.

Attach the intermediate face plate to a metal face plate and mount on the lathe spindle.

Set up the tool rest to turn the outside shape first. Use the tail stock spindle for support as you will be working against the glue line.

Use abrasive paper and carefully prepare the surfaces for finishing.

Turn the inside shape.

Apply a clear surface finish using the simple jig illustrated to support the platter while the lacquer or varnish is drying.

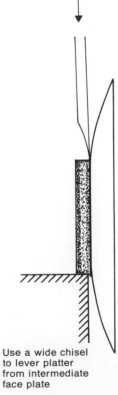

Turn the outside shape

Turn the inside shape

Use a wide chisel to lever platter from intermediate face plate

LAMINATING

...ITS PRINCIPLES, ITS USES AND ITS AESTHETICS

The art of laminating, dating back to the 15th century BC, is an essential part of present day industrial practice. The manufacture of sporting equipment, furniture components, and more recently structural laminates, such as roof beams, indicate some of the unique characteristics of timber.

In principle, laminating involves gluing together parallel-grained strips of timber, generally around a shaped 'former', to provide qualities not present in the initial material. With an increasing demand on what is now recognised as an exhaustible supply, the use of first grade, large dimensioned timber has become both expensive and wasteful. For this reason, coupled with the development in synthetic resin glues, manufacturers are now experimenting with new laminating techniques to enable a more economical use of the raw product.

Although the sophisticated machinery required for the mass production of laminated articles is not available to the amateur, often the ideas and designs involved may be adopted for single or 'one off' projects.

PRINCIPLES OF TIMBER LAMINATING

There are basically four main considerations involved in bending timber laminates to ensure a satisfactory end product: the correct selection of timber stock; a suitable softening process; an understanding of the stresses produced; the use of a suitable adhesive and drying time to prevent distortion.

Apart from the obvious economical implications, the lamination of timber occurs for the following reasons:

Aesthetics: This involves the use of timbers with similar bending characteristics but contrasting in colour. To ensure a pleasing appearance when using this method it is important to consider the concentricity or evenness of shaping in the resultant design of the finished article.

To Provide Timber of Larger Dimensions: When constructing 'formers' to enable the bending of large curves it is often necessary to 'build up' those formers by laminating smaller timber stock.

To Provide Increased Strength Properties: This includes the reduction of stresses where curves are involved, the controlling of movement by the alternation of growth rings in straight members, and the elimination of unnecessary and often non-functional joint detail.

A comparison of the strength to weight ratio reveals that laminated timber is considerably stronger than steel.

Selection of Timber Stock

In general it may be assumed that almost any species of timber is suitable for laminating. However, reference to the chart indicates that certain species are more suitable than others for particular purposes. Timbers selected for laminating must exhibit prescribed qualities. These should include strength, durability, freedom from defects, and a grain which is non-fissile, close, straight, and even.

The timbers may be used in one of two forms, either *solid* or *veneer*. Solid timber refers to strips of timber stock exceeding 2 mm in thickness, while veneer is defined as a thin wood sheet less than 2 mm in thickness.

The thickness of the laminate determines the minimum curvature through which it may be bent. Consequently it is important to make a 'dry run' to establish whether solid timber strips or veneer would be most suitable. This process enables the thickest possible material to be used, thereby allowing for fewer laminations. Moreover, experience has shown that the fewer the laminations the less the distortion following the removal of clamps.

The laminations should be cut approximately to size using a bandsaw or jigsaw. Where veneers are used, trimming may be done with a sharp knife, cutting with the best surface uppermost.

Where the laminates need to be of a certain thickness, obvious difficulties may arise in bending. In such cases they should be soaked in water, clamped around the former and allowed to dry. This process will 'pre-form' the laminates, but care should be taken to ensure that they are dry before gluing, to prevent a faulty glue line.

Solid timber strips may be produced by 'deep sawing' commercially available timber stock into 2 mm oversize strips, followed by passing it through a thicknesser to ensure an evenness of size. Veneers are obtainable from various plywood manufacturers or timber merchants and range from sliced to rotary peeled of varying lengths, widths, and thicknesses. Common thicknesses are .793 mm, 1.2 mm and 1.5 mm. Smaller veneers may be taped together, using specially prepared gummed paper, to provide a figured or multi-coloured surface.

When using veneers for larger projects, particularly cylindrical, it is necessary to 'cross band' internal veneers to provide rigidity.

Softening Process

The softening of timber laminates generally occurs only where it can be seen that the curvatures required may exceed the bending characteristics of the material. This can be easily ascertained by a dry run around a former of the desired shape. Veneer strips, for instance, may form most readily. However, thicker and wider laminates may indicate fracture lines when formed around similar shapes.

The most common method of softening timber laminates is by steaming. As most steaming is carried out at atmospheric pressure, a time allowance of one hour per 25 mm in thickness has proved adequate. Extended exposure to steaming may result in an increase in moisture content, causing problems of shrinkage and warping during re-drying.

A simple steam chamber may consist of a reasonably steam-tight wooden box large enough to accommodate the material being bent. The steam may be provided by a common urn connected to the steam chamber by means of a rubber hose. This type of steam chamber has a relatively short working life, but a thin copper lining suitably jointed will permit extended use.

The immersion of timber laminates in boiling water should be avoided as the moisture content is increased and the water may cause staining.

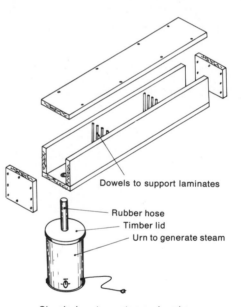

Dowels to support laminates

Rubber hose
Timber lid
Urn to generate steam

Simple box type steam chamber

The Forces of Tension and Compression

To understand the stresses incurred when bending timber refer to the two diagrammatic sketches. The first illustrates a parallel strip marked with parallel transverse lines 25 mm apart. In the second sketch, when the strip is bent, the lines do not remain parallel, but diverge on the convex edge and converge on the concave edge. However, along the centreline, or neutral axis, the lines remain 25 mm apart, indicating neither tension nor compression.

An important characteristic of timber is that it will compress considerably without fracture but will stretch only very little without fibre separation. Consequently it is necessary to protect the timber laminates from these tensile forces acting on the outside or convex surfaces.

One method is to use metal bands securely attached to adjustable end fittings to reduce the stretching force on the outside surfaces. Alternatively, as described in multiple piece formers, a number of sections having the correct outside curvature to apply against the shaped former are located as the laminates are bent.

Often when metal bands are used a lever is secured to the band to assist the bending.

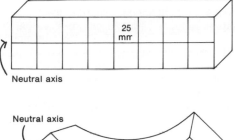

Neutral axis

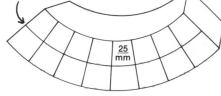

Neutral axis

Illustration of compression forces on the concave surface and the tension forces on the convex surface of a bent laminate

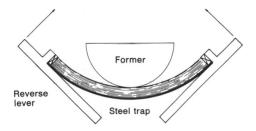

Diagramatic sketch of reversed lever bending machine

Adhesives

Adhesives are regarded as possessing adequate strength only if they can develop a shear strength higher than that of the timber. Because of the development of modern glues it is possible for timber members to be made into any required shape or size as well as making them adhere to other non-cellulose materials such as plastics and metals.

The characteristics of glue are widely variant and therefore careful consideration must be given to choosing the most suitable type for a particular purpose.

Thought should be given to the durability, ease of handling, setting requirements and cost of the glue.

The following precautions will assist in the gluing procedure:
- The moisture content of the components should be between 12% and 15%.
- A suitable glue correctly prepared should be used.
- The contact area of all surfaces to be bonded should be wet with glue.
- The meeting surfaces should be pressed firmly together while the glue is fluid.
- The glue line should be both continuous and very thin when set.
- Pressure should be maintained until the glue is sufficiently set to resist any parting.

Types of Glue

1. P.V.A.
2. *Casein* is available in the form of ready mixed powders requiring only the addition of water. These powders are frequently used as they give reliable bonds relatively easily, set at room temperature, and have good gap-filling qualities.
3. *Urea formaldehyde* is usually supplied as a 'two pot' mixture, one being the resin, the other the hardener. These glues normally provide a colourless glue line and exhibit controllable setting characteristics.
4. *Resorcinol formaldehyde* is used to make resorcinol based glues which are waterproof and suitable for the structural bonding of timber. They are produced as two components, one being the resin and the other usually a powder—the hardener and filler.
5. *Epoxy Resins* may be used where non-cellulose materials are glued to timber or where chemical resistance is required. However, they are difficult to use in comparison with orthodox woodworking glues as the mixed resins are not water-soluble.

Clamping Devices

In general sufficient and evenly distributed pressure is required to ensure uniform adherence of meeting surfaces. Research has provided evidence that a pressure of approximately 689 kilopascals is adequate for most timber species. For denser species of timber and glues with only fair gap-filling qualities, higher pressures may be required. It is important to check the position of laminates before and following clamping to eliminate undue slippage produced by clamp pressure and/or the application of glue. To this end pins or staples may prove more than helpful.

Suggested clamping devices include sash and bar clamps, G clamps, Webb clamps and bench vice, screw press, bolts and wing nuts. For clamping cylindrical veneers, rubber tubing cut into narrow strips is most satisfactory.

Waxed paper

To prevent the laminate from adhering to the 'former', waxed paper should be used as an intervening medium between the two

surfaces. This material facilitates easy removal of the laminate, prevents staining, but slows down the drying process.

Substances such as paraffin wax help prevent adhesion but may affect the surface finish of the laminate.

Formers

The function of the former is to provide a contoured surface against which the laminates may be firmly held while the glue is drying. This can vary from a piece of cylindrical stock, about which veneers have been wrapped to produce serviette rings, to sophisticated forming machines using hydraulic pressure and radio frequency glue-curing apparatus, as in the production of tennis racquets.

It is important that the formers be accurately shaped to allow the even distribution of pressure. A basic functional and aesthetic requirement of formers is that all curves be smooth and free flowing.

Two piece or male and female type formers should have a concentrically spaced material thickness allowance as well as location pins to ensure accurate positioning. The width of the former should exceed the finished laminates by 15 mm to 20 mm to ensure good glue lines on the outside edges.

Timber formers should be sealed, using a suitable polish or wax to prevent the laminates adhering to them.

METHODS OF LAMINATING

Butt-jointed Blanks

The simplest method of laminating consists of butt-jointing timbers of similar or differing colours to form built up blanks. The blanks can then be shaped to a predetermined design using either handtools or machines. It is important that the width and thickness of each laminate be controlled so as to maintain an evenness of appearance following shaping. Built up blanks to be lathe-mounted must have their centres accurately located to achieve the laminate concentricity of the finished article.

Projects using this method of laminating include cheese boards, table lamps, platters, bowls, and candle sticks.

Butt-jointed blank using blackwood and silver ash solid strips—suitable for use as a chopping board or cheese board

Project 23

LAMINATED CHOPPING BOARD

Chopping Boards are considered an essential item in any well laid-out kitchen. They are available in various shapes and sizes and generally the more functional and aesthetic boards are constructed wholly of timber.

The following design for a laminated chopping board provides for simplicity of construction and durability.

Procedure

Select a suitable pored timber and dress it to approximately 30 x 30 P.A.R. Mark off the required lengths, slightly oversize, and cut them off.

Plane the pieces edge to edge and check that the end grain is alternating from piece to piece. This helps to maintain the board in a flat condition (see end view). Check the face grain and mark the grain direction with an arrow to ensure that all pieces have their grain running in the same direction.

Using three bar clamps, two underneath and one on top, make a 'dry fit' to ensure that all edges pull up neatly. Using a waterproof glue, glue the strips of timber together and reclamp. Before fully tightening the bar clamps, check that the ends of the strips are flush and the top surface is similarly flush. If the glue is allowed to gel (that is, dry slightly), this helps to eliminate the problem of slippage.

Once the glue has dried, the top and bottom surfaces are planed flat—hence the need for all pieces to have their grain running in the same direction. Square one end with a smoothing plane and square the other end to the desired length.

Finishing

Using an orbital sander, clean up the top and bottom surfaces with 220 grit abrasive paper and the ends and edges using a cork block and similar abrasive paper. Since the chopping board is to come in contact with food, a vegetable oil of some description would best serve as a suitable finishing material. This may be readily applied using a brush or cloth.

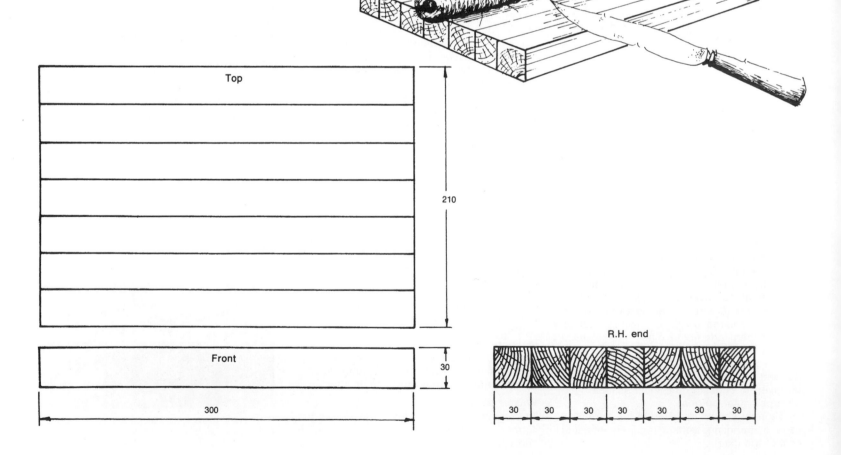

Project 24

LAMINATED CHEESE BOARD

As with chopping boards, cheese boards are also a most useful item in the kitchen/dining area. Cheese boards are generally more elaborate and smaller than chopping boards as they are often used as part of a dining-table setting.

The laminated design suggested, while similar in construction to the chopping board, has a few added refinements. There is some shaping and it is smaller, making it both functional and attractive.

Procedure

The basic rectangular laminated shape is produced in the same manner as the chopping board. Having planed the top and bottom surfaces flat, square one end using a smoothing plane. At the other end mark out a radius and using a jig saw or bandsaw, cut out the semicircle.

At the same end, bore a large hole using a Forstner bit. Again, through the same end, two holes may be drilled to run into the Forstner bit hole to allow a thick rope to be attached. This can be used to hang up the cheese board after use.

The semi-circle should be cleaned up using a flat-soled spokeshave and then with 180 grit abrasive paper. The top and bottom surfaces should be cleaned up using an orbital sander.

Finishing

Again the cheese board should be coated with a non-toxic vegetable oil.

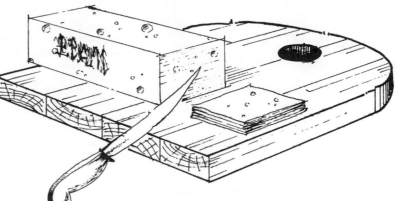

Hung up by rope through the end and knotted in hole

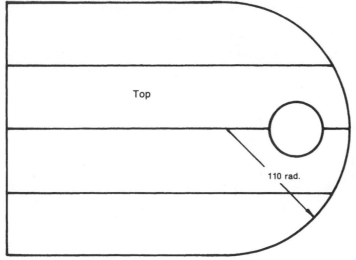

Top

110 rad.

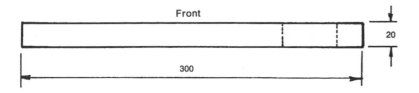

Front

300

20

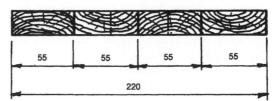

R.H. end

55   55   55   55

220

Project 25

MOBILE CHOPPING BOARD

The frame should then be assembled using three countersunk head screws in each corner joint and in conjunction with P.V.A. glue, with the shorter side planed between the longer sides. Once all screws are inserted and headed the ends of the longer sides should be planed flush with the outside surface of the shorter sides.

As a means of screwing the laminated top a small 25 mm x 25 mm cleat is screwed and glued to fit flush with the inside top edge of the frame. Finally the positions of the screws for attaching the legs should be marked and then the holes drilled, ready for assembly (see sketch).

Laminated Top

Although this is the most time-consuming section of the construction it is relatively simple. The strips of timber comprising the laminated board should be P.A.R. and laid edge to edge with their grain direction alternating. Ensure that each strip has its surface grain running in the same direction. The strips are then glued with preferably a waterproof glue and placed between two bar clamps. A third bar clamp should be placed on the top surface to assist in holding the laminated board flat.

While the clamps are only firm, the strips should be levelled at the ends and on the top surface. Once the clamps have been tightened, any excess glue should be removed.

When dry, the laminated board should be planed flat on both top and bottom surfaces and the ends placed to fit flush with the outside edge of the frame.

Assembly

Using countersunk head screws attach the laminated top to the cleats on the inside of the frame. The edges of the laminated board can now be easily planed flush with the outside of the frame (if required). The legs are then attached by using screws through the frame. It is advisable to position the screws into the legs first and then drill a pilot hole some 30 mm into the leg—this will prevent splitting as the screw is screwed home.

Finishing

All surfaces should be sanded using a range of abrasive paper between 120 grit and 240 grit. Since the top surface is to be in contact with food, vegetable oil or something similar should be used as the finishing medium. The frame and legs may have other appropriate clear finishes applied.

This easily constructed and useful kitchen aid consists basically of three components—legs, square outside frame, and laminated top. While the unit may be constructed of any desired timber species, it is recommended that timber properties such as taste, smell, resin content, etc., be considered prior to selection of the material. This is particularly essential for the material used in the laminated top.

Procedure

Legs

Assuming the timber for the legs is purchased in a planed all-round (P.A.R.) condition, very little preparation, other than cutting them to the required length, is required. Although the working drawing suggests a specific height, the height of the user should be considered and the subsequent length of the legs adjusted accordingly. The bottom ends of the legs should be prepared for screw on castors.

Outside Frame

As there are no rails connecting the legs, it is essential that the width of the outside frame sides be sufficiently deep to provide adequate support and rigidity for the legs. The two shorter sides of the frame should be squared to length using a smoothing plane while the two longer sides may be left sawn to length.

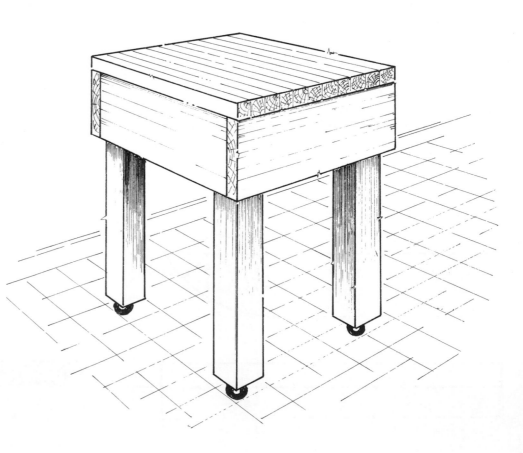

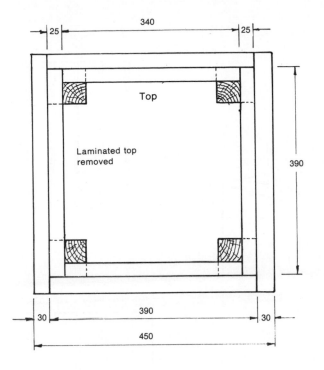

Top

25 — 340 — 25

Laminated top removed

390

30 — 390 — 30

450

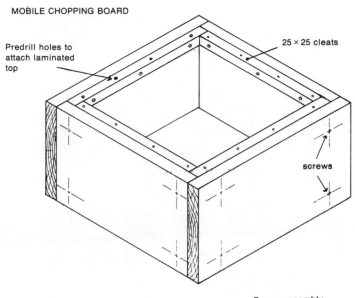

MOBILE CHOPPING BOARD

Predrill holes to attach laminated top

25 × 25 cleats

screws

Frame assembly

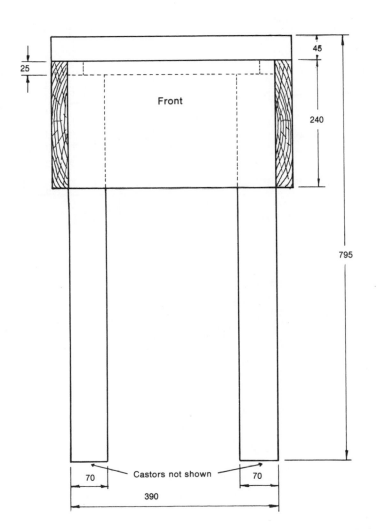

Front

45

25

240

795

70

Castors not shown

70

390

Note: Timber for top 45 × 45

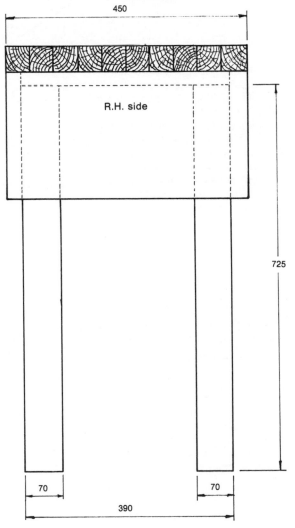

450

R.H. side

725

70

70

390

Project 26

BENCH KNIFE RACK

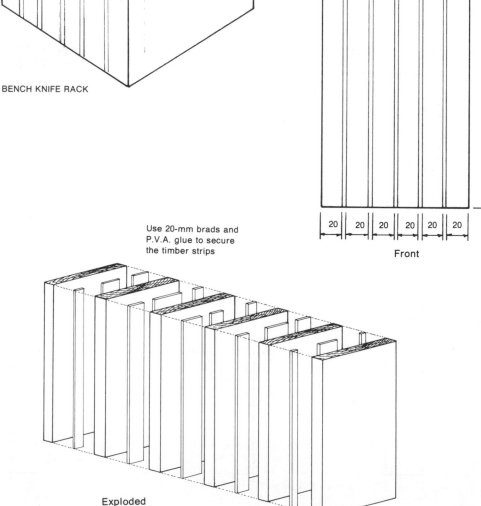

BENCH KNIFE RACK

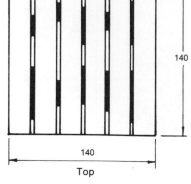

140

140

Top

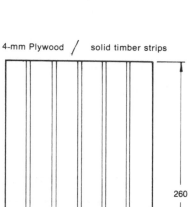

4-mm Plywood / solid timber strips

260

20 20 20 20 20 20

Front

Use 20-mm brads and
P.V.A. glue to secure
the timber strips

Exploded

This unit is made up of a series of 20 mm thick timber boards, separated by strips of 4 mm plywood. Initial planning depends on the number of knives to be stored, the width and length of their blades, the thickness of handles, and the type of timber to be used. It is suggested that a plan-view be drawn to illustrate the width of the gap between the plywood strips to accommodate each knife blade and to show the width of each plywood strip required. It may be found, for example, that the thickness of handles requires more than 20 mm thick timber boards. The longest knife blade is then measured and at least 20 mm added on to provide the overall height of the knife holder.

Timber Boards

From the working drawing it is possible to determine the number and size of the timber sections required. While the drawing illustrates a square knife holder, the size and number of knives to be stored may dictate that its shape be rectangular. Mark out and cut the appropriate number of timber sections and square both ends of each piece. This is best achieved by planing one end square to a knife-cut line, clamping all sections together, and planing the other end square, again to a knife-cut line. Each timber section should then be sanded, particular emphasis being given to the ends.

Plywood Strips

Again from the working drawing, determine the number and width of the various plywood

272

strips required and cut them to length. Sand each end using 240-grit garnet paper. It is possible, if facilities allow, to use 4 mm timber strips in lieu of plywood strips.

Assembly

Using 20 mm brads and P.V.A. glue, secure the appropriate number of plywood strips on to the first timber section. Care should be taken to ensure that the ends of the plywood strips and timber section are flush and that the edges are likewise.

The second timber section is then clamped into position over the glued surfaces of the plywood strips and allowed to dry. This timber section then has the next series of plywood strips glued and nailed into position and again the next timber section glued to these strips.

This process is continued until a sufficient number of slots have been produced to hold all knives required. One aspect of this particular design is that additions can be readily made as new knives are purchased.

Finishing

All outside surfaces, including the ends, should be sanded using 240 grit abrasive paper. A suitable clear finish should then be applied either by spraying or brush.

METHODS OF LAMINATING

Formers

The use of formers suggests the material being laminated is capable of bending to conform to the prescribed former shape. Consequently the laminates are considerably thinner than those used for butt-jointing blanks. For smaller projects, such as biscuit barrels, veneer 1 mm in thickness may be suitable, while dining chairs may require laminates of up to 4 mm in thickness. It should be realised that the laminate thickness is the controlling factor on the curvatures which may be applied to the formers.

Single Formers

(a) Wrapping (cylindrical)

Using a lathe, prepare a *slightly* tapered cylindrical former of the required proportions and cover it with waxed paper. The taper should be such that it assists the removal of the project from the former but small enough to permit accurate wrapping of the veneer strips.

Having dampened the initial veneer to provide suppleness, staple one end to the former and wrap it in a spiral fashion, making sure that the edges butt firmly together. Staple the other end to the former. A second veneer, glued on one surface, is spiralled over the first but running in the opposite direction. This procedure may be repeated for further layers depending on the wall thickness required.

Provided sufficient tension can be applied to the veneer strips, no additional clamping

pressure is necessary. However, stretching rubber strips tightly around the former will ensure that even pressure is distributed over the glued surfaces. Once the glue has dried, the ends may be trimmed and the surface sanded while being rotated on the lathe.

Tops and bases of suitable shapes are then turned to fit the veneered article.

Suggested projects applicable to the method include salt and pepper shakers, spice containers, and serviette rings.

(b) Wrapping (wide strips)

This method is often used where the formers are relatively large with various cross sectional shapes but with parallel sides. Consequently it is necessary to use wide strips of veneer with the grain running parallel with the vertical axis of the former. This allows the veneer to be wrapped around the former without splits occurring.

The length of each veneer strip is three and a half times that of the circumference of the former. In some instances it may be necessary to butt and tape together shorter lengths of veneer to obtain the required length.

Cylindrical former wrapped with wide strips of veneer—note slight overlap of veneer

The former is covered with waxed paper and the veneer, coated with P.V.A. glue on the inside surface, rolled tightly around it. Lengths of rubber strips are then wound firmly around the former to provide an even distribution of pressure.

Once the glue has dried, the rubber strips are removed and the lap joint is filed and glasspapered to blend in with the outside shape.

Circular projects may be cleaned up and parted to length while mounted in the lathe. Other shapes require cutting to length using

a tenon saw and sanding by hand.

Bases and lids may be turned or shaped to the appropriate proportions to fit the veneered form.

Veneer held firmly in position by lengths of rubber strips wrapped around the former

(c) Wrapping (diagonally)

Using a built up blank, turn a tapered former having 50 mm of waste material at each end. While the lathe is rotating, mark with a pencil the two diameters, indicating the length of the finished laminated article. These diameters, converted into circles, which are subsequently divided into an equal number of parts, provide the tapered shape of each veneer strip.

Turned lid fitted to the top of the canister

Built up blank of particle board turned to desired shape using a wood lathe

Particle board former wrapped with waxed paper

but not harden, the rubber strips are removed and the joint trimmed with a straight edge and a sharp knife. Both the waxed paper and rubber strips are replaced and the glue allowed to harden.

Attaching the second layer of tapered veneer strips at an angle opposing the first layer

Using this prepared paper shape as a templet the required number of veneers may be cut. Sufficient material at each end of the veneer strips should be left for stapling purposes. The former is then covered with waxed paper.

Attach the initial veneer strip to the former at the predetermined angle using the 50 mm waste material for stapling purposes. Continue this procedure until the first layer is complete. It will be necessary to trim the last veneer strip.

Subsequent diagonal layers may continue to be applied, depending on the strength requirements of the article.

The outside layer involves wrapping a good quality cartridge paper around the former to provide a development of the final shape. This pattern is used to build up a curved piece of veneer having its grain running towards the apex. The length of this veneer piece is cut to allow a small overlap. The outside layer is then glued, wrapped tightly around the second layer, and covered with waxed paper.

The trimming to length and cleaning up with abrasive paper may be carried out while the project is mounted in the lathe. It is then removed from the former and sanded on the inside surface.

To provide a more aesthetic and hygienic surface for the inside, a veneer is prepared similarly as for the outside but trimmed to the exact shape of the former. This veneer is coated with P.V.A. glue on the outside and firmly forced upwards into the cone-like shape of the veneered project.

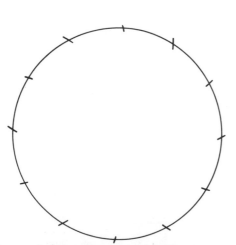

Larger diameter divided into twelve equal parts

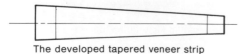

The developed tapered veneer strip

Initial tapered veneer strips stapled into position

Coating the initial veneer strips using a 12 mm brush and P.V.A. glue

To attach the second layer, first locate the veneer strip angle, which for strength and stability purposes must be opposite the first layer. Glue is now applied to the first layer and, using the reverse side of the veneer strips, locate and staple the second layer as before.

Strong rubber strips are now used to apply an even pressure over the full length of the former. Care should be taken to work in the same direction as the overlap of the outside veneer.

Allowing sufficient time for the glue to gel,

274

Using a large sheet of cartridge paper to provide a development of the outside shape

Wide veneer strips joined with gummed paper to form the developed shape

Applying P.V.A. glue to the developed veneer wrapping—note gummed paper on the outside

Wrapping the veneer around the former—note P.V.A. glue applied to both surfaces

Position the veneer evenly around the former with a small overlap

Trimming the joint with a straight edge and sharp knife

Former wrapped with rubber strips and allowed to dry

Trimming to length and cleaning up operations carried out on a wood lathe

Two Piece Formers

The simplest method of making two piece formers is to mark a free form line on the edge of a square or rectangular block of timber and cut the shape accurately using a bandsaw. The cuts are cleaned up with a plane or file and abrasive paper. Pressure may be applied with G clamps or, if these two piece formers are to be used often, metal bars attached by bolts may be more appropriate. This method, however, should be confined to simple shapes using thin laminates, as no provision has been made for laminate thickness.

To make a salad server, for example, develop a sectional shape of appropriate length and suitable curvature to function as a salad server; transfer this shape (paper templet if required) to a rectangular former; bandsaw as accurately as possible to this shape; clean up the curvature of the two sections of the former to ensure smooth surfaces; glue three or four layers of veneer together and place them between the wax paper-covered surfaces of the former; and clamp the former together using G clamps and allow them to dry. Then using a further paper templet, develop a plan view; attach this templet to the laminated veneers and bandsaw to shape; and clean up with a file and abrasive paper and polish with peanut oil.

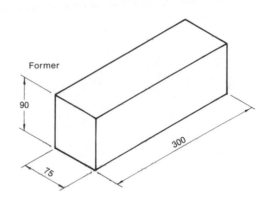

Former

90

300

75

Dress the material to size

Bandsaw to shape

Face veneers

Thicker core veneers

Prepare the laminates

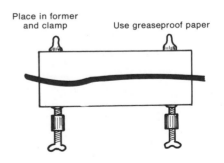

Place in former and clamp   Use greaseproof paper

For two piece formers providing laminate thickness allowance, it is recommended that they be cut from separate timber sections. The lower section or female shape is cut out and cleaned up to provide a flat surface square to both edges. Using this section as a pattern, the male former may be marked out. A pair of dividers adjusted to the correct clearance allowance and held against the female section will scribe the shape to be sawn. The male former is then cleaned up and checked against the female former for accuracy of the allowance.

For larger projects, such as waterskis, it is necessary to build up one or both ends of the former to accommodate the curvature required. Alternatively, for medium sized projects, a singular suitably shaped former may be used. This method involves clamping one

end of the laminates to the former and pulling them over the curved section, clamping them flat.

Sufficient pressure is applied by the laminates themselves over the curved section and further pressure if required may be applied by clamping on the straight sections.

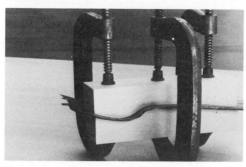

Two piece former suitable for salad servers with veneers clamped in position—note the use of waxed paper

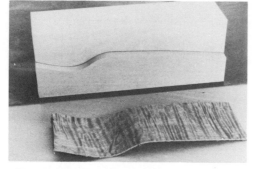

The shaped veneer on removal from the former

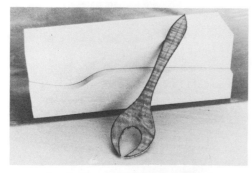

Laminate cut to the desired shape

Two piece former illustrating thickness allowance

Veneers and waxed paper located in position ready for clamping

Formed laminate on removal from the former

Cassette holder

Laminated water skis showing the two piece built up former

Built-up, two-piece form suitable for a large tray. Note the rounded corners of the male former and the corresponding radius on the female shape

The completed tray with black bean veneers and corresponding handles

Multiple Piece Formers

For projects involving complex or tight curves it is often an advantage to construct formers having a number of sections which may be applied as the laminate is shaped. This is particularly applicable in chair or table construction where the laminates may be bent through or past 90° or from a concave to a convex curve. Also, for this type of construction, solid timber laminates are desirable. Therefore some means of controlling the rate of bending is necessary if splitting is to be prevented.

One method of constructing multiple piece formers is to build up either the inside or outside shape, using solid timber or laminated particle board, and glue and screw this shape to a suitable base board. In practice, fixing the inside shape to the base board has proved most successful. The finished laminate thickness is determined and a line scribed using the fixed section of the former as a guide to indicate the shape of the movable former sections. The laminates are clamped at one end and drawn around the curves, positioning the movable former sections as required. To assist the bending of the laminates, they should be steamed and pre-formed to test their susceptibility to splitting. This method allows the inside and outside laminates—those under the most stress—to be relocated centrally when gluing is carried out.

Another type of multiple piece former is that used to construct chair backs and seats. This consists of a female former having a number of concave shaped members, preferably from solid timber, joined together to form an open frame. The male former, while constructed in a similar manner, has convex members shaped to provide laminate material allowance. Pressure may be applied using a series of G clamps or placing in a screw press.

This particular former is often used to glue and shape a number of plywood panels. Care should be taken to ensure that the grain direction runs parallel to the curvature.

Laminated dining chair of Radiata pine constructed with multiple formers, and with rubber webbing for the seat support

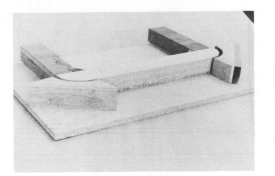
Multiple piece former suitable for bending a number of laminates through 90°

The bent laminates assembled to form a small occasional table

Occasional table laminated with teak veneers

Classification of Australian Timbers Used in Bending

Bending Quality	Species	Botanical Name	State of Origin
Excellent	Red tulip oak	*Tarrietia peralata*	North Queensland
	Myrtle beech	*Nothofagus cunninghamii*	Tasmania
	Southern sassafras	*Atherosperma moschatum*	Tasmania
	Celery top pine	*Phyllocladus rhomboidalis*	Tasmania
Very good	Northern silky oak	*Cardwellia sublimus*	North Queensland
	Silver quandong	*Elaeocarpus grandis*	North Queensland New South Wales
	Huon pine	*Dacrydium franklinii*	Tasmania
	King William pine	*Athrotaxis selaginoides*	Tasmania
	Southern blue gum	*Eucalyptus globulus*	Tasmania, Victoria
	Radiata pine	*Pinus radiata*	Plantation
Good	Silver ash	*Flindersia pubescens*	North Queensland
	Yellow siris	*Albizzia xanthoxylon*	Queensland
	Blackwood	*Acacia melanoxylon*	Tasmania, Victoria
	Mountain ash	*Eucalyptus regnans*	Tasmania, Victoria
	Messmate stringy bark	*Eucalyptus obliqua*	Tasmania, Victoria
	Karri	*Eucalyptus diversicolor*	Western Australia

ELEMENTARY CARPENTRY

...ADDING YOUR OWN TOUCHES AROUND YOUR HOME

Persons unfamiliar with trade nomenclature assume that people who work with wood are carpenters. This, however, is not so, as the carpenter's work is mainly confined to building construction, such as large buildings, housing industry and commerce, home building, and repairs and alterations.

The art of carpentry is thousands of years old, and for centuries the carpenter's work was almost entirely with wood. The modern carpenter, however, works with a variety of modern materials, including steel and plastic.

BUILDING LAWS

It is essential to check with the relevant authorities, and these may include the water and sewerage departments and local councils, regarding regulations which may concern any proposed project.

This will apply particularly if extensions to a house, carport, pergola, or other major alterations are contemplated. There are also regulations governing garages, toolsheds, and fences.

Building inspectors employed by local councils will explain relevant laws, and advice about building materials is freely available from suppliers.

Financing an addition, alteration, or perhaps a new fence, need not be a problem, as money is available through a number of sources. Initial enquiries could be made through a bank, or a finance company or credit union. Large department stores and handyman centres also provide credit.

In order to plan an addition so that it will harmonise with or match any existing structure it is essential to understand some of the methods and terminology used in the industry.

ROOF CONSTRUCTION

Roof Form

The most common forms are the pitched roof with gable and hipped ends.

With the traditional type of roof framing, total loads of roof covering and framing materials together with the fixing of top plates in timber or brick veneer construction would be more than sufficient to restrain the roof from being lifted in the most severe gales. Top plates may be tied down with hoop iron straps built into the walls.

Nailing

The important of nailing roof members is stressed. The failure to use sufficient nails of adequate length and gauge may result in defective structures. 75 mm x 9 g nails are recommended for general use.

Metal Framing Anchors

These are available commercially and may be used for any joints occurring in roof framing.

Pitch

The function of the roof is to exclude weather, and therefore it must be designed to shed rain water. This implies some degree of pitch even in a nominally flat roof. A flat roof may be considered as anything less than 5° pitch, and a low pitch from 5° to 22°. (See diagram over page.)

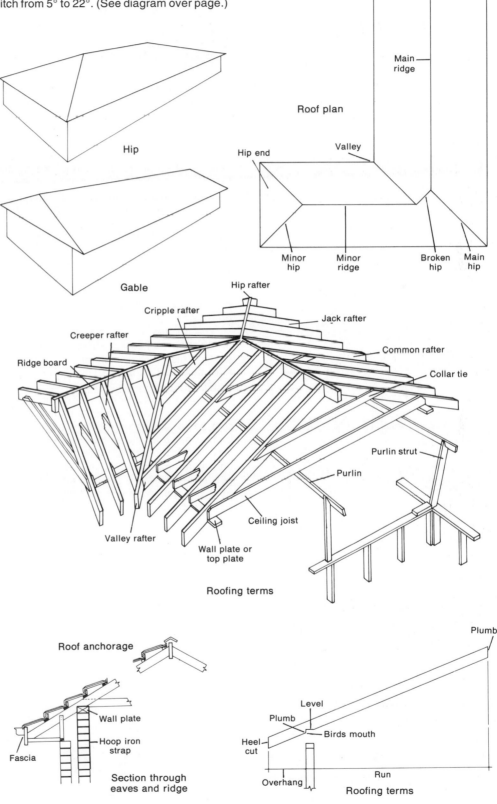

Hip

Gable

Roof plan

Gable end

Verge

Main ridge

Valley

Hip end

Minor hip

Minor ridge

Broken hip

Main hip

Hip rafter

Cripple rafter

Jack rafter

Creeper rafter

Common rafter

Ridge board

Collar tie

Purlin strut

Purlin

Ceiling joist

Valley rafter

Wall plate or top plate

Roofing terms

Roof anchorage

Wall plate

Hoop iron strap

Fascia

Section through eaves and ridge

Plumb

Level

Plumb

Birds mouth

Heel cut

Overhang

Run

Roofing terms

279

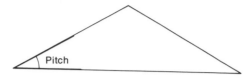

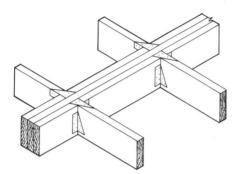

Pitch

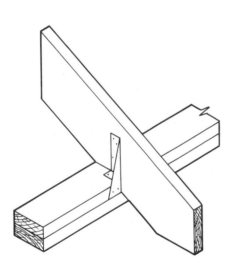

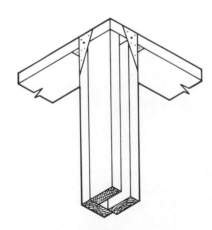

Typical applications of framing anchors

Covering Materials

Sheet Roofing
Corrugated galvanised iron
Cold rolled formed metal decking

Tiling
Cement roof tiles/Terracotta roof tiles
Shingles

Flashings
The finishing of roofs at points of abuttal with parapets, chimneys, and other such ancillary features is most likely to be the cause of leaks.

In most cases the projection through the roof will move independently of the roof and it is important that the roof covering material should not be attached to the projecting surface.

The gap between the roofing material and the projection is waterproofed with a cover flashing which is fastened to the projecting surface. Sheet metal makes the best cover flashing.

Roofs

If an attached carport or garage is contemplated, several alternatives may be considered.

The addition of a gable at right angles to an existing roof looks excellent but is quite costly. This involves cutting into the roof to add the new structure, and running new cladding up to the peak of the new gable.

A roof may also be added to an existing gable end. It is possible to tie into an existing roof, a method which will ensure harmony, and can be, as shown here, a gable within a gable.

It is also possible to tie into a roof, as shown, but this method can only be used with success if the eaves are high enough to have an acceptable pitch without bringing the new eaves too low.

Gable within a gable

Gable at right angles

A flat roof, with just enough pitch for drainage, is also suitable and somewhat cheaper.

Tying into a roof

Flat roof with just enough pitch for drainage

FOOTINGS AND SUB-FLOORING

The term foundation refers to the natural material of the site on which the building rests, while the term footing refers to the lowest part of the structure which bears the load of the structure and transfers this load in such a way as to ensure equilibrium of the structure.

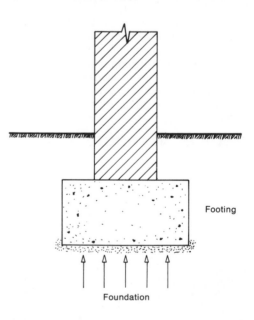

Footing

Foundation

Materials used for Footings

Reinforced Concrete
Is being used generally for reasons of economy, its strength, ease of handling, design flexibility, and availability.

Brickwork

Is still commonly used but should be reinforced with mild steel rods or hoop iron. Brickwork is particularly useful for underpinning work.

Stone

Is used in certain areas where suitable sandstone is readily available. Stable foundations are necessary where its use is proposed. For footing types, see diagram at right.

Protection of Sub-Flooring

This involves:

1. Proper drainage to prevent the moist conditions favourable to decay-causing fungi.
2. Adequate ventilation, a further safeguard against fungi.
3. The provision of termite shields.
4. The installation of damp-proof courses.
5. Site clearing.
6. Soil poisoning.

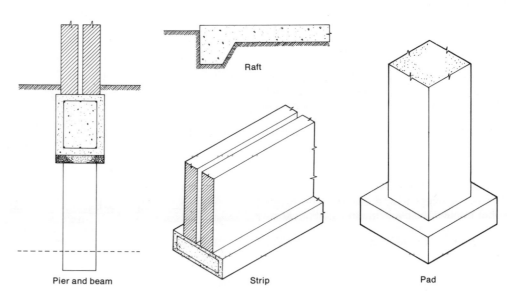

Pier and beam

Raft

Strip

Pad

Types of footing

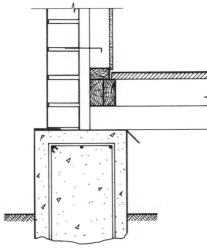

Floor framing

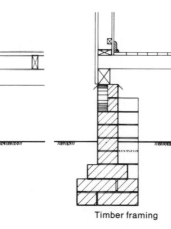

Brick veneer

Timber framing

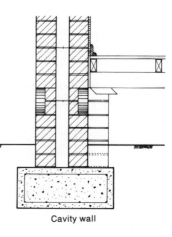

Cavity wall

Floor framing

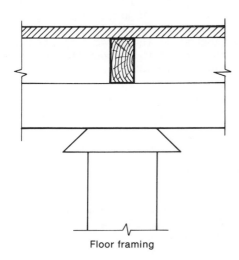

Floor framing

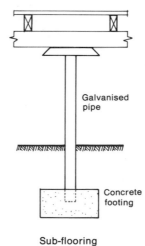

Brick pier

Galvanised pipe

Concrete footing

Sub-flooring

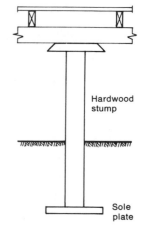

Hardwood stump

Sole plate

WALL FRAMING

Wall framing may be defined as the vertical framing constructed to support a roof, provide openings such as doors and windows, and to which cladding and linings are fixed.

Plates and studs are the main components, and when the frames are true they are braced diagonally to prevent racking. The horizontal member above a door or window opening is known as a door or window head. Vertical studs that form a door are known as jamb studs.

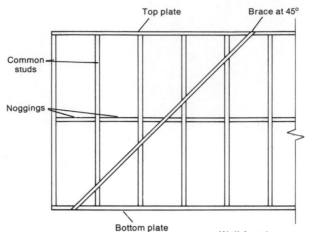

Wall framing

Fixing Studs to Plates

Two 75 mm nails should at each joint be driven either through the plate into the stud or skew-nailed through the stud into the plate. Nails should not be smaller than 75 mm x 9 swg.

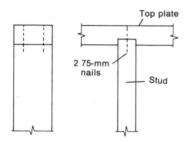

Fixing studs to top plate

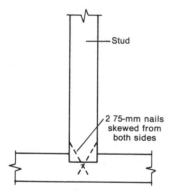

Trenched bottom plate

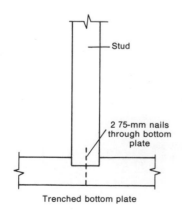

Trenched bottom plate

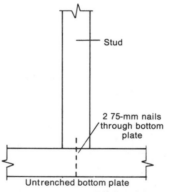

Untrenched bottom plate

Alternative fixing of studs to bottom plate

For plates thicker than 45 mm a longer nail is required.

Nogging

The studs in each panel of walling should be stiffened by means of closely fitted solid timber nogging pieces, spaced not more than 1300 mm centres. Closer spacing may be neces-

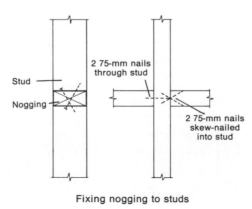

Fixing nogging to studs

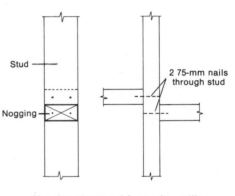

Nogging staggered for easier nailing

sary for support or fixing of cladding or linings.

Noggings should be nailed with two 75 mm nails driven through the stud at each joint. Skew-nailing should be used when through nailing is not practicable.

Ceiling joists should be in single lengths, where possible, and in the case of coupled roofs, similar in spacing and direction to the main roof rafters. This allows them to be fixed so that they act as ties between the feet of pairs of opposing rafters.

Cladding

Cladding is the outer covering of the external walls of a framed building.

Function

Cladding must:
1. Withstand the action of wind, rain, heat, and cold.
2. Provide the desired thermal insulation.
3. Provide acoustic insulation.
4. Prevent access.
5. Provide additional strength.

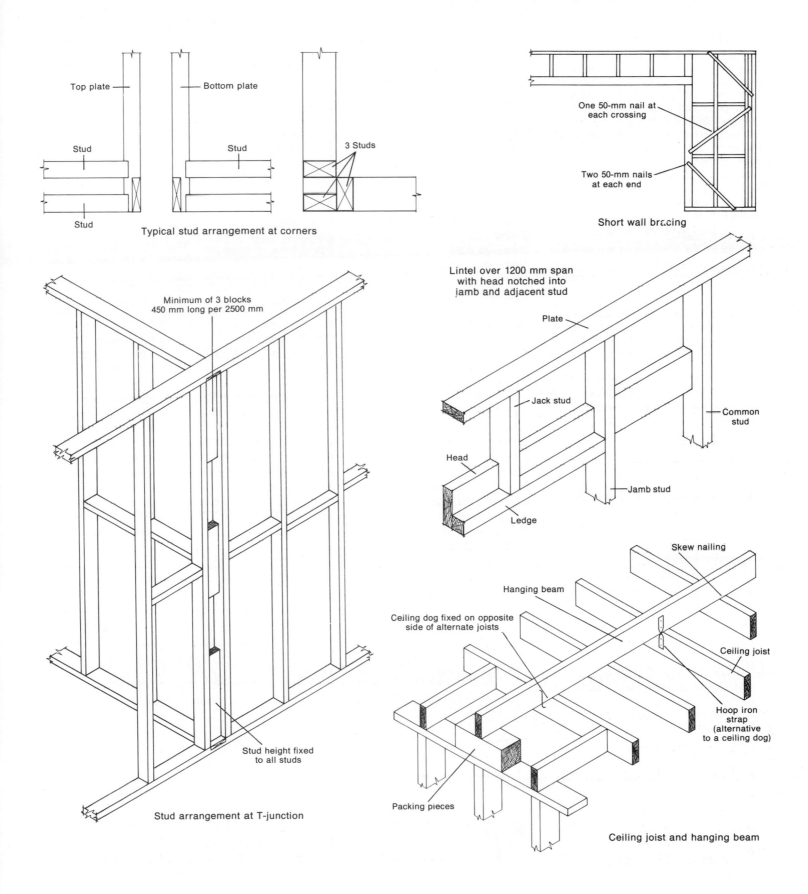

Top plate

Bottom plate

Stud

Stud

3 Studs

Stud

Stud

Typical stud arrangement at corners

One 50-mm nail at each crossing

Two 50-mm nails at each end

Short wall bracing

Minimum of 3 blocks 450 mm long per 2500 mm

Lintel over 1200 mm span with head notched into jamb and adjacent stud

Plate

Jack stud

Common stud

Head

Jamb stud

Ledge

Stud height fixed to all studs

Stud arrangement at T-junction

Skew nailing

Hanging beam

Ceiling dog fixed on opposite side of alternate joists

Ceiling joist

Hoop iron strap (alternative to a ceiling dog)

Packing pieces

Ceiling joist and hanging beam

Types of Cladding

1. Boards or sheets of a variety of material fixed by mechanical fastening or adhesive.
2. Veneer construction, where a single thickness of non-load bearing ceramic or concrete brick is supported on the footing and bonded to the frame with wall ties.

Other factors relating to cladding materials:
Aesthetics
Acoustics
Insulation
Joint design
Finishing and deterioration
Resistance to fire

Solid Timber Cladding

Weatherboards are available in a number of overlapping profiles and may, for vertical cladding, be built up with boards and battens or cover strips.

Joints in Solid Timber Cladding are used:

1. To join together adjacent boards.
2. To form expansion joints to allow for dimensional changes brought about by seasonal moisture change.
3. To prevent penetration of rain or rust.
4. To allow water to get away quickly so that it will not be absorbed by the cladding.

Cladding profiles

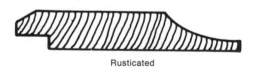

Rusticated

Semi-rusticated

Bevel siding

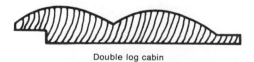

Double log cabin

Double teardrop

Cladding Timbers (By States)

The following schedule has been based on timbers appropriate to each State. Some are native to those States, others are imported, but all may be assumed to be more or less freely available. The listings are alphabetical.

SOUTH AUSTRALIA	VICTORIA	WESTERN AUSTRALIA
Cedar, Western red	Ash, mountain	Blackbutt, W.A.
Jarrah	Cedar, Western red	Cedar, Western red
Meranti	Oregon	Jarrah
Oak, Tasmanian (Australian Oak)	Pine, white Baltic	Karri
Oregon	Pine, red Baltic	Pine, radiata (treated)
Pine, radiata (treated and untreated)	Pine, Cypress	Tuart
Pine, red Baltic	Pine, radiata (treated)	Wandoo
Redwood, Californian	Redwood, Californian	
	Stringybark, messmate	

NEW SOUTH WALES	TASMANIA	QUEENSLAND
Ash, alpine	Beech, myrtle	Blackbutt
Ash, silvertop	Oak, Tasmanian	Box, brush
Blackbutt	Pine, radiata (treated)	Gum, forest red
Box, brush		Gum, grey
Cedar, Western red		Gum, rose
Gum, rose	NORTH QUEENSLAND	Gum, Sydney blue
Gum, spotted		Ironbark
Gum, Sydney blue	Gum, rose	Mahogany, red
Mahogany, red	Hardwood, Johnstone River	Mahogany, white
Oregon	Maple, scented	Pine, Cypress
Pine, white Baltic	Penda, brown	Pine, hoop (treated)
Pine, white Cypress	Satinash, grey	Pine, slash (treated)
Pine, radiata (treated)	Stringybark, white and other approved species	Satinay
Redwood, Californian		Stringybark, white
Stringybark, messmate		Tallowwood
Tallowwood		

Splayed, checked and nosed

Splayed

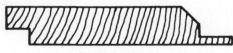

Ship lap with V joint

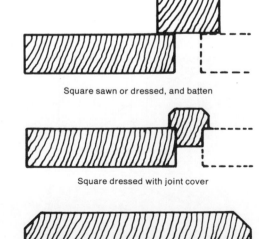

Square sawn or dressed, and batten

Square dressed with joint cover

Double grooved and chamfer

Joints

To meet the function mentioned above, the profile should be simple so that it will not trap moisture. It must be robust and complete in itself. The minimum lap allowed is generally between 11 mm and 15 mm but will depend on local regulations. The bottoms of vertical boards should be undercut or bevelled to assist drainage.

Finishing Cladding at Angles and Openings

Fixing

Solid timber cladding should be primed on faces and laps before being fixed in position. Side and end grain joints should be well coated.

Nails are the most economical, simple, and generally used form of fixing. In areas of high rainfall (500 mm) ordinary mild steel nails react with tannins in some timbers causing black stains around each nail hole. Other metals such as copper react to sea air and industrial atmospheric pollution. Punching the nails well below the surface and puttying over greatly reduces the staining. Opaque paint will completely hide the stain.

Recent tests have shown that hot-dipped galvanised nails do not cause staining and their use is strongly recommended.

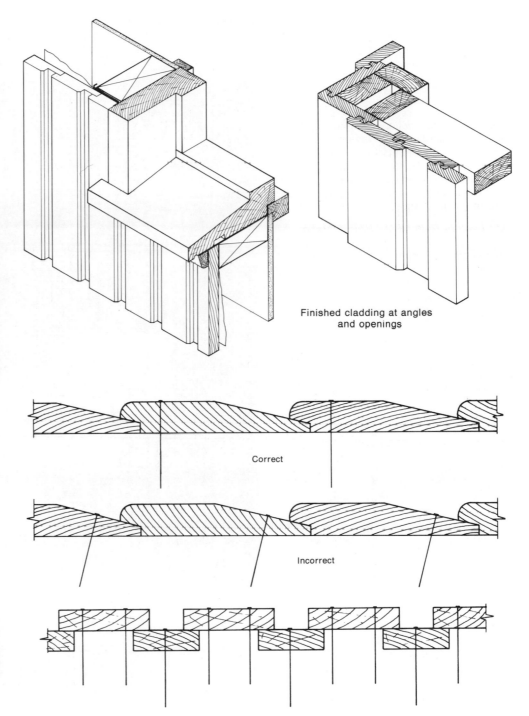

Finished cladding at angles and openings

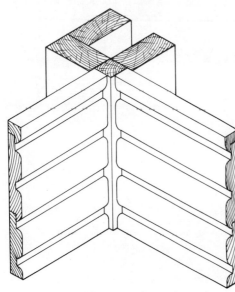

Finished cladding at angles and openings

Shingles and Shakes

Timbers suitable for shingles must be durable. Examples are:

Forest oaks and sheoaks, Western red cedar, Californian redwood, and treated softwoods.

Lining

Lining is the covering of the inner surfaces of a building and of the inner framework.

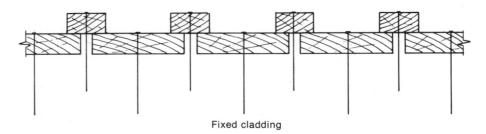

Fixed cladding

Function
1. To enclose the framing members and provide a suitable inner surface.
2. To provide stability on bracing.
3. To produce the required thermal and acoustic properties.
4. To provide an effective barrier.

Types of Lining
1. Milled timber sections or manufactured sheets fixed directly to the frame.
2. Factory made sheets fixed to the frame with the joints filled with a jointing material.
3. Material mixed on the site and applied to the wall or ceiling, where it undergoes chemical or physical change.

Other Factors Related to Lining Material
Aesthetics
Soundproofing or sound absorption
Insulation
Resistance to deterioration
Resistance to fire
Finishing and maintenance

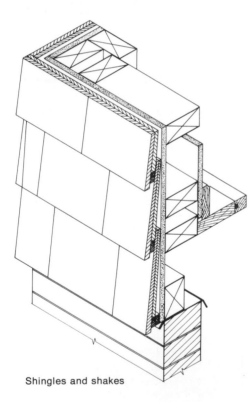

Shingles and shakes

Solid Timber Linings
Linings are not expected to transmit loads or absorb stresses. Their prime consideration should be availability and appearance.

Fixing
Lining boards are generally fixed to nogging or battens. Where fixing is to masonry, the battens are usually plugged to the wall at required intervals and directions. The battens are usually 42 mm x 19 mm material.

Wall lining

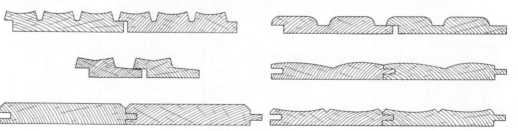

Typical sections of lining

Methods of Jointing a Corner

FACE NAILING: This is the quickest and easiest method of fixing. Double nailing is advisable for boards 75 mm wide or over. Some nail heads may contribute to the appearance, but it is usual to punch the nails and conceal the nail holes. Avoid nailing at eye level.

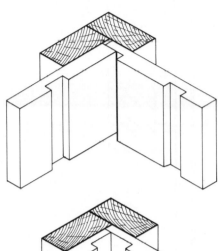

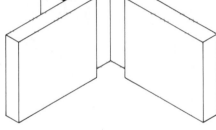

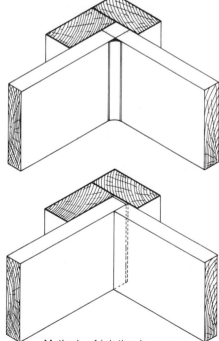

Methods of jointing in corners

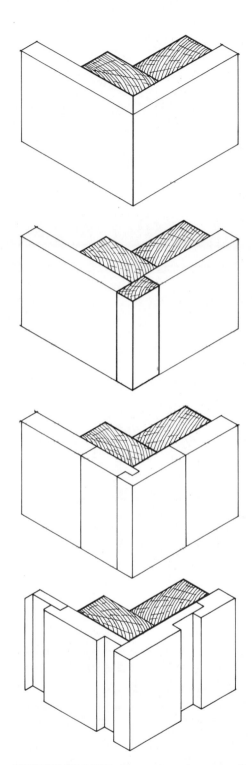

SECRET NAILING: These boards generally incorporate a tongue and groove profile.

Manufactured Boards

Plywood: There is a wide range of ply panelling available. The choice of face veneer, colour, and figure is almost unlimited.

The normal thickness for plywood lining is 6 mm, but the thickness may vary depending on the type of work being undertaken.

The available length of face veneers should be determined in the selection sequence. 2400 mm is usually the largest length available, but some species may be available in longer lengths.

Secret nailing

Joints

When considering the jointing system careful consideration of the compatibility of the figure is most important.

Joints should be made over battens.

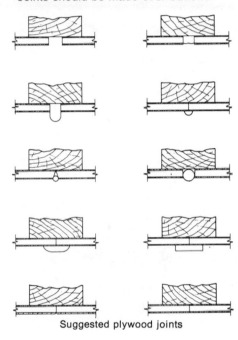

Suggested plywood joints

Suggested Plywood Joints

Internal and External Corners for Plywood Linings

Fixing: It is recommended that 6 mm plywood should be supported on battens at not greater than 450 mm centres in both directions.

Nailing of plywood may be carried out very close to the edge and should be at approximately 150 mm centre using 20 mm to 25 mm panel pins. The heads should be punched and the holes filled with coloured putty, plastic wood, or similar.

Where factory finished sheets are employed it is desirable to use an alternative method. Secret fixing may be achieved by adhesives, spider nails, or hanging clips. A spider nail is simply a 20 mm flat head nail on a serrated edge washer. The nails are driven into the battens and punched home. The plywood is then forced on to the spikes of the washer by hammering from the face side, using a softwood block to prevent bruising.

287

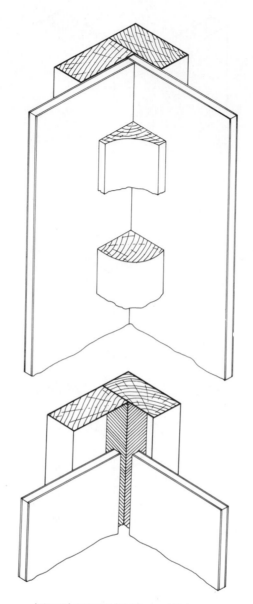

External corners for plywood linings

Internal corners for plywood linings

Spider nail

Fixing plywood with clips

Hardboards

Two basic types of hardboard are available, standard or tempered. The latter is less susceptible to moisture movement.

Preparation: To ensure permanently flat panels it is essential that all hardboards are brought to an equilibrium moisture content with the environment. This is achieved by scrubbing clean cold water on the back of each sheet. The sheets should then be stacked face to face for at least twenty-four hours.

Fixing: Nails should be 25 mm to 32 mm 16 g hardboard nails or panel pins, and should be driven at least 6 mm from the edge at 100 mm intervals.

Adhesives may also be used successfully.

Joints: Joints between sheets may be formed by planing the arrises to form a V joint. Timber, metal, or plastic mouldings may also be used.

Other Woodlining Materials

Softboards: These boards are manufactured from cane fibre or wood pulp. They have low impact resistance, but possess excellent acoustic and thermal insulating qualities. Joints may be treated with cover battens or V jointed.

Particle Boards and Medium Density Fibre Boards: These boards are manufactured from wood flakes. They are noted for their excellent thermal and acoustic insulation and dimensional stability. They may be faced with decorative veneers, laminates or hardboard.

Water emulsion paints are not recommended without first sealing the surface.

Project 27

FENCES

Treated radiata pine fence

Timber fences can be designed to match almost any architectural design, and their construction should present no problem to the competent handyman.

If naturally durable timber or pressure-treated preserved is selected the fence can be left in its natural state and no maintenance will be required.

A timber fence can fulfil a wide variety of functions. It may provide an attractive barrier for privacy and security. Fences may also control the effects of sun, wind, noise, or provide a background for shrubbery.

A wide variety of timber cladding for fences is readily available to complement adjacent buildings and fulfil the desired function.

Picket fences are most attractive and suit a wide range of situations. Lattice screens are easy to erect and look wonderful in gardens. Lattice panels on top of solid cladding also creates a most attractive fence.

A Basic Guide for Timber Fence Construction

Before building a fence:

Make sure the property line is correct.

Check against survey marks.

Check with the local council building inspector who will explain all relevant sections of the Building Act with respect to boundary fences affecting you and your neighbours.

Bear in mind that gates add distinctive character to any fence style.

Remember that timber gateposts should preferably be set in concrete to ensure permanent stability.

Use of preservatives will give additional protection to timber in contact with the soil. Preservatives may be brushed on or the post may be dipped. With some commercial timbers preservation is recommended.

Nails and hardware should be galvanised to prevent rust.

Fence Construction

Mark the fence line.

Set the posts solidly into the ground at 1.5 m centres.

Use the 3–4–5 rule for accurate square corners.

In the design shown below, the rails are fixed in line with posts. This method gives an attractive appearance from both sides. In this type of construction the rails are fixed to the post either with metal fixing brackets or by mortising the rail into the post.

In the alternative design the posts and rails are preservative-treated Radiata pine poles. The nails are sawn flat on both sides to take the pickets. The pickets are nailed on both sides of the rail to give the same appearance from both sides. The rails are bolted directly on to the posts.

Sawn finish pickets provide a better surface for staining, and are stronger.

Non-corrosive hot-dipped galvanised fixings are recommended.

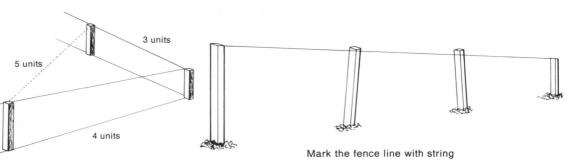

Use the 3–4–5 rule for accurate square corners

Mark the fence line with string

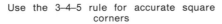

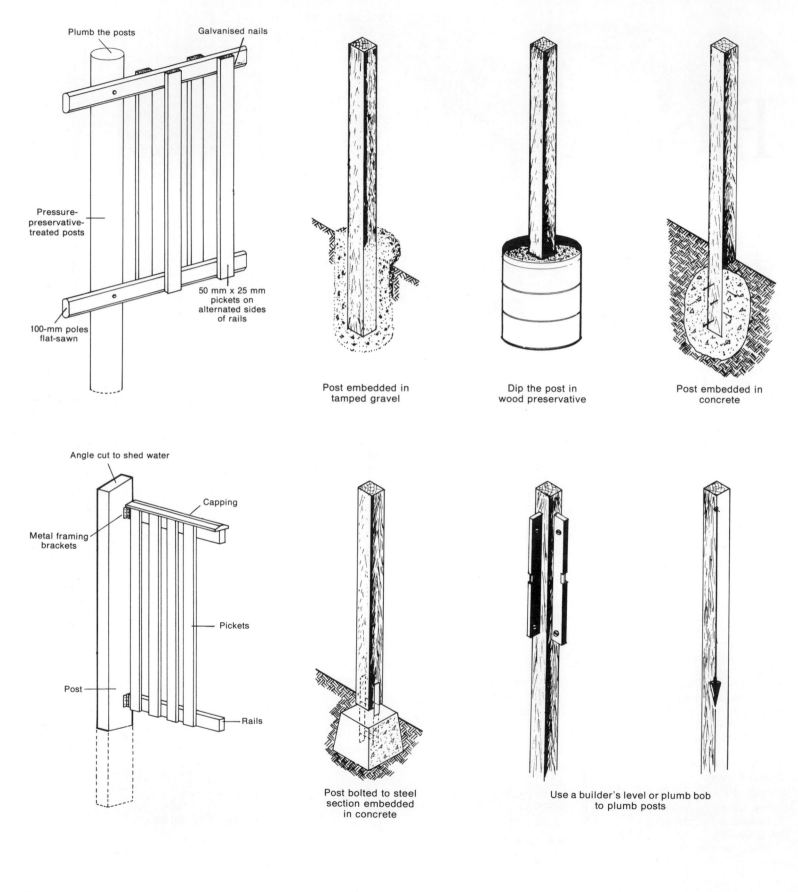

Plumb the posts

Galvanised nails

Pressure-preservative-treated posts

100-mm poles flat-sawn

50 mm x 25 mm pickets on alternated sides of rails

Post embedded in tamped gravel

Dip the post in wood preservative

Post embedded in concrete

Angle cut to shed water

Capping

Metal framing brackets

Pickets

Post

Rails

Post bolted to steel section embedded in concrete

Use a builder's level or plumb bob to plumb posts

Picket

Shapes of pickets

Lattice

Closed diagonal

Open square

Open diagonal

Closed square

Lattice above palings

70 x 35

90 x 45

Lattice surrounds are designed to trim any lattice setting. They fit well and give strength, and provide an easy method of fixing

Project 28

GATES

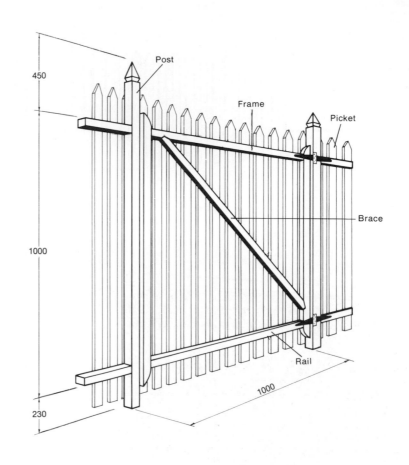

Post

Frame

Picket

Brace

Rail

450

1000

230

1000

A gate should be planned as an integral part of the fence. The gateposts should be the sturdiest of the fence posts and firmly embedded in concrete.

Using the basic frame shown here it is possible to vary the design by using pickets of varying shapes and arranging the pickets in various ways. A lattice panel could also be used by modifying the frame, and using lattice surrounds as shown.

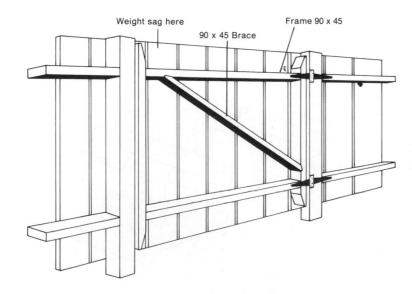

Weight sag here

90 x 45 Brace

Frame 90 x 45

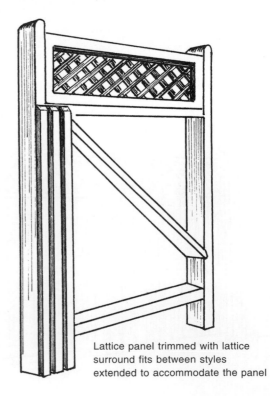

Lattice panel trimmed with lattice surround fits between styles extended to accommodate the panel

The gates illustrated are constructed on one basic frame. One diagonal brace is sufficient. Latches, hinges, and fastenings should all be corrosion-resistant and of the heavy duty type.

Construction

Because of the extra strain to which a gate is subjected, the posts should be firmly embedded in concrete.

A simple metre-wide gate which is to be installed between two fence posts can be constructed on a work bench. The frame is made of 90 x 45 mm material and cut as shown.

Because of the strain placed on the frame a gate must be constructed using mortise and tenon joints. Details are set out clearly in the section on joints.

Alternative joints, such as a halving joint, may be used but will not provide the same service or life as the mortise and tenon joints.

The brace is best fitted as set out in the diagram. If the brace is fitted diagonally across the corners it really only has the effect of pushing the joints apart.

Nail the first board in place flush with the edge of the stile on the hinge side of the frame. Nail additional boards from this point until the full width is covered.

Attach the hinges to the gate.

Fit the gate in the space in the fence. Check clearance. Make sure it will swing freely.

When correctly fitted place blocks beneath the gate, holding it clear of the ground, and attach the hinges to the fence post. Again check the fit.

Attach the gate latch.

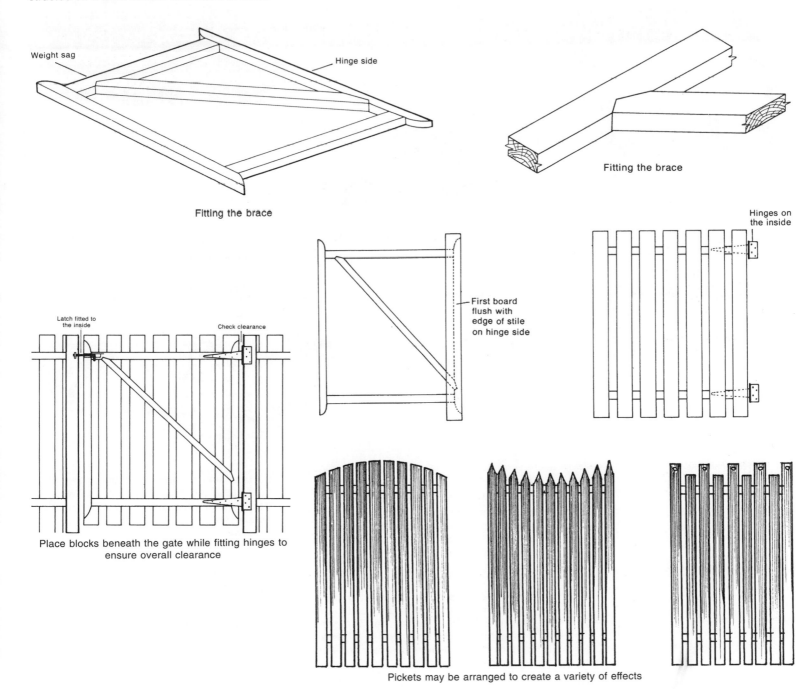

Fitting the brace

Fitting the brace

First board flush with edge of stile on hinge side

Hinges on the inside

Latch fitted to the inside

Check clearance

Place blocks beneath the gate while fitting hinges to ensure overall clearance

Pickets may be arranged to create a variety of effects

Project

29

DECKING

Flat land deck

Hillside deck

Roof top deck

Isolated deck

Deck Construction

The choice of deck type is largely a matter of personal taste but may be governed to a certain extent by factors such as the slope of the land and its relationship to the house. Decks fall into four main types.

Decks

For obvious reasons low-level or flat land decks are the easiest to plan and construct and are the least expensive. They usually extend from the house at floor level. This type of deck can be very convenient and lend an air of spaciousness.

Low-Level Deck Construction: To build a good-looking durable deck you need more than just a few nails and pieces of wood. A deck is within the reach of most competent handymen.

Study the area carefully, considering existing garden, trees, the deck's convenience in relation to your house or an area you may wish to obscure. Consider what other improvements you might wish to add to the property in the future.

Now sketch a plan. Check with your local council regarding building regulations. As with any other handyman project, go slowly and carefully. If you gain a full understanding of the job at this point, the work later on will be easier and quicker.

Timber Sizes

(based on pressure-treated Radiata pine—minimum stress grade F5)

Post Sizes

Post size mm	Maximum post height m
90 x 90	2.4
100 x 125	2.4
125 x 150	3.0

Bearers

Size mm	Span m	Spacing m
120 x 70	1.5	1.8–2.4
140 x 70	1.8	1.8–2.4
190 x 70	2.4	1.8–2.4

Joists

Size mm	Span m	Spacing mm
90 x 45	1.8	600
140 x 45	2.4	600

Decking (continuous over two or more spans)

Size mm	Maximum span mm
19 or 25	460
35 or 38	860
45 or 50	1090

Preparing the Site

First ensure that drainage is adequate to prevent any water remaining underneath the deck. In the case of low-level decks, action should be taken to prevent the growth of weeds between deck slats, either by treating the soil or by raking the area clear and laying polythene sheeting over the area. The plastic should be pierced at intervals with a nail to assist drainage.

Selecting the Timber

Posts: Timbers best suited for setting into the ground are Jarrah, Western red cedar, and pressure-preservative-treated Radiata pine. Oregon (Douglas fir) is also suitable provided it is fixed above ground level and is well painted or stained. Treated Radiata pine may be used in rounds or as sawn timber.

Sub-Structure Timbers: Beams and joists can be of Jarrah, Karri, or pressure-treated Radiata pine.

Decking Timbers: Jarrah and pressure-treated Radiata pine are suitable species for decking. All decking timbers should be dry when used (below 15% moisture content) and should be dressed on one face and two edges.

Timbers generally can be rough-sawn (undressed) if they are to be stained or left unfinished. The exceptions to this are Oregon and the decking timbers. Timbers which are to be painted should be planed (dressed) and must also be dry.

Setting Out

If you plan to position the deck alongside the house it is wise to make it free-standing. It can be close-butted to a wall so that it appears to be attached while free to allow minor movement and settling. When setting posts into the ground, squaring up with true right-angle corners can be simplified by using the 3–4–5 method. First establish one side (the wall of the house, a path, etc.) and drive two stakes (A and B) into the ground 3 units apart. Attach a string roughly the length of one side of the deck to point A and carry it out roughly at right angles from A and B. Take another string 5 units long at an angle from point B and adjust the first string so that it meets the string from point B exactly 4 units from point A. Thus a perfect right angle is established.

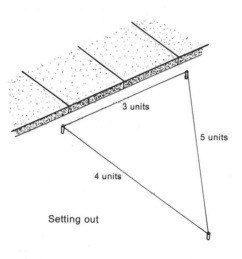

Setting out

Footings and Posts: Timber posts suitable for setting into the ground may be supported above ground level, or embedded to a depth not less than one third of their height above ground, with a minimum of 450 mm depth. They should rest on concrete sole plates of the following size:

Bearer Spacing	Concrete sole plate size
1.8 metre	250 mm diameter x 150 mm deep
2.4 metre	350 mm diameter x 150 mm deep

A concrete mix of 4:2:1 is suitable for sole plates. Backfilling of holes with suitable material should be done in 75 mm well rammed layers. Suitable filling materials include earth without clay or with a low clay content, gravel, or a cement-soil mixture of 1:6 proportions. Care should be taken to ensure that posts are plumb and in correct position during and after backfilling.

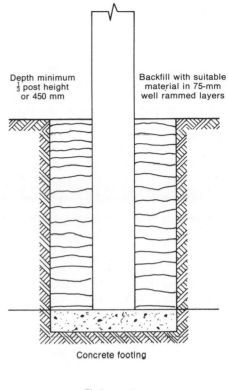

Depth minimum ⅓ post height or 450 mm

Backfill with suitable material in 75-mm well rammed layers

Concrete footing

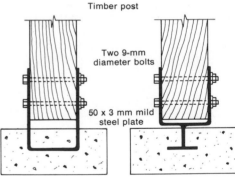

Timber post

Two 9-mm diameter bolts

50 x 3 mm mild steel plate

Footing and posts

As there is a possibility of termites climbing posts embedded in the ground, particularly short posts, some termite protection is desirable. Adequate protection can be achieved by adding a 50/50 mixture of creosote and sump oil to the last 6 inches of post hole backfill.

Where the height of posts above ground level exceeds twenty-four times the smallest dimension or the least diameter of the posts, bracing is required. Bracing is also necessary where the required depth of post embedding cannot be achieved.

Oregon posts may also be used, provided they are fixed above ground level only, and are well painted or stained. No termite protection is required with this type of support.

All metal fittings, including bolts and nails, should be galvanised.

Bearers and Joists: These may be secured to posts by skew-nailing or by using patent fastenings. Bearers should preferably be placed directly over the tops of posts. If this is not done, and the height of posts above ground exceeds twelve times the smallest dimension, then the post should be structurally designed or bracing should be provided.

Doubled bearers may also be used, provided they are blocked at suitable spacings. Shoulders may be formed on posts to provide temporary support for doubled bearers during construction. If the remaining post width at the shouldered section is less than 75 mm, larger bolts may be required.

Decking: The boards are fixed approximately 4 mm apart. A nail or a strip of wood this size can be used to check the spacing as you proceed. It is suggested that holes be drilled when nailing ends of some timbers. Treated Radiata pine can, however, be nailed close to the ends with little risk of splitting.

Use galvanised or non-ferrous nails to prevent staining.

Fasteners and Fixing

To avoid unsightly rust all fasteners should be galvanised.

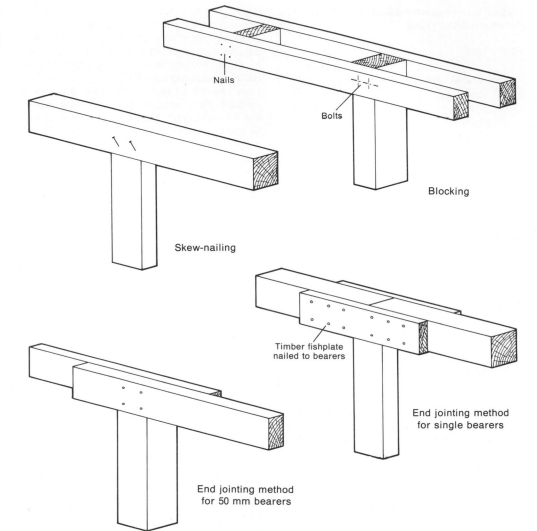

Nails

Bolts

Blocking

Skew-nailing

Timber fishplate nailed to bearers

End jointing method for single bearers

End jointing method for 50 mm bearers

Nails

Decking thickness (mm)	Nail size (mm)
19	65 x 3.75 diameter
35	75 x 3.75 diameter
45	100 x 3.75 diameter

Bolts

Post width	Spacing	Bolt diameter
100	38	10
125	44	16
150	48	20

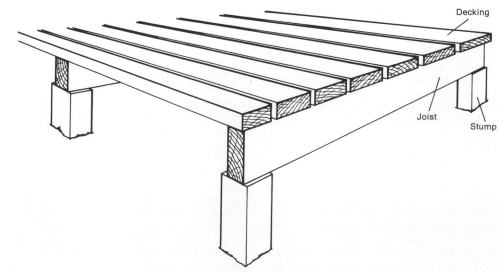

Decking

Joist

Stump

Components of low-level deck construction

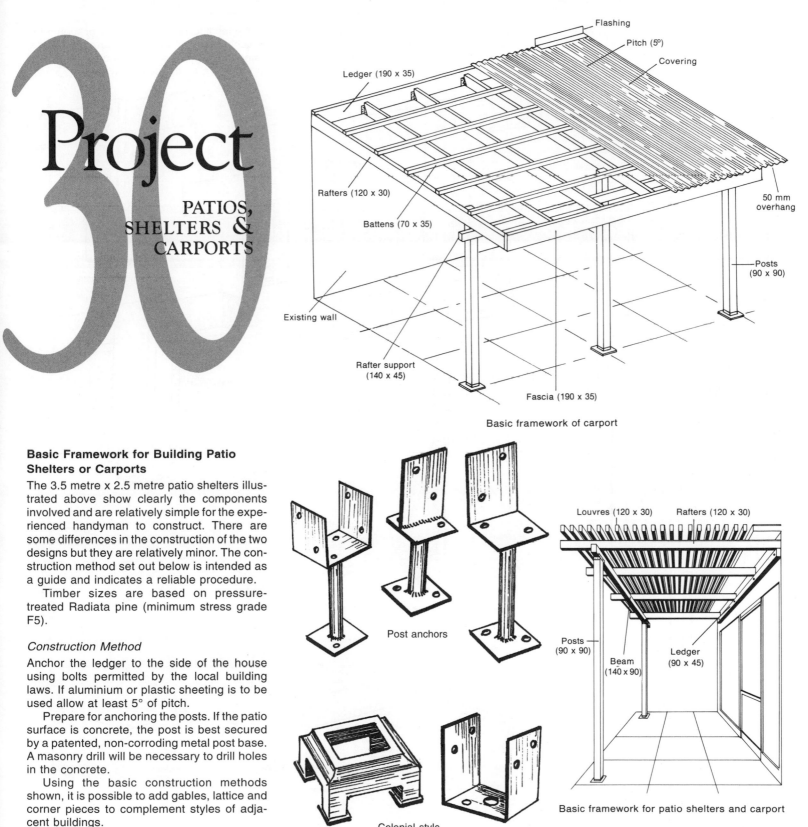

Project 30

PATIOS, SHELTERS & CARPORTS

Basic framework of carport labels: Flashing; Pitch (5°); Covering; Ledger (190 x 35); Rafters (120 x 30); Battens (70 x 35); 50 mm overhang; Posts (90 x 90); Existing wall; Rafter support (140 x 45); Fascia (190 x 35)

Post anchors

Colonial style

Basic framework for patio shelters and carport labels: Louvres (120 x 30); Rafters (120 x 30); Posts (90 x 90); Beam (140 x 90); Ledger (90 x 45)

Basic Framework for Building Patio Shelters or Carports

The 3.5 metre x 2.5 metre patio shelters illustrated above show clearly the components involved and are relatively simple for the experienced handyman to construct. There are some differences in the construction of the two designs but they are relatively minor. The construction method set out below is intended as a guide and indicates a reliable procedure.

Timber sizes are based on pressure-treated Radiata pine (minimum stress grade F5).

Construction Method

Anchor the ledger to the side of the house using bolts permitted by the local building laws. If aluminium or plastic sheeting is to be used allow at least 5° of pitch.

Prepare for anchoring the posts. If the patio surface is concrete, the post is best secured by a patented, non-corroding metal post base. A masonry drill will be necessary to drill holes in the concrete.

Using the basic construction methods shown, it is possible to add gables, lattice and corner pieces to complement styles of adjacent buildings.

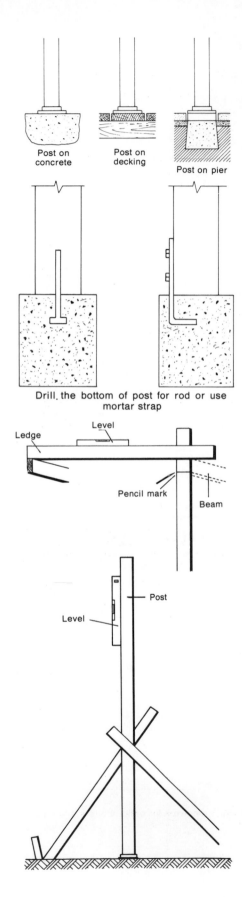

Post on concrete

Post on decking

Post on pier

Drill the bottom of post for rod or use mortar strap

Ledge

Level

Pencil mark

Beam

Post

Level

Trim the posts to the proper length.

With the posts trimmed, plumb them upright in their anchored positions and hold them with temporary supporting boards.

Depending upon the design or method of attaching post and beam, secure the beams, using either metal framing anchors or bolting to the beam as the case may be.

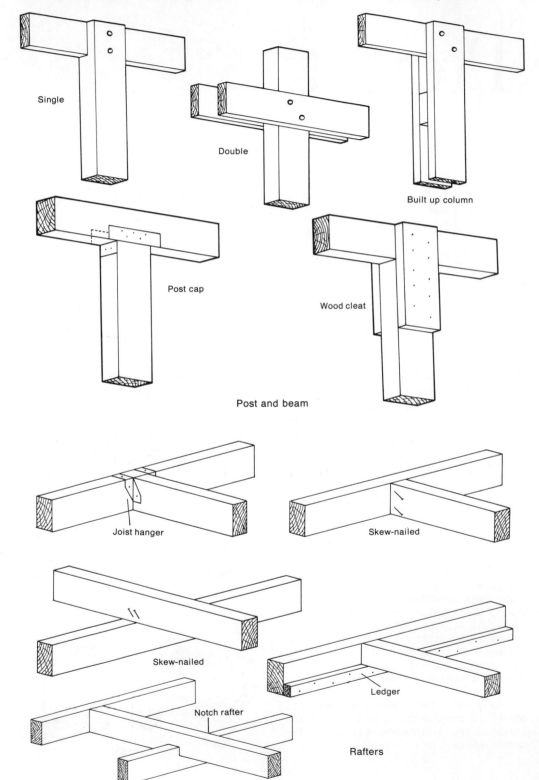

Single

Double

Built up column

Post cap

Wood cleat

Post and beam

Joist hanger

Skew-nailed

Skew-nailed

Ledger

Notch rafter

Rafters

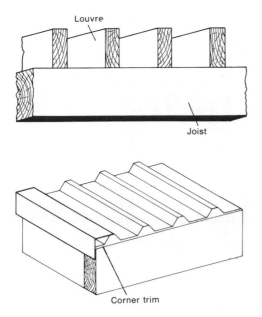

Louvre

Joist

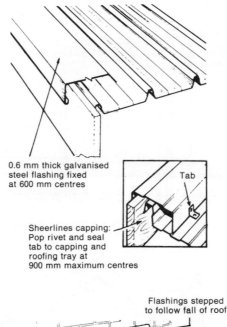

0.6 mm thick galvanised
steel flashing fixed
at 600 mm centres

Tab

Sheerlines capping:
Pop rivet and seal
tab to capping and
roofing tray at
900 mm maximum centres

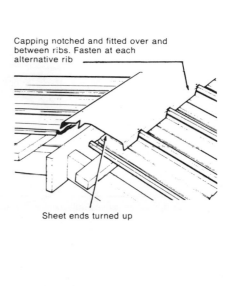

Capping notched and fitted over and
between ribs. Fasten at each
alternative rib

Sheet ends turned up

Corner trim

Fit the rafters at regular intervals, either skew-nailing or by using metal framing anchors.

If plastic or aluminium sheeting is to be used, sheet metal flashing must be attached to the wall and it may be desirable to fit guttering and downpipes.

If plastic or aluminium sheeting is to be used, battens must be laid across the rafters to support the sheet material at 450 mm intervals. The roofing nails are driven through the sheets into these battens.

Sheet metal flashing must be attached to the wall, and it may be desirable to fit guttering to downpipes.

With rafters in place, 120 mm x 30 mm louvres on edge may be skew-nailed to the rafters, leaving about 75 mm between louvres to allow filtered sunlight.

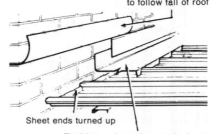

Flashings stepped
to follow fall of roof

Sheet ends turned up

Flashing and capping notched and
fitted over and between ribs.
Fasten at each alternate rib.

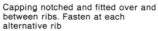

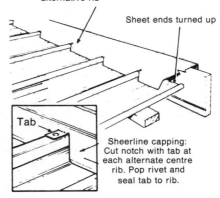

Capping notched and fitted over and
between ribs. Fasten at each
alternative rib

Sheet ends turned up

Tab

Sheerline capping:
Cut notch with tab at
each alternate centre
rib. Pop rivet and
seal tab to rib.

Crest fixing to timber

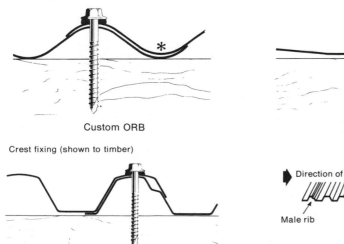

Custom ORB

Crest fixing (shown to timber)

Trimdek

Crest fixing (shown to timber)

Spandek

Klip-Lok

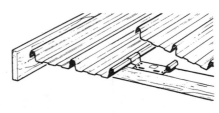

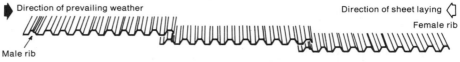

Direction of prevailing weather

Direction of sheet laying

Female rib

Male rib

Sheet laying procedure

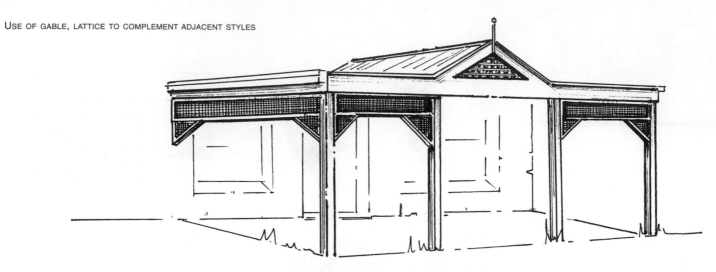

Patio shelter decorated with lattice and a gable

Garden arch incorporating a gable and corner pieces

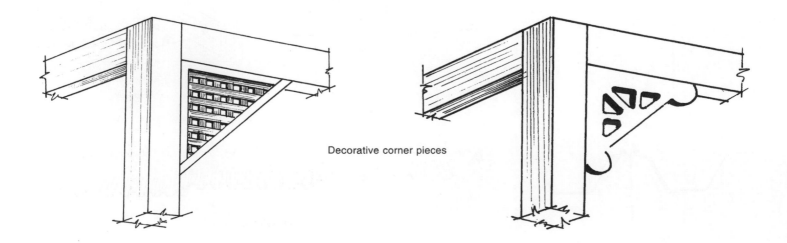

Decorative corner pieces

Project 31

OUTDOOR FURNITURE

In constructing outdoor tImber furniture, consideration must be given to the type of timber used, suitability of fasteners, the application of a preservative type finish, and the method of jointing.

Western red cedar, for example, has proved most durable when exposed to the elements, but requires galvanised fasteners for attaching purposes.

Joint structure needs to be simple but strong. Consequently, conventional joints are often ignored in preference to bolts, coach screws, screws, and knockdown connectors.

To provide a more aesthetic appearance as well as protection, various coloured stains containing preservatives may be applied to the timber surfaces.

Square or circular tables may also be constructed using the same method. Sizes, however, may be determined by the space available for the table and stools.

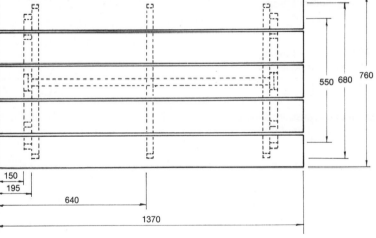

All material, except top,
70×45 mm

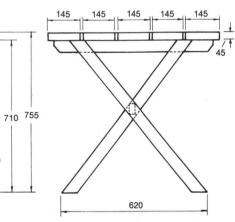

Outdoor table

Outdoor Table

Top

Cut the top members to length and radius all edges

Cut the required number of under cleats, splay the ends, and radius exposed edges.

Lay out the screw positions for the under cleats, drill and countersink, two screws for each top member.

With the good side downwards, clamp the top together, having 8 to 10 mm spacers placed between each member.

Position the under cleats and, using suitable fasteners, attach the top members.

Leg Frames

From a full size end view of the table lay out the position of the cross halving joints.

Similarly mark the bevel angle at the top and bottom of each leg.

Mark out in detail the cross halving joints, clearly indicating the waste material.

Cut out and fit the cross halving joints.

Saw-cut the leg bevels.

Position the leg frames against the end under cleats and attach, using suitable bolts.

Spreader Rail

Cut to length and radius all edges.

Centrally locate between the cross halving joints and secure, using suitable knockdown connectors.

Finishing

Apply a suitable stain containing water repellents and preservatives to the completed table.

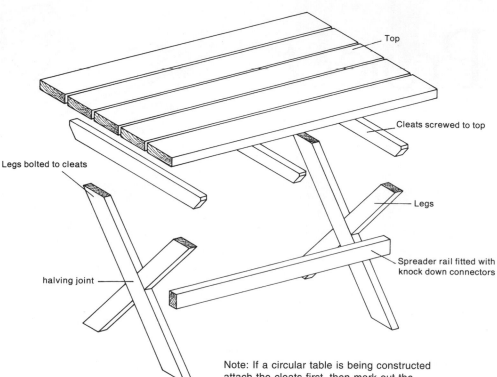

Top

Cleats screwed to top

Legs bolted to cleats

Legs

Spreader rail fitted with knock down connectors

halving joint

Note: If a circular table is being constructed attach the cleats first, then mark out the diameter required. The shape may be cut using a portable jig saw—radius all edges.

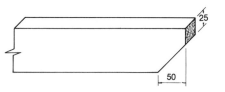

Ends of cleats

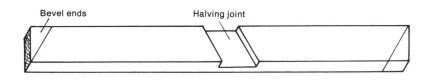

Bevel ends

Halving joint

Layout of leg shape

Radius all edges

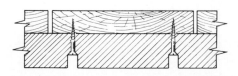

Method of attaching top to cleats

Using spacers to position the top

Stool

Construction as for the table—reduction in sizes.

Seat

Cleat

Legs

Cross halving

Spreader rail

Circular design

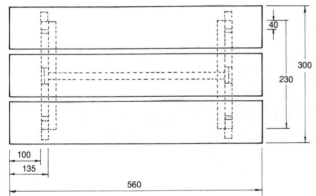

40

300

230

100

135

560

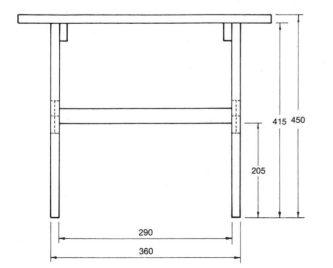

415 450

205

290

360

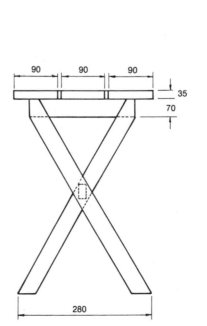

90   90   90

35

70

280

303

Project 32

PLANTER BOXES

These simply designed and easily constructed planter boxes will enhance the appearance of your favourite plants, be they indoor or outdoor. The units may be painted, stained, or clear varnished, depending on the surrounding decor. The rectangular planter box may also serve as a small room-divider. For protection against the leakage of water, a galvanized steel tray should be located in the bottom of the boxes.

SINGLE PLANTER BOX

Although the design illustrated will accommodate up to a 200 mm diameter pot, the appropriate increase or decrease in overall dimensions will allow a variety of pot sizes to be held.

Procedure

Legs

Choosing a timber having desirable characteristics, dress the leg material to finish 30 x 30 P.A.R. Mark out the four legs and cut to length, squaring both ends of each leg accurately.

Side Timbers

Prepare the required amount of timber stock for the sides of the planter box to finish 65 x 15 P.A.R. A look at the drawing will show that eight of the timber battens forming two sides of the planter box are longer than the eight battens forming the other two sides. Mark out and cut the timber battens according to length, and square the ends by planing of the shorter timber battens only.

On four of the battens, mark out and cut using a jig saw or bandsaw, a curve, as illustrated on the working drawing. This is best achieved by marking one batten, clamping the four together, cutting out, and then cleaning up using a flat-soled spokeshave and 240 grit abrasive paper (while still clamped).

From the sectional sketch, mark out and drill two holes in each end of the timber battens to accept 8-gauge brass screws.

NOTE

In the longer sides the holes are further back from the ends of the battens—refer to the orthographic sketch.

Assembly of Sides and Legs

Using 8-gauge brass screws, attach the shorter battens to the legs—the ends of the battens finishing flush with the outside edge of each leg and the first batten being located 60 mm up from the leg bottom.

Screw the longer battens to the legs, finishing flush with the outside of the shorter battens, starting level with the bottom of the shorter battens and again working upwards.

Base

The base member is cut from a 250 mm-wide P.A.R. board and cut to the template as indicated on the orthographic sketch. While 5 mm is left around each leg, the base member fits firmly against the side timbers. With the planter box turned upside down fit the base and attach by using two 8-gauge brass screws in each of the four sides.

Cleaning up and Finishing

Using a sharp smoothing plane, clean up the ends of the long sides to fit neatly against the face surfaces of the shorter sides. The whole unit is then sanded, using 240 grit abrasive to remove any remaining blemishes or arris. Depending on situation (indoors or outdoors) a suitable finish should be applied to provide protection. This should involve two or three brushed or sprayed coats, cut back between each coat.

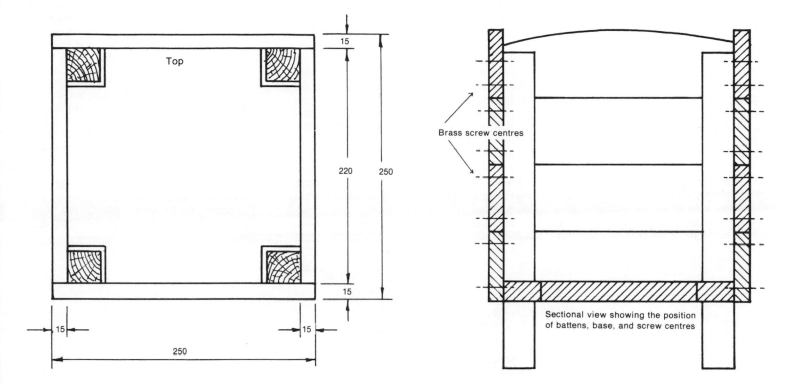

Top

250

220

250

15

15

15

15

250

Brass screw centres

Sectional view showing the position
of batten, base, and screw centres

WORKING DRAWING FOR FLOWER BOX

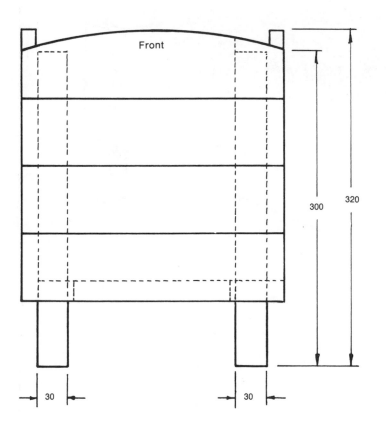

Front

300

320

30

30

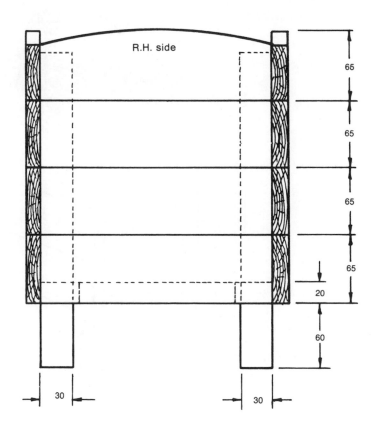

R.H. side

65

65

65

65

20

60

30

30

MULTIPLE PLANTER BOX

Although similar in construction to the single planter box, the multiple planter box has two leg frames at each end.

Procedure

Leg Frame

Again, using a durable species of timber, prepare the leg material to finish 30 x 30 P.A.R. Mark out and cut the four legs and plane them square to length. Using the same material, mark out and cut the two spreader rails to fit between the four legs. Both ends of these spreader rails should be accurately squared using a smoothing plane.

Join the two legs to a spreader rail, using screws, and check that the spreader rail is flush with the top surfaces of the legs. Repeat this process for the other legs and spreader rails.

Sides and Ends

Prepare sufficient material of dimension 80 x 15 P.A.R. to enable the longer sides and ends of the planter box to be obtained. Mark out and cut the six pieces required for the long sides. Mark out and cut the six pieces required for the ends and plane both ends square. Mark out, drill, and countersink all holes in the side pieces and end pieces, as indicated on the sketch, to accept 8-gauge brass screws.

Assembly

Screw the end timber pieces to the leg frames, the ends being flush with the outside of the leg frame and the top flush with the top of the leg frames.

Screw the side timbers to the leg frames, again ensuring that the ends are flush with the outside edges of the leg frames and the top edges are flush with the tops of the leg frames.

With a finely set smoothing plane, flush the ends and the top edges of the side timbers with the outside edges of the leg frame.

Base

Turning the unit upside down, cut out and fit from a 225 mm-wide board a base member to fit snugly inside the rectangle made by the sides and ends. Attach the base by means of screwing through the side and end timbers.

Cleaning Up and Finishing

Using 240 grit abrasive paper clean up all surfaces and remove all arris.

Depending on where the planter box is to be sited, select a suitable finish and apply two or three coats.

WORKING DRAWING FOR FLOWER BOX

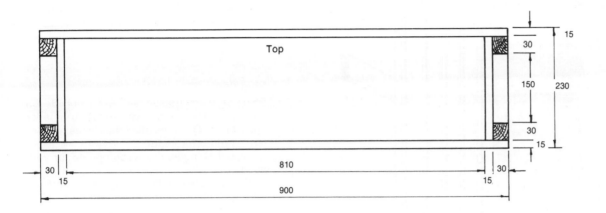

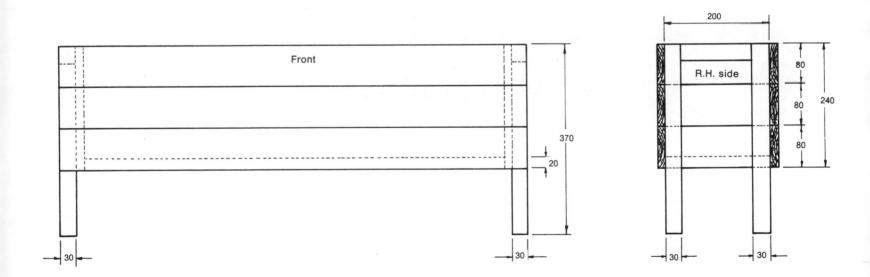

Project 33
PANELLING

Erecting a feature wall of solid timber panelling is not difficult for a competent handyman.

Solid Timber Panelling

For masonry walls 50 mm x 25 mm battens are fixed by wall plugs or special masonry nails. If panelling is to be fixed horizontally, battens should be placed vertically over the brickwork.

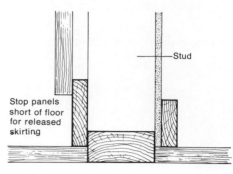

Stop panels short of floor for released skirting

Detail at floor

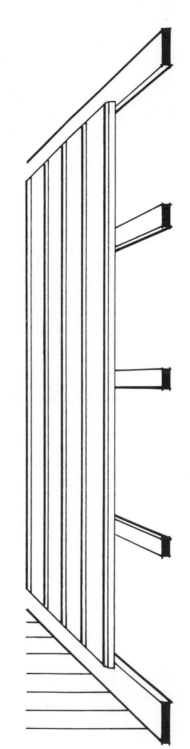

Fixing solid timber panelling

The battens are fixed at about 600 mm intervals.

Stop the panels short of the floor and ceiling. This recessed skirting and cornice detail is simple and avoids dust pockets.

Shingles

Shingles were traditionally used outside on roofs or walls but are well suited for interior application. Once installed they remain maintenance-free for years.

Select shingles most appropriate for your needs.

For masonry walls battens must be fixed with wall plugs or masonry nails, providing even spacing based on the desired exposure. Allowance must be made for skirting or cornice moulding if they are desired.

Start the application of shingles from the bottom. Nails should be placed so that they will be covered by the next row.

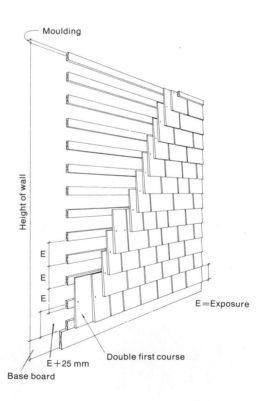

Moulding

Height of wall

E

E

E

E = Exposure

E + 25 mm

Double first course

Base board

A cornice moulding may be used to cover the top row.

The timber may be left in its natural state or it may be finished with a clear sealer.

Plywood Panelling

Each panel is individual in its grain characteristics. Before fixing, stand the panels side by side to ensure the best match.

Panels may be applied directly over some old walls. Check for undulations, irregularities, or protrusions. It is however a good idea to fix 42 mm x 19 mm battens to the wall at 450 mm centres to provide a framework for fixing.

The first panel is the key to the whole wall. Start in one corner, making sure the first panel is perfectly vertical. A spirit level held against the vertical edge is the best guide.

The simplest method of fixing is to use finishing nails or countersunk head wall board nails. Nails may be concealed in the grooves and spaced at about 200 mm centres.

If nailing through the face of the panel, the nail should be punched and the hole filled with a colour-matched putty.

Modern adhesives are particularly suitable for fixing plywood panels, but it is desirable to follow the manufacturers' instructions.

If the panel is to be cut, sharp, fine tooth saws give the bet results (see Hand Tools). For hand saws or bandsaws the finished face should be uppermost. For portable power saws the finish face should be down.

Turning corners presents little difficulty if corner mouldings are used.

Matching

Attach battens if necessary

Plumb the first sheet

Methods of cutting plywood sheet

Plywood panelling

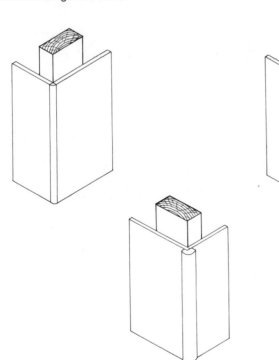
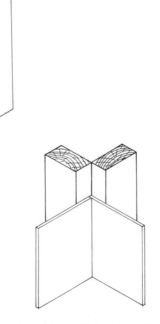
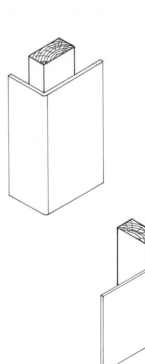

Methods of fixing plywood panelling at corners

309

Project 34
FITTING AND REPAIRING DOORS

Hinged Doors

There are many beautiful carved or glass panel doors available and many people may find it desirable to change an old door for a newer more attractive one.

Removing the Old Door

The old door is easily removed by simply unscrewing the butt hinges from the door jamb. It is desirable to remove the bottom screws initially, and finally the top screw. You may need some help in supporting the door while removing the screws.

Once the door is removed, the hinges may be unscrewed and used for the new door.

Fitting the New Door

The new door will probably be very close to the correct size, as doors are manufactured on a standard size basis. It will, however, need some attention if it is to fit correctly without jamming or perhaps rubbing on a carpet.

First stand the door in the opening with the hinged side located accurately against the jamb. Use a 2 mm spacer to provide a uniform clearance.

With the door supported in the correct position, mark carefully the areas to be removed; allow approximately 2 mm all the way around for adequate clearance.

Examples of double bi-fold doors

A plane is ideal for removing excess material along the edges. The door is best supported or its edge clamped to a saw stool to keep it vertical while planing.

If the door is too long, it is best to place the door flat on a pair of saw stools or remove the excess with a saw. If a hand saw is used, carefully saw to the outside of a line marked on the bottom of the door. If, however, a

Hinged doors are generally used for front and rear entrances and most interior doorways. However, it may be necessary or even desirable to convert the door so that it slides, or maybe even to replace it with one of more modern appearance. It is essential to measure the opening carefully before ordering the new door or doors.

Internal door   Entrance door

150

230

Position of hinges

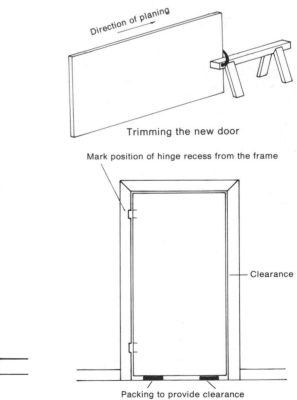

Direction of planing

Trimming the new door

Mark position of hinge recess from the frame

Clearance

Packing to provide clearance

portable electric saw is to be used, a guide to run along the end of the door will help to ensure a straight cut.

When sawing or planing is finished the arris should be removed.

Stand the door back in the opening and check the fit.

Pack up the bottom of the door so that it is in the correct position, and mark the position of the hinge sockets from the door jamb.

Fit the hinges to the door.

With the hinges fitted to the door, stand the door in position and screw the hinges to the door jamb using the original screw holes.

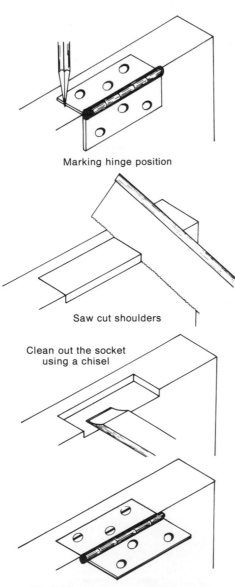

Marking hinge position

Saw cut shoulders

Clean out the socket using a chisel

Attach hinge using countersunk screws

It will also be necessary to fit a lock and some type of handle. These of course vary in design, function, and placement, and in the case of locks, manufacturers supply detailed fitting information. A hole saw or an expansive bit will probably be necessary to drill or bore through the door for the lock, while handles are generally screwed directly to the door.

The door is now ready for surface finishing.

Sliding Doors

If an interior door is to be converted to a sliding unit it will be necessary first to remove the door from the jamb.

With the door removed, the door stop battens must be levered from around the inside of the opening. Once removed, the nail holes and hinge recesses must be filled. The easiest method of filling and flushing off the hinge recesses is to use a plastic putty.

There are many types available but most are supplied as a two component mix. The putty will set by a chemical reaction, usually fairly rapidly, and it is then a simple matter to file or sand the surface until it is perfectly flush.

After applying some undercoat to the repaired areas the opening will be ready for refinishing. It will also be necessary to fix a piece of timber to the wall the same thickness as the architraves to accommodate the door runner.

So that the door will overlap the opening it will be necessary to glue and nail strips to each edge of the door.

The strips should be prepared so that they are as close as possible to the thickness of the door, requiring only a minimum of planing and sanding to flush the surface.

A wood stop putty is used to fill any holes or gaps before painting so that the edge strips are undetectable.

The old handle will also need to be replaced. Because it is a sliding door a special flush fitting handle will be required.

The door race is fitted to the door in accordance with the fitting instructions. It will be necessary to drill two holes to accommodate adjustment screws.

The door runner is fixed above the opening in accordance with the specifications.

Position the door on the runner and check the movement.

Position the nylon floor guide.

Position a door stop at the closing end.

Position a door stop at the opening end to suit the opening.

Bi-fold Doors

An attractive alternative to sliding doors are bi-fold doors, essentially a pair of hinged doors, one of which pivots along an aluminium slide attached to the head of the opening. The

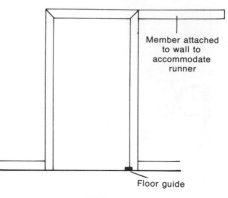

Member attached to wall to accommodate runner

Floor guide

Sliding door

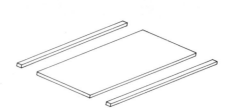

Glue and nail edge strips to the door to ensure the door overlaps the opening

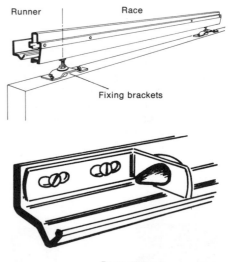

Runner   Race

Fixing brackets

Door stop

type illustrated is readily available and easily installed.

Cut the track to suit the opening width. If two lengths are required, cut to meet in the centre of the opening, e.g. four-door unit. Always cut the track to ensure that the guides do not pass over a joint.

Fit the top pivot sockets in the ends of the track. Final adjustment is made when the doors are hung.

Fix track to the head, parallel and level to the floor.

Plumb the centreline of the bottom jamb bracket from the centre top pivot socket and position for relevant application. Always fix the jamb adjusting screws in the centre of the slotted holes to allow for adjustment.

Prepare doors to the height and width indicated.

Drill holes for pivots and guide to dimension shown.

Be sure to work from the outside face of the door.

Drive the components into the correct holes using a timber block between nylon components and the hammer.

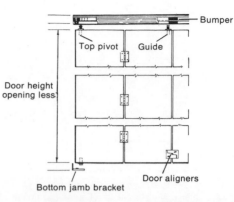

Adjustment screw

Bottom jamb bracket

Plumb centre line

Bumper

Top pivot　Guide

Door height opening less

Bottom jamb bracket

Door aligners

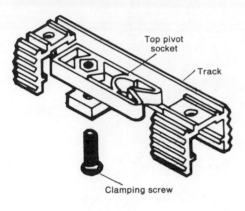

Top pivot socket

Track

Clamping screw

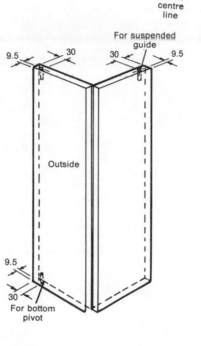

For suspended guide

9.5　30　　30　9.5

Outside

9.5

30

For bottom pivot

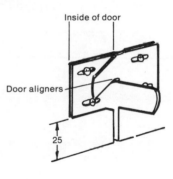

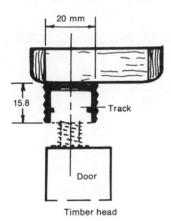

20 mm

15.8

Track

Door

Timber head

Inside of door

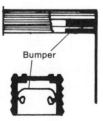

Door aligners

25

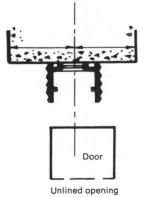

Door

Unlined opening

Lay the doors on a flat surface, inside faces up, and fix the hinges in the positions indicated.

Hold the doors together as shown; insert bottom pivot into the bottom jamb bracket. Enter the top pivot and suspended guide in the centre of the track, slide the doors towards the jamb until the top pivot snaps into the top socket. Repeat this procedure for the other doors if a four-door set is used.

In four-door sets door aligners are supplied and are positioned as indicated.

Bumpers are placed in the track at the opposite end to the top pivot socket.

Bumper

WOOD TECHNOLOGY

...A GUIDE TO TIMBER PROPERTIES

INTO THE TWENTY-FIRST CENTURY

During the last century, timber supplies were abundant, but now most timbers are in short supply. Australia is one of the many industrialised countries facing a timber shortage.

The world's forest resources are limited, and in most areas harvesting is subject to allocation. With the neglect of reafforestation and the 100 to 400 years required to produce suitable trees for quality furniture and building products, a serious threat to the long-term supply of timber has developed.

Rising prices throughout the world have made Australian timbers, with their inherent properties, competitive and thus popular on the world market.

This is particularly true of hardwoods, for which supply of furniture and building products is critical.

The use of hardwood sawn timber is anticipated to diminish. Softwood will receive more attention for structural purposes and furniture construction.

The high cost of timber products will lead to a greater emphasis on labour saving techniques and processes. This will encourage the use of decorative plastic finishes, e.g. table tops, drawer sides and linings and decorative mouldings.

Timber's natural attractiveness and workability assures it of a dominant place for furniture and building construction in the near future.

However, rising costs and a greater acceptance of alternative materials, will see a decline in the use of timber as we move further into the twenty-first century.

AUSTRALIAN FORESTS

The commercial forests of Australia are limited to the high rainfall areas of the eastern and south-eastern coastlines, the south-west corner of Western Australia and Tasmania. Travelling inland the prime indigenous forests merge into sclerophyllous woodland, savannah woodland, and mallee scrub. While few of the inland forest trees are considered suitable for sawmilling, they do provide timber for mining and agricultural purposes.

The genus Eucalyptus, a hardwood of over 500 species, reigns supreme in the Australian landscape and is renowned for its strength and durability. Species range from the magnificent grandeur of the Victorian Mountain Ash (90 m) to the dwarf ligno-tuberous specimens known as mallees. In areas of high rainfall other hardwood genera are found, including many highly prized cabinet timbers such as Red Cedar, Blackwood, Walnut, Rosewood, Silky Oak, and Queensland Maple.

The sparse occurrence of indigenous soft-wood forests has promoted the propagation of exotic non-pored timbers, in particular Radiata pine. Of the softwoods the few of any commercial value are the Huon, Celery Top, and King William pines of Tasmania, the Kauri and Bunya pines of Queensland, the Hoop pine of Queensland and New South Wales, and the Native or Cypress pine of inland areas.

Coastal and Highland Eucalypt Forests

These provide the main commercial timber source within Australia.

These forests are found in temperate latitudes having an average rainfall of between 750 to 1250 mm as do the eastern coast of Tasmania and the south-west corner of Western Australia. Marketable species include Blackbutt, Tallowwood, Spotted gum, and Ironbark of Queensland and New South Wales, Mountain ash and Stringybarks of Victoria and Tasmania, and Jarrah, Karri, and Tuart of Western Australia. Although some Eucalypt forests carry an understorey of Acacias and Casuarinas, others such as Karri and Mountain ash occur in relatively pure stands.

Rain Forests

These are found in areas having an average annual rainfall of 1250 mm or more and include tropical, sub-tropical, and temperate rain forests. Tropical rain forests with an average rainfall of 2500 mm occur in northern Queensland, while subtropical rain forests may be found in southern Queensland and northern New South Wales, with further areas extending along the eastern coastline of New South Wales.

The temperate rain forests are found on the west coast of Tasmania and in confined pockets in southern Victoria. Notable species from this type of forest include Myrtle beech, Blackwood, Southern Sassafras, Celery Top pine, King William pine, and Huon pine. Logging operations are expensive and difficult owing to the dense undergrowth and the often steep terrain coupled with a low volume per hectare return.

Inland Forests

These exist in areas receiving between 380 and 762 mm of rain per year. These forests comprise the Box, Ironbark, and Cypress pine forests of Queensland, New South Wales, and Victoria, the Red gum forests of the Murray Region, and the Wandoo forests of Western Australia. Although of little commercial value, the timber obtained from these area is extremely durable.

FORESTRY

Forestry, in broad terms, is the management of forests so that they return and provide maximum benefit for the community. Activities include controlled harvesting to provide structural timber, pulpwood, plywood, oils, and resins. Indirect benefits which affect the welfare of the community are the protection of water catchment areas, prevention of soil erosion, environment preservation, forest parks, flora and fauna reserves, and recreational facilities.

Forest Management

Forests are long term ventures managed by professional foresters who have undertaken special training in the Departments of Forestry at Australian universities, in particular the Australian National University. Most forests are government owned, although extensive plantations are privately owned by companies producing specialised products such as particle board, fibre board, and paper. To provide effective management, six major areas covering assessment, access, regeneration, tending, harvesting, and production are essential.

Assessment

Initially information is needed to provide details of a forest area. Land surveys and soil samples are undertaken to provide a general knowledge of the district. Measurement of trees necessary to provide an estimate of timber volume and the growth rate are other important activities. From this information the rate of harvesting can be determined and logging and regeneration may be controlled.

In plantations, on the other hand, the forest area is divided into site qualities or grades. This routine assessment of plantations is the basis upon which calculations are made of the growth rate and the classes of log material that can be made available to the sawmills.

Access

The construction of roads is essential. They enable foresters to make assessments, they allow logs to be removed quickly and easily, and fire protection units are able to move rapidly to the source of a fire. In addition, tourists are able to visit and enjoy the forest and the accompanying wildlife.

Australian forests may be classified as natural forest and plantations. The techniques of growing and tending trees, known as silviculture, varies and depends largely upon the forest, its location, and whether it is a plantation or a natural forest.

Logging Operations

Trees are harvested when they are thinned or when they are mature. Unless the forest is to be clear felled the trees to be harvested are marked by a forester in accordance with overall plans for regeneration and development of the area. Private contractors generally carry out logging operations which include felling, snigging, and transport.

Clear felling radiata pine using a chain saw

Felling

The fellers are rugged individuals who often work alone in a forest displaying skill and initiative in felling large trees sometimes 50 metres in height and with a girth of around 3 to 4 metres. The foresters not only mark the trees to be harvested, but will also indicate where the tree is to be placed, maybe to avoid new growth, or rocks that may damage the tree as it falls. The feller must study the land form, direction of the wind, and the shape and size of the stem before deciding where to put the scarf cut.

The scarf is a V-shaped cut made with a chain saw on the side the feller wishes the tree to fall. In effect it controls the direction of fall. The chain saw is then used to cut around the back of the tree. The feller makes good use of the defect that occurs in many Australian trees known as the pipe. This may be described as a hollowing caused by termites in the centre of the tree creating a tube-like effect.

The branches are removed from the felled logs which are then cut into lengths, depending upon market requirements.

Snigging

This term refers to the practice of dragging the logs from the stump to a log dump which is accessible to large semi-trailers for transport to a convenient sawmill.

Large crawler tractors equipped with a front end loader cut tracks into a forest. Rear-mounted winches are used to haul large logs from difficult terrain, such as steep valleys or gullies. Once clear, the logs are coupled to the tractor and dragged to the log dump.

Transport

From the log dump large semi-trailers generally haul the logs to a sawmill. The trucks travel on relatively good gravel roads made especially for the purpose. These roads usually feed on to major public roads. Once at the sawmill the logs are unloaded in a log yard ready for some form of specialised conveyance to the mill.

Plantation Forests

Valuable softwoods in Australia have been logged heavily since the early days of settlement, and in an effort to maintain supplies, plantations of various softwood species have been established. Of the early plantings only a few species indicated their suitability in terms of growth rate and quality. Probably the most notable of the species planted is Radiata pine (*Pinus radiata*). Radiata pine, together with other species of the same genus, have been planted throughout Australia with tremendous success.

Of the native softwoods, most of which have growth rates which tend to restrict their economic success, Hoop pine is a valuable softwood widely recognised in the plywood manufacturing industry. Because it has not been possible to establish a system of natural regeneration, plantations have been established in Queensland.

Modern mechanical tree harvesters have been developed for use in pine forests. These machines are capable of snapping off a tree, shearing off the branches, storing the stems in a rack, and later removing them to a dump to await transport.

Protection

As the manufacturing industry becomes more dependent upon the forest for its raw material so the forest must be able to survive agents of destruction. Fungal disease, insects, and fire are the main agents which are likely to reduce potential forest yields.

Nurseries and Plantation Establishment

Nursery techniques will depend upon the species being sown and the location of the nursery.

In the south-east of South Australia, Radiata pine cones are collected in early summer. Opened by the warmth of the sun in glass solar kilns, the seeds are collected, the wings removed, and they are stored ready for sowing.

Nurseries in New South Wales engaged in the raising of eucalypt species grow seedlings in peatmoss containers called jiffy pots. The jiffy pots are filled with forest soil, and the seeds collected from selected trees are inserted into the soil. The seedlings are planted out when they are about three to six months old. They are spaced at intervals of about 2 metres.

Research

Research is recognised as essential if the industry is to develop successfully. Each State Forestry Service retains research staff to investigate the immediate problems. In addition the Commonwealth Government is actively involved in assisting forestry research. The C.S.I.R.O. carries on research in a number of areas including building research, entomology, soils, and wildlife. The Bureau of Meteorology gives assistance on weather research involving fire protection. The Forestry and Timber Bureau supports a Forest Research Institute to study the problems of silviculture, forest management, and protection. Many problems are the subject of postgraduate studies in Universities.

As a result of silvicultural and forest management research many important practices have been introduced that will ensure the successful economic development of the industry.

SAWMILLING

The large modern sawmill of today is highly mechanised. The majority of the new mills have incorporated the most advanced techniques, enabling operators to sit at push button consoles and direct massive precision equipment with their fingertips.

Log carriages, capable of sawing accurately to specific dimensions, coupled with faster log handling equipment, have provided a considerable advance in breaking down operations. Selectively sized flitches produced by these breaking down machines reduce the sawing requirements of the subsequent operations. Electro-pneumatically controlled power feed benches capable of fast accurate sawing break down the flitches to the required timber sizes. Power docking saws, rollers, and improved mill layout have reduced heavy manual handling, thus making for further efficiency.

Sawmill Procedure

The aim of the sawmill is to convert round logs into timber of marketable sizes. The reduction in size of timber provides for quicker and more even drying. The order in sawing is to remove the curved outer surfaces of the log (slabs) and then to saw the squared cant or flitch into required sizes.

The flow pattern or sequence of operations is similar in all mills, regardless of size and degree of automation.

Logs reaching the mill landing are crosscut into suitable lengths. Breaking down occurs at the headsaw, where the log is cut lengthwise into manageable pieces with at least one flat face for use in further resawing.

Resawing means the timber from the headsaw is sawn into the required sizes. Defects are eliminated by a process of docking. Grading and sorting separates the cut pieces into groups of quality and size. These are then stored to await further processing.

Sawmill Layout

The initial requisites of a sawmill are log accommodation, unloading equipment, and a means of moving the logs into the mill. For mill entrance, each log is transferred to a log carriage for the primary breaking down at the headsaw. The saw and carriage serving the log are known as the headrig. The resulting products move to the smaller resaws to be cut into specified widths and thicknesses, docked in length, and finally finish at the sorting table.

The Small 'Bush' Mill

Logs are unloaded on to a raised bank of suitable height to allow for winching or rolling on to the log carriage. Any crosscutting of log length may be done by a portable chain saw prior to loading. Once on the carriage, the log is wedged and clamped for successive passes through the headsaw. The log carriage may be pulled back and forth by various mechanical means, with the log being moved manually into the next cutting position. The skill and experience of the operator determine the way the log is cut and hence the volume of usable timber produced from each log.

The breaking down headsaw is usually a large circular saw or, for large diameter logs, two circular saws may be mounted one above the other.

The resawing that follows may again be made by a circular saw but it is smaller than the breaking down saw. The usual docking saws in mills of this type are simple cross-cutting saws.

The banding together of small mills to form timber consortiums has made it possible to update the machinery. Bandsaws are being substituted for circular saws in both headsaws and resaws. The bandsaw saws faster, gives a better finish, and requires less power than a circular saw. Moreover, since it is much thinner, one extra 25 mm board may be obtained after every four, leaving far less waste.

The Modern Sawmill

Large mills are highly mechanised, with emphasis on speed and high volume production. Logs are unloaded in bulk by fork lifts or overhead cranes into a storage area. When required they are carried by these same machines ready for loading on to a conveyor known as a bull chain which lifts them into the mill.

Before entering the mill, logs may be washed to remove any grit, or completely debarked by a special machine. Logs are grouped according to diameter suitable for each production line and a small stock maintained close to the headsaw for each line. The flow pattern illustrates the passage of timber through successive stages and its separation from the waste by a series of power driven rollers and conveyors. Although the circular trimmer saws are mounted as a battery, only the two that crosscut most advantageously are used.

An alternative headrig for smaller diameter logs is the gang saw, consisting of a bank of saw blades moving up and down in a rectangular frame. The blades are so spaced as to cut the whole log into pieces of required width and thickness in one pass. The pieces move on to resawing, including edger saw and thinner saws with other types of headrig.

The trimmed pieces move on to the sorting table or 'green chain' where sizes and qualities are determined. This type of timber is referred to as green rough-sawn timber and may be sold or alternatively further processed by preservative treatment, seasoning, machining, or remanufacturing.

Sawing Methods

The sawing patterns or methods of conversion differ according to the type of timber, the quality and size of the logs, sawmill capabilities, and market acceptance. Often, logs may be live-sawn (sawing through and through), the taper of the log being removed in the slabwood and the outer boards cut roughly parallel to the growth rings. Other timbers are best cut along the line of taper as this produces boards less susceptible to distortion. These methods are known as 'sawing around' and involve turning the log to different positions as sawing progresses.

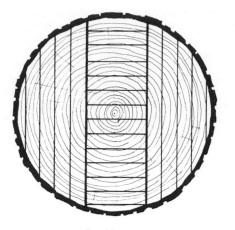

Double pass

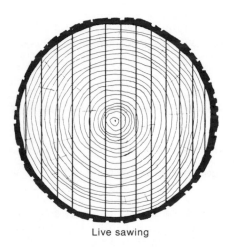

Live sawing

Live Sawing

Live sawing is the easiest and most economical way of converting logs into boards. In one operation a gang or frame saw, consisting of a body of vertical blades, breaks the log down by a series of parallel cuts. Milling costs are kept to a minimum since log handling is negligible and the recovery rate is extremely high.

Live sawing is often used where uniformity of log size and freedom of internal defects is assured. This applies to most plantation timbers and consequently this method is widely used in Australian and New Zealand pine plantations.

With the presence of sapwood in each live-sawn board care must be taken when seasoning to prevent distortion. For this reason live-sawn boards are mainly used for cheaper construction work, light framing, packing cases, fence palings, and crates.

An alternative method—double pass—is where the cant is resawn parallel to the growth rings.

Back Sawing (Tangential Cut)

In back sawing the log is turned so that the faces of the boards produced are tangential to the growth rings. This method is popular throughout Australia and New Zealand for converting non-pored and some pored timbers. For timbers susceptible to heart defects,

Back sawing

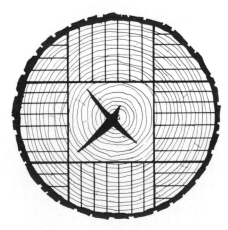

Back sawing (alternative method)

such as eucalypts, this method is highly suited, as it allows for sawing around any such fault, thus limiting the amount of waste. Although back-sawn boards season readily, tangential shrinkage will cause 'atmospheric movement' of timber when converted for use. Also of some concern is the 'cupping' away

from the heart because of the prominent tangential growth ring structure of each board.

Quarter Sawing (Radial Cut)

The ornamental grain peculiar to certain timbers may be best displayed if the log is sawn approximately at right angles to the growth rings. This method is known as quarter sawing. It requires the frequent changing of log position and produces more waste than normal methods but is compensated for by commanding a higher price for the highly figured wood produced.

For timbers possessing a distinct medullary ray, such as Silky oak, quarter sawing highlights a decorative figure called silver grain. In the case of Queensland maple, walnut, or those timbers with an interlocked grain structure, radial cutting produces a 'ribbon' or 'stripe' figure. It is logical, therefore, that valuable cabinet timbers possessing these qualities are fully quarter-sawn.

Although quarter-sawn boards have little tendency to cup, the seasoning process is much slower than for back-sawn boards.

The 'edge grain' produced by quarter sawing is most advantageous for use in exposed flooring where smooth, even wear is required.

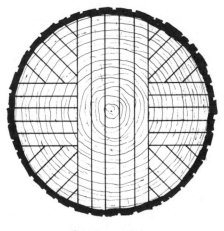

Quarter sawing

Timber Processing

The modern sawmill is no longer a producer of rough-sawn timber but is a wood processing unit converting logs into products ready for commercial use. This centralisation of processing has evolved with the establishment of sawmills large enough to carry expenditure on special production equipment. Procedures often carried out by timber merchants, joiners, and builders are being completed at the sawmills prior to distribution. This has reduced the capital investment problems of small woodworking businesses who would otherwise have to install costly machinery used only intermittently.

Manufacture at sawmills usually involves producing timber products either in a finished condition or as finished components ready for assembly. Typical manufactured products include glue laminated beams, box shooks, pre-cut house frames, and a range of timber fences.

The timber used is generally dried, preservative-treated, or planed.

SEASONING OF TIMBER

Seasoning is a process during which the moisture is dried from the timber until it ceases to lose moisture to the atmosphere. It is an essential part of the preparation of timber for commercial use.

The stem of the tree is made up of cells that resemble small tubes consisting of a cell wall enclosing a hollow cavity. In the living tree the cavity is filled with water and other materials essential to life. When felled and converted, the freshly sawn boards consist of numerous cells saturated with water.

In order to improve its properties the timber must be seasoned. Experiments have shown that compressive, tensile, bending, and shear strength are increased substantially. It is also well known that timber actually increases in hardness as it dries, as anyone who has tried to drive a nail into seasoned hardwood will testify. If Karri rails are used in fencing, the contractor will make sure they are delivered in the green state so that nails may be easily driven.

Increased hardness can be an advantage in the case of flooring where resistance to wear and bumps is essential.

The drying of timber results in a considerable loss of weight, an important factor when handling and transport costs are to be considered.

The durability is increased by seasoning. Timber kept at more than 20% moisture content is susceptible to attack by various fungi which destroy timber. Seasoning also limits the number of insects that are liable to attack, and is a prerequisite if preservative treatments are considered.

Wet timber is a good conductor of electricity, but dry timber becomes a good insulator and is often used for electrical installations.

Timber that is not fully seasoned will not take paint and other forms of surface finish satisfactorily. In addition, adhesives produce the strongest bonds on dry timber and break down rapidly if used on unseasoned timber.

Seasoned timber is also easier to work. Operations such as sawing, planing, chiselling and drilling are far easier in dry timber. Timber is not dried to the extent where all the moisture is removed; it will always contain some. The moisture content of the timber will depend on the relative humidity of the surrounding air.

The term moisture content put simply is the weight of water contained in the timber compared with the weight of the wood substance, expressed as a percentage.

A quick method of obtaining an approximate knowledge of the moisture content is to use a resistance type electrical meter. The electrical resistance of timber is directly related to the moisture content, and it follows then that by measuring the electrical resistance of a specific piece of timber the moisture content can be estimated. Since the relationship between resistance and moisture content is not the same for all species, correction factors are necessary as the meters are only calibrated against one species. Tables of correction factors are supplied by the manufacturers of the meters.

Combined Moisture and Free Moisture

Free moisture is the term applied to the water in the cell cavities, and the term combined moisture refers to the moisture saturating the cell walls. As the timber dries the free moisture evaporates first, producing a noticeable loss of weight, and as drying continues the combined moisture is removed producing dramatic changes in the properties of the timber.

Fibre Saturation Point

Fibre saturation point is that stage of drying where the moisture in the cell cavity has evaporated but the cell wall is still saturated. This is an important stage, as the moisture content of practically all timbers lies between 25 and 30% and it is at this stage also that changes commence which affect the properties of all timbers.

Moisture Gradient

Timber does not dry uniformly. It is generally recognised that drying has to occur at the surface before moisture will start moving from the centre or core to the surface so that it may in turn evaporate. The moisture will always flow from the wetter to the dryer areas, and it is this moisture gradient that eventually results in the drying of the centre.

Equilibrium Moisture Content

Timber will dry until the moisture content of the centre or core is approximately that of the surface layers of cells. The air to which the timber is exposed always contains moisture, so that the moisture content of the timber will depend on the relative humidity of the surrounding air. Timber dried to this state is said to be at its equilibrium moisture content and is fully seasoned.

Moisture content will vary with changes in relative humidity, and it follows that the location of the timber in service should be known in order to determine the extent of the seasoning process. For example in coastal areas

timber generally maintains moisture content of around 12% to 15%, but in extremely dry areas the moisture content of timber will drop to around 7%.

Shrinkage of Timber

All timber shrinks as it dries, and shrinkage is the direct cause of checks, cracks, and warping that too often occur when timber is seasoned.

When the timber reaches fibre saturation point it begins to shrink and will continue to do so until the timber reaches equilibrium moistener content.

Timber shrinks basically in three different directions. Shrinkage along its length is around 0.1%, although abnormal wood, such as reaction wood, sloping or spiral grained timber, has a higher level of shrinkage, usually around 1%.

Shrinkage in width and thickness depends largely on how the board is sawn from the log. A quarter-sawn board, one cut in a radial direction, will shrink at a rate approximately one half that of a board cut in a tangential direction.

Collapse

Many Australian timbers are susceptible to collapse, which is the phenomenon whereby the cell becomes flattened and distorted. Collapse occurs during the removal of the free water. If no collapse is apparent at fibre saturation point it can be assumed that the particular timber is not susceptible.

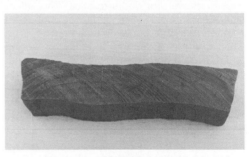

Collapse

Reconditioning Treatment for Collapsed Boards

Reconditioning is carried out in a reinforced concrete compartment designed for this purpose. The timber is subjected to steam treatment at temperatures of between 82°C to 109°C. The timber is left in the chamber until there is no obvious collapse. During treatment the moisture content of the timber is increased and the timber is returned to the kiln to complete the seasoning process.

Checks and Cracks

As already stated, a piece of timber dries gradually from the outside, and as this drying is taking place these drier outside layers are shrinking while the inner core remains saturated. This differential shrinkage sets up stresses within the timber, particularly if drying is too rapid. If these stresses are severe the surface may rupture, causing a separation of fibres along the lines of least resistance. This will show as checks or cracks.

Internal checking may occur in the latter stages of drying after the core has been dried below fibre saturation point.

Warping

When timber with straight grain is dried under optimum conditions the shrinkage is uniform and even. However, warping may be induced by uneven drying or poor stacking.

Timber with sloping grain, due to the presence of knots or other factors, will tend to dry unevenly and contribute to warping. Timber containing spiral grain will tend to twist as it is dried. Warping known as 'bow' is generally due to poor stacking techniques, usually where the ends of the boards are allowed to overhang.

Both checking and warping can be reduced by controlled drying and proper stacking. Carefully seasoned timber, when protected from weathering, will not shrink, warp, or check, and will remain serviceable for many years.

Movement of Seasoned Timber

Small amounts of 'movement' in timber is often observed in damp weather as a swelling which causes drawers or doors to stick. This effect disappears when the weather becomes warmer and the timber shrinks again. The basic cause is a change in moisture content and may be due to normal climatic variations, effects of modern airconditioning systems, or by wetting and drying of the timber that may occur if it is used outside.

Methods of Seasoning

Seasoning of timber is usually carried out by using one of three methods. However, comparatively recent developments by wood technologists have made alternative techniques available, and many are undergoing serious study by the industry to determine whether or not they are a viable proposition.
1. Kiln seasoning.
2. Air seasoning.
3. Air drying to fibre saturation point and completing the process in a kiln.

The method selected depends on many factors: the species to be dried, the size of material, and the economic considerations which involve the rate of air drying to that of kiln drying, and how much degrade is likely to occur.

Classification and Nomenclature

To appreciate and understand fully the properties of timber it is helpful to know something of the classification or grouping and the naming or nomenclature of plants and, in particular, trees.

An international system exists for the scientific classification and naming of plants and this is generally attributed to Carl Linnaeus (1707–1778), known as the founder of modern systematic botany. The many hundreds and thousands of plant species present a formidable problem. It is necessary to classify plants in an orderly fashion and it is general to group plants which share common features.

Recognisable types of plants are known as a species and are given a specific name, generally descriptive of the plant character, which always begins with a small letter. The most closely related species are then grouped to form a genus, the generic name being spelt with a capital letter. The closely related genera are then grouped into families.

There are hundreds of species of trees in Australia and each one varies in some way with respect to structure and properties. In an attempt to understand the material wood, it is necessary to consider the general structure of the wood and the structure of the wood cells and fibres.

The Tree

The tree consists of roots which anchor the tree to the ground and obtain water and mineral salts from the soil. The trunk or stem supports the crown. The crown consists of branches, twigs, and leaves.

Growth in height is confined to specialist cells at the extreme tip of the tree and branches. Vertical growth on a young tree is rapid, but as the tree matures the rate of growth slows down appreciably. The growth in diameter is due to the division of cells in the cambium layer and extends around the trunk from the roots to within a short distance of the growing tip. The cells of the cambium layer divide to form new wood and new bark. Growth in diameter is not regular. In cold climates growth may almost cease during winter, but in spring the growth rate increases and the wood cells formed are large in cross section. Towards the end of spring and summer the growth rate slows down, resulting in the formation of smaller, thick-walled cells.

The annual repetition of this type of growth rate produces growth rings.

In Australia growth rings generally indicate climatic change, and do not always mark years of growth. Growth rings in most eucalypts are often hard to distinguish due mainly to Australia's rather temperate climate. Trees grown in the tropics show little or no evidence of growth rings as growth rates remain regular throughout the year.

Sapwood and Heartwood

The cross section of a log usually shows the presence of two distinct zones of wood; a light coloured zone known as the sapwood and a darker coloured region known as the heartwood.

The function of the sapwood is the conduction of sap and food storage, while the heartwood's function is one of mechanical support. When the sapwood cells are first formed they are thin-walled, but they are slowly transformed as tannins, gums, resins, pigments, and other materials are deposited in the cell cavities. Gradually the sapwood cells are converted into thicker-walled darker coloured heartwood. These deposits also give the heartwood its characteristic colour and may add to its weight and hardness and may even increase its durability.

Sapwood generally represents around 25% of the total volume of the commercial log and clearly cannot be rejected if the industry is to remain viable. It has been found that the properties of sapwood and heartwood of similar moisture content and density are approximately equal. However, sapwood contains a large amount of plant food and as such is particularly prone to insect and fungal attack. Various preservation treatments have been developed to increase the durability of sapwood and in most cases treated sapwood is superior to heartwood.

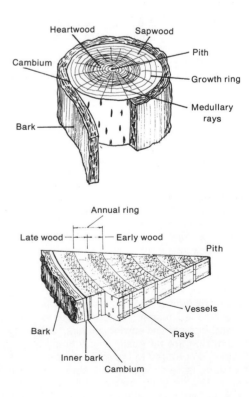

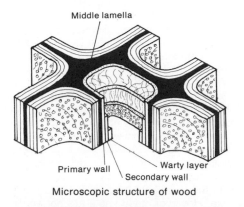

Middle lamella

Primary wall — Warty layer
Secondary wall

Microscopic structure of wood

Microscopic Structure of Wood

Wood is a porous material made up of many small cells derived from the cambium layer.

Hardwoods (pored wood)

Much of the timber used in Australia is classed as hardwood, the best known example perhaps being the many varieties of eucalypts.

Hardwoods have two distinct cell types. Large tubular vessels or pores are distributed throughout the early wood and late wood. These vessels are disposed longitudinally and conduct solutions to the leaves. Adjacent vessels are connected by pits. The second cell type provides mechanical support and is known as a wood fibre.

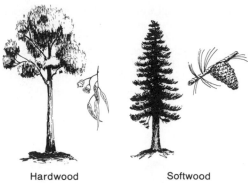

Hardwood
(Angiospermae)

Softwood
(Gymnospermae)

Softwood (non-pored wood)

Well known softwoods used in Australia include Radiata pine, Douglas fir, Hoop pine and Cypress pine.

In comparison with the cell structure of hardwood, that of the softwood is relatively simple.

Cells known as trachieds fulfil a double function in providing mechanical support and in conducting water.

Properties of Timber

Some timbers are soft, some hard, many are heavy and some light, others may be flexible or brittle. These characteristics are known as properties, and it is the properties of a timber which ultimately determine the use to which it is best suited. Many features must be studied to reveal a full picture of a timber's properties.

The properties of various species may vary considerably, some species being vastly stronger than others, while there may also be considerable differences within any one species.

Environmental factors, geographical location, soil, climatic conditions, spacing, age, and the position of the tree all have an important influence on the properties of a timber.

For the purpose of providing an accurate determination of a timber's properties standard conditions are set up for laboratory testing. Factors such as temperature and moisture content are controlled and standards are established by using accepted testing techniques.

Tests are usually made at 20°C and timber samples dried to 12% moisture content.

The influences of defects, duration of loading, moisture content, and temperature are tested separately and compared with a set of figures which represent the properties of a sample of clear timber for each species.

Strength and Density

The density of a timber is an indication of the amount of wood per unit volume (kg/cu metre) and is a guide to the strength of the timber. The rate of growth may have an important effect on these properties. For example a piece of Radiata pine viewed in cross section will show that the late wood trachieds are thicker and smaller than the early wood. They are denser and stronger, and it follows that if the tree is grown rapidly, that is with a greater proportion of early wood, the timber will not be as dense or as strong as timber from a tree which has grown at a more moderate rate. The density of timber may also depend upon the amount of deposits in the cell cavity such as resins, gums, etc.

Terms Used to Describe the Strength Properties of Timber Tested Under Laboratory Conditions

Tension: Straight-grained timber free of defects, such as knots and sloping grain, has a relatively high tensile strength. When knots are present the grain in the immediate vicinity is usually very steep and seriously affects its tensile strength. When timber is graded for structural purposes the effects of knots and grain angle are carefully considered.

Compression: The ability of a timber to resist crushing forces. These may be of two types, either parallel to the grain or perpendicular to the grain.

Bending: The ability of the timber to withstand compression and tension loads and return to its original shape.

Shear: Timber is much more likely to separate along the fibres than in a direction perpendicular to the grain. A timber's shear strength may be described as its ability to resist separation along the grain.

Impact: The ability of a timber to absorb a shock load. Many impacts show up defects not obvious to a visual inspection.

Cleavage: The ability of a timber to resist splitting. Arrangements such as growth rings, grain, resin, canals, and medullary rays are factors which will affect cleavage.

Hardness: The size of the cells and the thickness of the cell walls largely determine the hardness. The cells may also be filled with extraneous materials, such as resins or gums, and in addition mineral matter may be present. Mineral matter often has a serious effect upon cutting tools used to work the material. For example, the high silica content in Queensland walnut makes the timber extremely difficult to work as cutting tools quickly lose their edge.

Toughness: A timber is said to be tough if it shows a high resistance to shearing forces, a property generally found in timbers with small thick-walled cells.

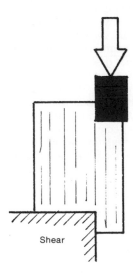

Shear

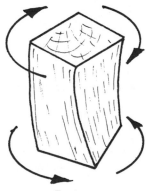

Torsion

Other Interesting Properties

Durability: A term used to describe the resistance of a timber to fungal and insect attack. This depends largely upon the nature of the chemicals present in the cells and cell walls. For example Turpentine (*Syncarpia glomulifera*) is resistant to the teredo, and it is believed that the presence of silica in the cells of the wood is largely responsible for its durability.

Figure: The attractive designs of texture, grain, and colour are referred to when one speaks of figure.

Texture depends largely upon the size of the wood cells.

Timber with small cells is said to have a fine texture and timber with large cells a coarse texture.

Structural features of timber such as growth rings, rays, and the methods of converting the log are factors which determine the figure. Knots may contribute in providing an interesting surface. A radially sawn board will show growth rings as parallel lines, while a tangentially sawn board will show growth rings in their characteristic cone shapes. Figure generally is more attractive in tangentially sawn boards, but some timbers have large medullary rays and are generally cut radially to feature the rays. Timbers such as silky oak (*Cardwella sublimis*) are cut in this way.

Interlocked grain is a term used to describe a double spiral grain where the fibres of adjacent growth rings are inclined at different angles to the axis. This particular abnormality is difficult to prepare but when cleaned up successfully produces a beautiful figure.

In some species the axial fibres grow in an undulating fashion rather than obliquely. When cut radially the varied reflection from the surface due to light striking the surface fibres at different angles produces a figure known as wavy grain. It is also commonly known as fiddleback grain because timber so figured is traditionally used for the backs of violins.

Figure due to colour or colour variation is not uncommon in timbers and provides a variety of interest. Colour is due largely to the extraneous substances in the walls of the cells, but it is not generally known what causes the colour variation. Colours may vary from the rich brown of walnut and blackbean to the pale cream colour of Radiata pine. Heartwood and sapwood of the same tree may contrast. Often colour effects may be produced by wood-staining fungi.

There are many other properties of timber which ultimately affect the use of various species. Fibre length is important if the wood is to be used for paper manufacture. Fibre direction too, can be significant if the property of resonance is important, as in the construction of musical instruments.

If the use of preservatives is considered the penetrability of a timber must be considered.

The deposits of extraneous substances may in some cases provide a timber with desirable properties. *Lignon vitae* is used for pulley blocks and bushings for propeller shafts in ships because resin deposits make the timber self-lubricating. Deposits of extraneous substances, because of distinctive colours, make some timbers entirely unsuitable for food containers.

Thermal Conductivity: In timber this is relatively low. That is why handles of tools and other items where insulation is required are often made of wood. Lower density timbers provide better thermal insulation than those of high density.

Timber is also resistant to a wide range of chemicals and is often used for vats and containers. It is also better suited for constructional purposes in coastal areas where steel rusts readily.

As the moisture content of timber varies so does its electrical resistance. Moisture meters have been developed to determine moisture content by measuring the electrical resistance. The electrical resistance of timber is relatively high and consequently cross arms on poles for power lines are often specified in timber.

The use of timber laminated beams for structural purposes is widely recommended by timber engineers, and supported by insurance companies, because of their behaviour in fires. Steel structures are known to bend and collapse, creating hazards and causing unnecessary damage, while timber beams show resistance to burning, charring only on the outside and retaining strength enough to support roof structures.

DEFECTS IN TIMBER

Defects in timber may be described as any abnormality which affects the strength, durability, or appearance. Defects are generally grouped as natural defects, defects due to seasoning, and defects due to decay and insect attack.

Natural Defects

This term refers to the irregularities that occur while the tree is growing. Knots, sloping grain shakes, gum veins and vein canals are the main natural defects which affect the quality of timber.

Knots

Knots are probably the most common defect in timber and are caused when branches are cut through in the milling process. They are common in timbers such as Radiata pine and Douglas fir. Fortunately they are rare in Australian timbers used for structural pur-

poses. Knots have an area of sloping grain around them and it is this that mainly affects the strength of timber. Standards are well established and it is possible to estimate the reduction in strength due to the type and size of knot.

The shape of a knot on a sawn board depends on the direction of cut. If it is cut at right angles a round knot results, if cut obliquely an oval knot, and when sawn along its length what is known as a spike knot. A knot may also be classified as a dead knot. This is the result of a branch dying and additional growth encasing the dead limb. When sawn, the dead knot is apt to fall out, leaving a hole. However, dead knots are not accompanied by an excess of sloping grain and have less effect on the strength of the board.

Sloping Grain

Sloping grain is where the fibres of a piece of timber are at an angle to the axis. It may be due to spiral growth about the trunk, incorrect milling procedures, or knots. A sawn board with sloping grain may be described as having cross grain or diagonal grain. Sloping grain also has the effect of warping the timber as it is seasoned. The strength of timber is greatly reduced by sloping grain. For example, the tensile and bending strength of timber is reduced by up to 40% if the slope of the grain is 1 in 10.

Reaction Wood

This is abnormal wood found in bent or leaning branches or trunks of trees. It is accompanied by marked eccentric growth.

Compression wood is the name applied to the abnormality as it occurs in Gymnosperms.

Tension wood is the term applied to the abnormality as it occurs in Angiosperms.

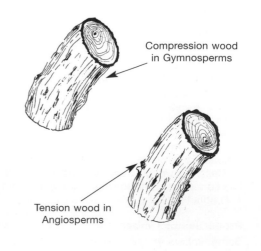

Compression wood in Gymnosperms

Tension wood in Angiosperms

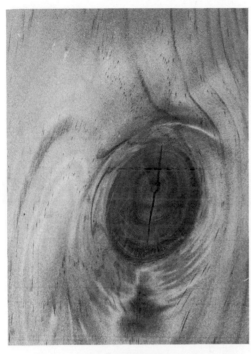

Round knot

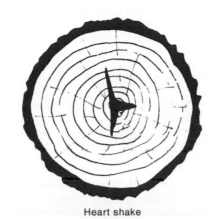

Heart shake

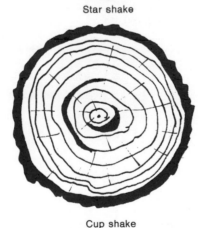

Star shake

Cup shake

Spike knot

the separation of fibres in the interior of the wood and is not visible at the surface. Again this is largely due to rapid or uneven drying. Blackbean is a difficult timber to season and often shows signs of collapse and honeycombing.

Gum veins and pockets

Honeycombing

Resin Canals, Gum Veins, Gum Pockets, and Shakes

Timbers belonging to the Gymnospermae contain a substance known as resin. The resin is found in the cells and between cells in cavities known as resin canals. The resin canals may be horizontal or parallel to the axis.

Gum veins or pockets are caused by a partial or complete separation of the fibres creating cavities containing dark coloured deposits of gum.

Shakes are also due to the separation of the fibres and arise in standing trees. The separation of the fibres occurring along the growth rings is known as ring shakes. Separation of the fibres along the medullary rays is known as heart or star shakes. Growth stresses or stress due to the effect of bending of the tree by the wind are said to be the cause of the fibre separation.

Defects due to Seasoning

Checks occur at the end and on the surface of a board. This type of defect is the separation of the fibres caused by rapid and uneven drying. Checks may create serious weakness and should be avoided if the timber is to be used for structural purposes.

Rapid and uneven drying will also result in the flattening and distortion of the cells, producing a defect known as collapse. This may be easily recognised, as the surface of the timber is undulating and uneven. Collapsed timber may be restored by steam treatment in a reconditioning kiln.

Honeycombing is a term used to describe

Warping

Warping is the broad term used to describe the distortion of sawn timber due to excessive stresses set up during seasoning. Warping may be accentuated by the presence of sloping grain or reaction wood. The main types of warping are cup, twist, bow, and spring. Generally, warping may be minimised by careful stacking and controlled seasoning.

Cup is a common defect in tangentially sawn boards. The board tends to shrink away from the heart, but may be controlled by careful stacking and seasoning.

Twist is a spiral distortion generally caused by sloping grain, but may also be caused by poor stacking.

323

Bow is a longitudinal curve.
Spring is a longitudinal curve where the face of the board remains flat.

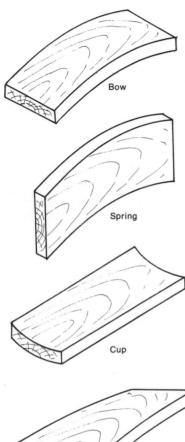

Bow

Spring

Cup

Twist

Warping

DEGRADE IN TIMBER

No timber is permanently resistant to degrade but a few like ironbark, teak, and red wood will endure for centuries under extremely severe conditions. There are many examples of timbers remaining in sound condition for thousands of years. Degrade in timber is caused by the attack of some outside agency and a set of conditions suitable for its development. Decay caused by the growth of fungi capable of attacking wood and using it for food, insect attack, and marine borer attack are the three most damaging of these agencies.

Decay in Timber

Wood-destroying fungi are not able to synthesise their own food so they depend on other organisms for their food supply. The wood-destroying fungi develop from spores which correspond to seeds of flowering plants. The spores are released when conditions are favourable for growth. The spores are light and are carried great distances on air currents.

The conditions which favour the growth of fungi may be listed:
1. A moisture content suitable for development, usually about 25% to 100% of the even dry weight of the wood.
2. A temperature range suitable for development. Most fungi thrive on warmth.
3. An adequate supply of oxygen.
4. A suitable food supply on which to grow. Wood-destroying fungi may be divided into three groups: brown rot, white rot, soft rot.

Brown Rot

The fungi feed mainly on the lighter coloured cellulose of the cell wall and leave the darker lignin as a loose dark brown powder. The destruction of the cellulose which gives the fibres longitudinal strength allows the wood to crack as easily across the grain as with the grain. Wood affected in this way often gives the appearance of wood recently charred in a fire. Brown rots are generally found in softwoods and lighter hardwoods.

Brown rot

White Rot

The breakdown of the wood material is more complex as both the cellulose and lignin are attacked. The timber eventually becomes much lighter in weight and colour and loses its strength properties. The timber breaks down in a longitudinal direction and is quite fibrous in appearance. White rots are generally found in hardwoods.

Soft Rot

Decay of this type is caused by a more primitive type of fungus or mould, and it flourishes in much wetter conditions as the mould requires less oxygen. These moulds attack only the cellulose. The moulds are progressive and as the wood breaks and crumbles away at the surface the decay travels inward.

White rot

Wood-staining Fungi

This type of fungus feeds on the food stored in the cell and not the cell walls. The strength of the timber is hardly affected although excessive discolouration occurs. Timbers seriously stained in this way are considerably reduced in value. The fungi can be easily controlled by seasoning of the sawn timber, and chemical sprays and dips are suitable for debarked logs. Both methods of control should be applied as soon as practicable after the log is felled.

Wood-destroying Insects

For convenience, wood-destroying insects may be broadly classified into two groups: wood borers and termites.

Wood Borers

Wood borers are beetles that at some stage of their life cycle bore into wood either for food or shelter. The life cycle of a beetle has four distinct stages of development: the egg, the larvae, the pupa or dormant stage, and the adult.

It is known that each species of borer has its own peculiar habits, and a knowledge of these factors assists in recognition so that appropriate steps may be taken for eradication. It is also possible to group wood borers into two groups: those that attack standing trees or green timber and those that attack seasoned timber.

Borers that Attack Green Timber and Standing Trees

The Pinhole Borers (Scolytidae and Platypodidae)

This group is so named because of the appearance of the surface of the wood. It appears to have been perforated by pins. These insects are known as Ambrosia beetles. They are unique because it is the adult beetle that causes the major part of the damage. The larvae live in galleries constructed by the parent and live on a mould which is introduced into the galleries by the adult. As the mould requires moisture for growth, it dies when the timber is seasoned and consequently the larvae do not survive. Pinhole borers of this species will not therefore reinfest once the timber is dry. There is, however, a species of pinhole borer where the larvae do not depend on a mould for food and actively bore into the wood. The borer dust, in the form of a light powder, is known as the frass and is ejected to the surface of the wood.

The Longicorn Beetles (Cerambycidae)

These borers are widely distributed throughout the world and are sometimes known as longhorns because of their feelers. They are essentially a forest pest, and although hundreds of species breed in Australia only a few (*Phymatodes testaceus*) are of importance to timber users.

In Australia these borers generally infect hardwoods where the larvae attack both heartwood and sapwood. These borers can complete the life cycle after the tree has been felled and emerge from dry wood.

The Bostrychid Borers (Bostrychidae)

Sometimes known as auger beetles their attack does not initiate in standing trees but in freshly felled logs and green timber. Attack often takes place during air seasoning before the timber reaches fibre saturation point. Dry timber is not attacked. The eggs are laid in tunnels and the grub bores into the sapwood, feeding on starch in the wood and subsequently emerging as an adult beetle.

Sirex Wood Wasp (Siricidae)

This insect is a wasp. (*Sirex noctillio*) not a beetle, originating in Europe but introduced into many other countries, including Australia. Sirex attack is limited to the softwood species and in particular pine. The wood wasp only attacks living trees, generally poor, damaged, or burnt trees, but once the wasp becomes established, quite healthy trees are also attacked.

The female lays her eggs via the egg-laying part of her anatomy known as an ovipositor, through the bark and into the wood. Wood-rotting fungus is also introduced, probably to soften the wood near the egg. It is thought that whenever the female inserts the ovipositor the fungus is also introduced, and it is this fungus which leads to the death of the tree.

The larvae are hatched after about two weeks and after initial feeding near the surface bore towards the heart. The larvae return to a position near the surface and after pupation the adult wasp chews its way clear leaving a hole approximately 6 mm in diameter.

Serious economic loss incurred by the death of living trees may be caused by these insects, and in Australia strict quarantine control is exercised.

Borers Attacking Dry Wood

The Lyctus Borer (Lyctidae)

Only the sapwood of seasoned hardwood is attacked by this insect (*Lyctus brunneus*). The susceptibility of the timber to attack depends on the starch content and the size of the pores.

The female lays her eggs in the pores of the sapwood. Timber that has pores too small to accommodate the ovipositor is immune from attack. The larvae bore into the sapwood and gain nourishment from the starch. If there is insufficient starch available the timber can be regarded as immune.

As the larvae bore into the wood the galleries become packed with a fine powder-like frass. The emerging beetles leave a flight hole of around 1 mm in diameter and the frass is often to be found in small piles on the surface.

If the cores are sealed with wax polish or paint the timber cannot be attacked. If on the other hand the timber is already infested, the adult can still emerge through the protective coating.

Kiln-drying will kill the lyctus but does not make the timber immune as this will not alter the starch content or the size of the pores.

The Anobid Borers (Anobiidae)

These borers (*Anobium punctatum*), commonly called furniture borers, attack furniture, flooring, and structural timber. They show preference for old, well seasoned timber and frequently it is old furniture they attack. These borers attack mainly softwood, but some hardwoods are susceptible.

Although not essential for its development, the borer prefers rather damp humid conditions and is therefore more likely to attack flooring timbers. The female beetle lays her eggs in cracks or old flight holes or on rough sawn surfaces. When the eggs hatch the larvae bore into the timber, haphazardly attacking both heartwood and sapwood. The emergence holes are small and usually surrounded by a granular-like frass.

Dry Wood Longicorns (Cerambycidae)

This group has been known to attack sapwood and heartwood in both softwood and hardwood. Two species (*Hylotrupes bajulus*) are known to be established in Australia after introduction from overseas. The borer is very common in Europe, U.S.A., and South Africa. Great damage can be caused to freshly felled logs and unseasoned timber if these insects are left unchecked.

Oval exit holes and granulated wood powder in the tunnels help to identify the borer.

Termites

Australia has about 200 species distributed throughout the country. White ants, as the termites are often called, utilise cellulose as a source of food. Termites feed upon the roots of plants, living trees, decaying vegetable matter, dry wood, building boards, and paper, in fact any wood tissue or wood product is susceptible to attack. Underground services such as telephone cables have also been attacked.

The classification and identification of the various species requires considerable experience and skill. The wood-user, however, seldom needs such detailed identification and is satisfied with descriptions based on the general habits of the insect. Of the many groups, the tree-dwelling and the subterranean termites cause the most concern.

Termite damage

Prevention of Termite Attack: Timber structures on buildings are protected by either mechanical barriers, such as metal shields placed on foundations, or by impregnating the soil surrounding the structure with a chemical such as dieldrin.

If the timber is to be used in the ground, resistant timbers or timber impregnated with a suitable wood preservative should be specified.

Eradication: When it is established that there is active termite attack in a structure the insects should be left undisturbed until the materials and equipment necessary for treatment have been assembled. If the termites are disturbed they may vacate the position and eradication procedure will be impossible.

Small quantities of white arsenic powder (arsenic trioxide) is blown into the occupied termite galleries. Particles of dust adhere to the insects and are subsequently removed by others as they groom each other. In due course the dead bodies are consumed and eventually the colony is exterminated.

The arsenic powder is extremely poisonous and should be handled with great care. The poison may be administered to the galleries by a suitable powder blower. A strong knife is used to slit the wood carefully to expose the galleries where the termites are working. The hole is then sealed, using masking tape, sticking plaster, or putty. This procedure is repeated in as many different galleries as possible. This treatment is most effective in the warmer months. When complete eradication is established, repairs may be carried out and precautions taken to prevent further attack.

Marine Borers

In the temperate waters of Australia two types of marine borers are of importance: the gribble (*Lemnoria* spp.) and the shipworm (*Teredo* spp.). Great damage by these organisms is caused annually to poles, jetties, and wharves, particularly to the parts between high and low water.

Prevention

Naturally Durable Timber: Few timbers are in fact immune to marine borer attack but many are highly resistant. The resistance is due largely to the presence of extraneous substances in the wood. The following three Australian hardwoods are recognised as highly resistant and give good service when used in the sea: Jarrah (*Eucalyptus marginata*), Brush box (*Tristania conferta*), Turpentine (*Syncarpia lauriflora*).

Mechanical Protection: Copper and plastic sheathing have been used successfully, and anti-fouling paints, provided they are regularly maintained, are relatively successful.

Timber Preservatives: Pressure-impregnation of timber preservatives will enable the timber to withstand marine borer attack. This impregnation is best done by the vacuum pressure process, using preservatives such as creosote and balanced mixtures of copper-sulphate and potassium dichromate.

DURABILITY AND PRESERVATION OF TIMBER

Durability

Reference is frequently made to the natural durability of certain timbers such as Jarrah, Ironbark, Gympie Messmate, Turpentine, and others, but the term really only applies to the heartwood. The sapwood of most timbers is not durable, but this does not mean it must not be used or treated, for in many species it is only a narrow section around the tree. The sapwood is often removed entirely during the milling operations.

Protection of Timber

Not all timbers require preservation treatment but all timbers need some form of protection.

Good building practice demands that a building site is cleared of logs and stumps which may attract termites and that a site is well drained before excavations for the footings are commenced. A free flow of air beneath the floors is vital if a reduction of the relative humidity is to be achieved. It is also important that a damp course be used to prevent water reaching timber by capillary action. Flashing is used to prevent the entry of water around windows, doors, and such things as chimneys which may protrude from a roof.

In order to make sure that the timber in any type of structure remains sound, adequate maintenance is necessary. Buildings should be inspected regularly for termite attack, changes in moisture conditions, and the flashing, gutters and downpipes checked for signs of deterioration.

Preservation Treatment

Painting and soaking were the original methods of applying preservatives. They achieved only limited penetration and their effectiveness decreased rapidly as the timber weathered.

Many types of treatment are available today, but by and large preservation is carried out by vacuum pressure-impregnation techniques. Also used are several methods of non-pressure treatment.

Non-Pressure Preservation Treatment

Brushing and spraying are widely used at the domestic level, but penetration under these conditions is extremely superficial. Preservatives generally used with these techniques include Pentachlorophenol and Copper naphthenate.

Solutions containing fungicides and water repellents are used in a dip process. They are essentially used to treat made-up joinery to give protection between delivery to the site and the final finish.

Preservative salts may be used to apply a salt solution, generally by a dip process to the outside of freshly sawn boards. The timber is stacked under moisture-retaining covers and the solution is allowed to diffuse into the sapwood. The salts are not fixed and may be leached out. This process is known commercially as dip diffusion.

Timber may also be immersed in a hot/cold bath system. Creosote is often used in this type of treatment. The timber is immersed in the preservative and heated for several hours. Some penetration is achieved during this time and in addition the air within the cells expands. When timber is subsequently cooled, air is expelled and the preservative will penetrate further into the timber.

Vacuum Pressure-Impregnation

Impregnation under pressure is generally regarded as the most effective and reliable system of preserving timber. A variety of preservatives may be applied giving lasting protection under the most difficult conditions.

The timber should be seasoned to about fibre saturation point if the best results are to be obtained.

Several methods of pressure-impregnation are used depending on the type of timber being treated and the use for which it is intended.

Types of Preservatives

Preservative Oils
These include preservatives such as creosote, which is derived from coal tar. Creosote treatment is applied to timber used where weatherproofing is essential. Timber treated with creosote is dirty to handle and cannot be painted.

Solvent type preservative in light oil, such as pentachlorophenol, can be readily painted and gives effective protection when used before painting of exterior joinery.

Water-Borne Preservatives
Non-fixed multi-salts consisting of boron compounds, sodium fluoride, arsenic, and chromium are generally used for dip diffusion methods. In New South Wales and Queensland non-fixed single salts are widely used in the control of the Lyctus (powder post beetle).

Fixed multi-salts are permanently fixed in the timber and remain effective. Timber treated in this way is odourless, non-toxic to humans and animals, and may be painted. The timber, however, is liable to weathering.

Copper-chrome-arsenic formulations are in general use throughout the world and are prepared from a mixture of organic salts, copper sulphate, potassium dichromate and arsenic pentoxide.

The dry powder is mixed with water to give a specific strength of solution which determines the retention rate. A characteristic effect of this treatment is that it confers a greenish colour on the treated timber.

Copper sulphate is used mainly to prevent attack from various fungi, while arsenic pentoxide is toxic to insects and also effective against fungi. Potassium dichromate changes the salts to an insoluble form which is retained within the timber structure.

It is desirable in most cases that the timber be machined to finished sizes before treatment, and where the timber is to be used where it must not shrink in service it is necessary to re-season to equilibrium moisture content.

Considerable care must be taken in the selection of metal fastenings and fittings. While modern timber preservatives are not corrosive it is advisable that for exterior use galvanised fittings are installed.

VENEER

The art of veneer inlay or decorating by laying a design on the surface is said to have originated in ancient Ethiopia. In relation to the timber industry, veneer is a thin sheet of wood of uniform thickness produced by the peeling, slicing, or sawing of logs or flitches. Veneers of valuable and exotic timbers may be glued to less expensive material, or thicker veneers of inexpensive timbers used to produce ice cream sticks, boxes, or packing cases. However, most veneer is bonded together, each layer called a ply, and so arranged that the plys are at right angles to each other to form plywood.

Veneers may be cut in a wide range of thicknesses ranging from 1.5 mm to 10 mm. Most rotary veneers are cut in thicknesses from 2.5 mm to 1.2 mm.

Species Used for Veneers

Timbers used within Australia for the production of veneers are in the main homegrown. From information supplied by the major plywood mills within all States of Australia it is possible to plot the predominantly used timbers of veneers. From reference to this information, 75% of all timbers used are found in Australia. Moreover, of that 75%, approximately 60% are to be found on the north-eastern coastline.

Imported timbers include species suitable for both rotary peeled and sliced veneers but their incoming quantity is severely controlled.

The locally grown timber Radiata pine, with the assistance of improved silviculture and harvesting, and permanent waterproof synthetic glues, is proving a boon for the home market.

Radiata structural plywoods for building and construction, floors, container making, and manufacturing uses are now available and are unaffected by steam, heat, moisture, or micro-organisms.

Type of Figure

The type of figure arrangement or pattern in veneer is influenced by a number of factors. Included in these are the colour, abnormalities of grain structure, predominance of medullary rays and annual rings, the species of timber, the section from which timber is removed, and the method used to produce the veneer.

From the following division of the tree the various types of veneers are obtainable:

Stump

Butt veneer—produced by slicing the butt or stump end of the tree. The resulting pattern is often distorted, producing variations of 'crossfire'. This veneer is generally heavily figured and of the cathedral type.

Fiddleback veneer (often termed 'crossfire' veneer) is traditionally used for the backs of violins, and is generally sliced from the butt end, giving rise to wavy and curly figure. For recognition purposes, large waves are referred to as wavy grain, medium waves as curly grain, and fine waves as fiddleback.

Trunk

Annual Ring veneer is produced by rotary peeling. Timbers having distinctive layers of autumn and spring wood and those not requiring expensive treatment are converted by this method.

Striped veneer has a figure generally running parallel and in a straight line with little or no crossfire.

Variations in striped veneer occur, including ribbon stripe and broken stripe. These may be produced by slice-cutting radially timbers with interlocked grain.

Quartered veneer is produced from timbers possessing distinctive medullary rays which have been slice-cut radially.

Burl veneer is produced from wart-like growths on tree trunks attributed to injury sustained in early maturity. The figure has no general direction but appears interwoven and is highly attractive.

Crotch veneer is obtained from the point immediately below where the crown branches out from the trunk. The figure obtained is not exactly parallel to the knife cut and is often described as an inverted V. Hence the term Cathedral.

Veneer Manufacture

Veneers may be produced by lathes, slicers, or saws and consequently the terms rotary, sliced, and sawn veneers refer to the method of cutting. For example, softwoods are usually rotary peeled, whereas hardwoods may be sliced, or if particularly hard they may be sawn.

Rotary Veneer

With the peeler block mounted in the veneer lathe, the most economical method of veneer manufacture is almost complete. Some 95% of all veneers produced are rotary peeled and are used extensively for the manufacture of ordinary 3-ply, multi-ply, and crossbands. With modern veneer lathes the knife nose bar assembly is automatically fed towards the log centre at a predetermined rate. This produces a continuous ribbon of veneer of uniform thickness. Since the veneer has been removed tangentially, lathe checks may be visible when the veneer is flattened out, particularly if the thickness exceeds 2 mm.

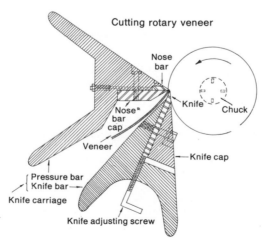

Cutting rotary veneer

Nose bar

Nose bar cap

Knife

Chuck

Veneer

Knife cap

Pressure bar
Knife bar

Knife carriage

Knife adjusting screw

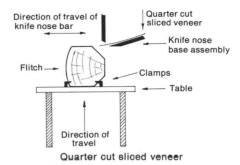

Direction of travel of knife nose bar

Quarter cut sliced veneer

Knife nose base assembly

Flitch

Clamps

Table

Direction of travel

Quarter cut sliced veneer

Sliced Veneers

Slicing is used for producing valuable, highly figured face veneers for use in furniture manufacture.

The logs, sawn into flitches generally by quarter sawing, are softened by steaming or cooking in boiling water for several hours. The flitch may be processed into veneer by one of two methods.

The first of these secures the flitch firmly to a base frame and the knife nose bar assembly passes backwards and forwards over the flitch, slicing one veneer with each forward pass. This method usually occurs in the horizontal plane, hence the term horizontal slicing. With the second method, the knife nose bar assembly is held rigid and the flitch is passed backwards and forwards over the knife. This method is performed in the vertical plane and consequently the term vertical slicing is applied.

Sliced veneers are numbered and stacked in order of cutting to allow for correct matching in pattern arrangement. Most Australian-produced sliced veneer is a standard 1 mm in thickness with imported veneers ranging from 0.25 mm to 1.2 mm.

Slicing enables numerous grain patterns and figure variations of timber structure to be advantageously exposed. Some of these include fiddleback, crossfire, and mottled grain.

Semi-Rotary Veneer

This is a combination of the rotary peeling and slicing methods. It produces decorative veneer with figures varying from quarter to tangential cut within the one veneer strip. A quarter-sawn flitch is mounted off-centre in a rotary veneer lathe and rotated past a knife nose bar assembly. This method is also adaptable for cutting crotch and burl veneers.

Sawn Veneers

Sawing is the oldest method of producing veneers but is rarely used since it produces less than half of a flitch as veneer. Extremely hard and brittle woods may sometimes be converted using bandsaws or large five-gauge circular saws.

Clipping and Drying

Following the peeling or slicing operation the veneer is either clipped to size and dried or continuously dried and then clipped.

Most veneer is mechanically dried in jet type box driers with air temperatures of 166°C blasted on to the veneer surface. For satisfactory results in subsequent gluing processes, the moisture content must be within the defined limits of 8% to 12%.

Finally the veneer is graded according to required standards.

PLYWOOD

Plywood is an engineered panel made up of an odd number of thin layers of wood glued together. These layers, called plys or veneers, are so arranged that the grain direction of each layer is at right angles to that of the layer next to it.

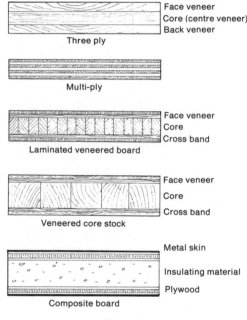

Three ply
Face veneer
Core (centre veneer)
Back veneer

Multi-ply

Laminated veneered board
Face veneer
Core
Cross band

Veneered core stock
Face veneer
Core
Cross band

Composite board
Metal skin
Insulating material
Plywood

Plywood

The outside plys are called face veneers and back veneers and the centre ply or plys the core. The veneers immediately below the faces and backs are known as crossbands. The simplest plywood is made up of three layers of veneer, but five, seven, nine, or more layers may be used.

Since the strength of timber is much higher and its shrinkage greatly lower along the grain, plywood produces a stable board that is strong in all directions.

For furniture construction use of this material is by no means modern, but as a building material it was not until the mid-1930s, with the development of synthetic resins, that its potential became evident.

Plywood Production

The production of plywood begins in the lay-up section. The graded or matched veneer faces and longbands are assembled with the crossbands in preparation for glue spreading.

Matching involves multiple face veneers being clipped and matched to give the requisite appearance. In general, the figure in plywood is produced by two different methods, rotary peeling or slicing. Normally it is not possible to match rotary figure, although in a few instances rotary sheets may be selected for their figure prior to manufacture into plywood. In the slicing process, however, the result is a number of narrow pieces of veneer usually 100 mm to 300 mm wide which must be joined to produce a sheet of veneer. Consequently the veneer edges must be made square and straight so that they may be butt-joined and taped or spliced with the least possible visible joint line.

Taping is achieved with gummed paper holding the required matched veneers together to form a full veneer sheet. Another method, a tapeless splicer, joints the glued edges by electrically curing the glue and has the added advantage of having no tape to be removed by sanding.

Common methods of matching face veneers include:

1. *Book leaf*—where the sheets of veneer are alternately folded out like the leaves of a book. Thus the back of one veneer meets the front of the adjacent veneer, giving a matching joint. All types of veneers may be used.
2. *Slip match*—where the veneer sheets are laid side by side to provide a consecutive repetitive figure. All types of veneers may be used but most common for quarter-sliced veneers.
3. *Random match*—where the veneers are joined to create a deliberate mis-match. Veneers from various flitches may be used.
4. *Diamond match*—this form of matching is generally given to stump, butt, or crotch veneers, since it highlights the beauty of grain formations. Variations of this theme include reverse diamond, herringbone, and V.

For most manufacturing techniques only the crossbands or cores are passed through the glue spreader, with the glue being conveyed to the contiguous veneers in the pressing operation.

The glue spreading operation allows the crossbands to be coated on both sides simultaneously. The thickness of adhesive applied is closely controlled by automatic adjustment of the spreader-doctor roll gap. These coated crossbands are arranged with the appropriate number of longbands to form packs of spread veneers ready for the first pressing operation.

Pressing
Pressing of the plywood sandwich ensures intimate contact of veneers and glue and may be carried out by a cold pressing or hot pressing process.

Cold Pressing
This is often associated with prepressing although it should be noted that a small amount of cold-pressed plywood is still manufactured.

Prepressing
This is performed in a cold press having one large daylight capable of accommodating two or three hot press loads. This operation conveys the adhesive from the spread to the unspread surfaces of the veneer, thereby promoting a more even glue bond.

In the hot press the spread sheets are bonded together under high temperature and pressure. Temperatures of the platens in normal hot presses range from 104° to 149°C with pressures between 827 and 1378 kilopascals being applied. The platens may be heated with steam, hot water, or oil. The spread pack remains for a predetermined time under conditions of pressure and temperature until curing of the glue has occurred.

Synthetic glues, because of their dielectric properties, may be cured with high frequency current. However, because of high installation and running costs presses of this type are very few in number.

The trimming and sanding of the panels which follows completes the production for most plywood. After curing, the sheets are passed through trim saws for accurate length and width dimensions.

Sanding is carried out by passing the sheets through a drum sander where both surfaces are sanded smooth to a predetermined and even thickness.

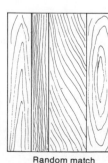

Book match
Slip match
Random match

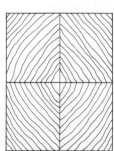

Diamond match

Common methods of matching face veneers

Sheets requiring repair are removed from the production line during the inspection and grading process. Checks, splits, and dead knots are removed and sound pieces of veneer inserted by means of passing the sheet through a special machine.

Finally the sheets are stamped with their type and quality identification and prepared for packaging.

Plywood adhesives are derived from synthetic resins and are all thermo-setting. To determine the differences in adhesive qualities a number of tests were formulated, graduating from type A to type D in descending order of permanence.

Type A bond has a glueline which will not deteriorate due to immersion or extremes of heat and cold. It is easily recognisable by the black colour of the glueline and is used for marine, exterior, and structural plywood.

Type B bond, due to the adhesive used, will break down under immersion. The glueline, therefore, is classified as not fully permanent. It is ideal for use as concrete formwork, having a limited life expectancy.

Type C and D bonds are manufactured for interior use only and should not be involved in structural applications where long term stresses may occur.

Classification of Plywoods

The standardised plywood products manufactured by the Australian industry fall into two broad groups: constructional and decorative.

Constructional Plywoods

1. Marine plywood is produced from timber species exhibiting properties applicable to marine situations. Some of these qualities include low water absorption for buoyancy, high strength-to-weight ratio, a surface texture suitable for clear finishing and durability. Restrictions are placed on the thickness of veneers relative to plywood thickness to provide uniformity and high two-way strength.

Further limitations include density between 448 and 720 kg/m^3, tangential shrinkage not more than 8%, and modulus of rupture not less than 75 834 kN/m^2.

Marine plywood is suitable for use where high strength and durability are required, as in commercial trawlers, or where medium strength but extreme lightness is necessary, as in racing class boats.

2. Exterior plywoods are available in type A bond suitable for permanent exposure, or in type B bond capable of withstanding similar exposure conditions but for a limited period. The face veneers of exterior plywoods are free from defects and suitable for painting or staining.

Exterior plywood may be specified for general purpose use subject to structural recommendations.

3. Structural plywood, consisting of pinus structural and hardwood structural plywoods, are standardised, low-cost engineered sheets, having extensive application in building, industrial, and agricultural projects.

The main variables controlling the strength of constructional plywoods are the veneer thickness and construction lay-up. The thick-face veneers (1.5 mm) provide better bending strength and stiffness, and higher abrasion and wearing surfaces than other wood-based panel products.

It is predicted that with the progressive maturity of the Australian forests the demand for low-cost structural plywood (in particular pinus structural) will develop enormously, with dramatic influence on future construction methods.

4. Overlaid plywoods are constructional plywoods that may be a number of materials that provide greater weathering and abrasive resistance peculiar to the requirement.

(a) High density overlays have a plasticised film fused to the plywood sheet during manufacture. This phenolic resin film overlay eliminates the absorption of water by the face veneers, thereby preventing any checking or swelling between uses. It is extensively used in concrete formwork.

SUMMARY OF STANDARD TYPES, SIZES, AND THICKNESSES

USE	BOND	FACE VENEER	Length mm	Width mm	Thickness mm
Marine	A	Selected rotary sliced	900 1200 2100	1800 2400 Larger s/s	3–25
Hardwood structural	A	Rotary hardwood veneers	900 1200	1800 2400 2100	7–17
Pinus structural	A	2.5 mm Pinus veneers	900 1200	1800 2100 2400 2700	7–22
Exterior	A or B	Most rotary and sliced species	900 1200	1800 2100 2400	3–25
Overlaid	A or B	Overlaid rotary species	900 1200	1800 2100 2400	2–19
Sliced faced plywood	D	All sliced species	900 1200	1800 2100 2400	3–20
Random grooved plywood	D	Selected rotary and sliced species	900	2100 2400 2700	4–6
Commercial plywood General purpose	C and D	All rotary species	900 1200	1800 2400 2700	25
Blockboard	C and D	All sliced and rotary species	900 1200	1800 2100 2400	20

(b) Medium density overlays provide similar properties to high density overlays but the phenolic resin is saturated with a fibrous film giving an overlay suitable for painting. The applied film is durable, highly resistant to chemicals, and will not flake under boiling, steaming, or extreme weather conditions. It is recommended for weatherboards, patio floors, garage doors, fascias, shipping containers, cool rooms, transport semi-trailers, and sheeting for heavy industrial chemical installations.

(c) Other overlays have been successfully bonded to plywood for particular applications. Materials such as aluminium, copper, stainless or galvanised steel, fibre glass, and polyester resins have been pressed on to plywood with the aid of selected adhesives.

Decorative Plywood

1. Rotary interior plywood has a face veneer consisting of one or more edge-jointed veneers of matching colour. It may be acceptable for transparent finishes but it is not intended for use where highly figured panels are required. Rotary interior plywood is used extensively in the building and furniture industries.

2. Sliced decorative plywood, although more expensive, has the advantage of allowing the grain pattern to be highlighted by the various matching techniques. In the case of some species, sliced veneer allows the natural figure to be represented in a manner not possible by rotary peeling.

3. Pre-finished plywoods. Random matched and grooved plywood is the only pre-finished decorative plywood produced that complies with industry standards. The face veneer, laid up in a mismatched form, is grooved in the joint lines to imitate the appearance of sawn timber. The panels are pre-finished with a clear plastic resistant to normal wear and tear. However, most applications suggest use in the vertical plane, indicating a limit to its wearing abilities. Pre-finished plywoods are popular for feature walls, interior linings, commercial uses in shops, and home renovations.

Commercial plywoods are used structurally in furniture manufacture but due to their glue-line are limited to interior usage.

Thin commercial plywoods are a lightweight sheeting used for drawer bottoms, wardrobe backs, toys, low cost furniture, coffins, and the like. Thick commercial plywood, with the introduction of particle board has declined in use. However, it does have the distinct advantage of superior strength and machinability, provides stronger joints, has better nail and screw holding power, and suffers less 'movement' than does particle board. For these reasons manufacturers often combine thick commercial plywood with particle board to take advantage of the combination of their individual properties.

PARTICLE BOARD

Particle board is also commonly known as chipboard, chipcore, chipcraft, shavings board, flake board, and wood waste board. (Note: This section covers the use of wood-derived material only. Estimates show that 25 to 30% of world production of particle board uses flax, straw, or other ligno-cellulose materials.)

Particle board, as defined by the Agricultural Organisation of the United Nations, 'is a sheet material manufactured from small pieces of wood or other ligno-cellulose materials, e.g. chips, flakes, strands, shives, agglomerated by the use of an organic binder together with one of the following agents: heat, pressure, moisture, or catalyst'.

Although competing with hardboards to some degree, particle board has taken to task timber corestock block boards and the thicker plywoods as used in the production of furniture. It is increasingly being used for purposes where utility or decorative panels are required.

Both raw board and veneered board are being used in the manufacture of bedroom, dining room, kitchen, built-in and occasional furniture, cabinet work, display fixtures, doors, desk, bench and bar tops, room or office partitions, room panelling and linings, flooring and pressed components, such as chair seats, radio and T.V. cabinets.

Particle board was first produced experimentally in Switzerland during the late 1930s by mixing thermo-setting adhesives with wood particles and pressing under heat, hence producing a flat homogeneous board. The first recorded commercial manufacture was in Bremen, Germany, in 1941 using a phenolic resin binder. This early production, however, proved unsatisfactory, but due to severe timber shortages immediately following the war, incentives were provided to solve basic production problems. By 1950 particle board had become an accepted product and further refinements had established it as the best board for furniture manufacture.

Raw Materials

Two materials only are required—wood particles and a synthetic resin adhesive. Optional additives may include paraffin wax for water repelling and dimensional stability, insecticides and fungicides, and fireproofing chemicals.

Although the wood particles form the bulk of the board, about 90% by weight, the synthetic resin is invariably the more costly item. *The Wood Particle:* Sawmill residue suitable for board production includes offcuts, slabs and edgings, dockings and round heart, planer shavings, and veneer cores. Sawdust and other fines are generally not acceptable and bark in particular is avoided due to excessive wear on cutting knives and detraction from appearance. Forest waste may include thinnings, low grade logs, and large limbs of suitable species.

Experiments have shown that the most suitable species are those of comparatively low density (480–640 kg/m^3) and of light colour. Australian manufacturers use extensively Radiata pine with a density of about 480 kg/m^3, while thinnings of Sydney Blue Gum have also proved to be most successful.

The Adhesive: For bonding the wood particles together synthetic resin adhesives are used exclusively. Those used are urea-formaldehyde, phenol-formaldehyde and various combinations of urea- and melamine-formaldehyde. The most popular in use at present are the urea-formaldehydes since they are generally the cheapest, cause little timber discolouration, and cure at moderate temperatures.

The phenol-formaldehydes are far more durable than the ureas but are costlier, darker in colour, and require higher pressing temperatures.

The melamine group are the dearest of these three resins but combine advantages of the other two. Hence the addition of a small quality of melamine resin to urea-formaldehyde resin improves water-resistance considerably and at a reasonable cost.

Types of Particle Board

The types of particle board may be classified according to their structure and method of production. For example:

Single Layer
The single layer board is produced by flat

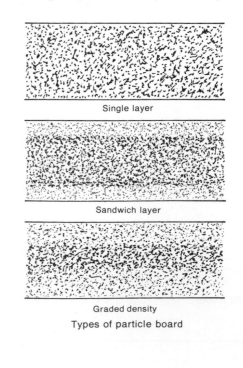

Single layer

Sandwich layer

Graded density

Types of particle board

platen pressing or by the extrusion method. Both of these boards are referred to as homogeneous boards.

Three Layer

The three layer or 'sandwich' board is manufactured by the flat platen pressing method only, and

Graded Density Boards

These are produced also by flat platen pressing only.

The single layer board produced by flat pressing is usually a medium quality general purpose board and requires crossbanding if used for veneered panels. Similarly, the extruded board requires the application of sheet materials to provide stability and extra strength while covering the edges and ends of face particles.

In the three layer or sandwich type board the outer layers of fine shred-like particles or thin flat flakes ('engineered flakes') knit closely together to form a high density smooth skin between 1 mm and 3 mm thick. The core may consist of a coarse form of engineered flake or a lower quality particle chip such as splinters from the hammer mill. This form of construction gives a very high quality board suitable for furniture construction or where stability, smoothness of face, and quality appearance is required.

Graded density boards are a balance between the single and three layer boards. Particles of similar type but varying in size are distributed throughout the board so as to increase in size towards the centre. Thus the smooth high density surfaces with low density cores are obtained without an abrupt change occurring.

Physical Properties

Density

Depending on the method of manufacture used, the board densities range from 240 to 1201 kg/m^3. Within this range three classes are acknowledged: The insulating group, covering from 240 to 400 kg/m^3, the medium density group, from 400 to 800 kg/m^3, and forming the main mass of particle board production the high density group, ranging from 800 to 1201 kg/m^3.

Elements affecting density comprise timber species, type of chip, adhesive resin content, and pressing pressure.

Shrinkage and Swelling

Under test conditions for flat pressed boards it was determined that the increase in length and width averaged 0.1 to 0.3% while thickness ranged from 2.22% to 8.62%. However, for extruded boards under the same conditions, increases in length to 12% and in thickness to 1% were found.

Thermal Conductivity

Particle board being ligno-cellulosic is combustible, but actual burning will be limited by charcoal formation on the surface.

Working Properties

Machining Characteristics

Particle board may be shaped by hand or machined in a similar manner to natural solid timber. However, since the bonding agent is a synthetic resin adhesive, there is a tendency for cutting edges to dull more quickly than they do on timber. Consequently, the use of high speed steel or preferably tungsten carbide tipped cutters is often recommended.

Fasteners and Holding Power

Experience has shown that particle board accepts nails and screws satisfactorily but the withdrawal resistance is *far less* than solid timber. Where possible, screw insertion should be limited to face surfaces of boards.

For increased screw holding power, when edge-screwing use long thread screws or edge-lip the board first with solid timber.

Uses

Because of its dimensional stability, uniformity of thickness, availability in large sizes, and working qualities, the majority of particle board produced is used by builders and furniture manufacturers. In general, the building industry uses the homogeneous boards, while the furniture trade uses the three-layer board.

MEDIUM DENSITY FIBRE BOARD

Medium Density Fibre Board (MDF) is a reconstituted wood product characterised by a smooth, high-density surface with excellent machining properties and is suitable for painting and staining. In Australia, plantation-grown radiata pine is the main species used in the manufacture of MDF, although many other non-pored timbers have suitable properties and characteristics. Other ligno-cellulose materials including bamboo have been successfully used in MDF production.

Manufacture

The initial process is that of *debarking* the log. This is generally achieved using a ring debarker to remove the majority of bark to assist in removing grit and providing a higher quality surface finish on the final product. The logs are then passed through a *chipper* to reduce them to a specified chip size. It is possible to blend chips from different timber species where certain properties are required. For example, eucalypt chips may be used to improve moisture resistant qualities.

The washed chips are then passed through a *defibrator* which, with the assistance of high pressure and high temperature, facilitates the fibre separation of the chips, resulting in a light and fluffy pulp.

Following defibration, the fibres are mixed with paraffin wax for water repellency and thermosetting synthetic resins as binders for board stability. Other chemicals such as insecticides, fungicides and fire-retardants can also be added to provide specific protection.

The fibres are spread uniformly onto a conveyer belt to form a *mat*. The mat may be cut to size ready for pressing or, as in the latest MDF plants, passed through a Continuous Press. After pressing, the boards are cooled in a dryer and finally trimmed and sanded.

Properties

MDF has become most competitive with traditional materials—in particular, particle board. Its moderate overall density gives it excellent machining characteristics. This property has seen many manufacturers of ornate furniture using MDF in lieu of solid timber or particle board, as it is readily shaped and accepts lacquer finishes very well on edges. MDF has a greater moisture tolerance than both particle board and timber.

Where possible, screw insertion should be limited to the face surfaces of boards. Experience has shown that screwing or nailing into the edges tends to cause the fibres to delaminate, thereby considerably reducing strength properties.

Uses

Due to its uniformity of thickness, dimensional stability, availability in large sizes and working qualities the majority of MDF produced is used by builders and furniture manufacturers.

HARDBOARD

Hardboard is a man-made panel material manufactured from natural timber fibres and retaining many of the characteristics of basic timber stock. It is without some of the physical disadvantages of timber, e.g. there are no knots or natural grain structure to allow splitting and only hardboard uses Lignin, the natural cohesive substance found in timber, to bind the fibre together.

Raw Materials

In Australia, low grade timber (particularly hardwood), which has previously been regarded as commercially useless, is the main constituent. This may include straight logs, sound material from misshapen trees, and residues from timber mills.

Approximately twenty species, mainly eucalypts, have been found suitable and classified as red wood or white wood, since the colour of the board is affected by the timbers used.

Most timbers have their own particular properties—long fibre, short fibre, high water content, and colour—some being desirable and others needing control.

Timbers used in other countries include Douglas fir in America, Firs in Sweden, Poplars in Italy, and Eucalypts and Acacias in South Africa.

Classification of Hardboards

Hardboards may be divided into the following three groups: natural Hardboards, Primed Hardboards, and Prefinished and Perforated Harboards.

Natural hardboards are available in standard or tempered and are designated as high density boards.

Natural Hardboards

Standard Hardboard: This is the board which is generally used for wall and ceiling linings and furniture construction. It is also the board produced in greatest quantity since it is basically the same as when it leaves the humidifier. Standard hardboard is also available pre-primed. This has proved most acceptable to the tradesman and amateur alike. Standard board has a relatively high strength factor and is resistant to water.

Tempered Hardboard: This type of hardboard evolves by soaking standard panels in various oils and then rebaking to lock in the absorbed oil. This produces a panel which is harder, stronger, smoother, and more water-resistant than the standard board. This board is useful in situations where moisture-resistance is required, such as kitchens and laundries.

Special tempered and thicker hardboard is available for vertical or flat forming where smooth concrete surfaces are required.

The oil mixture includes a polymer oil, acid linseed oil and ferric driers.

Primed Hardboards

These are natural hardboards which have been sealed with pigmented paints to limit the porosity of the board surface. The alkyd resin base and titanium dioxide pigment with extender of calcium carbonate enable the primed board to be recoated with melamine enamels, polyester resins, and other commonly used paints.

Prefinished Hardboards

These refer to the various surface finishes which may be applied to the natural hardboard. Surface treatments such as timber veneer, plastic film, plastic laminate, and metal cladding have been successfully applied to the appropriate hardboard surfaces.

Perforated Hardboards

Available in standard or tempered boards, these are die-punched under power presses to standard patterns. They are obtainable in a wide range of painted finishes.

Sandwich Panels

Hardboard cladding used in conjunction with a core material provides an efficient sandwich panel having numerous applications. The building industry, for example, uses panels of this construction where good acoustic and thermal properties are required as well as a high strength-to-weight ratio. Core materials include particle board, honeycomb paper, polyurethane, and polystyrene.

Post Forming

Using a heated mandrel to form relatively large radii, post forming has been the only exception to the concept of hardboard being a 'flat sheet board'. However, the Mitre Folding Process, using vinyl-faced hardboard, has shown experimentally that it is possible to form complex three-dimensional shapes from the flat sheet. The process involves V grooving the board down to the film, then folding and applying quick setting adhesives. Suggested applications include cabinets, carcass construction, speaker boxes, and mouldings.

Low Density Fibre Board

Softboard was first produced in Australia in 1939 using Bagasse, a by-product of the sugar cane industry, as the raw material. However, due to rising costs, the present day softboard is produced from pine wood fibres.

PLASTIC LAMINATES

The manufacture of plastic laminate incorporates the use of thermosetting resins. Brown paper is impregnated with phenol-formaldehyde, cut to length, and allowed to dry. Approximately eight sheets of paper are stacked together with a pattern sheet on top which has been impregnated with melamine-formaldehyde. The sheets are then pressed between heated plates until the resin cures.

Colours and printed patterns, together with a wide range of photographed wood grains, are readily available, and a choice of gloss or matt finish further increases the selection.

Laminated plastics are extremely tough and durable. They resist abrasion, household chemicals, and boiling water. They are ideal for use on kitchen units, children's furniture, table tops, desk tops, and bars. They are also manufactured for veneering furniture and for wall panelling.

Cutting and Bonding Plastic Laminate

A sharp panel saw, tenon saw, laminate cutter, or trimming knife are recommended for cutting plastic laminate. Particular care must be taken to support the offcut to avoid cracking. Plastic laminates are always cut from the decorative side and it is advisable to cut a little oversize.

Plastic laminates should never be bonded to solid timber. Plywood, hardboard, or particle board are ideal surfaces. Contact adhesive is spread on both surfaces using a special serrated edge applicator supplied with the can. The adhesive is allowed to dry for about twenty minutes. Do not bond while the adhesive is tacky, it should be touch-dry.

Contact adhesive will bond immediately on contact, so it is important to position the laminate correctly. Accurate alignment may be achieved by using dowels or timber strips to separate the adhesive-coated surfaces. When correctly aligned the dowels may be removed one at a time.

To ensure a good bond use a rolling pin or cork block or padded timber block tapped gently with a hammer.

It is best to allow the adhesive about thirty minutes to dry out before trimming. The edges may be trimmed with a file or plane. It is also desirable to remove the arris along the top edge as this will be very sharp.

A sharp panel saw, tenon saw or laminate cutter is recommended for cutting laminate

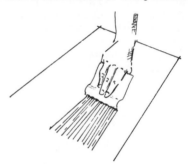

Contact adhesive is spread evenly with a serated-edge applicator to both surfaces

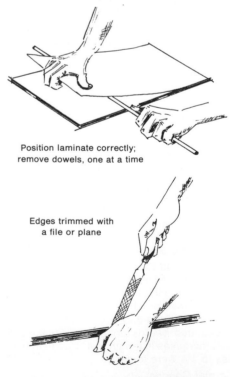

Position laminate correctly; remove dowels, one at a time

Edges trimmed with a file or plane

Cutting and bonding plastic laminate

COMMERCIAL TIMBERS

...KNOWING THE MATERIAL YOU ARE ABOUT TO WORK

TIMBERS USED COMMERCIALLY IN AUSTRALIA

The timbers available at any one time will vary. Some timbers are readily available while others are only available in the areas of occurrence.

The following notes indicate the standard trade name followed by the botanical name (reference *Nomenclature of Australian Timbers* and *Nomenclature of Commercial Timbers Imported into Australia*).

The timbers are listed in alphabetical order with brief notes about the timber, working qualities, and availability. The notes also indicate whether they are pored (hardwood) or non-pored (softwood).

African Mahogany   *Khaya* spp.
(pored)
Occurrence West Africa
Timber HARD Pinkish brown in colour, coarse texture, interlocking grain. Resistant to wood rotting fungi but susceptible to damage by borers
Working Qualities Works well with hand and machine tools; glues and finishes well
Weight Moderately heavy
Uses Furniture, joinery, boatbuilding
Availability Readily available

Australian Oak   *Eucalyptus obliqua*
(pored)
Occurrence Tasmania and Victoria
Timber HARD Pale brown in colour, usually straight grained, with rather an open texture. Growth rings are fairly prominent. It is tough and strong
Working Qualities Has relatively good bending qualities and turns rather well. Easily worked with handtools. Polishes well
Weight Heavy
Uses General building, furniture, joinery, cooperage, paper pulp
Availability Generally readily available

Balsa   *Ochroma pyramidale*
(pored)
syn. *Ochroma lagopus*
Occurrence Northern portion of South America, Central America, and the West Indies.
Timber VERY SOFT Almost white in colour, open textured. Lightweight, straight grained, with prominent medullary rays
Working Qualities Works easily, but fibres are likely to tear out
Weight Exceptionally light
Uses Insulation, model aeroplanes, floats, lifebuoys, life rafts
Availability Limited

Black Bean   *Castanospermum australe*
(pored)
Occurrence Northern New South Wales and Queensland
Timber HARD Very dark brown in colour, white sapwood. A rather open texture with a striking figure
Working Qualities Relatively easy to work
Weight Moderately heavy
Uses Furniture, joinery, carving, plywood
Availability Limited

Blackwood   *Acacia melanoxylon*
(pored)
Occurrence Tasmania, Victoria, and New South Wales
Timber HARD Golden brown in colour, with a fairly coarse texture. The grain is generally straight, occasionally interlocked and wavy
Working Qualities Easy to work, planes and turns well. Takes a high polish. Excellent bending properties
Weight Moderately heavy
Uses Furniture, panelling, boatbuilding, tennis racquets
Availability Generally readily available

Brush Box   *Tristania conferta*
(pored)
Occurrence Coast of northern New South Wales and Queensland
Timber HARD Light to dark red brown in colour, close textured. Is resistant to splintering
Working Qualities Relatively easy to work
Weight Heavy
Uses Flooring, panelling
Availability Commercial quantities

Coachwood   *Ceratopetalum apetalum*
(pored)
Occurrence In the rain forests of coastal New South Wales
Timber HARD Light to dark pinkish brown in colour. Close textured and tough
Working Qualities Easy to work
Weight Moderately heavy
Uses Furniture, joinery, plywood, turnery
Availability Commercial quantities

Japanese Oak   *Quercus mongolica*
(pored)
Occurrence Japan, China and other parts of Asia. It is imported into Australia chiefly from Japanese ports
Timber HARD Pale coloured, open textured wood with prominent medullary rays. Sapwood is susceptible to the powder post borer. Tough
Working Qualities Relatively easy to work. Bends well. Excellent carving timber
Weight Moderately heavy
Uses Furniture, carving, panelling, steam bending
Availability Adequate supplies available

Jarrah   *Eucalyptus marginata*
(pored)
Occurrence South-west corner of Western Australia
Timber HARD The sapwood is narrow and pale brown, the heartwood dark red. Coarse texture and usually straight grained. It is durable, tough, and heavy
Working Qualities Hard to work, but finishes and polishes well
Weight Heavy
Uses Heavy construction, railway sleepers, heavy furniture
Availability Usually readily available

Jelutong   *Dyera costulata*
(pored)
Occurrence Indonesia and Malaya
Timber SOFT and LIGHT Pale yellow to white in colour, the sapwood and heartwood not clearly defined. Straight grained with a fine even texture. Contains numerous latex deposits which detract from its appearance. Not durable
Working Qualities Easy to work. Chisels and carves exceptionally well
Weight Light
Uses Patternmaking, carving, interior joinery
Availability Readily available

Karri   *Eucalyptus diversicolor*
(pored)
Occurrence South-west corner of Western Australia
Timber HARD The sapwood is almost white, heartwood reddish brown and extremely hard. Fairly coarse texture. The grain is mainly straight but sometimes interlocked. It is a heavy and tough timber but not durable against termites
Working Qualities Difficult to work
Weight Heavy
Uses General building construction
Availability Generally readily available

Kauri   *Agathis palmerstonii*
(non-pored)
Occurrence Atherton Tableland of Northern Queensland
Timber SOFT Pale brown in colour, even close texture, straight grain, easy to work, accepts glue and polish well. Not durable in exposed positions
Working Qualities Easy to work with handtools
Weight Light
Uses Plywood, boatbuilding, patternmaking, indoor joinery
Availability Limited

Meranti   *Shorea* spp.
(pored)
Occurrence Malaya, Philippines, West Borneo
Timber SOFT to MODERATELY HARD Varies in colour from white to pale pink to a purple brown. White lines often show on longitudinal surfaces due to intercellular resin canals. Figure is not prominent. Grain is usually interlocked, with an even coarse texture
Working Qualities Saws and machines readily
Weight Varies from light to heavy
Uses Doors and windows, shelving, small boat construction, furniture, plywood

Availability Good supplies available

Myrtle Beech   *Nothofagus*
(pored)   *cunninghamii*
Occurrence South-east Victoria and Tasmania
Timber HARD Reddish brown in colour, straight or slightly interlocked grain. Fine and uniform texture. Not durable. Strong and tough
Working Qualities Works easily, turns well, and is an ideal bending timber
Weight Heavy
Uses Flooring, panelling, joinery, handles, plywood
Availability Limited quantities available

Nyatoh   *Palequium* spp.
(pored)   *Payena* spp.
Occurrence South-East Asia
Timber MODERATELY HARD Pale reddish brown in colour, even fine texture
Working Qualities Easy to work and finish
Weight Moderately heavy
Uses Furniture joinery
Availability Regular supplies

Oregon or Douglas Fir   *Pseudotsuga*
(non-pored)   *menziesii*
Occurrence West coast of North America
Timber MODERATELY SOFT A wide variation in colour from pale yellow to light reddish brown. Distinctive whitish sapwood. Usually straight grained, and rather uneven texture. Distinctive growth rings. A tough strong timber, with elastic qualities
Working Qualities One of the hardest of the softwoods. Relatively easy to work
Weight Moderately heavy
Uses General construction work, joinery
Availability Plentiful

Philippine Mahogany   Principally
(pored)   *Shorea* spp.
Occurrence South-East Asia
Timber MODERATELY HARD Reddish brown in colour. Coarse texture, interlocking grain
Working Qualities Easy to cut and plane. Holds nails and screws well
Weight Moderately heavy
Uses Furniture, joinery, panelling
Availability Regular supplies

Queensland Maple   *Flindersia*
(pored)   *brayleyana*
Occurrence Atherton Tableland in North Queensland
Timber HARD Pinkish brown in colour, close texture. A very highly figured timber, prized for veneers
Working Qualities Works easily, stains and polishes well
Weight Moderately heavy
Uses Veneers, plywood, high quality furniture, boatbuilding
Availability Generally available but needs to be ordered well in advance

Queensland Walnut   *Endiandra*
(pored)   *palmerstonii*
Occurrence Rain forests of North Queensland
Timber HARD Varies in colour from brown to dark chocolate, with lighter streaks. High silica content
Working Qualities Difficult to work with handtools. High silica content blunts cutting tools. Polishes well
Weight Moderately heavy
Uses Plywood, turnery, furniture
Availability Limited, generally only as plywood

Radiata Pine   *Pinus radiata*
(non-pored)
Occurrence Native of California, U.S.A. Extensively planted in New Zealand and most States of Australia
Timber SOFT Pale yellow-brown, with distinct growth rings. Even texture, resinous. Preservative treatment essential if used in exposed positions
Working Qualities Good
Weight Light
Uses General construction, flooring, cladding, joinery, furniture, plywood
Availability Readily available

Ramin   *Gonystylus* spp.
(pored)
Occurrence Malaya, Borneo, Sarawak, Philippines, Indonesia
Timber HARD White to pale yellow. Straight grain, with a fine even texture. Tough and strong
Working Qualities Works easily, polishes well
Weight Moderately heavy
Uses Furniture, joinery, turnery, plywood
Availability Regular supplies

Silky Oak   *Cardwellia sublimis*
(pored)
Occurrence Coastal areas of northern Queensland
Timber MODERATELY HARD Pinkish brown in colour, prominent medullary rays, and a rather open texture. Light in weight, tough
Working Qualities Works easily, carves, bends, and polishes well
Weight Moderately heavy
Uses Furniture, joinery
Availability Good

Silver Ash   *Flindersia*
(pored)   *pubescens*
Occurrence Rain forests of North Queensland coast
Timber HARD Almost white to pale brown in colour. Generally straight grained and close textured. Occasionally wavy or fiddleback figure
Working Qualities Works easily, takes a high polish

Weight Moderately heavy
Uses Furniture, joinery, sporting goods, boatbuilding, plywood
Availability Available in limited quantities

Sugar Pine   *Pinus*
(non-pored)   *lambertiana*
Occurrence West coast of U.S.A.
Timber SOFT Sapwood is creamy white, heartwood light brown. Straight and even grain with a coarse uniform texture. Preservative treatment essential if used in exposed positions
Working Qualities Excellent, very stable
Weight Light
Uses General construction, patternmaking, musical instruments, joinery
Availability Limited, imported almost exclusively for patternmaking

Teak   *Tectona grandis*
(pored)
Occurrence India, Burma, Thailand, Malaya
Timber HARD Golden brown, darkens on exposure to a deep brown. Texture is coarse and uneven. The grain may either be straight or irregular. Contains a resinous oil. Durable and strong
Working Qualities Relatively easy to work, but dulls cutting edges
Weight Heavy
Uses Shipbuilding, plywood, furniture
Availability Good supplies available

Western Red Cedar   *Thuja plicata*
(non-pored)
Occurrence West coast of North America, particularly British Columbia
Timber VERY SOFT Heartwood reddish brown to brown, sapwood white. Straight grained, coarse texture. Resistant to decay and borers
Working Qualities Easy to work
Weight Very light
Uses Shingles, fencing, panelling, joinery, boatbuilding
Availability Generally readily available

PHOTO AND DRAWING CREDITS

All photographs and drawings have been produced by Terry Smith and Brian Haines, with the exception of the following:

Australian Design Awards
Black & Decker A/Asia Pty. Ltd.
Brady Billiard Tables
Commonwealth Department of Agriculture, Fisheries and Forestry
David Trembath Agencies Pty. Ltd.
Department of the Environment and Heritage
Durden Machinery Co.
Ekornes
Guest, Keen & Nettlefield (Aust.) Pty. Ltd.
Hettich Australia
Makita (Australia) Pty. Ltd.
Norman Turner & Nottage Pty. Ltd.
Pine Australia
S.A. Brush Co.
Selleys Pty Ltd
Spear & Jackson Pty. Ltd.
Stanley Works Pty. Ltd.
Tessa Pty. Ltd.
Tharnet Bros. Ltd.
Timber Promotion Council
Triton Manufacturing and Design Co. Pty. Ltd.
Warburton Franki
Woodfast Machinery Co.

INDEX